Critical Theories, Radical Pedagogies, and Global Conflicts

Critical Theories, Radical Pedagogies, and Global Conflicts

Gustavo E. Fischman, Peter McLaren,
Heinz Sünker, and Colin Lankshear

ROWMAN & LITTLEFIELD PUBLISHERS, INC.
Lanham • Boulder • New York • Toronto • Oxford

ROWMAN & LITTLEFIELD PUBLISHERS, INC.

Published in the United States of America
by Rowman & Littlefield Publishers, Inc.
A wholly owned subsidiary of The Rowman & Littlefield Publishing Group, Inc.
4501 Forbes Boulevard, Suite 200, Lanham, Maryland 20706
www.rowmanlittlefield.com

PO Box 317, Oxford OX2 9RU, UK

British Library Cataloguing in Publication Information Available

Library of Congress Cataloging-in-Publication Data

Critical theories, radical pedagogies, and global conflicts / [edited by] Gustavo
Fischman . . . [et al.].
    p. cm.
Includes bibliographical references and index.
ISBN 0-7425-3071-X (cloth : alk. paper) — ISBN 0-7425-3072-8 (pbk. : alk. paper)
1. Critical pedagogy. I. Fischman, Gustavo.
LC196.C77 2005
370.11'5—dc22

2005008248

Printed in the United States of America

♾™ The paper used in this publication meets the minimum requirements of
American National Standard for Information Sciences—Permanence of Paper
for Printed Library Materials, ANSI/NISO Z39.48-1992.

Contents

Introduction

The twenty-first century appears to be marked not only by the bloody legacy of the previous century but with unprecedented levels of global injustice: the terrorist attacks of September 11, 2001, and March 11, 2004; the horrors of the wars in Afghanistan, Iraq, and Palestine; the repartitioning and savaging of the world market by globalized financial corporations with longer and longer fangs; the perfecting of empire building by the United States; the increasing opportunism of the transnational capitalist class; the heightened risks of ecological disasters and dangerous levels of global warming; the still-threatening spread of the HIV/AIDS epidemic with the daily deaths of thousands from preventable diseases and hunger. This undoubtedly is a time for mourning and reflection, but it is also a time for a renewal of our commitment to global justice, especially at this juncture of organic crisis when media pundits and high-level government leaders are calling for more blood to be spilled in the name of democracy and freedom. This is a time in which the hard-line politicians, popular syndicated columnists, and common citizens in the United States are supporting military crusades in the name of North American "moral superiority"; and it is a time in which the "doves" are calling for market crusades invoking the magical effects of capitalism. In this new scenario, there is an urgency in renewing efforts to fight against a new epidemic of authoritarian and violent measures, both military and economic.

We must remember, too, that we are being bombarded daily by the media, the results of which leave an indelible mark on the way we exercise critical judgment and act on such judgments. In shaping our attitudes and judgments, the media has transformed our political subjectivities into a self-regulatory system, cut off from developing a more critical conscious will and from rendering a high degree of permeability to our capacity to reason. In many cases, we are offered to live like parasites, enduring this constant media bombardment living in the digestive tracts of CNN and Fox News, as our host organisms attempt to shape our ability to deliberate. The only way to cheat the electronic homeostasis that produces us is to remove ourselves into another's situation. This is growing more difficult today, when, under the guise of "no spin" television commentary, we are trapped in webs spun from deceit and lies. To provisionally suspend ourselves from the complicity that unites us with mainstream ideology and the preoccupations and prerogatives of the American Empire takes a supreme effort.

In this context we find plenty in educational and social directions and practices to be critical about. Yet we often struggle to find a political or ethical base from which to launch critiques and oppositional practices. Nowadays many are suspicious of the role of big theory, and some even question our right to theorize—insofar as this might involve sketching some kind of blueprint for others, as well as ourselves, to follow.

At the same time, we inhabit a burgeoning educational planning and policy scene that follows what are now well-known patterns and contours. These are linked to the incurably iniquitous dimensions of global capitalism and include the commodification of life in general and education in particular, neoliberal governmentality, a fetish form of performativity, technocentrism, and so forth.

New questions we must raise include the following:

Is there a benign form of capitalism that can guarantee the universality of equality that the liberal parliamentary form of democracy—based on private property rights and a diminishing respect for social and human rights—has failed to bring about?
How do we move beyond the uncritical faith in constitutionalism which masks the control of the state by an increasingly concentrated and powerful ruling class?
Can the omnipresent power of the state be challenged by struggles at the level of civil society?
Are schools or universities the sites where critical consciousness can be agglutinated and transformed into anticapitalist and anti-imperialist social movements?

Many who have been persuaded by developments in poststructualism and postmodern social theory believe that they are operating off ambiguous ground when they pick out such trends and contours and subject them to critique. How can we be sure such critiques do not rest on commitment to values and assumptions associated with discredited positions hanging over from modernity? We often recognize only too well the legitimate points of critique leveled against these positions—among the best-known emerging from adherents of the critical theory tradition of the Frankfurt School.

Signs of disaffection with forms of poststructuralist and postmodern frameworks are beginning to surface, an awareness that we may have thrown out more than just the bathwater when we rejected the possibility of foundations for knowledge and joined the groundswell of incredulity toward metanarratives. It is becoming increasingly important and urgent to reassess the potential of critical theory's having a future as well as a past. For without some kind of critical theory that meets the legitimate charges of postmodern theory, how can we throw ourselves with conviction into broad-based social and political praxis on behalf of ideals, values, and purposes that transcend the merely local and particular?

It is in answer to these challenges that the authors of this book—a group of committed scholars and activists in the larger field of education—have contributed their efforts to produce an exploration of global conflicts and the prospects for critical theories and radical pedagogies as bases for engaging in the practice of critique under contemporary and foreseeable conditions. This book considers carefully and from a range of viewpoints—conceptual and thematic, transnational, cross-cultural, First World through Third World—the potential for a critical theory to revivify itself under neoliberal global conditions, including the emergence of new and old imperialisms, and to provide the basis for a viable future-oriented theory of education.

The book is organized into three parts. Part I addresses some recent educational developments linked to contemporary global conflicts and attempts to answer the following:

- What do the shifting social contexts of education look like from the perspective of a new critical theory standpoint, and how does a concern for education in its wider social context help us generate a new critical theory of education?

This part begins with the contribution of Mike Cole, who analyzes the current British government's proposals with respect to the processes of globalization of capital and presents his perspective of an educational program that contests current limitations of the social and educational programs of New Labour. Sharing a concern for the analysis of globalization, Dave Hill's chapter examines the adequacy of various theories of the state in relation to the restructuring of schooling and initial teacher education (ITE). The third chapter in part I is Henry Giroux's discussion of the politics of resistance and public pedagogy. Michael Peters's contribution proposes the need to develop an agenda for alternative globalizations that includes a focus on the notion of cultural globalization in relation to the university's critical function. In the last chapter, Douglas Kellner develops arguments for analyzing globalization, technological changes, and terrorism for the purpose of developing critical pedagogies adequate to the challenges of the current age.

Part II of this book is devoted to the exploration of critical theories. It is organized around the exploration of

- the possibility of a new critical theory of education—that is, components of a new critical theory that can serve as a theory of education. What might a new critical theory of education look like, and what concepts, priorities, purposes, and so forth might it build on and advocate?

This part begins with David Goldberg's inquiry into the possibilities of "postracial states" and transforming racialized state configurations from the dispositions of homogenizing exclusion and exclusivity to alternative organizational and conceptual state and racial formations. Also concerned with the concept of the "state," Heinz Sünker discusses the "illusions of equality of opportunity" and the need for rethinking the relationships between education and the state. Complementing Goldberg's discussion about the state but using a different perspective, Heinz Sünker from Germany inquiries about the fundamental question "How much does education need the state?" The next two chapters are also written by German scholars: Ludwig Pongratz, who discusses and proposes the work of Theodor W. Adorno and Max Horkheimer as the sociological basis for the development of a critical theory and praxis of education; and Albert Scherr, who discusses social subjectivity and mutual recognition as basic terms in the formulation of a critical theory of education.

Also in part II, Peter Mayo reviews Paulo Freire's later works and introduces the reader to some of the major themes preoccupying the late Brazilian educator and his conceptualizations of radical humanization in neoliberal times. Juha Suoranta, Tuukka Tomperi, and Robert FitzSimmons from Finland explore consumer-media culture within education's new capitalist order. Antonia Darder discusses the need to understand the manner in which the hidden ideology of dominion gives rise to the politics of standardized testing and its very real and present material consequences. Part II closes with the critical feminist perspective of Rhonda Hammer and her exploration of the limitations of the concept of domestic violence in these globalized times of "family terrorism."

The third and final part focuses directly on the question of rethinking critical pedagogy at a time of resurgent global conflicts and imperialistic tensions. It raises the question

- What are some of the key issues of pedagogy as seen from the perspective of a new critical theory standpoint, and how does a concern for pedagogical issues help us develop components of a new critical theory of education?

This part, devoted to radical pedagogies, begins with the contribution of Bernardo Gallegos, who examines the work of postcolonial and performance theorists exploring the political contours of indigenous identities and the authoring of Latina/o histories in classrooms, in academic and popular texts, and in museums. Peter McLaren and Ramin Farahmandpur's chapter addresses the importance of teachers' developing their abilities to engage students in discussions on terrorism and their creating pedagogical spaces inside classrooms in which students can express their concerns about the September 11 tragedy and their fears about the possibility of future attacks. Colin Lankshear and Michele Knobel's chapter explores aspects of Freire's pedagogy in relation to computer-mediated learning activities in a community setting in Australia. Erika Richter discusses the limits and possibilities of developing an "intercultural education" program, and Donna Houston and Laura Pulido present an example of the uses of performative strategies among food service employees in the University of Southern California in their struggle for justice and for a fair work contract in their workplace. Finally, and in closing this book, Gustavo Fischman and Peter McLaren explore the possibilities of hope and social justice in the age of globalization and terror.

I

GLOBAL CONFLICTS

1

New Labour, Globalization, and Social Justice: The Role of Education

Mike Cole

In this chapter, I begin by evaluating claims by influential world leader Tony Blair that globalization can be put in the hands of the many and, if combined with justice, can be a force for good. Referring to national and international data and drawing on Marxist theory, I find reason to reject this vision. I conclude by examining the role of education—actual and potential—in enabling citizens to make informed choices about major international and national processes such as globalization, as well as more national and local ones. I suggest that, currently, much of what goes on in schools in Britain (and elsewhere) amounts to miseducation and that there is an urgent need for education to be critical and emancipatory.

INTRODUCTION

> The next stage for New Labour is not backwards. It is renewing ourselves again. Just after the election, an old colleague of mine said: "Come on, Tony, now we've won again, can't we drop all this New Labour and do what we believe in?" I said: "It's worse than you think. I really do believe in it."
>
> —Tony Blair, speech to the British Labour Party Conference, October 2, 2001[1]

So what does British prime minister Tony Blair "really believe in"? What does this highly significant snippet from his speech to the Labour Party Conference tell us about Tony Blair and the ideology of New Labour? The answer to this question is important on at least two levels. First, following the terrorist attacks on the United States on September 11, 2001, Tony Blair has become second only to George W. Bush as a representative of world capitalist political power. Second, Blair, described by the *Wall Street Journal* as "America's chief foreign ambassador" (Rawnsley 2001, 29), appears to have the ear of the president of the world's only superpower and bastion of capitalist hegemony and may thus influence major U.S. policy decisions.[2]

"Renewing ourselves again," rather than going "backwards," means, for Blair, continuing "the modernization program." Modernization, a key component in Blairite rhetoric, is the conduit through which New Labour justifies ideologically the policy of continuing alignment to the needs of the global market (Cole 1998, 323). Modernization means embracing global neoliberal capitalism.[3] Modernization means a final break with "Old Labour" and an end to any speculation that Blair's second term might see a recommitment to social democratic, let alone Socialist values as New Labour's core guiding ideology.[4] Blair is, in fact, quite open about this break. The problem is not that trade has become too global, but that "there's too little of it" (Blair 2001, 4). His vision for the future is globalization,[5] but with "power, wealth, and opportunity" in "the hands of the many, not the few" (5), a globalization combined with justice; globalization as "a force for good." For Blair, this "commitment to the poor and weak . . . not the contentment of the wealthy and strong" is to be achieved by the vacuous concepts of "the power of community" (4) and "the moral power of a world acting as a community" (5).

I want to argue that globalization with "power, wealth, and opportunity . . . in the hands of the many, not the few" is an oxymoron and that globalization is, in fact, antithetical to social justice.[6]

GLOBALIZATION IN THE HANDS OF THE MANY AND AS A FORCE FOR SOCIAL JUSTICE AND THE COMMON GOOD?

That the "power, wealth, and opportunity" associated with globalization is not currently in the hands of the many, nor operating as a force for social justice and the common good, is self-evident. Let us take the case of the United States, a country implicated by Blair in his speech as a bastion of freedom and equality (2001, 5). During the 1980s the wealthiest 10 percent of U.S. families increased their average family income by 16 percent, the wealthiest 5 percent by 23 percent, and the top 1 percent by 50 percent. At the same time, the bottom 80 percent all lost something, with the poorest 10 percent of U.S. families losing 15 percent of their incomes (George 2000, cited in McLaren and Pinkney-Pastrana 2001, 208). According to the U.S. Census Bureau, the poverty rate rose from 11.3 percent in 2000 to 11.7 percent in 2001, and the number of poor increased by 1.3 million to 32.9 million.

In the United Kingdom, the latest figures show that the most wealthy 1 percent own 23 percent of wealth, while the most wealthy 50 percent own 95 percent (Summerfield and Babb 2004, 89). With respect to income, in Britain, the bottom fifth of people earn less than 10 percent of disposable income and the top fifth more than 40 percent (Summerfield and Babb 2004, 82). More than one in five children in Britain do not have a holiday away from home once a year because their parents cannot afford it (Matheson and Babb 2002, 87).

As far as the "developing world" is concerned, for two decades poverty in Africa and Latin America has increased, both in absolute and relative terms. Nearly half the world's population are living on less than two dollars a day and one-fifth live on just one dollar a day (World Development Movement 2001). The turning over of vast tracts of land to grow one crop for multinationals often results in ecological degradation, with those having to migrate to the towns living in slum conditions and working excessive hours in unstable jobs (Harman 2000). There are about one hundred million abused and hungry "street kids" in the world's major cities; slavery is reemerging; and some two million girls from the age of five to fifteen are drawn into the global prostitution market (Mojab 2001, 118). It was estimated that over twelve million children under five would die from poverty-related illness in 2001 (World Development Movement 2001). Approximately 100 million human beings do not have adequate shelter, and 830 million people are not "food secure"—that is, they're hungry (Mojab 2001, 118). It has been estimated that, if current trends persist, in the whole of Latin America apart from Chile and Colombia, poverty will continue to grow in the next ten years at the rate of two more poor people per minute (Heredia, cited in McLaren 2000, 39).

In fact, the world is becoming polarized into central and peripheral economies, with the gap between rich and poor, between the powerful and the powerless, growing so large that, by the late 1990s, the three hundred largest corporations in the world accounted for 70 percent of foreign direct investment and 25 percent of world capital assets (Bagdikan 1998, cited in McLaren 2000, xxiv). At the start of the twenty-first century, the combined assets of the 225 richest people was roughly equal to the annual incomes of the poorest 47 percent of the world's population (Heintz and Folbre 2000, cited in McLaren and Farahmandpur 2001, 345), and eight companies earned more than what half the world's population earned (World Development Movement 2001).

Today, 125 million children cannot go to school, and 110 million children, young people, and adults have to leave school before they have completely acquired the basic skills of reading and writing. At the same time, the global education market is estimated to be worth more than three thousand billion Euros (National Union of Education 2002, 4).

Blair's stated wish is to change all this; his vision of benign globalization needs to be seen in the light of the events of September 11, 2001. Among other things, these events increased awareness in "the developed world" that "we" cannot just forget about more than half of humanity. In Blair's words: "One illusion has been shattered on September 11: that we can have the good life of the west, irrespective of the state of the world" (*Guardian,* November 13, 2001, 10). So, is his vision of reversing global inequalities within the context of world capitalism a viable one?

First, I would argue that, rather than view "globalization" as a new epoch (the current orthodoxy), the global movement of capital might more accurately be seen as a cumulative process and one that has been going on for a long time—in fact, since capitalism first began four or five centuries ago. Second, one of the central features of capitalism is that, once rooted, it grows and spreads. This double movement is thoroughly explored by Marx in *Capital* and elsewhere (for a summary, see Sweezy 1997). For example, as Marx and Engels put it in *The Communist Manifesto*, when describing the development of capitalism:

> The markets kept ever growing, the demand ever rising. . . . The place of manufacture was taken by the giant, Modern Industry, the place of the industrial middle class, by industrial millionaires. . . . Modern industry has established the world-market. The need of a constantly expanding market for its products chases the bourgeoisie over the whole surface of the globe. It must nestle everywhere, settle everywhere, establish connexions everywhere. . . . In one word, it creates a world after its own image. (Marx and Engels [1868] 1977, 37–39)

Third, this expansion takes three main forms: first, spatially (globalization), as capital occupies all known sociophysical space (including outside the planet)—this is *extension*; second, capital expands as the differentiated form of the commodity, creating new commodities—this is *differentiation*; third, it expands through *intensification* of its own production processes (Rikowski 2001a, 14). Capitalism is thus a thoroughly dynamic system.

Capital is also out of control. As Rikowski has argued,

> Capital moves, but not of its own accord: the mental and physical capabilities of workers (labour-power) enable these movements through their expression in labour. Our labour enables the movements of capital and its transformations (e.g., surplus value into various forms of capital). The social universe of capital then is a universe of constant movement; it incorporates and generates a restlessness unparalleled in human history. . . . It is set on a trajectory, the "trajectory of production" . . . powered not simply by value but by the "constant *expansion* of surplus value." [It is a movement] "independent of human control." . . . It is a movement out of control. (Rikowski 2001a, 10)

Any idea of putting the control of globalized capital into the hands of the many is oxymoronic. Given its rapacious and predatory nature and, in particular, given the advances made since the 1980s neoliberal revolution—a revolution continued under Blair (e.g., Allen et al. 1999; Chitty 1998; Hatcher and Hirtt 1999) and in some ways exacerbated by New Labour (Cole 1999; Hill 1999, 24; 2001a; 2003)—capitalism will not retreat to its pre-1980s position.

My argument is not that capitalism cannot in theory be made more humane, nor that Blair's vision is insincere (this is neither here nor there). The point is that, in the words of Kevin Watkins of Oxfam, "Industrialised countries . . . have collectively reneged on every commitment made" (*Guardian,* November 12, 2001, 22). In fact, organizations such as the World Trade Organization (WTO), the World Bank, and the International Monetary Fund (IMF) are constitutionally destined to fail in any attempt at addressing the marginalization of "the developing world." The WTO can only set maximum standards for global trade, rather than the minimum standards that might restrain big corporations, while the World Bank and the IMF, entirely controlled by the creditor nations, exist to police the poor world's debt on their behalf. Rather than recognize these inherent defects, their backers blame the poor countries themselves. Peter Sutherland, former head of the WTO, has asserted that it is "indisputable that the real problem with the economies that have failed [is] their own domestic governments," while Maria Cattui, who runs the International Chamber of Commerce, insisted that the "fault lies most of all at home with the countries concerned" (Monbiot 2001, 17).

Any possible gain for poor and dispossessed workers in the developing countries and elsewhere as a result of increasing global political awareness after September 11 is likely to be minimalist and short-lived.

CAPITALISM AS NATURAL

For globalization to be seen as having the potential of being "a force for good," then capitalism itself must be a force for good or at least have this potential itself. In fact, not only is capitalism, like globalization, presented as "inevitable," but it is also hailed as natural and indeed coterminous with democracy and freedom. Capitalism presents itself as "determining the future as surely as the laws of nature make tides rise to lift boats" (McMurtry 2001, 2). The fetishization of life makes capitalism seem natural and therefore unalterable and the market mechanism "has been hypostatized into a natural force unresponsive to human wishes" (125).[7] Capitalism is praised "as if it has now replaced the natural environment. It announces itself through its business leaders and politicians as coterminous with freedom, and indispensable to democracy such that any attack on capitalism as exploitative or hypocritical becomes an attack on world freedom and democracy itself" (McLaren 2000, 32).

"Globalization," heralded as a new phenomenon, attempts to nail the lid on the coffin on any possibilities of running the world in any other way. Thus in Blair's (erroneous) vision, we can have a better world but only if globalization is taken as given. In this sense, globalization acts ideologically in that it mystifies what is really going on. The most important task it achieves, in presenting capitalist development as natural, is the reinforcement of the falsehood that nothing can be done. The world is now like this and certain measures have to be taken as a result; and in Blair's case, certain (unspecified) measures can be taken to alter its trajectory.

Whatever the case, any notion of workers' struggle, let alone Socialist revolution, is at the very least old-fashioned and inappropriate. Those who continue to talk about the overthrow of capitalism are seen as dinosaurs.[8] At the same time, the creative energy of the majority of the working class is being channeled away from confrontation with the global trajectories and into safer cultural pursuits. Marxists refer to this phenomenon as the creation of false consciousness.[9]

Thatcherism and Reaganomics were crucial not only in laying the foundations for the neoliberal revolution but, in Thatcher's case in particular, in discrediting Socialism. The collapse of the Soviet Union is used to back up the claim that Socialism is no longer viable.[10] Congruent with her success in championing the free market as the only viable way to run economies was the apparent success with which Margaret Thatcher seemed to wipe Socialism off the agenda of political change in Britain—essential if Britain were to move in the direction of labor market compliance and labor flexibility. Following the late 1980s revolutions in eastern Europe and the Soviet Union, Marxism, Thatcher argued, was now extinct. Therefore the Labour Party was also now extinct. It is precisely the success of this formulation which projected Tony Blair, a free marketeer, to center stage—a savior of the Labour Party—but only if the Labour Party became reformulated as "New Labour."[11]

"New Labour" was coined as part of an orchestrated campaign to distance the party from its Socialist roots, to modernize it—in other words, to establish an unequivocal procapitalist base for itself. For Blair, the "founding principle of New Labour" is "the partnership we have tried to build with [business] . . . and it will not change" (*Guardian*, November 6, 2001, 2). This underlines the crucial importance, for Blair, described and reported in Britain's most popular tabloid by Margaret Thatcher as "probably the most formidable Labour leader since Hugh Gaitskill" (*Sun,* July 21, 1995), of abandoning the anticapitalist clause IV from the party constitution.[12] In the same year, in Hayman Island, Australia, Tony Blair declared to Rupert Murdoch and the world that "the era of the grand ideologies, all encompassing, all pervasive, total in their solutions—and often dangerous—is over" (1995, 12).[13]

AN ALTERNATIVE VISION: THE CASE FOR SOCIALISM

In stark contrast to Blair's vision, Meiksins Wood (1995) has argued that

> the lesson that we may be obliged to draw from our current economic and political condition is that a humane, "social," truly democratic and equitable capitalism is more unrealistically utopian than socialism. (293)

Increased awareness of the plight of the majority of humanity in the aftermath of the events of September 11 provides some degree of space to argue for the alternative vision of Socialism as opposed to benign capitalism. For the Left, it is the Eastern European dictatorships that claimed to be Socialist that have been discredited rather than Socialism itself. As Callinicos has argued, Marxists must break through the bizarre ideological mechanism, in which every conceivable alternative to the market is seen as not viable because of the collapse of Stalinism (2000, 122).

Capitalism is, in reality, a messy business. Things rarely run smoothly. Indeed, the trajectory of capital's social universe forces it to continually crash against the limits of its own constitution and existence. However, this destructive movement rests entirely on workers' capacity to labor, their labor power. Hence, wherever capital is, so is labor, "aiding, abetting and nurturing its development . . . holding its hand as it bites us" (Rikowski 2001a, 11). Capital cannot become "not capital." It cannot become humanized in the way envisioned by Blair. "However, labour can become labour . . . unlocked from its value-form" (11). The only decent future for the working class is a Socialist one. "This is future *with* a future, a future that is possible for us on the basis of the implosion of capital's social universe" (11).

According to Marx's labor theory of value, the interests of capitalists and workers are diametrically opposed, since a benefit to the former (profits) is a cost to the latter (Hickey 2002, 168). Marx argued that workers' labor is embodied in goods that they produce. The finished products are appropriated (taken away) by the capitalists and eventually sold at a profit. However, workers are paid only a fraction of the value they create in productive labor; the wages do not represent the total value they create. We appear to be paid for every single second we work. However, underneath this appearance, the working day (as under serfdom) is split into two parts: first, into socially necessary labor (and the wage represents this); and, second, into surplus labor, which is not reflected in the wage. This is the basis of surplus value, out of which comes the capitalist's profit. While the value of the raw materials and of the depreciating machinery is simply passed on to the commodity in production, labor power is a peculiar, indeed unique commodity, in that it creates new value. "The magical quality of labour-power's . . . value for . . . capital is therefore critical" (Rikowski 2001d, 11). "Labour-power creates more value (profit) in its consumption than it possesses itself, and than it costs" (Marx [1894] 1966, 351). Unlike, for example, the value of a given commodity, which can only be realized in the market as itself, labor creates a new value, a value greater than itself, a value that previously did not exist. It is for this reason that labor power is so important for the capitalist in the quest for capital accumulation. It is in the interest of the capitalist or capitalists (nowadays, capitalists may, of course, consist of a number of shareholders, for example, rather than outright owners of businesses) to maximize profits, and this entails (to create the greatest amount of new value) keeping workers' wages as low as are "acceptable" in any given country or historical period without provoking effective strikes or other forms of resistance. Therefore, the capitalist mode of production is, in essence, a system of exploitation of one class (the working class) by another (the capitalist class).

Whereas class conflict is endemic to, and ineradicable and perpetual within, the capitalist system, it does not always or even typically take the form of open conflict or expressed hostility (Hickey 2002, 168). Revolution can only come about when the working class, in addition to being a "class in itself" (an objective fact because of the shared exploitation inherent as a result of the labor theory of value) becomes a "class for itself" (Marx 1976). By this, Marx meant a class with a subjective awareness of its social class position, that is, a class with "class consciousness"—including awareness of its exploitation and its transcendence of "false consciousness."

Capitalism is prone to cyclical instability and is subject to periodic political and economic crises. At these moments, the possibility exists for Socialist revolution. Marx argued that, if the working class has become a "class for itself," it has the potential to seize control of the means of production and the economy and take political power. Seizure of the economy would constitute such a Socialist revolution (Hill and Cole 2001b, 147).[14]

For Marx, Socialism (a stage before Communism—that form of existence when the state would wither away and we would live communally) was a world system in which "we shall have an association, in which the free development of each is the condition for the free development of all" (Marx and Engels [1868] 1977, 53). Such a society would be democratic (as such, Socialism as envisaged by Marx should be distanced from the undemocratic regimes of the former Soviet bloc)[15] and classless, and the means of production would be in the hands of the many, not the few. Goods and services would be produced for need and not for profit. This is in stark contrast to the capitalist "utopia" envisaged by Blair.

Given the huge benefits that accrue to capitalists in the process of global capital accumulation, any movements that are seen as challenging or even resistant to capitalism are met with intense state brutality, as witnessed by the reactions to the recent and ongoing anticapitalist protests (e.g., Rikowski 2001d; Vidal and Munk 2003). This however is not the reason mass movements for social change cannot be successful. As Callinicos puts it, despite the inevitable intense resistance from capital, the "greatest obstacle to change is not . . . the revolt it would evoke from the privileged, but the belief that it is impossible" (2000, 128). Education plays a major role in the process of fostering this ideology of impossibility; of keeping off the agenda any alternative vision of how societies might be run.

EDUCATION FOR COMPLIANCE OR EDUCATION FOR TRANSFORMATION

The tyranny of capitalism is masked by massive ideological apparatuses. Louis Althusser argued that in the current era, the educational ideological state apparatus is the most important apparatus of the state for transmitting capitalist ideology (1971).

As argued earlier, for it to function effectively and to protect its interests, capitalism needs to prevent the working class from becoming a "class in itself." This is a twofold process. First, a concept of the world is fostered in which capitalism is seen as natural and inevitable; second, "false consciousness" is nurtured, whereby consciousness is channeled into nonthreatening avenues (e.g., commercial ones; see Cole 2004b).

It is important for capitalism that the education system does not hinder this process. Indeed the current ideological requirements of capitalism are that the education system play an active role both in facilitating the growth of consumerism (a material as well as an ideological benefit for capitalists) and in naturalizing capitalism itself. This takes the form of bringing business into schools and in using schools to promote business values. This process has accelerated greatly under New Labour (Allen et al. 1999; Cole 2000; Hill 2001a, 2001b; Rikowski 2001c, 2003).[16]

In schools and colleges throughout Britain, people are being miseducated. However, the educational ideological state apparatus is neither total nor all-encompassing. While recognizing the limitations to the power of schools and teachers, I do consider that teachers have a valid role to play in challenging dominant inequalities and in raising consciousness in the quest for a more egalitarian economic, social, and educational system. Socialist teachers in Britain have consistently and constantly challenged and continue to challenge the "business-sification" of education and education for compliance. This takes the form of organized resistance from activists within the teacher unions, campaigning groups such as the Socialist Teachers Alliance and the Promoting Comprehensive Education Network. In addition, teachers in groups and individually are creating and opening up space within the national curriculum and the hidden curriculum to challenge education for compliance (Cole, Hill, and Shan 1997; Cole et al. 2001; Hill and Cole 1999b).[17] Since these remain marginal and relatively isolated pockets of resistance, what follows is meant to provide suggestions of how Socialist teachers might open further spaces of resistance in the current climate. It is not suggested, of course, that they could become generalized at the current conjuncture to the education system in Britain as a whole.

To move forward, it is sometimes useful to look to the past. There have been situations or even eras in the past from which we can learn as we plan for the future.[18] I would therefore like to address the popular educational traditions of 1790 to 1848, a time when at least sections of the working class were engaged in more radical (educational) pursuits than the aforementioned cultural ones.[19]

Drawing on four aspects of popular "radical education," identified by Richard Johnson—namely, *a critique of the existing system, alternative educational goals, education to change the world,* and *education for all*—and in the light of a dearth of popular radical Left thinking in Britain today, I argue that each of these have considerable relevance today. I will deal with each in turn and indicate how they might inform those who are agitating for a radical education for the twenty-first century.[20]

Critique of the Existing System

First, radicals conducted a running critique of all forms of "provided" education, which, in later phases of the period, involved a practical grasp and a theoretical understanding of cultural and ideological struggle in a more general sense

(Johnson 1979, 76). Schools and other educational institutions could be, and sometimes have been and are, centers of critical debate, involving the local trade unions, teaching and nonteaching staff, parents, and pupils/students (relative to age). Discussion fora could include the extent to which the community benefits from some New Labour measures that are clearly in the social democratic tradition, such as redistributive policy and financing through the agencies of the local and national state, on the one hand, and the effects of the continuation and extension of Conservative policy—in particular, burgeoning privatization—on the other (e.g., Allen et al. 1999; Cole 1998; Rikowski 2001d, 2003).

Questions about cultural and ideological struggle would arise naturally from such discussions. Such questions might include, for example, To what extent is the social democratic program meeting the needs of the population as a whole? To what extent is it meeting local needs? What are the effects of the privatization program? What are the reasons for the imposition of performance-related pay? What is the nature of the private finance initiative? What are the effects of league tables? At the center of the government's proposals for "autonomy" and "diversity" (Department for Education and Skills 2003) is the pursuance of privatization, a scenario opposed by 83 percent of the British public (according to a September 2001 public attitude survey by the National Opinion Polls) and a further attack on the principle of inclusive comprehensive education. What effect will this have on education communities? To what extent are Blair's references to globalization, modernization, and renewal ideological—to what extent do they occlude more than reveal? (See Cole 1998 for a discussion.)

Alternative Educational Goals: Really Useful Knowledge

Second, radicals were involved in the development of alternative educational goals: this entailed notions of how educational utopias could actually be achieved and a definition of "really useful knowledge," incorporating a radical content—a sense of what it was really important to know (Johnson 1979, 76). What knowledge is "really useful" in the promotion of equality? The school curriculum has for too long been structured to exclude, repress, and prevent the addressing of certain issues (Carrington and Troyna 1988, 208; Cole 1997, 68–69; Young 1984, 236). It is time to open it up. It is time to liberate the mind (Cole 2000).

Before the ascendancy of the radical Right in the 1980s, the dominant educational paradigm, the liberal progressive one, determined what happened in many, although not all, British primary schools and in some secondary schools (for a discussion and a historical contextualization, see Hill 2001b).

Debbie Epstein (1993) has offered a trenchant critique of what liberal progressivism often meant in practice (see also, Brehony 1992; Sarup 1983), in the context of the real critical potential of primary age children. The Plowden Report's (Plowden 1967) conceptualization of children as individuals rather than as members of groups (and the fact that social groups tended to be pathologized when they were mentioned) made it difficult to raise issues of power relations in primary schools. In addition, Plowden's deficit model of working-class children meant that efforts to promote equal opportunity focused on re-pairing the deficiencies of individual children rather than concentrating on structures and curriculum (Epstein 1993, 92).

The Plowden report contains two contradictory views about the relationship between children and society. Society is treated both as something from which children must be protected, and as an entity they will enter at some future date, and for which they therefore need to be molded. It is worth quoting Epstein (1993) at length:

> Both these views were aspects of Plowden discourse which diminished the likeli-hood that primary teachers working within their framework would try to consider and challenge social inequalities with the children they teach—for if the school is regarded as a safe haven from the ills of society, why allow disruptive ideas about inequality to enter the classroom? Furthermore, while "preparing" children to take their place in society (at some specified future date) might involve some ideas of liberal tolerance . . . it also carries the implicit assumption that the "nature" of soci-ety is fixed and that we can predict what kind of society children should be pre-pared for. Again, there is no compelling logic which says that predictions about a future society will not involve recognition of a need to combat inequalities but the notion does preclude the idea that children should be involved, in the here and now, in deconstruction of dominant ideologies. (92–93)

In place of the Plowden learning-process set of perspectives, Debbie Epstein advocates a cooperative, democratic learning process but in the mode of critical reflection, rather than Plowdenesque liberalism (see also Giroux 1988; Hill 1991, 1994, 1997). Judy Dunn has shown that children are aware of the feelings of oth-ers as early as their second year of life and can therefore "decenter" and are thus amenable to understanding issues of equality. As their understanding increases, they become more independent in their handling of concepts (Epstein 1993, 104). The implications for the possibilities for education to challenge all inequalities at a very early age are obvious. In Epstein's words, "It is essential to view every school as a site of struggle, where the negotiations taking place can either strengthen or weaken possibilities for developing education for equality" (Epstein 1993, 57).

Elsewhere (Cole, Hill, and Shan 1997; Hill and Cole 1999b), we and our co-authors have provided detailed practical advice on education for equality, with respect to issues of social class; "race," gender, sexuality, and disability, for each subject in the English and Welsh national curriculum from age five to sixteen. In the longer term, a new education act is required. From an early age, children have the right to know what it is really going on in the world.

Education to Change the World

Third, radicalism incorporated an important internal debate about education as a political strategy or as a means of changing the world (Johnson 1979, 76).

The pre-Thatcherite debates about whether education is political have not surprisingly subsided. As detailed in Hill (2001a), for example, not only is education in Britain political (lowercase *p*), it is also quite clearly Political (capital *P*). Hatcher (1995) argues that three developments can help in this context of popular self-activity. First, information technology can allow the pupil much greater choice and undermine the role of the teacher as gatekeeper of knowledge and at the same time enhance the latter's role as facilitator of the learning process. Second, there must be an increase in the rights of pupils. Effective citizenship in a democracy must begin at school. Although welcome, the extent to which the new citizenship component in the national curriculum will promote equality is open to question. Third, the school's isolation must be challenged. We must take seriously the concept of a "learning society" and open up all aspects of social, business, and industrial life to educational enquiry (1995, 3–4; this makes an interesting counterpoint to the opening up of schools to business and industry, including business *values*—see Allen et al. 1999; Rikowski 2001c, 2003). The combination of these three developments, Hatcher concludes, can place the classroom and the school at the center of a complex learning network and help create a new popular culture about education (Hatcher 1995, 4).

Essential to a new popular education is the replacement of the attempted inculcation of "facts" to be learned and tested, with a genuine dialogic education. Such a dialogic process needs to be differentiated from the postmodernist notion of multiple voices where "anything goes" (e.g., Lather 1991, 1998; for a critique, see Cole and Hill 2002).[21] Rather, dialogic education is empowerment education. It is pupil/student-centered but not permissive or self-centered. Like all education, dialogic education is not neutral, but aims to incorporate counterhegemonic themes into the classroom.

This is not to say that schools should replace capitalist propaganda with Socialist propaganda, rather that pupils be provided with alternative interpretations of why and how things happen and be constantly urged to ask whose history and literature is conventionally taught in schools and whose is left out, from whose point of view is the past and present examined? Empowerment education invites pupils and students to become thinking citizens but also to be change agents and social critics (Shor 1992, 15–16). Essential to dialogic education is critical thinking, but critical thinking needs imagination, where pupils/students and teachers practice anticipating a new social reality. Paulo Freire describes a conversation with a revolutionary in Bissau, in which she (the revolutionary) recounts a meeting with Amilcar Cabral. After an hour's discussion, evaluating the ongoing liberation movement, Cabral closed his eyes and talked for thirty or forty minutes of his dream of what life should be like in Guinea-Bissau after independence. When challenged by another revolutionary that this was a dream, Cabral opened his eyes, looked at the woman, smiled, and said, "Yes, it is a dream, a possible dream. . . . How poor is the revolution that doesn't dream" (Freire and Shor 1987, 186–87). Summing up the role of the radical Left educator, engaged in a pedagogy of liberation to change the world, Freire and Shor conclude:

This is imagination. This is the possibility to go beyond tomorrow without being naively idealistic. This is Utopianism as a dialectical relationship between denouncing the present and announcing the future. To anticipate tomorrow by dreaming today. The question is as Cabral said, Is the dream a possible one or not? If it is less possible, the question for us is how to make it more possible. (187)

Education for All

Finally, radical movements developed a vigorous and varied educational practice, which was concerned with informing mature understandings and on the education of all citizens as members of a more just social order. In this conception, no large distinction was made between the education of "children" and "adults" (in contrast to middle-class conceptions of childhood) (Johnson 1979, 77). As I have suggested, as a longer-term strategy, a new education act is required. I will outline here what I consider to be some major policy issues, inherent in such an act (cf. Cole 1992; for an extended analysis, see the Hillcole Group 1991, 1997).

Its main aims would be to provide a public education and training service, serving all citizens throughout their lives, to promote a democratically controlled and accountable education service at all levels and to apply the principles of equality and nondiscrimination to all parts of the service. To ensure equality a national unit should be established, with power to require reports of local monitoring in specific areas of practice, intake, provision, achievement, take-up, and outcome.

Section 28 of the Local Government Act of 1988, which discriminated against gays and lesbians, has now been repealed. It should be replaced by a requirement making it unlawful in the provision of education or training for any groups or individuals to be discriminated against by virtue of age; "race"; gender; lesbian, gay, bisexual, or transgendered (LGBT) orientation; social class; or disability.[22]

Parents and careers should have the right to have their children admitted to named local care and education facilities, starting with the age range three months to five years. School should continue to be compulsory from age five to sixteen, but there should be a major reorganization, based on the principle of excellent comprehensive schooling for all. As part of this reorganization, schools outside the state system should be brought back into a fully comprehensive state system. Charitable status should be removed from private schools.

As far as the curriculum for ages five through sixteen is concerned, this should have the core elements of English, mathematics, science, and physical education, but with the emphasis on critical reflection discussed earlier. Other subjects should be the subject of popular negotiation, with schools encouraged to integrate such subjects as geography and history, for example, and to synthesize them with the insights provided by such subjects such as sociology and politics. The reintroduction of media studies would provide a stimulating and exciting way for pupils and students to begin to critically understand the complexities of a vastly changing world.

Education for the twenty-first century should end the false distinction between education and work. Adults should be able to enter education or training at any time of life with the consent of their employers. It is time to move education away from the current destructive preoccupation with institutions as competitive private businesses divorced from localities and encourage them to serve their own as well as the wider national and global communities as positive agents of development (cf. Cole 1992).

CONCLUSION

Education should not exist for the glorification of capital, of consumption, of commodification. Teachers at all levels of the education system need to foster critical reflection. This is not an easy task. The iron fist of repression is ever-present in the velvet glove embrace of the ideological state apparatuses (Hill 2001c; see chapter 2, p. 23, Hill's "State Theory and the Neoliberal Reconstruction of Schooling and Teacher Education"). But the system needs to be challenged. Such transformative action needs to be linked with a grammar of resistance (Cole 2004b), to link with and articulate life outside the classroom.

With McLaren, I conclude the necessity to "transform schools into sites for social justice" (2000, 18) in which teachers, other school workers and pupils/students not only agitate for changes within the classroom and within the institutional context of the school but also support a transformation in the objective conditions in which students and their parents labor. A revolutionary pedagogy entails the struggle for macroeconomic policies favoring full employment and guaranteed support in the public sector for state schools, global labor rights, sustainable development, environmental protections, and the growth of movements for social and economic change (199). In other words, just as in the struggles of the period from 1790 to 1848, we must reclaim our education.

If this all sounds implausibly idealistic, it might be worth considering again which is the more utopian: the continued survival of anarchic and destructive and antidemocratic world capitalism; or a democratic world, planned for need and not profit (Meiksins Wood 1995; Kelly, Cole, and Hill 1999). The point is that "capital can never win, totally once and for all. It must [as we have seen] tolerate the continued existence of an alien subjectivity [the working class] which constantly threatens to destroy it" (Cleaver, cited in Rikowski 2001d, 8).

Whatever the twenty-first century has to offer, the choices will need to be debated:

> Each person and group should experience education as contributing to their own self-advancement, but at the same time our education should ensure that at least part of everyone's life activity is also designed to assist in securing the future of the planet we inherit. . . . Democracy is not possible unless there is a free debate about all the alternatives for running our social and economic system. . . . All societies will be struggling with the same issues in the 21st century. We can prepare by being bet-

ter armed with war machinery or more competitive international monopolies. . . . Or we can wipe out poverty . . . altogether. We can decide to approach the future by consciously putting our investment into a massive drive to encourage participation from everyone at every stage in life through training and education that will increase productive, social, cultural and environmental development in ways we have not yet begun to contemplate. (Hillcole 1997, 94–95)

As Callinicos has argued, challenging the current climate requires courage, imagination and will power inspired by the injustice that surrounds us. However, "beneath the surface of our supposedly contented societies, these qualities are present in abundance. Once mobilized, they can turn the world upside down" (2000, 129). It is the role of educators to foster critical reflection; to facilitate this process.

NOTES

I would like to thank Paula Allman and Gustavo Fischman for their comments on earlier drafts of this chapter and Dave Hill for his comments on a more recent draft. As always, of course, any inadequacies remain mine.

1. This is cited in the British broadsheet *Guardian*, October 3, 2001, 5. All future references to this speech refer to this edition. Blair's commitment to the New Labour program has been repeated since then on a number of occasions.
2. The occupation of Iraq is one obvious example of the Bush and Blair "double act." While this chapter deals primarily with economic issues, Naomi Klein (2003) has reminded us of the close connection between the brutal economic policies of the World Trade Organization (WTO; see note 3) and military conquest, the former itself engaged in a form of warfare against the poor and dispossessed (for a Marxist analysis of current U.S. imperialism, see Cole 2004a, 2005).
3. With its ideas embodied in the policies of the main international agencies such as the IMF, the World Bank, and the WTO, neoliberalism's thrust is to free itself from interference from nation states. In essence, it encompasses mass privatization of state-owned industries and services; reducing taxation on corporate profits and high personal incomes; an end to controls of the transfer of finances across frontiers; and the abolition of attempts to control imports (Harman 2000, 6). The adoption of neoliberalism is sweeping the globe, driven by capitalist imperatives and only minimally affected by national specificities, and, as has been argued, the changes represent only the beginning, not the end (e.g., Hatcher and Hirtt 1999, 21–2).
4. Traditionally, the British Labour Party has stood for social democratic policies. However, originally it was a socialist party, epitomized by the now-abandoned clause 4, which committed the party to democratic socialism (see below). Blair (and others) have adopted the term *New Labour* to distance the party finally from these socialist origins and significantly from the social democratic ones. This is not to say that there are no social democratic policies within New Labour's overall commitment to neoliberal global capitalism (for an analysis, see Hill 1999). For example, the New Labour government has introduced a national minimum wage and a working families tax credit. In addition, its stated intent is to abolish child poverty by 2020.
5. "Globalization" became one of the orthodoxies of the 1990s and continues to hold sway into the twenty-first century. It is proclaimed in the speeches of virtually all mainstream politicians, in the financial pages of newspapers and in company reports; it is common currency in corporation newsletters and shop stewards meetings (Harman 1996, 3). Its premises are that in the face of global competition, capitals are increasingly constrained to compete on the world market. Its argument is

that, in this new epoch, these capitals can only do this in so far as they become multinational corporations and operate on a world scale, outside the confines of nation states. This diminishes the role of the nation-state, the implication being that there is little, if anything, that can be done about it. The extent to which globalization is a new epoch is open to question. Meiksins Wood (1998, 47), for example, argues that what we are seeing is not a major shift in capitalism, but capitalism reaching maturity (see also Cole 1998). In addition, the degree to which it has transcended the nation state is debatable (e.g., Harman 1996; Cole 1998), Marxists are particularly interested in the way it is used ideologically to further the interests of capitalists and their political supporters (for an analysis, see Cole 1998), of the way in which it is used to mystify the populace as a whole and to stifle action by the left in particular (e.g., Murphy 1995; Gibson-Graham 1996; Harman 1996; Meiksins Wood 1997). Capitalists and their allies argue that, since globalization is a fact of life, it is incumbent on workers, given this globalized market, to be flexible in their approach to what they do and for how long they do it, to accept lower wages, and to concur with the restructuring and diminution of welfare states. The adoption of neoliberalism has given a major boost to globalization, both de facto and ideologically.

6. Within the rhetoric of "power, wealth, and opportunity," "in the hands of the many," of "social justice," there are, of course, progressive elements (see note 4). Moreover, such rhetoric does provide space for intervention by Left thinkers and Left-leaning campaigning organizations (Avis 1998, 262). While the longer-term solution, for socialists, is a new economic order, all socialists support reforms that benefit working people.

7. Ironically, the capitalist class and their representatives who used to deride what they saw as the metaphysic of "Marxist economic determinism" are the ones who now champion the "world-wide market revolution" and the accompanying inevitability of "economic restructuring" (McMurtry 2000).

8. This is not, of course, the case with Islamic fundamentalism, which is currently perceived as a real threat, at least to Western capitalism.

9. Current manifestations of false consciousness are signified by the diversion of the creative energy of the working class into pubs/alcohol and drugs, clubs, pop music, chat shows, football, soaps, play stations, and videos (Cole, 2004b). Significantly, ITV, the commercial terrestrial channel aimed specifically at Britain's working class, concerned about the general decline in news audiences, want the news to concentrate more on "leisure, consumer and show-business news" (Wells 2001, 1). At the same time, that technological supremo of our age, the Internet, which has enormous potential of playing a role in working-class liberation and can be used and, in many cases, is being used in progressive ways has enabled a further detour. Rather than being used as a source of liberatory knowledge, often it is being used in a further quest for trivia ("chat rooms" and "trainers"). On a much more sinister note, the Internet is being increasingly used as a site of oppression. Examples of this latter role are the numerous "race hate" websites and, in the case primarily of men, increasingly violent pornography (Amis 2001).

10. This was starkly reiterated by foreign secretary Jack Straw in an article titled "Globalisation Is Good for Us": "Since the collapse of the Soviet bloc, there is no longer a coherent ideology on offer" (*Guardian,* September 10, 2001). It is worth recalling that we were told by the spokespersons for capitalism (Margaret Thatcher and Ronald Reagan among them) that this collapse would bring freedom and democracy. If it has, it has also brought homelessness, unemployment, gangsterism, drugs, and child pornography. The following analysis is based on Cole (1998, 324).

11. At a speech to the Confederation of British Industry, the organization representing Britain's bosses, Blair twice paid tribute to the previous Tory government which had introduced "fundamental labour reforms" to give Britain "the most flexible labour market in Europe" (*Guardian,* November 6, 2001, 2).

12. In 1959, Hugh Gaitskill had attempted to abolish clause 4.

13. What Blair meant was that the grand ideology of socialism is over, but not the grand ideology of capitalism. He repeated this belief in his aforementioned speech to the (British) Labour Party Conference, on October 2, 2001, when, in reaffirming his belief in meritocracy, he declared that "ideology . . . in the sense of rigid forms of economic and social theory . . . is dead" (*Guardian,* October 3, 2001, 5).

14. Birchall addresses himself to the standard procapitalist argument that all revolutions lead to tyranny. As he points out, there have actually been only a few major revolutions in modern history, far too few to deduce any absolute principles from. "No self-respecting scientist would base a scientific law on so few experiments." As he puts it, "I can spin a coin and get 'tails' five times in a row—but that scarcely proves all coins will come down tails." Analyzing the French and Russian revolutions and the Spanish Civil War, Birchall concludes that if any general lesson can be drawn, it is not that revolution leads to tyranny but rather that failure to complete a revolution opens the way to tyranny (2000, 22).

15. It is ironic that the countries of the former Soviet bloc were termed *Communist* by the West. In reality (despite the fact that many had a number of positive features—full employment, housing for all, free public and social services, and so on) they were undemocratic dictatorships with special privileges for the elite and drudgery for the many. These Eastern European societies were far removed from Marx's vision of "the higher phase of communist society" (which would come after the temporary phase of Socialism). In Communist society, "labour is no longer merely a means of life but has become life's principal need. . . . All the springs of co-operative wealth flow more abundantly . . . [and the guiding principle is] from each according to his ability, to each according to his needs" (Marx 1875, *Critique of the Gotha Programme,* cited in Bottomore and Rubel 1978, 263). In a Communist world, the "original goodness" of humanity is realized, and "the private interest of each" coincides "with the general interest of humanity" (Marx 1845, *The Holy Family,* cited in Bottomore and Rubel 1978, 249).

16. In a speech embracing "inevitable globalization" in 2002, British chancellor Gordon Brown stated that teaching the "entrepreneurial culture" should start in schools (*Guardian,* March 29, 2002).

17. Since 1988, England and Wales has had a prescribed core national curriculum for students ages five to sixteen (this has been modified by successive New Labour legislation). The hidden curriculum refers to everything that goes on in educational institutions outside of this formal curriculum.

18. Marx and Engels, for example attempted to learn from the experiences of the Paris Commune of 1871 in their preface to the German edition (1872) of the *Manifesto of the Communist Party.* The *Manifesto of the Communist Party* is a seminal text that sets out the central tenets of Marxism and concludes with a program for action (Marx and Engels 1977, 31–32).

19. The following analysis draws on Cole (2000) and is summarized in Cole (2001).

20. Johnson points out that the traditions of this period (just like the aforementioned pockets of resistance in contemporary Britain) were springs of action unconnected to state provision. He also acknowledges (again as in contemporary Britain) that "we cannot assume that the attitudes of radical leaders and writers were those of 'the workers'" (1979, 75).

21. For an excellent Marxist critique of postmodernism, see Callinicos (1989). For Marxist critiques of postmodernism in educational theory, see Hill and colleagues (2002); see also Cole (2003).

22. For a discussion of education and equality and equal opportunity issues through history and in the present, see Cole (2005). For a discussion of these issues in relation to facts, concepts, and policy, see Hill and Cole (2001a).

REFERENCES

Allen, Martin, Caroline Benn, Clyde Chitty, Mike Cole, Richard Hatcher, Nico Hirtt, and Glenn Rikowski. 1999. *Business, business, business: New Labour's education policy.* London: Tufnell Press.

Althusser, Louis. 1971. *Lenin and philosophy and other essays.* London: New Left Books.

Amis, Martin. 2001. A rough trade. *Guardian Weekend,* March 17.

Avis, James. 1998. (Im)possible dream: Post-Fordism, stakeholding and post-compulsory education. *Journal of Education Policy* 13 (2): 251–63.

Birchall, Ian. 2000. "Revolution? You must be crazy!" *Socialist Review*, no. 247 (December): 20–22.

Blair, Tony. 1995. Speech at NewsCorp Leadership Conference, Hayman Island, Australia, July 7.

———. 2001. Quoted in the *Guardian*, October 3.

Bottomore, Tom, and Maximilien Rubel. 1978. *Karl Marx: Selected writings in sociology and social philosophy*. Harmondsworth, Engl.: Pelican Books.

Brehony, Kevin. 1992. What's left of progressive primary education? In *Rethinking radical education: Essays in honour of Brian Simon,* ed. Ali Rattansi and David Reeder, 196–221. London: Lawrence and Wishart.

Callinicos, Alex. 1989. *Against postmodernism: A Marxist critique*. Cambridge, Engl.: Polity Press.

———. 2000. *Equality*. Oxford: Polity Press.

Carrington, Bruce, and Barry Troyna. 1988. Combating racism through political education. In *Children and controversial issues: Strategies for the early and middle years of schooling,* ed. Bruce Carrington and Barry Troyna, 204–22. Lewes, Engl.: Falmer Press.

Chitty, Clyde. 1998. Education action zones: Test-beds for privatisation? *Forum* 40 (3): 79–81.

Cole, Mike. 1992. Winding up the studies business. *Education Guardian* 18 (February): 21.

———. 1997. Equality and primary education: What are the conceptual issues? In *Promoting Equality in Primary Schools,* ed. Mike Cole, Dave Hill, and Sharanjeet Shan, 48–75. London: Cassell.

———. 1998. Globalisation, modernisation and competitiveness: A critique of the New Labour project in education. *International Studies in Sociology of Education* 8 (3): 315–32.

———. 1999. Globalization, modernization and New Labour. In *Business, business, business: New Labour's education policy,* ed. Martin Allen et al., 4–11. London: Tufnell Press.

———. 2000. Time to liberate the mind: Primary schools in the new century. *Primary Teaching Studies* 2 (11): 4–9.

———. 2001. Conclusion. In *Schooling and equality: Fact, concept and policy,* ed. Dave Hill and Mike Cole, 265–70. London: Kogan Page.

———. 2003. Might it be in the practice that it fails to succeed? A Marxist critique of claims for postmodernism and poststructuralism as forces for social change and social justice. *British Journal of Sociology of Education,* 24 (4): 487–500.

———, ed. 2005. *Education, equality and human rights: Issues of gender, "race," sexuality, special needs and social class*. London: Routledge/Falmer.

———. 2004b. Rethinking the future; the commodification of knowledge and the grammar of resistance. In *For Caroline Benn: Essays in education and democracy,* ed. Melissa Benn and Clyde Chitty. London: Continuum

Cole, Mike, and Dave Hill. 2002. "Resistance postmodernism"—progressive politics or radical left posturing. In *Marxism against postmodernism in educational theory,* ed. Dave Hill, Peter McLaren, Mike Cole, and Glenn Rikowski. Lanham, Md.: Lexington Books.

Cole, Mike, Dave Hill, Peter McLaren, and Glenn Rikowski. 2001. *Red chalk: On schooling, capitalism and politics*. Brighton, Engl.: Institute for Education Policy Studies.

Cole, Mike, Dave Hill, and Sharanjeet Shan, eds. 1997. *Promoting equality in primary schools*. London: Cassell.

Department for Education and Skills. 2003. *Diversity in secondary education*. London: Stationery Office.

Epstein, Debbie. 1993. *Changing classroom cultures: Anti-racism, politics and schools*. Stoke on Trent, Engl.: Trentham Books.

Freire, Paulo, and Ira Shor. 1987. *A pedagogy for liberation: Dialogues on transforming education*. Basingstoke, Engl.: Macmillan.

Gibson-Graham, J. K. 1996. Querying globalization. *Rethinking Marxism* 9 (Spring): 1–27.

Giroux, Henry. 1988. *Schooling and the struggle for public life: Critical pedagogy in the modern age*. Minneapolis: University of Minnesota Press.

Harman, Chris. 1996. Globalization: A critique of a new orthodoxy. *International Socialism,* 73: 3–33.

———. 2000. Anti-capitalism: Theory and practice. *International Socialism* 88: 3–59.

Hatcher, Richard. 1995. Popular self-activity and state provision: The strategic debate in education. *Socialist Teacher* 23: 4.

Hatcher, Richard, and Nico Hirtt. 1999. The business agenda behind Labour's education policy. In *Business, business, business: New Labour's education policy,* ed. Martin Allen et al., 12–23. London: Tufnell Press.

Hickey, Tom. 2002. Class and class analysis for the twenty-first century. In *Education, equality and human rights,* ed. Mike Cole, 162–81. London: Routledge/Falmer.

Hill, Dave. 1991. Seven ideological perspectives on teacher education today and the development of a radical left discourse. *Australian Journal of Teacher Education* 16 (2): 5–19.

———. 1994. Initial teacher education and cultural diversity. In *Cross-curricular contexts, themes and dimensions in primary schools,* ed. Gajendra Verma and Peter Pumfrey, 218–41. Vol. 4 of *Cultural diversity and the curriculum.* London: Falmer Press.

———. 1997. Equality in primary schooling: The policy context, intentions and effects of the conservative "reforms." In *Promoting equality in primary schools,* ed. Mike Cole, Dave Hill, Sharanjeet Shan, 15–47. London: Cassell.

———. 1999. *New Labour and education: Policy, ideology and the third way.* London: Tufnell Press.

———. 2001a. Equality, ideology and education policy. In *Schooling and equality: Fact, concept and policy,* ed. Dave Hill and Mike Cole, 7–34. London: Kogan Page.

———. 2001b. Global capital, neo-liberalism, and privatization: The growth of educational inequality. In *Schooling and equality: Fact, concept and policy,* ed. Dave Hill and Mike Cole, 35–54. London: Kogan Page.

———. 2001c. State theory and the neo-liberal reconstruction of schooling and teacher education: A structuralist neo-Marxist critique of postmodernist, quasi-postmodernist, and culturalist neo-Marxist theory. *British Journal of Sociology of Education* 22 (1): 137–57.

———. 2003. Global neo-liberalism, the deformation of education and resistance. *Journal for Critical Education Policy Studies* 1, no. 1 (March), available online at www.jceps.com/?pageID= article&articleID=7 (accessed May 25, 2004).

Hill, Dave, and Mike Cole. 1999a. Introduction: Education, education, education—equality and "New Labour" in government. In *Promoting Equality in Secondary Schools,* ed. Dave Hill and Mike Cole, xi–xvi. London: Cassell.

———, eds. 1999b. *Promoting equality in secondary schools.* London: Cassell.

———. 2001a. *Schooling and equality: Fact, concept and policy.* London: Kogan Page.

Hill, Dave, Peter McLaren, Mike Cole, and Glenn Rikowski, eds. 2002. *Marxism against postmodernism in educational theory.* Lanham, Md.: Lexington Books.

———. 2001b. Social class. In *Schooling and equality: Fact, concept and policy,* ed. Dave Hill and Mike Cole, 137–59. London: Kogan Page.

Hillcole Group. 1991. *Changing the future: Redprint for education.* London: Tufnell Press.

———. 1997. *Rethinking education and democracy: A socialist alternative for the twenty-first century.* London: Tufnell Press.

Johnson, Richard. 1979. Really useful knowledge: Radical education and working-class culture, 1790–1848. In *Working class culture: Studies in history and theory,* ed. John Clarke, Chas. Critcher, and Richard Johnson, 75–102. London: Hutchinson.

Kelly, Jane, Mike Cole, and Dave Hill. 1999. *Resistance postmodernism and the ordeal of the undecidable.* Paper presented to the British Educational Research Association Annual Conference, University of Sussex.

Klein, Naomi. 2003. Activists must follow the money. *Guardian,* September 12, 26.

Lather, Patti. 1991. *Getting smart: Feminist research and pedagogy within the postmodern.* New York: Routledge.

———. 1998. Critical pedagogy and its complicities: A praxis of stuck places. *Educational Theory* 48 (4): 487–97.

Marx, Karl. [1894] 1966. *Capital,* vol. 3. Moscow: Progress Publishers.

———. 1976. *The Eighteenth Brumaire.* In *Selected works,* ed. Karl Marx and Frederick Engels, 94–179. London: Lawrence and Wishart.

Marx, Karl, and Frederick Engels. [1868] 1977. Manifesto of the Communist Party. In *Selected works,* ed. Karl Marx and Frederick Engels, 35–63. London: Lawrence and Wishart.

———. [1888] 1977. Preface to the German edition of the manifesto of the Communist Party. In *Karl Marx and Frederick Engels: Selected works in one volume,* 31–34. London: Lawrence and Wishart.

Matheson, Jil, and Penny Babb, eds. 2002. *Social Trends,* no. 32. London: Stationery Office.

McLaren, Peter. 2000. *Che Guevara, Paulo Freire, and the pedagogy of revolution.* Lanham, Md.: Rowman & Littlefield.

McLaren, Peter, and Ramin Farahmandpur. 2001. Educational policy and the socialist imagination: Revolutionary citizenship as a pedagogy of resistance. *Education Policy: An Interdisciplinary Journal of Policy and Practice,* no. 15: 343–78.

McLaren, Peter, and Jill Pinkney-Pastrana. 2001. Cuba, Yanquizacion, and the cult of Elian Gonzalez: A view from the "enlightened states." *Qualitative Studies in Education* 14 (2): 201–19.

McMurtry, Jim. 2000. Dumbing down with globalization: The ideology of inevitable revolution. *Economic Reform* (August): 8–9.

———. 2001. Education, struggle and the Left today. *International Journal of Educational Reform* 10 (2): 145–62.

Meiksins Wood, Ellen. 1995. *Democracy against capitalism: Renewing historical materialism.* Cambridge: Cambridge University Press.

———. 1997. A reply to A. Sivanandan. *Monthly Review Press* 48:21–32.

———. 1998. Modernity, postmodernity or capitalism? In *Capitalism and the information age,* ed. R. W. McChesney, E. M. Wood, and J. B. Foster. New York: Monthly Review Press.

Mojab, Shahrzad. 2001. New resources for revolutionary critical education. *Convergence* 34 (1): 118–25.

Monbiot, George. 2001. Tinkering with poverty. *Guardian,* November 20, 17.

Murphy, P. 1995. A mad, mad, mad, mad world economy. *Living Marxism* 80 (June): 17–19.

National Union of Education, Research, and Culture. General Confederation of Labour, France. 2002. Untitled paper presented at the European Social Forum, Florence, November 6–10.

Plowden, Lady Bridget. 1967. *Children and their primary schools: Plowden report.* London: HMSO.

Rawnsley, Andrew. 2001. Missionary Tony and his Holy British empire. *Observer,* October 7, 29.

Rikowski, Glenn. 2001a. After the manuscript broke off: Thoughts on Marx, social class and education. Paper presented at the British Sociological Association Education Study Group Meeting, Kings College London, June 23. Available from Rikowskigr@aol.com.

———. 2001b. *The battle in Seattle: Its significance for education.* London: Tufnell Press.

———. 2001c. The business take-over of education. *Socialist Future* 9 (4): 14–17.

———. 2001d. The importance of being a radical educator in capitalism today. Guest lecture in Sociology of Education, Gillian Rose Room, Department of Sociology, University of Warwick, Coventry, May 24. Available from Rikowskigr@aol.com.

———. 2003. The business takeover of schools, *Mediactive: Ideas, Knowledge, Culture,* no. 1: 91–108.

Sarup, Madan. 1983. *Marxism/Structuralism/Education.* Lewes: the Falmer Press.

Shor, Ira. 1992. *Empowering education: Critical teaching for social change.* Chicago: University of Chicago Press.

Summerfield, Carol, and Penny Babb, eds. 2004. *Social Trends,* no. 34. London: Stationery Office.

Sweezy, Paul. 1997. More (or less) on globalization. *Monthly Review* 49 (4): 1–4.

Vidal, J., and D. Munk. 2003. Farmer who got a hearing by paying the ultimate price. *Guardian,* September 12.

Wells, Matt. 2001. ITN cuts jobs and shifts towards lifestyle news. *Guardian,* November 22.

World Development Movement. 2001. *Isn't it time we tackled the causes of poverty?* London: World Development Movement.

Young, R. E. 1984. Teaching equals indoctrination: The dominant epistemic practices of our schools. *British Journal of Education Studies* 22 (3): 230–38.

2

State Theory and the Neoliberal Reconstruction of Schooling and Teacher Education

Dave Hill

This chapter examines the adequacy of various theories of the state, in relation to the restructuring of schooling and initial teacher education (ITE) and education more widely between 1979 and 2004 in England and Wales by both Conservative and New Labour governments.

The analysis advanced is structuralist neo-Marxist. I distinguish this from a culturalist neo-Marxist analysis, which lays greater stress on a number of aspects of agency and autonomy. I also briefly critique postmodernist analysis and, in more detail, what I term quasi-postmodernist analyses, associated with Stephen Ball.

In the first section of this chapter, Policy on Teachers and Teacher Education England and Wales, 1979–2004, I set out the major policy developments of the period and locate these within the progressively bigger pictures of schooling, education, and wider government policy. I then analyze the underlying hegemonic projects of capital. In the next section, How Do Different Theories Explain These Changes? I relate these policy changes to contemporary theories with their analyses of the relationships between capital, class, state, and government; and the role of discourse, agency, and resistance.

The theories discussed are postmodernism, quasi postmodernism, and culturalist neo-Marxism. This last analysis comprises a political economy variant (associated with Michael Apple and Geoff Whitty) and a resistance theory variant,[1] associated with Peter McLaren in his prestructuralist phase and with Henry Giroux in his prepostmodernist writing.[2] Both types of culturalist neo-Marxism stress the relative autonomy of institutions/apparatuses (such as schooling and initial teacher education) from and within the state and the relative autonomy of individual agents (such as teachers, teacher educators, students). I argue that these theories fail to explain the policy changes.

In the third section, Structuralist Neo-Marxism and Its Explanatory Value, I suggest a structuralist correction to Culturalist neo-Marxism, advancing a new concept—Althusser extended: economic determinism in the last resort. This observes and seeks to explain dominant shifts within global and domestic national state policies. In relation to the central issue of government changes to schooling and teacher education, I attempt to show that to explain the restructuring of education systems in late capitalist states, social class must be centrally placed. Social class is, ontologically, an aspect of what capital actually is. This is downplayed or ignored in alternative theories.

I conclude briefly with some implications for policy and agency.

POLICY ON TEACHERS AND TEACHER EDUCATION IN ENGLAND AND WALES, 1979–2004

The Importance of Teachers and Teacher Educators

Both Conservative and New Labour governments have attempted to "conform" both the *existing* teacher workforce and the future teacher workforce (i.e., student teachers) and their teachers, the reproducers of teachers—teacher educators. Why conform the teachers and the teacher educators at all? Like poets, teachers are potentially dangerous. But poets are fewer, and reading poetry is voluntary. Schooling isn't. Teachers' work is the production and reproduction of knowledge, attitudes, and ideology (Ainley 2000; Althusser 1971; Apple 1979; Harris 1979, 1982, 1994; Hill 2004a, 2004c, 2004d).

Successive government "reforms" of both the work of teachers and teacher education are an attempt to control and "mold" new teachers and student teachers, to prepare them for what governments have seen as the task of the economic, ideological, and cultural production (or reproduction) of future generations of labor power, cohorts of workers, and citizens.[3] To some extent teachers are, like doctors, relatively socially prestigious and have some power individually and collectively to legitimate or delegitimate the current hegemonic project of capital. They also have the power of effective organized resistance (through their trade unions and quasi unions) to government policy. Moreover, teachers are not widely perceived to be state functionaries, and may for this reason be attributed with extensive critical power.

The State and the Restructuring of Initial Teacher Education

To consider theoretical approaches to policy developments during the past twenty-one years, it is necessary to consider an account of these changes that relates them to the broader project of capital.

In education policy, restructuring of schooling such as No Child Left Behind in the United States and in Britain the Conservative governments' restructuring of schools and ITE between 1979 and 1997 has been described as part of a

"Conservative Restoration." This concept is developed, for example, in Apple (passim) and Shor (1986). But it is not exactly *restoration*. In the latest stage of capitalism, the contracting state is not so much a restoration, as a restructuring of the state into a contracting state in two senses of the word: concentration of power to the center, and contracting (i.e., franchising) as a mode of operation (Ainley and Vickerstaff 1993). This is part of a "neoliberal restoration."

Ideologically the policy changes have sought to orient, to reconstruct teachers away from supporting one-nation attitudes and policies and toward supporting a two-nation hegemonic project (Ainley 2000; Gamble 1983, 1988; Hall 1983; Jessop 1990). The British state, in the period of economic growth of the postwar three decades, focused on a one-nation hegemonic project—typified by welfarist, corporatist, social, economic, and fiscal policies—and by one-nation rhetoric. In the 1960s, especially, "education for education's sake" was widely supported for "the full flowering of the individual." In addition, education rhetoric and policy exhibited an avowed, social class–based social justice dimension. It claimed to be "education for a fairer society." Unlike New Labour, Conservative government and think-tank policy and discourse was, with very rare exceptions (Margaret Thatcher became leader of the Conservative Party in 1974), unmitigated two-nation rhetoric. The poor got poorer, the excluded got vilified, their benefits cut or withdrawn.

Currently, New Labour's rhetoric in education, as in wider policy areas, espouses a socially inclusive one-nation rhetoric. This, however, exists alongside and is contradicted by a two-nation moral authoritarian, exclusivist rhetoric, geared to reincorporating some of the socially excluded (the deserving poor) into the one (deserving) nation. Thus, at the same time as its "one-nation" rhetoric, it vilifies the "others," "the undeserving poor," those who refuse or fail to climb out of their social exclusionary status.

These contradictory discourses are matched in the policy arena by an *overall* adherence to, a continuation and a deepening of neoliberal (and neoconservative) education policies based on a regime of low public expenditure and privatization, and that are essentially competitive, selective, divisive, hierarchically elitist.[4] Indeed, both Conservative (1979–1997) and New Labour governments in Britain (1997–) since 1979 have identified themselves substantially in terms of their antisocialism.

Neoliberalism, through its stress on flexible, deregulated labor markets actually generates *more* of those described as "social excluded." Neoliberal and neoconservative policies are contradicted, but scarcely impeded, by some New Labour examples of inclusivist, redistributionist, Social Democratic micropolicies (Docking 2000; Gamarnikow and Green 1999; Hill 1999a, 2000a, 2000b, 2001a, 2001c, 2005b; Muschamp et al. 1999; Power and Whitty 1999) such as Chancellor Gordon Brown's largesse in his more recent public expenditure plans and budgets.[5] In education policy, the comprehensivist inclusivist, "one-nation" policy ideal has been demonized and replaced in policy terms—by both parties.

Ideological and Repressive State Apparatuses
in Schooling and Initial Teacher Education

Dale (1989) observed how the state reformulation of education policy since the 1970s has involved not merely the promotion of particular values but also the exclusion of others:

> There is a qualitative change in the nature of control over the education system . . .
> there is a change in the core problems of the State, bringing about a tighter—and quite
> possibly different—specification of the requirements of each of the state apparatuses,
> and the necessity, following the re-specification, of attempting to curtail all state ac-
> tivity which now appears to be irrelevant or non-effective. (38)

Changes to, and the curtailing of, schooling and initial teacher education have been effected through the *repressive* as well as *ideological* means available to the state (see Althusser 1971; Hill 1989, 1990, 2004a, 2004c, 2004d; Poulantzas 1972). As Althusser suggests, every ideological state apparatus is also in part a repressive state apparatus, punishing those who dissent: "There is no such thing as a purely ideological apparatus. . . . Schools and Churches use suitable methods of punishment, expulsion, selection, etc., to 'discipline' not only their shepherds, but also their flocks" (1971, 138).

Ideological state apparatuses have internal "coercive" practices (for example, forms of punishment, nonpromotion, displacement, being "out of favor"). Similarly, repressive state apparatuses attempt to secure significant internal unity and wider social authority through ideology (for example, through their ideologies of patriotism and national integrity). For Althusser, the difference between an ideological and a repressive apparatus of state is one of degree, a matter of whether force or idea predominates in the functioning of a particular apparatus (see Benton 1984, 101–2). It is a matter of debate as to whether Ofsted and the Teacher Training Agency (TTA) are primarily ideological or repressive state apparatuses.

Since 1979 the relative autonomy of education state apparatuses diminished remarkably. This is despite the increased autonomy and self-regulation which apparently derives from deregulation (as, for example, with "self-governing" universities, further education colleges and schools). Within this deregulation in the United States and in Britain are hugely increased surveillance and control mechanisms—compulsory and nationally monitored assessments, publication of performance league tables, and a policy emphasis on "naming and shaming," closing, or privatizing "failing" schools and local education authorities/school districts (Boesenberg 2003; Brosio 2003; Hursh 2002; Hursh and Martina 2003; Jeffrey and Woods 1998; Lipman 2004; Mathison and Ross 2002; Saltman and Gabbard 2003; Thrupp 1999; Woods and Jeffrey 1998). The capitalist agenda *for* education entails controlling the curriculum, teachers, and educational institutions through common mechanisms. Pauline Lipman (2004) notes that in the United States

George W. Bush's "blueprint" to "reform" education, released in February 2001, No Child Left Behind, crystallizes key neo-liberal, neo-conservative, and business-oriented education policies. The main components of Bush's plan are mandatory, high-stakes testing and vouchers and other supports for privatizing schools.

In England and Wales, by means of Ofsted, and the Council for the Accreditation of Teacher Education (CATE) and its replacement TTA, "providers" of ITE are rigidly controlled. They can now have their resources reduced, their staff contracted—made redundant, retired/pensioned off, dismissed, staff specializations thereby altered, and specialist centers, with their staffing expertise and resources, closed.[6] Alongside legislation and statutory circulars—such as the Education Reform Act of 1988, the 1994 Education Act (setting up the Teacher Training Agency), and the various requirements for initial teacher education—there has been:

1. A discourse of sustained criticism, under both Conservative and New Labour governments of "trendy" and "politically correct" liberal–progressive and socialist–egalitarian forms of schooling, and of teacher education (e.g., under New Labour; Blunkett, quoted in "Blunkett Attacks 'Elitist' Critics," BBC News, July 19, 1999; Woodhead, quoted in "Woodhead Joins Attack on 'Liberal' Attitudes," BBC News, July 20, 1999).[7] For Whitty, these two separate discourses, "both state and market forces imply a 'low trust' relationship between society and its teachers" (Whitty 1997, 307) with a resulting denigration of professional autonomy.
2. Sustained ministerial and media "spinning," slanted presentation of government advisory reports such as the HMI and Ofsted *New Teacher in School* reports of 1988 and 1993 respectively (Her Majesty's Inspectorate of Education 1988; Office for Standards in Education 1993; see Blake and Hill 1995).
3. The weakening of teachers' union power, the diminution of their national pay, conditions, and negotiating arrangements.
4. The diminution of the "core" of full time teachers on permanent contracts and the accompanying increase of the "peripheral" teachers on part-time and short-term contracts, and the stratification of the teaching force through the introduction of different pay scales and performance related pay (Ainley 1999; Allen 1999) and through the huge expansion of the numbers of "teaching assistants" who take on parts of teachers' jobs at far lower rates of pay under the 2003 Workload Agreement (still, in summer 2004, being opposed by the largest teachers, labor union in England and Wales, the National Union of Teachers).
5. The abolition of corporatist arrangements with a majority of teacher union members, such as the Schools Council, which from the 1960s to the 1980s endorsed and prioritized the input of teachers' unions and representatives to curriculum developments, *pace* New Labour's setting up of a General Teaching Council—a body with less powers and little intended corporatism.

6. The substantial control of teachers' work via the selection of educational content through the national curriculum and its associated publishable assessment results. This is even more apparent under New Labour with the heavily prescriptive "Literacy Hour" and "Numeracy Hour" in primary schools. This also applies to the evermore prescriptive "national curriculum for teacher training," with its very tightly prescribed "standards" under the Circular 4/98 (Department for Education and Employment [DfEE] 1998). These intensified the regulation of ITE "standards" (to be attained prior to qualified teacher status) of the 1992 (Circular 9/92; DfEE 1992) and of the 1993 (Circular 14/93; DfEE 1993a) criteria. They also followed, in most respects, the Conservative government criteria and their preelection proposals in 1997 (TTA 1997; see Hill 1999b, 2004a, 2005a).

7. The prescription of curriculum content has been accompanied by a virtual exclusion of the study of equal opportunities issues, and of the sociological, political, and psychological aspects and contexts of learning, teaching, and schooling. Spaces for the development of "critical reflection" virtually squeezed out,[8] a development exacerbated by the partial replacement of four-year by three-year and other, shorter, undergraduate ITE courses.

8. The insistence on subject, as opposed to topic-based interdisciplinary primary curriculum in schools (DfEE 1993b). New Labour has extended this pedagogical control by insisting that unless mixed-ability methods are being markedly successful in a particular school, then the setting of children by ability should become the norm (see U.K. Government 1999, 10; Woods and Jeffrey 1998).

9. The increased managerialization of schooling and intensification of teachers' work, with "teachers . . . driven to burnout" (Whitty 1997, 305), and the proletarianization of teachers in schools and in higher and teacher education (Ainley 1994, 2000; Allen et al. 1999; Carlson 1987; Harris 1982).

Why should the state's restructuring of education identified by Dale, and in particular by ITE and schooling, have taken this particular course since the late 1970s?

In response to the declining profitability of British capital within this increasingly competitive and deregulated international economy, the logic of capital has required that education and training systems should (a) be geared more directly to the perceived vocational and economic imperatives of national capital and (b) provide ideological support for the restructuring of the British state—the economy, polity, and society—in accordance with the needs of British capital (Cole 1998; Green 1997; Hill 2001d). Conservative government changes to schooling since 1979, and to ITE in the period 1984–1997, under both the Thatcher and Major Conservative governments, showed direct relation to international economic competition in their chosen strategy of attempting to create a low-wage, low-skill, neo-Fordist (Brown and Lauder 1997) offshore economy with increased levels of social and academic differentiation. New Labour is continuing a neoliberal competition/low public expenditure policy aimed at creating a modernized high-tech, "post-Fordist," "fast capitalist" economy (Neary and Rikowski 2000; Rikowski 1999, 2002a, 2002b). Indeed, "Britain under the Labour government has gone further than any other European country in adopting and implementing" the transnational business project for education generated and disseminated through key organizations of the international economic and political elite such as the Organisation for Economic Cooperation and Development (Hatcher 2001, 2002; see also Hatcher and Hirtt 1999; Rikowski 2002c).

HOW DO DIFFERENT THEORIES EXPLAIN THESE CHANGES?

I have so far associated policy changes with historical developments in the relationships between capitalism, state, and government. In pursuit of a wider theoretical explanation, I now evaluate aspects within postmodernist, quasi-postmodernist and culturalist neo-Marxist theories. Since I have written on the problems of postmodernist analysis elsewhere,[9] I simply summarise those criticisms. In addition, since some of the criticisms applied to quasi-postmodernist theory and to Culturalist neo-Marxist relative autonomy theory also apply to state autonomy theory, I do not refer specifically to state autonomy theory.[10]

The Problems with Postmodern Analysis

Capital, State, and Class

The limited analytical and political validity of postmodernism is evident in its account of the relationship between state and capital, particularly when this is applied to the restructuring of ITE, and to the bigger picture of the restructuring of education and of social and economic policy. In its reliance on post-Fordist "New Times" economic concepts (see Hall and Jacques 1989), postmodernism posits the death of class and diminishes the significance of the capital-state-government relationship in the implementation of policy, as well as in resistance to those policies.

Major aspects of recent and continuing policy changes in schooling and ITE are marketization and differentiation of schooling and of routes into teaching, apparent deregulation of schools, pseudoconsumer choice—where entry into school or "teacher training" is related, inter alia, to cultural capital (Hill 2001a, 2001c; Liljander 1998), the salience of quality control, and the end of "totalizing" mass provision and uniformity in schooling and initial teacher education. These appear to postmodernists to be a manifestation, and indeed, in some cases, a vindication, of postmodern fragmentation, of consumerization and heterogeneity.

However, "to regard the espousal of heterogeneity, pluralism, and local narratives as indicative of a new social order may be to mistake phenomenal forms for structural relations" (Whitty 1997, 300; see also Apple and Whitty 2002).

Post-Fordist changes in production and consumption, where they are taking place, are not fundamentally altering workers' relations to the means of production, even if many more are "self-employed" and/or now work at home. Postmodernist analysis, therefore, can be seen as a theoretical extrapolation of sectorally (and, indeed, on a global scale, geographically) limited economic and social change. State policy on education is neither free-floating nor a superstructural correspondence to what are mistakenly perceived to be overall changes in a post-Fordist economic base. Conservative government changes, substantially continued (indeed, deepened, see Hill 1999b, 2001a, 2005a; McLaren, Cole, Hill, and Rikowski 2001) by New Labour, are

> underpinned by market-led strategies . . . in line with the current requirements of late capitalist societies [a consideration] denied, ignored, or underplayed or else the changes are designated merely as "postmodern" in the discourse of postmodernism. [This omission] serves to uphold the Radical Right in their two-nation hegemonic project . . . incorporating the creation of a hierarchy of provision in the public services . . . in which education . . . has become a central target. (Cole and Hill 1996, 27–28; see also, Cole and Hill 2002)

The postmodernist shift of conceptual emphasis from capital, state, class, and solidarity affects the postmodernist view of the relationship between capital, the state, and education policy. Hartley, for example, is a postmodernist who locates ITE changes only partially within the economic imperatives of capitalism (1993, 92; cf. 1997). Like Usher and Edwards (1994), he profoundly underestimates both the intention and effects of government policy. For example, he suggests that the decline of academic disciplines in ITE is due to their "being rooted in the age of modernity," and that "in the culture of postmodernism, we should not be surprised by this" (91). Such passive acceptance of the displacement of theoretical tools for reflection on the social is highly questionable. Having expelled social class as a salient objective social phenomenon within contemporary society, Hartley (1993, 1997) cannot therefore recognize the essentially class-based policies of the British state within the educational arena.[11]

Localism, Contingency, Identity, and Resistance

Postmodernist analyses of educational, social, and cultural change clearly indicate the weakness of concentrating on the "small scale," the local, the specific, the contingent, and the microlevel. For example, the focus on fractured subjectivity and fractured solidarity, typical of postmodern and postmodern feminist writing (e.g., Biesta 1998; Butler 1990, 1998; Lather 1991, 1998, 2001) is rooted in postmodernism's theoretical refusal to recognise the validity of the concepts of solidarity for social class, or "women," or "race."

Since the refusal of solidaristic concepts also ensures the theoretical inability to construct a mass solidaristic oppositional transformatory political project, the "big picture" of overall state policy and capitalist oppression is necessarily ignored, along with the "big movement" of, for example, social class or women's solidarity, or, presumably, gay and lesbian solidarity, or, indeed, any mass movement.

In this respect, postmodernism's tunnel vision and myopic limitations have particular consequences when it comes to, first, the theoretical deconstructive analysis and assessment of developments within state policy, and, second, an inability to agree on and define a reconstructive socially and economically transformatory vision of the future. A third consequence is its inability to draw up and develop a politically and effective project and detailed program to work toward and actualize that social and economic vision; and a fourth, to define, or secure a politically effective agreement on a political strategy—to suggest how to get there. A fifth consequence is an inability to define what effective and solidaristic role radical educators might play in that political strategy. As far as I am aware, no postmodernist theorist, of any theoretical bent, has gone beyond *de*construction into constructing a coherent program for *re*construction. This is precluded by a postmodern theoretical orientation. This applies to Giroux's recent work (1999) as much as to his tentative suggestions of what a postmodern school might look like (in Aronowitz and Giroux 1991, critiqued in Hill 1993). It also applies to his first avowedly post-Marxist, postmodern book (1993). Similarly, Usher and Edwards (1994) suggest that any "reconfiguration is provisional and open to question." What this "reconfiguration" looks like, in both cases, is redolent of 1960s individualistic, student-centered ultrapluralism with its attendant dangers of separate (separatist) development. Theorists such as Giroux (and McLaren in his resistance postmodernist phase of the late 1980s and early 1990s) genuinely attempted to reconcile postmodern antifoundationalism with a modernist metanarrative and political project—but this is attempting to square the circle.

I now proceed to discuss in more detail the postmodern emphasis on localism, on discourse, and its analyses of social class, capitalism, and the capitalist state in relation to the quasi-postmodernist writings of Stephen Ball and his colleagues.

The Problems with Quasi-Postmodernist Analysis

Pluralism and the Attack on "Economic Reductionism"

Ball's specialisms within his sociological analysis are his focus on the micropolitics of schooling and education policy and his use of a (Barthian) concept of resistant human agency and autonomy in the transmutation of (government regulatory curricula) texts. He sees these as "writerly"—capable of being cowritten and transformed. He criticizes what he terms "reductionist Marxism" for adhering to

a theoretical analysis which is rooted in a conception of economic forms which have increasingly less relevance to the specifics of high-modernist, post-Fordist, multicultural western societies and a set of backward looking "possibilities" arising from the critique of those forms. . . . In practice there are no conceptual links in the theoretical chain which they stretch from capital to educational practice. Because their a priori position eschews or trivialises mediation and interpretation they must rest their case upon untheorised or invisible relations between capital and the state, the state and policy and practice. (Ball 1994, 178–79)

Ball finds this position susceptible to exactly those criticisms which Stuart Hall (Hall 1988, 170–71) aims at the "laborist left" because

it does not understand the necessarily contradictory nature of human subjects, of social identities. It does not understand politics as a production. It does not see that it is possible to connect with the ordinary feelings and experiences which people have in their everyday lives, and yet to articulate them progressively to a more advanced, modern form of social consciousness. It is not actively looking for and working upon the enormous diversity of social forces in our society. It doesn't see that it is in the very nature of modern capitalist civilisation to proliferate the centre of power, and thus draw more and more areas of life into social antagonism. It does not recognise that the identities which people carry in their heads—their subjectivities, their cultural life, their sexual life, their family life and their ethnic identities, are always incomplete and have become massively politicised. (cited in Ball 1994, 179–80)

In this instance, the pluralist perspective advocated by Ball is related to social identities, to forms of consciousness and principles of motivation, and is set against Marxist reductionism. This is in line with the "New Times" proposal, defined in 1989 by Hall and Jacques, that the transition from a Fordist to a post-Fordist economy has involved cultural changes which, in turn, have resulted, if not in the disappearance or "death" of class, than in its subsumption into and derogation into one identity among many. As they have no Marxist analysis of social class (because Marxism—for Hall and Jacques at least—is also "dead"), they are in no position to pronounce on the "death of class" from a Marxist perspective. As contemporary Marxist writers make clear, social class remains a necessary and defining feature of capitalist society (e.g., Callinicos and Haman 1987; Callinicos 1993a; German 1996; Hill, McLaren, Cole, and Rikowski 2002; Hill, Sanders, and Hankin 2002).

There are detailed data indicating the salience of class consciousness and of social class and its modern recomposition and redefinition (Crompton 1993; German 1996; Hill and Cole 2001; Kelly 1989; Marshall et al. 1988; Hill, Sanders, and Hankin 2002). Similarly, there is little denial of the existence of a small group of people owning tremendous material wealth, wielding immense power, sharing similar cultural backgrounds and aspirations, often (but not necessarily) reinforced by close family and other personal ties, who defend and promote their own interests within both the economic field of extraction of surplus value from their workforces and in the policy field—that is, the ruling capitalist class.

In fact, a theoretical reply to Ball's view of subjectivities needs a reference to the Marxist formulation of class theory, which perceives classes as internally differentiated entities. Class, for Marx, is not simply monolithic. Marx took great pains to stress that social class, as distinct from economic class, necessarily includes a political dimension that is in the broadest sense "culturally" rather than "economically" determined (see *The Poverty of Philosophy* [1847] in Tucker 1978).

Postmodernists object to a concentration on class and to an emphasis on class consciousness per se, on the grounds that it denies or suppresses the facts of "social difference." As Harvey (1993) observes: "Concentration on class alone is seen to hide, marginalise, disempower, repress and perhaps even oppress all kinds of 'others' precisely because it cannot and does not acknowledge explicitly the existence of heterogeneities and differences" (101).

One of the most influential aspects of postmodernist and poststructuralist writing has been the account of identity in terms of fragmented, decentered subjectivity. I have acknowledged, with Sanders and Hankin, that

> in some respects we recognise this as an advance on former monolithic "vulgar Marxist" accounts of social class which substantially ignored questions of ethnicity, sex, sexuality in both theoretical terms and in terms of political action and mobilisation. Thus, we would argue that the concept of decentred subjectivity is both correct and possesses useful explanatory power when we come to confront the question of declining class-consciousness. (Hill, Sanders, and Hankin 2002, 184)

Some postmodernists admit that class remains a possibly valid basis of identity (given that no identity is "essential" and all are constructed). Postmodern feminists strategically overprivilege cultural notions of identity and underprivilege material explanations of human and social class behavior. This emphasis on "identitarian" analysis and politics has reactionary implications—a case made out powerfully by Jenny Bourne (2002).[12]

Whereas sex or "race" identities and sexuality are exploitable (and admittedly are, on a near universal basis), the nature of class exploitation—a class exploitation that is gendered and "raced"—is fundamental to capitalism. Capitalism can survive with "race" equality, for example, or with gay rights. Indeed, for neoliberals, these are desirable meritocratic attributes of an economy and education/training system. But to conceive of social class equality and the continuance of capitalism is a contradiction in terms. Social class is necessary to the constitution of capitalist society. To show that social class is really "dead" *as the salient/primary form of social, economic, and political analysis*, or, at any rate, has lost its objective salience in society, postmodernists, and quasi postmodernists would have to assure us that expressions of antagonistic social class interests are not *fundamental* to the nature of capitalist society. Relying on strike statistics, voting patterns or survey evidence only scrapes the surface. Marxist analysis, on the other hand, goes beyond superficial "analyses" and seek to discover the new forms in which class antagonisms are expressed. Only if no concrete social expressions of antagonistic social interests could be found would the "death of class" start to make sense, but the evidence shows the contrary (see, e.g., Banfield 2003; Rikowski 1996, 2002a, 2002c).

Human Agency, Ball, and Barthes: Throwing
out the Baby with the Bathwater (Barthwater)

Ball and his cowriters concentrate on human agency, resistance, and what they see as the success of adapting and modifying, or colonizing, state policy. Using Barthian concepts of texts being "writerly" or "readerly," they talk of the national curriculum as a "writerly text," being "not so much 'implemented' in schools as being 're-created,' not so much 'reproduced' as being 'produced'"— a cycle that emphasizes the contextualization and recreation of policy.

Thus, the micropolitical processes of schools provide the milieu for policy recontextualization and mutual redefinition. This is expressed most emphatically in the summary of how the national curriculum has been "read" in various schools:

> While schools are changing as a result, so too is the National Curriculum. This leaves us with the strong feeling that the state control model is analytically very limited. Our empirical data do not suggest that the State is without power. But equally . . . such power is strongly circumscribed by the contextual features of institutions, over which the state may find that control is both problematic and contradictory in terms of other political projects. (Bowe and Ball with Gold 1992, 120)

Ball's pluralist revision includes the "writerly" emphasis on discourse and text, which leads him (1990) to consider the spoken and written intentionality of leading elite figures involved in the 1988 Education Reform Act. Evans and Penney (1995) criticize Ball's focus on the microanalysis of discourse. They focus in particular on the internal disagreements within what they term "the New Right" on the physical education curriculum working parties (set up to design the national curriculum subjects for schools), pointing out, however, the coercive role of the government and state, its use of nondiscursive forms of power. Thus they note:

> As in the making of other NC subjects, central government control over the curriculum was often exercised subtly through an expression of discursive power, but it also drew on positional and material forms of power. The actions of the members of the working group appointed by the Government to "advise" on an NCPE were consistently regulated by both discursive codes which contrived to establish a particular form of social order (cultural restoration), and production codes which reached out to a(n)(economic) context. (42; see also, Evans, Davies, and Penney 1994)

The same points about text, discourse, and state power can be made about teacher education policy. CATE and TTA circulars can be read in different ways. A degree of conversion/subversion can be made at the microlevel—in individual lectures, or staff appointments, for example. Yet this potential to coproduce, to subvert the intentions of these circulars is less potent than the power of the TTA and Ofsted to insist on their implementation (Hill 2005a). In a discussion of state policy, an emphasis on policy recontextualization within Ball's policy cycle thesis gives too much power to human agency and underestimates the Hillcole Group's judgment on the Radical Right in education, that "force, much more than consent has been the basis of its influence" (Hillcole Group 1993, 4).

Ball appears as a pluralist with added Foucault (the Foucauldian emphasis on the dispersal of power) and Barthes plus dashes of "critique"—that is, aspects of neo-Marxism—and therefore to occupy what Troyna and Hatcher describe as a "critical pluralist" position, "a revision of conventional pluralism designed to take account of the structured inequality of power in capitalist societies" (Hatcher and Troyna 1994, 157).

This particular aspect distinguishes Ball's approach from culturalist neo-Marxist theorists as well as from the more structuralist neo-Marxists, with whom he nonetheless shares several other critical concerns relating to his concern for social justice and his analysis of the effects of the market in schooling, such as the ways in which the middle classes secure positional advantage via the quasimarket in schools and education (e.g., Ball 2002; Ball, Maguire, and Macrae 2000; Gerwitz, Ball, and Bowe 1995). Unlike full-blown postmodernists, Ball and his quasi-postmodernist colleagues presumably regard the increasing inequality, for example in schools or, it might be argued, in the production of teachers within a status hierarchy of routes/institutions into teaching, not as an inevitable feature of postmodernity and of post-Fordism, but rather as a particular radical Right set of responses (by Conservatives and those in New Labour) to such post-Fordism.

Ball's difference from postmodernists is that, of the two broad types of postmodernist along the postmodern continuum (see Cole and Hill 1995, 1996, 1999, 2002; Cole, Hill, and Rikowski 1997; Giroux 1994; McLaren 1994a, 1994b) one end of the continuum (anchored by Nietzschean postmodernists of reaction) simply shrug their shoulders at antiegalitarian effects of postmodernity (poverty being just one aspect of difference). The second end of the continuum (resistance postmodernists), lacking both a theory of the state and a theory/project of solidarity would differ from Ball. They passionately share his distaste for the inequality of the Radical Right agenda, but virtually ignore the state in a movement of resistance, calling instead for resistance by ("nontotalitarian") coalitions of microinterests.

Delimitation: Capital, the State, and Autonomy

In a related critique of Ball's policy recontextualization thesis, Dale (1992) criticizes approaches similar to Ball's as "severing implementation from formulation of state policy (which) involves a serious misunderstanding of the role of the State in education policy" (393). For, on the crucial issue of state theory, Ball is ambivalent. On the one hand, he *does* theorize the state, locating the restructuring of education within a hegemonic project of capital. However, his emphasis on the degree of autonomy available to teachers to *co*produce and thereby recreate texts such as the national curriculum, marks a shared interest with—yet a theoretical distinction from—various forms of neo-Marxism, on the central question of the relative autonomy of the state. He attempts "to replace the modernist theoretical project of abstract parsimony with a somewhat more post-modernist one of localised complexity" (1990, 14). While he talks of post-Fordist education, he accepts that a postmodern culture is not dominant and repudiates notions of hyperreality, of fractured and commercially dominated individual selves. For these reasons, Ball's position is not fully postmodernist and, I suggest, is more appropriately comprehended as quasi postmodernist.

With regard to the economy-state-education relationship, Ball suggests:

> While the social composition of the state ensures a sympathetic hearing for the interests of capital, the state also responds to other interests and has other concerns. There is no absolute relationship here between the political and the economic: the state develops and pursues its own independent purposes. Thatcherite education policies, in particular, are marked by a combination of the ideological, technocratic, pragmatic and popular. (cited in Hatcher and Troyna 1994, 159)

The conventional Marxist riposte to the supposed autonomy of the state is that history is littered with the literal and figurative corpses of state rulers who were in fundamental conflict with the existing national dominant class and who attempted to assert their autonomy. As Ball's theory weakens the power of the state through the process of the local recontextualization of state policy, so it attenuates the link between the state and the interests of capital. These aspects relate to Ball's uncertainty regarding structural limitation as a whole:

> I am struggling here with not wanting to "give away" materialism—but neither wanting to accept an unproblematic, law-governed, normative version of social and educational change. We desperately need to account for the inconsistencies of social reproduction, and the "cracks, fissures and contradictions" . . . which appear within Thatcherism. . . . The reality of fiscal crises, changed strategies of accumulation and mode of production, and concomitant changes in the mode of regulation and the role of the state are not in question; but their effects in the field of education cannot just be read off (as many writers want to do). (Ball 1990, 16–17)

He suggests an important difference between recognizing that there are boundaries to the possibility of structure, and arguing that those possibilities are structurally preordained. He supports the idea that

> structural limitation . . . is especially important for understanding the sense in which economic structures "ultimately" determine political and ideological structures, and make some of these possible forms more likely than others, but they do not rigidly determine in a mechanistic manner any given form of political and ideological relations. (Wright 1979, 15–16, in Ball 1990, 13)

For Ball, the relative autonomy of the "political" and the "ideological" from the "economic" is best characterized and theorized as delimitation as opposed to determination. This issue of state power and effectiveness is a central problematic for Ball. It lies between the smaller and the bigger picture, the local story and the metanarrative, within the link this chapter is pursuing—that is, the link between the historical account and the wider analysis of the restructuring under consideration.

STRUCTURALIST NEO-MARXISM AND ITS EXPLANATORY VALUE

The Problems with Culturalist Neo-Marxism

If contemporary theories and analyses such as postmodernism and quasi postmodernism do not address the big picture, how then are recent and current changes to the structure and to formal and informal content/curriculum of initial teacher education and schooling to be explained?

Culturalist neo-Marxist theorists exhibit some of the same problems of underestimating the structural limitations on autonomy, as do quasi postmodernists, although to a lesser extent. Theorists such as Dale, Apple, and Whitty do illuminate how and where the current project, or intentions and activities of capital, and its discursive rhetoricians have resulted in the neoliberal and neoconservative restructuring of education systems (Apple, e.g., 1993a, 1996, 2001; Dale 1989; Whitty 1985, 1994, 1997). However, they do not adequately demonstrate the salience of economic determination within "the big picture." I will argue that they overemphasize the importance of culturalist–idealist (as opposed to structuralist–materialist) analysis and that they also overemphasize various aspects of autonomy and disarticulation in the relationships between capital, state, government, education, and teachers/teacher educators (see Farahmand-pur 2004 for a similar critique).

There are variations in specific projects of different fractions of capital, for example, between manufacturing and finance capital, between multinational and national capital, between Atlantic and Euro-centered capital, between post-Fordist and neo-Fordist capital (see, e.g., Cole 1998). However, culturalist neo-Marxists underestimate the ultimate and effective unity of capital in Britain regarding the extent and effectiveness of state intervention in making schooling and initial teacher education unashamedly fit for capital, with the consistent attempts at repressing social democratic, socialist, and liberal–progressive practices and ideologies in education. This underestimation casts doubt upon their claims about the relative autonomy of education state apparatuses and agents.

Articulations and Disarticulations in the Policy Process

There is, manifestly, a degree of relative autonomy attaching to education (and other) state apparatuses. They do not simply carry out all central or local state requirements. But teachers and teacher educators do carry out and "deliver" the curriculum. They do test for the "standards" and SATs and are, albeit frequently under protest and/or fear, complicit in the current neoliberal project for education. They are state agents. The spaces for oppositional activity within and by the educational state apparatuses have been squeezed tight, albeit not shut.

Schools and teacher education institutions do possess a degree of relative autonomy—from the Department for Education and Employment (DfEE) and the TTA—due to contradictions in government policy, discontinuities in micropolicy, disarticulations between the vertical and horizontal levels of government (Offe 1975; Therborn 1978), as well as the workings of the apparatuses of the education system itself. In addition, there is occasional ministerial backtracking on certain aspects of schools policy, internal inconsistency, competing claims, micro- and macropolitical, ideological, and economic considerations, short-term crisis management, long-term crisis management, refraction (Freeland, cited in Whitty 1985, 94), filtering (Offe 1975), and resistance (e.g., Giroux 1983a, 1983b). These can modify or disrupt policy—but not much.

Beyond this element of derived autonomy, contemporary theoretical analysis needs to answer the larger questions of the extent to which teachers and lecturers can exercise agency within educational contexts—and how much freedom individuals and apparatuses have for counterhegemonic, radical, or indeed revolutionary transformative action. At the theoretical level, a difficulty with culturalist neo-Marxist theory is that it diminishes not only the meta-explanation but also the meta-analysis, along with the importance of class, capitalism, and state power. This is due to the acceptance of the concepts of overdetermination (Althusser 1971; Lipietz 1993), and the post-Althusserian concept of delimitation (cf. Ball 1990; Dale 1989; Jessop 1990; Whitty 1985).

Such concepts overemphasize relative autonomy and the complexity and disarticulation in five ways. First, the relationships between capital and the state; second, within and between the economic, ideological/cultural, and the political regions of the state; third, between different factions of the capitalist class and their ideological and political representatives in the Radical Right; fourth, between different vertical levels and different horizontal sectors of state apparatuses—the autonomy of schools and education departments/schools; and, fifth, the autonomy of individual actors—teachers and teacher educators.

Culturalist neo-Marxist education theorists have moved too far away from economic determination, too far away from structuralist analysis, and therefore too far away from a concept of the big picture of capital, its attendant class conflict, and the policy and operations of the overall conglomeration of state apparatuses (Callinicos 1989; Cole, Hill, McLaren, and Rikowski 2001; Hatcher and Troyna 1994; McLaren, Cole, Hill, and Rikowski 2001).

Structuralist Neo-Marxism

Two problems are immediately apparent with the structuralist neo-Marxist analysis I am advancing. First, I recognize, in common with culturalist neo-

Marxists, that state apparatuses perform a variety of "sometimes conflicting" functions producing a labor force with the work skills necessary for continuing capital accumulation; legitimating the economic, social, and political status quo; and securing social cohesion (see Dale 1989, 28).

Second, this chapter itself focuses on the sectoral—the particular changes within initial teacher education and schooling. To deduce bold statements about the evolution of central state ideology from the activities in the evolution and activities of one particular state apparatus is not possible (as argued in Hill and Cole 1995). However, if the "reforming" of initial teacher education is contextualized within the larger scale policy and ideology—of the operationalizing and restructuring of the wider ensemble of ideological and repressive state apparatuses—then the theoretical analysis of such relationships is indeed possible.

A Structuralist Correction to Neo-Marxist Relative Autonomy Theory

I suggest here an economistic correction to what can be seen as the deficiencies of contemporary culturalist neo-Marxist theory and of its exaggerated notions of human agency and resistance. It is necessary to give greater weight in broad social explanation to the economic contra the political and the ideological. Callinicos (1993a) develops Althusser's concept of overdetermination[13] and elaborates the important concept of the hierarchy of determination:

> Althusser's genealogy of complex totality, his demonstration that the best Marxist thought has sought to understand social formations simultaneously as concrete wholes and as multiplicities of determinations, provides an important rebuttal of the argument that any totalisation necessarily involves the eradication of difference . . . conceiving a social formation as a multiplicity is not inconsistent with recognising a hierarchy of determination which materialist explanation seeks to respect. (44)

Policy analysis regarding the specific apparatuses of teacher education and schooling must be viewed in terms of Althusser's "complex totality" and "concrete wholes." Such analysis needs to include, first, the levels of state policy, and second, temporality, the long- or short-term aspect of policy. Whereas micropolicy and short-term policy may frequently exhibit the relative autonomy of state (e.g., education) policy from the logic of capital accumulation, macropolicy and long-term policy does not. (The 1970s rupture in the postwar political consensus, the break with social democracy, that Ainley [2000], Apple [1989], Dale [1989], Hill [1990], and Offe [1975] refer to, is inexplicable without reference to capital accumulation processes and crisis.)

In the global view, differences and similarities exist in the various national struggles between capital and labor. In the advanced capitalist states in the late twentieth and emerging twenty-first centuries, developments and hegemonic projects have differed, differences explained by mesolevel theories analyzing specific national political and economic circumstances. Yet the variation is limited.

It is possible to see that where the logic of capital as expressed in macropolicy and long-term policy is admitted, so aspects of the two-nation hegemonic project are becoming evident as part of the normal state response in relatively high-wage, Western, advanced capitalist economies (see Cole, chapter 1 in this volume; Hill 2001b, 2003, 2004d). There will, of course, be different levels of resistance in different states. Outcomes will vary. But they are varying, albeit in fits and starts, in a neoliberal direction, whatever the names and histories of the governing parties. It is that limited nature of the mesolevel (or national level) variation that is explained by the macrolevel theory advanced in this paper.

When a microlevel policy such as the reconstruction of teaching and of teacher education is seen in the context of "the big picture" of capital accumulation, when local and national changes in the curriculum and structuring/organization of teacher education and schooling are seen as part of a macrolevel and/or long-term overall policy, then the nature of those changes becomes comprehensible. Thatcherism's attempt to deal, for example, with a crisis of capital and its accompanying labor insubordination crisis involved a whole ensemble of state apparatuses, and included the quest for a more ideologically and politically compliant, economically low-wage, deunionized workforce. This explains how teachers and teacher educators as a whole have been perceived and persistently targeted as (actually or potentially) resistant members of oppositional sectors.

Althusser Extended: Economic Determination in the Last Resort

For Althusser, economic determination in the last instance means "in the last 'overdetermined' analysis." It is the bottom line. Although (and this is the fundamental difference of Marxist from non-Marxist analyses) Althusser did admit "economic determination in the last instance," he added the qualification that, in overdetermined form, "its bell never tolled."

This concept of economic determination is unduly minimalist. As Hatcher has noted, "It seems to me that we tend to operate with either temporal or spatial metaphors which distort the idea of determination. So, for example, Althusser's 'last instance' can imply that determinism only kicks in during prerevolutionary crises, and until that rare event autonomy has full play. This is not true—it's pervasive" (2000). Althusser's unduly minimalist concept also allows Resnick and Wolff to interpret Althusserian "overdetermination" as giving equal weight to political, ideological, and economic factors:

> Overdetermination offers a notion of base and superstructure as conditions of each other's existence. . . . It permitted the construction of a theory of society in which no process—economic, political, cultural or natural—and no site of processes—human agency, enterprise, state or household—could be conceived to exist as a cause without being itself caused. All, whether human agent or social structure, became defined—within a web of mutual overdeterminations. (1993, 68)

Althusser's concept is analytical and not related to any particular stage of capitalist development. However, the "bell," of economic determination, that (for Althusser) "never tolls," is, at the current neoliberal juncture of capitalism, now tolling. The theory of "economic determination in the last instance" is therefore inadequate. Yet it can be extended, by the concept of economic determination in the last resort.[14] This is a periodized concept, applying to particular stages in the development of capitalism (e.g., the early-nineteenth-century laissez-faire period in Britain and the post-1970s in Britain and the United States). Within such periodization, it is a concept referring to the nakedness of the primacy of the capital accumulation process. It is important to note, particularly with reference to Hatcher's point earlier, that this is not a millennial or prerevolutionary statement or stage. It refers to the current stage of capitalism.

There are three ways in which this nakedness is asserted: (a) in the intentionality of governmental discourse; (b) in media support for that intentionality; and (c) in creating general awareness of those intentions within the population at large, by conflating the interests of capital with those of society, where capitalism is "naturalized as the unquestioned backdrop to everyday global life" (McLaren 1999a, 171). This is recognized, for example in increased visibility and use of the term *capitalism* itself, by both its supporters (e.g., "venture capitalists") and by its opponents (e.g., the anticapitalism demonstrations in Seattle in 1999 and in many other cities since then; see Cole 2000; Rikowski 2001).

In contemporary terms, intentionality refers not only to the open recognition by the ruling group of the primary purpose and logic of the capitalist state, a recognition of which it is always aware, but also to its willingness to propagate the structural requirements of the current, latest stage of capitalism as a dominant (neoliberal) ideology, whatever the particular ideological nomenclature (e.g., "Third Way") in use.

The argument that I am advancing here is concerned with the extent of the nakedness of capital accumulation in a particular phase. In both the postwar boom of the late 1940s until the early 1970s, and post-1970s neoliberalism, the capital accumulation process was pursued with just as much ruthless determination. The difference is not only how it is "presented" in those two periods but also in the very different political project of the ruling class, partly as a result of a less competitive economic context in a period of boom, and partly because of the greater ability of the state to pay for reforms. In both periods the "economic" was equally determinant, but led to two very different ruling class projects, for explicable reasons relating to capital accumulation. I am not arguing that prior to the current period, state policy was less in the economic, political, and ideological interests of capital accumulation than today. What I am arguing is, first, that such state policy in the current period is more openly stated, and, second, that it is more repressive.

With this concept, applying economic determination in the last resort to (teacher-) education state apparatuses, suggests that the current logic of capital requires less room for dissent, less room for critique, less room for oppositional school and teacher education curricula, less room for "teachers as intellectuals," less room for revolutionary pedagogy "a rematerialized critical pedagogy" (McLaren 2001, 27; see also, McLaren 1998, 2001; McLaren and Farahmandpur 2001, 2004; McLaren and Rikowski 2002; McLaren et al., forthcoming) to challenge the hegemonic project of capital (see Aronowitz and Giroux 1993; Giroux 1988; Hill 1997a, 2004a, 2004c). Recent ideological and repressive changes in the schooling and teacher education state apparatuses can clearly be seen as elements of the economic determination of educational superstructural forms both in an overdetermined "last instance" and as determination "in the last resort."

CONCLUSION

There are a number of implications of this structuralist neo-Marxist analysis. The concept of "economic determination in the last resort" represents a greater recognition of the role of force and of the repressive aspects and effectiveness of state apparatuses, than that held by the alternative analyses examined here.

In terms of resistance to the hegemony of capital, I wish to briefly refer to two implications of this analysis. The first is the need for the development of a broad, solidaristic, political strategy of alliances, political activity, and organization centered on and with the class axiomatically oppressed and exploited by capital—the working class. The second relates to the role of teachers and teacher educators, whereby teachers and teacher educators act as public, critical, organic, transformative intellectuals, in activities that encompass and extend beyond the education state apparatuses and are part of a broader egalitarian political and economic program for economic and social justice. A structuralist neo-Marxist perspective recognizes its necessity, but lays less trust in the efficacy of individual, localized education sector specific action. It is more cautious about the space for autonomous agency by individuals, groups, and apparatuses such as schools or schooling. It is more cautious about the likely effectiveness of such action in changing the capitalist system. It ain't gonna be easy. It insists that, to strengthen this process—and the effectiveness of resistance and agency—an understanding of the relationships between national and global capital (capitalism), the state, the centrality of social class, and government policy (for example New Labour's "Third Way" in education and broader policy) is crucial.

NOTES

I should like to thank Mike Cole, Ted Hankin, Richard Hatcher, Peter McLaren, and Glenn Rikowski; and Pat Ainley and Geoff Whitty for comments on earlier versions, with the two anonymous reviewers for an earlier version of this article that appeared in *British Journal of Sociology of Education*, 22 (1): 137–57. Any inadequacies, of course, remain mine.

1. Lynch and O'Riordan (1998) analyze the two variants of Culturalist neo-Marxism.

2. Peter McLaren describes his brief "resistance" postmodern phase, as "flirtations" with "post-Marxism in some of my work in the late 1980s" (1999a, 179). His recent work, while acknowledging some strengths of some forms of postmodern analysis, is now unashamedly Marxist (see, in particular, McLaren 1997, 1998, 1999a, 1999b, 2000, 2001; McLaren and Baltodano 2000; McLaren and Farahmandpur 1999, 2000, 2004; McLaren and Rikowski 2002). For example, he criticizes cultural Marxism as "deemphasising the determining role of the economy in the production of hegemonic relations of domination and exploitation and [failing] to address a revolutionary praxis that included workers as wage-laborers" (1999a, 181).

3. For example, Rikowski's Marxist theory is based on an analysis of "labor power." He suggests, "Teachers are the most dangerous of workers because they have a special role in shaping, developing and forcing the single commodity on which the whole capitalist system rests: labour-power. Teachers are dangerous because they are intimately connected with the social production of labour-power, equipping students with skills, competences, abilities, knowledge and the attitudes and personal qualities that can be expressed and expended in the capitalist labour process. The pressure is on teachers and trainers to continually produce students with ever higher quality labour-powers. The State needs to control the process, therefore, for two reasons. First to try to ensure that this occurs. Secondly, to try to ensure that modes of pedagogy that are antithetical to labour-power production do not and cannot exist. In particular, it becomes clear, on this analysis, that the capitalist State will seek to destroy any forms of pedagogy that attempt to educate students regarding their real predicament—to create an awareness of themselves as future labour-powers and to underpin this awareness with critical insight that seeks to undermine the smooth running of the social production of labour" (Rikowski 2000, developing on Fielding and Rikowski 1997; Rikowski 1996, 1997, 2002a, 2002c).

4. Indeed, differentiation, facilitated, spurred on by the publication of test/SAT/GCSE results, also occurs within these sectors, as noted by Gerwitz, Ball, and Bowe (1995); Gillborn and Youdell (2000); Mathison (2003); Thrupp (1999, 2000); and Whitty, Power, and Halpin (1998). This results in highly differentiated local markets in schools.

5. In the United Kingdom, New Labour has kept to a regime of low public expenditure in comparison both to public spending in the rest of Western Europe and in comparison to its past record in government. Despite funding increases in the second New Labour term of office (2001–) by 2005 public spending will have risen to only 40.5 percent of GDP, which is a smaller share than in most other developed countries and considerably less than the 49.9 percent in 1976 (Toynbee 2000). Larry Elliott notes that spending on the nation's infrastructure has been lower in each of New Labour's first four years in office (1997–2001) than in the final twelve months of John Major's Conservative government—and only one quarter of what is was at the end of Old Labour Jim Callaghan's government in 1979 (Elliott 2001).

6. For example, at the same time that I (with my specialism in the politics and sociology of education) was made redundant from West Sussex Institute of Higher Education in 1996, the Centre for Racial Equality was also closed down and its resources dispersed. Staff specializing in "special educational needs" and "race" and education were partially redeployed (see Hill 1997a, 1997b). Reid (1993) has commented on the virtual disappearance of Sociology from courses of initial teacher education.

7. See Lawton (1992, 1995) and Hill (1994b, 1997c), for criticisms and examples of this discourse.

8. See Hill (1989, 1990, 1994b, 1997d); Reid (1993); Reid and Parker (1995); Whitty (1997); Wilkin (1996).

9. I have tried to develop some of these arguments concerning post-Fordism and postmodernism in Hill (1990); and, with Mike Cole, in Cole and Hill (1994, 1996, 1999, 2002); Cole, Hill, and Rikowski (1997); and Cole, Hill, McLaren, and Rikowski (2001). See also, the chapter by Mike Cole in this volume and Cole (2003, 2004).

10. For a critique of state autonomy theory in general (e.g., of Skocpol 1980 and Ben-Tovim et al. 1981), and, as applied to "race"—education in initial teacher education (by Gabe 1991, 1994; see Hill and Cole 1995).

11. Work by Aronowitz and Giroux (1991), Butler (1990, 1998), Giroux (1992, 1994), Hargreaves (1993, 1994), Hartley (1993, 1997) and Kenway and colleagues (1993) all underplay the state–capital relationship. This theoretical underplay by postmodernism is criticized, by culturalist neo-Marxist theorists such as Apple (1993b); Apple and Whitty (2002); and Whitty (1994, 1997).

12. See Bourne (2002); Cole and Hill (1999, 2002); Kelly (2002); Kelly, Cole, and Hill (1999); McLaren (1999a); and McLaren and Farahmandpur (1999, 2000) for a critique.

13. Althusser's ideological state apparatuses essay (Althusser 1971) has been criticized on two main grounds. The first is that it is internally inconsistent. Barrett (1993) has argued the ISA essay is in two halves. The first half functionalist, the second half (itself internally contradictory) developing the complexity of subjectivity. The second is that it is overly functionalist and overtly antihumanist (Barrett 1993; Callinicos 1993b; Giroux 1983a, 1983b) denying human agency, and denies class agency, explaining immobilism rather than change, failing to provide a motor for social change (Balibar 1993, 11; Benton 1984, 102; Callinicos 1993b, 41–42; Cole 1988, 1993b; Johnson 1979, 229–30; Larrain 1979, 154–61; Sarup 1984, 15–17, 146–47).

Althusser's analysis, while structuralist, was not economistically reductionist (Benton 1994; Kaplan and Sprinkler 1993). It was a reaction against a Stalinist, "vulgar" version of the economic base determining in a linear fashion the political/social/ideological superstructure. Althusser, followed by Poulantzas, did introduce into his post-Stalinist Marxism the notion of relative autonomy, of disjunctions and disarticulations within and between different "regions" of the superstructure, the juridico-legal, and the ideological. However, and this is where Marxist analyses differ essentially from non-Marxist, he did posit/accept "economic determination in the last instance."

14. This was first developed in Hill (1994a) and Cole and Hill (1995) and initially formulated with Cole and Williams, with subsequent reformulation following Hatcher's critique of the temporal metaphor.

REFERENCES

Ainley, P. 1994. *Degrees of difference: Higher education in the 1990s.* London: Lawrence and Wishart.

———. 1999. Left in a Right state: Towards a new alternative. *Education and Social Justice* 2, (1): 74–78.

———. 2000. *From earning to learning: What is happening to education and the welfare state?* London: Tufnell Press.

Ainley, P., and S. Vickerstaff. 1993. Transitions from corporatism: The privatisation of policy failure. *Journal of Contemporary British History* 7 (3): 541–56.

Allen, M. 1999. Labour's business plan for teachers. In *New Labour's education policy,* ed. M. Allen et al. London: Tufnell Press.

Allen, M., C. Benn, C. Chitty, M. Cole, R. Hatcher, N. Hirtt, and G. Rikowski. 1999. *New Labour's education policy.* London: Tufnell Press.

Althusser, L. 1971. Ideology and state apparatus. In *Lenin and philosophy and other essays.* London: New Left Books.

Apple, M. 1979. *Ideology and curriculum.* London: Routledge and Kegan Paul.

———. 1989. How equality has been redefined in the conservative restoration In *Equity in education,* ed. W. Secada. London: Falmer Press.

———. 1993a. *Official knowledge: Democratic education in a conservative age.* London: Routledge.

———. 1993b. What post-modernists forget: Cultural capital and official knowledge. *Curriculum Studies* 1 (3): 301–16.

———. 1996. *Cultural politics and education.* London: Open University Press.

———. 2001. *Educating the "right" way: Markets, standards, god, and inequality.* New York: Routledge/Falmer.

Apple, M., and G. Whitty. 2002. Structuring the postmodern in education policy. In *Marxism against postmodernism in educational theory,* ed. D. Hill, P. McLaren, M. Cole, and G. Rikowski. Lanham, Md.: Lexington Books.

Aronowitz, S., and H. Giroux. 1991. *Postmodern education: Politics, culture and social criticism.* Minneapolis: University of Minnesota Press.

———. 1993. *Education still under siege.* Westport, Conn.: Bergin & Garvey.

Balibar, E. 1993. The non-contemporaneity of Althusser. In *The Althusserian Legacy,* ed. E. Kaplan and M. Sprinkler. London: Verso.

Ball, S. 1990. *Politics and policy-making in education.* London: Routledge.

———. 1994. Some reflections on political theory: A brief response to Hatcher and Troyna. *Journal of Education Policy* 9 (2): 171–82.

———. 2002. *Class strategies and the education market: The middle classes and social advantage.* New York: Routledge/Falmer.

Ball, S., M. Maguire, and S. Macrae. 2000. *Choice, pathways and transitions post-16: New youth, new economics in the global city.* New York: Routledge/Falmer.

Banfield, G. 2003. Getting real about class: Towards an emergent Marxist education. *Journal for Critical Education Policy Studies* 1 (2), at www.jceps.com/index.php?pageID=article&articleID=14.

Barrett, M. 1993. Althusser's Marx, Althusser's Lacan. In *The Althusserian Legacy,* ed. E. Kaplan and M. Sprinkler. London: Verso.

Benton, T. 1984. *The rise and fall of structural Marxism: Althusser and his influence.* London: MacMillan.

Ben-Tovim, G., J. Gabriel, I. Law, and K. Stredler. 1981. *Race, left strategies and the state.* London: Routledge and Kegan Paul.

Biesta, G. J. J. 1998. Say you want a revolution. . . . Suggestions for the impossible future of critical pedagogy. *Educational Theory* 48 (4): 499–510.

Blake, D., and D. Hill. 1995. The newly qualified teacher in school. *Research Papers in Education* 10 (3): 309–39.

Boesenberg, E. 2003. Privatizing public schools: Education in the marketplace. *Workplace: A Journal for Academic Labor* 5 (2), at www.louisville.edu/journal/workplace/issue5p2/boesenberg.html.

Brosio, R. 2003. High stakes tests: Reasons to strive for better Marx. *Journal for Critical Education Policy Studies* 1 (2), at www.jceps.com/index.php?pageID=article&articleID=17.

Bourne, J. 2002. Racism, postmodernism and the flight from class. In *Marxism against postmodernism in educational theory,* ed. D. Hill, P. McLaren, M. Cole, and G. Rikowski. Lanham, Md.: Lexington Books.

Bowe, R., and S. Ball., with A. Gold. 1992. *Reforming education and changing schools.* London: Routledge.

Brown, P., and H. Lauder. 1997. Education, globalisation and economic development. In *Education, Culture and Economy,* ed. A. H. Halsey, H. Lauder, P. Brown, and A. Stuart Wells. Oxford: Oxford University Press.

Butler, J. 1990. *Gender trouble: Gender and the subversion of identity.* London: Routledge.

———. 1998. Merely cultural. *New Left Review* 227: 33–34.

Callinicos, A. 1989. *Against postmodernism: A Marxist critique.* Cambridge, Engl.: Polity.

———. 1993a. *The Revolutionary ideas of Karl Marx.* London: Bookmarcks.

———. 1993b. What is living and what is dead in the philosophy of Althusser. In *The Althusserian Legacy,* ed. E. Kaplan and M. Sprinkler. London: Verso.

Callinicos, A., and Haman, C. 1987. *The changing working class.* London: Bookmarcks.

Carlson, D. 1987. Teachers as political actors: From reproductive theory to the crisis of schooling. *Harvard Educational Review* 57 (3): 283–307.

Cole, M. 1988. Correspondence theory in education: Impact, critique and re-valuation. In *Bowles and Gintis revisited: Correspondence and contradiction in educational theory,* ed. M. Cole. London: Falmer Press.

———. 1998. Globalisation, modernisation and competitiveness: A critique of the New Labour project in education. *International Studies in Sociology of Education* 8 (3): 315–32.

———. 2000. Comments made to author on this chapter.

———. 2003. The "ordeal of the undecidable" vs. the "inevitability of globalized capital": A Marxist critique. In *Teaching Peter McLaren,* ed. M. Pruyn and L. Huerta-Carles. New York: P. Lang.

———. 2004. Fun, amusing, full of insights, but ultimately a reflection of anxious times: A critique of postmodernism as a force for resistance, social change and social justice. In *Discourse, power, resistance,* ed. E. Atkinson, W. Martin, and J. Satterthwaite. Stoke-on-Trent, Engl.: Trentham Books.

Cole, M., and D. Hill. 1995. Games of despair and rhetorics of resistance: Postmodernism, education and reaction. *British Journal of Sociology of Education* 16 (2): 165–82.

———. 1996. "Resistance postmodernism": Emancipatory politics for a new era or academic chic for a defeatist intelligentsia? In *Information Society: New Media, Ethics and Postmodernism,* ed. K. S. Gill. London: Springer-Verlag.

———. 1999. Into the hands of capital: The deluge of postmodernism and the delusions of resistance postmodernists. In *Postmodernism in educational theory: Education and the politics of human resistance,* ed. D. Hill, P. McLaren, M. Cole, and G. Rikowski. London: Tufnell Press.

———. 2002. Resistance postmodernism: Progressive politics or rhetorical left posturing? In *Marxism against postmodernism in educational theory,* ed. D. Hill, P. McLaren, M. Cole, and G. Rikowski. Lanham, Md.: Lexington Books.

Cole, M., D. Hill, P. McLaren, and G. Rikowski. 2001. *Red chalk: On schooling, capitalism and politics.* Brighton, Eng.: Institute for Education Policy Studies.

Cole, M., D. Hill, and G. Rikowski. 1997. Between postmodernism and nowhere: The predicament of the postmodernist. *British Journal of Education Studies* 45 (2): 187–200.

Crompton, R. 1993. *Class and stratification: An introduction to current debates.* Oxford: Pluto Press.

Dale, R. 1989. *The state and education policy.* Milton Keynes: Open University Press.

———. 1992. Whither the state and education policy? Recent work in Australia and New Zealand. *British Journal of Sociology of Education,* 13 (3): 387–95.

Department for Education and Employment (DfEE). 1992. *Circular 9/92: Initial teacher training (secondary phase).* London: Author.

———. 1993a. *Circular 14/93: The initial training of primary school teachers.* London: Author.

———. 1993b. *Curriculum organisation and classroom practice in primary schools. A discussion paper.* By R. Alexander, J. Rose, and C. Woodhead. London: HMSO.

———. 1998. *Circular 4/98: Teaching: High status, high standards—requirements for courses of initial teacher training.* London: Author.

Docking, J. 2000. *New Labour's policies for schools: Raising the standard?* London: David Fulton.

Elliott, L. 2001. It's about time Blair had a big idea. *Guardian,* April 2.

Evans, J., B. Davies, and D. Penney. 1994. Whatever happened to the subject and the state? *Discourse* 14 (2): 57–64.

Evans, J., and D. Penney. 1995. The politics of pedagogy: Making a national curriculum physical education. *Journal of Education Policy* 10 (1): 27–44.

Fielding, S., and G. Rikowski. 1997. Resistance of restructuring? Post-Fordism in British primary schools. In *Educational restructuring and teacher's political activism in the 1990s,* ed. S. Robertson and H. Smaller. Toronto: OurSchools/OurSelves.

Gabe, J. 1991. Explaining "race"—education. *British Journal of Sociology of Education* 12 (3): 347–76.

———. 1994. "Race"—education policy as social control? *Sociological Review* 42 (1): 26–61.

Gamarnikow, E., and A. Green. 1999. The third way and social capital: Education action zones and a new agenda for education, parents and community? *International Studies in Sociology of Education* 9 (1): 3–22.

Gamble, A. 1983. Thatcherism and conservative politics. In *The Politics of Thatcherism,* ed. S. Hall and M. Jacques. London: Lawrence & Wishart.

———. 1988. *The free economy and the strong state: The politics of Thatcherism.* London: Macmillan.

German, L. 1996. *A question of class.* London: Bookmarks.

Gerwitz, S., S. Ball, and R. Bowe. 1995. *Markets, choice and equity in education.* Buckingham, Engl.: Open University Press.

Gillborn, D., and D. Youdell. 2000. *Rationing education: Policy, practice, reform and equity.* Buckingham, Engl.: Open University Press.

Giroux, H. 1983a. Theories of reproduction and resistance in the new sociology of education: A critical analysis. *Harvard Education Review* 55 (3): 257–93.

———. 1983b. *Theory and resistance in education: A pedagogy for the opposition.* London: Heinemann.

———. 1988. *Teachers as intellectuals.* Granby, Mass.: Bergin & Garvey.

———. 1992. *Border Crossings.* London: Routledge.

———. 1994. Living dangerously: Identity politics and the new cultural racism. In *Between borders: Pedagogy and the politics of cultural studies,* ed. H. Giroux and P. McLaren. London: Routledge.

———. 1999. Border youth, difference and postmodern education. In *Critical Education in the New Information Age,* ed. M. Castells, R. Flecha, P. Freire, H. Giroux, D. Macedo, and P. Willis. Lanham, Md.: Rowman and Littlefield.

Green, A. 1997. *Education, globalisation and the nation state.* London: MacMillan.

Guardian. 1999. Brown's beneficence. July 17.

Hall, S. 1983. The great moving right show. In *The Politics of Thatcherism,* ed. S. Hall and M. Jacques. London: Lawrence & Wishart.

Hall, S. 1988. *The hard road to renewal: Thatcherism and the crisis of the Left.* London: Verso.

Hall, S., and M. Jacques. 1989. *New times: The changing face of politics in the 1990s.* London: Lawrence & Wishart.

Hargreaves, A. 1993. Teacher development in the postmodern age: Dead certainties, safe simulation and the boundless self. In *International Analyses of Teacher Education,* ed. P. Gilroy and M. Smith. London: Carfax.

———. 1994. Restructuring restructuring: Postmodernity and the prospects for educational change. *Journal of Education Policy* 9 (1): 47–65.

Harris, K. 1979. *Education and knowledge.* London: Routledge & Kegan Paul.

———. 1982. *Teachers and classes: A Marxist Analysis.* London: Routledge & Kegan Paul.

———. 1994. *Teachers: Constructing the future.* London: Falmer Press.

Hartley, D. 1993. Confusion in teacher education: A postmodern condition? In *International Analyses of Teacher Education,* ed. P. Gilroy and M. Smith. London: Carfax.

———. 1997. *Re-schooling society.* London: Falmer Press.

Harvey, D. 1993. Class relations, social justice and the politics of difference. In *Principled positions,* ed. J. Squires. London: Lawrence & Wishart.

Hatcher, R. 2000. Comments made to author on this chapter.

———. 2001. Getting down to the business: Schooling in the globalised economy. *Education and Social Justice* 3 (2): 45–59.

———. 2002. *The business of education: How business agendas drive labour policies for schools.* London: Socialist Education Association.

Hatcher, R., and N. Hirtt. 1999. The business agenda behind Labour's education policy. In *New Labour's education policy,* ed. M. Allen et al. London: Tufnell Press.

Hatcher, R., and B. Troyna. 1994. "The policy cycle": A ball by ball account. *Journal of Education Policy* 9 (2): 155–70.

Her Majesty's Inspectorate of Education. 1988. *The new teacher in school.* London: HMSO.

Hill, D. 1989. *Charge of the Right brigade: The radical Right's assault on teacher education.* Brighton: Institute for Education Policy Studies, at www.ieps.org.uk.cwc.net/hill1989.pdf.

———. 1990. *Something old, something new, something borrowed, something blue: Teacher education, schooling and the radical Right in Britain and the USA.* London: Tufnell Press.

———. 1993. Review of *Postmodern education: Politics, culture and social criticism,* by S. Aronowitz and H. Giroux. *Journal of Education Policy* 8 (1): 97–99.

———. 1994a. *The state and teacher-education: Capitalist teacher-education or postmodern teacher-education.* Conference paper to the Annual Conference of the British Educational Research Association, Oxford University.

------. 1994b. Teacher education and ethnic diversity. In *Cross-curricular contexts, themes and dimensions in primary schools,* ed. G. Verma and P. Pumfrey. Vol. 4 of *Cultural diversity and the curriculum.* London: Falmer Press.

------. 1997a. Brief autobiography of a Bolshie dismissed. *General Educator* 44: 15–17, at www.pipeline.com/~rougeforum/Newspaper/Summer2004/BriefAutobiography.htm.

------. 1997b. Critical research and the death of dissent. *Research Intelligence* 59: 25–26.

------. 1997c. Equality and primary schooling: The policy context intentions and effects of the conservative "reforms." In *Promoting Equality in Primary Schools,* ed. M. Cole, D. Hill, and S. Shan. London: Cassell.

------. 1997d. Reflection in teacher education. In *Teacher education and training,* ed. K. Watson, S. Modgil, and C. Modgil. Vol. 1 of *Educational dilemmas: Debate and diversity.* London: Cassell.

------. 1999a. *New Labour and education: Policy, ideology and the third way.* London: Tufnell Press.

------. 1999b. Social class and education. In *An introduction to the study of education,* ed. D. Matheson and I. Grosvenor. London: David Fulton.

------. 2000. The third way ideology of New Labour's educational policy in England and Wales. In *Combating social exclusion through education: Laissez faire, authoritarianism or some third way?* ed. G. Walraven, C. Day, C. Parsons, and D. Van Deen. Leuven-Apeldoon: Garant.

------. 2001a. Equality, ideology and education policy. In *Schooling and equality: Fact, concept and policy,* ed. D. Hill and M. Cole. London: Kogan Page.

------. 2001b. Global capital, neo-liberalism and privatisation: The growth of educational inequality. In *Schooling and equality: Fact, concept and policy,* ed. D. Hill and M. Cole. London: Kogan.

------. 2001c. The national curriculum, the hidden curriculum and equality. In *Schooling and equality: Fact, concept and policy,* ed. D. Hill and M. Cole. London: Kogan Page.

------. 2001d. New Labour's neo-liberal education policy. *Forum for Promoting 3–19 Comprehensive Education* 42 (1): 4–7.

------. 2002. Globalisation, education and critical action. *Educate: A Quarterly on Education and Development* (Sindh Education Foundation, Pakistan) 2 (1): 42–45, at www.sef.org.pk/educatewebsite/educate5fol/otherartedu5.asp.

------. 2003. Global neo-liberalism, the deformation of education and resistance. *Journal for Critical Education Policy Studies* 1 (1), at www.jceps.com/index.php?pageID=article&articleID=7.

------. 2004a. Books, banks and bullets: Controlling our minds—the global project of Imperialistic and militaristic neo-liberalism and its effect on education policy. *Policy Futures* 2 (3).

------. 2004b. Educational perversion and global neo-liberalism: A Marxist critique. *Cultural Logic: an Electronic Journal of Marxist Theory and Practice,* at http://eserver.org/clogic/2004/2004.html.

------. 2004c. Enforcing capitalist education: Force-feeding capital through in the repressive and ideological educational apparatuses of the state. In *Education and the Rise of the Security State,* ed. E. Wayne Ross and D. Gabbard. New York: Praeger.

------. 2004d. Global neo-liberalism, inequality and capital: Contemporary education policy in Britain and the USA. In *Neoliberalism and Education Reform,* ed. E. Wayne Ross and R. Gibson. Cresskill, N.J.: Hampton Press.

------. 2005a. *Charge of the right brigade.* Lampeter, Wales: Edwin Mellen Press.

------. 2005b. *New Labour and education: Ideology, (in)equality and capital.* London: Tufnell Press.

Hill, D., and M. Cole. 1995. Marxist theory and state autonomy theory: The case of "race"—education in initial teacher education. *Journal of Education Policy* 10 (2): 221–32.

------. 2001. Social class. In *Schooling and equality: Fact, concept and policy,* ed. D. Hill and M. Cole. London: Kogan Page.

Hill, D., P. McLaren, M. Cole, and G. Rikowski, eds. 2002. *Marxism against postmodernism in educational theory,* ed. D. Hill, P. McLaren, M. Cole, and G. Rikowski. Lanham, Md.: Lexington Books.

Hill, D., M. Sanders, and T. Hankin. 2002. Marxism, class analysis, and postmodernism. In *Marxism against postmodernism in educational theory,* ed. D. Hill, P. McLaren, M. Cole, and G. Rikowski. Lanham, Md.: Lexington Books.

Hillcole Group. 1993. *Falling apart: The coming crisis in conservative education.* London: Tufnell Press.

Hursh, D. 2002. Neoliberalism and the control of teachers, students, and learning: The rise of standards, standardization, and accountability. *Cultural Logic* 4 (1), at www.eserver.org/clogic/4-1/hursh.html.

Hursh, D. and Martina, C. 2003. Neoliberalism and schooling in the U.S.: How state and federal government education policies perpetuate inequality. *Journal for Critical Education Policy Studies* 1 (2), at www.jceps.com/index.php?pageID=article&articleID=12.

Jeffrey, B., and R. Woods. 1998. *Testing teachers: The effect of school inspections on primary teachers.* London: Falmer Press.

Jessop, B. 1990. *State theory: Putting capitalist states in their place.* London: Polity Press.

Johnson, R. 1979. Three problematics: Elements of a theory of working-class culture. In *Working Class Culture,* ed. J. Clarke, C. Critcher, and R. Johnson. London: Hutchinson.

Kaplan, E., and M. Sprinkler, eds. 1993. *The Althusserian legacy.* London: Verso.

Kelly, J. 1989. Class is still the central issue. *Communist Review* (3).

———. 2002. Postmodernism and feminism: The road to nowhere. In *Marxism against postmodernism in educational theory,* ed. D. Hill, P. McLaren, M. Cole, and G. Rikowski. Lanham, Md.: Lexington Books.

Kelly, J., M. Cole, and D. Hill. 1999. Resistance postmodernism and the ordeal of the undecidable: A Marxist critique. Paper presented at the Annual Conference of the British Educational Research Association, Sussex University, at http://www.ieps.org.uk.cwc.net/colehillkelly1999_1002.pdf.

Kenway, J., with C. Bigum and L. Fitzclarence. 1993. Marketing education in the post-modern age. *Journal of Education Policy* 8 (2): 105–22.

Larrain, J. 1979. *The concept of ideology.* London: Hutchinson.

Lather, P. 1991. *Getting smart: Feminist research and pedagogy within the postmodern.* New York: Routledge.

———. 1998. Critical pedagogy and its complicities: A praxis of stuck places. *Educational Theory* 48 (4): 487–97.

———. 2001. Ten years later, yet again: Critical pedagogy and its complicities. In *Feminist engagements: Reading, resisting and revisioning male theorists in education and cultural studies,* ed. K. Weiler. London: Routledge, 2001.

Lawton, D. 1992. *Education and politics in the 1990s: Conflict or consensus?* London: Falmer Press.

———. 1995. *The Tory mind on education, 1979–1994.* London: Falmer Press.

Liljander, J. P. 1998. Gains and losses on academic transfer markets: Dropping out and course switching in higher education. *British Journal of Sociology of Education* 19 (4): 479–95.

Lipietz, A. 1993. From Althusser to "regulation theory." In *The Althusserian Legacy,* ed. E. Kaplan and M. Sprinkler. London: Verso.

Lipman, P. 2004. Education accountability and repression of democracy post 9/11. *Journal for Critical Education Policy Studies* 2 (1), at www.jceps.com/index.php?pageID=article&articleID=23.

Lynch, K., and C. O'Riordan. 1998. Inequality in higher education: A study of class barriers. *British Journal of Sociology of Education* 19 (4): 445–78.

Marx, K. [1847] 1978. *The poverty of philosophy.* In *The Marx-Engels reader,* ed. R. Tucker. New York: W. W. Norton.

Mathison, S. 2003. The accumulation of disadvantage: The role of educational testing in the school career of minority children. *Workplace: A Journal for Academic Labor* 5 (2), at www.louisville.edu/journal/workplace/issue5p2/mathison.html.

Mathison, S., and E. W. Ross. 2002. Hegemony and "accountability" in schools and universities. *Workplace: A Journal for Academic Labor* 5 (1), at www.louisville.edu/journal/workplace/issue5p1/mathison.html.

McLaren, P. 1994a. Critical pedagogy, political agency and the pragmatics of justice: The case of Lyotard. *Educational Theory* 44 (3): 319–40.

——. 1994b. Multiculturalism and the postmodern critique: Towards a pedagogy of resistance and transformation. In *Between borders: Pedagogy and the politics of cultural studies,* ed. H. Giroux and P. McLaren. London: Routledge.

——. 1997. Epilogue—beyond the threshold of liberal pluralism: Towards a revolutionary democracy. In *Revolutionary multiculturalism: Pedagogies of dissent for the new millenium,* ed. P. McLaren. Boulder, Colo.: Westview Press.

——. 1998. Revolutionary pedagogy in post-revolutionary times: Rethinking the political economy of critical education. *Educational Theory* 48 (4): 431–62.

——. 1999a. The educational researcher as critical social agent: Some personal reflections on Marxist criticism in postmodern deeducational climates. In *Multicultural research: A reflective engagement with race, class, gender and sexual orientation,* ed. C. Grant. London: Falmer Press.

——. 1999b. Traumatizing capital: Oppositional pedagogies in the age of consent. In *Critical education in the new information age,* ed. M. Castells, R. Flecha, P. Freire, H. Giroux, D. Macedo, and P. Willis. Lanham, Md.: Rowman & Littlefield.

——. 2000. *Che Guevara, Paolo Freire and the pedagogy of revolution.* Oxford: Rowman & Littlefield.

——. 2001. Marxist revolutionary praxis: A curriculum of transgression. *Journal of Critical Inquiry into Curriculum and Instruction* 3 (3): 27–32.

McLaren, P., and M. Baltodano. 2000. The future of teacher education and the politics of resistance. *Teacher Education* 11 (1): 31–44.

McLaren, P., M. Cole, D. Hill, and G. Rikowski. 2001. Education, struggle and the left today: An interview with three UK Marxist educational theorists: Mike Cole, Dave Hill, and Glenn Rikowski, by Peter McLaren. *International Journal of Education Reform* 10 (2): 145–62.

McLaren, P., and R. Farahmandpur. 1999. Critical pedagogy, postmodernism, and the retreat from class: Towards a contraband pedagogy. In *Postmodernism in Educational Theory: Education and the Politics of Human Resistance,* ed. D. Hill, P. McLaren, M. Cole, and G. Rikowski. London: Tufnell Press.

——. 2000. Reconsidering Marx in post-Marxist times: A requiem for postmodernism? *Education Researcher* 29 (3): 25–33.

——. 2001. The globalization of capitalism and the new imperialism: Notes towards a revolutionary critical pedagogy. *Review of Education, Pedagogy, and Cultural Studies* 2 (22): 271–315.

——. 2004. *Capitalists and conquerors: Critical pedagogy against empire.* Lanham, Md.: Rowman and Littlefield.

McLaren, P., G. Martin, R. Farahmandpur, and N. Jaramillo. Forthcoming. Teaching in and against empire: Critical pedagogy as revolutionary praxis. *Teacher Education Quarterly.*

McLaren, P., and G. Rikowski. 2002. Pedagogy for revolution against education for capital: An e-dialogue on education in capitalism today. *Cultural Logic* 4 (1), at http://eserver.org/clogic/4-1/mclaren&rikowski.html.

Marshall, G., D. Rose, H. Newby, and C. Vogler. 1988. *Social class in modern Britain.* London: Unwin Hyman.

Muschamp, Y., I. Jamieson, and H. Lauder. 1999. Education, education, education. In *New Labour, New Welfare State: The "Third Way" in British social policy,* ed. M. Powell. Bristol, Engl.: Policy Press.

Neary, M., and G. Rikowski. 2000. *The speed of life: The significance of Karl Marx's concept of socially necessary labour-time.* Paper presented at the British Sociological Association Annual Conference, University of York, April 17–20.

Offe, C. 1975. The capitalist state and the problem of policy formation. In *Stress and contradiction in modern capitalism,* ed. L. J. Lindberg et al. Lexington, Mass.: Lexington Books.

Office for Standards in Education. 1993. *The new teacher in school: A survey by HM inspectors in England and Wales.* London: HMSO.

Poulantzas, N. 1972. Problems of the capitalist state. In *Ideology and social science,* ed. R. Blackburn. London: Fontana.

Power, S., and G. Whitty. 1999. New Labour's education policy: First, second or third way? *Journal of Education Policy* 14 (5): 535–46.

Reid, I. 1993. The lost opportunity? The relative failure of British teacher education in tackling the inequality of schooling. In *Inequality and teacher education,* ed. G. Verma. London: Falmer Press.

Reid, I., and F. Parker. 1995. Whatever happened to the sociology of education? *Educational Studies* 21 (3): 395–413.

Resnick, S. A., and R. Wolff. 1993. Althusser's liberation of Marxist theory. In *The Althusserian Legacy,* ed. E. Kaplan and M. Sprinkler. London: Verso.

Rikowski, G. 1996. Left alone: End time for Marxist educational theory? *British Journal of Sociology of Education* 17 (4): 415–51.

———. 1997. Scorched Earth: Prelude to rebuilding Marxist educational theory. *British Journal of Sociology of Educational Studies,* 18 (4): 551–74.

———. 2000. Comments made to author on this chapter.

Rikowski, G. 2001. *The battle in Seattle: Its significance for education.* London: Tufnell Press.

———. 2002a. Education, capital and the transhuman. In *Marxism against postmodernism in educational theory,* ed. D. Hill, P. McLaren, M. Cole, and G. Rikowski. Lanham, Md.: Lexington Books.

———. 2002b. Fuel for the living fire: Labour-power! In *The labour debate: An investigation into the theory and reality of capitalist work,* ed. A. Dinerstein and M. Neary. Aldershot, Engl.: Ashgate.

———. 2002c. *Globalisation and education.* A paper prepared for the House of Lords Select Committee on Economic Affairs. HL Paper 5-1, November 18, at http://education.portal.dk3.com/article.php?sid=21.

Saltman, K. J., and D. Gabbard. 2003. *Education as enforcement: The militarization and corporatization of schools.* New York: Routledge.

Sarup, M. 1984. *Marxism/structuralism/education.* London: Falmer Press.

Shor, I. 1986. *Culture wars: School and society in the conservative restoration, 1969–1984.* London: Routledge and Kegan Paul.

Skocpol, T. 1980. Political response to capitalist crisis: Neo-Marxist theories of the state and the case of the New Deal. *Politics and Society* 10 (2): 155–201.

Teacher Training Agency. 1997. *Consultation on the revised requirements for all courses of initial teacher training.* London: Teacher Training Agency.

Therborn, G. 1978. *What does the ruling class do when it rules?* London: New Left Books.

Thrupp, M. 1999. *Schools making a difference: Let's be realistic!* Buckingham, Engl.: Open University Press.

———. 2000. Compensating for class: Are school improvement researchers being realistic? *Education and Social Justice* 2 (2): 2–11.

Toynbee, P. 2000. Gordon Brown speaks. And, as they say, money talks. *Guardian,* July 19.

Tucker, R. 1978. See Marx ([1847] 1978).

U.K. Government. 1999. *The government's annual report 98/99.* London: Stationery Office.

Usher, R., and R. Edwards. 1994. *Postmodernism and education: Different voices, different worlds.* London: Routledge.

Whitty, G. 1985. *Sociology and school knowledge: Curriculum theory, research and politics.* London: Methuen.

———. 1994. Education reform and teacher education in England in the 1990s. In *International analyses of teacher education,* ed. P. Gilroy and M. Smith. Abingdon: Carfax.

———. 1997. Marketization, the state, and the re-formation of the teaching profession. In *Education, culture and economy,* ed. A. H. Halsey, H. Lauder, P. Brown, and A. Stuart Wells. Oxford: Oxford University Press.

Whitty, G., S. Power, and D. Halpin. 1998. *Devolution and choice in education: The school, the state and the market.* Buckingham: Open University Press.

Wilkin, M. 1996. *Initial teacher training: The dialogue of ideology and culture.* London: Falmer Press.

Woods, P., and B. Jeffrey. 1998. Choosing positions: Living the contradictions of OFSTED. *British Journal of Sociology of Education* 19 (4): 547–70.

3

War Talk and the Shredding of the Social Contract: Youth and the Politics of Domestic Militarization

Henry A. Giroux

To understand how the social contract is being shredded, it is crucial to focus on the way in which the militarizing language of war now dominates public discourse. The concept of war occupies a strange place in the current lexicon of foreign and domestic policy. It no longer simply refers to a war waged against a sovereign state such as Iraq, nor is it merely a moral referent for engaging in acts of national self-defense. The concept of war has been both expanded and inverted. It has been expanded in that it has become one of the most powerful concepts for understanding and structuring political culture, public space, and everyday life. Wars are waged against crime, labor unions, drugs, terrorism, and a host of alleged public disorders. Wars are not declared against foreign enemies but against alleged domestic threats. The concept of war has also been inverted in that is has been removed from any concept of social justice—a relationship that emerged under President Lyndon Johnson and is exemplified in the war on poverty.

War is now defined almost exclusively as a punitive and militaristic process. This can be seen in the ways in which social policies have been criminalized so that the war on poverty is now a war against the poor, the war on drugs is now a war waged largely against youth of color, and the war against terrorism is now largely a war against immigrants, domestic freedoms, and dissent itself. In the Bush, Perle, Rumsfeld, and Ashcroft view of terrorism, war is individualized as every citizen becomes a potential terrorist who has to prove that he or she is not dangerous. Under the rubric of the never-ending terrorist apocalypse, which feeds on government-induced media panics, war provides the moral imperative to collapse the "boundaries between innocent and guilty, between suspects and non-suspects."[1]

War provides the primary rhetorical tool for articulating a notion of the social as a community organized around shared fears rather than shared responsibilities and civic courage. War is now transformed into a slick, Hollywood spectacle designed to both glamorize a notion of hypermasculinity fashioned in the conservative oil fields of Texas and fills public space with celebrations of ritualized militaristic posturing touting the virtues of either becoming part of "an Army of one" or indulging in commodified patriotism by purchasing a Hummer. Within the undemocratic confluence of politics, propaganda, and advertising, public space is militarized and everyday life becomes an advertisement for a hyperaggressive image of masculinity. For instance, a number of major fashion designers are now dressing their models in commando gear and combat fatigues.[2] Sony takes aim at the youth market by patterning the term *shock and awe*—made famous by President Bush to describe the initial bombing strategy to be used against Baghdad—for a computer game. War as spectacle easily combines with the culture of fear to divert public attention away from domestic problems, define patriotism as consensus, and further the growth of a police state. The latter takes on dangerous overtones not only with the passage of the Patriot Act and the suspension of civil liberties, but also in the elimination of laws that traditionally separated the military from domestic law enforcement and offered individuals a vestige of civil liberties and freedoms. The political implications of the expanded and inverted use of war as a metaphor can also be seen in the war against "big government," which is really a war against the welfare state and the social contract itself—this is a war against the notion that everyone should have access to decent education, health care, employment, and other public services. But more important, it is a war against the most fundamental principles of democracy and raises important questions about whether this society is on the road to a new form of authoritarianism in which the only contract that matters is between the state and corporate power.

Wars are almost always legitimated to make the world safe for "our children's future" but the rhetoric belies how their future is often denied by the acts of aggression put into place by a range of state agencies and institutions that operate on a war footing. This would include the horrible effects of the militarization of schools, the use of the criminal justice system to redefine social issues such as poverty and homelessness as criminal violations, and the subsequent rise of a prison–industrial complex as a way to contain disposable populations such as youth of color who are poor and marginalized. Under the rubric of war, security, and antiterrorism, children are "disappeared" from the most basic social spheres that once provided the conditions for a sense of agency and possibility, as they are rhetorically excised from any discourse about the future. What is so troubling about the current historical moment is that youth no longer symbolize the future. And yet, any discourse about the future has to begin with the issue of youth because, more than any other group, youth embody the projected dreams, desires, and commitment of a society's obligations to the future. This echoes a classical principle of modern democracy in which youth both symbolize society's responsibility to the future and offer a measure of its progress. For most of this century, Americans have embraced as a defining feature of politics that all levels of government would assume a large measure of responsibility for providing the resources, social provisions, security, and modes of education that simultaneously offered young people a future as it expanded the meaning and depth of a substantive democracy. In many respects, youth not only registered symbolically the importance of modernity's claim to progress, they also affirmed the centrality of the liberal, democratic tradition of the social contract in which adult responsibility was mediated through a willingness to fight for the rights of children, enact reforms that invested in their future, and provide the educational conditions necessary for them to make use of the freedoms they have while learning how to be critical citizens. Within such a political project, democracy was linked to the well-being of youth, while the status of how a society imagined democracy and its future was contingent on how it viewed its responsibility towards future generations.

Yet, at the dawn of the new millennium, it is not at all clear that we believe any longer in youth, the future, or the social contract, even in its minimalist version. Since the Reagan/Thatcher revolution of the 1980s, we have been told that there is no such thing as society and, indeed, following that nefarious pronouncement, institutions committed to public welfare have been disappearing ever since. Rather than being cherished as a symbol of the future, youth are now seen as a threat to be feared and a problem to be contained. A seismic change has taken place in which youth are now being framed as both a generation of suspects and a threat to public life. If youth once symbolized the moral necessity to address a range of social and economic ills, they are now largely portrayed as the source of most of society's problems. Hence, youth now constitute a crisis that has less to do with improving the future than with denying it. A concern for children is the defining absence in almost any discourse about the future and the obligations this implies for adult society. To witness the abdication of adult responsibility to children we need look no further than the current state of children in America.

Instead of providing a decent education to poor young people, American society offers them the growing potential of being incarcerated, buttressed by the fact that the United States is one of the few countries in the world that sentences minors to death and spends "three times more on each incarcerated citizen than on each public school pupil."[3] Instead of guaranteeing them food, decent health care, and shelter, we serve them more standardized tests; instead of providing them with vibrant public spheres, we offer them a commercialized culture in which consumerism is the only obligation of citizenship. But in the hard currency of human suffering, children pay a heavy price in the richest democracy in the world: 20 percent of children are poor during the first three years of life and more than 13.3 million live in poverty; 9.2 million children lack health insurance; millions lack affordable child care and decent early childhood education; in many states more money is being spent on prison construction than on education; the infant mortality rate in the United States is the highest of any other industrialized nation.

When broken down along racial categories, the figures become even more despairing. For example, "In 1998, 36 percent of black and 34 percent of Hispanic children lived in poverty, compared with 14 percent of white children."[4] In some cities, such as Washington, D.C., the child poverty rate is as high as 45 percent.[5] While the United States ranks first in military technology, military exports, defense expenditures and the number of millionaires and billionaires, it is ranked eighteenth among the advanced industrial nations in the gap between rich and poor children, twelfth in the percent of children in poverty, seventeenth in the efforts to lift children out of poverty, and twenty-third in infant mortality.[6] One of the most shameful figures on youth as reported by Jennifer Egan, a writer for the *New York Times*, indicates that "1.4 million children are homeless in America for a time in any given year . . . and these children make up 40 percent of the nation's homeless population."[7] In short, economically, politically, and culturally, the situation of youth in the United States is intolerable and obscene. It is all the more unforgivable since President Bush insisted during the 2000 campaign that "the biggest percentage of our budget should go to children's education." He then passed a 2002 budget in which forty times more money went for tax cuts for the wealthiest 1 percent of the population rather than for education.[8] In his more recent budget, President Bush is doing something no other president has done. He is pushing through an immense tax cut, estimated at three trillion—that largely benefits the rich—in the midst of a war whose cost down the road is staggering. At the same time, he is cutting veterans programs, including money for disabilities caused by war, and benefits in education health care for their kids. He is also cutting $93 billion from Medicaid, making huge environmental cuts, and cutting a vast array of domestic programs that directly benefit children.

Under this insufferable climate of increased repression and misplaced priorities, young people become the new casualties in an ongoing war against justice, freedom, citizenship, and democracy, and this can be seen in the images this society provides of children in trouble, which should but rarely strike at the heart of a society's conscience. In a society that appears to have turned its back on the young, what we are increasingly witnessing on prime time media are images of children, such as Alex and Derek King, ages 12 and 13, handcuffed, sitting in adult courts before stern judges, facing murder charges. These images are matched by endless films, videos, ads, documentaries, television programs, and journalistic accounts in which urban youth—depicted largely as gang bangers, drug dealers, and rapists—are portrayed as violent, dangerous, and pathological.

No longer seen as a crucial social investment for the future of a democratic society, youth are now demonized by the popular media and derided by politicians looking for quick-fix solutions to crime. In recent times, a whole generation of youth have been labeled as superpredators, spiraling out of control. One vivid example of such an attack can be seen in a provocative antidrug–antiterrorism advertising campaign sponsored by the Bush administration's

White House Drug Control Office and run extensively in both print media and on telelvision. Driven by a dead-end moralism as it taps into a culture of fear, the campaign serves to both punish youth and prevent any reasonable analysis about the causes of terrorism. Shot in stark black and white, the ads begin with close-ups of the faces of exclusively dark-haired teenagers (no blond, suburban kids in this group). Their faces appear in rapid succession on the television screen. Each teenager admits matter-of-factly in short staccato sentences a litany of horrendous crimes they allegedly helped people commit. The mantra includes: "I helped murder families in Columbia," "I helped kids learn how to kill," "I helped a bomber get a fake passport," and "I helped blow up buildings." After each admission, a different youthful face repeats any one of the following refrains: "It was just innocent fun," "Hey, some harmless fun," or "All the kids do it." The ad ends with the message: "Drug money supports terror. If you buy drugs, you might too."

A succeeding batch of antidrug ads were even more offensive. Using the same signature message "Drug money supports terror. If you buy drugs, you might too," they demonize youth in more extreme fashion. Here is one example from an ad titled, "Timmy." In this ad a young boy facing the camera says matter-of-factly "I kill mothers; I kill fathers; I kill grandmothers; I kill grandpas; I kill sons; I kill daughters; I kill firemen; I kill policemen. [pause] Technically, I didn't kill these people, I just kind of helped." It is difficult to tell whether the qualification is for added effect or whether the insanity of the charge became clear, if only as an afterthought.

Ostensibly a blow against the war on drugs but framed as part of the war against terrorism, the ad campaign suggests that children are, in part, responsible for promoting terrorist campaigns being waged all over the world, including those directed at the United States on September 11, 2001. The goal of the campaign is to shame young, casual drug users by leading them to believe that the drugs they purchase help pay for terrorist activities, especially those acts engaged in by the al Qaeda terrorists who attacked New York's World Trade Center and the Pentagon. What is so disturbing about these ads is the presupposition that American youth who casually engage in drug use are somehow responsible for such terrorist acts. According to this logic, people who fill up their cars with gasoline or buy diamonds would also be responsible for such acts since terrorist groups make millions from both the diamond trade and oil profits. But don't expect any ads to appear soon condemning suburban moms who buy gas-guzzling SUVs or Hollywood starlets who wear diamonds for sponsoring terrorist campaigns around the globe. Adults would not tolerate such an irresponsible, blanket accusation. But an accusation that appears irresponsible and fallacious when applied to adults seems quite reasonable when applied to young people.

In a society deeply troubled by their presence, youth prompts in the public imagination a rhetoric of fear, control, and surveillance—made all the more visible with the 2002 Supreme Court decision upholding the widespread use of random drug testing of public school students. Such random drug testing of all junior and senior high school students who desire to participate in extracurricular activities registers a deep distrust of students and furthers the notion that youth should be viewed with suspicion and treated as potential criminals. Police and drug-sniffing dogs now are a common fixture in public schools as schools increasingly resemble prisons, and students are treated as suspects who need to be searched, tested, and observed under the watchful eye of administrators who appear to have less interest in education than in policing. Trust and respect now give way to fear, disdain, and suspicion. Moreover, this perception of fear and disdain is increasingly being translated into social policies that signal the shrinking of the democratic public sphere, the hijacking of civic culture, and the increasing militarization of public space.

In many suburban malls, young people (coded as youth of color) cannot even shop or walk around without either appropriate identification cards or being in the company of their parents. Excluded from public spaces outside of schools that once offered them the opportunity to hang out with relative security, work with mentors in youth centers, and develop their own talents and sense of self-worth, young people are forced to hang out in the streets, while increasingly subject to police surveillance, antigang statutes, and curfew laws, especially in poor, urban neighborhoods. Gone are the youth centers, city public parks, outdoor basketball courts, or empty lots where kids can play stick ball. Play areas are now rented out to the highest bidder, "caged in by steel fences, wrought iron gates, padlocks and razor ribbon wire."[9]

Liberals, conservatives, corporate interests, and religious fundamentalists are waging a war against those public spaces and laws that view children and youth as an important social investment, and it includes a full-scale attack on social services, the welfare state, and the public schools. For instance, Peter Cassidy argues that young people are being subjected to forms of emotional violence and privacy intrusions that were unimaginable twenty years ago, except for prison inmates. He claims that "a veritable Kindergulag has been erected around schoolchildren, making them subject to arbitrary curfews, physical searchers, arbitrarily applied profiling schemes, and . . . random, suspicionless, warrantless drug testing. . . . If you're a kid in the U.S. today, martial law isn't a civics class lecture unit. It is a fact of life as the war on drugs, the war on violence and a nearly hysterical emphasis on safety has come to excuse the infliction of every kind of humiliation upon the young."[10] Youth have become the central site onto which class and racial anxieties are projected. Their very presence represents *both* the broken promises of capitalism in the age of deregulation and downsizing *and* a collective fear of the consequences wrought by systemic class inequalities and a culture of "infectious greed" that has created a generation of unskilled and displaced youth expelled from shrinking markets, blue-collar jobs, and any viable hope in the future. It is against this growing threat to basic freedom, democracy, and youth that I want to address the related issues of democracy, zero-tolerance policies, and public schools.

ZERO TOLERANCE AND THE POLITICS/COLOR OF PUNISHMENT

When the "war on poverty" ran out of steam with the social and economic crisis that emerged in the 1970s, there was a growing shift at all levels of government from an emphasis on social investments to an emphasis on public control,
social containment, and the criminalization of social problems. The criminalization of social issues—starting with President Ronald Reagan's war on drugs,[11]
the privatization of the prison industry in the 1980s, and escalating to the war
on immigrants in the early 1990s and the rise of the prison–industrial complex
by the close of the decade—has now become a part of everyday culture and
provides a common referent point that extends from governing prisons and
regulating urban culture to running schools. This is most evident in the emergence of zero-tolerance laws that have swept the nation since the 1980s, and
gained full legislative strength with the passage of the Violent Crime Control
and Law Enforcement Act of 1994. Following the mandatory sentencing legislation and get-tough policies associated with the "war on drugs," this bill calls
for a "three strikes and you're out" policy, which puts repeat offenders, including nonviolent offenders, in jail for life, regardless of the seriousness of the
crime. As has been widely reported, the United States is now the biggest jailer
in the world. Between 1985 and 2001 the prison population grew from 744,206
to 2.1 million (approaching the combined populations of Idaho, Wyoming, and
Montana), and prison budgets jumped from $7 billion in 1980 to $40 billion in
2000.[12] Put another way, the United States is "spending $35,000 a year to main-
tain one prisoner in a minimum-security cell. . . . [while] it costs nearly $80,000
a year to confine a prisoner in a maximum-security cell. [In addition,] we are
building over a hundred new prison cells a day."[13] Yet, even as the crime rate
plummets dramatically, more people, especially people of color, are being arrested, harassed, punished, and put in jail.[14] Of the two million people behind
bars, 70 percent are people of color with 50 percent being African Americans,
while 17 percent are Latinos.[15]

A Justice Department report points out that on any given day in this country
"more than a third of the young African American men aged 18–34 in some of
our major cities are either in prison or under some form of criminal justice su-
pervision."[16] The same department reported in April 2000 that "black youth are
forty-eight times more likely than whites to be sentenced to juvenile prison for
drug offenses."[17]

Domestic militarization in the form of zero-tolerance laws, in this instance,
not only functions to contain "minority populations," deprive them of their electoral rights (13 percent of all black men in the United States have lost their right
to vote),[18] and provide new sources of revenue from a system that "evokes the
convict leasing system of the Old South,"[19] it also actively promotes and legitimates retrograde and repressive social policies. For example, an increasing
number of states, including California and New York, are now spending more
on prison construction than on higher education. They are also hiring more

prison guards than teachers. In California, the average prison guard now earns $10,000 more than the average public school teacher, and increasingly more than many professors working in the state university system.[20]

What is one to make of social policies that portray youth, especially poor youth of color, as a generation of suspects? What are we to make of a social order—headed by a pro-gun, pro–capital punishment, and pro–big business conservative such as George W. Bush—whose priorities suggest to urban youth that American society is willing to invest more in sending them to jail than in providing them with high-quality schools and a decent education? How does a society justify housing poor students in schools that are unsafe, decaying, and with little or no extracurricular activities while spending five times more annually—as high as $20,000 in many suburban schools—on each middle-class student, housing them in schools with Olympic swimming pools, the latest computer technology, and well-cared-for buildings and grounds? What message is being sent to young people when in a state such as New York "more Blacks entered prison just for drug offenses than graduated from the state's massive university system with undergraduate, masters, and doctoral degrees combined in the 1990s."[21] What message is being sent to youth when, as federal deficits are soaring, the Bush administration provides tax cuts for the rich— in one instance $114 billion in corporate tax concessions—while children face drastic cuts in education and health aid as well as other massive cuts in domestic programs such as job training and summer employment opportunities. In this instance, the culture of domestic militarization, with its policies of containment, brutalization, and punishment become more valued to the dominant social order than any consideration of what it means for a society to expand and strengthen the mechanisms and freedoms of a fully realized democracy.[22]

Zero-tolerance policies have been especially cruel in the treatment of juvenile offenders.[23] Rather than attempting to work with youth and make an investment in their psychological, economic, and social well-being, a growing number of cities are passing sweep laws—curfews and bans against loitering and cruising—designed not only to keep youth off the streets, but also to make it easier to criminalize their behavior. For example, within the last decade, "45 states . . . have passed or amended legislation making it easier to prosecute juveniles as adults," and in some states "prosecutors can bump a juvenile case into adult court at their own discretion."[24] In Kansas and Vermont, a ten-year-old child can be tried in adult court. A particularly harsh example of the draconian measures being used against young people can be seen in the passing of Proposition 21 in California. This law makes it easier for prosecutors to try teens fourteen and older in adult court who are convicted of felonies. These youth would automatically be put in adult prison and be given lengthy mandated sentences. The overall consequence of the law is to largely eliminate intervention programs, increase the number of youth in prisons, especially minority youth, and keep them there for longer periods of time. Moreover, the law is at odds with a number of studies that indicate that putting youth in jail with adults both increases recidivism and poses a grave danger to young offenders who, as a recent Columbia University study suggested, are "five times as likely to be raped, twice as likely to be beaten, and eight times as likely to commit suicide than adults in the adult prison system."[25]

Paradoxically, the moral panic against crime and now terrorism that increasingly feeds the calls for punishment and revenge rather than rehabilitation programs for young people exists in conjunction with the disturbing fact that the United States is currently one of only seven countries (Congo, Iran, Nigeria, Pakistan, Saudi Arabia, and Yemen are the other six) in the world that permit the death penalty for juveniles, and that in the last decade it has executed more juvenile offenders than the other six countries combined.[26] In many states, youth cannot get a tattoo, join the military, get their ears pierced, or get a marriage license until they are eighteen, but a ten-year-old can be jailed as an adult and condemned to death in some states. The prize-winning novelist Ann Patchett recently suggested in the *New York Times* that perhaps the problem is that "as Americans, we no longer have any idea what constitutes a child."[27] This strikes me as ludicrous. The ongoing attacks on children's rights, the endless commercialization of youth, the downsizing of children's services, and the increasing incarceration of young people suggest more than confusion. In actuality, such policies suggest that, at best, adult society no longer cares about children and, at worse, views them as an object of scorn and fear.

As the state is downsized and basic social services dry up, containment policies become the principal means to discipline youth and restrict their ability to think critically and engage in oppositional practices. Within this context, zero-tolerance legislation within the schools simply extend to young people elements of harsh control and administration implemented in other public spheres where inequalities breed the conditions for dissent and resistance. Moreover, as David Garland points out, "Large-scale incarceration functions as a mode of economic and social placement, a zoning mechanism that segregates those populations rejected by the depleted institutions of family, work, and welfare and places them behind the scenes of social life."[28] Marginalized students learn quickly that they are surplus populations and that the journey from home to school no longer means they will next move into a job; on the contrary, school now becomes a training ground for their "graduation" into containment centers such as prisons and jails that keep them out of sight, patrolled and monitored so as to prevent them from becoming a social canker or political liability to those white and middle-class populations concerned about their own safety. Schools increasingly resemble other weakened public spheres as they cut back on trained psychologists; school nurses; programs such as music, art, and athletics; and valuable after-school activities. Jesse Jackson argues that under such circumstances, schools not only fail to provide students with a well-rounded education, they often "bring in the police, [and] the school gets turned into a feeder system for the penal system."[29] I now want to switch my focus a bit to analyze zero-tolerance policies and practices as they are applied more specifically in public schools.

SCHOOLING AND THE PEDAGOGY OF ZERO TOLERANCE

Across the nation school districts are lining up to embrace zero-tolerance policies. According to the U.S. Department of Education, about 90 percent of school systems nationwide have implemented such policies to deal with either violence or threats.[30]

Emulating state and federal laws passed in the 1990s, such as the federal Gun-Free Schools Act of 1994, that were based on mandatory sentencing and "three strikes and you're out" policies, many educators first invoked zero-tolerance rules against those kids who brought guns to schools. But over time the policy was broadened and now includes a gamut of student misbehavior ranging from using or circulating drugs, harboring a weapon, to *threatening* other students—all broadly conceived. Under zero-tolerance policies, forms of punishments that were once applied to adults now apply to first-graders. Originally aimed at "students who misbehave intentionally, the law now applies to those who misbehave as a result of emotional problems or other disabilities" as well.[31]

Unfortunately, any sense of perspective or guarantee of rights seems lost, as school systems across the country clamor for metal detectors, armed guards, see-through knapsacks, and in some cases armed teachers. Some school systems are investing in new software to "profile" students who might exhibit criminal behavior.[32] Overzealous laws relieve educators of exercising deliberation and critical judgment as more and more young people are either suspended or expelled from school, often for ludicrous reasons. For example, two Virginia fifth-graders who allegedly put soap in their teacher's drinking water were charged with a felony.[33] A twelve-year-old boy in Louisiana who was diagnosed with a hyperactive disorder was suspended for two days after telling his friends in a food line, "I'm gonna get you" if they ate the all the potatoes. The police then charged the boy with making "terroristic threats" and he was incarcerated for two weeks while awaiting trial. A fourteen-year-old disabled student in Palm Beach, Florida, was referred to the police by the school principal for allegedly stealing two dollars from another student. He was then charged with strong-arm robbery and held for six weeks in an adult jail, even though this was his first arrest.[34] There is also the equally revealing example of a student brought up on a drug charge because he gave another youth two lemon cough drops.[35]

As *Boston Globe* columnist Ellen Goodman points out, zero tolerance does more than offer a simple solution to a complex problem, it has become a code word for a "quick and dirty way of kicking kids out" of school rather than creating safe environments for them.[36] For example, the *Denver Rocky Mountain News* reported in June 1999 that "partly as a result of such rigor in enforcing Colorado's zero-tolerance law, the number of kids kicked out of public schools has skyrocketed since 1993—from 437 before the law to nearly 2,000 in the 1996–1997 school year."[37] In Chicago, the widespread adoption of zero-tolerance policies in 1994 resulted in a 51 percent increase in student suspensions for the next four years, and a 3,000 percent increase in expulsions, jumping from 21 in 1994–1995 to 668 the following year.[38] Within such a climate of disdain and intolerance, expelling students does more than pose a threat to innocent kids, it also suggests that local school boards are refusing to do the hard work of exercising critical judgment, trying to understand what conditions undermine school safety, and providing reasonable support services for all students and viable alternatives for the troubled ones. As the criminalization of young people finds its way into the classroom, it becomes easier for school administrators to punish students rather than listen to them or, for that matter, to work with parents, community programs, religious organizations, and social service agencies.[39] Even though zero-tolerance policies clog up the courts and put additional pressure on an already overburdened juvenile justice system, educators appear to have few qualms about implementing them. And the results are far from inconsequential for the students themselves.

Most insidiously, zero-tolerance laws, while a threat to all youth and any viable notion of equal opportunity through education, reinforces in the public imagination the image of students of color as a source of public fears and a threat to public school safety. Zero-tolerance policies and laws appear to be well tailored for mobilizing racialized codes and race-based moral panics that portray black and brown urban youth as a frightening and violent threat to the safety of "decent" Americans. Not only do most of the high-profile zero-tolerance cases involve African American students, but such policies also reinforce the racial inequities that plague school systems across the country. For example, the *New York Times*, has reported on a number of studies illustrating "that black students in public schools across the country are far more likely than whites to be suspended or expelled, and far less likely to be in gifted or advanced placement classes."[40] Even in a city such as San Francisco, considered a bastion of liberalism, African American students pay a far greater price for zero-tolerance policies. Libero Della Piana reports, "According to data collected by Justice Matters, a San Francisco agency advocating equity in education, African Americans make up 52 percent of all suspended students in the district—far in excess of the 16 percent of the general population."[41] Marilyn Elias reported in a recent issue of *USA Today,* "In 1998, the first year national expulsion figures were gathered, 31% of kids expelled were black, but blacks made up only 17% of the students in public schools."[42]

Feeding on moral panic and popular fear, zero-tolerance policies not only turn schools into an adjunct of the criminal justice system, they also further rationalize misplaced legislative priorities. And that has profound social costs. Instead of investing in early childhood programs, repairing deteriorating school buildings, or hiring more qualified teachers, schools spend millions of dollars to upgrade security, even when such a fortress mentality defines the simplest test of common sense. For example, school administrators at Fremont High School in Oakland, California, decided to build a security fence costing $500,000 "while the heating remained out of commission."[43] Young people are quickly realizing that schools have more in common with military boot camps and prisons than they do with other institutions in American society. In addition, as schools abandon their role as democratic public spheres and are literally "fenced off" from the communities that surround them, they lose their ability to become anything other than spaces of containment and control. In this context, discipline and training replace education for all but the privileged as schools increasingly take on an uncanny resemblance to oversized police precincts, tragically disconnected both from the students who inhabit them and the communities that give meaning to their historical experiences and daily lives. As schools become militarized, they lose their ability to provide students with the skills to cope with human differences, uncertainty, and the various symbolic and institutional forces that undermine political agency and democratic public life itself.

SCHOOLING AND THE CRISIS OF PUBLIC LIFE

Zero-tolerance policies suggest a dangerous imbalance between democratic values and the culture of fear. Instead of security, zero-tolerance policies in the schools contribute to a growing climate of bigotry, hypocrisy, and intolerance that turns a generation of youth into criminal suspects. In spite of what we are told by the current Bush administration, conservative educators, the religious right, and the cheerleaders of corporate culture, the greatest threat to education in this country does not come from disruptive students, the absence of lock-down safety measures, and get-tough school polices. Nor are young people threatened by the alleged decline of academic standards, the absence of privatized choice schemes, or the lack of rigid testing measures. On the contrary, the greatest threat to young people comes from a society that refuses to view them as a social investment, that consigns 13.5 million children to live in poverty, reduces critical learning to massive testing programs, refuses to pay teachers an adequate salary, promotes policies that eliminate most crucial health and public services, and defines masculinity through the degrading celebration of a gun culture, extreme sports, and the spectacles of violence that permeate corporate-controlled media industries. It also comes from a society that values security more than basic rights, wages an assault on all nonmarket values and public goods, and engages in a ruthless transfer of wealth from the poor and middle class to the rich and privileged.

We live in a society in which a culture of punishment, greed, and intolerance has replaced a culture of social responsibility and compassion. We have increasingly become a society in which issues regarding persistent poverty, inadequate health care, racial apartheid in the inner cities, and the growing inequalities between the rich and the poor have been either removed from the inventory of public discourse and progressive social policy or factored into talk-show spectacles. This is evident in ongoing attempts by many liberals and conservatives to turn commercial-free public education over to market forces, dismantle

traditional social provisions of the welfare state, turn over all vestiges of the
health-care system to private interests, and mortgage social security to the whims
of the stock market. Emptied of any substantial content, democracy appears im-
periled as individuals are unable to translate their privately suffered misery into
public concerns and collective action. The result is not only silence and indifference, but the elimination of those public spaces that reveal the rough edges
of social order, disrupt consensus, and point to the need for modes of education
and knowledge that link learning to the conditions necessary for developing
democratic forms of political agency and civic struggle. This is a society in which
biographical solutions are substituted for systemic contradictions, and as Ulrich
Beck points out institutions "for overcoming problems" are converted into "institutions for causing problems."[44]

Within such a climate of harsh discipline and moral indifference, it is easier
to put young people in jail than to provide the education, services, and care
they need to face problems of a complex and demanding society.[45] The notion
that children should be viewed as a crucial social resource who present for any
healthy society important ethical and political considerations about the quality
of public life, the allocation of social provisions, and the role of the state as a
guardian of public interests appears to be lost in a society that refuses to invest
in its youth as part of a broader commitment to a fully realized democracy. As
the social order becomes more privatized and militarized, we increasingly face
the problem of losing a generation of young people to a system of increasing
intolerance, repression, and moral indifference.

The growing attack on youth and public education in American society may
say less about the reputed apathy of the populace than about the bankruptcy of
the old political languages and the need for a new language and vision for expanding and deepening the meaning of democracy and making the education
of youth central to such a project. Made over in the image of corporate culture,
schools are no longer valued as a public good but as a private interest; hence,
the appeal of such schools is less about their capacity to educate students according to the demands of critical citizenship than it is about enabling students
to master the requirements of a market-driven economy. This is not education
but training. Under these circumstances, many students increasingly find themselves in schools that lack any language for relating the self to public life, social
responsibility, or the imperatives of democratic life. In this instance, democratic
education with its emphasis on social justice, respect for others, critical inquiry,
equality, freedom, civic courage, and concern for the collective good is suppressed and replaced by an excessive emphasis on the language of privatization, individualism, self-interest, and brutal competitiveness. Lost in this commercial and privatizing discourse of schooling is any notion of democratic
community or models of leadership capable of raising questions about what
public schools should accomplish in a democracy and why they fail under certain circumstances, or, for that matter, why public schools have increasingly
adapted policies that bear a close resemblance to how prisons are run.

I want to conclude by arguing that the growth and popularity of zero-tolerance policies within the public schools have to be understood as part of a broader crisis of democracy in which the market is now seen as the master design for all pedagogical encounters and the state is increasingly geared to measures of militarization, containment, and surveillance rather than expanding democratic freedoms and social investments. In this sense, the war in Iraq, the corporatizing of public schooling, and the war against youth cannot be disassociated from the assault on those public spheres and public goods that provide the conditions for greater democratic participation in shaping society. As the state is downsized and basic social services dry up, containment policies become the principal means to discipline youth and restrict their ability to think critically and engage in oppositional practices. Within this context, zero-tolerance legislation within the schools simply extend to young people elements of harsh control and administration implemented in other public spheres where inequalities breed dissent and resistance. What has become clear in the policies enacted by Bush administration is that there is no discourse for recognizing the obligations a democratic society has to pay its debts to past generations and fulfill its obligations to future generations.

Zero tolerance has become a metaphor for hollowing out the state and expanding the forces of domestic militarization, reducing democracy to consumerism, and replacing an ethic of mutual aid with an appeal to excessive individualism and social indifference.[46] Within this logic, the notion of the political increasingly equates power with domination, and citizenship with consumerism and passivity. Under this insufferable climate of manufactured indifference, increased repression, unabated exploitation, and a war with Iraq that Senator Robert Byrd believes is rooted in the arrogance of unbridled power, young people have become the new casualties in an ongoing battle against justice, freedom, social citizenship, and democracy. As despairing as these conditions appear, they increasingly have become the basis for a surge of political resistance on the part of many youth, intellectuals, labor unions, educators, and social movements.[47] Educators, young people, parents, religious organizations, community activists, and other cultural workers need to rethink what it would mean to both interrogate and break away from the dangerous and destructive ideologies, values, and social relations of zero-tolerance policies as they work in a vast and related number of powerful institutional spheres to reinforce modes of authoritarian control and turn a generation of youth into a generation of suspects. This suggests a struggle both for public space and the conditions for a public dialogue about how to imagine reappropriating a notion of politics that is linked to the creation of a strong democracy while simultaneously articulating a new vocabulary, set of theoretical tools, and social possibilities for revisioning civic engagement and social transformation. Under such circumstances, it is time to remind ourselves that collective problems deserve collective solutions and that what is at risk is not only a generation of young people now considered to be generation of potential troublemakers, but the very promise of democracy itself. The issue is no longer whether it is possible to invest in the idea of the schooling as a democratic public sphere and the social order as a vibrant and substantive democracy, but what are the consequences for not doing so.

NOTES

1. Ulrich Beck, "The Silence of Words and Political Dynamics in the World Risk Society," *Logos* 1, no. 4 (Fall 2002): 1–18, 3.

2. Cathy Horyn, "Macho America Storms Europe's Runways," *New York Times,* July 3, 2003, A1, A10.

3. Heather Wokusch, "Leaving Our Children Behind," *Common Dreams News Center,* July 8, 2002, available online at www.commondreams.org/views02/0708-08.htm.

4. These figures are taken from Child Research Briefs, "Poverty, Welfare, and Children: A Summary of the Data." Available online at www.childtrends.org.

5. These figures are taken from Childhood Poverty Research Briefs 2, "Child Poverty in the States: Levels and Trends from 1979 to 1998." Available online at www.nccp.org.

6. These figures largely come from Children's Defense Fund, *The State of Children in America's Union: A 2002 Action Guide to Leave No Child Behind* (Washington, D.C.: Children's Defense Fund Publication, 2002): iv–v, 13.

7. Jennifer Egan, "To Be Young and Homeless," *New York Times Magazine,* March 24, 2002, 35.

8. Heather Wokusch, "Leaving Our Children Behind," 1.

9. Cited in Robin D. G. Kelley, *Yo' Mama's Disfunktional! Fighting the Culture Wars in Urban America* (Boston: Beacon Press, 1997), 44.

10. Peter Cassidy, "Last Brick in the Kindergulag," online at alternet.org/print.hgml? StoryId=13616.

11. For an insightful commentary on the media and the racial nature of the war on drugs, see Jimmie L. Reeves and Richard Campbell, *Cracked Coverage: Television News, the Anti-cocaine Crusade, and the Reagan Legacy* (Durham, N.C.: Duke University Press, 1994).

12. These figures are taken from the following sources: Gary Delgado, "'Mo' Prisons Equals MO' Money," *Colorlines* (Winter 1999–2000): 18; Fox Butterfield, "Number in Prison Grows Despite Crime Reduction," *New York Times,* August 10, 2000, A10; Lewis, "Number in Prison Grows Despite Crime Reduction," *New York Times,* August 10, 2000, A1.

13. Manning Marable, "Green Party Politics," transcript of speech given in Denver, Colorado on June 24, 2000, 3.

14. For some extensive analyses of the devastating affects the criminal justice system is having on black males, see Michael Tonry, *Malign Neglect: Race, Crime, and Punishment in America* (New York: Oxford University Press, 1995); Jerome Miller, *Search and Destroy: African-American Males in the Criminal Justice System* (Cambridge: Cambridge University Press, 1996); David Cole, *No Equal Justice: Race and Class in the American Criminal Justice System* (New York: New Press, 1999).

15. Cited in David Barsamian, "Interview with Angela Dais," *Progressive* (February 2001), 35.

16. Donziger in Barsamian, "Interview with Angela Dais," 101.

17. Lisa Featherstone, "A Common Enemy: Students Fight Private Prisons," *Dissent* (Fall 2000), 78.

18. Paul Street, "Race, Prison, and Poverty: The Race to Incarcerate in the Age of Correctional Keynesianism," *Z Magazine* (May 2001), 26.

19. Featherstone, "A Common Enemy," 81.

20. Cited from Eric Lotke, "The Prison–Industrial Complex," *Multinational Monitor* (November 1996), available online www.igc.org/ncia/pic.html.

21. Paul Street, "Race, Prison, and Poverty," 26.

22. Even more shameful is that fact that such discrimination against African Americans is often justified from the Olympian heights of institutions such as Harvard University by apologists such as lawyer Randall Kennedy who argue that such laws, criminal policies, and police practices are necessary to protect "good" blacks from "bad" blacks who commit crimes. See Randall Kennedy, *Race, Crime, and the Law* (New York: Pantheon, 1997).

23. For a moving narrative of the devastating effects of the juvenile justice system on teens, see Edward Humes, *No Matter How Loud I Shout: A Year in the Life of Juvenile Court* (New York: Touchstone, 1996).

24. Margaret Talbot, "The Maximum Security Adolescent," *New York Times Magazine,* September 10, 2000, 42.

25. Cited in Evelyn Nieves, "California Proposal Toughens Penalties for Young Criminals," *New York Times,* March 6, 2000, A1, A15.

26. Cited in Sara Rimer and Raymond Bonner, "Whether to Kill Those Who Killed as Youths," *New York Times,* August 22, 2000, Al6.

27. Ann Patchett, "The Age of Innocence," *New York Times Sunday Magazine,* September 29, 2002, 17.

28. David Garland, cited in Melange, "Men and Jewelry; Prison as Exile; Unifying Laughter and Darkness," *Chronicle of Higher Education* July 6, 2001, B4.

29. An interview with Jesse Jackson, "First Class Jails, Second-Class Schools," *Rethinking Schools,* (Spring 2000), 16.

30. Kate Zernike, "Crackdown on Threats in School Fails a Test," *New York Times,* May 17, 2001, A21.

31. Quoted from a report on zero-tolerance laws by the American Bar Association. Available at www.abanet.org/crimjust/juvius/zerotolreport.html.

32. See Brian Moore, "Letting Software Make the Call," *Chicago Reader* 29, no. 49 (September 8, 2000): 18.

33. Ellen Goodman, "'Zero Tolerance' Means Zero Chance for Troubled Kids," *Centre Daily Times.* January 4, 2000, 8.

34. These examples are taken from a report on zero-tolerance laws by the American Bar Association. Available at www.abanet.org/crimjust/juvius/zerotolreport.html

35. An interview with Jesse Jackson, "First Class Jails, Second-Class Schools," 16.

36. Ellen Goodman, "'Zero Tolerance,'" 8.

37. Editorial, "Zero Tolerance Is the Policy," *Denver Rocky Mountain News,* June 22, 1999, 38A.

38. Gregory Michie, "One Strike and You're Out: Does Zero Tolerance work? Or Does Kicking Kids Out of School Just Make Things Worse?" *Chicago Reader* 29, no. 49 (September 8, 2000): 24.

39. It was reported a few years back in the *New York Times* that, in responding to the spate of recent school shootings, the FBI has provided educators across the country with a list of behaviors that could identify "students likely to commit an act of lethal violence." One such behavior is "resentment over real or perceived injustices." The reach of domestic militarization becomes more evident as the FBI takes on the role of monitoring potentially disruptive student behavior, even to the degree that teachers are positioned to become adjuncts of the criminal justice system. The story and quotes appear in Editorial, "FBI Caution Signs for Violence in Classroom," *New York Times,* September 7, 2000, A18.

40. Tamar Lewin, "Study Finds Racial Bias in Public Schools," *New York Times,* March 11, 2000, A14.

41. Libero Della Piana, "Crime and Punishment in Schools: Students of Color Are Facing More Suspensions Because of Racially Biased Policies," *San Francisco Chronicle,* February 9, 2000, A21.

42. Marilyn Elias, "Disparity in Black and White?" *USA Today,* December 11, 2000, 9D.

43. Libero Della Piana, "Crime and Punishment in Schools," A21.

44. Ulrich Beck, *The Reinvention of Politics,* trans. Mark Ritter (Cambridge: Polity Press, 1995), 7.

45. As has been widely reported, the prison industry has become big business with many states spending more on prison construction than on university construction. See Anthony Lewis, "Punishing the Country," *New York Times,* December 2, 1999, A1.

46. For a provocative analysis of the relationship between what Norman Geras calls "the contract of mutual indifference," the Holocaust, and neoliberalism's refusal of the social as a condition for contemporary forms of mutual indifference, see Norman Geras, *The Contract of Mutual Indifference* (London: Verso Press, 1998).

47. For some recent commentaries on the new student movement, see Lisa Featherstone, "The New Student Movement," *Nation,* May 15, 2000, 11–15; David Samuels, "Notes from Underground: Among the Radicals of the Pacific Northwest," *Harper's Magazine,* May 2000, 35–47; Katazyna Lyson, Monique Murad, and Trevor Stordahl, "Real Reformers, Real Results," *Mother Jones,* October 2000, 20–22; Liza Featherstone, "Sweatshops, Students and the Corporate University," *Croonenbergh's Fly,* Spring/Summer 2002, 107–17; Imre Szeman, ed. *Review of Education, Pedagogy, and Cultural Studies* (special double issue, *Learning from Seattle*) 24, nos. 1–2 (January–June 2002).

4

The Posthistorical University? Prospects for Alternative Globalizations

Michael A. Peters

This chapter reviews Bill Readings's argument (1996) concerning the three grand narratives of the modern university: the Kantian, the Humboldtian, and the neoliberal university based on the discourse of "excellence." It identifies and discusses two neoliberal or corporate forms of the "posthistorical" university as they have been defined in the recent reviews of higher education in the United Kingdom (the Dearing report; National Committee of Inquiry into Higher Education 1997) and Australia (the West report; West Committee 1997). Readings (1996, 119) asks how we might reimagine the university once its guiding idea of culture has been overtaken and superceded by the forces of globalization that threaten a cultural homogenization. He asks us to ponder the question of what it means to dwell in the ruins of the university without falling back on romance or nostalgia. This paper acknowledges the force of his question but provides a different answer, suggesting in programmatic terms an agenda for alternative globalizations that includes a focus on the notion of cultural globalization in relation to the university's critical function.

"Structural adjustment" policies of the World Bank and International Monetary Fund, international "free trade" agreements, the development of new communications and information technologies, and so-called new growth theory are important factors that have led Western governments recently to restructure their systems of higher education to enhance their national competitiveness in the global economy. There has been a consequent shift in national economic policy to focus on the relations between higher education, human capital, and knowledge production, as the favored nexus necessary for encouraging greater growth, productivity, and providing the basis for participation in the global "knowledge economy." It could be argued, that under these new conditions, the founding discourses of the modern university—those of Kant, Humboldt, and Newman—have been ruptured by the emergent discourse of "excellence" that reflects this logic of performativity (to use Lyotard's phrase).

Taking my lead from Bill Readings, I shall argue that three ideas of the university dominate the modern era: the Kantian idea of reason, the Humboldtian idea of culture, and the technobureaucratic idea of excellence. The idea of the modern university, historically speaking, is to be identified with a set of founding discourses initiated by Kant, the Humboldt brothers, John Newman, and others. While the University of Excellence is still modern in the sense that it is both regulated and unified through the force of a single idea, nevertheless, it significantly breaks with the set of founding historical discourses of the university.

I differ from Readings because I think the founding discourses of the modern university have been ruptured by the discourse of excellence. The combined pressures of globalization, managerialism, and marketization have stripped the university of its historical reference points and threatens to permanently change its mission and to jettison both the academic freedoms and institutional autonomy characteristic of the traditional liberal university. I use the term *posthistorical* to describe this state of affairs. I hasten to add that my use of the term *posthistorical* is not meant to suggest an "end of history" or "end of ideology" thesis: these are the melodramatic tropes of Hegelians who believe that history is motored by a dialectical struggle of opposing forces that ends when one side prevails over the other. Thus, right Hegelians like Francis Fukuyama, believe that the collapse of Communism after 1989 and the end of the Cold War signals the triumph of capitalism, and, therefore, the "end of history," in much the same way that doctrinaire Marxists believed that history ended with establishment of the "classless" society and the rule of the proletariat. My use of *posthistorical*, however, is meant to signify an "end of modernity" and, consequently, an institutional transformation of the modern university (see, for example, Peters 1996b; Vattimo 1988, 1991, 1992).

First, I trace Readings's argument concerning the three dominant ideas or grand narratives of the university, in terms first crystallized by French philosopher Jean-François Lyotard, who died in April 1998. I would like to dedicate this chapter to him.[1]

Second, I identify two neoliberal or corporate forms of the posthistorical university as they are defined in the recent reviews of higher education in the United Kingdom (the Dearing report) and Australia (the West report). Finally, I return to Readings (1996, 119), who asks the question, How are we to reimagine the university, once its guiding idea of culture has ceased to have an essential function? He suggests that the university is in ruins and he asks us to ponder the question of what it means to dwell in the ruins without falling back on romance or nostalgia. By "nostalgia" in this context, Readings means to question modernity's preoccupation and search for "the primordial unity and immediacy of a lost origin" (169). I acknowledge the force of his question but provide a different answer to the question.

THE MODERN (HISTORICAL) UNIVERSITY

Timothy Bahti discusses the historiography of the modern university in terms which not only emphasize its historical break with the medieval university but also echo the theme of the posthistorical:

> Standard histories of the university distinguish the "older" and modern versions according to a chronology that is familiar from other such histories as the history of literature, the history of industrialization and modernization (urbanization, rationalization, etc.), and the history of warfare. Somewhere between the eighteenth and the early nineteenth centuries, the model at hand changes: whether the opposition is (neo)classical/romantic, early capitalist/high capitalist, or manual/mechanized, the switch is made, the revolution occurs, and we are all henceforth *post*—postromantic, postrevolutionary, postfeudal—which is to say *modern*. With respect to the university, the opposition is medieval/modern, the place is Germany and the time is the end of the eighteenth century. (Bahti 1987, 438)

Bahti indicates that whereas the seventeenth century had been heyday for the European academies of sciences, the eighteenth had been the lowpoint for German universities, with student rioting and drunkenness, dropping enrollments, and little relationship between subjects taught and vocations. In the last decade of the eighteenth century there was talk of abolishing the university altogether, allowing the academies of sciences and the new practical vocational schools to take its place. And then in 1810, the University of Berlin was founded. In the intervening years following the defeat of Prussia by Napoleon, the reorganization of the Prussian bureaucracy occurred and, as Bahti (1987, 439) points out, also the discourse of German idealism becomes established with "the philosophical writings on and for the university, from Kant and Schelling and then from Fichte, Schleiermacher, and Humboldt."

For Kant it was the idea of reason that provided an organizing principle for the disciplines, with "philosophy" as its home. Reason is the founding principle of the Kantian university: it confers universality upon the institution and, thereby, ushers in modernity. As the immanent unifying principle of the Kantian university, reason displaces the Aristotelian order of disciplines of the medieval university based on the seven liberal arts, and substitutes a quasi-industrial arrangement of the faculties.[2] In *The Conflict of the Faculties* Kant writes:

> It was not a bad idea, whoever first conceived and proposed a public means for treating the sum of knowledge (and properly the heads who devote themselves to it), in a quasi-*industrial* manner, with a division of labour where, for so many fields as there may be of knowledge, so many public teachers would be allotted, professors being trustees, forming together a kind of common scientific inquiry, called a university (or high school) and having autonomy (for only scholars can pass judgement on scholars as such); and, thanks to its faculties (various small societies where university teachers are ranged, in keeping with the variety of the main branches of knowledge), the university would be authorized to admit, on the one

hand, student-apprentices from the lower schools aspiring to its level, and to grant, on the other hand—after prior examination, and on its own authority—to teachers who are "free" (not drawn from members themselves) called "Doctors," a universally recognized rank (conferring upon them a degree)—in short *creating* them. (Kant [1789] 1979, 23)

The free exercise of a self-critical and self-legislating reason controls the higher faculties of theology, law, and medicine, establishing autonomy for the university as a whole. Readings (1996, 59) argues that there is, in Kant, a problem or paradox that haunts the constitution of the modern university: how to institutionalize reason's autonomy, or how to unify reason and the state, institution, and autonomy? Kant attempts to reconcile this conflict through the republican subject, the universal subject of humanity, who incarnates this conflict. Thus, while it is one of the functions of the university to produce technicians or men of affairs for the state, the state must protect the university to ensure the rule of reason in public life. Philosophy, as the tribunal of reason, must protect the university from the abuse of power from the state and must act to distinguish legitimate from illegitimate conflict, that is, the arbitrary exercise of authority.

Humboldt's project for the foundation of the University of Berlin in 1810 is decisive for the modern university up until the present day. Once the idea of reason is replaced with the idea of a national culture, the university becomes pressed into service of the state. For the German idealists the unity of knowledge and culture has been lost and needs to be reintegrated into a unified cultural science (*Bildung*). The university is assigned the task of producing and inculcating national self-knowledge and as such becomes the institution charged with watching over the spiritual life of the people.

The British, under John Henry Newman and Matthew Arnold, substitute literature for philosophy as the central discipline of the university, and, therefore, also of national culture. The possibility of a unified national culture is defined explicitly in terms of the study of a tradition of national literature (or canon, as in the case of the United States). Literature and the function of criticism is entrusted with a social mission in the Anglo-American university. In England, the idea of culture gets its purchase in opposition to science and technology, partly as a result of the threat posed by industrialization and mass civilization. Newman gives us a "liberal education" as the proper function of the university, which educates its charges to be gentlemen, not through the study of philosophy, but through the study of literature. Readings argues that "For Arnold, as for Eliot and Leavis after him, Shakespeare occupies the position that the German Idealists ascribed to the Greeks: that of immediately representing an organic community to itself in a living language" (Readings 1996, 78). In "The Idea of a University," F. R. Leavis proposes that all study should be centered in the study of literature, centered in the seventeenth century, and based on Shakespeare as the natural origin of culture. Leavis believes that the University of Culture can provide the lost center and heal the split between organic culture and mass civilization.

In "Literature: A Lecture in the School of Philosophy and Letters," delivered in 1858, Newman (1968, 201–21) "explicitly positions as the site of the development both an idea of the nation and the study of literature as the means of training national subjects" (Readings 1996, 76). Newman suggests that "a literature, when it is formed, is a national and historical fact; it is a matter of the past and present, and can be as little ignored as the present, as little undone as the past" (Newman 1968, 230). National language and literature defines the character of "every great people," and Newman speaks of the classics of a national literature by which he means "those authors who have had the foremost place in exemplifying the powers and conducting the development of its language" (240).

The grand narrative of the university, centered on the cultural production of a liberal, reasoning, citizen subject, in the wake of globalization, is no longer credible. As Readings argues: "The University . . . no longer participates in the historical project for humanity that was the legacy of the Enlightenment: the historical project of culture" (Readings 1995, 5). Excellence has become the last unifying principle of the modern university, yet the discourse of excellence brackets out the question of value in favor of measurement and substitutes accounting solutions for questions of accountability. As an integrating principle excellence is entirely meaningless: it has no real referent. Under corporatization universities have become sites for the development of "human resources." As Readings remarks: "University mission statements, like their publicity brochures, share two distinctive features nowadays. On the one hand, they all claim that theirs is a unique educational institution. On the other hand, they all go on to describe this uniqueness in exactly the same way" (Readings 1996, 12).

He goes on to tell the true story about of how Cornell University Parking services received an award recently for "excellence in parking." The discourse of excellence is contentless: it does not enable us to make judgments of value or purpose and it does not help us to answer questions of what, how, or why we should teach or research.

THE POSTHISTORICAL UNIVERSITY

Anyone with a passing familiarity with Readings's thesis as I have presented it must recognize the traces of Jean-François Lyotard's influence (see also Clark and Royle 1995; Crittenden 1997; Derrida 1983; Habermas 1987; Smith and Webster 1997). Lyotard's *The Postmodern Condition: A Report on Knowledge* (1984), originally published in Paris in 1979, became an instant cause célèbre because Lyotard analyzed the status of knowledge, science, and the university in way that many critics believed signaled an epochal break not only with the so-called modern era but also with various traditionally "modern" ways of viewing the world. It was written, Lyotard asserts, "at this very Postmodern moment that finds the University nearing what may be its end" (xxv).

In *The Postmodern Condition,* Jean-François Lyotard was concerned with grand narratives which had grown out of the Enlightenment and had come to mark modernity. In *The Postmodern Explained to Children,* Lyotard mentions, "The progressive emancipation of reason and freedom, the progressive or catastrophic emancipation of labour . . . , the enrichment of all through the progress of capitalist technoscience, and even . . . the salvation of creatures through the conversion of souls to the Christian narrative of martyred love" (1992, 29). Grand narratives are the stories that cultures tell themselves about their own practices and beliefs in order to legitimate them. They function as a unified single story that purport to legitimate or found a set of practices, a cultural self-image, discourse, or institution.

Lyotard writes in a now famous formulation: "I will use the term *modern* to designate any science that legitimates itself with reference to a metadiscourse . . . making explicit appeal to some grand narrative, such as the dialectics of the Spirit, the hermeneutics of meaning, the emancipation of the rational or working subject, or the creation of wealth" (1984, xxii). By contrast, he defines *postmodern* simply as "incredulity toward metanarratives" (xxiv). Lyotard holds that capitalist renewal after the 1930s and the postwar upsurge of technology has led to a "crisis" of scientific knowledge and to the internal erosion of the very prospect of legitimation. He locates the seeds of such "delegitimation" in the decline of the legitimating power of the grand narratives of the nineteenth century. The speculative narrative of the unity of all knowledge held that knowledge is worthy of its name only if it can generate a second-order discourse that functions to legitimate it, otherwise such "knowledge" would amount to mere ideology. Lyotard claims that the process of "delegitimation" has revealed that not only does science play its own language game (and consequently is both on a par with and incapable of legitimating other language games) but also it is incapable of legitimating itself as speculation assumed it could. In particular, the process of European cultural disintegration is symbolized most clearly by the end of philosophy as the universal metalanguage able to underwrite all claims to knowledge and, thereby, to unify the rest of culture. By European cultural disintegration Lyotard is referring, first, to the collapse of the European monarchies and the two world wars, and, second, what Nietzsche calls the question of European nihilism (see Shapiro 1991).

Since the late 1970s neoliberalism has become the dominant global narrative. (The publication of Lyotard's *The Postmodern Condition* coincided with the election to power of Margaret Thatcher's Conservative government in Britain). The discourse of neoliberalism revitalizes the master discourse of economic liberalism and advances it as a basis for a global reconstruction of society. A form of economic reason encapsulated in the notion of *homo economicus,* with its abstract and universalistic assumptions of individuality, rationality, and self-interest, has captured the policy agendas of Western countries. Part of its innovation has been the way in which the neoliberal global narrative has successfully extended the principle of self-interest into the status of a paradigm for understanding politics itself, and, purportedly, all behavior and human action. In the realm of higher education policy at every opportunity the market has been substituted for the state: students are now "customers" and teachers are "providers." The notion of vouchers is suggested as a universal panacea to problems of funding and quality. The teaching/learning relation has been reduced to an implicit contract between buyer and seller. As Lyotard argued prophetically in *The Postmodern Condition,* "Knowledge is and will be produced in order to be sold, it is and will be consumed in order to be valorized in a new production: in both cases, the goal is exchange" (1984, 4).

TWO CORPORATE FORMS OF THE POSTHISTORICAL UNIVERSITY

Fundamental to understanding the new global economy has been a rediscovery of the economic importance of higher education and structural shifts in the production of knowledge. The Organization for Economic Cooperation and Development and the World Bank have stressed the significance of education and training for the development of "human resources," for upskilling and increasing the competencies of workers, and for the production of research and scientific knowledge, as keys to participation in the new global economy. Both Peter Drucker (1993) and Michael Porter (1990) emphasize the importance of knowledge—its economics and productivity—as the basis for national competitive advantage within the international marketplace. Lester Thurow suggests that "a technological shift to an era dominated by man-made brainpower industries" is one of five economic tectonic plates that constitute a new game with new rules: "Today knowledge and skills now stand alone as the only sources of comparative advantage. They have become the key ingredient in the late twentieth-century's location of economic activity" (Thurow 1996, 68; see also Delanty 1998; Papadopoulos 1994).

Equipped with this central understanding and guided by neoliberal theories of human capital, public choice, and new public management, Western governments have begun the process of restructuring universities, obliterating the distinction between education and training in the development of a massified system of higher education designed for the twenty-first century. Recently, the governments of the United Kingdom, Australia, and New Zealand have convened reviews of higher education to determine the shape and imperatives of the sector for the twenty-first century. I shall briefly describe the underlying visions of the Dearing report (United Kingdom) and the West report (Australia) as two corporate forms of the posthistorical university.

The Dearing Report: The Corporate University in the Service of Global Capital and National Culture

The Dearing report recognizes globalization as the major influence upon the U.K. economy and the labor market with strong implications for higher education.

Analyzing the Dearing report it is possible to talk of the globalization of tertiary or higher education, according to three interrelated functions: the knowledge function, the labor function, and the institutional function (see box 4.1). We can talk of the primacy of the knowledge function and its globalization, which has a number of dimensions: knowledge, its production, and transmission or acquisition, is still primary as it was with the idea of the modern university, but now its value is legitimated increasingly in terms of its ability to attract global capital and its potential labor service functions to transnational corporations. Knowledge is valued for its strict utility rather than as an end in itself or for its emancipatory or enlightenment effects.

The developments described here under the banner of globalization which accentuate the primacy of knowledge, are further underwritten by recent advances in so-called growth theory. Neoclassical economics does not specify how knowledge accumulation occurs. As a result there is no mention of human capital and there is no direct role for education. Further, in the neoclassical model there is no income "left over" (all output is paid to either capital or labor) to act as a reward or incentive for knowledge accumulation. Accordingly, there are no externalities to knowledge accumulation. By contrast, new growth theory has highlighted the role of education in the creation of human capital and in the production of new knowledge. On this basis it has explored the possibilities of education-related externalities. In short, while the evidence is far from conclusive at this stage there is a consensus emerging that education is important for successful research activities (e.g., by producing scientists and engineers); education creates human capital, which directly affects knowledge accumulation and therefore productivity growth. (See report 8, "Externalities in Higher Education," of the Dearing report.)

The globalization of the labor function is formulated in terms of both the production of technically skilled people to meet the needs of transnational corporations and the ideology of lifelong learning, where individuals can "re-equip themselves for a succession of jobs over a working lifetime." The institutional function is summed up in the phrase "higher education will become a global international service and tradeable commodity." The competitive survival of institutions is tied to the globalization of its organizational form (emulating private sector enterprises) and the globalization of its "services." With this function already a stronger and closer alliance between global corporations and universities has developed, especially in terms of the funding of research and development, and, in some cases, universities have become global corporations with international sites for teaching and research. The latter is a trend likely to develop further with the world integration and convergence of media, telecommunications, and publishing industries. It is important to note that the Dearing report still acknowledges the British university as a site for the development, preservation, and transmission of national culture, albeit in its commodified, tradeable, and exportable forms. A commissioned paper for the West report, by contrast, is even more unremitting.

Box 4.1 Globalization (World Economic Integration)

1. Main causes
   - Technological changes in telecommunications, information, and transport
   - Political promotion of free trade and the reduction in trade protection
2. Main elements
   - Organization of production on a global scale
   - Acquisition of inputs and services from around the world, which reduces costs
   - Formation of cross-border alliances and ventures, enabling companies to combine assets, share their costs, and penetrate new markets
   - Integration of world capital markets
   - Availability of information on international benchmarking of commercial performance
   - Better consumer knowledge and more spending power—hence, more discriminating choices
   - Greater competition from outside the established industrial centers
3. Consequences for the labor market
   - Downward pressure on pay, particularly for unskilled labor
   - Upward pressure on the quality of labor input
   - Competition increasingly based on quality rather than price
   - People and ideas assuming greater significance in economic success because they are less mobile than other investments, such as capital, information, and technology
   - Increased unemployment rates of unskilled workers relative to skilled workers
   - More small companies whose business is knowledge and whose ways of handling knowledge and information are needed
4. Implications for higher education
   - High-quality, relevant higher education provision will be a key factor in attracting and anchoring the operations of global corporations.
   - Institutions will need to be at the forefront in offering opportunities for lifelong learning.
   - Institutions will need to meet the aspirations of individuals to reequip themselves for a succession of jobs over a working lifetime.
   - Higher education must continue to provide a steady stream of technically skilled people to meet needs of global corporations.
   - Higher education will become a global service and tradable commodity.
   - Higher education institutions, organizationally, may need to emulate private sector enterprises to flourish in a fast-changing global economy.
   - The new economic order will place a premium on knowledge and institutions; therefore, it will need to recognize the knowledge, skills, and understanding that individuals can use as a basis to secure further knowledge and skills.
   - The development of a research base to provide new knowledge, understanding, and ideas to attract high-technology companies.

SOURCE: Compiled from "The Wider Context," in the Dearing report.

The West Report: The Hollowed-Out University

The West Committee's discussion paper "Review of Higher Education Financing and Policy," released in late November 1997, begins with a preface by its chairman, Roderick West, who asserts two "certainties": first, "the twenty-first century will mark the era of tertiary education and lifelong education for everybody" and, second, there are "extraordinary possibilities in the provision of education through ever expanding technological advance." These two elements dictate the approach to financing and policy.

The paper spells out a vision for "learning for life," a seamless postsecondary education environment with commitments to building a culture of learning, civic values, scholarship, preparing graduates, advancing knowledge and skills, "developing the industry," and equity. It lists the principles on which the future should be built, including a commitment to universal access, a consumer-driven system emphasizing student choice, outcome-based assessment of quality, cost-effectiveness, and greater levels of competition from the private sector.

The vision of a corporate form of the posthistorical university is provided in a commissioned paper entitled "Australian Higher Education in the Era of Mass Customisation" by Global Alliance Limited, which is is a Tokyo-based investment bank established in 1995 specializing in providing investment and corporate advisory services, mainly to Japanese and Taiwanese companies, especially in relation to the information technology sector. It has investments on its own account in Internet service providers and related companies.

The report proclaims both the end of "the era of homogeneity" under state planning and the beginning of another era that will be consumer-oriented, more diversified, and exposed to international competition. The remnants of an era of state planning show that while costs of production are world competitive, productivity incentives are poor and capital management requires reform. The existing providers, protected in the Australian domestic market, will be opened up to the forces of international competition as a result of changes taking place in the global economy.

The report identifies the following forces for change: the reducing government fee structure, the associated shift of power to the consumer, increasing international competitive exposure and changes in the technology of production and consumption. Computers will lower costs of marketing and the provision of customer services while at the same time as promoting greater access to learning and enhancing the quality of the learning experience. Back-end systems will be automated and learning systems will increasingly apply computers so that courses can be delivered over the web. The effects of these forces will lead to "the hollowing out of the university." The report is worth quoting at some length here:

> The vertically integrated university is a product of brand image, government policy, history and historical economies of scale in support services. If government policy is no longer biased in favour of this form, and technology liberates providers from one location, then we would expect to see new forms arising such as multiple outlet vertically integrated specialist schools and web based universities. . . . Specialist service providers,

such as testing companies and courseware developers will arise, as will superstar teachers who are not tied to any one university. Many universities will become marketing and production coordinators or systems integrators. They will no longer all be vertically integrated education versions of the 1929 Ford assembly plant in Detroit. (12)

The overall result of these combined forces will be an increased segmentation of markets, an increased specialization and customization of supply of courses, and an increased specialization of providers. The new university business system will take the form of one of a series of possible business models: low-cost producer university; Asia middle-class web university; Harvard in Australia university; world-specialist school university.

REIMAGINING THE UNIVERSITY

Readings asks how we might reimagine the university once we have had to relinquish the notion of culture as the unifying idea: how should we attempt to live in the ruins of the university without romance or nostalgia. Since Kant the university has operated as a privileged model of free and rational discussion, one based upon a notion of communication, that ties the individual to the nation-state. Readings provides us with a different answer. He offers us a new community of dissensus as a model for the posthistorical university: not one based upon consensus and transparency but rather upon openness, opacity, incompleteness, and difference. I argue a very similar line in my "Cybernetics, Cyberspace and the University: Hermann Hesse's *The Glass Bead Game* and the Dream of an Innocent Language" (1996a), except I use the notion of a universal and transparent language rather than a model or mode of communication.

I have some sympathy for Readings's view but rather than explore the underlying notion of community at stake—its political dimensions and exclusions—I want to take a different tack. I want to suggest a form of the posthistorical university that does not break with the founding historical discourses and their single unifying ideas but preserves them, reinterprets and adapts them to new conditions, reinvents, and redefines these ideas as an imaginative basis for resistance against the narrowing of thought.

The university becomes modern when all of its activities are organized in terms of a single regulatory and unifying idea: the "uni" of the "versity," so to speak. The founding historical discourses are the primary intellectual resources from which it is possible to reimagine the university: on what other possible basis might we reimagine the university? Yet I am suggesting a sense of the "posthistorical" that is a return to the past which is critical rather than innocent or romantic: of moving from a single unifying idea to a constellation or field of overlapping and mutually self-reinforcing forces that constitute the university tradition. In short, the discourses of the modern university, themselves, exercise a unifying narrative that needs to be reworked and reinvented with each successive generation as effective history. Let me briefly sketch what I have in mind by reference to the ideas of the modern university (see box 4.2).

Box 4.2 Reimagining the University

From a single unifying idea to a constellation or field of overlapping and mutually self-reinforcing ideas.

1. The Kantian University and the Idea of Reason
   Kant's critical philosophy or critical reason as a source of criticism, critique, and reflection—self-criticism, self-reflection, and self-governance. "The thread which may connect us to the Enlightenment is not faithfulness to doctrinal elements but, rather, the permanent reactivation of an attitude—that is, of a philosophical ethos that could be described as a permanent critique of our historical era" (Michel Foucault, "What Is Enlightenment?" in *Michel Foucault: Ethics. The Essential Works,* ed. Paul Rabinow [London: Allen Lane & Penguin, 1996], 312).
2. The Humboldtian University and the Idea of Culture
   • From Bildung as self-cultivation and moral self-formation to learning processes (pedagogy) based on an ethical relation of self and other.
   • From national culture to cultural self-understandings and reproduction which implies a recognition of indigenous cultures and traditional knowledges; an awareness of "nation" as a sociohistorical construction; an acceptance of the reality of multiculturalism.
3. The University of Literary Culture (Newman-Arnold-Leavis)
   National culture as a literary culture revealed in the tradition of a national literature or canon. The shift from a literary to postliterary culture: the modern western university was a print culture shaped by print technologies for the creation, storage, and transmission of knowledge. The shift to a new technoculture is being shaped by digital technologies for the storage and exchange of information.
4. The Corporate "Massified" University
   From cultural élite formation to mass access and participation.

The Kantian University and the Idea of Reason

Kant's critical philosophy or critical reason as a source of criticism, critique, and reflection inaugurates the modern discourse of the university and becomes the basis for self-criticism, self-reflection, and self-governance (or autonomy). As the French philosopher Michel Foucault argues (1996, 312): the thread that may connect us to the Enlightenment is not faithfulness to doctrinal elements but, rather, the permanent reactivation of an attitude—that is, of a philosophical ethos that could be described as a permanent critique of our historical era.

The Humboldtian University and the Idea of Culture

There are two critical reappraisals or returns in respect of the Humboldtian university: first a move from Bildung as self-cultivation and moral self-formation to learning processes (or pedagogy) based on the ethical relations of self and other; and, second, a move from the notion of "national culture" to "cultural self-understandings" and social reproduction which implies a recognition and valuing of indigenous cultures and traditional knowledges; an awareness of "nation" as a sociohistorical and political construction; and an acceptance of the reality of a global multiculturalism. For Aotearoa/New Zealand, there has been a slow and grudging acceptance of the significance of Maori knowledges as a basis for academic study that has gained some momentum only in recent years (Walker 1999). The development of *wananga*—both iwi-based and urban— with state funding on an equal basis to pakeha institutions, will in years to come provide, perhaps, the most distinctive characteristic differentiating the national system.[3]

The University of Literary Culture (Newman-Arnold-Leavis)

This idea concerns national culture as a literary culture revealed in the tradition of a national literature or canon and, critically, examines the structural shift from a literary to postliterary culture. The modern western university was primarily a print culture shaped by print technologies for the creation, storage, and transmission of knowledge; the shift to a new technoculture is being shaped by digital technologies for the storage and exchange of information and the radical concordance of image, text, and sound in new multimedia forms of communication. In terms of this critical reappraisal the national canon is not restricted to literature or the realms of élite high culture but is interwoven with a diversity of cultural products and traditions in film, music, and television that reflect an acceptance of local and popular culture.

The Corporate "Massified" University

It may be surprising to some that I should want to rescue or maintain anything at all from the corporate university and yet I believe there have been some positive changes. I shall mention only one here: the move away from the university's cultural élite formation function to principles of mass access and participation. It is this idea which still distinguishes the era of the state-funded university based on the idea of modern democracy and the one that promises the greatest institutional transformation of the university.

THE UNIVERSITY AND CULTURAL GLOBALIZATION

With these resources and with this constellation of ideas and their imaginative reconstruction, the university might be able to preserve its historical commitments to reason and to culture (albeit a different notion) and, thereby, to play its part, alongside other international agencies, international movements, and world-oriented bodies, in establishing and maintaining what I call an agenda for alternative globalizations, based on three planks: the promotion of a global social contract, arrangements for global governance, and cultural globalization (see box 4.3).

Box 4.3 Agenda for Alternative Globalizations

1. Promotion and development of a global social contract
   - Promoting sustainable development
   - Promoting ecological standards
   - Consolidating the democratic process
   - Enhancing the development of international labor standards
   - Promoting world trade union rights
   - Monitoring the social dimension of global and regional trade agreements
2. Promotion and encouragement of global governance
   - Building standards of global governance
   - Protecting the public institutions of civil society
   - Developing transparency and accountability of international fora and world institutions
   - Developing approaches to institutions of an international civil community
   - Encouraging greater North/South dialogue and better world representation
3. Promotion and development of cultural globalization
   - Promoting cultural diversity and exchange
   - Developing genuine multicultural structures and processes
   - Promoting and enhancing the notion of cultural rights
   - Protecting indigenous property rights
   - Promoting political and cultural self-determination

The university faces a critical historical transition concerning culture as the guiding idea: it must confront its liberal and statist legacy of "one culture, one language, one nation" and its implicit support of a neoliberal global cultural homogeneity to embrace a critical multiculturalism that recognizes a number of potent forces: the revitalization of traditional cultures and knowledges; the internal differentiation of Western culture since World War II along lines of age, gender, and ethnicity and, in particular, the growth and globalization of youth subcultures, and, the development of postliterary (image-based) media cultures.

The agenda of alternative globalizations is meant to begin the intellectual task of refashioning the university's role as the critic and conscience society in a global context by focusing upon three interrelated themes: a global social contract, standards and mechanisms for the promotion of global government, and the development of modes for the encouragement of cultural globalizations. The modern university has always been an internationally oriented institution, even if this has meant it has played an important part in the process of colonization. In a globally integrated world environment universities can continue to operate as something more than simply labor service centers for multinational corporations or circuit in the world commodity exchange of ideas: they have an important role in their historic commitments to reason and to culture and yet at the same time they must also assume new critical roles.

There is not space to develop this programmatic outline in detail in this chapter. I shall end by offering some philosophical observations and critical remarks concerning new critical roles that universities might play in relation to the question of cultural globalization, though I wish to emphasize that the future role of the university in supporting this third plank of alternative globalization depends upon simultaneous advances with the other two planks identified in box 4.3.

The critical role of the modern Kantian university was very much tied to a notion of universal reason and the development of the idea of the modern university, including the idea of emancipation, which helped to structure the coherence of the nineteenth- and twentieth-century narratives or philosophies of world history, that had as their end or *telos*, freedom. To rework or reimagine this critical tradition in relation to the question of globalization it is necessary to return to these ideas and to examine their status in the new context. To what extent historically was the modern university implicated in the process of colonization and the suppression of traditional cultures and knowledges? To what extent historically has the university, as an institution of liberal society, really protected cultural diversity? To what extent has the promotion of cultural diversity been part of the mission of the modern university, especially in the "new world" and, if so, how successful has it been? These historical and philosophical questions are important aspects of a critical rather than a memorial history of the modern university. Answers to these questions will provide better self-understandings of the university in its capacity to resist the neoliberal project of globalization as world economic integration, on the one hand, and, to develop strategies to promote and encourage cultural globalization, on the other. In other words, are there possibilities for a university based on the principle of cultural difference: a kind of institution that can turn the growing importance of "soft" power (i.e., cultural and technological) of informational globalization against commercial forces of cultural homogenization in order to preserve, promote and develop cultural diversity? What might affirmative answers to this question imply for universalist and humanist constructions of the modern university?

What might it imply, for instance, for the notion of emancipation? Lyotard comments that within the tradition of modernity the movement toward emancipation "is a movement whereby a third party, who is initially outside the *we* of the emancipating avant-garde, eventually becomes part of the community of real (first person) or potential (second person) speakers" (1989, 319). He raises the question concerning the status of this *we* and examines whether it arises independently of the idea of a history of humanity. Lyotard's answer to the question of this *we* in relation to problems concerning the "insurmountable diversity of cultures" impinges both upon on the legitimating power of local versus the great narratives.

The great narratives of legitimation that characterize modernity and the university are cosmopolitical in the Kantian sense, transcending particular cultures in favor of a universal civic identity. Lyotard wants to draw our attention to how this transcendence takes place through the structure of narrative as it was shaped syntactically in modernity. He writes, "The humanist presupposes the Idea of a universal history and inscribes particular communities within it as moments within the universal development of human communities. This is also, *grosso modo,* the axiom of the great speculative narrative as applied to human history. But the real question is whether or not there is a human history" (1989, 321).

Lyotard suggests that many universalist movements, including that of labor, derived their legitimacy from an idea yet to be realized rather than local or popular traditions, and he sees the new independence movements and nationalist struggles to be a retreat into local legitimacy as a reaction against the effects of cultural imperialism.

Certainly, the game of the global market, as Lyotard points out, has little to do with cosmopolitical ends in Kant's sense, nor does it concern itself with reducing international inequalities. In other words, "The world market is not creating a universal history in modernity's sense of that term. Cultural differences are . . . being promoted as touristic and cultural commodities" (Lyotard 1989, 323). In this new environment, utilizing the principle of cultural difference, the university must help to build a cosmopolitical civic culture which, while protecting cultural rights and diversity, can develop parameters for world democracy and global citizenship.

NOTES

This chapter is dedicated to Jean-François Lyotard. I would like to thank James Marshall, Peter Roberts, and Matthew Fitzsimons for comments on an earlier version. A version of this paper was presented as the concluding lecture at the University of Auckland's Winter Lectures Series, "The University in the Twenty-First Century," Maidment Theatre, August 25, 1998; and a revised version appeared as "Globalization: Prospects, Paradoxes and Ruptures," *Jahrbuch fur Bildings- und Erziehungphilosophie* 2 (1999).

1. Both Lyotard and Readings exercised a strong direction on my thought and have been supportive of my work. Lyotard (1995) wrote the foreword to the collection I edited called *Education and the Postmodern Condition* (1995), to which Readings (1995) contributed the final chapter. Readings invited me in 1994 to give a paper (what became 1996a) at his multidisciplinary seminar at the Université de Montreal "L'Université et la Culture: La Crise Identitaire d'une Intsitution," on which his book was based. He died tragically in an air accident on October 31, 1994.

2. The Aristotelian order of the disciplines was divided into the trivium (grammar, rhetoric, and knowledge) and the quadrivium (arithmetic, geometry, astronomy, and music).

3. Maori are the indigenous people of Aotearoa/New Zealand and *wananga* are teaching and research institutions that maintain, advance, and disseminate knowledge, develop intellectual independence, and assist the application of knowledge regarding *ahuatanga* Maori (Maori tradition) according to *tikanga* Maori (Maori custom). Three *wananga* in New Zealand are established tertiary institutions: Te Wananga o Aotearoa, Te Wananga o Raukawa, and Te Wananga o Awanuirangi (Walker 1999).

REFERENCES

Bahti, Timothy. 1987. Histories of the university: Kant and Humboldt. *MLN* 102 (3): 437–60.

Clark, Timothy, and Nicholas Royle, eds. 1995. The university in ruins: Essays on the crisis in the concept of the modern university. Special issue, *Oxford Literary Review*, 15.

Crittenden, Brian. 1997. Minding their business: The proper role of universities and some suggested reforms. Occasional Paper Series 2/1996, Academy of the Social Sciences in Australia, Canberra.

Dearing report. See National Committee of Inquiry into Higher Education.

Delanty, Gerard. 1998. The idea of the university in the global era: From knowledge as an end to the end of knowledge. *Social Epistemology* 12, no. 1: 3–26.

Derrida, Jacques. 1983. The principle of reason: The university in the eyes of its pupils. *Diacritics* (Fall): 3–20.

Drucker, Peter. 1993. *Post-capitalist society.* New York: Harper.

Foucault, Michel. 1996. What is enlightenment? In *Michel Foucault: Ethics. The Essential Works,* ed. Paul Rabinow, 303–20. London: Allen Lane and Penguin.

Habermas, Jürgen. 1987. The idea of the university—learning processes. *New German Critique* 41 (Spring–Summer): 3–22.

Humboldt, Wilhelm von. 1970. On the spirit and the organisational framework of intellectual institutions in Berlin. *Minerva* 8, no. 2: 242–50.

Kant, Immanuel. [1789] 1979. *The conflict of the faculties.* Trans. M. Gregor. New York: Abaris Books.

Lyotard, Jean-François. 1984. *The postmodern condition: A report on knowledge.* Trans. G. Bennington and B. Massumi. Minneapolis: University of Minnesota Press.

———. 1989. Universal history and cultural differences. In *The Lyotard reader,* ed. Andrew Benjamin. Oxford: Blackwell.

———. 1992. *The postmodern explained to children: Correspondence, 1982–1985.* Trans. and ed. J. Pefanis and M. Thomas. Sydney: Power Publications.

———. 1995. Foreword: Spaceship. In *Education and the postmodern condition,* ed. Michael A. Peters, xi–xx. Westport, Conn.: Bergin & Garvey.

National Committee of Inquiry into Higher Education. 1997. *Higher education in the learning society.* London: HMSO.

Newman, John Henry. 1968. *The idea of the university.* Introduction and notes by M. Svaglic. New York: Holt, Rhinehart & Winston.

Papadopoulos, George. 1994. *Education, 1960–1990: The OECD Perspective.* Paris: OECD.

Peters, Michael A., ed. 1995. *Education and the postmodern condition.* Westport, Conn.: Begin & Garvey.

———. 1996a. Cybernetics, cyberspace and the university: Herman Hesse's the glass bead game and the dream of a universal language. In *Poststructuralism, politics and education.* Westport, Conn.: Bergin & Garvey.

———. 1996b. Vattimo, postmodernity and the transparent society. In *Poststructuralism, politics and education.* Westport, Conn.: Bergin & Garvey.

Porter, Michael. 1990. *The competitive advantage of nations.* New York: Free Press.

Readings, Bill. 1995. From emancipation to obligation: Sketch for a heteronomous politics of education. In *Education and the postmodern condition,* ed. Michael A. Peters, 193–208. Westport, Conn.: Bergin & Garvey.

———. 1996. *The university in ruins.* Cambridge, Mass.: Harvard University Press.

Shapiro, Gary. 1991. Nietzsche and the future of the university. *Journal of Nietzsche Studies* 1: 15–28.

Smith, Anthony, and Frank Webster. 1997. *The postmodern university? Contested visions of higher education in society.* Buckingham, Engl.: SRHE and Open University Press.

Thurow, Lester. 1996. *The future of capitalism: How today's economic forces will shape tomorrow's future.* New York: Morrow.

Vattimo, Gianni. 1988. *The end of modernity: Nihilism and hermeneutics in post-modern culture.* Trans. J. Snyder. Cambridge: Polity Press.

———. 1991. The end of (hi)story. In *Zeitgeist in Babel: The postmodernist controversy*, ed. I. Hoesterey, 132–43. Bloomington: Indiana University Press.

———. 1992. *The transparent society.* Trans. D. Webb. Baltimore, Md.: Johns Hopkins University Press.

Walker, Ranginui. 1999. The development of Maori studies in tertiary education. In *After the disciplines? Disciplinarity, culture and the emerging economy of studies*, ed. M. Peters. Westport, Conn.: Bergin & Garvey.

West Committee. 1997. *Review of higher education financing and policy.* Discussion paper. Canberra, Austral.: Author.

West report. See West Committee.

5

Globalization, September 11, and the Restructuring of Education

Douglas Kellner

The September 11, 2001, terrorist attacks have generated a wealth of theoretical reflection as well as repressive political responses by the Bush administration and other governments. The attacks and subsequent global terror war have dramatized once again the centrality of globalization in contemporary experience and the need for adequate conceptualizations and responses to it for critical theory and pedagogy to maintain their relevance in the current age. In this article, I want to argue that critical educators need to comprehend globalization, technological revolution, and the prospects and obstacles to democratization to develop pedagogies adequate to the challenges of today. Accordingly, I begin with some comments on how the September 11 terrorist attacks call attention to certain dimensions of globalization, and then provide a critical theory of globalization, after which I suggest some pedagogical initiatives to aid in the democratic reconstruction of education in the contemporary era.[1]

SEPTEMBER 11 AND GLOBALIZATION

The terrorist acts on the United States on September 11 and the subsequent terror war throughout the world dramatically disclose the downside of globalization, and the ways that global flows of technology, goods, information, ideologies, and people can have destructive as well as productive effects. The disclosure of powerful anti-Western terrorist networks shows that globalization divides the world just as it unifies, that it produces enemies as it incorporates participants. The events reveal explosive contradictions and conflicts at the heart of globalization and that the technologies of information, communication, and transportation that facilitate globalization can also be used to undermine and attack it, and generate instruments of destruction as well as production.[2]

The experience of September 11 points to the objective ambiguity of globalization, that positive and negative sides are interconnected, that the institutions of the open society unlock the possibilities of destruction and violence, as well as democracy, free trade, and cultural and social exchange. Once again, the interconnection and interdependency of the networked world was dramatically demonstrated as terrorists from the Middle East brought local grievances from their region to attack key symbols of American power and the very infrastructure of New York. Some saw the terrorism as an expression of "the dark side of globalization," while I would conceive it as part of the objective ambiguity of globalization that simultaneously creates friends and enemies, wealth and poverty, and growing divisions between the "haves" and "have nots." Yet, the downturn in the global economy, intensification of local and global political conflicts, repression of human rights and civil liberties, and general increase in fear and anxiety have certainly undermined the naïve optimism of globaphiles who perceived globalization as a purely positive instrument of progress and well-being.

The use of powerful technologies as weapons of destruction also discloses current asymmetries of power and emergent forms of terrorism and war, as the new millennium exploded into dangerous conflicts and military interventions. As technologies of mass destruction become more available and dispersed, perilous instabilities have emerged that have elicited policing measures to stem the flow of movements of people and goods across borders and internally. In particular, the Patriot Act has led to repressive measures that are replacing the spaces of the open and free information society with new forms of surveillance, policing, and repression, thus significantly undermining U.S. democracy.

Ultimately, however, the abhorrent terror acts by the bin Laden network and the violent military response by the Bush administration may be an anomalous paroxysm whereby a highly regressive premodern Islamic fundamentalism has clashed with an old-fashioned patriarchal and unilateralist Wild West militarism. It could be that such forms of terrorism, militarism, and state repression will be superseded by more rational forms of politics that globalize and criminalize terrorism and that do not sacrifice the benefits of the open society and economy in the name of security. Yet the events of September 11 may open a new era of terrorism that will lead to the kind of apocalyptic futurist world depicted by cyberpunk fiction.

In any case, the events of September 11 have promoted a fury of reflection, theoretical debates, and political conflicts, and upheaval that put the complex dynamics of globalization at the center of contemporary theory and politics. To those skeptical of the centrality of globalization to contemporary experience, it is now clear that we are living in a global world that is highly interconnected and vulnerable to passions and crises that can cross borders and can affect anyone or any region at any time. The events of September 11 also provide a test case to evaluate various theories of globalization in the contemporary era. In addition, they highlight some of the contradictions of globalization and the need to develop a highly complex and dialectical model to capture its conflicts, ambiguities, and contradictory effects.

Consequently, I argue that to properly theorize globalization one needs to conceptualize several sets of contradictions generated by globalization's combination of technological revolution and restructuring of capital, which, in turn, generate tensions between capitalism and democracy, and "haves" and "have nots." Within the world economy, globalization involves the proliferation of the logic of capital, but also the spread of democracy in information, social movements, and the diffusion of technology (see Friedman 1999; Hardt and Negri 2000). Globalization is thus a contradictory amalgam of capitalism and democracy, in which the logic of capital and the market system enter ever more arenas of global life, even as democracy spreads and more political regions and spaces of everyday life are being contested by democratic demands and forces. But the overall process is contradictory. Sometimes globalizing forces promote democracy and sometimes inhibit it, thus either equating capitalism and democracy, or simply opposing them, are problematical. These ambiguities are especially evident, as I will argue, in the domain of the Internet and the expansion of technologically mediated communication, information, and politics.

The processes of globalization are highly turbulent and have generated new conflicts throughout the world. Thomas Friedman (1999) makes a more benign distinction between what he calls the "Lexus" and the "olive tree." The former is a symbol of modernization, affluence, and luxury, and Westernized consumption, contrasted with the olive tree, which is a symbol of roots, tradition, place, and stable community. Barber (1997), however, is too negative toward McWorld and Jihad, failing to adequately describe the democratic and progressive forces within both. Although Barber recognizes a dialectic of McWorld and Jihad, he opposes both to democracy, failing to perceive how both generate their own democratic forces and tendencies, as well as opposing and undermining democratization. Within Western democracies, for instance, there is not just top-down homogenization and corporate domination, but also globalization-from-below and oppositional social movements that desire alternatives to capitalist globalization. Thus, it is not only traditionalist, non-Western forces of Jihad that oppose McWorld. Likewise, Jihad has its democratizing forces as well as the reactionary Islamic fundamentalists who are now the most demonized elements of the contemporary era, as I discuss below. Jihad, like McWorld, has its contradictions and its potential for democratization, as well as elements of domination and destruction (see Kellner, 2003b).

Friedman, by contrast, is too uncritical of globalization, caught up in his own Lexus high-consumption lifestyle, failing to perceive the depth of the oppressive features of globalization and breadth and extent of resistance and opposition to it. In particular, he fails to articulate the contradictions between capitalism and democracy, and the ways that globalization and its economic logic undermine democracy as well as encourage it. Likewise, he does not grasp the virulence of the premodern and Jihadist tendencies that he blithely identifies with the olive tree, and the reasons that globalization and the West are so strongly resisted in many parts of the world.

Hence, it is important to present globalization as a conflicted amalgam of both homogenizing forces of sameness and uniformity *and* heterogeneity, difference, and hybridity, as well as a contradictory mixture of democratizing and antidemocratizing tendencies. On one hand, globalization unfolds a process of standardization in which a globalized mass culture circulates the globe creating sameness and homogeneity everywhere. But globalized culture makes possible unique appropriations and developments all over the world, thus proliferating hybrids, difference, and heterogeneity.[3] Every local context involves its own appropriation and reworking of global products and signifiers, thus proliferating difference, otherness, diversity, and variety (Luke and Luke 2000). Grasping that globalization embodies these contradictory tendencies at once, that it can be both a force of homogenization and heterogeneity, is crucial to articulating the contradictions of globalization and avoiding one-sided and reductive conceptions.

My intention is to present globalization as conflictual, contradictory, and open to resistance and democratic intervention and transformation and not just as a monolithic juggernaut of progress or domination as in many other discourses. This goal is advanced by distinguishing between "globalization from below" and "globalization from above" of corporate capitalism and the capitalist state, a distinction that should help us to get a better sense of how globalization does or does not promote democratization. "Globalization from below" refers to the ways in which marginalized individuals and social movements resist globalization and/or use its institutions and instruments to further democratization and social justice.

Yet, one needs to avoid binary normative articulations, since globalization from below can have highly conservative and destructive effects, as well as positive ones, while globalization from above can help produce global solutions to problems like terrorism or the environment. While on one level, globalization significantly increases the supremacy of big corporations and big government, it can also give power to groups and individuals that were previously left out of the democratic dialogue and terrain of political struggle. Such potentially positive effects of globalization include increased access to education for individuals excluded from sharing culture and knowledge and the possibility of oppositional individuals and groups to participate in global culture and politics through gaining access to global communication and media networks and to circulate local struggles and oppositional ideas through these media. The role of new technologies in social movements, political struggle, and everyday life forces social movements to reconsider their political strategies and goals and democratic theory to appraise how new technologies do and do not promote democratization (Kellner 1997, 1999a).

In their book *Empire*, Hardt and Negri (2000) present contradictions within globalization in terms of an imperializing logic of "Empire" and an assortment of struggles by the multitude, creating a contradictory and tension-full situation. As in my conception, Hardt and Negri present globalization as a complex process that involves a multidimensional mixture of expansions of the global economy and capitalist market system, new technologies and media, expanded judicial and legal modes of governance, and emergent modes of power, sovereignty, and resistance.[4] Combining poststructuralism with "autonomous Marxism," Hardt and Negri stress political openings and possibilities of struggle within Empire in an optimistic and buoyant text that envisages progressive democratization and self-valorization in the turbulent process of the restructuring of capital.

Many theorists, by contrast, have argued that one of the trends of globalization is depoliticization of publics, the decline of the nation-state, and end of traditional politics (Boggs 2000). While I would agree that globalization is promoted by tremendously powerful economic forces and that it often undermines democratic movements and decision making, I also argue that there are openings and possibilities for both a globalization from below that inflects globalization for positive and progressive ends, and that globalization can thus help promote as well as destabilize democracy.[5] Globalization involves both a disorganization and reorganization of capitalism, a tremendous restructuring process, which creates openings for progressive social change and intervention as well as highly destructive transformative effects. On the positive ledger, in a more fluid and open economic and political system, oppositional forces can gain concessions, win victories, and effect progressive changes. During the 1970s, new social movements, emergent nongovernmental organizations (NGOs), and novel forms of struggle and solidarity emerged that have been expanding to the present day (Burbach 2001; Foran 2002; Hardt and Negri 2000).

But not only the anticorporate globalization of the 1990s emerged as a form of globalization from below, but also al Qaeda and various global terror networks intensified their attacks and helped generate an era of terror war. This made it difficult simply to affirm globalization from below while denigrating globalization from above, as clearly terrorism was an emergent and dangerous form of globalization from below that was attacking hegemonic global forces and institutions. Moreover, in the face of Bush administration unilateralism and militarism, multilateral approaches to the problems of terrorism called for global responses and alliances to a wide range of present-day problems.

The current conjuncture is marked by a conflict between growing centralization and organization of power and wealth in the hands of the few contrasted with opposing processes exhibiting a fragmentation of power that is more plural, multiple, and open to contestation. As the following analysis will suggest, both tendencies are observable and it is up to individuals and groups to find openings for progressive political intervention and social transformation that pursue positive values such as democracy, human rights, ecological preservation and restoration, and social justice, while fighting poverty, terror, and injustice. Thus, rather than just denouncing globalization, or engaging in celebration and legitimation, a critical theory of globalization reproaches those aspects that are oppressive, while seizing on opportunities to fight domination and exploitation and to promote democratization, justice, and a forward-looking reconstruction of the polity, society, and culture.

Against capitalist globalization from above, there have been a significant eruption of forces and subcultures of resistance that have attempted to preserve specific forms of culture and society against globalization and homogenization, and to create alternative forces of society and culture, thus exhibiting resistance and globalization from below. Most dramatically, peasant and guerrilla movements in Latin America, labor unions, students, and environmentalists throughout the world, and a variety of other groups and movements have resisted capitalist globalization and attacks on previous rights and benefits.[6] Several dozen people's organizations from around the world have protested World Trade Organization policies and a backlash against globalization is visible everywhere. Politicians who once championed trade agreements such as GATT (General Agreement on Tariffs and Trade) and NAFTA (North American Free Trade Agreement) are now often quiet or critical about these arrangements. For example, at the 1996 annual Davos World Economic Forum, its founder and managing director published a warning titled "Start Taking the Backlash against Globalization Seriously." Reports surfaced that major representatives of the capitalist system expressed fear that capitalism was getting too mean and predatory, that it needs a kinder and gentler state to ensure order and harmony, and that the welfare state may make a comeback (*New York Times*, February 7, 1996, A15).[7] One should take such reports with the proverbial grain of salt, but they express fissures and openings in the system for critical discourse and intervention.

Indeed, by 1999, the theme of the annual Davos conference was making globalization work for poor countries and minimizing the differences between the "haves" and "have nots." The growing divisions between rich and poor were worrying some globalizers, as were the wave of crises in Asian, Latin American, and other "developing countries." In James Flanigan's report in the *Los Angeles Times* (February 19, 1999), the "main theme" is to "spread the wealth. In a world frightened by glaring imbalances and the weakness of economies from Indonesia to Russia, the talk is no longer of a new world economy getting stronger but of ways to 'keep the engine going.'" In particular, the globalizers were attempting to keep economies growing in the more developed countries and capital flowing to developing nations. U.S. vice president Al Gore called on all countries to spur economic growth, and he proposed a new U.S.-led initiative to eliminate the debt burdens of developing countries. South African president Nelson Mandela asked: "Is globalization only for the powerful? Does it offer nothing to the men, women, and children who are ravaged by the violence of poverty?"

As the new millennium opened, there was no clear answer to Mandela's question. In the 2000s, there have been ritual proclamations of the need to make globalization work for the developing nations at all major meetings of global institutions like the World Trade Organization (WTO) or G-8 convenings. For instance, at the September 2003 WTO meeting at Cancun, organizers claimed that its goal was to fashion a new trade agreement that would reduce poverty and boost development in poorer nations. But critics pointed out that in the past years the richer nations of the United States, Japan, and Europe continued to enforce trade tariffs and provide subsidies for national producers of goods such as agriculture, while forcing poorer nations to open their markets to "free trade," thus bankrupting agricultural sectors in these countries that could not compete. Moreover, major economists like Joseph Stiglitz (2002), as well as anticorporate globalization protestors and critics, argued that the developing countries were not making progress under current corporate globalization policies and that divisions between the rich and poor nations were growing. Under these conditions, critics of globalization were calling for radically new policies that would help the developing countries, regulate the rich, and provide more power to working people and local groups.[8]

THE GLOBAL MOVEMENT AGAINST
CAPITALIST GLOBALIZATION

With the global economic recession and the terror war erupting in 2001, the situation of many developing countries has worsened. As part of the backlash against globalization over in recent years, a wide range of theorists have argued that the proliferation of difference and the shift to more local discourses and practices best define the contemporary scene. In this view, theory and politics should shift from the level of globalization (and its accompanying often totalizing and macro dimensions) in order to focus on the local, the specific, the particular, the heterogeneous, and the microlevel of everyday experience. An array of theories associated with poststructuralism, postmodernism, feminism, and multiculturalism focus on difference, otherness, marginality, the personal, the particular, and the concrete in contrast to more general theory and politics that aim at more global or universal conditions.[9] Likewise, a broad spectrum of subcultures of resistance have focused their attention on the local level, organizing struggles around identity issues such as gender, race, sexual preference, or youth subculture.

It can be argued that such dichotomies as those between the global and the local express contradictions and tensions between crucial constitutive forces on the present scene. It may be a mistake to focus on one side in favor of exclusive concern with the other (Cvetkovitch and Kellner 1997). Hence, an important challenge for a critical theory of globalization is to think through the relationships between the global and the local by observing how global forces influence and even structure an increasing number of local situations. This requires analysis as well of how local forces mediate the global, inflecting global forces to diverse ends and conditions, and producing unique configurations of the local and the global as the matrix for thought and action in today's world (see Luke and Luke 2000).

Globalization is thus necessarily complex and challenging to both critical theories and radical democratic politics. But many people operate with binary concepts of the global and the local, and promote one or the other side of the equation as the solution to the world's problems. For globalists, globalization is the solution and underdevelopment, backwardness, and provincialism are the problems. For localists, globalization is the problem and localization is the solution. But politics is frequently contextual and pragmatic, and whether global or local solutions are most fitting depends on the conditions in the distinctive context that one is addressing and the specific solutions and policies being proposed.[10]

For instance, the Internet can be used to promote capitalist globalization or struggles against it. One of the more instructive examples of the use of the Internet to foster movements against the excesses of corporate capitalism occurred in the protests in Seattle and throughout the world against the WTO meeting in December 1999. Behind these actions was a global protest movement using the Internet to organize resistance to the WTO and capitalist globalization, while championing democratization. Many websites contained anti-WTO material and numerous mailing lists used the Internet to distribute critical material and to organize the protest. The result was the mobilization of caravans from throughout the United States to take protestors to Seattle, many of whom had never met before and were Internet recruits. There were also significant numbers of international participants in Seattle which exhibited labor, environmentalist, feminist, anticapitalist, animal rights, anarchist, and other protests against aspects of globalization while forming new alliances and solidarities for future struggles. In addition, protests occurred throughout the world, and a proliferation of anti-WTO material against the extremely secret group spread throughout the Internet.[11]

Furthermore, the Internet provided critical coverage of the event, documentation of the various groups' protests, and debate over the WTO and globalization. Whereas the mainstream media presented the protests as "antitrade," featured the incidents of anarchist violence against property, and minimized police violence against demonstrators, the Internet provided pictures, eyewitness accounts, and reports of police brutality and the generally peaceful and nonviolent nature of the protests. Mainstream media framed the protests negatively and privileged suspect spokespersons like Patrick Buchanan, an extreme right wing and authoritarian critic of globalization; the Internet provided multiple representations of the demonstrations, advanced reflective discussion of the WTO and globalization, and presented a diversity of critical perspectives.

The Seattle protests had some immediate consequences. The day after the demonstrators made good on their promise to shut down the WTO negotiations, Bill Clinton gave a speech endorsing the concept of labor rights and trade sanctions. This effectively made any agreement or consensus impossible during the Seattle meetings. In addition, at the World Economic Forum in Davos a month later there was much discussion of how concessions were necessary on labor and the environment if consensus over globalization and free trade were to be possible. Importantly, the issue of overcoming divisions between the information rich and poor, and improving the lot of the disenfranchised and oppressed, bringing these groups the benefits of globalization, were also seriously discussed at the meeting and in the media.

More significantly, many activists were energized. They formed new alliances, solidarities, and militant groups, and continued to cultivate the antiglobalization movement. The Seattle demonstrations were followed in April 2000 with struggles in Washington, D.C., to protest the World Bank and International Monetary Fund (IMF), and later in the year against capitalist globalization in Prague and Melbourne; in April 2001, an extremely large and militant protest erupted against the Free Trade Area of the Americas summit in Quebec City and in summer 2001 a large demonstration took place in Genoa.

In May 2002, a surprisingly large demonstration took place in Washington against capitalist globalization and for peace and justice. It was clear that a new worldwide movement was in the making uniting diverse opponents of capitalist globalization. The anticorporate globalization movement favored globalization-from-below, which would protect the environment, food and agriculture, labor rights, national cultures, democratization, and other goods from the ravages of an uncontrolled capitalist globalization (see Brecher, Costello, and Smith 2000; Steger 2002).

In February 2003, some of the largest peace demonstrations in history took place in response to the impending U.S.- and British-led war against Iraq, and while the demonstrations did not stop the invasion, they helped produce global resistance to militarism and war. Initially, the incipient antiglobalization movement was precisely that—an antiglobalization movement. The movement, itself, became increasingly global, linking a diversity of movements into global solidarity networks and was using the Internet and instruments of globalization to advance its struggles. Moreover, many opponents of capitalist globalization recognized the need for a global movement to have a positive vision and be for such things as social justice, equality, labor, civil liberties and human rights, and a sustainable environmentalism. Accordingly, the anticapitalist globalization movement began advocating common values and visions.

In particular, the movement against capitalist globalization used the Internet to organize mass demonstrations and to disseminate information to the world concerning the policies of the institutions of capitalist globalization. The events made clear that protestors were not against globalization per se, but were against neoliberal and capitalist globalization, opposing specific policies and institutions that produce intensified exploitation of labor, environmental devastation, growing divisions among the social classes, and the undermining of democracy. The emerging anticorporate globalization movements are contesting the neoliberal model of market capitalism that extols maximum profit with zero accountability and have made clear the need for democratization, regulation, rules, and globalization in the interests of people, not just profit.

The new movements against capitalist globalization have thus placed the issues of global justice, human rights, and environmental destruction squarely in the center of important political concerns of our time. Hence, whereas the mainstream media had failed to vigorously debate or even report on globalization until the eruption of a vigorous antiglobalization movement, and rarely, if ever, critically discussed the activities of the WTO, World Bank, and IMF, there is now a widely circulating critical discourse and controversy over these institutions. Stung by criticisms, representatives of the World Bank, in particular, are pledging reform and pressures are mounting concerning proper and improper roles for the major global institutions, highlighting their limitations and deficiencies, and the need for reforms like debt relief from overburdened developing countries to solve some of their fiscal and social problems.

To capital's globalization-from-above, cyberactivists and a multitude of groups have thus been attempting to carry out globalization-from-below, developing networks of solidarity and propagating oppositional ideas and movements throughout the planet. To the capitalist international of transnational corporate-led globalization, a Fifth International, to use Waterman's phrase (1992), of computer-mediated activism is emerging, that is qualitatively different from the party-based socialist and communist Internationals. Such networking links labor, feminist, ecological, peace, and other anticapitalist groups, providing the basis for a new politics of alliance and solidarity to overcome the limitations of postmodern identity politics (see Burbach 2001; Dyer-Witheford 1999; Hardt and Negri 2000).

Of course, right wing and reactionary forces can and have used the Internet to promote their political agendas as well. In a short time, one can easily access an exotic witch's brew of websites maintained by the Ku Klux Klan, myriad neo-Nazi assemblages, including the Aryan Nation and various militia groups. Internet discussion lists also disperse these views and right-wing extremists are aggressively active in many computer forums, as well as radio programs and stations, public access television programs, fax campaigns, video and even rock music productions. These organizations are hardly harmless, having carried out terrorism of various sorts extending from church burnings to the bombings of public buildings. Adopting quasi-Leninist discourse and tactics for ultraright causes, these groups have been successful in recruiting working-class members devastated by the developments of global capitalism, which has resulted in widespread unemployment for traditional forms of industrial, agricultural, and unskilled labor. Moreover, extremist websites have influenced alienated middle-class youth as well (a 1999 HBO documentary titled *Hate on the Internet* provides a disturbing number of examples of how extremist websites influenced disaffected youth to commit hate crimes).

A recent twist in the saga of technopolitics, in fact, seems to be that allegedly "terrorist" groups are now increasingly using the Internet and websites to promote their causes. An article in the *Los Angeles Times* (February 8, 2001, A1,

A14) reports that groups like Hamas use their website to post reports of acts of terror against Israel, rather than calling newspapers or broadcasting outlets. A wide range of groups labeled as "terrorist" reportedly use e-mail, listservs, and websites to further their struggles, causes including Hezbollah and Hamas, the Maoist group Shining Path in Peru, and a variety of other groups in Asia and elsewhere. The Tamil Tigers, for instance, a liberation movement in Sri Lanka, offers position papers, daily news, and free e-mail service. According to the *Times*, experts are still unclear "whether the ability to communicate online worldwide is prompting an increase or a decrease in terrorist acts."

There have been widespread discussions of how the bin Laden al Qaeda network used the Internet to plan the September 11 terrorist attacks on the United States, how the group communicated with each other, got funds, and purchased airline tickets via the Internet, and used flight simulations to practice their hijacking. In the contemporary era, the Internet can thus be used for a diversity of political projects and goals ranging from education, to business, to political organization and debate, to terrorism.

Moreover, different political groups are engaging in cyberwar as an adjunct of their political battles. Israeli hackers have repeatedly attacked the websites of Hamas and Hezbollah, while pro-Palestine hackers have reportedly placed militant demands and slogans on the websites of Israel's army, foreign ministry, and parliament. Likewise, Pakistani and Indian computer hackers have waged similar cyberbattles against the opposing nation's websites in the bloody struggle over Kashmir, while rebel forces in the Philippines taunt government troops with cell-phone calls and messages and attack government websites.

The examples in this section suggest how technopolitics makes possible a refiguring of politics, a refocusing of politics on everyday life, and using the tools and techniques of new computer and communication technology to expand the field and domain of politics. In this conjuncture, the ideas of Guy Debord and the Situationist International are especially relevant with their stress on the construction of situations, the use of technology, media of communication, and cultural forms to promote a revolution of everyday life, and to increase the realm of freedom, community, and empowerment.[12] To some extent, the new technologies *are* revolutionary, they *do* constitute a revolution of everyday life, but it is often a revolution that promotes and disseminates the capitalist consumer society and involves new modes of fetishism, enslavement, and domination, yet to be clearly perceived and theorized.

The Internet and emerging forms of technopolitics also point to the connection between politics and pedagogy. Paulo Freire has long argued that all pedagogy is political and politics contains a pedagogical dimension (which could be manipulative or emancipatory). Critical educators need to devise strategies to use the Internet and new technologies to enhance education and to produce more active democratic and global citizens.

The Internet is thus a contested terrain, used by members of the Left, Right, and Center to promote their own agendas and interests. The political battles of the future may well be fought in the streets, factories, parliaments, and other sites of past struggle, but politics is already mediated by broadcast, computer, and information technologies and will increasingly be so in the future. Those interested in the politics and culture of the future should, therefore, be clear on the important role of the new public spheres and intervene accordingly, while critical pedagogues have the responsibility of teaching students the skills that will enable them to participate in the politics and struggles of the present and future.

THE CONTRADICTIONS OF GLOBALIZATION AND CHALLENGES FOR THE LEFT

And so, to paraphrase Foucault, wherever there is globalization-from-above, globalization as the imposition of capitalist logic, there can be resistance and struggle. The possibilities of globalization-from-below result from transnational alliances between groups fighting for better wages and working conditions, social and political justice, environmental protection, and more democracy and freedom worldwide. In addition, a renewed emphasis on local and grassroots movements has put dominant economic forces on the defensive in their own back yard. Often, the broadcasting media or the Internet have called attention to oppressive and destructive corporate policies on the local level, putting national and even transnational pressure upon major corporations for reform. Moreover, proliferating media and the Internet make possible a greater circulation of struggles and the possibilities of new alliances and solidarities that can connect resistant forces who oppose capitalist and corporate-state elite forms of globalization-from-above (Dyer-Witheford 1999).

In a certain sense, the phenomena of globalization replicates the history of the United States. In most so-called capitalist democracies tension between capitalism and democracy has been a defining feature of the conflicts of the past two hundred years. In analyzing the development of education in the United States, Bowles and Gintis (1986) have analyzed the conflicts between corporate logic and democracy in schooling; I (Kellner 1990, 1992, 2003a) and others have articulated the contradictions between capitalism and democracy in the media and public sphere. Joel Cohen and Joel Rogers (1983) and others argue that contradictions between capitalism and democracy are defining features of the U.S. polity and history.

On a global terrain, Hardt and Negri (2000) have stressed the openings and possibilities for democratic transformative struggle within globalization, or what they call "Empire." I am arguing that similar arguments can be made in which globalization is not conceived merely as the triumph of capitalism and democracy working together as it was in the classical theories of Milton Friedman or, more recently, in Francis Fukuyama (1992) and Thomas Friedman (1999). Nor should globalization be depicted solely as the triumph of capital as in many despairing antiglobalization theories. Rather, one should see that globalization unleashes conflicts between capitalism and democracy. In its restructuring processes this creates new openings for struggle, resistance, and democratic transformation.

I would also suggest that the model of Marx and Engels as deployed in the "Communist Manifesto" could also be usefully employed to analyze the contradictions of globalization (Marx and Engels 1978, 469ff.). From the historical materialist optic, capitalism was interpreted as the greatest, most progressive force in history for Marx and Engels, destroying a backward feudalism, authoritarian patriarchy, backwardness and provincialism in favor a market society, global cosmopolitanism, and constant revolutionizing of the forces of production. Yet, in Marxist theory, so too was capitalism presented as a major disaster for the human race, condemning a large part to alienated labor, regions of the world to colonialist exploitation, and generating conflicts between classes and nations, the consequences of which the contemporary era continues to suffer.

Marx deployed a similar dialectical and historical model in his later analyses of imperialism arguing, for instance, in his writings on British imperialism in India, that British colonialism was a great productive and progressive force in India at the same time it was highly destructive (Marx and Engels 1978, 653ff.). A similar dialectical and critical model can be used today that articulates the progressive elements of globalization in conjunction with its more oppressive features, deploying the categories of negation and critique, while sublating (*Aufhebung*) the positive features. Moreover, a dialectical and transdisciplinary model is necessary to capture the complexity and multidimensionality of globalization today that brings together in theorizing globalization, the economy, technology, polity, society and culture, articulating the interplay of these elements and avoiding any form of determinism or reductivism.

Theorizing globalization dialectically and critically requires that we both analyze continuities and discontinuities with the past, specifying what is a continuation of past histories and what is new and original in the present moment. To elucidate the latter, I believe that the discourse of the postmodern is useful in dramatizing changes and novelties of the mode of globalization. The concept of postmodern can signal that which is fresh and original, calling attention to topics and phenomena that require novel theorization, and intense critical thought and inquiry. Hence, although Manuel Castells has the most detailed analysis of new technologies and the rise of what he calls a networked society, by refusing to link his analyses with the problematic of the postmodern, he cuts himself off from theoretical resources that enable theorists to articulate the novelties of the present that are unique and different from previous modes of social organization.[13]

Consequently, although there is admittedly a lot of mystification in the discourse of the postmodern, it signals emphatic shifts and ruptures in our era, as well as novelties and originalities, and dramatizes the mutations in culture, subjectivities, and theory which Castells and other theorists of globalization or the information society gloss over. The discourse of the postmodern in relation to analysis of contemporary culture and society is just jargon, however, unless it is rooted in analysis of the global restructuring of capitalism and analysis of the scientific–technological revolution that is part and parcel of it.[14]

As I have argued in this study, the term *globalization* is often used as a code word that stands for a large diversity of issues and problems and that serves as a front for a variety of theoretical and political positions. While it can function as a legitimating ideology to cover over and sanitize ugly realities, a critical globalization theory can inflect the discourse to point precisely at these deplorable phenomena and can elucidate a series of contemporary problems and conflicts. In view of the different concepts and functions of globalization discourse, it is important to note that the concept of globalization is a theoretical construct that varies according to the assumptions and commitments of the theorist in question. Seeing the term *globalization* as a construct helps rob it of its force of nature, as a sign of an inexorable triumph of market forces and the hegemony of capital, or, as the extreme right fears, of a rapidly encroaching world government. While the term can both describe and legitimate capitalist transnationalism and supranational government institutions, a critical theory of globalization does not buy into ideological valorizations and affirms difference, resistance, and democratic self-determination against forms of global domination and subordination.

Globalization should thus be seen as contested terrain with opposing forces attempting to use its institutions, technologies, media, and forms for their own purposes. There are certainly negative aspects to globalization which strengthen elite economic and political forces over and against the underlying population, but, as suggested previously, there are also positive possibilities. Other beneficial openings include the opportunity for greater democratization, increased education and health care, and new opportunities within the global economy that open entry to members of races, regions, and classes previously excluded from mainstream economics, politics, and culture within the modern corporate order.

GLOBALIZATION AND EDUCATION

Consequently, critical pedagogy needs to develop new educational strategies to counter the oppressive forces and effects of globalization to empower individuals to understand and act effectively in a globalized world, and to struggle for social justice. This requires teaching skills such as media and computer literacy, as well as helping to empower students and citizens to deploy multiple technologies for progressive purposes (Kellner 1998). Globalization and new technologies *are* dominant forces of the future and it is up to critical theorists and activists to illuminate their nature and effects, to demonstrate the threats to democracy and freedom, and to seize opportunities for progressive education and democratization.

The project of transforming education will take different forms in different contexts. In the postindustrial or "overdeveloped" countries, individuals must be empowered to work and act in a high-tech information economy, and thus must learn skills of media and computer literacy, to survive in the new social environment. Traditional skills of knowledge and critique must also be fostered, so that students can name the system, describe and grasp the changes occurring in it the defining features of the new global order, and can learn to engage in critical and oppositional practice in the interests of democratization and progressive transformation. This requires gaining vision of how life can be, of alternatives to the present order, and the necessity of struggle and organization to realize progressive goals. Languages of knowledge and critique must thus be supplemented by the discourse of hope and praxis.

In much of the world, the struggle for daily existence is paramount and meeting unmet human and social needs is a high priority. Yet, everywhere, education can provide the competencies and skills to improve one's life, to create a better society, and a more civilized and developed world. Moreover, as the entire world becomes a global and networked society, gaining the multiple literacies necessary to use a range of technologies becomes important everywhere as media and cyberculture become more ubiquitous and the world economy requires people with ever more sophisticated technical skills.

It is interesting that one of the godfathers of critical pedagogy, Paulo Freire, was positive toward media and new technologies, seeing technologies as potential tools for empowering citizens, as well as instruments of domination in the hands of ruling elites. Many critical pedagogues, however, are technophobes, seeing new technologies solely as instruments of domination. In a world inexorably undergoing processes of globalization and technological transformation, one cannot, however, in good conscience advocate a policy of clean hands and purity, distancing oneself from technology and globalization, but must intervene in the processes of economic and technological revolution, attempting to deflect these forces for progressive ends and developing new pedagogies to advance the project of human liberation and well-being.

A critical theory of technology maintains that there is utopian potential in the new technologies as well as the possibility for increased domination and the hegemony of capital. While the first generation of computers were large mainframe systems controlled by big government and big business, later generations of "personal computers" and networks created a more decentralized situation in which ever more individuals own their own computers and use them for their own projects and goals. A new generation of wireless communication could enable areas of the world that do not even have electricity to participate in the communication and information revolution of the emergent global era. This would require, of course, something like a Marshall Plan for the developing world which would necessitate help with disseminating technologies that would address problems of world hunger, disease, illiteracy, and poverty.

In relation to education, the spread and distribution of information and communication technology signifies the possibility of openings of opportunities for research and interaction not previously open to students who did not have the privilege of access to major research libraries or institutions. The Internet opens more information and knowledge to more people than any previous institution in history, despite its many problems and limitations. Moreover, the Internet enables individuals to participate in discussions, to circulate their ideas and work, that were previously closed off to many excluded groups and individuals.

A progressive reconstruction of education that is done in the interests of democratization would demand access to new technologies for all, helping to overcome the so-called digital divide and divisions of the "haves" and "have nots" (see Kellner 2000 and 2002). Expanding democratic and multicultural reconstruction of education forces educators and citizens to confront the challenge of the digital divide, in which there are divisions between information and technology "haves" and "have nots," just as there are class, gender, and race divisions in every sphere of existing of societies and cultures. Although the latest surveys of the digital divide indicate that the key indicators are class and education and not race and gender, nonetheless, making computers a significant force of democratization in education and society will require significant investment and programs to assure that everyone receives the training, literacies, and tools necessary to properly function in a high-tech global economy and culture.[15]

As a response to globalization and technological revolution, I propose that transformations in pedagogy must be as radical as the technological transformations that are taking place. Critical pedagogy must thus rethink the concepts of literacy and the very nature of education in any high-tech and rapidly evolving society. At the same time that we are undergoing technological revolution, important demographic and sociopolitical changes are occurring in the United States and throughout the world. Emigration patterns have brought an explosion of new peoples into the United States in recent decades and the country is now more racially and ethnically diverse, more multicultural, than ever before. This creates the challenge of providing people from diverse races, classes, and backgrounds with the tools to enable them to succeed and participate in an increasingly complex and changing world.

In my previous work, I have delineated the multiple literacies necessary to respond to new technology including an expanded role for media literacy, computer and information literacies, and multimedia literacies that provide literacy in reading, researching, and producing in the emergent multimedia world (see Kellner 1998, 2000). Radically reconstructing education requires a wide range of other literacies often neglected in the current organization of schooling. Since a multicultural society is the context of education for the contemporary moment, novel forms of social interaction and cultural awareness are needed that appreciate differences, multiplicity, and diversity. Therefore, an expanded *cultural literacy* is needed, one that appreciates the cultural heritage, histories, and contributions of a diversity of groups. Whereas one can agree that we need to be literate in our shared cultural heritage, we also need to become culturally literate in cultures that have been hitherto invisible.

Social literacy should also be taught throughout the educational systems, ranging from a focus on how to relate and get along with a variety of individuals, how to negotiate differences, how to resolve conflicts, and how to communicate and socially interact in a diversity of situations. Social literacy involves ethical training in values and norms, delineating proper and improper individual and social values (which may well be different in various regions and countries). It also requires knowledge of contemporary societies and thus overlaps with social and natural science training. In fact, given the significant role of science and technology in the contemporary world, given threats to the environment, and the need to preserve and enhance the natural as well as social and cultural worlds, it is scandalous how illiterate the entire societies are concerning science, nature, and even peoples' own bodies. An *ecoliteracy* should thus appropriately teach competency in interpreting and interacting with our natural environment, ranging from our own body to natural habitats, like forests and deserts.

The challenge for education today is thus to develop multiple literacies to empower students and citizens to use new technologies to enhance their lives and to create a better culture and society based on respect for multicultural differences and aiming at fuller democratic participation of individuals and groups largely excluded from wealth and power in the previous modern society. A positive postmodernity would thus involve creation of a more egalitarian and democratic society in which more individuals and groups were empowered to participate. The great danger facing us, of course, is that globalization and the new technologies will increase the current inequalities based on class, gender, and racial divisions. So far, privileged groups have had more direct and immediate access to new technologies. It is therefore a challenge of education today to provide access to the technologies and to the literacies needed for competence to excluded or oppressed individuals and groups to overcome some of the divisions and inequalities that have plagued contemporary societies during the entire modern age.

Radical educators must attempt to connect the phenomenon of the technological revolution and the multicultural explosion and drama of conflicting ethnicities, classes, genders, and so on, so that differences can create diversity, tolerance, and an enhanced and strengthened democracy and society and not conflict, intolerance, division, and violence. It is not just a question of talking about media literacy, computer literacy, or other multiple literacies from a technological viewpoint, but thinking together new technologies and multiculturalism, with technological and social transformation. Thus, a challenge for critical pedagogy is to discover how the new technologies and literacies can serve the interests of multiculturalism, making teachers, students, and citizens aware of how the new technologies are transforming everything from education to work to war, the challenges involved, the literacies needed, and the opportunities for educational reform and social reconstruction.

To be sure, legitimate concerns have been raised in regard to the possibilities that computer and multimedia technologies will increase the regnant inequalities in relation to privileged class, gender, and racial groupings. As is well known, the original computer culture was largely composed of white middle- to upper-class male "geeks" or "nerds," a culture that tended to exclude women, people of color, and members of classes without access to computer technologies. As new technologies become a more central aspect of schooling, work, and everyday life, however, more and more women and members of groups previously excluded from computer culture are now becoming participants as they gain access to computers and multimedia technologies in schools, in the workplace, and at home. Of course, the question of access to new technologies becomes increasingly important as work, education, and every other aspect of social life is undergoing transformation, making multiple literacies essential to work, cultural, educational, and political exigencies of the future. If the previously disadvantaged and marginalized groups will not gain access to the emergent technologies, class, gender, race, and other divisions will exponentially grow, creating ever more virulent divisions and the prospects of social upheaval and turbulence.

Yet there are aspects of the forms of literacy being spawned by information technologies and multimedia culture that are potentially democratizing and empowering for individuals and groups previously on the bottom end of prevailing configurations of class, gender, and racial power. The increased informality, closeness to speech patterns, and spontaneity of e-mail composition and participation in chat rooms and computer-mediated communications and forums provide access to individuals and groups whose literacies and modes of writing were deemed inferior or deficient from more standard classical print-media perspectives. Indeed, the openness of many forums of computer-mediated communication, the possibility of ever more individuals able to produce their own websites, and access to volumes of information previously limited to those who had access to elite libraries potentially democratize education, cultural production, and participation in cultural and political dialogue.

Thus, issues of access and exclusion in relation to new technologies and multiple literacies are crucial to realizing the promises of democracy. Yet, there are potential threats in the proliferation of seductive technologies of information and entertainment. There is the danger that youth will become totally immersed in an alluring world of high-tech experience and lose its social connectedness and ability to interpersonally communicate and relate concretely to other people. Statistics suggest that more and more sectors of youth are able to access cyberspace and that college students with Internet accounts are spending as much as four hours a day in the novel realm of technological experience.[16] Moreover, the media have been generating a moral panic concerning allegedly growing dangers in cyberspace with lurid stories of young boys and girls lured into dangerous sex or running away from home, endless accounts of how pornography on the Internet is proliferating, and the publicizing of calls for increasing control, censorship, and surveillance of communication—usually by politicians or others who are computer illiterate. The solution, however, is not to ban access to those technologies, but to teach students and citizens how to use them so that they can be employed for productive and creative, rather than problematical, ends.

To be sure, there are dangers in cyberspace as well as elsewhere, but the threats to adolescents are significantly higher through the danger of family violence and abuse than seduction by strangers on the Internet. And while there is a flourishing trade in pornography on the Internet, this material has become increasingly available in a variety of venues from the local video shop to the newspaper stand. So, it seems unfair to demonize the Internet. Attempts at Internet censorship are part of the attack on youth, which would circumscribe their rights to obtain entertainment and information, and create their own subcultures.[17] Consequently, devices like the V-chip that would exclude sex and violence on television, or block computer access to objectionable material, is more an expression of adult hysteria and moral panic than genuine dangers to youth which certainly exist, but much more strikingly in the real world than in the sphere of hyperreality.

Throughout this century, there has been a demonization of new media and forms of media culture, ranging from comic books to film to popular music to television and now to the Internet. As Jenkins argues this demonization is supported by an assumption of the innocence of childhood, that children are merely passive receptacles, easily seduced by cultural images, and in need of protection from nefarious and harmful cultural content. But as he also contends (1997, 30–31), the myth of "childhood innocence" strips children of active agency, of being capable of any thoughts of their own, and of having the ability to decode and process media materials themselves. Of course, children need media education. They need to be involved in an active learning process concerning their culture. But censorship and vilification of media does not help young people become active critics, and participants in their culture.

Accordingly, children's "cyber-rights" have been argued for in that our youth's access to Internet cyberculture and media culture in general is necessary for their participation in the larger culture and their own education and development. Mastery of the culture can be the difference between economic success and hardship. The Internet, in particular, allows participation in many dimensions of social and cultural life as well as the cultivation of those technical skills that can help children in later life.

Therefore, it is necessary to divest ourselves of myths of childhood innocence and the passivity of children's media consumption, positing instead the possibility of active and creative use of media material in which media education is seen as part of youth's self-development and constitution. Rather than demonizing and rejecting out of hand all new technologies, we should criticize their misuse, but also see how they can be used constructively and positively. In studying the kaleidoscopic array of discourses which characterize the evolving technologies,

I am rather bemused by the extent to which they expose either a technophilic discourse which presents new technologies as our salvation, that will solve all our problems, or they embody a technophobic discourse that sees technology as our damnation, demonizing it as the major source of all our problems. It appears that similarly one-sided and contrasting discourses greeted the introduction of other new technologies this century, often hysterically. It is indeed curious that whenever an innovative technology is introduced a polarized response emerges in relation to its novelty and differences from previous technologies. New technologies seem to attract both advocates and champions and critics and detractors. This was historically the case with mass media, and now computers.

Film, for instance, was celebrated by early theorists as providing a marvelous documentary depiction of reality. Siegfried Kraucauer published a book on film as the "redemption of reality," and it was described early on as a new art form, as well as providing new modes of mass education and entertainment. Likewise, it was soon demonized for promoting sexual promiscuity, juvenile delinquency and crime, violence, and copious other forms of immorality and evil. Its demonization led in the United States to a production code that rigorously regulated the content of Hollywood film from 1934 until the 1950s and 1960s—no open-mouth kissing was permitted, crime could not pay, drug use or attacks on religion could not be portrayed, and a censorship office rigorously surveyed all films to make sure that no subversive or illicit content emerged (Kellner 1995b).

Similar extreme hopes and fears were projected onto radio, television, and now computers. It appears whenever there are new technologies, people project all sorts of fantasies, fears, hopes, and dreams onto them. This is now happening with computers and new multimedia technologies. It is indeed striking that if one looks at the literature on computer and information technologies it is either highly celebratory and technophilic, or sharply derogatory and technophobic. A critical theory of technology, however, and critical pedagogy, should avoid either demonizing or deifying emergent technologies and should instead develop pedagogies that will help us use technology to enhance education and life, and to criticize the limitations and false promises made on behalf of new technologies.

Certainly there is no doubt that the cyberspace of computer worlds contains as much banality and stupidity as real life. One can waste much time in useless activity. But compared to the bleak and violent urban worlds portrayed in rap music and youth films like *Kids* (1995), the technological worlds are havens of information, entertainment, interaction, and connection where youth can gain valuable skills, knowledge, and power necessary to survive the postmodern adventure. Youth can create alternative, more multiple and flexible selves in cyberspace as well as their own subcultures and communities. Indeed, it is exciting to cruise the Internet and to discover how many interesting websites that young people and others have established, often containing valuable educational and political material. There is, of course, the danger that corporate and commercial interests will come to colonize the Internet, but it is likely that there will continue to be spaces where individuals can empower themselves and create their own communities and identities. A main challenge for youth (and others) is to learn to use the Internet for positive cultural and political projects, rather than just entertainment and passive consumption (see Best and Kellner 2001).

Reflecting on the growing social importance of computers and new technologies makes it clear that it is of essential importance for youth today to gain various kinds of literacy to empower themselves for the emerging new cybersociety (this is true of teachers and adults as well). To survive in a postmodern world, individuals of all ages need to gain skills of media and computer literacy to enable ourselves to negotiate the overload of media images and spectacles. We all need to learn technological skills to use media and computer technologies to subsist in the high-tech economy and to form our own cultures and communities. Youth, especially, need street smarts and survival skills to cope with the drugs, violence, and uncertainty in today's predatory culture, as well as new forms of multiple literacy.

It is therefore extremely important for the future of democracy to make sure that youth of all classes, races, genders, and regions gain access to information and multimedia technology. This requires receiving training in media and computer literacy skills in order to provide the opportunities to enter the high-tech job market and to fully participate in the society of the future, so as to prevent an exacerbation of class, gender, and race inequalities. And while multiple forms of new literacies will be necessary, traditional print literacy skills are all the more important in a cyberage of word processing, information gathering, and Internet communication. Moreover, what I am calling multiple literacy involves training in philosophy, ethics, value thinking, and the humanities which is necessary today more then ever. In fact, *how* the Internet and emergent technologies will be used depends on the overall education of youth and the skills and interests they bring to the technologies, which can be used to access educational and valuable cultural and political material, or pornography and the banal wares of cybershopping malls.

Thus, the concept of multiple literacies and the postmodern pedagogy that I envisage maintains that it is not a question of "either/or" (e.g., either print literacy or multimedia literacy, either the classical curriculum or a new curriculum), but rather a question of "both/and" that preserves the best from classical education, enhances emphasis on print literacy, and develops new literacies to engage the emergent technologies. Obviously, cyberlife is just one dimension of experience and one still needs to learn to interact in the "real world" of school, jobs, relationships, politics, and community. Youth—indeed all of us!—need to negotiate many dimensions of social reality and to gain a multiplicity of forms of literacy and skills that will enable individuals to create identities, relationships, and communities that will nurture and develop the full spectrum of their potentialities and satisfy a wide array of needs. Our lives are more multidimensional than ever, so part of the postmodern adventure is learning to live in a variety of social spaces and to adapt to intense change and transformation (Best and Kellner 2001). Education, too, must meet these challenges and both utilize new technologies to improve education and devise pedagogical strategies in which new technologies can be deployed to create a more democratic and egalitarian multicultural society.

CONCLUSION

To conclude, a critical theory of globalization presents it as a force of capitalism and democracy, as a set of forces imposed from above, in conjunction with resistance from below. In this optic, globalization generates new conflicts, struggles, and crises, which, in part, can be seen as resistance to capitalist logic. In the light of the neoliberal projects to dismantle the welfare state, colonize the public sphere, and control globalization, it is up to citizens and activists to create alternative public spheres, politics, and pedagogies. In these spaces, that could include progressive classrooms, students and citizens could learn to use information and multimedia technologies to discuss what kinds of society people today want and to oppose the society against which people resist and struggle. This involves, minimally, demands for more education, health care, welfare, and benefits from the state, and to struggle to create a more democratic and egalitarian society. But one cannot expect that generous corporations and a beneficent state are going to make available to citizens the bounties and benefits of the globalized information economy. Rather, it is up to individuals and groups to promote democratization and progressive social change.

Thus, in opposition to the globalization-from-above of corporate capitalism, I would advocate globalization-from-below, which supports individuals and groups using the information and multimedia technologies to create a more multicultural, egalitarian, democratic, and ecological globalization. Of course, the new technologies might exacerbate existing inequalities in the current class, gender, race, and regional configurations of power and give major corporate forces powerful tools to advance their interests. In this situation, it is up to people of good will to devise strategies to use the new technologies to promote democratization and social justice. For as the emergent technologies become ever more central to the domains of everyday life, developing an oppositional technopolitics in alternative public spheres will become increasingly important (see Kellner 1995a, 1995b, 1997, 2000). Changes in the economy, politics, and social life demand a constant rethinking of politics and social change in the light of globalization and the technological revolution, requiring new thinking as a response to ever-changing historical conditions.

NOTES

1. This study is part of a larger theoretical project. For my perspectives on globalization and new technologies that inform this study, see Best and Kellner (2001) and Kellner (2002). For my perspectives on education, new technology, and new literacies that I expand upon in this study see Kellner (1998, 2000, 2002). On September 11 and the subsequent terror war, see Kellner (2003b).

2. I am not able in the framework of this paper to theorize the alarming expansion of war and militarism in the post–September 11 environment. For my theorizing of war and militarism, see Kellner (2002, 2003b).

3. For example, as Ritzer argues (1993), McDonald's imposes not only a similar cuisine all over the world, but circulates processes of what he calls "McDonaldization" that involve a production/consumption model of efficiency, technological rationality, calculability, predictability, and control. Yet as Watson has (1998) argued, McDonald's has various cultural meanings in diverse local contexts, as well as different products, organization, and effects. Yet the latter goes too far toward stressing heterogeneity, downplaying the cultural power of McDonald's as a force of a homogenizing globalization and Western corporate logic and system; see Kellner (1999a).

4. While I find *Empire* an impressive and productive text, I am not sure, however, what is gained by using the word *empire* rather than the concepts of global capital and political economy. While Hardt and Negri combine categories of Marxism and critical social theory with poststructuralist discourse derived from Foucault and Deleuze and Guattari, they frequently favor the latter, often mystifying and obscuring the object of analysis. I am also not as confident as Hardt and Negri that the "multitude" replaces traditional concepts of the working class and other modern political subjects, movements, and actors, and find the emphasis on nomads, "New Barbarians," and the poor as replacement categories problematical. Nor am I clear on exactly what forms their poststructuralist politics would take. The same problem is evident, I believe, in an earlier decade's provocative and post-Marxist text by Laclau and Mouffe (1985), who valorized new social movements, radical democracy, and a postsocialist politics without providing many concrete examples or proposals for struggle in the present conjuncture.

5. I am thus trying to mediate in this paper between those who claim that globalization simply undermines democracy and those who claim that globalization promotes democratization like Friedman (1999). I should also note that in distinguishing between globalization from above and globalization from below, I do not want to say that one is good and the other is bad in relation to democracy. As Friedman shows (1999), capitalist corporations and global forces might very well promote democratization in many arenas of the world, and globalization-from-below might promote special interests or reactionary goals, so I am criticizing theorizing globalization in binary terms as primarily "good" or "bad." While critics of globalization simply see it as the reproduction of capitalism, its champions, like Friedman, do not perceive how globalization undercuts democracy. Likewise, Friedman does not engage the role of new social movements, dissident groups, or the "have nots" in promoting democratization. Nor do concerns for social justice, equality, and participatory democracy play a role in his book.

6. On resistance to globalization by labor, see Moody (1997); on resistance by environmentalists and other social movements, see the studies in Mander and Goldsmith (1996), while I provide examples below from several domains.

7. Friedman (1999, 267–68) notes that George Soros was the star of Davos in 1995, when the triumph of global capital was being celebrated, but that the next year Russian Communist Party leader Gennadi A. Zyuganov was a major media focus when unrestrained globalization was being questioned—though Friedman does not point out that this was a result of a growing recognition that divisions between "haves" and "have nots" were becoming too scandalous and that predatory capitalism was becoming too brutal and ferocious.

8. On the Cancun meetings, see Chris Kraul, "WTO Meeting Finds Protests Inside and Out," *Los Angeles Times,* September 11, 2003, A3; Patricia Hewitt, "Making Trade Fairer," *Guardian*, September 12, 2003; and Naomi Klein, "Activists Must Follow the Money," *Guardian,* September 12, 2003. On the growing division between rich and poor, see Benjamin M. Friedman, "Globalization: Stiglitz's Case," *New York Review of Books,* August 15, 2002; and George Monbiot, "The Worst of Times," *Guardian,* September 12, 2003.

9. Such positions are associated with the postmodern theories of Foucault, Lyotard, Rorty, and have been taken up by a wide range of feminists, multiculturalists, and others. On these theorists and postmodern politics, see Best and Kellner (1991, 1997, 2001), and the valorization and critique of postmodern politics in Hardt and Negri (2000) and Burbach (2001).

10. In a report on the 2002 World Social Forum event in Porto Alegre, Michael Hardt suggests that protestors divided into antiglobalization groups that promoted national sovereignty as a bulwark against globalization and local groups connected into networks affirming an alternative democratic globalization. See "Today's Bandung?" *New Left Review* 14 (March–April 2002): 112–18. Not all countries or regions that oppose specific forms of globalization should be labeled "antiglobalization." Moreover, one might also delineate a category of localists who are simply antiglobalization and focus on local problems and issues. There is accordingly a growing complexity of positions on globalization and alternative political strategies.

11. As a December 1 abcnews.com story titled "Networked Protests" put it: "Disparate groups from the Direct Action Network to the AFL-CIO to various environmental and human rights groups have organized rallies and protests online, allowing for a global reach that would have been unthinkable just five years ago. As early as March, activists were hitting the newsgroups and listservs—strings of e-mail messages people use as a kind of long-term chat—to organize protests and rallies."

In addition, while the organizers demanded that the protesters agree not to engage in violent action, there was one website that urged WTO protesters to help tie up the WTO's web servers, and another group produced an anti-WTO website that replicated the look of the official site (see RT-Mark's website, http://gatt.org/; the same group had produced a replica of George W. Bush's site with satirical and critical material, winning the wrath of the Bush campaign). For compelling accounts of the anti-WTO demonstrations in Seattle and an acute analysis of the issues involved, see Paul Hawkens, "What Really Happened at the Battle of Seattle," available at www .purefood.org/Corp/PaulHawken.cfm; and Naomi Klein, "Were the DC and Seattle Protests Unfocused, or Are Critics Missing the Point?" available at www.shell.ihug.co.nz/~stu/fair.

12. On the importance of the ideas of Debord and the Situationist International to make sense of the present conjuncture see Best and Kellner (1997, chap. 3), and on the new forms of the interactive consumer society and Debordian critique, see Best and Kellner (2001).

13. Castells claims that Harvey (1989) says about as much about the postmodern as needs to be said (1996, 26–27). With due respect to their excellent work, I believe that no two theorists or books exhaust the problematic of the postmodern which involves mutations in theory, culture, society, politics, science, philosophy, and almost every other domain of experience, and is thus inexhaustible (Best and Kellner 1997, 2001). Yet one should be careful in using postmodern discourse to avoid the mystifying elements, a point made in the books just noted as well as Hardt and Negri (2000).

14. See Best and Kellner (1997, 2001).

15. The "digital divide" has emerged as the buzzword for perceived divisions between information technology have and have nots in the current economy and society. A U.S. Department of Commerce report released in July 1999 claimed that the digital divide in relation to race is dramatically escalating and the Clinton administration and media picked up on this theme (see the report "Americans in the Information Age: Falling through the Net" at www.ntia.doc.gov/ntiahome/ digitaldivide/). A critique of the data involved in the report emerged, however, claiming that it was outdated; more recent studies by Stanford University, Cheskin Research, ACNielson, and the Forester Institute claim that education and class are more significant factors than race in constructing the divide (see http://cyberatlas.internet.com/big-picture/demographics for a collection of reports and statistics on the divide). In any case, it is clear that there is a gaping division between information technology "haves" and "have nots," that this is a major challenge to developing an egalitarian and democratic society, and that something needs to be done about the problem. My contribution involves the argument that empowering the have nots requires the dissemination of new literacies and thus empowering groups and individuals previously excluded from economic opportunities and sociopolitical participation; see Kellner (2002).

16. *Wired* magazine is a good source for statistics and data concerning growing computer and Internet use among all sectors of youth and documents the vicissitudes of cyberculture. Studies of Internet addiction, however, raise concerns about negative implications of excessive usage. The *Chronicle of Higher Education* has reported that "Students are unusually vulnerable to Internet addiction according to a new quarterly journal called *Cyberpsychology and Behavior*" (February 6,

1998, A25). The study indicated that students aged eighteen to twenty-two are especially at risk and point to a correlation between high Internet use and a dropout rate that more than doubled among heavy users. Accordingly, the University of Washington has limited the amount of Internet time available to students to cut down on overuse and several other colleges have set up support groups for Internet addiction. But such studies do not record the benefits of heavy Internet use or indicate potentially higher productive uses than, say, watching television, drinking, or engaging in traditional forms of collegiate socializing.

17. On the attack on youth in contemporary society and culture, see Manes (1996).

REFERENCES

Best, S., and D. Kellner. 1991. *Postmodern theory: Critical interrogations.* London: MacMillan and Guilford.
———. 1997. *The postmodern turn.* London: Routledge and Guilford Press.
———. 2001. *The postmodern adventure.* London: Routledge and Guilford Press.
Boggs, C. 2000. *The end of politics.* New York: Guilford Press.
Bowles, S., and H. Gintis. 1986. *On democracy.* New York: Basic Books.
Brecher, J., T. Costello, and B. Smith. 2000. *Globalization from below.* Boston: South End Press.
Burbach, R. 2001. *Globalization and postmodern politics. From Zapatistas to high-tech robber barons.* London: Pluto Press.
Castells, M. 1996. *The rise of the network society.* Oxford: Blackwell.
Cvetkovich, A., and D. Kellner, eds. 1997. *Articulating the global and the local: Globalization and cultural studies.* Boulder, Colo.: Westview Press.
Dyer-Witheford, N. 1999. *Cyber-Marx: Cycles and circuits of struggle in high-technology capitalism.* Urbana: University of Illinois Press.
Foran, J., ed. 2002. *The future of revolutions: Rethinking radical change in the age of globalization.* London: Zed Books.
Friedman, T. 1999. *The Lexus and the olive tree.* New York: Farrar, Straus & Giroux.
Fukuyama, F. 1992. *The end of history and the last man.* New York: Free Press.
Hardt, M., and A. Negri. 2000. *Empire.* Cambridge, Mass.: Harvard University Press.
Harvey, D. 1989. *The condition of postmodernity.* Cambridge: Blackwell.
Kellner, D. 1990. *Television and the crisis of democracy.* Boulder, Colo.: Westview Press.
———. 1992. *The Persian Gulf TV war.* Boulder. Colo.: Westview Press.
———. 1995a. Intellectuals and new technologies. *Media, Culture, and Society* 17: 201–17.
———. 1995b. *Media culture.* London: Routledge.
———. 1997. Intellectuals, the new public spheres, and technopolitics. *New Political Science,* 41–42 (Fall): 169–88.
———. 1998. Multiple literacies and critical pedagogy in a multicultural society. *Educational Theory* 48 (1): 103–22.
———. 1999a. Globalization from below? Toward a radical democratic technopolitics. *Angelaki* 4 (2): 101–13.
———. 1999b. Theorizing McDonaldization: A multiperspectivist approach. In *Resisting McDonaldization,* ed. B. Smart, 186–206. London: Sage.
———. 2000. New technologies/new literacies: Reconstructing education for the new millennium. *Teaching Education* 11 (3): 245–65.
———. 2003a. *Media spectacle.* London: Routledge.
———. 2003b. *From September 11 to terror war: The dangers of the Bush legacy.* Lanham, Md. Rowman & Littlefield.
Laclau, E., and C. Mouffe. 1985. *Hegemony and socialist strategy: Toward a radical democratic politics.* London: Verso.

Luke, A., and C. Luke. 2000. A situated perspective on cultural globalization. In *Globalization and education*, ed. N. Burbules and C. Torres, 275–98. London: Routledge.

Mander, J., and E. Goldsmith. 1996. *The case against the global economy*. San Francisco: Sierra Club Books.

Marx, K., and F. Engels. 1978. *The Marx-Engels reader*. 2nd ed. Ed. by R. Tucker. New York: Norton.

Moody, K. 1997. Towards an international social-movement unionism. *New Left Review* 225: 52–72.

Ritzer, G. 1993. *The McDonaldization of society*. Thousand Oaks, Calif.: Pine Forge Press.

Steger, M. 2002. *Globalism: The new market ideology*. Lanham, Md.: Rowman & Littlefield.

Stiglitz, J. 2002. *Globalization and its discontents*. New York: Norton.

Waterman, P. 1992. *International labour communication by computer: The fifth international?* Working Paper Series 129. The Hague: Institute of Social Studies.

Watson, J., ed. 1998. *Golden arches east: McDonald's in East Asia*. Palo Alto, Calif.: Stanford University Press.

II

CRITICAL THEORIES

6

Postracial States

David Theo Goldberg

Why, one might ask, has modern state formation been predicated principally upon the artifice of homogeneity as an *idee fixe?* Recall that in posing the challenge of state formation at the outset of modernity, Hobbes characterized the state of nature as driven by individualized force and fraud. Force and fraud framed the supposed sources of the natural condition, and in doing so revealed the "rational necessity" of modern state formation, namely, the capacity to make war and to develop capital's resources. Force and fraud, for Hobbes, are the re-*sources* of survival in the absence of state control, the abilities and facilities rational choice would have us maximize in the absence of social security and in the drive to individualized survival. Well, if force and fraud are the virtues of presocial nature, comfort and control are the social conditions—the virtues of state formation—rationality would have the state maximize as sources (resources) of establishing social security and abating the perceived need for individualized force and fraud. Comfort and control—comfort as a form of control, and social control as the underpinnings of social comfort—are to the modern state then what force and fraud are to lonely and threatened individuals in the state of nature: the virtues of survival, individuated and social. Comfort, feeling at ease with one's surroundings and so neighbors, is both presupposition and rational implication of commitment to minimized state intervention to sustain public security. And comfort, so the story goes, is most easily reproduced in the setting of those one best knows, kin and extended kin, family and friends, cultural brethren, and common citizens.[1]

Race is taken to be the "natural" extension of this social narrative, questionable not least because, once the circle extends beyond those one literally knows, comfort becomes at best an artifice, in the intermediate a rationalization, and at worst the grounds of exclusion and expulsion, material and moral.

And, of course, sometimes those one knows best, those closest to one, might make one feel the most uncomfortable. Homogeneity, and in particular racial homogeneity, thus is considered as among rationality's most effective means of social control, a key governing biotechnology in what Gramsci came to characterize as the reproduction of consent in one's social conditions and surroundings. What I have elsewhere characterized and analyzed as racial naturalism—the longstanding racial claim that those not European or of European descent are inherently (naturally) inferior to those who are—as a prevailing mode of modern biogovernance grew out of this set of assumptions. Racial naturalism gave way later to the mandates and management of racial historicism, what ultimately took over as the prevailing presumptions of racially predicted rule not of inherent inferiority but historical immaturity of Europe's others (Goldberg 2002).

So, what sort of state best represents the commitments of heterogeneities, demographically and culturally, politically and economically, socially and legally? What, in short, might be the shape of contemporary and future states, their principal modes of rule and representation, their social contours and lines of governance in the absence of and resistance to racist formation and in the aftermath of homogenizing logics? This is a question connected to but emphatically to be distinguished from that of the shape of *raceless* states (Goldberg 2002, chap. 8; 2002).

One way of posing this question of postracist states is to address what modern social formations might have emerged had they not been so racially conceived and weighted in various ways? How, one might ask in other words, would modern states have formed but for race as an ordering principle? The shape of this question, however, as hinted in the close of the previous paragraph, is consistent with the presumptions of racelessness articulated in Goldberg (2002, chap. 8), now universalized not just geographically but as a matter of nostalgic retrospection, historical memory in denial. The obvious response, if the question is taken on face value, is that class formation and exploitation would now be barer and balder, perhaps less mitigated, more intense on its own terms but precisely for that reason less sociologically defensible and defended. If that were so one could imagine that class conditions without the modalities and arrangements of racial configurations conceivably would have conjured more explicit, vigorous, sustained, and ultimately successful counters. But conceivably because balder and bolder and so more questionable and questioned, they also might have been tempered in ways making such class distinctions more palatable because less expressly and extremely exploitative, divisive, and exercised.

The deeper point here, however, is that it is impossible in the final analysis to tell which way it would have gone had race not so marked modern state and social formation. So the very call to imagine the alternatives to a history racially turned serves discursively to draw us away from the more compelling question of imaginative politics in the present and facing the future. Here the concern is not with what might have been but, given how we now understand what indeed has been and now is, with what the possibilities of transformation to social conditions and spaces of justice could yet be. So the question is not whether we can erase race—as we have seen, that only renders the structures of racist exclusion and derogation less visible—but with how we might be able to shape race and its social orderings in ways that are socially attractive and interactive. How, in short, can we transform racial configuration from the dispositions of homogenizing exclusion and exclusivity to the disposing toward heterogenizing openness and incorporation, social engagement and shaping to reflect the interests and conceptions of all?

In asking to what states without racism might amount, notice then that a number of concerns are being raised. First, what is being placed in question is the common contemporary call, at least as the first-level commitment, the causal condition, to erase race from our conceptual apparatus and frame of reference, from all state characterization and concern (Appiah and Gutmann 1996; Gilroy 2000; McWhorter 2000). The historical invocation of race by the state to exclusionary and discriminatory purpose or outcome ought to be eliminated from state design and practice, implicit or explicit. It does not follow from this critical commitment, however, that racial record keeping for the sake of monitoring and redressing past and present forms of historical discrimination ought to be abandoned as a consequence, as Ward Connerly would do in the Californian context (Selingo 2001). The point is not so much the bald concern with racial reference and invocation, no matter the implications, but the purpose to which race is invoked and the work to which it is being put by and in the name of the state. The principal aim is—or ought to be—*states without racism*. Whether that commitment entails states without race will turn on whether race inherently or instrumentally causes or conspires to racist states, racist conditions of being and rule. So second, the principal concern is to withdraw the state from exclusionary racial definition and arrangement, to render state instrumentalities and instrumental state and institutional apparatuses unavailable to discriminatory racial usage. This entails, third, that it remains an open question whether and how race is usable or invokable outside of state force or enforcement, state determination or orchestration. Is it possible to engage racial arrangement, as Foucault suggested in his lectures on racism, sometimes as a counterhistory (*contre-histoire*), a critical counterhistory to dominating state formation, a mode of self-determining political and cultural resistance (Stoler 1995, 68–72), or indeed as a creative but nonexclusionary mode of cultural (re)formation? Or is racial arrangement, wherever and whenever, inherently an imposed mode of controlling governance and self-surveillance?[2]

THE RACE TO STATE HOMOGENEITY

One thing could be said with confidence, consequently: a state without *racism* would be one in and for which whiteness has retreated, has been fractured and fissured, has dissipated and dissolved. If, as I have argued elsewhere, whiteness stands for the relative privilege, profit, and power of those occupying the structural social positions of whites in a hierarchically ordered racial society, racist states are states of whiteness (Goldberg 2002, chap. 7). The elimination of such states accordingly must mean the demise of the associated privilege, profit, and power. But, it must be emphasized, a state without racism in the wake of the long and vicious racist histories of the present cannot simply be a raceless state. Postracist (in contrast to merely postracial) states must be those for which state agencies, and most notably law, are vigorous both in refusing racist practice and in public representation of the unacceptability of all forms of discriminatory expression. I am not so naive or romantically utopian as to think this would amount to the end of all social privilege, power, and profit. But it would mean the end of a particularly vicious variety, the sort that has served both as modality of expression for and a kind of multiplier of class and gender, national and indeed state-based advantage and disadvantage. It would mean, in short, a very different sort of state personality, a different demeanor to those inside and outside the state cast (caste), a different disposition to population definition and characterization, to law and law en-*force*ment, to power and policy making, to kith and kin, "legitimate" family and the shape of class, to sociospatial configurations and schooling, social engagement and accessibility, to national culture (most notably in and through language, the "mother tongue") and historical memory (Balibar 1991b, 98–100).

States after racism would mean in short a deep transformation in state personality. Etienne Balibar is right thus to insist that "[d]estruction of the racist complex" requires "the transformation of the racists themselves" (though not just in *any* way), and so "the internal composition of the community created by racism" (Balibar 1991b, 18). Implicit within Balibar's imperative is more than just an exhortation to individuals to change their racist ways. Balibar here hints by extension at the social dynamics by which modern "community" is composed. And in the context of nation formation, these dynamics bear the label, the (not so) hidden hand (Comaroff and Comaroff 2000), of state "juris-diction," of the forms and contents of legality and justice (injustice), in national self-narration. But postracist states would mean also very different dispositions to other states, states of otherness, and state othering. Entailed would be not simply some extended circulation through racism's polyvalent mobilities (Stoler 1995, 69), reinscriptions of racist modes and manners, racist "bearers" and "targets" mobilized from one crisis moment to another (Balibar 1991a, 219). They would mean, rather, a different set of global arrangements where racial dispositions or calculations no longer determined or set the formative background to international relations, no longer determined or even descriptively characterized the general flows of capital, commodities, workers and executives, refugees and im/migrants, or the radically uneven distribution of human and economic costs of AIDS and its treatment. It is these radically transfigured sets of assumptions and dispositions, characterizations and (institutional) arrangements, spatialities and chronicities that I mean to reference in urging the shift from prevailing presuppositions of homogeneity and fixity in state conception and personality to those of heterogeneity and flow.

Modern states, by their (modern) nature, systematically produce and reproduce "political and cultural homogeneity" (Parekh 2000, 184) as a matter of their institutional logic. The modernity of the state turns on the drive both to codify and to represent a general will, on the classification schemas invoked to order and administer (to) the population masses that make them up. This homogeneity is a function, by extension, of the bureaucratic insistence on formal equality sociopolitically and legally (though perhaps less so economically).[3] States thus assume their modernity in and through producing and reproducing sameness, definitively squeezing out the different, the very heterogeneity which modernity's logic of spatiotemporal compression (Eagleton 1998, 50; Harvey 1989) has been instrumental paradoxically in effecting. In the name of justice, democracy, and equality—of a people with a common will, interests, and character—the modern state creates a population, a "community," cut from the same cloth.

Modern states administratively promote coherence of civil society and social structures, and through them the cohering of their populations. This coherence is ramified throughout the economy, polity, law, culture, modes of representation, and social narratives. In this sense, the modern state is a form of institutional reinforcement, the enforcing mechanisms of institutional arrangements and conditions. The state thus conceived is a sort of conductor. It orchestrates but also serves as a conduit and symbol for the conduct—the disciplinary consistencies—of the institutions and individuals in virtue of which it is constituted, over which it ranges. But the state is also a conductor of culture—of institutional and social values and meanings, the generator and shaper of historical memory through schools, museums and monuments, public art and ceremonies, rituals and symbols. And as a conductor shapes the orchestra and arranges the score without necessarily making the music, so the state fashions citizens, those representative individuals at once able to play responsibly, by themselves but in concert (Lloyd and Thomas 1998). States accordingly are at once spaces and media of affiliation between governing bodies and populations. Race, as I have argued, is the oil between state and society, the black and white formal wear turning critical attention away from the players and toward enjoyment of the music, the social welfare of the "audience."

Modern states are thus "structured in racial (and interactively in gendered and class) dominance" (Hall 1980). So the state is not neutral but structurally reproduces and regulates the hierarchies it has helped institutionally to constitute. The liberal state professes neutrality between its members—between groups ethnoracially defined, between men and women, and members of social classes—and enacts laws and regulations predicated on such assumptions. It follows that state apparatuses such as law can be invoked to mobilize for more equitable treatment on the part of those the state hitherto has served to dispossess or disenfranchise, to disqualify from equal treatment or to disempower. In insisting on materializing what otherwise is projected as ideological rationalization, the marginalized are able to empower themselves though always subject to the limiting and homogenizing terms of state definition and design. Angela Davis (1998) comments that when those once actively resistant to state imposition, control, and definition of the political and socioeconomic arrangements later become representatives of state institutions—morphing in effect into state agents—there is something about the state apparatus, about its definition and functions, that delimits, constrains, and transforms the disposition and outlook of even the best intentioned. Thus, former Black Panthers or members of SNCC (Student Nonviolent Coordinating Committee) have become political representatives in Congress, and anticolonial revolutionaries such as Robert Mugabe, Kwame Nkrumah, or ANC (African National Congress) leaders have assumed state power. They are constrained in their agency not just by the fact of their electoral representation but also by the institutional logic of state formation, agency, and incorporation into the modern world system.

Hence the inevitable ambiguities in modern state commitments. For instance, a commitment to freedom for all may be discounted by interpreting it as opportunity, not outcome. The expressed commitment to equality may be discounted as the formality of rights to speech or property with no attention paid to the substantive conditions rendering materialization or manifestation of those rights possible or even probable (cf. Waylen 1998). In insisting on equal treatment before the law, equal state promotion or resources, those subjected to state or social exclusions may advance their interests by invoking the neutrality principle of the liberal state on behalf of those not so readily benefited in the past. Of course, the formalism of state neutrality leaves it open equally to those hitherto in control or benefiting from the state of patriarchal whiteness to extend or redefine the structures of opportunity in their favor. The (at least implicit) characterizations of the state as black or as representing the interests of those not white are deeply connected to the now common call for shrinking state power and influence. The contemporary insistence on state commitments to racelessness is a case in point (Goldberg 2002, chap. 8).

Two points follow concerning characterization of modern racial states. The first is to note a distinction between strong racial states and weak racial states, or between strongly and weakly racist states. A state unambiguously committed to insistent and reductive racial definition, a state in which racial definition is routinized through its state apparatuses and penetrates its agencies, is likely a state committed to strongly explicit and enforced forms of racist exclusion. A state that is weakly racial—that may invoke racial classification in record keeping, say, with an eye to tracking historical discrimination—does not necessarily promote racist exclusions, though it may sustain (at least by ignoring) a culture of racist derogation in civil society and social institutions. Obviously the particular shapes and expressions of racial and racist states run the gamut between these two poles.

Second, I do not mean to suggest that modern states lack all virtues. Unlike premodern states that rested on multiple sources of authority and rules applied differentially to various social classes, modern states at least in principle rest on a singular authoritative body and source of law applied equally to all citizens. Modern (at least liberal) states enshrine a unitary code of rights protecting all members positioned and placed in suitably similar ways. Individuals are both equally incorporated into the state and reasonably protected not just from each other but from state incursion. The so-called arbitrary characterizations of individuals—in group terms such as race, gender, class—are deemed at least juridically illegitimate considerations in state disposition and treatment of individuals. Goods and services, rights and powers, the distribution of burdens and responsibilities are to be open to all at least to compete (cf. Parekh 2000, 181–83). And modern liberal democracies seem more ready than most contrasting societies to tolerate if not to promote criticism, challenge, and revision, even if within implicit and definitive limits. There are accordingly wide and deep benefits of state modernization, both in the principles of arrangement and materially, that it would be silly and self-defeating to deny or to overlook. The virtues of liberal modernizing are real, to be sure, even as they are partial (Hall 2000, 228; Smith 1997, 10–11).

These virtues of modern states are considered to represent indices of progress over earlier state forms, and in many ways they can be considered to do so. And yet, the celebration of modernization also denies its inevitable burdens, either by ignoring them completely or discounting them as inevitable but limited costs of progress. Bearing this very consciously in mind, it must be pointed out that the claim to *racial* progress trades on a misconceived measure as a consequence. The state of racial progress—the progress of states *now* on race—is not to be measured against states of racist repression in the past.[4] That calculus too easily produces contemporary complacency and self-congratulation. The proper measure of "racial progress"—of the distance from racially fashioned or indexed exclusions—concerns assessment at the common historical moment ("the present") of the relative experience and conditions of each group racially defined and positioned, refined and conditioned against each other one. The historical contrast can only tell us how far we have come and convey a sense of what still has to be achieved, not that we have completed the task. Looking exclusively to the rear blinds us to seeing both how far there is to go or indeed to a reconsideration of what routes to adopt and signposts to pursue. Historical reconstruction and retrospection are crucial not as a fixation nor as contemporary celebration or rationalization but as indicating how we have come to the present, what the contemporary moment amounts to and on what it rests, and for revealing roadmaps to the future.

COUNTERRACIAL QUESTIONS

Given my characterization of the modern racial state as a will to power, as a particular sort of empowering self-assertion, the pressing question accordingly is not some version of the currently popular one in liberal circles, namely, whether a modern constitutional state can "recognize and accommodate cultural diversity" (Tully 1995, 1; Kymlicka 1996; Kymlicka and Norman 2000). That question presupposes as more or less given the very set of suppositions and structured ordering of the state marked so deeply by the histories of racial conception and formation. The question looks to embrace into the very fabric of social arrangements those hitherto excluded and denied, defined in cultural terms as "strange multiplicity," as outsiders or strangers. It leaves unquestioned the prevailing assumption of institutional and structural homogeneity, and the accompanying codification of existing racial powers and frames of reference. It manifests recognition of difference in speech and cultural expression, in "a just form of constitutional discussion in which each speaker is given her or his due" (Tully 1995, 6). But it is open to addressing only indirectly at best the institutional structures and material conditions shaping social possibilities and access, actual political arrangements and constitutive practices, and their long histories of constitution and reproduction. These histories have been marked constitutively for the most part by racially predicated exclusion and marginalization.

The counterquestion, I am suggesting, from an assumption of radical and reiterative heterogeneity, of unsettlement and entanglement (Tully 1995, 11), is not simply one in the reactive frame concerning recognition and accommodation of and into the state's own historically limiting schemas. It concerns the grounds of its constitutive conditions themselves. Can a state be predicated on assumptions of heterogeneities? Can a state constitutively be open to the flows not simply of capital but of human beings recognized equally and with equal sensitivity, on and in equal terms, as belonging in their flows to the body politic, when both here and there, so to speak? Can heterogeneity in social arrangements coexist with the justice of the state and fair treatment of its citizens? What would state citizenship in a state so conceived come to look like? Indeed, what would such a state itself look like?[5]

Conceived thus, the question is less about belonging than it is about the state and its form. Or at least it is about the relation of citizenship to state form and shape. Is citizenship necessarily a condition—a *state*—of the state? Is the notion of belonging, both cultural and administrative, that citizenship implies tied inextricably to the structures of the state as we have come to know that institutional arrangement? For if it is so connected then there may be very distinct—indeed, undermining—constraints on a notion of "flexible citizenship" (Ong 1999). These limiting assumptions may pose sharp limits to the possibilities of conceiving citizenship predicated on flows rather than fixity, on mobilities (Urry 2000, 159–87) rather than on the given of modern stasis and the static implications of statehood. Is it possible, in short, to speak of citizenship in a robust sense in relation to multiple and intertwining ("entangled") commitments—social, familial, economic, cultural, political? And to what would such commitment amount institutionally, administratively, socially, personally?

TRACELESS CITIZENSHIPS

Now *deracializing* concerns undoing the processes and structures of white dominance and rule through antiracisms. It involves the unstitching of white rule, picking apart the fabric of world wide whiteness, decolonizing global imaginaries of white dominance (Pieterse and Parekh 1995). And it calls for reimagining a world in which norms, standards, practices, relations, and structures fashioned historically by and associated with white dominance and dominating whiteness are no longer (conceived and ordered to be) singular. Deracializing amounts to dehomogenizing the state, heterogenizing forms of governance and being, loosening if not splintering the grip, the vice, of the racial imaginary on the state and of the state on racial configuration. So a state without racism would be part of a global arrangement of states not marked by racial configuration. And this, it would follow, would be a world breaking dramatically with the global racial orderings of the past half-millenium, processes that began with decolonization a half century ago in checkered and all too often checked ways. If a contemporary state without blackness (in the extended political sense) would be one subjected to a terrible holocaust, biological or cultural, a state without whiteness would be one, in a worldly scheme of things, without racism as historically configured. It would not be a state in which black (or white) people necessarily would *not* be recognized as black (or white), nor one in which the norms of regulation and governance were set by and in terms of "black" interests, whatever they might amount to. Rather, such a state would be one in which people of color in general, like white people generally, would be recognized as fully human (Fanon 1965, 250; Gordon 1995, 60). The salient point here is not the self-absorption of whiteness in its own demise, as is so much the case with whiteness studies, but the undoing of states of racial being and forms of governmentality in their global profusions. The aim is to deroutinize and desystematize interlocking worlds of race historically produced and the racially figured exclusions and derogations they entail.

In the latter sense, post*racist* states would not only abandon state-prompted, state-based, or state-promoted racial taxonomies, categorizations, and censal classifications (save in the latter case for tracking discrimination, past and present). States after racism would demand that the debilitating and distorting impacts of the histories of racial exclusions, institutional and individual, be transformtively addressed, with sensitivity and civility. Thus deracializing the state entails critically evaporating the hold of race on state powers over defining borders, the profiles of immigration, and on the body of citizenship. It requires undoing the hold of race on policing and incarceration as well as on the shape, scope, and implementation of law. And it means "erasing" the determinations of race on the space, place, and design of residence and education, work and recreation.

All this, in turn, presupposes a dramatically altered conception of citizenship. The question with which I am concerned thus becomes how we can conceive of state engagement and citizenship (of citizenship as state engagement and interaction rather than as state belonging and identification) outside of the constitutive oppositions identified above. Here citizenship is to be premised rather on openness and flows than on stasis and fixity, on heterogeneities rather than homogeneity. Aiwha Ong (1999) has begun usefully to theorize these concerns in a critical context as "flexible citizenship(s)."

Crossing borders must now be understood a staple both of social and economic arrangements and of political debates. Transnational population movements are engaged in a dynamic of sending and receiving, prompting new networks of demographic circulation and transformed conditions of existence at each end of the movement. These conditions include changing implications for settled communities as well as compressed impacts on lived conditions for those left behind in sending societies and hometowns. Lives are effected through job and service provision, the experiences of everyday racism in receiving societies, family formation and dissolution, community networks, and the composition of religious groups. Established social values are impacted dramatically, as well as material and lived cultures (Agamben 2000; Essed 1991; Hannerf 1996; Menjivar 2000; Portes, Guarnizo, and Landolt 1999). The new immigration/migration studies have offered valuable insight into the political conditions and impacts of these dramatic population movements in both sending and attracting societies, played out in debates concerning changing immigration law and conditions of settlement and movement, as well as policing practices and prison demographics.

The "push–pull" conditions of earlier migrations are no longer simple or simply unidirectional (Roberts, Frank, and Lozano-Ascencio 1999). The political concern over transnational population movements in the past twenty years or so, in contrast if related to the economic considerations, principally has been about the composition of citizenship. It has concerned who properly belongs in and to the society and who does not, of the constitution of the social fabric and the implications for social formation. The modernist model considered people to belong statically to just one nation-state, to have interests in, obligations to, and principal political and economic rights in a single state. This national belonging was both predicated on and served to reify the underlying assumption that nation-states were institutional manifestations of cultural homogeneity, natural developments of an inherent commonality preexisting among groups imagined to have some extended form of kinship to and so common understanding of each other.

Modern nation-states can no longer be considered homogeneously constituted, if they ever could. Heterogeneity is not new, only so much more dramatic and evident. Nation-states are made up more or less dramatically of various groups and cultures, ethnically and racially conjured and constituted, as the 2000 U.S. census data has begun to reveal, for instance. Groups and cultures are themselves internally dynamic and often at odds in assumption and practice, sometimes with multiple citizenship allegiances, constantly moving between countries and cultures (Faist 2000), if not individually certainly where the family, nuclear or extended, is taken to offer the basic social referent point. For two centuries now the state has fashioned as the license of national projection a conception of state personality as singular, as fixed fast. No longer can that myth be sustained.

Political theory and social thought of late have been consumed with reconsidering the bases of citizenship and political and cultural commitment. These renewed concerns are of course directly linked to concerns over globalization and the forms of transnational migratory mobilities, movements, and settlements thus prompted (Baubock 1994; Castles and Davidson 2000; Kymlicka 1996; Parekh 2000; Soysal 1994). The presumptions of homogeneity and stasis underpinning the modernist conception of citizenship have been undermined by the processes of intensified globalization and the spatiotemporal compressions fueled as a consequence. Questions of equal membership have become especially pressing in the face of the fact that globalizing economic, social, and geopolitical processes have so exacerbated the divides between the wealthy and the poor, not just on a global scale but within especially the wealthiest of nations such as the United States. These divisions have assumed even more complex ethnoracial composition than the old model dividing black from white.

The container state of Fordist capitalism produced a conception of citizenship as inherited or insistent belonging. The container state, in contrast to the segregating state of the late nineteenth century, enacted a rationality of state control expressed through encapsulated containment. It enacts an evacuation of the space of those regarded as racially dangerous or threatening so long as the periphery of that space is fenced off by a "military cordon" (Taussig 1997, 56–57; Agamben 2000, 39–42). Because the boundaries are clearly cordoned off and ringed, militarized and policed, symbolically as much as concretely, the interior for the most part can be abandoned to its own anarchic and self-destructive practices.

The modernist conception of citizenship, accordingly, has built into it as a constitutive (if not foundational) condition the *identification* of individual citizen with the state. Implicit in this identification is a triple logic: first, of the disposition to frame citizenship in identity terms; second, of the state taken as a coherent, a singular entity; and by implication third, of citizen-members as settled and more or less statically located within the space of the state. Settlement was supposed the rule, movement and mobility exceptional, exciting, and excitable. National character equates with state personality in the figure of the citizen. The classic modern conception of citizenship, then, most effectively articulated in T. H. Marshall's famous lecture (1950), concerns the claim to represent the social heritage of the nation-state. Citizenship in these terms is the abstract embodiment of the complementary right—liberty, interest, claim, empowerment—to participate in and benefit from social practices, collective benefits, and responsibilities of state belonging.

This classic conception of citizenship (what I have characterized as the modernist one) is predicated on stasis and state territorial sovereignty, on borders and interiorized burghers, spatial fixity and introspection. The modernist sense of citizenship is static, at basis immobile. It also, in a sense, bristles at its borders, antagonistically excluding those taken not to belong, not already a member. By contrast, I am asking with John Urry (2000, 167ff.) what a conception of citizenship (and by extension the state)—of civic engagement and commitment, interests and investments, powers and responsibilities—would amount to if taking as first principles social flow and flexibilities, mobilities and movements, transformativity and transition. What conception of citizenship and state fabric might one offer as an horizon of possibility for postracist, postregulator, postregulated states on such assumptions?

Restrictions on capital movement and on the class of financial managers guaranteeing capital flows increasingly have evaporated. At the same time, traffic cop states have maintained more or less firm restrictions on the movement and mobility of those marked as ethnoracially different or threatening: "Muslim or Arab terrorists," "helpless (if not sometimes murderous) Africans," "economically challenged or trafficking Central Americans," "overabundant Asians," and indeed any and all mistaken for these cutout characters. A postracist cosmopolitanism will have to face up to open movements of people unhindered by ethnoracial restriction. Such open movement and mobility cannot be realized without the prospects of full sociomaterial, sociocultural, and sociopolitical participation locally and globally. This includes the prospects for developing vigorous social movements to represent general interests in the face of powerful opposition from those who continue to exercise the power to shape economic, political, legal, and cultural representation. Above and beyond all else, perhaps, the power of social movements serves as the limit to the self-arrogation of those commanding significant sociomaterial and political resources. Such concerns link up with interests in developing and sustaining relatively risk-free environments of habitation and work wherever people pass their lives. Where risks and dangers do exist they would be distributed as evenly and representatively (materially and demographically) across classes and powers as factors reasonably beyond control allow. This likewise necessitates a commitment to educational access, definition, encouragement, and the conditions for self-advancement for all wherever people might find themselves. And it presupposes openness about cultural expression without the privileging of some and the degradation of others, as well as mutual cultural interactions, engagement, and influence.

Serious civil commitments are now interwoven, as Urry indicates (2000, 174–75), with sets of global dispositions and commitments. For one, they presuppose a global or planetary in contrast with a parochial outlook and range (rather than frame) of reference. Risks and dangers as well as rewards and benefits, it follows, are to be considered on global and interactive scales rather than provincially and in isolation. Sources of meaningful information are increasingly diffuse and expansive regarding social impacts and implications of significant events, natural and social, and most every significant event now impacts well beyond the reach of its local occurrence. Ecological considerations necessitate, even from a local point of view, that resources be used sustainably and with planetary implications in consideration. The concerns in turn suggest as a presupposition that people individually and collectively consider each other with a sensitive respect whether in direct interaction or in extended and more distanced sociocultural reference.

Sensitivity within the circle of ethnoracial considerations, as more generally, is deeply intertwined with civility and trust. Social sensitivity, respect, and civility presuppose and promote trusting those with whom one interacts. Trust— especially ethnoracial trust historically located—has traditionally been localized to those in some more or less literal or abstract sense close to one, those about whom one has experience and those one takes to be like one, who speaks the same language linguistically and culturally. The mobilities prompted by and generating (regenerating) globalizing dispositions call forth expanded circles and cycles of civic trust by recognizing and acknowledging the sources (re-sources) of their promotion. By contrast, we increasingly lose trust in states whose leaders express or convey ethnoracial disdain of one sort or another, for this disdain, if sustained, is often identified with state personality. Consider Yu-goslavia under Milosevic.

It has been popular recently, as much in cultural as in commercial terms, to conceive of regional and transregional connectivities, networks and lines of re-lation (interrelation), to conjure, in short, nets that capture and captivate but also the open lines that work to instill sensitivity, civility, and trust. There are no magic pills here. Every disposition to closure and self-absorption threatens and is threatened by the lure of heterogeneous polyvalence. Every call to hybridity and the transformative is open to challenge in light of the limits of our collec-tive visions and vocabularies, by existing structures and forms, and ultimately by the threat of the anarchic and formlessness.

The line of critical and promissory argument I have pursued throughout, then, leads not so much to anarchic conclusions, though the radical tensions between bald state terror and romantic anarchism offer always the limit cases that likewise require rethinking in the wake of global pressures. The state, as James Scott notes, "is the vexed institution that is the ground of both our free-doms and unfreedoms" (1998, 7). The response to racist states is as little a call to anarchism as it is to racelessness. Rather, it is the call to rethink again and again, without end or closure, the modern (modernizing) terms of social rela-tion: of statehood and citizenship, of race and its intersected modalities, of democracies and public spheres; of freedoms and private spheres; of rights and responsibilities, civilities and incivilities.

Individuals as citizens of the state continue to be endowed racially (there's a sense in which as citizens they consensually are made to endow themselves as such, most notably under conditions of racelessness), just as racial configura-tion acquires individuated expression through the media of the state. What "modern" state does not conceive itself, or is not conceived by others, in eth-noracially tinged terms? It is this notion of self-endowment and self-regulation that raises the question of democracy in relation to racially conceived states and their global arrangement.

Democratizing Race, Heterogenizing Democracies

Wendy Brown (1995) characterizes democracy as about governing together that we may govern ourselves. The regulation (self-regulation) at the heart of govern-mentality is made obvious by inverting this neat formula: to govern ourselves so that we may govern together. That logic of regulation (self-regulation) is already there, one might say and as Brown's book makes clear, in governing per se. So democracy is about ways of governing that (either) delimit the impositions of reg-ulation or render governing acceptable—justifiable—precisely because more or less noncoercively (or uncoercively) engaged. I have expressed democratic gov-ernance thus without reference to self-governance (the imposition of governance upon oneself by oneself) not simply because of the difficulties in formulating a coherent conception of the self (Taylor 1992). Rather, it is because self-governance may be mediated—informed, encouraged, imposed—by externalities internalized, through the self on the self, so to speak, thus blurring the distinction between self-regulation and imposed regulation (cf. Butler 1997).

Roughly speaking, a democratic state would be one where all the competing interests share state power, resources, and media of representation in a repeatedly renewable negotiation of balance (Dolan 1994, 55) without any one, or any alliance—racially or otherwise configured—dominating to the exclusion of or control over others. And a democratic state so conceived would be part of a global web of similarly conceived states. A totalitarian state involves the domination of all institutions and culture in and of the state by a single representative interest over all others. One could give similar readings, for instance, in conceptualizing authoritarian or fascist or racist states. A racist state would be one where a racially conceived (self-conceived) group (usually the one controlling the terms of racial subjectification, including definition) dominates the power, resources, and representational media of the state to the relative exclusion, subjection, or subordination of other groups racially conceived. And, as we have seen, such a state is sustained by global networks of similarly ordered and ordering states, or at least of states easy with interactions with such states, what I have called "states of whiteness." A state engaged in racial configuring (a "racializing" state in the contemporary cliché) is one where groups within the state are racially conceived and defined especially by the state and its agents to various purposes and ends.

It is important to contextualize modes of democratic states in relation to relative access to and power over resources and voice, to the media to speak and be heard or listened to. There are many ways of being democratic, related in part to questions of how accessible are channels of expression, how even the distribution of resources and power, and how (how heavily and in what ways) such access and expressibility are mediated (Cunningham 2000; Gould 2000; Mills 2000). But there is also an outcome consideration that needs to be attended in considering the nature of democratic states that has to do with what elsewhere I have conceptualized under the name of "incorporation" (Goldberg 1995). Here the question becomes whether and in what ways, thin or thick, less powerful interests and groups have been able to transform the principles, rules, norms, modes of organization, and terms of conception and expression—in short, the material culture—of state formation.

Instead of speaking of racial democracies, an antiracist politics might better speak of democracies in more or less heterogeneous societies, of heterogeneous democracies. Homogeneous societies, I have argued, either are or certainly remain homogenous via imposition, through enforcement in modern states not the least racially configured.[6] And so the question becomes how the definitions offered above can be tailored to reflect degree and kind of access and expressibility on the part of heterogeneous groups (sometimes racially characterized) and heterogeneous populations homogenized (through restricting racial configuration). More generally, how might democracy for heterogeneous conditions be fashioned in nonfoundational terms?[7] How do we think anew the shifting spaces and expressive conditions for democracy in ethnoracially heterogeneous societies? Democracy is understood to have no fixed foundations, no settled center, only the more or less unstable balance of shifting, negotiated, and revisable interests and powers within and beyond state purview, locally and regionally, state-bounded and globally. The constant negotiations, cultural and political, economic and legal, take place precisely in the wake and face of "split affiliations" and radical "undecidabilities" attendant to so much of everyday life in the "slipstreams of late capitalism" and the cross-sections of millenial regulator states (Bhabha and Comaroff 2002). Here the interests and powers are rendered more complex precisely in and through their racial making.

To these ends, I conceive of rights as generalizations of claims and interests, expressions of liberties and drives to powers of and from local customs and practices. As these generalizations face increasingly outward, as in their broadening they embrace more and more of the generally human (which is to say not the individual but the social characteristics of human being), I am suggesting that rights so conceived are projections outward of the "human in us." And in return one could say the local and specific in part is the inward imbrication or instantiation of the general or generalizable, the specific embodiment of general social conditions. There are no absolute universals ontologically outside of abstraction from particulars, and no local instance (not even the radically idiosyncratic or idiolectic) completely cut off from representing manifestations of more generalized conception (Hall 2000, 234–35). The relation between the individual and the social, the social constitution of individuals and the social horizons of individuality, encourages as a result a conception of "cosmopolitan connection."

This picture amounts to a social citizenship constituted by a specificity and generalizability. It requires a connectedness both locally to those about one, to those sharing a culture more or less broadly ("cultural rights"), but also more and more outwardly to those linked together by the broadest of social—which is now at the very least to say global or planetary—conditions ("human rights"). So the insistence on rights locally, at least normatively, is at once also the realization of rights more generally, tentatively more globally. If rights are generalizations from local practice and local embodiments of generalized extensions, then my right—the right of those like me, of "my people"—at once contain the kernel of the rights (or their restriction and lack) for all. The challenge is to open up those self-interestedly invested in their own (restricting) rights to the claims, interests, liberties, and powers of others not just similarly situated but equally embodiments of extended social spaces of "overlapping, multiple and intersected modernities" (Ong 1999), developed and developing, we now call the planet.

I am pointedly not claiming that the connections and commitments I have identified here will magically reconfigure the state in their image, will open up the state to the erasure of its own bounded limits. State powers massage rights to

their definition and purpose. I mention these rights and configurations as parameters of possibility. If we are to learn anything from reading in tension the likes of
race critical theories (Essed and Goldberg 2001) and John Rawls (1971) together,
it is that the available means are to be deployed to advance the interests of the
most dispossessed and degraded in the society. In doing so, the very character,
the personality, of state formation will be transformed. But it is also that the parameters, the "repertoires of meaning" (Hall 2000), no matter how diminished or
expansive, are to be enlarged through collective and individual efforts against the
grain, in the face of regulation and repression (Scott 1990). Throughout modernity those most dispossessed and degraded have tended overwhelmingly to be
positioned as such through the stated configurations of race. And it is now undeniable that "society" has global reach, and the global has local social embodiment.
These efforts accordingly assume racial reference and global reach.

Rather than conceiving states as "pastoral regulators" committed to controlling social conditions and populations, is it possible to reconceive states as facilitators coping and coordinating social practices, as the nodal points and contact zones between flows? Can we think of states to be not as structures of
imposed governmentalities but as the principal terrains in which social life is
played out in all its cultural—what one might characterize as ethnoracial—
thickness? In this context, "flexible citizenship" is not limited just to the case of
"refugees and business migrants who work in one location while their families
are lodged in 'safe havens' elsewhere" (Ong 1999, 214). What Aihwa Ong properly captures by this characterization is the ethnographic description of increasingly widespread practices prompted by and expressive of global lures
and pushes. But the characterization requires an opening up to a more general
set of conditions as a consequence of all sorts of flows, political and existential
terror, commercial and work-seeking opportunity, and recreational lure. It
raises the possibility of giving to the conception of "flexible citizenship" a va-
lence of desirable because valuable normativity.

In this light, it is possible surely to be a part of and play a part in multiple sites
of identification. Here the commitments would amount to respectful and sensitive consideration in the free flows and movements at and between each of
those sites. Responsibilities and commitments as well as freedoms are (to be)
exercised both at and between the point(s) of residence. Flexibility to date has
been exercised more robustly by those economically best positioned to be mobile, as Ong points out. I am suggesting that the claims on, commitments in
relation to, and responsibilities regarding citizenship are to be opened up to
reflect the dramatically transformed conditions now facing much of the world's
population. And to do this requires thinking in a different light, in more open
(opened) and flexible forms, about both state and ethnoracial definition.

Modern political theory, at least in the social contract strain from Hobbes onward, restricts heterogeneity to the state of nature (or in more contemporary
terms, to one side of a veil of ignorance). The challenge this delimiting assumption poses is to find a form of social order excising what are perceived on
the account as the dangerous challenges of the different. The resultant structure

came to be understood as the modern state, homogeneously fashioned. Much of contemporary liberal political theory regarding multicultural states has sought to open outward the defining principles to make them responsive and responsible to what has been understood as the demanding diversity, the descriptive "multicultural" (Hall 2000, 209), of latter-day social life. I have been concerned throughout to challenge the very presuppositions of this picture. The principal questions, by contrast, concern whether it is conceivable to conjure social conditions—a "state"—against the formative background conditions of constitutive, contrasting, and fluctuating heterogeneities, of flexible citizenships, and mobile or "fugitive" democracies (Wolin 1996)? And how far would these conceptions bring us toward not just postracial but post- and (renewably) antiracist states, public spheres, and modes of governance?

It is apt to point toward an ending by posing the dilemma critical to the entanglements of ethnoracial and state formation I have discussed throughout. Against the thick hierarchical and exclusionary histories of racial configuration, potentially any invocation of race in state creation and formation is implicated in reproducing, extending, and renewing racist exclusions and derogations. Against this background even raceless commitments ignore the history of racially predicated exclusions and the fact that contemporary racially skewed conditions were produced by such histories. Thus any undertaking to address these exclusions and the skewed conditions they generate (regenerate) must be predicated on recognizing and redressing racially prompted and indexed exclusions. The seemingly paradoxical pursuit is that the "adjectival" (Hall 2000, 209) and causal categories of subjection and subordination are necessarily implicated, though as media of redirection, in the conditions of addressing and redressing the grounds of such subjection and subordination. A vigorous commitment to root out all forms of racist discrimination would be hard pressed to abjure any use of racial categories. Setting agendas by states in racial terms limits possibilities of conception and action to those terms, but absent those terms the programmatic address will tend to miss the mark. The terms accordingly seem to delimit possibilities even as the state's recognition of its own restrictions is a necessary condition for its transformation.

My concern then has not been with laying out the details of a counterconception of fugitive or mobile cultures of democratic social arrangements. By fugitive democracies (Wolin 1996) I am suggesting democratic cultures in flight, in all of the complex meanings thus conjured. This includes flight from the histories of ethnoracial constraint; forms of social existence outside of the law of racial derogation and exclusion as well as from cloning cultures individually, biologically and institutionally fashioned; mobilities between worlds of belonging and commitment, work and social relation that mark the histories of almost all in the world now. Fugitive democracies would seek sets of social arrangements hospitable to flight and flux, mobilities and motilities, multiplicities and "metis-friendly institutions" (Scott 1998, 352 ff.), the complexities of countermemories vested in cultures of the heterogeneous. "Democracy is a rebellious moment," Sheldon Wolin (1996, 43) rightfully insists, open to the transformative and unbounded, heterogeneities and uncontainability, and to limitless and reiterative negotiation (Hall 2000, 235).

I have been concerned consequently to shift the space of presumption in social conception, intellectual and material, from heterogeneity as state externality, as the outside of modern state formation, and homogeneity as the given, the infrastructure, in state grounding and foundation. My aim has been to reveal the racial forms of state erected upon those presumptions and the logics of modern political theory licensed in those terms. And to press the counterquestion about the implications for social arrangements and political theorizing of the pervasiveness of heterogeneities as following from global flows and interfaces, of erasing the imposed boundaries between inside and externality, of group belonging and the spatial grounds for citizenship. How are we to conceive both formatively and substantively the shapings of heterogeneous social worlds beyond racial states without leaving racist states unaddressed? What will states and world systems of states amount to that are no longer regulated through race? How are we to elaborate social commitments and arrangements open to global flows, multiple and overlapping and interfacing modernities, "multi-identifications" (Essed 2000, 53–56), and flexible citizenships while sustaining trusting and respectful, sensitive and reasonable, just and equitable, free and fair social arrangements? For these are the marks and manifestations of the social beyond not just race but racist states.

NOTES

This is a much shortened version of the concluding chapter, "Stating the Difference," to my book *The Racial State* (2002). It first appeared in a festschrift to Peter Caws in the journal *Janus Head*.

1. Sheldon Wolin argues that already in Locke, homogeneity had been read back into the state of nature as an initiating assumption, but a homogeneity, he writes, that "turns out to have been the suspension of heterogeneity" (1996, 40–41).
2. James Scott's terrifically insightful reading of the "public and hidden transcripts" of resistance to domination is suggestive of the various responses that might be made, individually and collectively, to racist imposition (see especially 1990, 39–40). But the book leaves open a response to the questions I am raising here.
3. The variability and proliferation in the content of contemporary economic practices has taken itself to require for its own sense of possibility and stability precisely the sorts of political and bureaucratic homogenization we are now witnessing. Contemporary economic practices in turn seem to transform the very cultural heterogeneities they seek out for new opportunities into the sorts of bland homogenization with which economic managers appear most comfortable.
4. Stephen Steinberg makes this point usefully in a thorough critique of American social science, from Booker T. Washington and Gunnar Myrdal to Orlando Patterson and the Thernstroms (1998, 70ff.).
5. James Tully (1995), to his credit, recognizes the contemporary manifestations of heterogeneity, albeit interpreted strictly in terms of cultural difference, and offers an account of constitutional transformation in postliberal democratic societies vested solely in these terms.
6. I suspect that this enforced imposition is quite deeply related to what Dolan (1994), following Lyotard, characterizes as the "'pietistic' theory of politics" and what by extension I might refer to as piety in modern state conception.
7. Dolan (1994) provocatively though in perhaps problematic historical terms calls this the "pagan" conception of the political.

REFERENCES

Agamben, Giorgio. 2000. *Means without end: Notes on politics.* Minneapolis: University of Minnesota Press.

Appiah, K. Anthony, and Amy Gutmann. 1996. *Color conscious: The political morality of race.* Princeton, N.J.: Princeton University Press.

Balibar, Etienne. 1991a. Class racism. In *Race, nation, class: Ambiguous identities,* ed. Etienne Balibar and Immanuel Wallerstein, 204–16. London: Verso.

———. 1991b. The nation form: History and ideology. In *Race, nation, class: Ambiguous identities,* ed. Etienne Balibar and Immanuel Wallerstein, 86–106. London: Verso.

Baubock, Rainer, ed. 1994. *From aliens to citizens.* Aldershot, Engl.: Avebury.

Bhabha, Homi, and John Comaroff. 2002. Speaking of postcoloniality in the continuous present. In *Relocating Postcolonialism,* ed. David Theo Goldberg and Ato Quayson, 15–46. Oxford: Basil Blackwell.

Brown, Wendy. 1995. *States of injury: Power and freedom in late modernity.* Princeton, N.J.: Princeton University Press.

Butler, Judith. 1997. *The psychic life of power: Theories of subjection.* Stanford, Calif.: Stanford University Press.

Castles, Stephen, and Alastair Davidson. 2000. *Citizenship and migration: Globalization and the politics of belonging.* London: Routledge.

Comaroff, Jean, and John L. Comaroff. 2000. Naturing the nation: Aliens, apocalypse and the postcolonial state. *HAGGAR: International Social Science Review* 1 (1): 7–40.

Cunningham, Frank. 2000. Democratic theory and racist ontology. *Social Identities: Journal for the Study of Race, Nation, and Culture* 6 (4): 463–82.

Davis, Angela. 1998. Reflection on race, class, and gender in the USA: Interview with Lisa Lowe. In *The Angela Y. Davis Reader,* ed. Joy James, 297–328. Oxford: Basil Blackwell.

Dolan, Frederick. 1994. *Allegories of America: Narratives, metaphysics, politics.* Ithaca, N.Y.: Cornell University Press.

Eagleton, Terry. 1998. Five types of identity and difference. In *Multicultural states,* ed. David Bennett, 48–52. London: Routledge

Essed, Philomena. 1991. *Understanding everyday racism.* London: Sage.

———. 2000. Beyond antiracism: Diversity, multi-identifications, and sketchy images of new societies. In *The semiotics of racism: Approaches in critical discourse analysis,* ed. Martin Reisigl and Ruth Wodak, 17–40. Vienna: Passagen Verlag.

Essed, Philomena, and David Theo Goldberg, eds. 2001. *Race critical theories: Text and context.* Boston: Basil Blackwell.

Faist, Thomas. 2000. Transnationalization in international migration: Implications for the study of citizenship and culture. *Ethnic and Racial Studies* 23, no. 2 (March): 189–222

Fanon, Frantz. 1965. *The wretched of the earth.* Preface by Jean-Paul Sartre. Trans. Constance Farrington. New York: Grove Press.

Gilroy, Paul. 2000. *Against race: Imagining political culture beyond the color line.* Cambridge, Mass.: Harvard University Press.

Goldberg, David Theo. 1995. The prison house of modern law. *Law and Society Review* 29 (3): 541–51.

———. 2002. *The racial state.* Oxford: Basil Blackwell.

Gordon, Lewis. 1995. *Fanon and the crisis of European man: An essay on philosophy and the human sciences.* New York: Routledge.

Gould, Carol. 2000. Racism and democracy reconsidered. *Social Identities: Journal for the Study of Race, Nation, and Culture* 6 (4): 425–39.

Hall, Stuart. 1980. Race, articulation and societies structured in dominance. In *Sociological theories: Race and colonialism.* Paris: UNESCO.

———. 2000. The multi-cultural question. In *Un/settled multiculturalisms: Diasporas, entanglements, transruptions,* ed. Barnor Hesse, 209–41. London: Zed.

134 David Theo Goldberg

Hannerf, Ulz. 1996. *Transnational connections: Culture, people, places*. London: Routledge.
Harvey, David. 1989. *The condition of postmodernity*. Oxford: Basil Blackwell.
Kymlicka, Will. 1996. *Multicultural citizenship: A liberal theory of minority rights*. Oxford: Oxford University Press.
Kymlicka, Will, and Wayne Norman, eds. 2000. *Citizenship in diverse societies*. Oxford: Oxford University Press.
Lloyd, David, and Paul Thomas. 1998. *Culture and the state*. New York: Routledge.
Marshall, T. H. 1950. *Citizenship and social class and other essays*. Cambridge: Cambridge University Press.
McWhorter, John. 2000. *Losing the race: Self-sabotage in black America*. New York: Free Press.
Menjivar, Cecilia. 2000. *Fragmented ties: Salvadoran immigrant networks in America*. University of California Press.
Mills, Charles. 2000. Race and the social contract tradition. *Social Identities: Journal for the Study of Race, Nation, and Culture* 6 (4): 441–62.
Ong, Aiwha. 1999. *Flexible citizenship: The cultural logics of transnationality*. Durham, N.C.: Duke University Press.
Parekh, Bhikhu. 2000. *Rethinking multiculturalism: Cultural diversity and political theory*. London: Macmillan.
Pieterse, Jan Nederveen, and Bhikhu Parekh, eds. 1995. *The decolonization of the imagination: Culture, knowledge and power*. London: Zed.
Portes, Alejandro, Luis Guarnizo, and Patricia Landolt. 1999. Introduction: Pitfalls and promises of an emergent research field. *Ethnic and Racial Studies* 22 (2): 217–37.
Rawls, John. 1971. *The theory of justice*. Cambridge, Mass.: Harvard University Press.
Roberts, Bryan, Reanne Frank, and Fernando Lozano-Ascencio. 1999. Transnational migrant communities and Mexican immigration to the U.S. *Ethnic and Racial Studies* 22 (2): 238–66.
Scott, James. 1990. *Domination and the arts of resistance*. New Haven, Conn.: Yale University Press.
———. 1998. *Seeing like a state: How certain schemes to improve the human condition failed*. New Haven, Conn.: Yale University Press.
Selingo, Jeffrey. 2001. Foe of affirmative action seeks to bar colleges in California from collecting data on race. *Chronicle of Higher Education,* February 14.
Smith, Rogers. 1997. *Civic ideals: Conflicting visions of citizenship in U.S. history*. New Haven, Conn.: Yale University Press
Soysal, Yasemin. 1994. *The limits of citizenship: Migrants and postnational membership in Europe*. Chicago: University of Chicago Press.
Steinberg, Stephen. 1998. Up from slavery: The myth of black progress. *New Politics* 7, no. 1 (Summer): 69–81.
Stoler, Ann Laura. 1995. *Race and the education of desire: Foucault's history of sexuality and the colonial order of things*. Durham, N.C.: Duke University Press.
Taussig, Michael. 1997. *The magic of the state*. New York: Routledge.
Taylor, Charles. 1992. *Sources of the self: The making of the modern identity*. Cambridge, Mass.: Harvard University Press.
Tully, James. 1995. *Strange multicplicity: Constitutionalism in an age of diversity*. Cambridge, Engl.: Cambridge University Press.
Urry, John. 2000. *Sociology beyond societies: Mobilities for the 21st century*. London: Routledge.
Waylen, Georgina. 1998. Gender, feminism and the state: An overview. In *Gender, politics and the state*, ed. Vicky Randall and Georgina Waylen, 1–17. London: Routledge.
Wolin, Sheldon. 1996. Fugitive Democracy. In *Democracy and difference*, ed. Seyla Benhabib, 31–45. Princeton, N.J.: Princeton University Press.

7

How Much Does Education Need the State?

Heinz Sünker

I

Despite talk of the "illusion of equality of opportunity" in education (Bourdieu and Passeron 1971), educational policy is social policy. This is why questions surrounding the "interdependence of societal constitution and educational institutions" (Heydorn 1979), the determination of the relationship between schooling and society, educational policy and the reproduction of social inequality have been widely discussed and numerous social scientific analyses and explorations in educational theory advanced during the past forty years. The debate on the state and education continues to be captured here in terms of "education's state of emergency" (*Picht*) or the "civil right to education" (*Dahrendorf*). It gains in contemporary relevance in view of recent sociopolitical disputes around innovations which also attempt to introduce the market and economic forms structuring broader social relations into the field of education (Henig 1994; Meiksins Wood 1995; Whitty 1997).

The German twentieth-century tradition, which can already be called "classical," includes above all the contributions to a critical educational theory—dealing with the famous German term *Bildung* which is different from *Erziehung* (education) because it aims at emancipation and maturity of every man and woman—organized around a theory of society of Heydorn (1979), Siemsen (1948), and Adorno (1972). The subsequent decline of educational thought and productive efforts in educational theory in the shape of a "theory of *Bildung*" (cf. Sünker 1997b) has been analyzed in an exemplary way by Adorno in his "theory of half-education" (*Halbbildung*), where he identifies the relationship between social history and educational theory in the shape of the ruling of instrumental reason:

What Education has turned into, sedimented as a sort of negative objective spirit, and not only in Germany, was itself derived from social laws of movement, even from the concept of education itself. It has become socialised half-education, the ever-presence of the alienated spirit. (1972, 93)

Adorno's analysis ends with the statement of a practical task in the following words:

If in the meantime the spirit only does what is socially correct, as long as it does not dissolve into society in an undifferentiated identity, anachronism is upon us: clutching to education (Bildung) after society has destroyed its foundations. But it has no other means of survival than critical reflection on half-education, which becomes essential for it. (1972, 121)

The Anglo-Saxon and French discussions, on the other hand, concentrate on contributions to a sociology of education oriented toward social policy. While the French analyses are integrated with a critique of power and domination, and Anglo-Saxon analyses are linked to a critique of current market ideology in the educational field, they nonetheless complement each other. The discussion of the related issues of "state, society, education, and individual" reveals that it is still overwhelmingly a matter of the functions of the education system for the reproduction of the societal status quo. What remains debatable is the way in which the dialectic inherent in the institutionalization of education (Heydorn 1979) can be developed in the direction of transcending this simple function of reproducing relations of social inequality. This requires a theory of education processes that begins from the societal constitution of subjectivity and at the same time can establish a capacity for resistance against societal relations of power and domination grounded in that very subjectivity itself.

On one hand, at the structural level, Bourdieu can argue in his views on the relevance of the education system to the "structure of class relations"—a leitmotif running consistently through all his analyses—that among all the solutions to the problem of the transmission of power and privilege recurring throughout history, none "is better disguised, and thus more suited to those societies inclined towards the denial of the more obvious forms of the traditional transmission of power and privilege, [than] those which guarantee the school system, in that it contributes to the reproduction of the structure of class relations, and at the same time hides under the mantle of neutrality the fact that it fulfills this function" (1973, 93; cf. Apple 1982a, 1982b, 1990; Cole 1988; Giroux and McLaren 1989; McLaren and Giarelli 1995; Wexler 1987; Young and Whitty 1977).

On the other hand, von Friedeburg's (1989) text *Educational Reform in Germany: History and Social Contradiction* takes as its starting point the social contradiction between the European Enlightenment's individual claim to education ("education as human right") and the functional processes of "integration and conformity" with society, which is always manifested through the education system—generally under state control. He concludes that in relation to social and educational policy

> the civil right to education cannot be realised in the market of systemic competition, through the rivalry between different school forms over increasingly scarce school pupils, irrespective of whether they assume the older three-tiered form or the newer four-tiered form taken on by the standard comprehensive school. The idea that the selective schools combine a number of tiers in one also leads no further, but simply reestablishes the old two-tiered division between higher and lower schools, with all its consequences for social selection. However, the history of school reform has shown that it is not pedagogic insights and organisational concepts which determine its progression, but social relations of power. Individual demands grow regardless of overwhelming status differences. Constant school expansion hollows out the credentialing system, and the social instrumentalisation of public education gets increasingly more difficult. Education reform remains on the agenda. (476–77)

II

From his early writings in the 1950s Heinz-Joachim Heydorn tried to respond to the task inherent in the "state-education problematic" of identifying or investigating the mediations between social structures, the structuring of social relations between the members of a society, and the conditions of the constitution of subjectivity. He did so by pointing to the connections between the priority of a capitalist utilitarian logic, the market form of social relations, and the reduction of social existence to "bare functionality" (1994a, 232). This underlying functionalism leads to the "question of a schooling that secures maximum human efficiency in a technological society, a society resting on conformity, exchange and mobility within largely determined social boundaries" (1994b, 284). This means that "education, as always throughout history, secures the ideology and power of an existing society"; it has to avoid those reflections that might bring about the demythologization of power. This is how it ends up caught in a clear contradiction (285).

According to Koneffke the task of radical educational theory involves reflection "on the contradiction between education and society, the incorporation of the objective compulsions both emanating from the capitalist system itself and questioning it at the same time, is the task of radical educational theory" (1981, 188). This led Koneffke to a thesis that helps us identify ways in which the transformation of society and the education system are related to each other. The patent transformation of education into training is determined in bourgeois capitalist society by the requirement that "the dependent masses . . . also be empirical bourgeois subjects" (1982, 946). To invoke Marx, this occurs in the wake of their splitting into both "Bourgeois" and "Citizen." This further demands an analysis of the dialectic of the institutionalization of education of the kind undertaken by Heydorn as done via an overview of societal and educational history. The analysis must include a reconstruction of the possibilities of development of the original attempt at a concept of education as discourse among people about their own freedom (Heydorn 1979, 32) out of their evolving sociohistorical conditions. The dialectic of the institutionalization of education leads to the class aspects of education, and the connection between them has to be related to the figurations of homo faber and homo ludens (Heydorn 1980b, 285). The conceptual universality and simultaneous empirical restrictions of education which arose with the bourgeois world radicalized the disintegration of the concept of education produced by the mass education required by the industrial revolution; this radicalization can in turn be understood in terms of class history. This historical development leads to the conclusion that "Institution and maturity find themselves in an unbridgeable opposition to each other" (Heydorn 1979, 317; Harvey 2000, 182ff.; Sünker 2000).

Heydorn proposes that "institution is domination; institution becomes superfluous" (1979, 331) and that "maturity is the transcendence of all institutions as tutelage through domination" (335). In opposition to the domination characterizing the dialectic of the institutionalization of education, Heydorn argues that "education will once again become what it first was: self-help" (1979, 324). This is Heydorn's substantive finding from his analysis of social reality dealing with the interdependence of societal constitution and educational institutions (Sünker 1994, 1997b, 1999). Accordingly, it is necessary to situate educational history and conceptualize educational theory within the framework of the history of society, in order to develop insights into the mutual mediations between micro-, meso-, and macrosocial processes. To avoid subjective or objective misinterpretations, we need a critical theory of education that works with the help of an impetus toward cultural revolution and a resolution of the concept of totality informed by the concept of contradiction (Sünker 1989, 25ff., 69ff.).

The concept of cultural revolution refers here to a revolutionization of everyday life, the basis of individual and social existence. This enables us to conceive of the abolition of superfluous structures of domination as well as to insist on the possibility of unfolding emancipatory human needs, accompanied by the competencies required for constituting social relationships, something which cannot be achieved in the framework of the existing social formation (Adorno 1973, 92–93; Heydorn 1979, 12–13; 1980b, 165; Lefebvre 1995). Heydorn links this perspective, which he calls the "totality of becoming a subject" (1980a, 297), to a general sociopolitical conception that connects the transcendence of alienation, the "revolutionising of human labour," leisure time and needs, with the development of a radical democracy (295). He also takes up this position to oppose the metaphysical tendencies of educational theory with the principle of immanence, and thus the capacity for history to be changed through human praxis.

If "education for agency" is to be understood as a "means of liberation (Heydorn 1979, 45, 324), we need both an analysis of the connections between schooling and the constitution of society and a theory of history that links its analysis to an examination of concrete historical relationships and forms of human interaction. Analysis of the history of relations between education and society affirms that education remains unrealized, because to this day the human condition is constituted by "determination" (31, 115, 300, 335). The issue of the potential for human history to encompass freedom remains on the agenda (1980a, 178). Insofar as education is understood as the "actualisation of potential" enabling people to realize their humanity, becoming "their own actor" (1980a, 164), the educational ideal can be interpreted as promoting human understanding of our own freedom: "as an attempt to end one's submission to authority" (1979, 32). Maturity in the form of human self-disposition thus constitutes the primary reference point, being the "fulfilment of the human dream and the dialectical correlate of development" (322). For this reason Heydorn believes that "education is rationally mediated spontaneity" (24).

This line of argument encompasses the field of human subjectivity and praxis as well as the historical and social structural context. Heydorn insists that education can become comprehensive and universal. This in turn rests on the possibility of an institutionalized process of education for ever-increasing numbers of people (Heydorn 1980a, 287), and is supported by recent research in industrial sociology. Even if the relationship between practical domination and people's simultaneous subjectification is undermined within the socially determined empirical restriction of the potential for maturity, a development is nonetheless occurring in the underlying structure of society.

The degree of structural rationality it ends up achieving is linked to the abstract character of production in the sense that "the comprehensive character which education has acquired in view of technical development" corresponds to a comprehensive paralysis of its potential for enlightenment and for establishing individuals as self-determining actors (1980b, 290). Society's contradictory constitution and reality encompasses education. Consequently, "The universality which education has achieved shows that the moment education overcomes its historical class divisions, it can become universal for a liberated species" (291).

To make this perspective more precise and explain the extent to which the growing significance of institutionalized education and the increasing achievement of human content are related to each other (1980b, 287–88), it is necessary to identify anew the contemporary dimensions of the hidden content of the concept of education (291), and to sketch the contours of a concept of education "demanded by the present" (295). Reference to the formation of consciousness thereby assumes unprecedented historical significance (294). Heydorn ends his article on survival with "Consciousness is everything" (301). This rests partly on the idea that thought processes which demythologize society—supported by its *rational* structure—(300) are both necessary and possible. It also builds on a train of thought in Hegel's analysis of the master–slave relationship (Sünker 1989, 103ff.) that humans only become subjects by mentally penetrating their material conditions and, thus, transforming them (Heydorn 1980a, 294).

For Heydorn education is only one rather than an independent revolutionary element in the movement of history (1980b, 100). He therefore insists that the institution of education offers "a self-transforming contribution which cannot be exchanged" (167) for the realization of a perspective that keeps this freedom in view. To counter the strategies of the paralysis of consciousness we need to examine ways in which educational theory can be used to concretize the identification of the dialogic structure of pedagogic processes and relationships that revolve around mutual recognition.

III

In the context of the problem of hegemony wherein the state is seen as "contested terrain," the debates and processes of deregulation in education take on particular significance to the extent that our focus is on marketization and its associated disempowerment. Because of their experience with Thatcherism and Reaganism and the accompanying renaissance of neoliberal economics, with its consequences for all social relations, Anglo-Saxon theorists particularly have analyzed the ideology of market apologists, the consequences of market strategies in the educational field, and the "seductive appeal" of the market metaphor (Henig 1994; see also, Dale 1990; Fiske and Ladd 2000).

Given globalization of the capital relationship and associated strategies of the capitalistic formation of world society or the world system (Amin 1992; Wallerstein 1991, 227–72), and the ever-intensifying divisive processes with Western–capitalist societies (the "two-thirds society") particular strategic significance attaches to strategies of depoliticization in the educational field that accompany market ideologies (Whitty 1998). As Heydorn suggested more than thirty-five years ago (1994b, 291; see also, McLaren 1993, 81–144), the leitmotif of strategies aiming at securing domination remains on an interest in adaptation to the production process on the one hand and the development of a socially conformist worldview on the other.

Market strategies always lead to intensified disparities. Because of their weak market position, the disadvantaged fall behind in their social position, and are certainly not able to improve it. What is "improved" in a market-oriented education system is, rather, the reproduction of social inequality. The discourse of market relations provides the deepening of social distinctions with a new rhetoric of legitimation (Whitty 1998, 97–98; Henig 1994, 188ff.). It also promotes fundamental redefinitions of the understanding of the state and state activity, and of the possible forms to be taken by the relationships between state and "civil society."

> The growing tendency to base more and more aspects of social affairs on the notion of consumer rights rather than upon citizen rights involves more than a move away from public-provided systems of state education towards individual schools competing for clients in the marketplace. While seeming to respond to critiques of impersonal over-bureaucratic welfare state provision, this also shifts major aspects of education decision-making out of the public into the private realm with potentially significant consequences for social justice. (Whitty 1998, 100)

Pointing in same direction is the identification of the danger of a destruction of social and political institutions and the public sphere that provide the preconditions for real changes in the social system (Henig 1994, 193; Barber 1998, 225ff.). Propagating the ideology of the market can thus clearly be seen as contributing to processes of the paralysis of consciousness which, according to Heydorn, become necessary for securing power and domination because of the rationality of social processes and forms of production under late capitalism.

The "return" of a public or government-run education system (the distinction can only be indicated here) to a "marketised civil society" decisively undermines the potential for democratic debates and decision-making processes, as well as collective action (Whitty 1998, 101). It can also be said that "atomized decion making within an already stratfied society may appear to give everyone formally equal opportunities but will actually reduce the possibility of collective struggles that might help those least able to help themselves" (100; see also, Giroux and McLaren 1992, 101–2).

Against the background of an analysis of hegemonic relationships, we can conclude that the ideology of the market and marketization strategies achieve their aim to the extent that they destroy a public sphere in which general interests do not simply stand in the shadow of private interests. This creates a need to think about possible alternatives in the field of education, beginning with a defense of structures that are founded on universalistic principles (Gutmann 1988; Shor 1992; Whitty 1997, 33ff.).

Steinvorth (1999) invokes this kind of perspective. He is concerned with institutions and rights that are integral to securing equal freedoms and democratic equality. These range from systems of education to insurance, from the right to work to health care. His ideas are organized around two legal images. These are the generational participation in the culture of the "previous generation" and the "elementary education" in everything "which enables one to participate in political decision-making processes" (Steinvorth 1999, 221; see also, Hill and Cole 1999; Kincheloe 1999; Sünker 1997a).

This is a matter of the "principle of democratic minimalism." This principle forbids a distribution of resources that falls below the standard required to secure "the capacity to participate in the culture and politics of one's own society" (Steinvorth 1999, 277). Recognizing this principle is urgently necessary in view of the state of the world, mass unemployment, environment destruction, and the scarcity of natural resources. In addition, "without this capacity, people are excluded from all decisions which concern them and which constitute the framework for their self-determination" (277).

Correspondingly, the state is obliged to achieve social justice, in the sense of institutionally securing these resources and making them universally accessible in the form of social rights—including in opposition to property rights and with the help of taxation (Steinvorth 1979, 222). In opposition to the "illusion of equality of opportunity," the task facing us in terms of state and society is to fight for educational conditions and educational processes that enhance the interests of *all* members of society. This is no less than to fight for a substantively democratic society (Sünker 2002).

Heydorn's cautious optimism about the possibilities for the future—even in a time where "the end of politics" (Boggs 2000) has been stated—is based on the hope that "with this experience [of self-determination and happiness] we are already set free, even while we are still subordinated" (Heydorn 1980b, 298). There are good reasons, I believe, to argue that precisely the development and experiences of civil rights movements in Eastern Europe and the former German Democratic Republic, as well as old and new social movements in the West, support this optimism.

REFERENCES

Adorno, Theodor W. 1972. Theorie der Halbbildung. In *Soziologische Schriften I,* 93–121. Frankfurt: Suhrkamp.
———. 1973. *Negative dialectics.* New York: Continuum.
Amin, S. 1992. *Das Reich des Chaos: Der Neue Vormarsch der Ersten Welt.* Hamburg: VSA.
Apple, M., ed. 1982a. *Cultural and economic reproduction in education.* London: Routledge and Kegan Paul.
———. 1982b. *Education and power.* Boston: Routledge and Kegan Paul.
———. 1990. *Ideology and curriculum.* London: Routledge.
Barber, Benjamin J. 1998. Education for democracy. In *A passion for democracy,* 225–36. Princeton: Princeton University Press.
Boggs, C. 2000. *The end of politics: Corporate power and the decline of the public sphere.* New York: Guilford Press.
Bourdieu, P., and J.-C. Passeron. 1971. *Die Illusion der Chancengleichheit.* Stuttgart.
Bourdieu, Pierre. 1973. Cultural reproduction and social reproduction. In *Knowledge, education and cultural change,* ed. Richard Brown, 71–112. London: Tavistock.
Cole, Mike, ed. 1988. *Bowles and Gintis revisited: Correspondence and contradiction in educational theory.* London: Falmer.
Dale, R. 1990. The Thatcherite project in education: The case of the city technology colleges. *Critical Social Policy* 9: 4–19.
Fiske, E. B., and H. F. Ladd. 2000. *When schools compete: A cautionary tale.* Washington, D.C.: Brookings Institute Press.

Giroux, H., and P. McLaren, eds. 1989. *Critical pedagogy, the state, and cultural struggle.* Albany, N.Y.: State University of New York Press.

———. 1992. America 2000 and the politics of erasure: Democracy and culture difference under siege. *International Journal of Educational Reform* 1: 99–110.

Gutmann, Amy. 1988. Distributing public education and democracy. In *Democracy and the welfare state,* ed. Amy Gutmann, 107–30. Princeton, N.J.: Princeton University Press.

Harvey, David. 2000. *Spaces of hope.* Berkeley: University of California Press.

Henig, J. R. 1994. *Rethinking school choice: Limits of the market metaphor.* Princeton, N.J.: Princeton University Press.

Heydorn, Heinz-Joachim. 1979. *Über den Widerspruch von Bildung und Herrschaft.* Frankfurt: Syndikat.

———. 1980a. Überleben durch Bildung. Umriß einer Aussicht. In *Ungleichheit für alle. Bildungstheoretische Schriften,* 282–301. Frankfurt: Syndikat.

———. 1980b. Zu einer Neufassung des Bildungsbegriffs. In *Ungleichheit für alle. Bildungstheoretische Schriften,* 95–184. Frankfurt: Syndikat.

———. 1994a. Zur inneren Schulverfassung. Elemente einer Kritik der deutschen Bildungsideologie. In *Werke,* 283–96. Vaduz: Topos.

———. 1994b. Zur pädagogischen Situation unserer Zeit. In *Werke,* 231–38. Vaduz: Topos.

Hill, D., and M. Cole, eds. 1999. *Promoting equality in secondary schools.* New York: Cassell.

Kincheloe, J. 1999. *Toil and trouble: Good work, smart workers, and the integration of academic and vocational education.* New York: Lang.

Koneffke, G. 1981. Überleben und Bildung. In *Argument-Sonderband AS 58,* 163–93. Berlin.

———. 1982. Wert und Erziehung. Zum Problem der Normierung des Handelns in der Konstitution bürgerlicher Pädagogik. *Zeitschrift für Pädagogik* 28: 935–50.

Lefebvre, H. 1995. *Introduction to modernity.* London: Verso.

McLaren, P. 1993. *Schooling as ritual performance: Towards a political economy of educational symbols and gestures.* New York: Routledge.

McLaren, P., and J. M. Giarelli, eds. 1995. *Critical theory and educational research.* Albany: State University of New York Press.

Meiksins Wood, E. 1995. *Democracy against capitalism.* Cambridge: Cambridge University Press.

Shor, I. 1992. *Empowering education.* Chicago: University of Chicago Press.

Siemsen, A. 1948. *Die gesellschaftlichen Grundlagen der Erziehung.* Hamburg.

Steinvorth, U. 1999. *Gleiche Freiheit. Politische Philosophie und Verteilungsgerechtigkeit.* Berlin: Akademie Verlag.

Sünker, Heinz. 1989. *Bildung, Alltag und Subjektivität.* Weinheim: Deutscher Studien Verlag.

———. 1994. Pedagogy and politics: Heydorn's survival through education and its challenge to contemporary theories of education. In *The Politics of Human Science,* ed. S. Miedema et al., 113–28. Brussels: Vubpress.

———. 1997a. After Auschwitz: The quest for democratic education. In *Education and fascism,* ed. H. Sünker and H.-U. Otto, 161–70. London: Falmer.

———. 1997b. Heydorn's Bildungs theory and content as social analysis. In *The politics, sociology and economics of education,* ed. R. Farnen and H. Sünker, 113–26. Basingstoke: McMillan.

———. 1999. Kritische Bildungstheorie und Gesellschaftsanalyse: Bildung, Arbeit und Emanzipation. In *Kritische Erziehungswissenschaft am Neubeginn?!* ed. Heinz Sünker and H-H. Krüger, 327–48. Frankfurt: Suhrkamp.

———. 2000. Bildung, Emanzipation und Reflexivität beim Übergang von der Arbeits—zur Wissensgesellschaft. In *Wissen und Nichtwissen,* ed. H. G. Homfeldt and J. Schulze-Krüdener, 41–53. Weinheim: Deutscher Studien Verlag.

———. 2002. Democracy, participation and education. In *Participation, globalisation and culture,* ed. G. Széll, D. Chetty, and A. Chouraqui, 186–206. Frankfurt: Lang.

von Friedeburg, L. 1989. *Bildungsreform in Deutschland. Geschichte und gesellschaftlicher Widerspruch.* Frankfurt: Suhrkamp.

Wallerstein, Immanuel. 1991. *Unthinking social science.* Cambridge, Engl.: Cambridge University Press.

Wexler, Phillip. 1987. *Social analysis of education. After the new sociology.* London: Routledge and Kegan Paul.

Whitty, G. 1997. Creating quasi-markets in education. *Review of Research in Education* 22: 3–47.

———. 1998. Citizens or consumers? Continuity and change in contemporary education policy. In *Power/knowledge/pedagogy: The meaning of democratic education in unsettling times,* ed. D. Carlson and M. Apple, 92–109. Boulder: Westview.

Young, M., and G. Whitty. 1977. *Society, state and schooling.* Barcombe: Falmer.

8

Social Subjectivity and Mutual Recognition as Basic Terms of a Critical Theory of Education

Albert Scherr

This text develops a basis for a critical theory and praxis of education. Such a theory must show the possibilities, aims, and the legitimization of a specific understanding of the perspective of pedagogy. Critical pedagogy cannot be reduced to teaching useful knowledge and skills for professional life, training for social demands, or an education that tries to suppress nonconforming behavior. Hence, a critical theory of education needs a theoretical foundation: its possibilities and tasks do not simply result from expectations of politically and economically influential individuals, groups and organizations.

The central principles of a theory and praxis of critical pedagogy are to support development of subjectivity and enable mutual recognition. Education in the sense of *Bildung* finds its central perspective in enabling individuals to pursue more self-aware and self-determined ways of life and giving them access to experiences of recognition, attention, respect, and esteem of their history, abilities, need dispositions, interests, and life plans. Critical pedagogy seeks to contribute by challenging unquestionable validity of habitual routines of daily life, widespread ways of thinking, certainties of common sense and self-evident ideas. Critical pedagogy seeks to encourage and prepare individuals to understand and critically question views about themselves, society, and nature. In Paulo Freire's words (1998) it involves a "praxis of freedom," which enables individuals to pursue self-determined ways of living.

A BRIEF ACCOUNT OF BASIC TERMS

The idea that human individuals should be autonomous and independent subjects was formulated by the philosophy of enlightenment in criticism of structures of political and religious power. Enlightenment philosophy, based on a particular understanding of human nature, asserted that individuals become subjects when they are capable of acting self-responsibly and making rational and morally justifiable decisions.

The Frankfurt School of Critical Theory adopted this idea of subjects believing that education toward self-responsibility is absolutely essential for countering a return to fascism. Adorno states that "Education after Auschwitz" only makes sense as an "education towards critical self-reflection" (1970, 90). Education should help individuals maintain objective distance from social expectations, to critically question ideologies, prejudices, and attitudes of hostility, to become conscious of their own fears and feelings of hate and rage and judge based on the consideration of a moral point of view. Subjectivity is defined as capability to judge and to act in self-determined ways, on the basis of critical and rational thinking and under consideration of moral principles, and to enter equal-rights relationships with others, who are recognized as autonomous subjects.

"Subjectivity" has a central role within the theory of society and the theory and praxis of education of the Critical Theory of the Frankfurt School. Central to this is the idea that "the human being as an individual can only find himself in a just and humane society" (Adorno 1956, 48). A just and humane society and pedagogy are identifiable by their respect for and furtherance of self-determination and independence. The "supremacy of the society over the individual" and the reduction of the latter to a "simple specimen of its kind, which is not so important" (45) becomes the central targets of Adorno's criticism of contemporary society.

Subjectivity characterizes an elementary quality of human sensations, reflections, and actions. It does not equate with individual autonomy in the sense of a total independence from social conditions. The idea that "the human being exists from its beginning through corresponding with others and is fellow-creature before also being individual" (Adorno 1956, 42) is self-evident for the critical theory of Adorno and for the theory of George H. Mead ([1932] 1980, 168) alike. In Frankfurt School Critical Theory, subjectivity does not mean individual independence but, rather, the fact that inborn instincts and social fixations do not determine human individuals in their sensations, reflections, and actions. Social and mental limitations are not the same as social and mental determinations. Human individuals can be characterized by an open and reflexive relation to themselves and their social contexts. Four separate dimensions can be differentiated here:

- Human individuals experience themselves as beings equipped with certain need dispositions and emotions (A: subjectivity as an individual's feeling about himself).
- They take up an evaluating position toward their qualities, capabilities, need dispositions, and interests (B: subjectivity as self-esteem).

- They communicate and act on the basis of a certain knowledge about themselves (C: subjectivity as self-awareness).
- They are capable of judging between alternatives, to take or not to take chances, in general to act self-determined on the basis of decisions (D: subjectivity as the ability of self-determination).

Human individuals, then, are no "trivial machines" reacting to changes in their natural and social surrounding by fixed patterns of behavior. They rather deal with impulses and information on the basis of complex emotional and cognitive structures, in a manner that is not determined and likewise is not predictable. Individuals as subjects are principally capable of opposing expectations, breaking with habits, questioning statements, ignoring norms, and doing the unexpected.

Yet subjectivity does not mean that individuals are independent and socially unconditioned beings with respect to their sensations, reflections, and actions. Individuals develop their subjectivity in conflict with the expectations of significant others (Habermas 1994, chap. 8; Mead 1962). To achieve this they rely on social relations and the communicative consideration of their need dispositions and abilities. The ways individuals experience themselves emotionally (their feelings about themselves) and evaluate themselves (self-esteem), are based on experience of social esteem and disregard. Erving Goffman (1961) has shown that the image of the own person can be extensively destabilized and questioned by labeling. Even knowledge of oneself (self-awareness) develops in relation to images of oneself communicated by others. Subjectivity is therefore necessarily social subjectivity, which means that it is in its development dependent from social relations. Self-perception, self-evaluation, self-awareness, and self-determination are qualities of individual praxis of life within social relations, and presume social coexistence.

Individuals strive to maintain and enforce a positive self-esteem (Elias and Scotson 1993, 307). To do this they rely on social relations, which give them access to experiences of esteem of their need dispositions, qualities, and capabilities. Such experiences are necessary for individuals to develop the ability to speak and act, to understand themselves, the world, and others in this world through participation in social relations comprising structures of mutual recognition. All social relations in which individuals are more than an instrument for external objectives and in which their right to and capacity for self-determination is respected, can be characterized as structures of mutual recognition (for it essentially; Honneth 1992). Accordingly, subjectivity, self-esteem, self-awareness, and self-determination are not inherent qualities of human individuals but outcomes of social coexistence. Individuals are incapable of maintaining their self-image and ability to act in total isolation.

A critical theory of education must put these basic ideas to sociological and empirical use and ask to what extent given social structures, especially power structures, improve or decrease the ability of self-determination, what kind of conditions they establish for the self-understanding of individuals, and under which conditions they support positive self-esteem through social esteem. A critical theory and praxis of education has the task of contributing to preventing individuals from being reduced to objects of government power required to senselessly comply with social conditions.

Critical Pedagogy in Modern Society

Education is a socially situated praxis. Each pedagogic action is embedded in the structures and dynamics of society. Education, as a planned and pedagogically justified attempt to influence the sensation, reflection, and action of individuals, is but one of many factors in the socialization process. Familial and professional education compete with other social influences on the knowledge and beliefs of children, teenagers, and adults. These include churches, sects, political organizations, and commercial culture industries which, besides selling their products, supply complete lifestyle and identity blueprints.

Moreover, education does not take place in a vacuum, but in particular social and local contexts. It faces individuals who have grown up under particular social conditions and acquired particular experiences, need dispositions, and expectations. Education must define its possibilities and aims in competition with learners' situations and connect with their need dispositions, hopes, knowledge, norms, and life plans.

If education renounces this and limits itself to mediate the official stock of knowledge it risks becoming irrelevant to its participants. The central processes of learning for the individual are then left to what is supplied by common culture through daily communication and the mass media (Willis 1990, 147).

Critical pedagogy must examine the social conditions of living, which form the frame for the individual experience and praxis of living and enable or disable certain chances to shape this praxis. Critical pedagogy finds its point of contact in the experiences of individuals, in their discontent with and their suffering caused by the social conditions of living that they are exposed to, and in their fears and unanswered hopes. It is the task of critical pedagogy to make the connection between individual sensation and reflection and social conditions, and the possibilities of a changed reflection and action, clearly visible.

This requires theoretical effort. The conditions and problematic of their own life situations are not entirely transparent to individuals themselves. Rather, seeking the reasons for one's own problems remains confined within the bounds of ideologies, prejudices, and hostile attitudes. Discontent articulates itself in hate for oneself, or hate toward whatever social group is thought responsible.

The following argument proposes to examine social structures and processes as conditions that structure possibilities for development of individual subjectivity and access to chances of social recognition. On the basis of a theory of subjectivity social and governmental power structures and social inequalities have to be criticized not only because they lead to inequalities in distribution of income, wealth, and political efficacy, but also because they limit the options for a self-determinated praxis of life and access to chances for social esteem. *From this standpoint power and social disadvantages centrally consist in limited chances for self-determination and in denial of social esteem, experiences, social identities, and life plans of individuals. Such limitations are a key analytical starting point of critical pedagogy.*

If one looks at the situation of individuals in the developed, industrial (postindustrial) societies of the Northwest the need for a critical pedagogy that seeks to enlarge the chances of social recognition and individual self-determination is not evident. The statement, "The objective conditions of Western capitalism . . . appear . . . completely incompatible with the realization of freedom and liberation" (McLaren 1994, 192) provokes evident resistance. Moreover, modern societies understand themselves to be societies of free and equal individuals that have overcome traditional power structures. While this claim is negated daily by the situations of the poor and socially excluded, such a self-understanding is plausible insofar as modern societies renounce comprehensively regulating individual ways of living by religious or political orders. Preferences of nourishment or consumption, sexual orientation, religious beliefs, and so on are not dictated to the individual or social group by a central authority. Freedom of speech and press are socially recognized. In modern society the place of such comprehensive regulations of ways of living have been replaced by the compulsion to orient oneself to conditions of participation and success determined by businesses as organizations of the economic system, schools as organizations of the educational system, parties as organizations of government politics, hospitals as organizations of the health care system, and so on. Whoever cannot or does not want to adapt their way of living to the prevailing conditions will sink or, at least, not rise (Weber [1920] 1972, 61).

In developed welfare states such failure is made more or less bearable by compensations from the government. Modern societies as a whole can be described as societies in which the situation of the individuals is best characterized as "exclusionary individuality" (Luhmann 1997). The individual's life no longer takes place within a comprehensive and indissoluble social context—be it family, social standing, or an organization—that determines their conditions and chances of living for the long term.

Memberships can be chosen and possibilities for decision are available. At the same time individuals must find access to multiple social systems, partnerships, families, schools, professions, information spread by the mass media, institutions of legal representation, and so on. Chances of social recognition and of a self-determinate way of living are, consequently, limited in various respects.

1. Based on the destruction of economically subsistent forms of living the individual has become extensively dependent on services of organizations of the economic system, the legal system, the health care system, and the

educational system. Many goods and services that are essential for or beneficial to the shaping of the individual way of living are only available in exchange for money. The unequal distribution of income and wealth therefore limits the chances of a self-determining way of life in a manner that divides social classes. As Pierre Bourdieu (1984, 597) puts it, "The space of opportunities is finite."

2. As various studies of professional and industrial sociology have shown (e.g., Braverman 1974; Sennett 1998) professions are differentiated according to the possibilities they offer for self-responsible action and decision during work, and the extent to which they stimulate and further or limit the development of individual qualities, capabilities, and self-responsibility.

3. Organizations tie access to their services to specific conditions. Schools require that pupils sufficiently discipline and motivate themselves in accordance with regulations and teacher demands. Businesses determine standards for the qualities of their employees. Many legal claims can only be enforced if one is in a legal state of residence.

4. Possibilities of self-determination are further dependent on access to "cultural capital" (Bourdieu 1984, 171ff.), to available knowledge and to culture. The mass media and consumer goods industries exert much effort in creating a fascination for a way of living oriented toward professional success, possessing and using consumer goods, particular ideals of beauty, and middle-class values.

5. In modern society social esteem is related to positions in hierarchies. A person who fails school or university is not only excluded from career opportunities, but also encounters social disregard. Unemployment leads not only to loss of income, but also commonly results in a negative evaluation of the unemployed person and his or her abilities, as well as imputation of self-responsibility for the failure.

What Does Education Mean in Terms of Development of Subjectivity

Individuals perceive themselves and others on the basis of patterns of perception and interpretation, which they find within the cultures of society and appropriate in processes of socialization. The ideas individuals have of themselves and the world are only partly the result of their material life conditions. They are also partly the result of autonomous acts of construction, based upon socially provided patterns (Bourdieu 1985). Such patterns comprise fundamentally distinct types (Schütz 1974) that enable us to perceive social and natural reality as ordered and comprehensible and to act purposefully on them. For example, cultures differentiate between eatable and noneatable animals, thereby establishing consequential patterns for the experience of and behavior toward animals. Individuals experience themselves and others as men or women, based on the socially valid knowledge of the qualities of men and women that are believed to be typical, yet have in fact been appropriated in daily communication. Such distinctions of types also comprehend distinctions of groups of humans as members of social classes or ethnic groups, which exist in combination with extensive suppositions about characteristic qualities and abilities. Distinctions of types also include basic valuations, which permit us, for example, to distinguish between beautiful and ugly bodies. From this point of view cultures have an enormous influence on individuals, since they extensively determine the ways individuals experience and evaluate themselves and others, what they think to be normal or abnormal, what they consider worth striving for and what they despise.

Yet theories in the tradition of the symbolic interactionism have repeatedly shown, that individuals are no cultural dopes who merely embrace a culture's patterns of interpretation, behavior and evaluation as unequivocal rules. Rather sensations, reactions, and actions consist of creative and obstinate modes of dealing with the patterns and rules provided in different cultures. These do not determine the ways concrete individuals could or should experience concrete situations, think, or act. Rather these schemes and rules constrain the space of opportunities in which individuals can move. Accordingly Stuart Hall (2000, 106) sees cultures as "a weaving of limitations . . . without which we do not speak" and are not able to come to an understanding of our identity. Anthony Giddens's (1984, 1ff.) theory of structurization points to the fact that social structures limit as well as enable individual sensation, reflection, and action. Pierre Bourdieu (1987, 97ff.; 1992) has shown that they work as generative structures, which are the basis of the creative, productive output of individuals. For example, language limits what can be said and how it can be said, yet does not determine what we say in a concrete situation.

Individuals, then, are always subjects of their praxis of living. Their sensation, reflection, and action are not genetically or socially determined in their concrete realization. They emerge as active performances. This, however, does not mean that individuals are autonomous in relation to the styles of thinking, norms, and values that they find in society. We always grow up in a certain cultural context, which provides us with a certain knowledge, and certain patterns of perception, evaluation, and interpretation and excludes others. The space of opportunities for individual "obstinacy" is, therefore, limited by cultural frames.

The task of a critical pedagogy aimed at development of subjectivity can be seen then, *primarily*, to be one of giving individuals access to knowledge and patterns of perception, evaluation, and interpretation that are not otherwise accessed in the normal process of growing up, via socialization in the family, schools, businesses, and participation in mass media. It is about opening new horizons of sensation, reflection, and action. Therefore critical pedagogy does not accept the dominant culture as inevitable. Rather, it seeks to enable individuals to question facts they thought to be self-evident. It can basically be characterized as a pedagogy that enables opportunities for different sensations, reflections, and actions (Grossberg 1994, 18).

Second, pedagogy aimed at developing subjectivity does not conceive itself as a one-way transmission of knowledge seen as worthy of being implanted in the heads of learners. Rather its subject is the basic relations between individuals and themselves, others, social structures, and nature. It sees its task as offering individuals chances to clarify, check, and change these relations.

Third, critical pedagogy seeks to fulfill the task of supporting individuals in the process of dealing with their life story and helps them to check and clarify their identity. It does not presume, that individuals possess a cultural identity determined by social and ethnic origin and cannot be changed. Rather, it seeks to enable individuals to critically deal with identifications and memberships.

Fourth, such pedagogy can be characterized by the fact, that it does not regard subjective experiences, life knowledge, and the fears and hopes of its addressees to be unimportant and ignore them. Instead, it considers them important and takes them up. If critical pedagogy is supposed to be about opening individuals' minds to opportunities for different understanding of themselves and the world, then alternative offers have to prove their worth when it comes to helping its addressees to a better understanding of their concrete experiences and life situations. This is only possible if educational themes and content are related to previous knowledge.

Fifth, for that reason critical pedagogy must understand itself as a dialogic practice that "aims to allow the silenced to speak" (Grossberg 1994, 16). If it is about clarifying experiences, enabling other ways of seeing one's experiences, breaking up solidified patterns of perception, interpretation, and evaluation, then it can only take place in processes that provide chances to bring up such experiences in dialogue. Recognizing individuals as subjects, as persons capable of self-awareness and self-determination is, then, both an aim and a method of critical pedagogy. Its praxis takes place in small steps aimed at enabling opportunities for a self-determining praxis of living and for overcoming limitations that are imposed on individuals and that they impose on themselves. For this, a basic respect for the self-responsibility of individuals to shape their way of living is absolutely necessary.

REFERENCES

Adorno, Theodor W. 1956. Individuum. In *Institut für Sozialforschung: Soziologische Exkurse*, 40–49. Frankfurt: Suhrkamp.
———. 1970. *Erziehung zur Mündigkeit*. Frankfurt: Suhrkamp.
Bourdieu, Pierre. 1984. *Die feinen Unterschiede*. Frankfurt: Suhrkamp
———. 1985. *Sozialer Raum und Klassen*. Frankfurt: Suhrkamp.
———. 1987. *Sozialer sinn. Kritik der theoretischen Vernunft*. Frankfurt: Suhrkamp.
———. 1992. *The logic of practice*. Stanford, Calif.: Stanford University Press.
Braverman, Harry. 1974. *Labor and monopoly capital: The degradation of work in the twentieth century*. New York: Monthly Review Press.
Elias, Norbert, and John L. Scotson. 1993. *Etablierte und Außenseiter*. A German translation of their *The established and the outsiders* (1965). Frankfurt: Suhrkamp.

Freire, Paulo. 1998. *Pedagogy of freedom: Ethics, democracy, and civic courage.* Lanham, Md.: Rowman & Littlefield.

Giddens, Anthony. 1984. *The constitution of society.* Cambridge, Engl.: Polity Press.

Goffman, Erving. 1961. *Asylums: Essays on the social situation of mental patients and other inmates.* New York: Doubleday Books.

Grossberg, Lawrence. 1994. Introduction: Bringin' it all back home—pedagogy and cultural studies. In *Between borders: Pedagogy and the politics of cultural studies:* ed. Henry A. Giroux and Peter McLaren, 1–28. New York: Routledge.

Habermas, Jürgen. 1994. *Postmetaphysical thinking: Philosophic essays.* Cambridge, Mass.: MIT Press.

Hall, Stuart. 2000. Ein Gefüge von Einschränkungen. In *Die kleinen Unterschiede. Der Cultural-studies-reader,* ed. Jan Engelmann Hg., 99–122. Frankfurt: Campus.

Honneth, Axel. 1992. *Kampf um Anerkennung. Zur moralischen Grammatik sozialer Konflikte.* Frankfurt: Suhrkamp.

Luhmann, Niklas. 1997. *Die Gesellschaft der Gesellschaft.* Frankfurt: Suhrkamp.

McLaren, Peter. 1994. Multiculturalism and the postmodern critique: Toward a pedagogy of resistance and transformation. In *Between borders: Pedagogy and the politics of cultural studies,* ed. Henry A. Giroux and Peter McLaren, 192–224. New York: Routledge.

Mead, George Herbert. [1932] 1980. *The philosophie of the present.* Ed. Arthur E. Murphy. Chicago: University of Chicago Press.

———. 1962. *Mind, self and society.* Ed. C. W. Morris. Chicago: University of Chicago Press.

Schütz, Alfred. 1974. *Der sinnhafte Aufbau der sozialen Welt.* Frankfurt: Suhrkamp.

Sennett, Richard. 1998. *The corrosion of character.* New York: W. W. Norton.

Weber, Max. [1920] 1972. *Die protestantische Ethik und der Geist des Kapitalismus.* Tübingen, Ger.

Willis, Paul. 1990. *Common culture.* Boulder, Colo.: Westview Press.

9

Critical Theory and Pedagogy: Theodor W. Adorno and Max Horkheimer's Contemporary Significance for a Critical Pedagogy

Ludwig Pongratz

THE DEVELOPMENT OF CRITICAL PEDAGOGY IN GERMANY

Dubiel's introduction to critical theory (Dubiel 1988) relates an anecdote about an American student getting off the train in Frankfurt looking for the Frankfurt School. Seeking the right building on the Frankfurt University campus, the student eventually locates the Institute for Social Research, but receives the friendly advice that the Frankfurt School can at best be located in a symbolic sense, since the Frankfurt School lies "both nowhere and simultaneously in many places" (16).

Important Frankfurt School texts were not written in Frankfurt, but in the United States. The period in which Max Horkheimer gathered together a group of young, critical scholars in Frankfurt around the Institute for Social Research (and their theoretical organ, the *Zeitschrift für Sozialforschung*) was quite brief. The group—including Theodor W. Adorno, Erich Fromm, Otto Kirchheimer, Leo Löwenthal, Herbert Marcuse, Franz Neumann, Friedrich Pollock—was first formed in the early 1930s. Its central task was pursuing social scientific and interdisciplinary social analysis. The group took up Hegel's philosophy of history and Marx's critique of political economy to, in Hegel's oft-cited words, "grasp their era in thought."

"Their era" comprised the final years of the Weimar Republic. They prepared for emigration upon Hitler's rise to power, and by 1935 most were in the United States, where the institute was hosted by Columbia University. Only the first issue of the institute's journal appeared in Germany itself.

From the second issue onwards the *Zeitschrift für Sozialforschung*, which was to run to nine volumes, was no longer published in Germany. Horkheimer's most im-

154

portant articles were written in New York. The same is true of Leo Löwenthal's work in the sociology of classical literature, Adorno's sociology of music, Marcuse's social philosophy, Fromm's social psychology, and Pollock, Kirchheimer and Neumann's theory of the state. *The Dialectic of Enlightenment* and the *Critique of Instrumental Reason* were written in California, where the research for *The Authoritarian Personality* was also undertaken. In short, the intellectual capital that Horkheimer and Adorno transferred in the 1950s to post-Fascist West Germany was largely not even built up in Germany. (Dubiel 1998, 14)

In this sense our American student could have spared himself the detour through Frankfurt. The most important information about the Frankfurt School can be found in any well-stocked university library (Dubiel 1988; Held 1980; Jay 1973; Kellner 1989; Slater 1977; Türcke and Bolte 1994; van Reijen 1984; Wiggershaus 1994).

A succinct summary of the impact of critical social theory on German educational theory could be given as follows. "Critical educational theory" is concerned with an approach to the theoretical problems of a pedagogy inspired by "critical theory." Critical educational theory is inspired not only by the intellectual circle surrounding Horkheimer, but even more by the following generation, which has developed the inheritance of the "Frankfurt School" in quite diverse ways. Among the second generation theorists such as Negt, Offe Schmidt, and Wellmer, Jürgen Habermas clearly takes the leading place. All of these philosophers and social theorists share a common interest, namely, a critical reconstruction or transformation of social theory under the leitmotif of individual and social emancipation. This means in particular that the theorist's view on social structures and processes cannot remain content with recording and sketching the pure facticity of the societal status quo. Their task is equally to bring to consciousness the illegitimate domination and violence of this situation, and to bring to expression the real-existing, but as yet unarticulated, potential for liberation (Keckeisen 1983).

The emphasis placed by critical theory on enlightenment, critique of domination, and emancipation does not arise from the theorist's arbitrary, subjectively determined interests, but from the movement of historical processes themselves, brought to consciousness. In other words, the cultural achievements and political institutions of bourgeois society (such as in the idea of the integrity of the individual, universal and equal law, the autonomy of art) encompass a "moment of reason" which continues to contain their truth claims, even when the bourgeois class utilizes it for its own purposes. Critical theory thus aims to reveal the inner contradictions of the bourgeois world, without lapsing into the traditional mistake of suggesting its own recipes to the society it is criticising. This is because all critique which is concerned with the concrete form of social actuality passes together with the transcendence of this society. For this reason, critical theorists have always refused to explicate the concept of a reconciled society (van Reijen 1984, 35).

This has significant consequences for the problematics and research logic of pedagogic theory. A pedagogy informed by a critical orientation can be satisfied neither with bringing about harmonious integration into bourgeois society, nor with viewing pedagogic institutions simply in terms of their efficiency, functionality, or instrumental utility. Critical educational theory is more concerned with a constantly renewed, critical questioning of pedagogic goals, institutions, and practices. This critical reflection is inextricably linked to a normative concern with individual and social emancipation. Its impact is based on the analysis of ever-changing social contradictions in the field of pedagogic praxis. Accordingly, dialectical concepts are central to its research logic, and concepts like critique, autonomy, resistance, ego strength, identity, and maturity become key concepts of critical educational theory.

Critical educational theory dominated German pedagogic discussion in the 1960s and 1970s (e.g., Blankertz 1979; Heydorn 1970, 1972; Klafki 1976; Mollenhauer 1968). It has been argued that the end of reform policies in German schooling since the 1980s has led to stagnation and decline in what used to be the leading theoretical approach in pedagogy. How valid is this view and what has become of the impulse toward critical theory in pedagogy?

First the intellectual climate has indeed changed dramatically since the 1980s. The current mood in German educational theory might be expressed as "the future isn't what it used to be." A creeping disillusionment characterizes the pedagogic field. Postmodern critiques of Enlightenment narratives dominate the scene. General doubts have been radicalized into doubts about everything in general: reason, subjectivity, and maturity. European Enlightenment ideals are again caught in the crossfire of critique.

That reason and social rationalization do not simply coincide with general happiness accompanied the modern enlightenment process as a permanent, irrepressible uncertainty. Romanticism, historicism, the cultural critique of the fin de siécle and critical theory's antimodernist philosophy of history made that clear in every possible way. "Every attempt to break the natural thralldom, because nature is broken, enters all the more deeply into that natural enslavement" (Adorno and Horkheimer 1979, 13). This applies to all extensive forms of domination of inner, subjective nature, not only to modern economy and technology.

In Germany's period of optimistic reform in the late 1960s and the 1970s Horkheimer and Adorno's insight fell on barren ground. Today it has become increasingly clear how problematic the exaggerated expectation of a pedagogically led process of human emancipation actually was. With a sharper insight into the deep ambivalence characterizing the modern process of emancipation, however, Adorno—widely apostrophized as an "eternal naysayer"—gains a new, unexpected contemporary relevance (Pongratz 1986, 1989). His provocative thesis, formulated in connection with the work of Freud, that barbarism is already anchored in the civilizing process itself, gains in plausibility given modernity's far-reaching self-blockages. The question that was central to the *Dialectic of Enlightenment,* why it is that humanity, "instead of entering into a truly human condition, is sinking into a new kind of barbarism" (Adorno and Horkheimer 1979, xi) strikes more than ever at the heart of the social condition of the present.

German pedagogy's intellectual engagement with critical theory initially passed its founders by, and was essentially mediated by (perhaps, even, peculiarly restricted to) Jürgen Habermas. In the 1960s and 1970s his work, more than that of any other theorist of the Frankfurt School, stood at the center of interest. His support for emancipatory reason suited the numerous reform-oriented pedagogues. Habermas, however, expected more from rationalism and reflection than Adorno. The history of the modern process of enlightenment is not only the history of the universalization of rationality, but also of increasing societal domination. Horkheimer and Adorno gave this particular emphasis in the *Dialectic of Enlightenment*. Not surprisingly, critical educational theory in its initial reception phase largely refused to engage with this work.

> This would not have been possible without a destabilisation of its own self-understanding. The critique of the civilizing process articulated by Horkheimer and Adorno is linked to a no less radical critique of individual socialization processes. The civilizing process in general and the individual socialization process in particular underlie in the same way the dialectic of subjectification and reification. This has become a central theme in contemporary social science. (Wulf and Wagner 1987, 30)

It remains for critical educational theory to address this insecurity. Horkheimer and Adorno anticipated in the *Dialectic of Enlightenment* that enlightenment forfeits its power of illumination, that reason loses its inner telos and deteriorates into the dumb machinery of mind, and that advancing mastery of nature expresses itself as advanced natural decay. Today this engenders a new pedagogic reflection on the subtle forms of the subjugation of human nature (Pongratz 1987, 1995).

DOMINATION OF HUMAN NATURE—PEDAGOGIC ASPECTS OF THE DIALECTIC OF ENLIGHTENMENT

Adorno's pedagogic reception in Germany essentially took place via a small number of essays. "Education after Auschwitz" (1998) is the most frequently cited. His claim that Auschwitz has posed a central demand for all education—that Auschwitz never be repeated—has encouraged the search for the backgrounds to the modern holocaust. The insightful demand that Auschwitz never be repeated motivates a more detailed look at why Auschwitz happened at all, and why atrocious industrialized death continues.

For Horkheimer and Adorno, the history of the European bourgeois civilizing process became manifest in Auschwitz. Auschwitz was possible because in the realm of traditional culture as well as in the material life process, society, through its own historical development, had made impossible that which according to Horkheimer and Adorno was alone capable of resisting Auschwitz—namely, autonomy.

Instead of seeing twentieth-century fascism as a simple mistake of an otherwise untarnished historical progression toward constant improvement, they studied it in terms of the subterranean, "underground" processes (Adorno and Horkheimer 1979, 231) in which "reason itself reveals itself as unreason" (Horkheimer 1970). Accounts are thereby settled with the Western European emancipation process. Expansion of the playing fields of subjective autonomy is ultimately paid for with a never-ending history of repressed, degenerated passions, a dumb embodiment robbed of its own speech, and the growing suppression of inner nature. In contrast to "official history," the *Dialectic of Enlightenment* assumes the ethnographer's stance. It views modernity with methodical surprised estrangement (much as Foucault did later, in his own way). As long as one remains within the framework of the process of enlightenment, its unavoidable costs remain hidden.

In the advanced industrial nations, collective repression of the "dark side" of the process of enlightenment seems to have begun to exhaust itself only in the 1980s. It is increasingly impossible to sidestep the alarming results of advancing natural exploitation and environmental destruction, or the absurdity of technological development alongside the simultaneous wastage of human resources. The apocalyptic accusations of the *Dialectic of Enlightenment* resound in contemporary debates around modernity and postmodernity. Yet, the pessimism running through the darkest pages of the *Dialectic of Enlightenment* and echoed again today derives not only from the horrors of the real world. It is simultaneously the "expression of a profound disappointment, the inevitable reverse side of the all-too confident rational utopias which characterized early modernity" (Hesse 1984, 9).

To understand why the project of modernity went awry from the very beginning, Adorno and Horkheimer (1979, 54) sought to expose the "prehistory of subjectivity." They reconstruct the origins of modern rationality (231), arguing that the original constitution of a resilient, self-supporting ego resulted from the dissolution of a sympathetic (and murderous) fused relationship with Nature. Civilizatory rationality arises from the hard-won and fiercely defended distinction of the subject from its life circumstances. Subjects distance themselves from surrounding objects to better master them. Calculative rationality organizes its relationship to the world around maximizing control. Its perspective is thoroughly contained; its object is universality. Civilization's reason is formed as "the organ of calculation, of planning, indifferent to ends, its element is coordination" (Adorno and Horkheimer 1979, 88, translation modified).

Human beings pay for their incontrovertible gain in power, however, "with alienation from that over which they exercise their power over" (Adorno and Horkheimer 1979, 9). Things lose their color, their playful multiplicity, their surprising peculiarities. Their nature "as a substratum of domination is revealed as always the same. This identity constitutes the unity of nature" (9). The rational subject cannot stop itself from permanently shoring up its "unity" and at the same time constantly putting itself in "brackets" in relation to the rest of the world. These brackets become the cage of the subject's self-mastery. Constantly haunted by anxiety about losing their self, subjects always have to demonstrate to themselves that they are "keeping up."

All identity established within the civilizing process thus contains traces of compulsory renunciation: "Human beings had to do fearful things to themselves before the self—the identical, instrumental, and masculine nature of humans—was formed, and some part of that is repeated in every childhood" (Adorno and Horkheimer 1979, 33, translation modified). For Horkheimer and Adorno, then, the history of civilization can be read as a the history of the inversion of sacrifice. Beneath "official" history, which misunderstands itself as a history of liberation, there is a history of the repressed "shadows" of reason, the split-off drives and passions, the abstractions from the body. The self constructs itself around a certain clarity which excludes everything material, spontaneous, embodied, pushing it to the fringe zones. Ultimately the subject becomes unrecognizable to parts of itself.

"Mastery of nature is chained to the introjected violence of humans over humans, to the violence of the subject exercised upon its own nature" (Habermas 1983, 101). And this chain of the subject's self-discipline cannot—paradoxically—be cut loose from the search for freedom. This contradictoriness does not touch pedagogy only at its edges. Since the eighteenth century, pedagogy in Germany has played a growing and vital role in the process of modernity, constituting the "core elements" of modernity (rationality, subjectivity, identity, and self-mastery).

Currently, with the crisis of modernity particularly in consciousness, pedagogy has come under considerable legitimation pressure. Polarizations characterizing the field of pedagogy are organized around three typical tensions representing the modern enlightenment process in its pedagogic turn: imagination—reason; embodiment—abstraction; sensuousness—stereopathy of experience.

Imagination and Reason

A long tradition in German pedagogy of protest against a rationalistic–instrumental approach to understanding reality can be discerned in the pedagogic discourse of romanticism and in German reform pedagogy of the early twentieth century. What is sought here is a preservation of the child's soul, nature, and genius. Appeal is made to an authenticity seen as having been wrested from the process of modernity. Most recent works on topics like creativity, spontaneity, and play in the socialization process reside in this tradition. Criticisms are made against the sterility of children's fantasy, the disappearance of productive imagination in favor of muddled fantasy, the handicapping of the imagination. In their place are offered an atmosphere of relaxed spontaneity, the informal "ambience" of the social group process, the "sense of possibility," which is meant to be released by creativity techniques, brainstorming, and so on. All this aims at freeing up the blocked imagination, to correct the relationship between imagination and reason. This, however, seems a pious hope that fails to grasp pedagogically the depth of the problem.

Embodiment and Abstraction

Numerous works address pedagogical dilemmas and problems arising in the process of modernity through its increasing abstraction from the body in the interests of its "civilization." These include the mechanization, formalization, and disciplining of the body. There exists a counterdiscourse that seeks to mobilize other experiences and desires, aiming at intensive encounters and bodily experience. This pedagogic goal of the "return of the body" is also questionable.

Sensuousness and Stereopathy of Experience

The "disappearance of the senses," the "destruction of sensuousness," the lack of a sense for the unmediated are subjects of numerous studies (particularly of "everyday life"). Orientation toward "experience" has correspondingly become a pegagogic formula. It characterizes the learning processes capable of resisting the logic of abstraction and subsumption, in order to return to "the thing itself," and revive a sophisticated conception of the experiential process.

Such attempts to activate an original experiential potential generally orient themselves around what Foucault has analyzed as the "repression hypothesis" (Foucault 1980). Beneath disturbed or destroyed sensuousness, a "human potential," a subjective factor, waits for liberation to resist modernity's processes of abstraction.

PEDAGOGY AS TRANSGRESSION—AESTHETIC ASPECTS OF CRITICAL EDUCATIONAL THEORY

These three endeavors (reinvigorating the imagination, return of the body, reawakening sensuousness) labor under a basic misapprehension. They conceive their theoretical and practical critique of the process of enlightenment as a backward movement and an attempt to step outside modernity. This backward look invests hope in some sort of ancient, prehistorical "exterior." Retreat to the prerational, to reason's excluded and "Other" certainly tries to expose rationality as modernity's unacknowledged fetishism. But it equally runs the danger of sliding into irrationality, revoking reason, to the extent that it revives a new form of *Ursprungsdenken*.

Besides the insight into the contradictions of the enlightenment process, contemporary pedagogy can acquire from Horkheimer and Adorno a skepticism about the idea that these contradictions can be somehow "resolved" with good will and pedagogic skill. We first need to establish

- whether the "blocked" imagination we are supposed to release has not been damaged in the process of being split off, such that its "liberatory potential" might no longer exist and be merely a fiction;
- whether the "return of the body" rests on a questionable myth of the "natural body" existing beneath its alienation, awaiting liberation; and
- whether sensuousness is not being regarded as a quasinatural potential that has only emerged historically as a product of assemblages of power.

The point at issue is the theoretical value of concepts like imagination, embodiment, or sensuousness as the foundations of a critique of modernity. This discussion has generated an "aesthetic turn" in the critical educational theory of the 1990s (Mollenhauer 1986, 1995).

The aesthetic dimension of pedagogic theory and practice did not receive undivided support. It did implicitly offer the opportunity for a radical change of perspective. Unlike critiques of modernity that argued in terms of withdrawing from modernity, an alternative emerged, which was to transcend modernity's horizon of reflection, in the sense of taking Enlightenment intentions at their word. This perspective aims at opening up the new, unfamiliar, unheard, and unsaid that spring from breaches in modernity's erosion process. They open up a transcending movement of reflection that subjects the Enlightenment itself to enlightenment critique.

Every attempt to grasp what is new in our social situation and to make it productive compels the critic to self-critique. Sociologically this inversion has been thematized in terms of "reflexive modernisation" (Beck 1992; Beck, Giddens, and Lash 1994). Enlightenment, says the critic of Enlightenment, does not simply mean blind reproduction of social relations of force, but also their negation via their own means.

Such critique of enlightenment aims at a responsive reflexion and a reflexive responsiveness that tries to open up violence-free routes for those regarded as different, excluded, and alien. Its criterion for truth no longer finds this form of thought in an identificatory approach which overwhelms the object to contain it within the idea. It concentrates more on collecting concepts around the thing they refer to, so that they can appear within a constellation, for only then does the gaze open up "something" which does arise from the concept itself. Benjamin (1977) and Adorno (1973, 1999) have provided an exemplary expression of this type of "thinking in constellations." They show the extent to which thought constellations correspond with forms of aesthetic design. "Thinking in constellations" essentially links art and critical thought.

All art, when it succeeds, places the given within constellations so that "more" becomes visible. This "more" is neither fictional appearance nor bare factuality. It is more a "rip" in the tissue of dominant reality, an "astonished glance" at the world which reveals its injuries and stiffnesses, producing what is still becoming. Art enables, like all critical thought, the reading of "things in being . . . as a text of their becoming" (Adorno 1973, 53).

The thematizing of pedagogy's aesthetic dimension in the 1990s has often been characterized as a privatizing retreat and depoliticization of critical educational theory. Such interpretations are, however, based on a consequential misinterpretation of art nourished by the contemporary culture industry. It may be that art is ineffectual and toothless as long as it remains contained within the reserves of art galleries and museums. However, the moment that aesthetic productions seek their expression in social contexts—such as Jenny Holzer's "Images of Disruption" (Holzer and Waldman 1990)—irritations come into play which cut across the apparent normativity of actuality. Art in public, urban contexts is political in a very fundamental sense. In a pedagogic sense this means that the sharpening of the political content of pedagogic theory runs these days in ways which include the unfolding of its political–aesthetic dimension (Leyh 1999).

Seen in this way, engagement with aesthetic theory appears neither as an unrealistic detour nor as a dead end. It is more the case that it makes recognizable the potential critical theory has for current pedagogic discourse. The question of political–aesthetic education makes it possible to draw out crucial core elements of critical educational theory. Critical pedagogy is based on its power of distinction, the capacity to make visible differences and ruptures, and the ability to perceive more in phenomena than the pure identity of concept and object allows for. It follows an innovative movement toward transcending existing social relationships.

If we are to redefine the role of educators against this background, the most appropriate description is that expressed by Paulo Freire (1981): "The pedagogue is both politician and artist." Certainly, the model of the technical "constructor of learning worlds," the concept of economically efficient "managers," and the image of the disillusioned "player" are woefully inadequate.

REFERENCES

Adorno, Theodor W. 1973. *Negative dialectics*. London: Routledge & Kegan Paul.
———. 1998. Education after Auschwitz. In *Critical models: Interventions and catchwords*. New York: Columbia University Press.
———. 1999. *Aesthetic theory*. London: Athlone.
Adorno, Theodor W., and Max Horkheimer. 1979. *Dialectic of enlightenment*. London: Verso.
Beck, Ulrich. 1992. *Risk society*. London: Sage.
Beck, Ulrich, Anthony Giddens, and Scott Lash. 1994. *Reflexive modernisation*. Cambridge: Polity.
Benjamin, Walter. 1977. *The origin of German tragic drama*. London: NLB.
Blankertz, H. 1979. Kritische Erziehungswissenschaft. In *Erziehungswissenschaft der Ggegenwart*, ed. K. Schaller. Bochum, Ger.: Kamp.
Dubiel, Helmut. 1988. *Kritische Theorie der Gesellschaft: Eine einführende Rekonstruktion von den Anfängen im Horkheimer-Kreis bis Habermas*. Weinheim/München, Ger.: Juventa.
Foucault, Michel. 1980. *History of sexuality*. Vol. 1, *An introduction*. New York: Vintage/Random House.
Freire, Paulo. 1981. *Der Lehrer ist Politiker und Künstler*. Reinbek, Ger.: Rowohlt.
Habermas, Jürgen. 1983. Theodor Adorno: The primal history of subjectivity self-affirmation gone wild. In *Philosophical-political profiles*, 99–109. Cambridge, Mass.: MIT Press.

Held, David. 1980. *Introduction to critical theory: Horkheimer to Habermas*. London: Hutchinson.

Hesse, Heidrun. 1984. *Vernunft und Selbstbehauptung*. Frankfurt: Fischer.

Heydorn, Heinz Joahim. 1970. *Über den Widerspruch von Bildung und Herrschaft*. Frankfurt: EVA.

———. 1972. *Zu einer Neufassung des Bildungsbegriffs*. Frankfurt/M: Suhrkamp.

Holzer, Jenny, and D. Waldman. 1990. *Protect me from what I want*. New York: Guggenheim Museum.

Horkheimer, Max. 1970. *Vernunft und Selbsterhaltung*. Frankfurt/M: Fischer.

Jay, Martin. 1973. *The dialectical imagination: A history of the Frankfurt school and the institute for social research, 1923–1950*. Boston: Little, Brown.

Keckeisen, Wolfgang. 1983. Stichwort Kritische Erziehungswissenschaft. In *Enzyklopädie Erziehungswissenschaft*, vol. 1, ed. D. Lenzen. Stuttgart: Klett-Cotta.

Kellner, Douglas. 1989. *Critical theory, Marxism and modernity*. Cambridge, Engl.: Polity.

Klafki, Wolfgang. 1976. *Aspekte kritisch-konstruktiver Erziehungswissenschaft*. Weinheim/Basel: Beltz.

Leyh, Anette. 1999. Ästhetische Konstellationen—Umrisse einer Konzeption politisch-ästhetischer Bildung. In *Politik, Disziplin und Profession in der Erwachsenenbildung*, ed. K. Derichs-Kunstmann, P. Faulstich, and J. Wittpoth. Frankfurt/M: DIE.

Mollenhauer, Klaus. 1968. *Erziehung und Emanzipation*. München: Juventa.

———. 1986. *Umwege: Über Bildung, Kunst und Interaktion*. Weinheim/München: Juventa.

———. 1995. *Grundfragen ästhetischer Bildung*. Weinheim/München: Juventa.

Pongratz, L. A. 1986. *Bildung und Subjektivität. Historisch-systematische Studien zur Theorie der Bildung*. Weinheim: DSV.

———. 1987. Bildungstheorie im Prozess der Moderne—Perspektiven einer theoriege-schichtlichen Dekonstruktion. *Bildungsforschung und Bildungspraxis* 3:244–62.

———. 1989. *Pädagogik im Prozess der Moderne. Studien zur sozial—und Theoriegeschichte der Schule*. Weinheim: DSV.

———. 1995. Freiheit und Zwang—Schulische Strafformen im Wandel. *Die deutsche Schule* 2: 183–95.

Slater, Phil. 1977. *Origin and significance of the Frankfurt school*. London: Routledge and Kegan Paul.

Türcke, C., and G. Bolte. 1994. *Einführung in die kritische Theorie*. Darmstadt, Ger.: Wiss. Buchgesellschaft.

van Reijen, W. 1984. *Philosophie als Kritik. Einführung in die kritische Theorie*. Königstein, Ger.: Athenäum.

Wiggershaus, R. 1994. *The Frankfurt school: Its history, theories, and political significance*. Cambridge, Mass.: MIT Press.

Wulf, C., and H J. Wagner. 1987. Lebendige Erfahrung und Nicht-Identität. Die Aktualität Adornos für eine kritische Erziehungswissenschaft. In *Kritische Theorie und Pädagogik der Gegenwart*, ed. F. Paffrath. Weinheim, Ger.: DSV.

10

Education for Radical Humanization in Neoliberal Times: A Review of Paulo Freire's Later Work

Peter Mayo

With the posthumous publication of a number of his last writings, Paulo Freire's oeuvre is almost complete. It therefore seems to be an appropriate time to take stock of Freire's later work, to indicate, among other things, the light it sheds on the evolution of his thought and its significance in an age in which cynicism is rife. It seems to have become unfashionable, in this age, to dream of a world that is different from and better than the current one. Remaining steadfast, till the very end, to his cherished principles of radical humanization and democracy, Freire continued to produce work that provides resources of hope, agency, and reinvigoration in these neoliberal times. To many of us cultural workers, engaged in a constant search for emancipatory possibilities, his work stands as a crag of sanity facing the contemporary tide of nihilistic madness.

FACTORS INFLUENCING LATER WORK

The fatalism brought about by neoliberalism is one of several factors that influenced Freire's later output in what is a very large oeuvre. As his widow, Nita Freire, told Carmel Borg and me in an interview at her São Paulo residence, one year after Freire's death: "He was concerned with the number of persons who let themselves be deceived by neoliberal slogans and so become submissive and apathetic when confronted with their former dreams. Paulo used a metaphor for this situation: 'They have gone to the other side of the river!'" (Nita Freire, in Borg and Mayo 2000, 109).[1]

There were, of course, other important factors that influenced his later work. These include his involvement as founding member of the Partido dos Trabalhadores (PT; Workers' Party) in Brazil and his work as education secretary in São

Paulo after the party won the municipal elections there. One other important factor was the emergence of important social movements in Brazil, especially the Movimento dos Trabalhadores Rurais Sem Terra (Movement of Rural Workers without Land; the abbreviated title is Movimento dos Sem Terra [MST; Movement of Landless Peasants]). This is arguably one of the two most vibrant movements in Latin America, the Frente Zapatista in Chiapas being the other. The MST allies political activism and mobilization with important cultural work, including highly inspiring music and poetry.[2] As in the period that preceded the infamous 1964 coup, Freire's work and thinking must also have been influenced and reinvigorated by the growing movement for democratization of Brazilian society. Only a few days before his death, he stood enthralled at the huge MST march into Brasilia (Borg and Mayo 2000, 109). There was also his marriage, following a period of desolation caused by the death of his beloved Elza, to Dr. Ana Maria (Nita) Araújo Freire, his former student, a fellow academic, and daughter of Paulo's teacher. Like Elza, Nita contributed to his output. An accomplished scholar in her own right, she often provided important editorial work, in the form of detailed and illuminating annotations, besides writing prefaces to a number of works by or on Freire (see, for example, Allman et al. 1998; Freire 2000; McLaren 2000). Nita's annotations contribute to the reader's (particularly the non-Brazilian reader's) understanding of the contexts that gave rise to the ideas in question. The later period of Freire's life also included collaborative projects with international scholars and activists, especially key figures in the North American critical pedagogy movement.

The Watershed

It is very difficult and arbitrary to establish a cutoff point to indicate the later period of Paulo Freire's works. There are those who would argue that, as far as his English texts go, the *Politics of Education*, ably translated by Donaldo Macedo (Freire 1985), and the conversational text with Ira Shor (Shor and Freire 1987), represent a watershed. Ideas that were implicit in his early work, including his most celebrated work, were revisited and developed further in these books (see Allman et al. 1998, 9). One of these two books (Freire 1985) is a compendium of old and new pieces. It includes, for instance, the early "Adult Literacy Process as Cultural Action for Freedom" alongside a highly illuminating conversation with Donaldo Macedo. For heuristic purposes, I shall concentrate, in the rest of this essay, on works published in the final seven years of Paulo's life. These are works published in the 1990s. Of course, there will be passing references to and quotes from earlier works, since many of the ideas recur throughout Paulo's writings.

THE 1990s

The work of the 1990s starts off with a continuation of his "talking books" series. The first book, edited by Brenda Bell, John Gaventa, and John Peters, involves a conversation between Freire and one of North America's much respected radical educators, Myles Horton of the Highlander Folk School (Horton and Freire 1990). This is followed by the book marking the period in which Paulo Freire served as education secretary in São Paulo during Mayor Luiza Erundina de Souza's term of office. The book is aptly titled *Pedagogy of the City* (Freire 1993) and includes interviews and a fine postscript by his close collaborator, Ana Maria Saul. His work as education secretary was also documented in other places, including a taped 1991 AERA session in Chicago, studies by Ana Maria Saul, Carlos Alberto Torres, Pia Wong, Maria del Pilar O'Cadiz, and Moacir Gadotti (see Gadotti 1994; O'Cadiz et al. 1997; Torres 1994, 1995) and essays by Freire published in a variety of works (Freire 1998b, 1999). These were followed by the largely autobiographical *Pedagogy of Hope* (1994) and *Letters to Cristina* (1996), both providing the reader with an expanded and often detailed knowledge of the concrete contextual background concerning the genesis and development of his ideas. These expositions of the context, in which Freire's work was immersed, bring to the fore the various personalities and movements that played or are still playing an important role in the larger struggle for the democratization of Brazilian society. We learn of the group of Brazilian exiles in Chile and their Chilean counterparts who engaged in discussions that were central to the development of *Pedagogy of the Oppressed*, namely, Plinio Sampaio, Paulo de Tarso Santos, Marcela Gajardo, and Ernani Fiori (Freire 1994, 62). We learn of Paulo's childhood dreams and nightmares, about the stark reality of oppression, and not just the pain of exile but also the brutality and bestiality of torture. We learn of the publication of such key works as *Brasil Nunca Mais* (Brazil Never Again), published after Argentina's *Nunca Mas*[3]—a strong reminder of the coercive, apart from the ideological/consensual, basis of power. We learn of the courage of such radical ecclesiastics as the inspirational Paulo Evaristo Arns, incidentally the person who, following the *abertura*, visited Freire in Geneva to persuade him to return to his homeland.[4] *Brasil Nunca Mais* was prepared under the auspices of Cardinal Arns.[5] This is an account of the horrors of torture by the military regime, details of which are provided by Nita Freire in an extensive footnote in *Letters to Cristina* (Freire 1996). We also hear about the courageous activism of other key figures such as the Nobel prize nominee, Betinho (Herbert Jose de Souza) who died the same year as Paulo (see Martin 1998). He started a very important social movement in Brazil, the Movement of Citizens Action against Hunger and Misery and for Life (Araújo Freire, in Freire 1996, 247). To these one can add the lay Dominican popular educator, journalist, activist Carlos Alberto Libanio Christo, better known as Frei Betto. He is the coauthor with Freire (and Ricardo Kotscho) of a splendid conversational book in the mid-1980s, which, in my view (I read the Italian version), deserves to be translated into English (Freire and Betto 1985; or Betto and Freire 1986). These figures and many others convey to us the sense of a large movement for democratization in Brazil, of which Paulo Freire was just one, albeit key, representative.

Around the same time as *Pedagogy of Hope*, State University of New York Press published a book-length exchange between Paulo Freire and a group of scholars from the National Autonomous University of Mexico (Escobar et al. 1994). This is a most interesting work focusing on a variety of topics, including, as the title suggests, the role of institutions of higher education. A related issue is that concerning the role of intellectuals operating as cultural workers in both the academic and public spheres. In between these two 1994 books and *Letters to Cristina*, we saw the publication of such books or booklets as *Paulo Freire at the Institute* (de Figueiredo-Cowen and Gastaldo 1995) and *Education and Social Change in Latin America* (edited by Carlos Alberto Torres 1995) ,which included pieces (interviews, talks, responses to discussants) by Freire. Significant papers were also produced, such as an exchange with Carlos Alberto Torres in a book on Freire edited by Peter McLaren and Colin Lankshear (1994) and exchanges with Donaldo Macedo, in McLaren and Leonard (see Freire and Macedo 1993), *Harvard Educational Review* (see Freire and Macedo 1995), and most recently Steiner and colleagues (see Freire and Macedo 2000). I would also refer, for good measure, to an interview with Carlos Alberto Torres in a book dealing with biographies of leading, predominantly North American, academics (Torres 1998). Around the time of his death, we saw the publication of *Pedagogy of the Heart*. Later, *Teachers as Cultural Workers: Letters to Those Who Dare Teach* (1998a) and *Pedagogy of Freedom* (1998b) were published. The latter is the English version of the much-acclaimed *Pedagogia da Autonomia: Saberes necessários à prática educativa*. We await the publication of *Ideology Matters* (with Donaldo Macedo).

HOW MUCH IS LOST IN TRANSLATION?

All of the books mentioned are in the English language, often translations of works originally written by Paulo in Portuguese. Those who read his works in English must keep in mind that this is only a part, albeit a substantial one, of Freire's later output. Some still await translation. We also have to ask ourselves an important question: how much is lost in translation? Carmel Borg and I posed the question, in an interview, to Paulo's widow, Nita. She replied unequivocally that those who read Paulo only in translation miss much of the beauty and emotional resonance of his work.

> He used words of such beauty and plasticity, organized in phrases and these in turn in the context of the totality of the text, with such aesthetic and political force that, I repeat, they cannot be transposed so easily into other languages because a language cannot be translated literally. And it is important to emphasize that his language is extraordinarily beautiful, rich, and full of his particular way of being. . . . Another problem for translators who did not know Paulo well is the fact that his language is loaded with his feelings, since he never provided a dichotomy between reason and emotion. Paulo was a radically coherent man: what he said contained what he felt and thought, and this is not always easy to translate. There are emotions whose meaning can only be well perceived, understood, and felt inside a certain culture. And we Brazilians are unique in this way. I think this is so, isn't it? Without

any prejudice, I think it is difficult for translators who have only studied the Portuguese language, albeit accurately, to express Paulo in all his aesthetic and even cultural-ideological richness. (Nita Freire, in Borg and Mayo 2000, 110–11)

The emphasis on Freire's constant fusion between reason and emotion ought to be noted. Many of us experience this sense of an absolute fusion between the two human elements even when reading Freire in translation. I had stated, a year before our interview with Nita in São Paulo, that Freire has communicated with me both at an intellectual and emotional level (Mayo 1997a, 121; 1997b, 369).[6] One can imagine how great our sense of this fusion would be if we read Paulo in the beautiful Brazilian variant of Portuguese. And yet I have come across a few North American feminists who refer to the "separation between reason and emotion" as one of the problematic polarities in Freire's work. There are those who would argue that his work promotes the rational to the exclusion of other domains of experience and knowing. One wonders whether they would hold the same opinion were they to read him in the original.

WHAT IS NEW IN FREIRE'S LATER WORKS?

I would argue that, in his later work, Freire stresses and elaborates on points that were already present in his early work. In a collaborative piece (Allman et al. 1998), it was argued that "these positions were also revised in the light of the new experiences of oppression and emancipation to which he was exposed in the later years of a highly eventful life as educator, activist, consultant to revolutionary governments (Guinea Bissau, Nicaragua, Grenada) and ultimately educational policy maker and administrator. His life was lived across different borders and different geographical contexts" (9). Very few, if any, of his later works have that "unity of dialectical thought and style" (10), which remains the distinctive feature of *Pedagogy of the Oppressed*. This having been said, it would be foolish to attempt to do justice to Freire's work and ideas by referring only to this celebrated piece. Freire was, like most critical intellectuals, a "person in process" constantly in search of greater coherence.

He has offered us ideas and conceptual tools that constantly warrant further elaboration, in view of the new experiences and challenges encountered across different borders. These experiences and challenges shed new light on Freire's concepts. Some elements, which are considered to be central to the Freirean concept of "authentic dialogue," are revisited and given expanded treatment in later works. Take the basic concept of "listening." To engage in dialogue, educators must stop suffering from "narration sickness" and become "listeners." This, we would assume, is basic to a Freirean conception of teaching. For how can one engage in genuine dialogue without being able to listen, to resist the urge to speak (as Freire puts it)? Otherwise, one would be simply talking past the other. And yet, I would still find refreshing Freire's and Nita's illuminating reflections on the notion of "listening," in *Pedagogy of Freedom* and *Convergence* (Araújo Freire 1998, 4, 5) respectively:

Listening is an activity that obviously goes beyond mere hearing. To listen, in the context of our discussion here, is a permanent attitude on the part of the subject who is listening, of being open to the word of the other, to the gesture of the other, to the differences of the other. This does not mean, of course, that listening demands that the listener be "reduced" to the other, the speaker. This would not be listening. It would be self-annihilation. (Freire 1998a, 107)

Works like *Pedagogy of Freedom* abound with reflections on some of those concepts or themes, which recur throughout Paulo's oeuvre, including "methodological rigor," "praxis" ("critical reflection on practice"), "respect for what students know," "risk," "autonomy and dignity," and "agency" (this is based on the "conviction that change is possible" and the notion that we are conditioned but not determined beings). One finds new meanings, experiences new sensations, and discovers new sources of inspiration each time one rereads a piece of good poetry. Likewise, one discovers new sensations, new meanings, and fresh sources of inspiration when being led by Freire himself and Nita to revisit some of the basic concepts in the Freirean pedagogical approach.

One cannot help being struck by the emotional impact of the following evocative account by Nita, again focusing on the basic concept of listening. Like Paulo, Nita captures the tactility of the experience involved, fusing reason with emotion. And here we experience this only in translation!

Paulo's act of touching while looking at people made the act of touching, an act so natural in our Brazilian culture, more than body to body contact. Touching with his hand and with his look, Paulo somehow connected his whole being, his reason and emotion, to the whole being of another. . . . His ability to listen, not just to hear the other person, but that way of listening mentioned in the *Pedagogy of Autonomy* [*Pedagogy of Freedom*—author's insertion]—also noticeable in his look signalled the moment when he accepted and gathered within himself what he was hearing from the other. . . . In Paulo, to touch, to look, and to listen become moments of *me and you in dialogue* about something which he and the other person wanted to know. (Araújo Freire 1998, 4, 5)

Similar basic concepts are resorted to, elaborated on, and refined not just by Paulo and Nita but also by many cultural workers and researchers who draw on Freire when grappling with a variety of phenomena. The idea of praxis and of "reading the word and the world" is taken up by others within the context of, say, "redemptive memory" (see McLaren and Tadeuz Da Silva 1993; Mayo 1999, 147–51). In this context, the codification is the means to recuperate collective histories. After all, the collective process of praxis involved within a cultural circle entails a critical engagement with historically accumulated concepts and practices (Mayo 1996, 156; 1999, 147).[7] And the same applies to many others who, like Freire, resort to these concepts to *reinvent* them within such areas as cultural studies, community theatre, feminist and antiracist pedagogy, anticolonial or postcolonial pedagogy (in a variety of different sites), gay/lesbian studies, critical multicultural pedagogy, and even such unlikely areas as museum studies (this involves the quest to transform traditionally colonizing spaces into decolonizing ones). The list is by no means exhaustive.

Furthermore, the explications and reformulations of positions already present in his early work were probably rendered necessary because of the constant misappropriations of his ideas. Misconceptions concerning Freire abound, the sort of misconceptions that irked Paulo Freire and led him, after 1987, to stop using such terms as *conscientização*. He claims to have used it, for the last time, in a Geneva seminar with Ivan Illich (Freire, in Escobar et al. 1994, 46). He thought the term had been bandied about freely and loosely. As a result, it gradually lost its significance (Freire 1993, 110; Freire, quoted in Escobar et al. 1994, 46).

The assumed nondirectiveness of a genuinely democratic education is another misconception that was strongly refuted by Freire. His insistence on the directiveness of education is, in fact, a recurring theme in his later works (see, for instance, Freire, in Freire and Macedo 1995, 394). It was already emphasized in works published in the mid- and later 1980s, *The Politics of Education* (1985) and the conversational book with Ira Shor, *Pedagogy for Liberation: Dialogues on Transforming Education* (1987), being cases in point. The idea that a nonneutral education has, perforce, to be directive was, however, already implied in his earlier work, most notably his much celebrated *Pedagogy of the Oppressed*. What later works do is explicate this position further, also in view of many criticisms leveled at Freire's work, often based on a misconception of his position in this regard. Take Frank Youngman (1986) as an example. In an otherwise masterly contribution to the historical materialist literature in adult education,[8] Youngman provides a critique of Freire's pedagogy that is analyzed within the context of its potential suitability or otherwise for a socialist pedagogy. In my view, he seemed bent on lopping off the feet that would not fit his Procrustean bed (a set of abstracted concepts for a Marxist education). He maintains that Freire is "ambivalent about saying outright that educators can have a theoretical understanding superior to that of the learners" (179). Freire might not have said this outright in his early work but this is certainly implied in his contention that education is not neutral and that educators/activists must ask themselves on whose side are they when they teach/act. Furthermore, in books published around the same time that Youngman's work saw the light, Freire wrote explicitly that educator and learner are not on an equal footing: "Obviously we also have to underscore that while we recognise that we have to learn from our students . . . this does not mean that teachers and students are the same. I don't think so. That is, there is a difference between the educator and the student. This is a general difference. This is usually also a difference of generations" (Freire 1985, 177). Shortly after, he would tell Ira Shor: "At the moment the teacher begins the dialogue, he or she knows a great deal, first in terms of knowledge and second in terms of the horizon that he or she wants to get to" (Freire, in Shor and Freire 1987, 103).

These writings seem to have been overlooked in a number of studies on Freire. Paul V. Taylor's book-length study on Freire's texts is a case in point (Taylor 1993). Had he been familiar with these works, Taylor would probably have refrained from including the following statement (see Mayo 1993, 283) in his otherwise in-depth and insightful analysis of Freire's decodification process:

"The most obvious (contradiction) is the overtly directive manner of the teaching. There is no hint here of a learning partnership, of a dialogue between equals. Rather, what is evident is the clear distinction between the teacher and the taught" (Taylor 1993, 129). What we are presented with here is yet another formulation based on the common misconception that Freirean pedagogy is nondirective and involves a "dialogue among equals." And there is no mention of Freire's emphasis on directivity and the need to "teach" in another book-length analysis of Paulo Freire's work, that by John Elias (Elias 1994). If anything, the author reminds us, as a criticism of Freire, that there are "areas which entail careful teaching and even testing" (Elias 1994, 116). So these important misconceptions concerning the nature of Freirean pedagogy abound even in full, book-length studies on Freire. In my view, these studies deserve to be consulted, since they have their strengths.[9] However, for a more accurate and up-to-date explanation of Freire's pedagogical approach, one which does justice to Freire's actual thought, I would strongly recommend two books. One of them is an introductory study by Freire's companion, Moacir Gadotti (1994). The other is a comprehensive and in-depth study of Freire's work by the New Zealand scholar, Peter Roberts (2000). The authors of these two books engage holistically with Freire's work.[10]

One term that is dropped from the Freirean lexicon—it was probably used not by Freire but by commentators—is that of "facilitator." In an illuminating exchange with Macedo (Freire and Macedo 1995), Freire categorically refutes this term because of its connotation of laissez faire pedagogy. *Teacher* is the term used. This comes across quite strongly in his series of letters to teachers "who dare teach" (Freire 1998c). Teachers are presented as people who need to be competent, who teach when necessary, at times being 50 percent a traditional teacher (when circumstances warrant this—Freire, in Horton and Freire 1990, 160), and who require opportunities for ongoing teacher formation as well as professional recognition (which includes the provision of adequate pay).

This brings us to one important contribution that Freire's later work has made. The one book I would single out here is *Teachers as Cultural Workers: Letters to Those Who Dare Teach* (1998a). This is one of the finest books in English in Freire's later output, an output which, alas, is characterized by too much repetition (one gains the impression that, latterly, Freire produced one book too many). It is a pity that the book has been published only in hardcover. A paperback version would render the book more accessible and therefore an important source for prospective teachers undergoing preservice preparation as well as teachers currently in service. What this book places on the agenda is that there is no contradiction between a Freirean approach to an authentically dialogical education and the quest for professional recognition. By professional, Freire is not referring to the excesses of the "ideology of professionalism," based on the trait model of professionals, which often result in the following arrogant posture: I know what's best for you. Freire is using *profession* in the sense of people who are competent, both in terms of the subject matter taught and in terms of pedagogical disposition, and who engage in very important work that demands respect and adequate re-muneration. He obviously has in mind the plight of teachers in the Brazilian pub-lic school system. Freire worked hard as education secretary to improve the con-ditions of underpaid teachers in São Paulo during Mayor Erundina's tenure. For Freire, teachers were not to be regarded as coddling aunts or mothers, a position which can sound problematic in that it somehow smacks of a *machista* devalua-tion of what has often been termed a "feminized profession" (see Fischman 1999, 557, 558). Equally problematic is his reference to the fact that teaching proves at-tractive to women during the short period of their working life prior to marriage (Freire 1998c, 36). Unfortunately, Freire raises this issue without any engagement, on his part, in a critique of the normalizing discourse, regarding women's role in the family, generated by and supporting the existing patriarchal structures of eco-nomic oppression. This is, after all, a discourse that continues to limit women's involvement in the public domain since it continues to channel them, for the greater part of their working life, into the domestic sphere. In this so-called post-Fordist period, the domestic sphere also constitutes an important site for casual-ized work. It is therefore a normalizing discourse that limits women's chances of embarking on a career rather than simply a job.

Freire regarded teachers not as coddling figures but as people who are en-gaged in work that necessitates the delicate balancing between freedom and authority, to which an entire section is devoted in *Pedagogy of Freedom*. And this brings me to what strikes me as an important theme in Freire's later work—a point which, in my view, was implied in his early work but was rendered more pronounced in his later ones. The issue of *authority and freedom* is broached time and again in Freire's works (see, for example, Freire 1998a, 95–99; 1998c, 88). Indeed, such repetition is necessary. Witness Diana Coben's (1998) insistence on a fundamental "contradiction" in Freire's work where dia-logue and democratic social relations are preached while it is always the teacher who "holds the cards" (186).

What is the alternative to this? Laissez-faire pedagogy? This, as I have argued, is pedagogical treachery of the worst kind which often results in the violence meted out to learners by members of an "in-group" in possession of the required cultural capital allowing them to abuse a pseudo-dialogical process (Mayo, in McLaren and Mayo 1999, 402). Freire has been arguing, at least since his book with Shor, for an authentically dialogical process in which the teacher has authority, deriving from his or her competence, and the respect generated by this competence. "Teachers maintain a certain level of authority through the depth and breath of knowledge of the subject matter that they teach." (Freire, in Freire and Macedo 1995, 378). This however does not degenerate into authoritarianism (Freire, in Shor and Freire 1987, 91; Freire, in Horton and Freire 1990, 181; Freire 1994, 79).

The educator's "directivity" should not interfere, in Freire's view, with the "creative, formulative, investigative capacity of the educand," for, if this were to be the case, this directivity degenerates into "manipulation, into authoritarian-ism" (Freire 1994, 79). Stanley Aronowitz forcefully states, in his brilliant intro-ductory essay to *Pedagogy of Freedom*, that "the educator's task is to encourage human agency, not mold it in the manner of Pygmalion" (1998, 10). The position regarding "authority and freedom" has similarities with that expressed by Antonio Gramsci in his piece on the Unitarian School. In this piece, Gramsci calls for a balance to be struck between the kind of authority promoted by the old classical school (without the excess of degenerating into authoritarian education) and the freedom put forward by proponents of the Rousseau school. The latter school, for Gramsci, had to develop from its romantic phase (predicated on unbridled freedom for the learner, based on her or his spontaneity) and move into the classical phase, classical in the sense of striking a balance. This is the balance between freedom and authority (see Gadotti 1996, 53).

One of the themes that recurs throughout Freire's later work is the need for teachers to extend their work outside the sphere of the classroom, adult education setting, cultural circle, or university and to connect with what goes on in the "public sphere."

> In reality, when you work toward convincing the students, your effort is in relation to a political victory that takes place outside of the university. Your act of convincing seeks to obtain support for your greater dream, not simply to be a good professor. If you accept that your teachings do not go beyond the walls, in my opinion you are making a mistake, that of elitism. You will be a Marxist who only knows Marx through books and who restricts Marxism to the classroom, outside of which he [*sic*] claims to be only an academic. This is denying Marx and denying education itself. (Freire, in Escobar et al. 1994, 37)

It was important for Freire to engage with the system and not shy away from it for fear of co-optation (see, for instance, the discussions in Horton and Freire 1990 and Escobar et al. 1994 on this). Holding on to a conception that denotes strong Gramscian overtones, Freire did not regard the system as monolithic. On the contrary, it offered spaces for counterhegemony, for "swimming against the tide" (see Freire, quoted in Escobar et al. 1994, 31–32). Teachers and other social actors who see themselves as transformative intellectuals and cultural workers should, to use a popular Freire phrase, "be tactically inside and strategically outside" the system. Here the theme of social movements is given prominence (a recurring theme in most of, if not all, his books from the mid-1980s onward), attesting to Freire's recognition of the role of social movements as agents of change. The emergence of MST in Brazil and other movements elsewhere, including Europe, captured his imagination. He himself was part of, and indeed contributed to, a movement striving for an important process of change, of radicalization, within an important institution in Latin America and beyond—the church. Cardinal Arns told Carmel Borg and me, in São Paulo, something to the effect that Paulo changed not only people's lives but also the church.[11] Furthermore, Freire strove to bring social movements and state agencies together in São Paulo when education secretary there (see O'Cadiz et al. 1997).

The idea of a wide public sphere in which teachers must engage is in keeping with Freire's insistence that education should not be romanticized. Education does not change things on its own and should therefore not be attributed

powers it does not have (see Freire, in Shor and Freire 1987, 37). This contention by Freire should have put paid to the, by now, hackneyed criticism that
"conscientization" does not necessarily lead to change, a criticism that persisted
throughout the 1990s (e.g., Elias 1994).

Of course, the idea of educators working within the contexts of social movements has gained prominence in the literature on transformative education, most
particularly in the area of adult education (for a critical review of this, see Foley
1999, 135–38). In this literature, the discussion centers on a very non-Gramscian
use of the concept of "civil society." In his later work, however, Freire sought to
explore the links between movements and the State (Freire 1993) and, most significant, movements and party, a position no doubt influenced by his role as one
of the founding members of the PT. The latter is quite interesting given the criticism often leveled at social movement theorists, namely that they tend to ignore
the role of the party (see Holst 1999). In a position that echoes Raymond
Williams, Freire argues that the party for change, committed to the subaltern,
should allow itself to learn from and be transformed through contact with progressive social movements. It had "to reconnect with the general interest" (McIlroy 1993, 277), as John McIlroy puts it, with reference to Raymond Williams's
ideas in this regard. Williams was here referring not only to the party but to all
organizations traditionally associated with the working class.

One important proviso Freire makes, in this respect, is that the party should do
this "without trying to take them over." Movements, Freire seems to be saying,
cannot be subsumed by parties; otherwise they lose their identity and forfeit their
specific way of exerting pressure for change. In terms of the links between party
and movements, and with specific reference to the possible links between the PT
and such movements as MST, Paulo has this to say: "Today, if the Workers' Party
approaches the popular movements from which it was born, without trying to
take them over, the party will grow; if it turns away from the popular movements,
in my opinion, the party will wear down. Besides, those movements need to
make their struggle politically viable" (Freire, quoted in Escobar et al. 1994, 40).

Freire's later work and biographical elements help to elucidate themes that
have always been connected with his work. The major contribution here is that
of rendering the concepts more concrete. The theme of connecting with the
lifeworlds of the learners, the "concrete knowledge of the reality" of the community in question (Freire 1998a, 122) as the basis for genuine democratic
teaching, is a recurring one. "Educands'" concrete localization is the point of
departure for the knowledge they create of the world" (Freire 1994, 85). It is the
starting point, however, and not the be all and end all of the pedagogical encounter (84). In remaining there and not moving beyond (through coinvestiga-
tion of the object of inquiry), one would be engaging in "basism," the romanti-
cization (or "mythification") of the vernacular. We must start, however, by
connecting with the learners' "concrete context" (Freire 1998c, 78), including
the child's dreams (in the case of young learners) or possibly nightmares (Freire
repeats, throughout at least three of his last books, the response of a child from

the slums who states: I do not have dreams, only nightmares). To ignore this is "elitism" (Freire 1994, 84).

The central theme of praxis constitutes the leitmotif in Freire's later work (see the ninth letter in Freire 1998c, 75–85; see also, Freire 1998a, 44), as in all of his work. He regards exile as a form of praxis, in the sense of enabling Freire and others to gain critical distance from their native land, to view it in a critical light. This can lead to transformative action. This is a recurring theme in his later works (see Freire 1997a, 67–72). Perhaps one of the first instances is provided in his 1989 exchange with fellow Latin American exile, Antonio Faundez (Freire and Faundez 1989). There were many experiences to which Freire was exposed during exile, including his involvement with workers' education circles in Italy and Spain (see Freire 1994) as well as the postcolonial experiences in Portugal's former African colonies (see Freire 1978; Freire and Faundez 1989; Freire and Macedo 1987). This notwithstanding, exile meant for Freire a cruel severing from his Brazilian roots during the best years of his life, "when he was at the peak of his activist energies, intimately linked to a society roused for transformation" (Shor 1998, 78).

This brings the age factor into consideration. Of course, Freire raises the issue of "returning old" in *Pedagogy of the Heart* (Freire 1997a, 72), affirming how his return was a form of reinvigoration: "I was returning hopeful, motivated to relearn Brazil, to participate in the struggle for democracy" (Freire 1997a, 72). Given the "lost years," he had to feel young to be able to make the most, in terms of activism, of his remaining years. The more recent works are full of accounts of this later activism that was jolted by the loss of his beloved Elza in the fall of 1986 and possibly reinvigorated through his ten years of marriage to Nita. These are described as ten years of love and passion and are captured by Nita Freire in *Nita e Paulo: Cronicas di Amor,* recently published in English. The sense of "making up for one's lost years" is what runs through these later works that project the image of Freire as a role model for people in their Third Age: "As I write this at seventy-five, I continue to feel young, declining—not for vanity or fear of disclosing my age—the privilege senior citizens are entitled to, for example, at airports. . . . People are old or young much more as a function of how they think of the world, the availability they have for curiously giving themselves to knowledge" (Freire 1997a, 72).

Love and humility continue to remain recurring themes in his later work. He constantly exhorts teachers to engage in their work with humility, tolerance, and love (see Freire 1995b; 1998a, 65; 1998c, 39–41). Love was always a key feature of his work. It reflects several key elements in the genesis of Freire's work, not least its Christian overtones. Love is also, for Freire, one of the emotional elements that drive a person forward in any humanizing activity. For Freire, there could be no teaching and other humanizing activity without love: "I could never think of education without love and that is why I think I am an educator first of all because I feel love" (Freire, quoted in McLaren 1997a, 37). The concept of love becomes arguably even stronger in his later work. Paulo states, in response to a question, by Carlos Alberto Torres, regarding his legacy, that he would like people to say the following: "Paulo Freire was a man who loved, who could not understand a life existence without love and without knowing. Paulo Freire lived, loved, and he tried to know" (Freire 1995a, 181). Strongly connected with love is the value of humility. For all their competence and authority, teachers must be humble to relearn that which they think they already know from others, and to connect, through learning ("there is no teaching without learning"—Freire 1998a, 29–48), with their learners' lifeworlds.

Tolerance is a word that strikes me as being somewhat condescending, and I would much prefer the term *solidarity* in this context. Solidarity becomes an important issue in Freire's writings of the late eighties and nineties, writings which stress the need for persons to gain greater coherence throughout life (see Freire 1998a, 58). The quest for life and for living critically becomes an ongoing quest for greater *coherence* as a human being—an elaboration on his earlier modernist contention that a person's ontological vocation is that of becoming "fully human." Gaining coherence, for Freire, entails gaining greater awareness of one's "unfinishedness" (Freire 1998a, 51, 66) and one's "multiple and layered identities" (Freire 1997b). These identities are often contradictory, rendering a person oppressed in one context and an oppressor in another, in the latter case being a manifestation of the "oppressor within," a very important theme in his most celebrated work. This makes nonsense of the criticism, often leveled at Freire in U.S. circles, that he fails to recognize that one can be oppressed in one situation and an oppressor in another and that he posits a binary opposition between oppressor and oppressed. If anything, the relations between oppressor and oppressed have always been presented by Freire as *dialectical* rather than as binary opposites (see Allman 1999, 88–89, for an insightful exposition in this regard).

Gaining greater coherence entails getting to know and engaging in solidarity with, as well as learning from, the "other." This theme becomes all the more pertinent given the quest, among democratic educators/cultural workers, to press for a revolutionary, critical form of multiculturalism (see McLaren 1997b).

The theme of gaining coherence is a recurring one in his later work, especially in a brilliant piece that constitutes a response to a number of commentators on his work (Freire 1997b). It reflects a recognition, on Freire's part, that forms of domestication can emerge from an ostensibly emancipatory practice. The contradictions arising from our multiple and layered subjectivities render this a constant possibility. Rather than indulging in a nihilistic renunciation of attempts at an empowering pedagogical practice, Freire sees this as one of the strengths of critical pedagogy, the approach to pedagogy which Henry Giroux associates with Paulo Freire, stating: "I think that anyone who took up that field, in some way, had to begin with [Freire] whether they liked him or not" (Giroux, quoted in Torres 1998, 141). Being based on praxis, on the recognition of our "unfinishedness" as human beings and as pedagogues and on the constant need to engage in annunciation and denunciation, genuine critical pedagogy involves an ongoing struggle of reflecting on oneself, on the social collectivity involved and on the pedagogical practice. This is done with a view to transformative action—action intended to enable one to confront one's contradictions to become less "unfinished"/

incomplete, less incoherent. This emerges quite clearly from the piece by Freire in *Mentoring the Mentor* (Freire 1997b), but I would submit that it was always present in his work. It is implied in Freire's exhortation, in *Pedagogy of the Oppressed*, to recognize the presence of and to confront the "oppressor within" (the "oppressor consciousness"—the internalization of the oppressor's image).

The response to commentators in *Mentoring the Mentor* is a piece that throws into sharp focus Freire's later concerns with forms of oppression that are not just related to class issues but which also include matters concerning race and gender. As he states, time and again in his later works, one cannot explain anything under the sun in terms of the class struggle. At the same time, he has often argued that perestroika did not have the power to suppress the existence of social class (Freire 1991). With respect to his discussions on race, gender, and other forms of identity, Freire's contact with the North American critical pedagogical milieu strikes me as having been instrumental. Collaborators like Donaldo Macedo and the contributors to the *Mentoring the Mentor* volume have pressed him hard on these issues, as have writers like Kathleen Weiler (1991), through her criticisms of Freire's writings, and the largely sympathetic bell hooks (1993).

One ought to refer here to his discussions on machismo (Freire 1994, 1996; Freire and Macedo 1993, 1995) and racism (see Freire and Macedo 2000). In the latter case, he and Macedo condemn the scientism that is often a hallmark of Eurocentric regimes of truth. Having said this, I winced at his statement "I am too a woman" (Freire and Macedo 1993, 175), concerning solidarity with women. I feel that there is a limit to which we men can be at one with women in their struggles, not being able to feel the pain of this specific form of oppression (Mayo 1999, 115). This notwithstanding, Freire has gone to great lengths to rectify the totalizing gender discourse of his earlier works, thus responding positively to the numerous American feminists who took up issue with him on this matter. Perhaps, a talking book in English between Freire and a woman or a person of color would not have been out of place in this context. bell hooks expressed her desire to engage in such a book with Freire (hooks 1993), but for some reason or other, this never materialized.

Perhaps, the greatest contribution of Freire's later works lies in the demonstration of the ability to introduce concepts connected with popular education in the context of a municipal state school system (see Freire 1991; 1993; 1997a, 59–63; Saul 1995). The theme of a democratic, popular public school is a recurring one in his works. It is a community school (Freire 1998b, 1999) that is not the exclusive domain of teachers and educational administrators but which is open to many other people with a stake in education, including parents and other guardians, community representatives, students, janitors, cooks, and so on. And all those who are in contact with children in schools are to be formed as educators, including the cooks and janitors (see Freire 1991). Those educators who are involved worldwide in democratizing the face of the public schools and education in general would do well to read Freire's works on the subject of "changing the face of the schools."[12] This process might have been interrupted in São Paulo following the PT's loss of government there but has continued in at least one other city in Brazil, Porto Alegre in Rio Grande do Sul, where the PT has been in government at the municipal and state levels. It is likely to be resumed in São Paulo and introduced in a number of other localities following the string of victories, including victory in São Paulo, registered by the PT in the fall 2000 municipal elections.[13] The ideas connected with the São Paulo reforms remain influential in different parts of Brazil. This renders such books as *Pedagogy of the City* and *Pedagogy of Hope* of great importance to cultural workers, policy makers, and educational administrators who work toward the democratization of the public educational system. If one looks at the printed literature (in English) connected with the Porto Alegre experience, one can immediately detect the Freirean influence. The spirit of his São Paulo reforms runs through this municipal project in Rio Grande do Sul (City Secretariat of Education of Porto Alegre 1999). *Pedagogy of the City* strikes me as a publication worth recommending for any educational policy or educational administration course. Of course, this raises the question regarding spaces available for such reforms within the context of the hegemonic neoliberal state whose funding policies are closely monitored by the International Monetary Fund and the World Bank. And, of course, as Freire would argue, these experiences cannot be transplanted but have to be reinvented in the contexts in question.

Another important theme, emerging from Freire's later works, which requires underlining in this chapter, is that of postcolonialism. This is more than just a theme. Postcolonialism, or more appropriate, anticolonialism, is that to which Paulo has always given voice. His early work, including his most famous book, is rooted in the history of the Brazilian colonial experience, while the Guinea Bissau, Cape Verde, and São Tome and Principe writings (see Freire 1978; Freire and Faundez 1989; Freire and Macedo 1987) reflect a concern with a national, postcolonial educational strategy for "decolonizing the mind." In his later work, the issue of colonialism is addressed in many ways. One gathers that Freire uses the term *colonial* in the broader Foucauldian sense of "colonized subject." One obvious example here is his reference to the oppression of women, through sexist discourse and enfleshment in "concrete practices," as "colonial" (1994, 67). He also deals, in his work, with the legacy of colonial structures and thinking in countries that went through long historical periods of foreign colonial occupation/domination. For instance, he regards the policies affecting the establishment of priorities with regard to salaries in Brazil as a colonial hangover (1998c, 37). The theme of colonialism was also developed in a manner that is in keeping with the situation of most countries worldwide—neocolonialism in its most predatory (McLaren 1995) form. For Freire, the struggle for decolonization had to be an ongoing one. Analyzing Freire's work in relation to that of Ernesto (Che) Guevara, Peter McLaren underlines that

> Freire acknowledges that decolonization is a project that knows no endpoint, no final closure. It is a lifetime struggle that requires counterintuitive insight, honesty, compassion, and a willingness to brush one's personal history against the grain of "naive consciousness" or commonsense understanding. After engaging the legacy

of revolutionary struggles of the oppressed that has been bequeathed to us by Freire, it remains impossible to conceive of pedagogical practice evacuated of social critique. Freire has left stratified deposits of pedagogical insight upon which the future development of progressive education can—and must—be built. There is still reason to hope for a cooperative pedagogical venture among those who support a Freirean, class-based, pedagogical struggle, feminist pedagogy, or a pedagogy informed by queer theory and politics, that may lead to a revival of serious educational thinking in which the category of liberation may continue to have and to make meaning. (2000, 170)

It is fitting therefore to conclude this chapter the way it started. In confronting the fatalism of neoliberalism, Freire embarked on his latest attempt to confront the most recent form assumed by colonialism. For colonialism is a constant feature of the capitalist mode of production which is characterized by restructuring, and the search for new markets. Colonialism takes on different forms and the one it is assuming at present is predicated on neoliberalism with its concomitant ideology of the marketplace.

The fatalism of neoliberalism (Araújo Freire 1997, 10) is an important theme in Freire's later English language books. He speaks of the nihilism of what he calls reactionary postmodernity that denies people the chance to dream of a better world. The kind of nefarious and insidious thinking that becomes the subject of his attack is what he terms the ideological negation of ideology: "the ideology of ideological death" (Freire 1998c, 14). Freire's thinking in this regard, predicated on the sense of agency and the constant unmasking of ideologies characterized by *denúncia* and *anúncio*, strikes me as being in keeping with what Frei Betto anticipates to be "a world movement to rescue utopias" (Betto 1999, 45). In Frei Betto's words:

> This is exactly it: it is an ideology that preaches the death of ideology. I think this is all nonsense, because human beings need dreams, need utopia and there is no ideology, no system that can stop this force. Dostoyevski was right when he said: "The most powerful weapon of a human being is his [*sic*] conscience" and this nobody can destroy. I think it ridiculous when they preach that there is no ideology any more, in order to be able to state that the only ideology is the neo-liberal one. I think that it is a matter of time before we witness the eruption of a world movement to rescue utopias.

Of course, in these later works, Freire seems to be expressing his immediate reactions to an ideology that is fatalistic and contradictory. These reactions are sporadic and, at the time they were written, had yet to be developed into a coherent and systematic work. This is precisely the kind of work Freire was contemplating at the time of his death. Freire expresses his anger at this ideology, in *Letters to Cristina*, where he argues:

> We therefore don't have to continue to propose a pedagogy of the oppressed that unveils the reasons behind the facts or that provokes the oppressed to take up critical knowledge and transformative action. We no longer need a pedagogy that

questions technical training or is indispensable to the development of a professional comprehension of how and why society functions. What we need to do now, according to this astute ideology, is focus on production without any preoccupation about what we are producing, who it benefits, or who it hurts. (1996, 84)

And yet, as I have argued elsewhere (Mayo 1999), the scenario of general impoverishment, often bordering on destitution, in various parts of the world, especially those under the sway of structural adjustment programs, with an ever widening gap between North and South, necessitates that we remain preoccupied with *how* (an addition to Freire's phrase) and "what we are producing, who it benefits, or who it hurts" (5). We need a pedagogy concerned not only with the above but which, in response, enables us to imagine and strive collectively toward the realization of a world which can and ought to be different. This would be a world governed by life centered rather than market driven values (see Miles 1996; 1998, 256). The quest for such a pedagogy by Freire, the anticolonial or postcolonial pedagogue par excellence, is in keeping with his long search for the refinement of pedagogical approaches that confront colonialism in its different forms (see Giroux 1993, 1996). Freire was exploring the ingredients for what would have been his next major and timely book project. Alas, it was not to be!

One wonders whether his new work would have extended beyond the anthropocentric framework that characterizes much of his output and that of many other authors whose work he inspired. The point concerning Freire's "anthropocentrism" is raised also by Stanley Aronowitz (1998, 11). In confronting neoliberalism by positing life-centered values in contrast to market-driven ones, we require a radicalism which extends beyond the realm of social relations, to embrace the larger domain of human–Earth relationships. There is need for the *eco* prefix to be added to the title of any of the radical *isms* we embrace, as in *ecofeminism* (see Mies and Shiva 1993). The *eco* prefix is not simply an "add on" but an integral feature of the struggle involved. With regard to human–Earth relationships, we can draw sustenance from the works of people like Metchild Hart (1992) and Maria Mies and Vandana Shiva (1993). Among the most recent works, I would cite that by Edmund O'Sullivan (1999) and the one by Francisco Gutierrez and Cruz Prado (2000), the term *Ecopedagogia* being used in the latter case. It is also heartening to note that the Instituto Paulo Freire in São Paulo, officially founded on September 1, 1992, has a program in ecopedagogy, intended to promote the construction of a planetary citizenship, and is working assiduously in the context of the Earth Charter (Carta da Terra), something similar to the Universal Declaration of Human Rights (Instituto Paulo Freire 2000, 11, 12).

O'Sullivan forcefully expresses the point, concerning the anthropocentric nature of much critical pedagogy, in his highly inspiring book:

Probably one of the most prominent omissions in the critical pedagogical approaches to education at this juncture of its formulations is its lack of attention to ecological issues. My major criticism of a critical perspective is their preeminent emphasis on inter-human problems frequently to the detriment of the relations of humans to the wider biotic community and the natural world. The general direction of critical perspectives is toward anthropocentrism. The criticism of anthropocentrism is by no means a reason for dismissal of the vital concerns that critical perspectives pose for contemporary education. These issues must be taken forward and fused into wider biocentric concerns. (O'Sullivan 1999, 63, 64)

This requires our building on and going beyond the struggle commenced by Freire. Freire has however thrown down the gauntlet. It is left to others to pick it up, reconstituting his work and ideas in the process. For, once again, these cannot be simply "transplanted" across time, geographical boundaries, and different struggles, but need to be "reinvented."

NOTES

This chapter is from *Remaining on the Same Side of the River: A Critical Commentary on Paulo Freire's Later Work,* by Peter Mayo. Copyright 2001. Reproduced by permission of Taylor & Francis, www.routledge-ny.com. This paper was originally published in the *Review of Education/Pedagogy/Cultural Studies* 22, no. 4 (2001): 369–97.

1. The interview took place in São Paulo, April 1998. Transcribed by Frei Sergio Abreu and translated by Lilia Azevedo. Frei Joao Xerri acted as interlocutor throughout the interview. It was published as Borg and Mayo (2000).

2. See for instance the following compact discs: *Terra* by Chico Buarque; and *Arte em Movimento* (nineteen pieces of music and a poem), interpreted by Ires Escobar, Marcos Monteiro, Ze Pinto, Ze Claudio, and Protasio Prates.

3. It was published in the mid-1980s by the Comisión Nacional sobre la Desaparición de Personas (Conadep; National Commission Concerning Disappeared Persons), led by one of Argentina's most important public intellectuals, writer Ernesto Sabato. I am indebted, for this information, to my good friend, Daniel Schugurensky, from the Ontario Institute for Studies in Education, University of Toronto.

4. Carmel Borg and I are indebted to Cardinal Arns for this information—private conversation, in the presence of Frei Joao Xerri, in the Sacristy of São Paulo Cathedral, April 1998. The point was confirmed to me by Nita Freire at the Pedagogy/Theatre of the Oppressed Conference, New York, June 1999.

5. I am indebted to Lilia Azevedo for confirming and clarifying facts surrounding this document and other matters referred to in this chapter. I am also indebted to Frei Joao Xerri for having picked up lots of information, referred to in this chapter, from him.

6. In my "Tribute to Paulo Freire" (1997b, 369n5), I mention that my good friend and colleague Mary Darmanin had reminded me of this most important feature of Freire's work. Like me, she read Freire in translation.

7. I am indebted for this point to David W. Livingstone, from the Department of Sociology and Equity Studies in Education at the Ontario Institute for Studies in Education, University of Toronto.

8. At the risk of sounding apologetic, I would like to reiterate, in fairness sake, the point I make elsewhere (2000, 105). For my money, Frank Youngman (1986) provides the finest text in English to date for a comprehensive analysis of the potential contribution of Historical Materialist tenets to the development of a socialist approach to adult education. The book contains, among other things, a brilliant and lucid second chapter, "Marxism and Learning."

9. Taylor's text is full of erudition, extremely informative, and quite thought provoking. It challenges Freire-inspired adult educators to reflect critically on their practice and recognize the emerging contradictions (Mayo 1993, 283). Elias's strength lies in his discussion on the Marxist humanist and theological underpinnings to Freire's work. See my review (1996) of *Paulo Freire: Pedagogue of Liberation.*

10. Roberts's book has the advantage of being a most recent publication which, therefore, takes on board some of the key ideas in Freire's latest publications that are available in English. It provides, among other things, illuminating discussions on such important issues as the directive and interventionist nature of Freirean pedagogy.

11. Conversation with Cardinal Arns, mentioned in note 4.

12. The phrase derives from Nita Freire and is taken from the source in note 1.

13. I thank Daniel Schugurensky for providing feedback in this regard.

REFERENCES

Allman, Paula. 1999. *Revolutionary social transformation: Democratic hopes, political possibilities and critical education*. Gramby, Mass.: Bergin & Garvey.

Allman, Paula, with Peter Mayo, Chris Cavanagh, Chan Lean Heng, and Sergio Haddad. 1998. . . . the creation of the world in which it will be easier to love. *Convergence (a tribute to Paulo Freire)* 31: 9–16.

Araújo Freire, Ana Maria. 1997. A bit of my life with Paulo Freire. *Taboo: The Journal of Culture and Education* 2: 3–11.

———. 1998. Paulo Freire: To touch, to look, to listen. *Convergence (A tribute to Paulo Freire)* 31: 3–5.

Aronowitz, Stanley. 1998. Introduction. In *Pedagogy of freedom. Ethics, democracy and civic courage,* by Paulo Freire, 1–19. Lanham Md.: Rowman & Littlefield.

Betto, Frei. 1999. Liberation theology "no longer a ghetto in the church." Frei Betto interviewed in São Paulo by Carmel Borg and Peter Mayo in *Sunday Times* (Malta), October 17.

Betto, Frei, and Paulo Freire. 1986. *Una scuola chiamata vita* [A school called life]. Bologna: E.M.I.

Borg, Carmel, and Peter Mayo. 2000. Reflections from a third age marriage: A pedagogy of hope, reason and passion. An interview with Ana Maria (Nita) Araújo Freire. *McGill Journal of Education* 35, no. 2 (Spring): 105–20.

City Secretariat of Education of Porto Alegre. 1999. *Cycles of formation: Politic-pedagogical proposal for the citizen's school*. Porto Alegre, Braz.: Prefeitura de Porto Alegre.

Coben, Diana. 1998. *Radical heroes: Gramsci, Freire and the politics of adult education*. New York: Garland Press.

de Figueiredo-Cowan, Maria, and Denise Gastaldo, eds. 1995. *Paulo Freire at the institute*. London: Institute of Education, University of London.

Elias, John. 1994. *Paulo Freire: Pedagogue of liberation*. Malabar, Fla.: Krieger.

Escobar, Miguel, Alfredo L. Fernandez, and Gilberto Guevara-Niebla, with Paulo Freire. 1994. *Paulo Freire on higher education: A dialogue at the National University of Mexico*. Albany: State University of New York Press.

Fischman, Gustavo. 1999. Review of *Teachers as cultural workers: Letters to those who dare teach*. *Comparative Education Review* 43: 556–59.

Foley, Griff. 1999. *Learning in social action. A contribution to understanding informal education*. London: Zed.

Freire, Paulo. 1970. *Pedagogy of the oppressed*. New York: Seabury Press.

———. 1978. *Pedagogy in process: The letters to Guinea Bissau*. New York: Continuum.

———. 1985. *The politics of education*. Gramby, Mass.: Bergin & Garvey.

———. 1991. The work of Paulo Freire as secretary of education in São Paulo. In *Educational policy and social change in Brazil*. AERA session audiotape. Chicago: Teach 'em Inc.

———. 1993. *Pedagogy of the city*. New York: Continuum.

———. 1994. *Pedagogy of hope*. New York: Continuum.

———. 1995a. Learning to read the world: Paulo Freire in conversation with Carlos Torres. In *Education and social change in Latin America*, ed. Carlos Alberto Torres, 175–81. Melbourne: James Nicholas.

———. 1995b. The progressive teacher. In *Paulo Freire at the institute*, ed. Maria de Figueiredo-Cowan and Denise Gastaldo, 17–24. London: Institute of Education, University of London.

———. 1996. *Letters to Cristina: Reflections on my life and work*. New York: Routledge.

———. 1997a. *Pedagogy of the heart*. New York: Continuum.

———. 1997b. A response. In *Mentoring the mentor: A critical dialogue with Paulo Freire*, ed. Paulo Freire, with James W. Fraser, Donaldo Macedo, Tanya McKinnon, and William T. Stokes, 303–29. New York: Peter Lang.

———. 1998a. *Pedagogy of freedom. Ethics, democracy and civic courage*. Lanham, Md.: Rowman & Littlefield.

———. 1998b. *Politics and education*. Los Angeles: University of California, Latin American Center Publications.

———. 1998c. *Teachers as cultural workers: Letters to those who dare teach*. Boulder, Colo.: Westview Press.

———. 1999. Education and community involvement. In *Critical education in the information age*, ed. Manuel Castells, Ramon Flecha, Paulo Freire, Henry A. Giroux, Donaldo Macedo, and Paul Willis, 83–91. Lanham, Md.: Rowman & Littlefield.

———. 2000. *Pedagogia da indignação: Cartas pedagógicas e outros escritos*. São Paulo: Editora UNESP.

Freire, Paulo, and Frei Betto. 1985. *Essa escola chamada vida*. São Paulo, Braz.: Atica.

Freire, Paulo, and Antonio Faundez. 1989. *Learning to question: A pedagogy of liberation*. Geneva: World Council of Churches.

Freire, Paulo, and Donaldo Macedo. 1987. *Literacy: Reading the word and the world*. Gramby, Mass.: Bergin & Garvey.

———. 1993. A dialogue with Paulo Freire. In *Paulo Freire: A critical encounter*, ed. Peter McLaren and Peter Leonard, 169–76. London: Routledge.

———. 1995. A dialogue: Culture, language and race. *Harvard Educational Review* 65: 377–402.

———. 2000. Scientism as a form of racism. In *Freirean pedagogy, praxis and possibilities: Projects for the new millenium*, ed. Stan Steiner, Mark Krank, Peter McLaren, and Robert Bahruth, 33–40. New York: Falmer Press, 2000.

Gadotti, Moacir. 1994. *Reading Paulo Freire: His life and work*. Albany: State University of New York Press.

———. 1996. *Pedagogy of praxis. A dialectical philosophy of education*. Albany: State University of New York Press.

Giroux, Henry. 1993. Paulo Freire and the politics of postcolonialism. In *Paulo Freire. A critical encounter*, ed. Peter McLaren and Peter Leonard, 177–88. New York: Routledge.

———. 1996. *Disturbing pleasures*. London: Routledge.

Gutierrez, Francisco, and Cruz Prado. 2000. *Ecopedagogia e cittadinanza planetaria*. Bologna: EMI.

Hart, Metchild. 1992. *Working and educating for life: Feminist and international perspectives on adult education*. London: Routledge.

Holst, John D. 1999. The affinities of Lenin and Gramsci: Implications for radical adult education theory and practice. *International Journal of Lifelong Education* 18: 407–21.

hooks, bell. 1993. bell hooks speaking about Paulo Freire: The man, his works. In *Paulo Freire: A critical encounter*, ed. Peter McLaren and Peter Leonard, 146–54. New York: Routledge.

Horton, Myles, and Paulo Freire. 1990. *We make the road by walking: Conversations on education and social change*. Philadelphia: Temple University Press.

Instituto Paulo Freire. 2000. *Curriculo institucional: Projeto, perfil e percurso* [Institutional curriculum: Project, profile and trajectory]. São Paulo: Instituto Paulo Freire.

Martin, Darcy. 1998. Learning from the south. *Convergence (a Tribute to Paulo Freire)* 31: 117–27.

Mayo, Peter. 1993. Review of *The Texts of Paulo Freire*, by Paul V. Taylor. *Adults Learning* 4: 283.

———. 1996. Review of *Paulo Freire: Pedagogue of liberation*, by John Elias. *Convergence* 29: 63–68.

———. 1997a. Reflections on Freire's work: A Maltese contribution. *Taboo: Journal of Culture and Education* 2: 120–23.

———. 1997b. Tribute to Paulo Freire (1921–1997). *International Journal of Lifelong Education* 16: 365–70.

———. 1999. *Gramsci, Freire and adult education: Possibilities for transformative action.* London: Zed Books.

———. 2000. Marxism's impact on adult education. *Educational Practice and Theory* 22 (2): 95–110.

McLaren, Peter. 1995. *Critical pedagogy and predatory culture: Oppositional politics in a post-modern era.* London: Routledge.

———. 1997a. Paulo Freire's legacy of hope and struggle. *Taboo: Journal of Culture and Education* 2: 33–38.

———. 1997b. *Revolutionary multiculturalism: Pedagogies of dissent for the new millenium.* Boulder, Colo.: Westview Press.

———. 2000. *Che Guevara, Paulo Freire, and the pedagogy of revolution.* Boulder, Colo.: Rowman & Littlefield.

McLaren, Peter, and Colin Lankshear, eds. 1994. *Politics of liberation: Paths from Freire.* New York: Routledge.

McLaren, Peter, and Peter Mayo. 1999. Value commitment, social change and personal narrative. *International Journal of Educational Reform* 8: 397–408.

McLaren, Peter, and Tomaz Tadeuz Da Silva. 1993. Decentering pedagogy: Critical literacy, resistance and the politics of meaning. In *Paulo Freire. A critical encounter,* ed. Peter McLaren and Peter Leonard, 47–89. New York: Routledge.

McIlroy, John. 1993. Community, labour and Raymond Williams. *Adults Learning* 4: 276.

Mies, Maria, and Vandana Shiva. 1993. *Ecofeminism.* London: Zed Books.

Miles, Angela. 1996. *Integrative feminisms: Building global visions, 1960s–1990s.* New York: Routledge.

———. 1998. Learning from the women's movement in the neo-liberal period. In *Learning for life: Canadian readings in adult education,* ed. Sue M. Scott, Bruce Spencer, and Alan Thomas, 250–58. Toronto: Thompson Educational Publishing.

O'Cadiz, Maria del Pilar, Pia Lindquist Wong, and Carlos Alberto Torres. 1997. *Education and democracy: Paulo Freire, social movements and educational reform in São Paulo.* Boulder, Colo.: Westview Press.

O'Sullivan, Edmund. 1999. *Transformative learning: Educational vision for the 21st century.* London: Zed Books and the University of Toronto Press.

Roberts, Peter. 2000. *Education, literacy, and humanization: Exploring the work of Paulo Freire.* Westport, Conn.: Bergin & Garvey.

Saul, Ana Maria. 1995. Municipal educational policy in the city of São Paulo, Brazil (1988–1991). In *Education and social change in Latin America,* ed. Carlos Alberto Torres, 155–62. Melbourne: James Nicholas.

Shor, Ira. 1998. The centrality of beans: Remembering Paulo. *Convergence (a Tribute to Paulo Freire)* 31: 75–80.

Shor, Ira, and Paulo Freire. 1987. *Pedagogy for liberation: Dialogues on transforming education.* Gramby, Mass.: Bergin & Garvey.

Taylor, Paul V. 1993. *The texts of Paulo Freire.* Buckingham, Engl.: Open University Press.

Torres, Carlos Alberto. 1994. Paulo Freire as secretary of education in the municipality of São Paulo. *Comparative Education Review* 38: 181–214.

———, ed. 1995. *Education and social change in Latin America.* Melbourne: James Nicholas.

———. 1998. *Education, power, and personal biography: Dialogues with critical educators.* New York: Routledge.

Weiler, Kathleen. 1991. Freire and a feminist pedagogy of difference. In *Politics of liberation: Paths from Freire,* ed. Peter McLaren and Colin Lankshear, 12–40. New York: Routledge.

Youngman, Frank. 1986. *Adult education and socialist pedagogy.* Beckenham: Croom Helm.

11

Revolutionary Pedagogy in Media Culture: Reading the Techno-Capitalist Order of Education

Juha Suoranta, Tuukka Tomperi, and Robert FitzSimmons

I have pride in my voice, but it lacks power.

> —Finnish writer and leftist critic Christer Kihlman,
> *Epätoivon toivo* (The hope of despair)

The nature of capitalistic business is the nature of war. That business operates by seduction, with private property and illusory individual freedom, on seemingly voluntary base, only makes it that much more dangerous. To be exploited without really knowing it is in the long run more harmful than to be openly enslaved. In the latter you know the reason for your hurt, and can locate the violators and then work against them. In the former it's difficult to even realize that you are being castrated, decapitated, when the blade is nowhere to be seen and your misery is covered with quick-fix surrogate pleasures.

> —Finnish artist Teemu Mäki, *Teemu Mäki*

What do you do when you sought? / well, you hide—the Hell you died! / L-i-e is how I spell you lie / Paleface is here to tell you why / The Land of the Brave became / the Land of the Slaves.

> —Finnish hip-hop artist Paleface

Our everyday practices in education and in other related fields signify the triumph of capitalism and its "laws of gravitation" that have been validated for the last two centuries. Schools have always been political institutions. In the capitalistic regimes institutional education has sought to preserve and strengthen the existing mode of domination and hegemony.

185

At this particular moment of capitalist reality, this translates into the commodification of the lifeworld through increasing penetration of corporate interests into every aspect of individual and social life. Corporate capitalism has become a major player not only in the macro levels of political power play, but also in our very intimate and private politics of identity and personal life. It portrays itself as the collective heart of society; not only the source of wealth and well being, but also the source of dreams and longing. We seem to be living a myth in which business corporations portray themselves as "public servants," as instruments for a common cause and "common good."

The myth is not new to the capitalist social structure, and it has always been used to legitimate the presence of business interests in schooling. It is in the direct interest of corporate power to influence the form and the content of schooling. As nation-states begin to shy away from investing in education as a form of civic education for the public interest, and as the role of education is no longer seen as a "guardian" of "educational equality and through it social equality" (Rinne 2000), the corporate sector is eager to take its place. Also, schools are now encouraged to take on a corporate persona which, according to Rinne, requires schools to function as enterprises (6). The two trends create a powerful capitalist presence within the sphere of education, thus reformulating the suspicion that schools function as ideological state apparatuses.

In our view, the basic idea of such developments is to convince the working class that their own public and social interest is directly tied to the interests of corporations and the capitalist system that it propagates. It should come as no surprise that these developments do serve a purpose for the ruling elite in terms of positions of power and social privilege. This is accompanied by a strong tendency toward a more exclusive and repressive political atmosphere, described by Noam Chomsky (2000, 36):

> We do have a welfare state, but it is a welfare state for the rich. To maintain a well-functioning welfare state for the rich you have to have a highly conscious business class. The rest of the people have to be convinced that they live in a classless society. Schools have always played a role in keeping this myth alive.

Thus it is in the class interests of the newborn super-rich class to keep schools as sites of irrelevant information. As Stephen Haseler (2000, 1) writes, the new class of super-rich "commands wealth beyond the imagination of ordinary working citizen." So it is their interest to have an educational ideology that supports their greedy needs by strengthening consumeristic hustler lifestyles. This new class is also "assuming the proportions of overlordship, of an overclass—as powerful, majestic and antidemocratic as the awesome, uncompromising imperial governing classes at the height of the European empires." Haseler emphasizes that the one dimension of today's super-rich that separates them drastically from earlier economic elite is that "they owe no loyalty to community or nation." Compared with the situation when the wealthy of the super-rich class was under some control of the laws of nation states, there are now no control mechanisms anymore, and, in consequence, their social responsibility is next to zero. The super-rich are free to move themselves as well as their money around the world, as Haseler states, "to the most productive haven." This is a very familiar form of rhetoric pressure in Finland too, much used by the cluster of industry, finance, and rightist politicians.

As we are writing this text at troubled times we are trying to find out what is going on outside and inside of us. Sure, we are customers if nothing else. Certainly we still reflect the madness of September 11, 2001, and its ongoing aftermath in Afghanistan, and Iraq. Willingly or unwillingly, we are representatives of a dominant culture reproducing it with our daily acts of random violence, orgasmic shopping, and consumerist orgies. Advertisers and sale personnel are teasing us with their endless offers, seducing us to buy lot of unnecessary goods and commodities. They know our dreams and secret wishes because our inner selves, images, ideas, thoughts, and visions are all media mediated.

The media-mediated world floods everyday life as Norman Denzin (1994, 458) writes: "It makes the social constructions of reality that people create, constructions stitched out of meanings previously given in the media and elsewhere." But our fellow sales personnel also are victims of capitalistic circumstances as they are forced to do their jobs for the best of their ability under lousy salaries, zero benefits, and without securities for a better tomorrow. How could we become victims a little less, not innocent but at least conscious consumers? How could we be fearless as teachers and critical educators? How could we teach others to be like that?

THE NEOLIBERAL TRENDS IN POLITICS AND EDUCATION

We believe that answering these questions demands a rethinking of our pedagogical practices from a revolutionary viewpoint, and taking seriously a pedagogy of revolution recently emphasized by critical scholars (McLaren 2000; McLaren and Farahmandpur 2001a, 2001b; Trifonas 2000). Revolutionary pedagogy seeks out alternatives to capitalist schooling—alternatives that would be concerned with the "intellectual, aesthetic, social and physical development of all children" (Levitas 1974, 187). This will involve not only educational and social but also political initiatives. For education can be nonpolitical only in dreams and there is no neutral side to be taken. Teaching has to become self-reflexively political in its theory and practice for an educator to be revolutionary.

In the overwealthy and overweighty West where liberal democracy has a beachhead, the philosophy of revolutionary pedagogy can easily receive a Cold War welcome. A pedagogy that is critical about capitalist development will experience roadblocks from educational administrators, parents, students, academics, and teachers. The solution to this problem can be difficult to find but even so, revolutionary educators need to join forces to remain committed to social change and political action. We need to have confidence in others, disregarding the obstacles that are to be expected. Obstacles are rather the real contradictions and conflicts that preside in the capitalist society.

It is important that the revolutionary teacher and educator work with the antagonisms that they may experience. For, as Marx stated, consciousness is "explained rather from the contradictions of material life, from the existing conflict between the social productive forces and the relations of production" (in Lenin 1976, 24). Thus the educators with a revolutionary consciousness understand not only their own moral commitments but also the contradictions that persist inside the capitalist system.

Of course, the word *revolution*—like other words—gets its meaning from the specific use. For many, images of violence and destruction come first into mind, for *revolution* can symbolize and remind people of blood and death, as is the case in many countries, including Finland (see McLaren 2001, 163–64). In this regard, the word itself can have various negative meanings. But in the context of revolutionary pedagogy it must be understood that the word "revolution" does not mean the brutal act of violence. Rather, the word can become synonymous for change and hope. In this regard, William Morris, an early British socialist, wrote in 1884: "The word revolution, which we Socialists are so often forced to use, has a terrible sound in most people's ears, . . . it may frighten people but it will at least warn them that there is something to be frightened about, which be no less dangerous for being ignored; and also it may encourage some people, and will mean to them at least not a fear, but a hope" (Morris 2000).

It has become more and more difficult to talk about revolution and to use terms like *revolution*. In a way the whole word seems out of place. The discursive transformations that the media culture has effected in the prevailing common sense have undermined discussions on real and serious social change on several different forms and levels. In the current hegemonic capitalistic discourse this has happened at least in four aspects.

First, and as mentioned earlier, the concept of citizenship has been undermined, thus stealing the political agency and autonomy of people. It is easy to agree with Henry Giroux (2000, 102) who claims that "in the new world order citizenship has little to do with social responsibility and everything to do with creating consuming subjects." Second, the meaning of public space has accordingly changed, and the properly political public space has diminished considerably, as pointed out by Naomi Klein (2000, 130), for instance:

> Everyone has, in one form or another, witnessed the odd double vision of vast consumer choice coupled with Orwellian new restrictions on cultural production and public space. We see it when a small community watches its lively downtown hollow out, as big-box discount stores with 70,000 items on their shelves set up on their periphery. . . . It is there again when protesters are thrown out of shopping malls for handing out political leaflets, told by the security guards that although the edifice may have replaced the public square in their town, it is, in fact, private property.

So there are less and less opportunities and spaces for people to put their political deliberation into use, even if they have managed to hold on to their political integrity and autonomy. Giroux (2000, 102) also suggests that the notion of consuming subjects legitimates a hyperindividualistic ethos and substitutes the freedom of choice for a concerted respect for the common good.

Third, media culture has colonized the language of change, making its preferred and reactionary use of words once full of transformative power. It is interesting that corporate vocabularies of media culture have become "radicalized" as they incorporate radical terminology into their wholesale vocabularies. It is not uncommon to read in corporate publications when referring to corporate strategy and tactics such words as *saboteur, change insurgent, change agent, social entrepreneur, tempered radical,* and *revolutionary Bolshevik.* But the corporate "change agents" are clever, and sometimes it is worth to listen to them to learn from their rhetoric.[1]

Fourth, there has been a considerable shift from political to economic power at the macrolevel of political and economic institutions. Political structures have been made to retreat in front of market mechanisms, and political decision makers in front of market players, thus diminishing the legitimate sphere of democratic politics. This can be seen as an assault on the fundamental democratic principles. According to Chomsky (2000, 136), "corporate entities" are more "totalitarian in internal structure, increasingly interlinked and reliant on powerful states, and largely unaccountable to the public." It is this antidemocratic corporate wave that swallows up and drowns alternative public discourse in social, political, and economic relations.

The Nordic welfare states under the thumb of their own perestroika and neoliberal politics seem unable to provide for various social programs and services that were taken for granted during the period of welfare capitalism throughout Western Europe. The all-encompassing ideological shift from welfare to "helpcare" has already had dramatic impacts on public health care, social services, and educational practices. There are already separate markets of private welfare services for the rich and public welfare services for the poor at the same time as we are witnessing a polarization between the rich and the poor in wealth accumulation.

Accordingly, we are witnessing the concentration of power in the hands of political elite that may be few in number (the International Monetary Fund and World Trade Organization) but prominent in implementing economic and social policy. For the most part, the economic and social programs benefit a relative few in the middle class as labor productivity, efficiency, and cost-cutting become buzzwords for the unregulated free market.

The streamlining of education goes along with the globalized economy and its traumatic effects on people's well being. In the modern era education and training were seen as productive forces and the tools for the nation to compete in the still relatively covered international markets. In the globalized world, as the role of the nation states have weakened, education has become an ever important factor in the competition between corporations which now preach such ideologically laden and individualized terms as human capital, core skills, or flexible competencies. There is a current trend within the public and corporate sphere to view education, especially at higher levels, as a corporate enterprise that produces knowledge as goods and services for the market (Gumport 2000, 70–71).

It is thus clear that education is under immense pressures to adjust to ideological shifts that stress privatization, free market forces, and laissez-faire competitive practices. Neoliberalism has made tremendous inroads in redefining the basic premise of educational discourse. In this respect, education is now less concerned with social justice and social equality and more under pressure of economic imperatives focused on corporate power structures and competitive imperatives.

Finnish critical sociologist of education, Risto Rinne (2000) has listed the recent changes from the welfare to neoliberal educational policy from the Nordic viewpoint. According to Rinne, in the welfare model the following values, among others, were emphasized: educational and social equality, publicly funded common school system for all, centralized state control and bureaucratic administration, great autonomy for education, uniform curricula, and teachers' authority to knowledge. However, in the neoliberal model the values look very different: competition between individual pupils and schools, diversification and stratification of the school system, growth of regional and school-specific decision-making power, increase in parental choice, private competition and private funding for education, and constant evaluation and testing of pupils and schools, and so on. Rinne lists these changes in an objective manner and by the liberal bystander-look demonstrated in his *Some Words for the Future*:

> From this point of view it is not at all surprising that as economic competition increases and as we become an even more integral part of the global world village or supranational network and media society the small northern periphery has a very difficult time maintaining its educational policy or its culture and educational ideology which would support its own traditional values.

From our view it is not enough to describe the change but to counter it by exposing its hidden ideological values, and explaining its pitfalls and evident social anomalies. This is not to suggest that we would not see and admit many problems in the welfare educational policy model, such as a too heavy bureaucracy in the educational administration, the loss of sense of community at schools and in the neighboring communities, and certain uniformism of curricula. But still we are ready to proclaim that the welfare ideology in education is a far better way to make educational policy than the neoliberal or, as we would like to call it, techno-capitalist model of education.

THE TECHNO-CAPITALIST ORDER OF EDUCATION: THE CASE OF CYBER-LEARNING

Along with capitalist educational policy the new order of education includes talk about virtual education, application of information and communication technologies in learning, network training, and web schooling, all referred to here as cyber-learning. All these learning contexts are designed to work and become established in the timeless and spaceless worlds of electronic communications media. Cyber-learning refers to all those practices in which new information technologies are used in order to participate in and complete different learning tasks whether formal or informal in nature. These learning tasks can be as different as searching for information using web engines or traditional electronic databases; surfing the Internet as a leisure time activity; writing e-mails; attending a virtual school; playing virtual reality games; studying via diverse forms of distance education; or participating in projects that call for organizational learning with the help of different information and communication media.

When the possible benefits of Internet, e-mail, and other information technology (IT) solutions began to show themselves in their entirety, there first was a lot of enthusiasm and optimism. At one point some critical educators were ready to see the electronic communication as a possible tool of democratic advancement: "assuming access to a modem, and the wish to do so, it is not at all difficult to envisage a peasant-born woman of color from a remote village conversing on equal terms with a white male professor located in one of the world's most prestigious universities" (Lankshear, Peters, and Knobel 1996, 164).

After a while it started to become obvious that the cyber-communication not only retained many of the basic obstacles to equal dialogue—due to differences in cultural and linguistic contexts, backgrounds, and expectations—but also brought along others that had to do with the unequal access to high-tech applications. Who would buy a modem and a computer if the choice had to be made between that and daily food or a dose of crack? Would the participants in an intercontinental electronic communication really understand each other even if they spoke the same language? How would the differences in cultural expectations and beliefs be overcome? What would the people outside the wealthy West do with information technology? What is the meaning of cyber-learning in circumstances that lack electricity, food, and, from our perspective, the basic elements of well being, thus resembling a premodern situation?[2]

In addition, there may be forms of structural imbalance even without the obvious one of wealth and technological resources. Some critics have drawn attention to the fact that the cyber-society is not only "an almost all-male society," as John Brockmann (1996) writes, "but it's a little-boy society, part of an ongoing infantilization of the society over the past half century." This is the reason that some feminist thinkers such as Dale Spender feel uneasy about the new gender gap in the boyish wonderland of cyber-learning. For it is a fact that "the world of computers and their connections is the world of men" (Spender 1995, 165). However, as much as we share Spender's general concern, we feel reserved toward the implicit technological determinism in the following words:

> If computer competence were an optional leisure skill, or just another means of collecting your mail, the gender gap might be merely a fascinating phenomenon. But there is nothing optional any longer about computer involvement. The electronic

medium is the way we now make sense of the world, and this is why women have to be full members of the computer culture. Women have to take part in making and shaping that cyber-society, or else they risk becoming the outsiders: they will be the information-poor, as they were for so long after the introduction of print. (168)

If we understand Spender's argument right, there once was a time when computers were no more than little details, but this is not the case any longer. Have computer competence and cyber-learning in general thus become absolute necessities? For many policy makers and educational institutions the answer seems to be positive.

New vocabularies are invented and new concepts created in the fields of educational practice and educational theory. It seems like cyber-learning as a core part of the new order of capitalist education is finally redeeming promises of old utopias of educational engineering. As Michael Apple (1988, 150) has put it, "A considerable number of parents and educators believe that the computer will revolutionize the classroom and their children's chances of a better world." Or, as Neil Postman (1996, 38) has asserted, "Nowhere do you find more enthusiasm for the god of Technology than among educators." Thus, in the West— even globally—we have a whole new and demanding discourse of high-tech learning in the field of education.

The new discourse of learning is so powerful and exciting that it nearly seems like heaven on earth and penetrates not only individual computer screens but also official national policies of education. Furthermore, it has become one of the leading strategies of the European Union in its desperate fight to ensure continuous growth and political stability in the world of economic chaos. This eagerness and desire for technological discourse as a new belief system is deeply problematic also from a more historical and philosophical point of view, as it is based on the great narrative of human being as the ruler of the world.

The keywords here seem to be *control through technology:* Control of the natural environments, control of the society, control of the economy, control of the future. But the more we pay attention to our attempts to control and enhance the economy through resourcing the research, development, and schooling of the new technologies, the more we may become blind to the basic inequalities in society.

On behalf of the e-learning discourse, the problem seems to be that today's theorizing and conceptualizing often resembles preaching or advocating. It amounts to selling commodities that are really not needed. It is as Zygmunt Bauman (1995, 12) writes: "If stated repeatedly, with authority, and with the support of adequate resources, propositions tend to become true in the end— and the training aim at making us 'expert-dependent' cannot but bring its fruit." In our media culture expert-dependent advocating blooms at the expense of critical or even analytical approaches. Therefore it is sometimes difficult to separate sound academic research from politics or pure money making. The newly formed and strengthening alliance between commercial enterprises, private funds, and universities and polytechnics in the R and D of cyber-learning is a threat to the autonomy and critical spirit of the academy.

The PR work for cyber-learning includes disseminating certain positive rhetoric around the uses of communications technologies in education. It is commonplace to describe it with positive terms like *freedom, flexibility, autonomy, self-direction, openness, effectivity, productivity, "high" technology,* and so on. However, this vocabulary has its counterpart in much gloomier visions, if we look at it from a different angle: free and autonomous choosers may actually mean individualized and isolated customers; flexibility and effectivity may mean submission to chaotic changes in economy; "high" technology can bind pedagogical visions tightly to the "lowly" business interests of the media, information and communication technologies (ICTs), and entertainment conglomerates.

It goes without saying that technology itself does not foster revolutionary learning (see Bowers 1993; Streibel 1998). Media machines are not the key to students' and teachers' liberation; it depends on the teachers' pedagogical visions, their willingness to trust on their students' imagination, and their skill in building a committed and collectively responsible atmosphere. Information and communication technologies may be part of the liberation, but they are by no means a necessary condition. Media machines can be powerful tools, but not only tools, for in many ways they mediate our experience and thus affect our worldview. As Bowers (1993) notes, the design of the computerized learning tools tends to view knowledge as propositional, symbolic, and factual in contrast to more tacit and embodied modes of knowing and thinking. In consequence, this brings with it a biased concept of human: "The view of thinking as information processing seems to fit nicely with the liberal view of the individual as an autonomous, self-directing being" (74).

Bowers also claims that computers (and technology in general) can reinforce the subject-centered, individualistic, and solipsistic ways of thinking, and subject-object-separation as its epistemological root. It can reverberate in a misrecognition of the self as individualized and isolated instead of culturally and historically constructed in social groups and communities. Thus these different conceptualizations of the self have several effects on the concept of responsibility, the sense of belonging, and the possibility of solidarity.

The rhetoric that presents users of information and communications technology as customers, clearly shows how the neoliberal governmentality builds on the old trick of binding together the ideals of individual freedom and responsibility with a sociobiological conception of human being. Flexibility of the technological learning environments is marketed as a boundless realm of freedom, accompanied, naturally, with the proper responsibility of the results. Again we can see how the purported autonomy and freedom may boil down to nothing more than an arbitrary ability and coerced need to choose one's place and standing in the preestablished hierarchies of capitalism and the "free" market economy: labor market, educational market, domestic market, global economic market. Those unwilling or unable to play this game of choosing and competition, as learners, producers, and customers, will be marginalized.

Considering this, it becomes even more problematic that a large part of the cyber-learning research and development is closely associated with the IT—and entertainment—business. Whatever good or evil the cyber-learning brings us, one certain outcome will be the dependence of educational institutions on the high technology in the form of hard- and software. If libraries once were an idealistic project of publicly funded enlightenment in the name of public interest, free and open for all, then cyber-learning serves directly the interests of business. High technology is very expensive, and in the end it is ordinary people who pay the bill.

For instance, the constant "advancement" in the form of new programs and abilities, and the need to upgrade old programs and hardware, is one of the most ingenious capitalistic inventions to boost consumption. High technology is an effective way to bind teachers, students (families), institutions, and whole national economies to the needs of the commercial sector. Students and their parents as well as teachers become convinced that technology is our future, and that technoliteracy is about the only key to the success and pursuit of happiness. At the same time the IT business benefits from all efforts to teach IT skills to students. They not only get qualified workers trained by public money but also consumers able and willing to consume what they have produced, whether computers, accessories, programs, or more generally just entertainment.

Thus the world of cyber-learning is in many ways the world of enter- and infotainment. Hans-Peter Martin and Harald Schumann (1996) use the term *tittytainment* to refer to the world order created by the global entertainment business. *Tittytainment* means the same as what the old Romans meant by *panem et circenses*, bread and circus. In addition, *titty* refers not only to soft porn (*tits*) but also to maternal care and compensatory support offered by prime time television. Now, instead of a circus, we have videos, action movies, and virtual toys. From a Foucauldian perspective these forms of "tittytainment," or forms of cultural industry are parts of biopower since they offer us preconstructed feelings, such as comfort, pleasure, and joy. They normalize the soul and seduce people to think that this is what life is and should be all about.

And what is it all about? When the late Pierre Bourdieu (1996) claimed that television presents an obvious danger to the possibility of democracy, he meant that "fast food" journalism in television decides and determines—on behalf and in front of us—the order and relevance of common things and the meaning of publicity. In other words, as spectators in society we give the media industry the right to manufacture representations of the world that in turn reproduce views of decent life using stereotypes and contradictions. Questions of good and evil are reduced to the personal level; politicians are shown as heroic individuals in an ideological vacuum. Complex moral questions look like simplistic games that are stopped when the time is up.

All this oversimplification and ideological whitewashing in the form of entertainment and media consumerism becomes elemental also from the point of the view of education. The role of schools as learning contexts is declining rapidly in the new order of capitalist education. Classroom learning is taken over by diverse informal learning sites and the school as an institution is losing the game for meaningful learning. As Henry Giroux (2000, 99) writes:

> Kids no longer view schools as the primary source of education, and rightfully so. Media texts—videos, films, music, television, radio, computers—and the new public spheres they inhabit have far more influence on shaping the memories, language, values, and identities of young people. The new technologies that influence and shape youth are important to register not merely because they produce new forms of knowledge, new identities, new social relations, or point to new forces actively engaged in new forms of cultural pedagogy, but also because they point to public spheres in which youths are writing and creating their histories and narratives within social formations that are largely ignored or only superficially acknowledged in trendy postmodern symposiums on music, youth, and performance.

Informal learning contexts such as Hollywood's teaching machine not only reflect reality but carry with them "a language of ethics and a pedagogy" (Giroux 1995, 311) of their own. Thus, if and when these teaching machines of media industry are replacing or challenging schools as meaningful places for learning and socialization, from the point of view of critical pedagogy we must ask: What kind of a pedagogical machine is it? What kind of moral authority does it represent? What kind of models for identity construction does this new and powerful teaching machine offer? What kind of a better tomorrow does it imply? When Jerome Bruner (1996, 22) writes, "just as the omniscient narrator has disappeared from modern fiction, so will the omniscient teacher disappear from the classroom of the future," he does not mean to say that institutional education should disappear. Trying to improve education is a different thing from trying to claim that schooling is about to vanish into thin air of the consumer-driven cyber-culture. Therefore, the question whether societies should be deschooled or not, should be followed by the question: Are we ready to let the profit-oriented media culture and market forces decide the contents and goals of learning—and if not, what are the alternatives?

UNDERWORLD: RESISTANCE WITHIN THE SPHERE OF INFORMATION AND COMMUNICATION TECHNOLOGIES

To answer, we should first look and see whether there is any hope to be found in the developments among the youth and their cultures of information technology. To start with, we propose that these IT cultures should be divided into two different realms. The first and faster expanding realm consists of what we would call the "bulk-culture of cyber-learning." It is stuffed with video games and mixtures of info-, enter-, and tittytainment and dominated purely by economic interests. It is ruled by the principles of capitalist economy, growth orientation of the media industry, and "nerd barons" such as Bill Gates. It is a reasonable fear that the new information technologies such as the Internet are becoming more and more under the pressure to obey the commercial and manipulative interests of mainstream media industry. And it is a field of industry, furthermore, that is undergoing a startling process of consolidation. As Mark Crispin Miller (2002) shows, the ten biggest multinational conglomerates reign supreme, from television and music to movies and theme parks, through magazine and book publishing: "The rise of the cartel has been a long time coming (and it still has some way to go). It represents the grand convergence of the previously disparate U.S. culture industries—many of them vertically monopolized already—into one global super-industry providing most of our imaginary 'content.'"

This high-tech consumption- and corporate-oriented antidemocratic bulk culture of cyberlearning is in sharp contrast with the picture Ivan Illich (1971, 84) draws in his utopia of tomorrow's learned society where public places are equipped with various learning facilities which can be used without charge. Cyber-learning thus has many faces. On one hand, it is an ideological apparatus inside another ideological apparatus, namely institutional education and corporate media-entertainment industry. On the other hand, it is yet another mode of distinction that increases symbolic capital for those who already possess skills and competencies in new technology, and who, for example, have computers at their disposal.

But, at the same time it is clear that the commercial cyberculture is not the whole story. Some writers even believe that there is a subculture of cyber-activism that contains too much restless spirit and "too much creative energy for corporate interest to ever control it" (Bronson and Katz 1997, 29). Fittingly, Douglas Kellner (2001) calls the Internet "a contested terrain," which is used by both the right and the left, by media corporations and by radical media and activist groups. Whatever results eventually from these struggles remains to be seen, but it seems inevitable that political activism must take presence in the new media and use the new information technology if it is to be effective:

> Deploying computer-mediated technology for technopolitics, however, opens new terrains of political struggle for voices and groups excluded from mainstream media and thus increases potential for resistance and intervention by oppositional groups. Hence, if revolution is to have a future in the contemporary era it must incorporate technopolitics as part of its strategy, conceiving of technopolitics, however, as an arm of struggle and not an end in and of itself. (3)

Thus we could call this second and radical realm the counterculture of cyber-learning, which consists of the activities of different socialist, feminist, ecological, peace and human rights movements, communities, groups of activists, and subcultures. This cultural field tries to maintain the lifeworld free of corporate colonization and fit for living, and many activists are striving for this goal through digital and other kind of networking. Yet, we must avoid false optimism, which means being able to discern between forces that are nothing apart of alternative subcultures and the ones that have the critical potential to be oppositional countercultures: "between someone who finds a different way to live and wishes to be left alone with it, and someone who finds a different way to live and wants to change society in its light. This is usually the difference between individual and small group solutions to social crisis and those solutions which properly belong to political and ultimately revolutionary practice" (Williams 1980, 41–42).

Most of the technosavvy youth—romanticized by many teachers and theorists—are in fact just participants in different alternative subcultures, happy to live in their specialized pockets of IT communities, without further ado of the state of the world outside those pockets. They seek their pleasures, perhaps independently, inventively, and free of prefabricated contents of entertainment, but still within the ideological boundaries of the consumer capitalism and with the same rationale of legitimated hedonism and egoism. Their highly developed technoliteracy per se does not turn them into any kind of technorevolutionaries. Changing the world is not their goal—quite the contrary, they sign into the relativistic logic of "live and let live," championed by libertarian right-wingers as well.

This will not suffice for those of us who are willing to build on the ideals of revolutionary education. Instead, part of our hope may reside in two groups branded as "criminals" or "terrorists" and "hooligans" by the conservative establishment and the leading media: the hackers and the antiglobalization activists. First of all, it is a good sign that such misguided brand names have been so eagerly placed on them, because it shows that the establishment has understood their ability to threaten the fabricated consensus and silence around serious issues. It is time for critical intellectuals, theorists, and teachers to understand this potential too. What unites these otherwise very different movements is their resistance to and explicit criticism of the logic of making profit and their vision of high technology as a medium of social transformation. They do not trade in money, but in information, data, code, ideas and ideals, knowledge, action, and of course, also pleasures.

The original hacker communities were born out of the idea that the tools of communication should be free and open for all in the new ICT world as well. It had, as the genuine hacker ethics still has, strong democratic and also anticapitalistic determinations, and its goal was to keep the code free.[3]

But to keep the code free and channels open and existing will not suffice in itself: "A key to developing a robust technopolitics is articulation, the mediation of technopolitics with real problems and struggles, rather than self-contained reflections on the internal politics of the Internet" (Kellner 2001, 15). We have to encourage people to bring out their message and put critical issues on the agenda.

This is exactly what the new globally oriented social movements and international activism today are about. Primarily they are also struggling to keep the channels of communication open, as freedom of speech and expression is gradually being connected to wealth and to the interests of media conglomerates. This has been one the major issues for activists in Seattle, in Prague, in Gothenburg, and in Genoa—and the reason why they have had to take their message to the streets in order to reclaim lost public space and make visible the democratic deficit so typical of formally free Western societies today. And, we must add, the organized violence of the police has only helped to emphasize their argument.

Another step is that, in order to create real countercultural and political effects, this movement needs to join forces with other social and anticapitalist movements— both new and traditional—such as the workers' unions, the Socialists, the Greens, Third Worldists, anarchists, ATTAC, and the like, as well as the critical theorists and academics. Counterpositions among anticapitalism, labor, and other movements, or activists and theorists, are useless. As protest against economic globalization around the world clearly show (see Kellner 2001; Suoranta and Tomperi 2002), "those engaged in different kinds of collective action are increasingly motivated by a sense that, beyond their specific concerns or grievances, lies a common enemy—global capitalism" (Callinicos 2001, 116). Moreover, it is the multitude and incoherence of various movements that finally "encourage the elaboration of different, mutually incompatible alternative models" of society, and through theoretically articulating and practically implementing "these models we are likely to develop a much clearer sense of how we can transcend capitalism" (119).

Hopefully, these developments and movements in different sectors of IT culture will form an antidote against the neoliberal biopower and the rapidly forming capitalist technocracy. Theories on cyber-learning are still often based on naïve assumptions about the omnipotence of information technologies that will increase democracy and equal opportunities. The belief that social, political, and educational problems could be solved and qualitative improvements made through technological development only amounts to technocracy. This is the ultimate threat: if we give way for technocracy, we will surrender our individual and collective autonomy and initiative to those whose interests the technology already serves, and they will make sure it will remain that way. Therefore radical revolutionary pedagogy must be able to see mutual interests with the IT activists and ready to form resistance and effective alliances of everyday learning with cyborg guerillas. We must also theorize the larger contexts of the movements to see the fundamentally important connections between the new and the older forms of activism.

WHAT IS TO BE DONE? RECLAIMING THE POLITICS OF EDUCATION

One of the most problematic issues in democratization of the media and IT culture is the balance between positive and negative effects of decentralized information systems. The Internet resists centralization and hierarchization, which has led many theorists to celebrate its democratic potential. However, decentralization can also hinder effective resistance (Dillinger 2001). As long as communities remain small and share some common standards in ethics and in evaluation of knowledge, decentralization works for egalitarian initiatives. But when the amount of information (or data) grows and the participants of communication can potentially be anywhere in the world, as in the case of the Internet, then the problems begin to show. As noted earlier, we should not trust the liberal and bourgeois myth of humans as rational, autonomous choosers who individually view their world and wisely select information to make the most rational choices based on apparently pure facts and logic.

If we are to create subversive and revolutionary practices, it will take more than just grassroots struggles to keep the channels of communications open and to disseminate essential information—repressed by the leading media—of the prevailing conflicts and antagonisms, and the state of the world and society. This is the calling for a coherent, revolutionary theory and the pedagogy to go with it. We still need the theoretical attempts to form effective, coherent and even synoptic interpretations of what is going on in the world. Lenin's famous statement in his "What is to be done?" is relevant for all critical teachers today now more than ever: "Without a revolutionary theory there can be no revolutionary movement" (Lenin 1976, 109). We believe that at its best, institutional education can be an effective and revolutionary counterforce to the consumer-media form of capitalism. But, to be a revolutionary power, education needs a revolutionary theory.

In the Freirean spirit Finnish sociologist Matti Hyvärinen (1984) has claimed that to overcome the abyss between orthodox Marxism (as a ready-made belief system) and people's possibilities to reach their full potential and act upon their own goals, it is imperative to create dialogical practices where people can meet each others as openly as possible with as little orthodoxy as possible. Perhaps the forms of civic activism today are openings for radical pedagogy in the vein of dialogical practices longed for by Hyvärinen. They can transgress the boundaries between formal and informal education and bring up essential issues and real learning needs, instead of instrumental educational contents that are filling the formal and institutional schooling. Here, if anywhere, the Freirean idea of problem-posing pedagogy becomes a reality, understood as learning in action, a movement toward an emancipatory praxis: "the action and reflection of human beings upon their world in order to transform it" (Freire 1970, 66). The learning in civic activism is more than "problem-based" education present in school pedagogy today, which usually means just learning through problems or using problems as just another method of teaching, as if problems were external both to the world and the inner sense of learning. Paulo Freire's message was that we can learn by dealing with real social problems, and we must deal with social problems by learning. This reciprocal relation of the word and the world, of the need to learn and the need to change the world lays the foundation of an education that is revolutionary and creative, as well as dialogic and dynamic, and, thus, links theory and practice firmly together.

When searching for alternatives, the first issue that must be addressed is the neoliberal hegemony of setting the agenda in public discussion on politics, economy, and schooling. Often this hegemony makes it look like there was no alternative to the current system. The public has become extremely passive in outlook as a result; also they share the "TINA" syndrome: "There is no alternative." The question that should be asked is why has the public become lethargic. It is true that there have been sporadic outbursts of discontent but in general collective action has been scarce and, for example, in Finland, practically nonexistent.

Critical educators must work to deconstruct the manufactured consent on the surface and to bring out the underlying real conflicts of class, race, gender, ethnicity, and age. Michael Yates has argued for a radical transformation in how we educate students inside a neoliberal globalized world. For Yates (1998, 1), it is important that students understand the underlying principles of political economy. This understanding must be in such a way "that they come to see it as one driven by class conflict, driven by the exploitation of wage labor by the capitalist class, and in need of radical transformation."

What is important for revolutionary pedagogy is for human beings to apprehend their reality as social beings and to equate knowledge with power. Knowledge should not passively reflect the real world but rather knowledge should allow the human being to actively influence reality and its development. The basic premise for the revolutionary educator is to create the social environment and social consciousness necessary for the human being to reach their full potential in social capacities. In this way "workers must develop the social capacity to dream, to understand, to participate, and to act politically" (Gindin and Panitch 2000, 4). Classrooms and schools of education need to become institutions where "dangerous" ideas are formulated and debated. Marshall Berman (2000) has referred to this concept as "jaytalking" (as in "jaywalking"). Jaytalking is an ability to question assumptions and evidence. It is an ability to speak provocatively about issues of substance and to question what you are taught and also to put into question your belief patterns. In other words, jaytalking is the ability to critically think your way through the maze that envelopes our society.

IN PLACE OF TECHNO-CAPITALISM: OUTLINES FOR A DIFFERENT SOCIETY

The time of ready-made utopias might be over, and there might not be any point in reviving the rigid, rationally guided utopian planning, neither in education nor in any other field of governance. But, on the other hand, the utopian imagination and sensibility must always play part in the revolutionary approach to education. In addition to the utopian aspect of hope, as developed by Ernst Bloch and other writers in critical theory, we are referring to the necessary sensibility to recognize positive developments toward the ultimate goal of egalitarian and unalienated society.

Concerning the structural transformation of society, we could borrow R. G. Peffer's (1990) principles toward a theory of social justice that could be incorporated into the general governance of economic well being by revolutionary pedagogical practice. Peffer's first principle of social justice states: "Everyone's security rights and subsistence rights shall be respected" (418). This principle is extremely important if a theory of social justice is to be implemented as a core part of a well-developed human society that truthfully cares about Marx's (1970) famous notion in his *Critique of the Gotha Program*: "From each according to his ability, to each according to his needs!"

A person's *humanitas* is directly tied to the essence of economic and social security. The basic needs of the human are formed around the simple moments of life like food, clothing, shelter, work, and education. Other human rights become expanded when these five simple truths are given priority in human life engagement. Full employment with job security creates favorable conditions for the social community of individuals whereas common education prepares for responsible contributions for the common good. For Peffer, security and subsistence rights provide the "minimum floor of well-being" (1990, 420). The goal is to build a solid foundation on the minimum in order to construct more floors for the maximum of human development not just for us in the North corner of the globe but also throughout the world.

Peffer's second principle concerns "a maximum system of equal basic liberties" that would include the freedom of speech, assembly, conscience, and thought; freedom to possess personal property and most importantly "freedom from arbitrary arrest" as being defined by the "rule of law" (418). As important qualities for human society, equal basic liberties are precisely those that are distributed equally throughout it. Thus in capitalism there is no true understanding of equal basic liberties; there is only the word, not the deed. For liberties cannot be divorced from social practices nor can they become passively received. Thus it is the ultimate task of the revolutionary educators to foster social practices inside and outside the classroom that promote equal liberties to nourish.

True liberty, one that is separated from inner and outer falseness in word, can only occur through a dignified existence of human beings that are engaged in active deeds for humankind. As Simone Weil (2001, 81) opined: "True liberty is not defined by a relationship between desire and satisfaction, but by a relationship between thought and action; the absolutely free man [*sic*] would be he whose every action proceeded from a preliminary judgment concerning the end which he set himself and the sequence of means suitable for attaining this end."

Furthermore, the human being must be free to act in what Weil terms "common wisdom." It is this common wisdom that takes us away from the arbitrary and centers our thinking in practical reflection and critique. The idea would be to take the concept of liberty away from the consumerist use and put it squarely in use of collective good and action. It is through collective action that society reaches a free community of individuals where human beings work for a wholesome social capacity on behalf of the social commons.

It is obvious that in terms of equal human development there are unequal basic liberties manifesting in various categories throughout the world. This trend of development will need to be reversed if we are to build a society where true human liberty will begin to develop. Mechanisms for such development are not just found in freedom of speech, freedom of assembly, freedom of thought, and other basic human rights under capitalism associated with liberal thinking. Rather, a healthy organic social commons would emphasize more fundamental basic liberties. Such liberties would focus on good quality health care (regardless of place of residence), the prospects for employment, a basic right to work without fear of being unemployed due to market fluctuations, and good quality public schooling regardless of one's social class, gender, and ethnicity.

Peffer's (1990, 418) third principle for social justice states that there "is to be (a) a right to an equal opportunity to attain social positions and offices and (b) an equal right to participate in all social decision-making processes within institutions of which one is part." The principle would also need to focus on making us the subject and not the object of our social, political, educational, or economic environments. For us to be free and feel free in a genuine definition of liberty we must be included in the decision-making processes, which govern our own lifeworld. This would be true not just for the political arena but also for self-governance inside the family as well as for work and learning communities.

Peffer's fourth and last principle states: "Social and economic inequalities are justified if, and only if, they benefit the least advantaged, consistent with the just savings principle, but are not to exceed levels that will seriously undermine equal worth of liberty or the good of self-respect" (Peffer 1990, 418). For Peffer, the "just savings principle" would ensure that the generation to which the human being belongs "will not inherit a completely impoverished and/or polluted environment" (422). We can no longer forget that ecology sets the ultimate boundaries for human world and that these boundaries are already transgressed massively. In these circumstances the growth of inequality is fatal to the least advantaged, who are incapable of sheltering themselves in times of crises. It is the poor who always suffer the most during economic and ecological catastrophes caused by the conspicuous consumption of the privileged.

Unfortunately, inequality is a normal part of capitalism's moral development and its communicative imperative "not to do you good, to educate you, to inform you, to develop you, but to sell your buying power and buying capacity on the largest possible scale" (Willis 2000, 49). When gross inequalities reside in a society, no amount of increase in the buying power of the poor will offer a solution alone. It is a question of ensuring human dignity, liberty, and sustainable living conditions for all, and this calls not only for higher living standards for the poor but also a radical redistribution of wealth and a newborn sense of social solidarity between all the segments of a society. It is thus our urgent task as critical revolutionary educators to lay the seeds for democratic and inclusive learning. By encouraging the active participation of all the people, regardless of their social status, we will help them to regain their collective memory and imagination. Fostering people's ability to analyze capitalism's hydra-headed dimensions should take central place in all initiatives toward critical thinking and collective political action. For Kamenka, a Marxist definition of dignity means "a society in which labor acquires dignity and becomes free because it is carried out by full and conscious participants in a community given over to cooperation and common aims" (in Peffer 1990, 119). It is in this area of even development of cooperation and common aims where a "just savings principle" could take affect and be successful.

Here we are reminded of Francis Noel Babuef and his Society of Equals. In the heydays of the French Revolution Babuef (in Goldston 1966, 31-32) declared that "we can no longer endure, with the enormous majority of men, labor and sweat in the service and for the benefit of a small majority." For Babuef, the struggle was about economic and political justice rooted deeply in economic and political equality. For advocating these basic human rights he was guillotined in the year 1796. The struggle of Babuef's, and so many others before and after him, continues today in many colors, forms, and practices also through revolutionary learning that supports active participation of people in shaping their political, cultural, and ecological futures.

NOTES

1. In his management book *Leading the Revolution* Gary Hamel (2000, 188–93) has written extensively about being a revolutionary in the workplace to institute change and transformation for a more productive, efficient, and profitable company. According to Hamel, a revolutionary needs a "point of view." This point of view must be well-developed, coherent, and emotionally compelling. For Hamel, a revolutionary must speak to the hearts and intellect of the people. A revolutionary also needs to be aware of "what is changing in the world; what opportunities do these changes make possible and what are the . . . concepts that would profitably exploit these changes" (188). Hamel also stresses the need for a revolutionary to write a manifesto which "speaks to timeless human needs and aspirations," draws "clear implications for action," convincingly demonstrates "the inevitability of the cause," and elicits support from the people (191). This manifesto, however, "must capture peoples' imagination" and build a case not only for the revolutionary intellectual's authority but also for the moral authority of the revolutionary (193). Hamel's book seems to be filled with wonderful strategies for corporate "revolutionaries." Someone would even think that revolutionary educators have much to learn from the business world in terms of strategy and tactics. However, the strategies must be radicalized. In other words, revolutionary educators need not only to develop but also open new and revolutionary social, economic ,and political dialogues inside the classroom. A true saboteur and change insurgent inside the classroom thus challenges corporate ideologies and tactics, and creates her classroom as a place of *critical economic literacy* (about the term, see Buckingham 2000, 167).

2. The International Telecommunication Union (2004) publishes worldwide reports on the indicators of the use of information and communication technologies. The statistics and case studies easily show how enormous the "digital divide" still is: for instance, in sub-Saharan Africa (and thus in the majority of African countries) less than 7 percent of the population have access to telephones and less than 1 percent have access to the Internet. Accordingly, the well-known "How Many Online?" report of the Nua Internet Surveys (2004) estimates that in 2002 there were around 190.91 million Internet users in Europe and 182.67 million in the United States and Canada, compared to only 6.31 million in the whole of Africa. There is a real danger that as the technology develops, those who have less opportunities now will be left even more behind when the wealthy North steps up to the next stage of techno-capitalism. The solution lies not in high-tech but in "low-tech" innovations to fill the need for basic communication tools in the circumstances of poor infrastructure—but as with Medicare, the companies are not interested in these low-profit markets.

3. One of the achievement of the movement has been the nowadays quite popular GNU/Linux operating system. The movement itself has been divided over opinions on the commercialization of software and the "open source," and despite the many early pioneers who have traded their idealism to cash, a certain side of the hacker community has kept up the high ideals of the free distribution and the open source code. Richard M. Stallman became and remains the most renowned advocate of this radical freedom of the information branch of hackerism. Central points of democratic hackerism are obviously important to any programs of social change: to secure the freedom of information and to increase diversity of opinions, and the tolerance of diversity. These are first steps toward a truly democratic society, and the freedom of information; they also mean struggles over the ownership and control of the forms of media. Whereas the consolidation of big media and the corporate hold of educational institutions, technologies, and learning spaces work against democracy, the hackers work for democracy, for democratic control of media technology, hard- and software and through them also contents and communication. So the hackers and the activists of the "free software" movement, as well as many other movements of freedom of speech within cyberspace (for instance, the FOS, free online scholarship movement), are trying to secure the preliminary, structural conditions for democratic transformation of the capitalistic societies.

REFERENCES

Apple, M. 1988. *Teachers and texts: A political economy of class and gender relations in education.* New York: Routledge.
Bauman, Z. 1995. *Life in fragments.* Oxford: Blackwell.
Berman, M. 2000. *Blue jay way: Where will critical culture come from?* Available at www.dissentmagazine.org/archive/w100/berman.html.
Bourdieu, P. 1996. *On television.* New York: New Press.
Bowers, C. A. 1993. *Critical essays on education, modernity, and the recovery of the ecological imperative.* New York: Teachers College Press.
Brockman, J. 1996. *Inter-not.* Available at www.utne.com/lens/mt/19minternot.html.
Bronson, P., and J. Katz. 1997. Why William Bennett is a blockhead. *At Random* 6 (1): 27–31.
Bruner, J. 1996. *The culture of education.* Cambridge, Mass.: Harvard University Press.
Buckingham, D. 2000. *After the death of childhood.* Cambridge, Engl.: Polity Press.
Callinicos, A. 2001. *Against the third way.* Cambridge, Engl.: Polity Press.
Chomsky, N. 2000. *Chomsky on miseducation.* Lanham, Md.: Rowman & Littlefield.
Denzin, N. 1994. Postpragmatism: Beyond Dewey and Mead. *Symbolic Interaction* 17 (4): 453–63.
Dillinger, B. 2001. *Controlling the Internet: Cyberdemocracy or just more channels?* Available at lingua.kie.utu.fi/bredelli/elearning/internet_control.htm.
Freire, P. 1970. *Pedagogy of the oppressed.* New York: Continuum.

Gindin, S., and L. Panitch. 2000. Rekindling socialist imagination: Utopian vision and working-class capacities. *Monthly Review* 51, no. 10. Available at www.mothlyreview.org/300gind.htm.

Giroux, H. 1995. Pulp fiction and the culture of violence. *Harvard Educational Review* 65 (2): 299–313.

———. 2000. Representations of violence, popular culture, and demonization of youth. In *Smoke and Mirrors*, ed. S. Spina, 93–105. Lanham, Md.: Rowman & Littlefield.

Goldston, R. 1985. *The Russian revolution.* New York: Ballentine Books.

Gumport, P. 2000. Academic restructuring: Organizational change and institutional imperatives. *Higher Education* 39 (1): 67–91.

Hamel, G. 2000. *Leading the revolution.* Boston: Harvard Business School Press.

Haseler, S. 2000. *The super-rich: The unjust new world of global capitalism.* London: Macmillan Press and St. Martin's Press.

Hyvärinen, M. 1984. *Alussa oli liike* [In the beginning there was a movement]. Tampere, Finland: Vastapaino.

Illich, I. 1971. *Deschooling society.* New York: Harper and Row.

International Telecommunication Union. 2004. ICT indicators: Africa (2003) and telecom projections; Africa (1995–2005). Available at www.itu.int/ITU-D/ict/.

Kellner, D. 2001. *Globalization, technopolitics and revolution.* Available at www.gseis.ucla.edu/faculty/kellner/papers/GlobTPRev-Foran.htm.

Klein, N. 2000. *No logo.* London: Flamingo.

Lankshear, C., M. Peters, and M. Knobel. 1996. Critical pedagogy and cyberspace. In *Counternarratives,* ed. H. Giroux, C. Lankshear, P. McLaren, and M. Peters, 149–88. New York: Routledge.

Lenin, V. 1976. *Selected works.* Vol. 1. Moscow: Progress Publishers.

Levitas, M. 1974. *Marxist perspectives in the sociology of education.* London: Routledge and Kegan Paul.

Martin, H. P., and H. Schumann. 1996. *Die globalisierungsfalle.* Hamburg, Ger.: Rowohlt Verlag.

Marx, K. 1970. Critique of the Gotha program. In *Selected Works,* Vol. 3, ed. K. Marx and F. Engels, 13–30. Moscow: Progress Publishers. Available online www.marxists.org/archive/marx/works/1870/gotha/ch01.htm.

McLaren, P. 2000. *Che Guevara, Paulo Freire, and the pedagogy of revolution.* New York: Rowman & Littlefield.

———. 2001. The killing field and the necessity of memory [interview with Juha Suoranta]. *International Journal of Educational Reform* 10 (2): 163–75.

McLaren, P., and R. Farahmandpur. 2001a. Educational policy and the socialist imagination: Revolutionary citizenship as a pedagogy of resistance. *Educational Policy* 15 (3): 343–78.

———. 2001b. Teaching against globalization and the new imperialism: Toward a revolutionary pedagogy. *Journal of Teacher Education* 52 (2): 136–50.

Miller, M. C. 2002. What's wrong with this picture? The media cartel and its cultural effects. *Nation,* January 7, 2002. Available at www.thenation.com/issue.mhtml?i=20020107.

Morris, W. 2000. *How we live and how we might live.* Available at www.marxist.org/archive/morris/1884/hwl/hwl.htm.

Mäki, T. 2002. *Teemu Mäki.* Jyväskylä, Finland: Like.

Nua Internet Surveys. 2004. How many online? Available at www.nua.com/surveys/how_many_online/index.html.

Peffer, R. G. 1990. *Marxism, morality, and social justice.* Princeton, N.J.: Princeton University.

Postman, N. 1996. *The end of education.* New York: Vintage Books.

Rinne, R. 2000. The globalisation of education: Finnish education on the doorstep of the new EU millenium. *Educational Review* 52 (2): 131–42.

Spender, D. 1995. *Nattering on the net.* North Melbourne: Spinifex Press.

Streibel, Michael. 1998. A critical analysis of three approaches to the use of computers in education. In *The curriculum: Problems, politics, and possibilities,* ed. L. Beyer and M. Apple. New York: State University of New York.

Suoranta, J., and T. Tomperi. 2002. From Gothenburg to everywhere—bonfires of revolutionary learning. *Review of Education/Pedagogy/Cultural Studies* 24, (1–2): 29–47.

Trifonas, Peter Pericles, ed. 2000. *Revolutionary pedagogies.* New York: RoutledgeFalmer.

Weil, S. 2001. *Oppression and liberty.* London: Routledge.

Westö, M., and C. Kihlman. 2000. *Epätoivon toivo* [The hope of despair]. Jyväskylä, Finland: Tammi.

Williams, R. 1980. *Base and superstructure in marxist cultural theory: Problems in materialism and culture.* New York: Verso.

Willis, P. 2000. *The ethnographic imagination.* Cambridge, Engl.: Polity Press.

Yates, M. D. 1998. An essay on radical labor education. *Cultural Logic* 2, no. 1. Available at www.eserv.org/clogic/2-1/yates.html.

12

Schooling and the Culture of Dominion: Unmasking the Ideology of Standardized Testing

Antonia Darder

Since its inception in the United States, the public school system has been seen as a method of disciplining children in the interest of producing a properly subordinate adult population. Sometimes conscious and explicit, and at other times a natural emanation from the conditions of dominance and subordinacy prevalent in the economic sphere, the theme of social control pervades educational thought and policy.

—S. Bowles and H. Gintis, *Schooling in Capitalist America*

It became considerably more clear to me that the notion of hegemony is not free floating. It is in fact tied to the state in the first place. As part of the state, education, then, must be seen as an important element.

—Michael Apple, *Education and Power*

Most Americans are probably unaware of how Washington exercises its global hegemony, since so much of this activity takes place . . . under comforting rubrics. Many may, as a start, find it hard to believe that our place in the world even adds up to an empire. But only when we come to see our country as both profiting from and trapped within the structures of an empire of its own making will it be possible for us to explain many elements of the world that otherwise perplex us.

—Chalmers Johnson, *Blowback: The Costs and Consequences of American Empire*

Public education in the United States has consistently presented itself in the last century as a liberal democratizing force for the world that operates in the name of justice, freedom, and excellence. However, closer examination of schooling practices reveals a culture of dominion at work—a "structure of an empire" that systematically reproduces, reinforces, and sustains the hegemonic forces of social control and regulation linked to class oppression, gender inequalities, and the racialization of populations. Hence it should not be surprising to discover that popular myths related to meritocracy, the rights and privilege of the elite, and the need for state consensus, have all served well to conserve an ideology that readily supports the current craze over high stakes testing in public schools today.

This rapidly growing phenomenon can be understood in connection to major changes in the socioeconomic landscape of U.S. society—changes that potentially could ignite greater class conflict and social unrest than modern history has ever known. And this condition continues to worsen for the growing numbers of working-class people, given recent events associated with the global political economy that have resulted in thousands of workers being laid off with fewer options for employment. This theme was echoed in a speech given at the Asia-Europe-U.S. Progressive Scholar's Forum: Globalization and Innovation of Politics in Japan by Jeff Faux (2002) of the Economic Policy Institute in Washington, D.C. In his comments, he confirmed that inequality has become worse. "In the short term, we can expect the U.S. unemployment rate . . . to rise. . . . In the long term, the U.S. economy is clearly headed for a financial crisis," with an account deficit of more than $400 billion (4, 8). Moreover, preliminary findings from *State of Working America* (Economic Policy Institute 2002) predict that unless the economy reverses course soon, working families can look forward to high and rising unemployment that will generate wage stagnation, higher poverty rates, and rising inequality. The response of workers to the impact of this economic decline on their lives is well-illustrated in a recent front page story in *The Christian Science Monitor* titled "Labor More Militant as Economy Teeters," which reports that "the nation's economic slowdown is threatening millions of ordinary workers' paychecks and jobs" (Belsie 2002).

Alex Molner (1996) in *Giving Kids the Business* points out that simultaneously with a depressed economy and worsening condition for workers, we find "the rhetoric about the catastrophic failure of American public schools [has] become even more feverish." Business leaders clamor for free-market solutions to educational problems, alleging that these solutions can improve education at no additional cost. What lies hidden is that these reforms "offer a public-spirited justification for introducing education to the profit motive and giving educators a healthy dose of the 'real world' in the form of competition. Most important, they keep the focus on schools and off the failure of business to promote the well-being of most of the countries citizens" (10).

In response to the pressure of business, the enterprise of education has become more and more fixated on making claims of scientific authority to carry out its instrumentalized policies in response to the academic problems faced by students from working class and communities of color. As such, it is interesting to note the historical parallels that exist between contemporary "accountability experts" in education and the "cost-efficiency consultants" of the early part of the twentieth century. Conditions that parallel these two historical eras include increasing immigration, burgeoning student enrollments in urban centers, economic decline, and overt military action overseas. Moreover, the same rhetoric of corruption and declining efficiency of public schools, so prevalent among corporate elites today, was utilized to legitimate the move by big business leaders to take control of public education in the early 1900s. At that time, elite businessmen ran for school boards and solicited the advice of efficiency experts like Frederick Taylor, in their misguided effort to make schools function like well-oiled factory machines.

THE POLITICS OF ACCOUNTABILITY

In today's world, corporate leaders again hold the enterprise of education hostage, in exchange for support of tax hikes and budget increases. The tactics of these businessmen are closely aligned to the idea that schools should now function with the efficiency of a for-profit business, with a chief executive officer-type holding the reins of the district and the language and practices of schooling translated into the technical realm of accountability. Accordingly, they insist that measurable, scientifically based objectives should be the primary impetus for making decisions, designing curricula, and articulating the pedagogical imperatives of the classroom.

Hence, business leaders advocate fervently for an increase in standardized testing, arguing "that emphasis on testing ensures that (a) schools and teachers are accountable to communities and students are accountable for their lessons, (b) quality of education is increasing as scores increase, (c) economic and academic opportunities are expanding for students that attain higher scores, and (d) schools are accountable to a patriotic curriculum. Using standardized tests as a hammer, many of these leaders tell students to be accountable for their classwork and homework, parents to be accountable for their children's performance and teachers to be accountable for their students' performance. In doing so, they effectively marginalize discussion of the real problems in education" (Caputo-Pearl 2001, 4).

In the process, the singular indicator of tests scores has achieved an overarching prominence, seriously limiting educational debates to that of numbers and categories of students to be tested. Consequently, the majority of questions welcomed and legitimated within this narrow discourse of quality and accountability uphold an uncritical adherence to standardized testing as the most effective and legitimate means for assessing academic achievement. Rather than entertaining questions regarding student abilities and overall performance, the current questions that dominate educational debates all loop back to the issue of testing and the improvement of test scores. Thus, it is not unusual for educators to primarily ponder questions such as: How soon can recent immigrant students be tested? What subjects and grade levels should be tested? What scores should be used to determine grade promotion or graduation? What degree of movement in the improvement of scores should be required to grant principal bonuses? What scores should determine teacher merit pay?

Within the current discourse of accountability, rarely is there any serious or substantive mention of academic success outside test score indicators. In this closed system of accountability, dialogue related to the very conditions under which schooling functions, its unexamined assumptions, and its effect on students is negated, as such questions are deemed irrelevant or scientifically irrational. Hence, any issue not captured by the measurement of test scores is considered simply anecdotal or, worse, ideological prattle, justifying its dismissal as inconsequential to public policy and educational debates. And nowhere is this change more evident than in California, where the reform movement in support of testing and the standardization of knowledge has openly and unabashedly turned the education of working-class and poor students of color into "drill and kill" exercises of teaching-to-the-test and highly scripted literacy instruction such as Open Court, which is being widely used by many districts. The exceedingly prescriptive nature of these practices leaves little doubt that state testing and test-driven curricula are, directly or indirectly, linked to an academically limiting system of social control—a system that successfully sustains the reproduction of class formation within *both* public schools and the larger society.

Moreover, to ensure compliance, school funding, principal tenure, and teacher incentive pay are being determined more and more by performance contracts linked to performance as measured on a single indicator—the aggregation of student standardized test scores. Hence, standardized testing is increasingly being used as the central mechanism for decisions about student learning, teacher and administrative practice, and overall school quality (Heubert and Hauser 1999). This is exemplified by a supplementary section published in the *Rocky Mountain News* (August 1, 2002) titled CSAP (Colorado Student Assessment Program) 2002: A Guide to Results of the Student Assessment Tests. The twenty-four-page supplement (of which eighteen pages consist of test scores for Colorado schools) reported "Colorado's largest-ever release of state scores" (2E). Story headlines reveal the problems with standardized testing in the Denver Public Schools (DPS): "Test Scores Hit the Wall" (2E); "Schools Fare Better, Worse in DPS" (3E); "Affluent Districts Score at Top. Spotty performance to cost Jeffco $4.5 million. Tax Dollars are tied to results in state's largest school districts" (4E).

The consequence here is that the institutionalized locus of control over curriculum, teaching, and assessment, all based on a tightly regimented set of prescriptions, not only locates authority of educational decisions at the state level but also, as mentioned earlier, locates the power over those decisions in the domain of business leaders. The insidious nature of this hegemonic mechanism of control is glaringly evident in a national commission report issued in the early 1990s by the Ford Foundation, which estimated that nearly 130 million standardized tests were being administered to elementary and secondary students, at an estimated cost of $500 million per year (Toch 1991). This has resulted in the preponderance of testing within public schools, and the reform movement so invested in it, "that increasingly it is in terms of standardized test scores alone that the nation judges its schools and educators judge themselves" (206).

Yet, despite its key role in the accountability reform movement, studies repeatedly show that standardized tests are flawed when used as a single measure of progress, because they fail to measure students' ability to judge, analyze, infer, interpret, or reason—namely, engage in critical thought. Standardized tests have been found even less useful in measuring students' more advanced academic knowledge. One reason for their failure is associated with the purpose behind norm-referenced tests, such as the Stanford 9 that has been widely administered in California Public Schools. These tests are designed to rank students against one another, rather than to measure student's knowledge of the material. Many of the questions "are intentionally developed so that a relatively high percentage of students will be tricked by them. This is an important method of differentiating one student from another in the rankings. Further because test scores are supposed to fall into a bell curve pattern in comparing one to the other, 50 percent of students will always be considered 'below average' or 'below middle ground' " (Caputo-Pearl 2001, 7). Other reasons associated with student failure are directly tied to questions of cultural relevancy and class biases hidden in the conceptual construction and language use of standardized tests.

If these were not enough to raise concerns, widespread testing problems related to the administration and scoring of tests is rampant. In New Mexico, 70 percent of superintendents recently reported a variety of testing errors. In Georgia, Harcourt Educational Measurement could not deliver accurate results from last spring's Stanford 9 tests in a timely fashion. In Nevada, officials reported that 736 sophomores and juniors had mistakenly been told they had failed the math portion of a test, although they had actually passed. And even states, such as North Carolina, "considered models of accountability are struggling to come up with reliable tests" (Jonsson 2002, 11).

Even more disconcerting here is the manner in which the politics of standardized testing functions to silence and prevent greater public engagement within communities. When the only language of currency for the construction of educational policy is linked to accountability, this language impedes and jeopardizes the capacity for critical civic interaction among parents, communities, and educators, in order to raise significant and more complex questions related to student academic success. Excluded are critiques based on democratic values, children's development, cultural differences, class privilege, and other critical questions that could potentially unveil the social and economic consequences tied to standardized testing. In the current political climate, the only conversations that are deemed meaningful are those that are linked directly to raising test scores.

In, *Contradictions of School Reform: Educational Costs of Standardized Testing*, Linda McNeil (2000) sheds light on the manner in which this insidious system of accountability is operationalized. First, the tenure for principals is replaced by "performance contracts." Their contract renewal, assignment, and annual bonuses are predicated on test scores results in their school—this reinforces the role of the principal as compliance officer and justifies the principal's intervention and control over the labor of teachers. Second, newspaper ratings and state rankings of schools disaggregate by race and ethnicity. Scores of all must "improve." "This disaggragating of scores gives the appearance that the system is sensitive to diversity and committed to improving minority education. This reporting, however, actually exacerbates . . . a focus on test to the exclusion of many other forms of education. Increasingly common is the substitution of commercial test-prep materials in place of traditional curricula and instructional activities for these students" (233). As a consequence, teachers are held captive to the accountability protocols set forth by the state, which leave little room to generate or execute more effective criteria for assessing the academic progress of their students.

DE-SKILLING OF TEACHERS

The requirements for standardized tests for students also sets into motion a series of state mandated curricula, all aimed at minimum skills that result from long-term pedagogical practices of social control and regulation within schools. Increasingly the curricula and tests are divorced from any serious consideration of critical forms of pedagogies or learning theories. More often than not, the development of standardized curriculum, assessment instruments, and high-stakes testing fails to consider the wealth of research and literature on teaching and learning to inform its execution. There is no question that an educational system that willingly ignores curriculum theory and child development research—not to mention the social, political, and economic realities of students' lives—has the veiled organizational objective to serve as a regulatory mechanism to control teacher work and student outcomes.

Testing and teaching-to-the test serve as mechanisms to instill a teacher-proof curriculum which in many cases may include narrowly prescribed checklists for assessing teaching and student minimum skills. Undoubtedly, such regimentation makes schooling exceedingly simple for less skilled teachers. Many of these teachers are happy to teach routine lessons according to a standard sequence and format, preferring to function as deskilled laborers who do not have to do much thinking or preparation with respect to their practice. In contrast, a teacher-proof instructional approach makes it extremely uncomfortable and disturbing for those teachers who know their subjects well, who teach in ways that critically engage their students, and who want teaching to be linked to the realities of students' lives. Moreover, this "controlling, top-down push for higher standards may actually produce a lower quality of education, precisely because the tactics constrict the means by which teachers most successfully inspire students' engagement in learning, and commitment to achieve" (Ryan and La Guardia 1999, 46).

The standardization of the curriculum at the state level echoes the distrust of teachers by the public and legislators—a fabricated distrust that is widely used to rally sentiment and support for high-stakes testing. Consequently, standardized testing results are used to support principal efforts to hold greater power over teachers, since test scores are deemed as a legitimate and objective way to measure teacher performance. The primary goal of the standardized curriculum then is to provide all teachers with the exact course content to which they must adhere. Hence, any variation in the quality of student performance, according to the current logic of accountability, can be tied directly to the quality of teaching. In this way, low student scores can be justified to fire teachers without further discussion and high student scores can be used to grant merit pay to teachers for their compliance.

This is an example of how a system of rewards and punishment works in schools to preserve the status quo, through a practice of using what people need or want (i.e., salary increase) as an incentive or motivation for compliance, whereby insuring teacher regulation and social control within the classroom. However, it is imperative to recognize that such a pervasive system of rewards and punishment is not predicated on a law of nature. It reflects a particular ideology or set of assumptions that must be questioned within education, particularly in terms of dismantling social agency and reinforcing dependency on school officials.

Alvy Kohn (1993), a staunch critic of the rewards and punishment system endemic to public school, views this system of social control and regulation as rooted in the legacy of behaviorism and scientism. Kohn laments that "we are a nation that prefers acting to thinking, and practice to theory, we are suspicious of intellectuals, worshipful of technology and fixated on the bottom line. We define ourselves by numbers—take home pay, percentiles (how much does your baby weigh), cholesterol counts, and standardized testing (how much does your child know). By contrast we are uneasy with intangibles and unscientific abstractions such as a sense of well-being or an intrinsic motivation to learn" (9–10).

In the urgency to test students, seldom are the disempowering effects and negative impact of the testing situation itself and the removal of students from the classroom several times during the year for testing discussed. At issue here is the manner in which such practices disrupt the developmental momentum of student learning, provoke enormous unnecessary stress and tension in students, and interfere with the quality of interaction in the classroom. In many ways, the politics of testing, along with the prescribed curriculum it inspires ultimately functions to erode teacher autonomy and creativity, as well as their authority within their classrooms. In the process, teachers are socialized to become highly dependent on prepackaged materials and the authority of state sanctioned educational experts to provide the next curricular innovation.

McNeil (2002) argues that the bottom line is that the state mechanism for assessing teacher quality like proficiency testing must be cheap, quick, generalizable across all subjects and school settings and capable of being used by school-level administrators independent of their knowledge of the subjects being taught. In many cases what is generated is a factory-like checklist reminiscent of the social efficiency era, reducing teaching to specific observable and thus, measurable behaviors; many having little or nothing to do with the classroom content being taught, nor the particular pedagogical needs of students. Typically, behaviors found on teacher assessment checklists can include such items as eye contact with students, having the daily objective written on the board, having a catchy opening phrase and definite closure to the lesson, and the number of times teachers vary their verbal responses to students.

A major consequence of standardized testing and teaching-to-the-test, is the manner in which the emphasis of learning shifts away from intellectual activity toward the dispensing of packaged fragments of information. Meanwhile, students and teachers as subjects of classroom discourse, who bring their personal stories and life experiences to bear on their teaching and learning, are systematically silenced by the need for the class to "cover" a generic curriculum at a prescribed pace established by the state. In making the case against standardized testing, Kohn (2000) argues that

> high-stakes testing has radically altered the kind of instruction that is offered in American schools, to the point that "teaching to the test" has become a prominent part of the nation's educational landscape. Teachers often feel obliged to set aside other subjects for days, weeks, or (particularly in schools serving low-income students) even months at a time in order to devote to boosting students' test scores. Indeed, both the content and the format of instruction are affected; the test essentially *becomes* the curriculum. (29)

It is significant to note that through the hegemonic process of standardized testing, teachers, as workers, have become the new scapegoat of the system. As a result of the political struggles in education rooted in the civil rights era, it became unfashionable to blame students, their parents, or their culture. Teachers, whose status is located at the next lowest rung of the educational hierarchy, became the most likely suspects. State and national teacher tests, constructed upon the very same premise as those administered to their students, are now being used as a primary indicator of teacher labor, rather than the quality of their actual teaching. Such a mechanism of assessment could now more easily be used to support the notion that the problem of student failure is the fault of poor teachers.

So, once again, educational debates have shifted from the quality of teaching and the schooling process to that of "quality control"—a shift that is closely linked with conservative political efforts to dictate the agenda of public education. Inherent in this debate is a justification for taking further control of their labor away from the hands of teachers. In the process, there is no consideration for increasing classroom resources; nor provisions made for instructional materials and ongoing teacher development that is linked to enhancing the quality of children's learning or teacher-parent relationships. There is little attention given to engaging communities and interest groups in a plan to rectify persistent inequalities. More clearly, there is little willingness to openly challenge the asymmetrical relations of power that result in the racialized reproduction of class formations, a strategy that must be central to efforts geared toward dismantling the educational injustices prevalent in public schools.

SCHOOLING AND THE CULTURE OF DOMINION

More disturbing is the use of this system of accountability to justify the undemocratic governance of urban public schools. In many ways, one can trace how the old efficiency rhetoric was brushed off and revamped into the new accountability rhetoric. This "new" rhetoric was quickly seized and embraced by those mainstream educators and researchers who felt they were losing control of schooling debates to progressive multicultural educators who clamored for greater democratic participation of teachers, students, parents, and communities. The language of scientific accountability with its narrow focus on test scores was seen as a sure way to replace the messiness of "interest group" participation in schools; that is, the participation of those who had historically been excluded from debates in the first place.

In this way, the politics of testing within public schools has historically played an insidious role in the perpetuation of underachievement among working-class students and students of color. Bowles and Gintis (1976) argue that "the educational system legitimates economic inequality by providing an open, objective, and ostensibly meritocratic mechanism for assigning individuals to unequal economic positions. Through the construction of testing instruments as value-free scientific tools, considered to produce objective, measurable, and quantifiable data, predefined skills and knowledge have been given priority at the expense of the cultural knowledge and experience of students from economically disenfranchised communities" (103).

As mentioned earlier, the evaluation and assessment of students (as well as teachers) then is predicated on the results of standardized tests, which are used to sort, regulate, and control students. Thus, the testing of students more and more drives the curriculum and prescribes both teaching and the role of students in their learning. This prescriptive teaching hardens and intensifies the discrimination already at work in schools, as teaching of the fragmented and narrow information on the test comes to substitute for substantive curriculum in the schools of poor and minority students. This intensified discrimination and widespread pattern of substituting test-prep materials, devoid of substantive content and respect for the ways children learn is most at work in schools where the majority of economically oppressed children attend. Hence, standardized testing has historically functioned to systematically reproduce, overtly and covertly, the conditions within schools that perpetuate a culture of elitism, privilege, and exploitation.

One of the most insidious dimensions tied to the preservation of a culture of dominion within schools is the unexamined philosophical assumptions and values, or ideology, that undergird and hence, legitimate educational policies and practices associated with standardized testing. Many of the values and assumptions at work in sustaining asymmetrical relations of power within the larger society have been engaged substantially in the work of radical educators, psychologists, sociologists, political scientists, economists, and other social critics during the last century. However, given the limitation of this essay, it is impossible to provide more than a brief glance at some of the primary values and assumptions operating within the context of schooling. Nevertheless, it must be emphasized that the interrelatedness of these assumptions often function in concert, to successfully veil the ideological contradictions that exist between a rhetoric of democratic ideals and the undemocratic practices at work in U.S. public schools today—assumptions that teachers may seldom connect to their teaching practice but nevertheless underlie what they do within their classrooms (Kohn 1993).

An overarching philosophical assumption that undergirds the ideology of public schooling today is the unbridled, but veiled, acceptance of Darwinian conclusions related to the belief in the "survival of the fittest." As a consequence, substantial educational rhetoric functions to justify the existence of economic inequality, sexism, racialized notions of humanity, and good old U.S. self-promotion at the expense of the greater good. Such rhetoric is well-disguised in the false benevolence at work in the discursive justifications for standardized testing, tracking, and the competitive and instrumentalizing curricular practices found within classrooms today.

As such, "common sense" beliefs about human nature, deeply rooted in racialized and class notions of normalcy, are actively at work in the assessment of student intellectual abilities and their potential for academic success. For example, racialized beliefs about the inferior or superior abilities and potential of particular student populations are often utilized to justify the so-called objective measurement of student knowledge and then to use these measures to justify the unequal distribution of educational resources and opportunities. Such racialized notions are at work in the disturbing "scientific" assertion that "race" determines academic performance made by Richard J. Hernstein and Charles Murray (1994) in their book *The Bell Curve.* "The term 'race' serves to conceal the truth that it is not 'race' that determines academic performance; but rather, that academic performance is determined by an interplay of complex social processes, one of which is premised on the articulation of racism . . . to affect exclusion in the classroom and beyond" (Darder and Torres 1999, 181). The fact that such practices effectively work to perpetuate class interests is well-hidden by an educational rhetoric that glorifies expediency in learning, dichotomizes theory from practice, heralds the conquest of nature, and objectifies time and human experience in the name of scientifically fabricated assessment criteria.

Also at work within this culture of dominion is an overwhelming penchant for unbridled individualism, at the expense of greater collective well-being. Hence, competition among students within the context of knowledge construction is strongly reinforced and well-rewarded. Students learn very quickly to acquiesce to the wiles of competition, if they are to be deemed as material for academic success in the future. In the process, knowledge is reified and objectified in such a way that students are socialized to accept the belief that somehow knowledge actually exists objectively disconnected from the subjective realm of human experience. This is in contrast to a view of knowledge that connects its construction and evolution to the realities of the larger social milieu. The consequence is that students become convinced, particularly as they advance in the educational hierarchy of achievement, that their goal is to independently construct some "original" notion, thought, idea, theory, and so on, in order to gain prominence within their chosen field. What seldom is acknowledged here is the organizational regimes of power or the hegemonic forces at work in the legitimation of knowledge and the institutional assignment of both "originality" and worthiness. It is most disturbing to note that these very qualities which are considered so essential in the education of elite students and then later, so crucial to the dictums of graduate school success, are virtually absent and almost entirely negated within the context of standardized testing within public schools.

Further, the individualistic and economist language so prevalent in the educational rhetoric of public school testing is deeply rooted in the ideological tenets of advanced capitalism. Its materialist emphasis on private property is extended to the domain of knowledge, where intellectual ideas become the property of an individual or the state. Hence, the pedagogy of the elite very early teaches students that they are the owners of their intellectual products with rights to sell or buy at their discretion. In contrast, poor and working class students are socialized to accept, accommodate, and comply to the knowledge deemed "truth," even when that knowledge is diametrically in opposition to their experience and their well-being. The emphasis of academic socialization then for these students is not to be creators of knowledge, but consumers of specific knowledge forms as prescribed by the dominant class. Nowhere is this prescription of knowledge for the oppressed more readily visible than in the politics of standardized testing—a prescription that is steeped in the rhetoric of scientism.

SCIENTISM AND MERITOCRACY

The scientific claim of accountability experts is one of the most devious and fallacious elements at work in the testing mania. An overemphasis on "hard" science and "absolute objectivity" gives rise to scientism, rather than any real

In the process, extensive field-based research on standardized testing that has documented its negative effects on teaching and learning, particularly to working class and students of color, is categorically ignored. Even worse is the lasting harm that imbedded controls, the legitimization of "accountability" as the language of school policy, and the elimination of the real possibilities for wider public debates on the purpose of schooling for poor, working class, and racialized students, has on concrete educational efforts to democratize schooling practices.

Scientism also supports a carte blanche adherence to the educational practice of meritocracy—a practice that functions as one of the primary hegemonic mechanisms implicated in the inequitable achievement and advancement of students within the educational system. It constitutes a form of systemic control by which the culture of dominion is naturalized and perpetuated. Public schools persistently tout this myth to guarantee that successful participation in the educational system becomes the most visible and legitimate process by which individuals are allocated or rewarded higher status within the society at large. Through a system of merit tied to high stakes testing for example, the process of unequal privilege and entitlement is successfully smoke-screened under the guise of "fair and equal" opportunity for all students.

Common practices of meritocracy linked to social promotion (or demotion) and graduation function as a twofold justification for the undemocratic distribution of wealth in this country and around the world. First, it establishes the merit of those in power as the legitimate criterion for achieved social position. And second, it persists in blaming those who fail for their underachievement (whether the blame is placed on to the teachers, the students, or the parents) by implying they do not have the necessary intelligence, motivation, or drive to partake of what is freely being offered them by the educational system. In other words, if students fail it's their own damn fault!

TESTING AND THE POLITICS OF SCHOOLING

Within a context of dominion, schools and educators as agents of the state are viewed as neutral and apolitical, whose sole purpose is to educate students with the necessary knowledge and skills to render them functional in and to society—in other words, to fulfill their place in the process of consumption and capitalist accumulation. Hence, ideas and practices that are in concert with dominant knowledge forms are generally perceived as neutral and acceptable, shrouding the authoritarianism of the status quo. Conversely, knowledge forms that in any substantive way might bring into question the "official" curriculum, methods or pedagogy are deemed "political" and unacceptable. To make things even more perplexing, the function of neutralizing contesting views is generally carried out simultaneously by a variety of social agents including: (a) those who knowingly support the limits and configuration of "official" authority within the fundamental order of public schools for their own personal gains; (b) those who are complicit as a consequence of insufficient knowledge and skills to contest; (c) those who protect their class interest by "playing the game" with a rhetoric of helping the oppressed; and (d) those who consent due to their overwhelming fear of authority.

Unfortunately, there are many educators and advocates from all walks of life, who confidently support the propagation of testing as a legitimate educational strategy within public schools, irrespective of the volumes that have been written linking standardized testing to cultural invasion and economic exploitation. The rallying cry of testing advocates is often tied to the question: "If we take away testing how will we have the objective criteria to demand better schools?" What is disturbing about this argument is that this myopic view fails to link an acceptance and adherence to such educational policies and practices with capitalist interests that perpetuate undemocratic life in this country and around the globe. Even more disturbing is the negative impact that such practices continue to have on students of all ages.

In the process, many well-meaning educators and advocates, who are content with playing the "race card" to rally support for their views, can actually obstruct the possibility for teachers, parents, and communities to publicly question and critique those ideas, practices, and events that go contrary to community self-determination and the construction of a genuinely democratic political movement in education. Many go so far as to propose that any discourse that puts into question racialized arguments in defense of testing as a good thing for students of color is somehow falling prey to white, bleeding-heart liberal tendencies. Radical efforts then to expose the long-term damage of testing to all oppressed students is rendered suspect, rather than recognizing that a concerted search for a wider range of information from which we can struggle (beyond identity politics) is crucial to dismantling the structures of capitalist domination and inequality at work in schools and society today.

What the history of civil rights struggles in the United States should have taught us is that our understanding of racialized practices within schools can never be separated from the reproduction of class relations. As such, practices of high-stakes testing must be understood as systematically implicated in the reproduction of racialized economic inequality and injustice. For it is precisely through the uncontested acceptance of such mechanisms of social control and regulation that students from the dominant class consistently end up at the top of the hierarchy and students from subordinate communities at the bottom—a factor that readily and unjustly fuels common-sense belief in the legitimacy of a hierarchically racialized, gendered, and class-stratified society.

It is no secret that in the United States, the most politically powerful are those who retain control over the bulk of society's wealth and resources. This economic and institutional control is clearly perpetuated from generation to generation through the process of schooling. The ruling class, with its bureaucratic system of managerial officials, strives to retain control of schooling through the construction of educational public policies. As such, curriculum and pedagogical practices that support the standardization (and control) of knowledge—knowledge that functions in the interest of capitalist relations—effectively sustain the culture of dominion within schools. Moreover, through control of teacher certification and such schooling practices as curricular policies, literacy instruction, pedagogy, and testing requirements tied to educational opportunities, the stratification of populations so necessary to capitalist accumulation is successfully maintained. As a consequence, even working-class students and students of color learn to furiously compete for the limited "top" positions in society, rather than work to alter the social, political, and economic conditions that defy the future well-being of their communities.

TESTING AND A POLITICS OF SILENCE

Schools produce and perpetuate knowledge that serves as a silencing agent, in that it relegates legitimacy to the abstract reality developed by prescribed knowledge, rather than to the actual lived daily experiences that shape the knowledge that students bring to the classroom. Nowhere was this more evident than in the manner in which the majority of public schools responded to the events of September 11. Here the actual experiences of students predicated upon what they were hearing and feeling about this historical moment were marginalized and suppressed. A politics of silence was the solution for a return to normalcy, with expectations that little to no discussions be held regarding this issue. And if discussions did ensue, these were to echo the language of a most superficial and vulgar patriotism, in concert with the official public discourse of the government.

As a consequence, blind flag-waving nationalism substituted for any real critical dialogue. Teachers were told that the attitude in classrooms was to be "business as usual," as students were being ushered in and out of their beginning-of-the-year standardized testing sessions. Meanwhile, administrative pressures on teachers to keep up with the prescribed curriculum and to prepare students for future testing, worked to silence the possibility for critical inquiry into the initial and subsequent events connected with the "war on terrorism." So while the practice of high-stakes testing effectively contributed to an ahistorical and fragmented response to such a significant historical event in the lives of students, book sellers were rushing to develop and insert the official historical reading into traditional social studies textbooks to generate new sales. By the time the events of September 11 and the "war on terrorism" are officially documented and taught in social studies classrooms across the country, the lived impact of the events will have been buried and lost for many, with only the prescribed curricula and its sanitized interpretation of the events remaining.

Last, an aspect of the culture of dominion that is seldom discussed within education but very much at work in the politics of silence is a dichotomized view of good and evil so prevalent in conservative and liberal political discourses on schooling and society. The "good" are those who conform and accept to fulfill their rightful place in the process of capitalist accumulation. From this perspective, all problems in schools and society are approached from the standpoint of how the "evil" (or deviance) may be eliminated in students, teachers, or parents. Through linking notions of evil consequences (pregnancy, drug abuse, crime, dropout, unemployment, etc.) to academic failure, students who fail are justifiably excluded and rendered disposable. In the testing madness, this notion has been interjected into the definition of good schools, good students, good teachers, good parents, where the level of "goodness" is determined by the measurable outcomes of standardized testing. The "good" are then all considered worthy of rewards by the state for their achievement.

This veiled moralism that unwittingly permeates educational discourse and the acceptance of high stakes testing actually socializes populations to accept uncritically the inferiority of the other and the need for corrective action, in order to assure the participation of the majority within the labor market and as rightful citizens of this nation. Hence, many unexamined assumptions that give rise to an ideology enmeshed in the nobility of "good versus evil" shape many of the uncritical, common sense perceptions of whole populations as "evil" and in need of punishment and/or corrective action—whether the action be loss of opportunity, incarceration, or military intervention. No where is this more evident than in the demonizing "good versus evil" arguments being disseminated at this historical moment to justify the expansion of U.S. military intervention in the Middle East. So whether it be the contrived political wars waged in public schools or the fabricated military wars waged over seas, it is economically dispossessed people who are most destructively affected by the policies and practices of those who seek to retain dominion over their destinies.

222   *Antonia Darder*

REFERENCES

Apple, A. 1995. *Education and power.* 2d ed. New York: Routledge.
Belsie, L. 2002. Labor more militant as economy teeters. *Christian Science Monitor,* August 22.
Bowles, S., and H. Gintis. 1976. *Schooling in capitalist America.* New York: Basic Books.
Caputo-Pearl, A. 2001. *Challenging high-stakes standardized testing: Working to build an anti-racist progressive social movement in public education.* Working paper for Coalition for Educational Justice, Los Angeles, Calif.
Darder, A., and R. Torres. 1999. *Shattering the race lens: Toward a critical theory of racism.* In *Critical Ethnicity,* ed. R. Tai and M. Kenyatta. Lanham, Md.: Rowman & Littlefield.
Economic Policy Institute (EPI). 2002. *The state of working America, 2002/2003.* Armonk, N.Y.: M. E. Sharpe.
Faux, J. 2002. *Rethinking the global political economy.* Speech given at the Asia-Europe-U.S. Progressive Scholar's Forum: Globalization and Innovation of Politics, Japan, April 11–13.
Hernstein, R., and C. Murray. 1994. *The bell curve: Intelligence and class structure in American life.* New York: Free Press.
Heubert, J., and R. Hauser. 1999. *High stakes: Testing for tracking, promotion and graduation.* Committee on Appropriate Test Use, Board on Testing and Assessment, Commission on Behavioral and Social Sciences and Education, and National Research Council. Washington D.C.: National Academy Press.
Johnson, C. 2000. *Blowback: The costs and consequences of American empire.* New York: Owl Books.
Jonsson, P. 2002. When the tests fail. *Christian Science Monitor,* August 20.
Kohn, A. 1993. *Punished by rewards.* Boston: Houghton Mifflin.
———. 2000. *The case against standardized testing: Raising scores, ruining schools.* Portsmouth, N.H.: Heinemann.
McNeil, L. 2000. *Contradictions of school reform: Educational costs of standardized testing.* New York: Routledge.
Molner, A. 1996. *Giving kids the business: The commercialization of American schools.* Boulder, Colo.: Westview Press.
Rocky Mountain News. 2002. CSAP 2000: A guide to results of the student assessment tests. August 1.
Ryan, R., and J. La Guardia. 1999. Achievement motivation within a pressured society: Intrinsic and extrinsic motivations to learn and the politics of school reform. In *Advances in motivation and achievement,* vol. 11. Stanford, Conn.: JAI Press.
Toch, T. 1991. *In the name of excellence.* New York: Oxford University Press.

13

Patriarchal Family Terrorism and Globalization: A Critical Feminist Pedagogical Approach

Rhonda Hammer

The ongoing terror wars that have marked the twenty-first century have dramatized the centrality of globalization and the dangers and vulnerabilities of the entire world to destructive violence. These events have provoked widespread discussions of terrorism that generally fail to recognize that terrorism finds its basis in patriarchal values and relations that permeate and organize political, social, economic, and cultural domains of everyday life. In this chapter, I want to explore the phenomenon of patriarchal family terrorism as an essential constituent to dimensions of globalization. I employ a critical feminist pedagogy which presents broad perspectives on terrorism that include its roots in patriarchal violence and domination to address dimensions of terrorism at individual, local, and global levels, neglected in many current discussions.

I use the term *patriarchal family terrorism* to demonstrate the far-reaching, multidimensional quality, as well as massive quantity of abuse, terror, and torture, often described as "domestic abuse" which is not, I will argue, exclusive to nuclear familial relations. "Domestic abuse" is far too benign and limited to signify the real complex nature of family violence that, I argue, is better articulated by the expression "patriarchal family terrorism." Indeed, this term far better represents the contextual and systemic nature of relations of subordination, domination, and violence through which those in hierarchical positions of power control others. It is these kinds of inequitable power relations, which include the politics of gender, race, class, and ethnicity that underlie overlapping and multileveled theories and practices of critical transformative, feminist pedagogies.[1]

The emphasis on "praxis," as espoused by Paulo Freire (1972), which involves the transformation of consciousness as a process of "reflection and action," is embraced in Chandra Mohanty's radical pedagogy.[2] She describes her approach, in part, as an "antiracist feminist framework," anchored in decolonization, anticapitalist critique, and solidarity (2003, 3). With Mohanty, I envision that "political education through feminist pedagogy should teach active citizenship in such struggles for justice" (243). And many would argue that "citizenship" and social justice are becoming lost rights, especially for the marginalized, in the escalating terror wars that are characterizing relations in much of the overdeveloped and developing worlds.

Indeed, these kinds of critical feminist approaches assist in understanding the complexities and far-reaching implications of patriarchal family terrorism, by showing how the multidimensional nature of individual and collective abusive relations is situated in their sociopolitical, economic, and cultural context. Moreover, myriad interrelated forms of family terrorism must be perceived and located within a dialectical understanding of the reality of patriarchal codes and ideology, which are hardly unidimensional or exclusive to capitalism. For, as Enloe reminds us: "Feminists have shown in their research and in their campaigns for reform that ideas about what constitutes acceptable behavior by men can share patriarchal tendencies and yet vary in surprising ways across cultures. Patriarchy does not come in 'one size fits all'" (Enloe 1993, 5).

In this chapter, I have added the prefix "patriarchal" to what I am calling "family terrorism." With bell hooks, I believe that it is crucial for the "feminist movement to have as an overriding agenda ending all forms of violence. Feminist focus on patriarchal violence against women should remain a primary concern. However emphasizing male violence against women, in a manner that implies that it is more horrendous than all other forms of patriarchal violence, does not serve to further the interests of feminist movement. It obscures the reality that much patriarchal violence is directed at children by sexist women and men" (2000, 62). In other words, patriarchal terrorism is not the sole domain of men, and is often appropriated by individual and collective women. It is, in this sense, a pathological ideology that mediates multiple dimensions of sociopolitical, psychic, and economic relations.

It is within this multileveled context that I reexamine the notion of the domestic and private spheres in relation to patriarchal privilege and abuse and battery of women and children, and contextualize these atrocities within the wider context of the community, state, global, and public spheres. I conclude with comments on how critical feminist pedagogies should address issues of patriarchal family terrorism.

PATRIARCHAL VIOLENCE AND COLONIZATION

Critical scholars like Manual Castells emphasize that it is "analytically, and politically essential" to recognize "the roots of patriarchalism in the family structure" (1997). "Patriarchalism," he contends, "is a founding structure of all contemporary societies" and is characterized "by the institutionally enforced authority of males over females and their children in the family unit." This authority is exercised through the permeation of the entire economic, political, and social organization of society by patriarchalism. Hence "interpersonal relationships and thus personality are marked, as well, by domination and violence originating from the culture and institutions of patriarchalism" (134). Yet it is the patriarchal family, Castells argues, that shields recognition of the "sheer domination" of patriarchalism.

bell hooks points out that there is a popular myth, which is perpetuated by antifeminists, that feminists have an antimale bias. She argues that critical feminists have always recognized that "men were not the problem, that the problem was patriarchy, sexism, and male domination" (hooks 2000, 67). She and others have demonstrated the harmful effects of patriarchal values and beliefs on men and women in a variety of cultural, localized, and global environments, a theme that has been a significant part of transformative feminisms, critical theories, and radical pedagogies.

In addition, many antiracist global feminists, critical theorists, and radical pedagogues have argued that colonization has become globalized in our contemporary society and that collaborators play an important role in this. The employment of colonization theory, which is applied by many transformative and/or transnational feminists to dissect terror relations that take place at local/global levels, provides for a deeper understanding and analyses of the complexities and multidimensional nature of patriarchal family terrorism. Translating from classic works on colonization illuminates the multifarious relationships of violence and terror, especially those directed against women, children, and the elderly. In reality, colonization is not just restricted to physical deprivation, legal inequality, economic exploitation, and classist, racist, and sexist unofficial or official assumptions, but also has a psychological dimension. Sandra Bartky identifies a pathological dimension that is essential to the process of colonization and terrorisms that Frantz Fanon, who was trained as a psychologist before taking up revolutionary writings and practice, described as "psychic alienation" (Bartky 1990). "To be psychologically oppressed is to be weighed down in your mind; it is to have a harsh dominion exercised over your self-esteem. The psychologically oppressed become their own oppressors; they come to exercise harsh dominion over their own self-esteem. Differently put, psychological oppression can be regarded as the "internalization of intimations" (22).

Indeed, the complexities of psychological states of the mind-set of peoples involved in the pathologies of colonization and terrorisms are often subordinated or ignored in many analytical discussions of these kinds of relations. Yet, understanding patriarchal family terrorism necessitates recognition of hidden pathologies of colonization. These pathological characteristics of colonization and its role in family terrorisms reveal the complexities involved in what is often called a "master/slave dialectic."[3] Moreover, the distinctions between patriarchal codes and values and erroneous essentialized behaviors of a generalized class of "men" become even more apparent when discussed within the context of colonization as an elaborate process which usually involves colonizer, colonized, and collaborator. In relation to women and children's situations, for example, transformative feminists, like Cynthia Enloe maintain:

> To describe colonization as a process that has been carried on solely by men overlooks the way male colonizers' success depended on some women's complicity. Without the willingness of "respectable" women to see that colonization offered them an opportunity for adventure, or a new chance of financial security or moral commitment, colonization would have been even more problematic. (Enloe 1990, 16)

Moreover, colonization cannot be addressed in simplistic Manichaean, reductionist terms, that essentializes men as oppressors and women as oppressed, or to infer that all women suffer the same degrees of subordination; for women can be both colonizer and colonized and can be instruments of family terrorism against children, the elderly, as well as instruments of colonization in relation to other women and even men. Hence, colonization is a dialectical set of hierarchical relations which involves class, race, ethnicity, gender (sexuality), age, nationalism, and other determinations, which are often interconnected and multiple.

It is, in this sense, that a critical feminist approach expands upon the notions and realities of battery, terrorization, and abuse of women and children to include relations of state, cultural, and global terrorism of women and children in the forms of the feminization of poverty, hunger, exploited labor and slavery, prostitution, and the sex trade, arguing that these are expansive forms of the ideology of patriarchal family terrorism, especially given that family members, cultural communities, and the family of the state are actively involved in these kinds of atrocities. Moreover, as many transformative feminists argue violence against men—especially during war—is often mediated through the abuse, murder, rape, and torture of familial women and children of the enemy.

The theory of colonization proves relevant for understanding the complexities of these kinds of physiological and psychological dimensions of terror and terrorism. It also serves to examine the complex and often collaborative role of women in what hooks describes as "patriarchal violence" (2000, 61). Hence, I argue for the ongoing development of transformative global feminisms which are dialectical and critical in both theory and practice and are against an ahistorical and noncontextual feminism and antifeminism that reify theoretical abstractions and any acute contemporary problems. Instead, I am proposing an emergent critical feminist epistemology that embraces a subject/object dialectic that views all forms of behavior in contextual and materialist terms. In other words, feminisms that embrace a dialectical epistemology and stress a transnational politics, inclusiveness, and activism which address concrete contemporary issues in theoretical and practical fashion.

"TERRORISM": MULTIPLE REALITIES, IDEOLOGICAL CONSTRUCTS, AND HUMAN RIGHTS

A discussion of the effectiveness of the polysemic term *patriarchal family terrorism* for understanding a multiplicity of social, political, psychic, and economic relations is especially relevant given the contentious nature of the meaning and use of "terrorism" in light of George W. Bush's initial 2001 declaration of a war against terrorism and "evil,"[4] which was endorsed and supported by a so-called coalition of other nations. Bush's decision to evoke "a war on terrorism," many argue, demonstrates widespread misunderstandings and misrepresentations of the nature of terrorisms. In fact, there has been extensive U.S. and international opposition to the Bush administration policy on terrorism, which is far too often silenced or ignored by government and commercial media forms. As the editors of the *Progressive* demonstrate, in response to Bush and Blair's terror war against Afghanistan, a wide range of peoples from every walk of life contested this warfare strategy as the appropriate manner in which to address the terrorist attacks on the United States. As they perceive it:

> It's a mission which is doomed from the start. The United States cannot kill every terrorist in the world. . . . What's more, the war is probably already creating more terrorists who will be willing to kill and die to stand up to an America they see as the aggressor. . . . Yes, the United States needs to secure itself against future attacks. Yes, Osama bin Laden and al Qaeda, or whoever were the authors of the atrocity of September 11, need to be brought to justice. They should be apprehended and hauled before an international tribunal for committing a crime against humanity.[5]

These insights are especially relevant given the devastating consequences of the escalation of these terror wars into Iraq.

Indeed, there are many critics of Bush's military strategy, which wages war against an enemy that is neither declared nor clearly identified, but designated as "evil." Critics argued that this is a war directed against the entire populations of nations. For example, Mark Weisbrot, codirector of the Center for Economic and Policy Research, in Washington, D.C., is one of many individuals and organizations who perceive this and many other U.S. military actions and/or interventions as "terrorism." Drawing on Wharton School of Business emeritus professor Edward Herman's definition of *terrorism* as "the use of force or the threat of force against civilian populations to achieve political objectives," which he argues is "politically neutral" and "straightforward." Weisbrot argues that previous U.S. actions, as well as Bush's contemporary escalating war, is encompassed by this definition. As he explains it, "This is not the first time that our government has used collective punishment, or terrorism, in order to achieve its political goals. . . . In fact, by any objective definition of terrorism—one that includes the terrorism of states as well as individuals—the United States has been its largest single sponsor over the last half-century."[6] Weisbrot goes on to specify the difference of the "war on terror," in that "it originated with a horrific terrorist attack on Americans" but goes on to argue that "the collective punishment of the people of Afghanistan [and Iraq, I might add] is no more excusable than the crimes of September 11." Indeed, a growing social justice movement continues to critique and challenge the Bush administration's escalation of global terror wars. Weisbrot eschews, like so many other experts, the ineffectual and counterproductive nature of military action against terrorism, and astutely advises: "There is no military solution to the problem of terrorism within our borders. We will have to change our foreign policy, so that the government does not make so many enemies throughout the world. Those who collaborated in the crimes of September 11 will have to be pursued through legal and political channels, including the United Nations."

In fact, the Bush government's escalating "war on terror," which distracts from the realities of domestic and international concerns, has been successful, due, in large part, to a patriarchal ideology which depicts Bush as the all-knowing "father" to the U.S. family/nation. And in America, as in most other nations, father continues "to know best." Yet, there has been a long-term historical and contemporary contestation over the appropriate definition of the highly controversial term of terrorism. Its conflicting meanings have allowed for a plethora of changing delineations, which are not only contradictory, but are being used by some to serve particular hegemonic political interests. These kinds of limited definitions of terrorism are seriously damaging the true impact and contextual meaning of the term, as well as concealing and ignoring the multidimensionality of terrorism in regards to individual and global human rights including multiple forms of violence directed at massive numbers of disenfranchised peoples, especially women, children, and the elderly.

For example, the gender politics and relationship between family terrorism (which encompasses or is associated with other terrorist forms) is rarely discussed in terms of violence against women and children within pathological patriarchal situations. Yet violence against women by men escalates during conditions of war, and many experts argue that modern or contemporary wars are in themselves acts of terrorism. For example, Howard Zinn argues that "terrorism and war have something in common. They both involve the killing of innocent people to achieve what the killers believe is a good end" (2001, 16). "Collatoral damage," as it is now euphemistically called, has been extensive in contemporary wars, especially within the Bush administration war against terror in Afghanistan and Iraq. Indeed, as Julie Mertis and Jasmina Tesanovic demonstrate, "in contemporary warfare, 95 percent of the casualties are civilians, the majority of them women and children (Rycenga and Waller 2001, xvii).

Regarding these events and what many consider to be a decontextualized reading of "terrorism," Edward Said identifies a serious lack of "analysis and reflection" on the complexities of the realities of terrorism within a global context. The absence of this kind of critical thinking and evaluation have had grave consequences in that "terrorism" has become synonymous now with anti-Americanism, which, in turn, has become synonymous with being critical of the United States, which, in turn, has become synonymous with being unpatriotic. That's an unacceptable series of equations" (Said, in Barsamian 2001, 44).

In fact, Ruth Conniff notes that much of the "media flag waving" in the United States since September 11 has in fact been motivated by cynicism and fear, "specifically of being deemed unpatriotic by self-appointed conservative watchdogs . . . who are armed with lists of the unpatriotic compiled by the right-wing Media Research Center" (2002, 15) and Lynne Cheney's Committee to Protect American Civilization (Clinton 2002, 11).[7] It would seem that not only journalists but educators and intellectuals are especially at risk given that Ms. Cheney and Senator Joseph Lieberman's American Council of Trustees and Alumni issued a report after September 11 called "Defending Civilization: How our Universities are Failing America, and What Can Be Done About It." Their neo-McCarthyist report "cited 100 examples of what it considers unpatriotic acts by specific academics" (Rothschild 2001, 23).[8] It appears that the lines have become so blurred and the connotation of "patriotism" has become so obscured, within the new American ideology of terrorism, that Democrat Barbara Lee, the sole member of Congress who voted against the September 14 House Bill (SJ-Resolution 23) that "granted President Bush broad authority to use force to counter the terrorist attacks on the World Trade Center and the Pentagon," has had death threats as well as being attacked as anti-American and a "traitor" (Nichols 2001, 28).[9] Indeed, many writers, scholars, and activists are equating these contemporary attacks on those deemed unpatriotic, in that they are critical of U.S. policies, as the new McCarthyism.

Furthermore, the "hastily drafted," complex antiterrorism legislation, which is known as the U.S. Patriot Act, was signed by Bush on October 26, 2001, after being passed by the U.S. House and Senate with virtually no public hearings, debates, or committee reports. The text has been described as the most unpatriotic act ever enacted—for example, by Nancy Chang of Center for Constitutional Rights (2001) and by Congressman Ron Paul (R-Tex.; 2002). Employing a vague and indeterminate definition of terrorism, which was clearly associated with so-called anti-American behavior and actions, the draconian legislation circumvents and negates the very constitutional rights whereby American freedom and democracy were established (Nancy Chang, November 2001). This criticism is hardly particular to liberals or the Left, as Ron Paul, who voted against the act, characterizes the antiterrorist law as "a clear violation of the civil liberties of all Americans" (2002). He goes on to describe how this expansive, complicated, inaccessible, and often unread bill, "which undermined the principles of individual freedom and liberties in this country" was forced through by Bush and his executives: "It was called Patriot Act because they didn't want anyone to vote against it, claiming that if you didn't vote for it you weren't a patriotic American citizen" (Paul 2002).

According to Nadine Strossen, president of the ACLU, these kinds of antiterrorism mandates have serious implications, in that the "term *terrorism* is taking

on the same kind of characteristics as the term *communism* did in the 1950s. It
stops people in their tracks, and they're willing to give up their freedoms. People are too quickly panicked. They are too willing to give up their rights and to
scapegoat people, especially immigrants and people who criticize the war"
(Rothschild 2002, 19).

These kinds of so-called antiterrorist legislation, domestic and international
policies, and military actions are being identified by many leading scholars, activists, and legislators as "terrorist." Within the context of the United States, for
example, they would seem to fall within the framework of classical American
definitions of terrorism in "official U.S. documents: 'the calculated use of violence to attain goals that are political, religious, or ideological in nature. This is
done through intimidation, coercion, or instilling fear'" (Chomsky 2001, 90).
However, as Chomsky points out, this appropriate meaning of the term has
been displaced by an expanding global "propagandistic usage" which is "used
to refer to terrorist acts committed by enemies against our allies." Indeed, this
kind of propagandistic employment of terrorism not only negates the real
essence and realities of the term, but can also reify what are essentially terrorist ideologies and praxis within an imaginary antiterror mind-set. For it was this
characterization of terrorism which delineated Nazi "counter-terrorism against
terrorist partisans." As Howard Zinn (2002, 12) explains it, new U.S. legislation
allows the secretary of state to designate any organization as terrorist, "and his
decision is not subject to review." According to Zinn, the current U.S. government appears to be implementing laws and practices that meets with the country's own established definitions of terrorism in that

> the USA Patriot Act defines "a domestic terrorist" as someone who violates the law
> and is engaged in activities that "appear to be intended to . . . influence the policy
> of government by intimidation or coercion." This could make many activist organ-
> izations subject to designation as terrorist organizations. As for noncitizens—and
> there are twenty million of them in the United States—they can now be subject to
> indefinite detention and deportation. (12)

Moreover, the pernicious military order, which George W. Bush signed on
November 13, 2001, that "authorized extra-constitutional military tribunals" allows Bush to arrogate "the right to apprehend 'any individual who is not a
United States citizen' and subject that person to a secret military trial and then
impose the death penalty."[10] In this outrageous order, which supersedes the
American constitution, Bush has further ignored traditional usage of terrorism
and expanded on his propagandized doublespeak version of the term, which
makes further mockery of any just U.S. usage and has further altered its meaning and the powers it affords him and his junta. Not only can he "round you up,
try you, and fry you" even if you're a legal immigrant, but he has the power to
travel anywhere in the world and "nab any citizen of a foreign country, and
drag that person into a kangaroo court, which he can hold outside or within the
United States." With further elaboration on the now highly Orwellian and ex-

tremely dangerous prose describing terrorism in his previous acts, legislations, and public pronouncements, Bush can now arrest, hold, detain, extradite, and try anyone "if there is reason to believe" you have "engaged in, aided or abetted, or conspired to commit acts of international terrorism, or acts in preparation therefore, that have caused, threaten to cause, or have as their aim to cause injury to or adverse effects on the United States, its citizens, national security, foreign policy, or economy" and if there is reason to believe that you "knowingly harbored" such a person, you're also "toast."[11] Furthermore, there appears to be no appeals process to any U.S. or world court (except to Donald Rumsfeld, the secretary of defense, or to Bush himself). The order states, "Military tribunals shall have exclusive jurisdiction with respect to offenses by the individual" nor will the individual be "privileged to seek any remedy or maintain any proceeding, directly or indirectly, or to have any such remedy or proceeding sought on the individuals behalf, in any court of the United States, or any State thereof, any course of any foreign nation, or any international tribunal." The omnipotence of global power, intimidation, and dominance underlying the Bush hegemony demonstrates the totalitarian terrorist influence of the U.S. government and the powerful elites and institutions who have failed to contest his efforts and/or have collaborated in blatantly antidemocratic behavior. Indeed Amnesty International states that the new U.S. order "violates fundamental principles of justice in any circumstances, including in times of war, and is contrary to the Geneva Convention."

The ambiguous nature of the term *terrorism* has serious consequences for human rights at a global level and for, ironically, the escalation of all forms of terrorisms. United Nations diplomats' work on a counterterror convention is being impeded by the lack of agreement on who or what constitutes a terrorist and/or terrorism. Moreover, demands "by the Security Council that U.N. members act against global terrorism are being used to justify repression of domestic dissent, U.N. officials and independent human rights advocates say." In fact: "The anti-terrorism campaign has been used by authoritarian governments to justify moves to clamp down on moderate opponents, outlaw criticism of rulers and expand the use of capital punishment."[12]

Hence, many scholars are arguing that this kind of propagandistic "terrorism" is being employed by Western mass media and certain governmental organizations in a particularly restrictive sense. George Shultz, who was Ronald Reagan's secretary of state, for example, described terrorism as "a threat to Western civilization" and a "menace to Western moral values" (Ahmad 1998). Michael Kinsley (2001) points out that defining *terrorism* was a major industry of Washington during the 1980s and that there remains no adequate or agreed upon explanation. This lacunae in conjunction with the everchanging propagandistic definitions of the term, by the United States in particular, could be viewed as self-serving in that it appears to exclude particular U.S. actions.

Indeed, the U.S. government's commitment to ending terrorism appears especially hypocritical given that in 1997 the government rejected the jurisdiction of the International Court of Justices which "condemned the U.S. for the 'un-lawful use of force,' ordering Washington to cease its *international terrorism*, violation of treaties, and illegal economic warfare, and to pay substantial repa-rations" (Chomsky 1999, 73; emphasis mine).[13] Yet, as Chomsky notes, this court judgment was rarely reported by mainstream mass media. Although ap-palling, it is hardly surprising given the escalating corporate concentration and monopolies of ownership of Western and U.S. mass media, in particular. It ap-pears that much of the media has flagrantly collaborated with hegemonic gov-ernment and business forces to perpetuate propagandistic versions of terrorism and antidemocratic global policies, hostilities, and conflicts. The responsibilities of the Fourth Estate, many argue, have been co-opted especially during the Bush Jr. regime and undeclared "war" against terror.

> During the Gulf War, journalists used to challenge government news managers and insisted they wouldn't just accept the official version of events. It seems that with the war in the Balkans and now this, journalists have accepted the official version. Journalists go to press briefings at the Ministry of Defense in London or the Penta-gon in Washington, and no critical questions are posed at all. It's just a news-gath-ering operation, and the fact that the news is being given by the governments who are waging war doesn't seem to worry any journalists too much. (Tariq Ali, in Barsamian 2002, 33)

Susan Douglas notes that the lack of critical, informed, unbiased news report-ing, in the wake of September 11, is due in large part to the heavy reliance, of the news media "on official sources" (2001, 3). To even further manage mainstream media and public perceptions, the Bush government has obstructed the basic rights of Americans to fairly judge its country's military actions. The incredible be-havior of the current government's suppression of information is, in fact, remi-niscent of George Orwell's terrifying description of the totalitarian regime in his classic novel *1984* in that the U.S. Defense Department bought up all the rights to "high-resolution pictures of Afghanistan taken by commercial satellite" (Con-niff 2002, 15).[14] Rather than barring the media from access to these visuals, on na-tional security grounds and risking a legal battle, the military paid Space Imaging $1.9 million per month of U.S. tax dollars for this crucial documentation (15).

In 2003, the Bush administration pushed for an expansion of the so-called Pa-triot Act (nicknamed Patriot Act II) that would give the government further powers of surveillance, arrest, and detention, and further erode U.S. citizens' rights and democracy.[15] And on December 13, 2003, the day Saddam Hussein was captured, Bush signed into law "a bill that grants the FBI sweeping new powers" (Martin 2003). As Martin explains it, the leak of the proposed expan-sion of the Patriot Act and "ensuing public backlash frustrated the Bush admin-istration's strategy, so Ashcroft and Co. disassembled Patriot Act II, then re-assembled its parts into other legislation. By attaching the redefinition of 'financial institution' to an Intelligence Authorization Act, the Bush Administra-tion and its Congressional allies avoided public hearing and floor debates for the expansion of the Patriot Act." The current Bush administration manipulation of the discourse of terrorism and media complicity in its war policy makes it all the more urgent to clarify modes of terrorism and to focus on what I am calling "family terrorism."

PATRIARCHAL FAMILY TERRORISM

I have developed the expression *patriarchal family terrorism* to provoke a dialectical shift in addressing issues of violence against women, children, and the elderly that is far more extensive and interrelated to social, political, economic, and global dimensions (which necessarily includes relations of gender, race, ethnicity, caste, class, and sexuality) than conventional thinking about what violence or abuse of women and children usually signifies. Family terrorism, in its first sense, reveals and critiques the problematic nature of such inept ideological descriptions as "domestic violence" or its latest incarnation "intimate partner abuse"—which even further neutralizes and reduces the real complexity of relationships it is allegedly delineating. As Ann Jones explains it: "*Domestic violence* is one of those gray phrases, beloved of bureaucracy, designed to give people a way of talking about a topic without seeing what's really going on. Like *repatriation* or *ethnic cleansing*, it's a euphemistic abstraction that keeps us at a dispassionate distance, far removed from the repugnant spectacle of human beings in pain" (1994, 81).[16]

According to bell hooks, *domestic violence* has been used to cover up the severity and systematic nature of family terrorism. She argues that it is "a 'soft' term that suggests it emerges in an intimate context that is private and somehow less threatening, less brutal, than the violence that takes place outside the home" (2000).

> This is not so, since more women are beaten and murdered in the home than on the outside. Also most people tend to see domestic violence between adults as separate and distinct from violence against children when it is not. Often children suffer abuse as they attempt to protect a mother who is being attacked by a male companion or husband, or they are emotionally damaged by witnessing violence and abuse. (62)

Ann Jones points out that it was during the Carter administration (1976–1980) that discourse such as *wife beating*, was replaced with highly neutral "professional vocabularies" such as *spouse abuse, conjugal violence, marital aggression,* and of course *domestic violence* (1994, 82). "A great renaming took place, a renaming that veiled once again the sexism a grassroots women's movement had worked to uncover." The term *partner abuse* or *intimate partner violence* (which is widely used in contemporary studies) further neutralizes violent relations in terms of both gender and sexuality.[17] For example, note the ambiguous and potentially misleading statistical findings cited from the U.S. National Violence

Against Women (NVAW), cosponsored by the National Institute of Justice and the Centers for Disease Control:

> Intimate partner violence is pervasive in U.S. society. Nearly 25 percent of surveyed women and 7.6 percent of surveyed men said they were raped and/or physically assaulted by a current or former spouse, cohabiting partner, or date at some time in their lifetime. (Tjaden and Thoennes 2000, iii)

Not only does this finding, in conjunction with the language used, misconstrue the real sexual politics of male violence, but it also makes it appear as if women's violence against men is normalized and even prevalent. Moreover, the inclusion of same-sex violence in homosexual relationships is inadequately addressed in much research findings. Further, the distinctions between lesbian and gay partner violence is not always apparent, although this was documented in subsections of the later parts of the NAVW study, which many people might overlook. Indeed, much later in the study it is documented that "intimate partner violence is more prevalent among male same-sex couples than female same-sex couples. . . .These findings indicate that intimate partner violence is perpetrated primarily by men, whether against same-sex or opposite-sex partners" (Tjaden and Thoennes 2000, 56).

Ann Jones points out that the usefulness of the term *intimate partner violence* "lies in its gender neutrality, for it conveniently hides one undeniable fact: that despite the real problem of violence committed by women against women, the assailant in [most] heterosexual *and* homosexual violence is a man" (1994, 84). It is within this context that my employment of the term *patriarchal family terrorism* is used to emphasize the torture, abuse, neglect, and murder of children and the elderly, as well as male battery of women and men. Moreover, this term draws on work of critical antiviolence feminists like Linda Gordon who sees family violence as "a political issue" (Gordon 1988, 5). She is concerned with the abuse and neglect of children and discusses this within a contextual framework that includes the roles of women in terrorizing and/or neglecting their children. This, of course, includes traditional, "alternative" and/or single-mother families. Central to her analysis is the mediating effects of class and money in relations of family violence. It is in this sense that bell hooks employment of the term *patriarchal violence* is especially appropriate. As she explains it: "The term *patriarchal violence* is useful because unlike the more accepted phrase *domestic violence* it continually reminds the listener that violence in the home is connected to sexism and sexist thinking, to male domination" (2000, 61–62).

The abuse of children and elderly, as well as the escalating nature of global violence against women and children, must therefore be understood as a systemic process. Gordon points out that even a "a mother who might never be violent, but who teaches her children, especially her sons, that violence is an acceptable means of exerting social control, is still in collusion with patriarchal violence" (1988, 64). She clarifies the relationship of patriarchal violence to parental violence and women's role as collaborator and/or colonizer in this relationship.

Riane Eisler argues, in her discussion of how we must begin to analyze the events of September 11 and fundamentalist terrorist extremism, with examining gender and parent–child relations since these "are the critical, formative relations . . . where we first learn what's normal and moral, where we learn values and behaviors" (2001, 33). She asserts that you must examine the context of hate and terror, which involves a transformative and dialectical analysis: "Clearly most women do not use violence to dominate men (even though small numbers of women batter the men in their lives) but lots of women believe that a person in authority has the right to use force to maintain authority" (hooks 2000, 64). Moreover,

> Since women remain the primary caretakers of children, the facts confirm the reality that given a hierarchical system in a culture of domination which empowers females (like the parent–child relationship) all too often they use coercive force to maintain dominance. In a culture of domination everyone is socialized to see violence as an acceptable means of social control. Dominant parties maintain power by the threat (acted upon or not) that abusive punishment, physical or psychological, will be used whenever the hierarchal structures in place are threatened, whether that be in male-female relationships, or parent and child bonds. (64)

Yet, as Marcia Ann Gillespie points out, mainstream feminism, and I would add, many other feminist forums, have paid only lip service to addressing this "plague of violence" against children and "society's ongoing policy of 'benign' neglect" (Gillespie 1994b).[18] Gillespie asks why there have been no marches on Washington to demand "that this nation make children—*all* children and their right to safety—a priority."

> This women's movement has consistently denounced our antichoice foes as caring more about fetuses than they do living children. Time and again we proclaim our movement's commitment to ensuring children's well-being. So why have we primarily left it up to women living in the communities where the violence is most out of control, especially to women of color, to be the ones marching, the ones calling out to this nation to save the children?

Moreover, as Barbara Ehrenreich documents, poverty and class play a significant role in the lives of the disenfranchised and privileged, especially in regard to children. As she insightfully points out: "The 'working poor,' as they are approvingly termed are, in fact the major philanthropists of our society. They neglect their own children so that the children of others will be cared for; they live in substandard housing so that other homes will be shiny and perfect; they endure privation so that inflation will be low and stock prices high."[19]

Given that violence, abuse and/or terrorism against children and teenagers is escalating, especially given globalization's emphasis on the commoditization of people (primarily women and children), current "politics of greed," and rising government cutbacks, downsizing, and dismantling of the so-called welfare state in much of the first-world north and west, it is mandatory that many feminisms expand upon their definitions of family violence. For example, Amnesty International's *Children's Report for the 2000 Campaign to Stamp out Torture* provides us with a shocking pronouncement on the global state of family terrorism, specifically violence against children: "violence against children is endemic: children are tortured by the police or security forces; detained in appalling conditions; beaten or sexually abused by parents, teachers or employers; maimed, killed or turned into killers by war."

Some are victims many times over, first of the chronic poverty and discrimination that renders them vulnerable to torture and ill-treatment, then to the injustice and impunity that allows it to continue unpunished (www.stoptorture.org). The systemic nature of family violence is further established by the escalating rate of violence against the elderly.

The National Elder Abuse Incidence Study (NEAIS) found that an estimated total of 550,000 elderly persons experienced abuse, neglect, and/or self-neglect in domestic settings in 1996. The NEAIS estimated that for each new incident of elder abuse, neglect, and/or self neglect reported in 1996, four or five incidents went unreported. Almost 62 percent of the substantiated reports were incidents of maltreatment by other persons, while 38 percent were self-neglect incidents. The most common types of elder abuse, in order of frequency, are neglect, emotional/psychological abuse, financial/material exploitation, and physical abuse. The majority of victims are among the oldest elders (eighty years and older) and are more likely to be women. Abusers are more likely to be male and family members, especially adult children (Soto-Aquino 1999, 2).[20]

Indeed, as Sabah Bahar warns: "As long as the relation between the public and the private sphere, the state and the family is not re-theorized, many human rights violations against women will remain undocumented, regardless of avowed commitments" (1996, 109). Her admonition, however, is hardly exclusive to women, but necessarily includes children, the elderly and/or the marginalized and disenfranchised. Hence it becomes necessary to recognize that terror and hate have a context, and that the notion of family and/or patriarchal terrorisms begins to identify these complex systems of relations in a dialectical manner.

THE PUBLIC/PRIVATE DICHOTOMY: THE MULTIDIMENSIONALITY OF PATRIARCHAL FAMILY TERRORISM

Classical understandings of family relations, as well as much critical feminist analyses and activism, are related to the treatment of women and children within the patriarchal structure of the family which is relegated to the private domain. Much of feminist research and critical feminist concerns regarding the subordination of women and children is related to "the organization of societies into public and private spheres, the organization of economies into the spheres of production and reproduction, and the ways that these have articulated with gender and class, as well as with ethnicity and race" (Moghadam 2001). Indeed, Moghadam reveals how the subordinated status of women and their labor within the patriarchal family crosses the borders, of the so-called public–private divide and how oppressive and often violent relations within the family are simultaneously manifested within the public sphere. "Feminist analyses, and women's activism, have been concerned with the broad implications of the identification of women with the private sphere of the family, including their exclusion from the public sphere, their varied experiences of marginalization, exploitation, and integration in the sphere of production, and their undervalued location within the sphere of reproduction, whether as paid or unpaid labor" (1).

In fact, many critical feminists argue that rather than being restricted to the private or domestic domain, women and children's active roles and work within the public sphere are being treated as privatized and subordinate. And the permissible role of hierarchical violence within the patriarchal family translates into public domains. For example, Patricia Hill Collins describes how the "family values" that underlie the organization of the traditional family "naturalize U.S. hierarchies of gender, age, and sexuality" (1998, 65). It is within this context that male authority, leadership, and masculinity is not only privileged but naturalized. Many anthropologists, sociologists, and human rights activists do not equate this kind of hierarchical relations with overdeveloped northern and western nations, but also with a multiplicity of often divergent patriarchal cultures and nation states. She goes on to argue that this kind of family system and structure simultaneously reinforces and lays the foundation for "many social hierarchies" (64). As Hill Collins puts it:

In particular hierarchies of gender, wealth, age, and sexuality within actual family units correlate with comparable hierarchies in U.S. societies. Individuals typically learn their assigned place in hierarchies of race, gender, ethnicity, sexuality, nation, and social class in their families' origin. At the same time, they learn to view such hierarchies as natural social arrangements, as compared to socially constructed ones. Hierarchy in this sense becomes "naturalized" because it is associated with seemingly "natural" processes of the family. (64)

Eisenstein argues that the success of many transnational capitalist relations lies in the renegotiation of the nation, globe, and home since earlier forms of familial patriarchal privilege were relocated into "class divisions between men and women" (1998, 111). For example, many "domestic and familial responsibilities are transplanted into the market itself. So McDonald's and Pizza Hut do their own sort of family cooking for profit" (111).

It is hardly surprising that when dissonance arises and chaos ensues lost family values becomes the rationale for all forms of political, social, and economic problems and that women, children, teenagers, and marginalized and disenfranchised peoples are generally identified as culpable. Marcia Gillespie

(1994a) points out how the "keepers of patriarchy" identify the secrets of world peace, or at least the key to solving almost all of our internal problems is "family values."

> Lost family values, not militarism and the legacies of cold war policies. Not racism and the capitalist reverence for market forces. . . . Not the plethora of guns and the steady diet of violence spooned up as entertainment. Not the male rage that makes so many homes unsafe. And most definitely not patriarchy. (Gillespie 1994a, 1)

For conservatives, it is the loss of family values and the abandonment of "the patriarchal family with daddy firmly entrenched at the head" that has weakened the "moral" of the nation. And "of course, women are to blame: women failing to keep to our anointed place and uppity feminists who suggest that family model is flawed, who offer alternatives and talk about valuing families, not repressive family values" (1).

An idealized notion of the family is becoming even more unrealistic given that "the borders between public and private become further skewed and the lines between politics and culture are muted . . . as the nation is reconfigured for globalism" (Eisenstein 1996, 111). Indeed, the patriarchal family is more than apparent in the public sphere, nation states, and corporate organizations. In fact, Eisenstein goes on to identify how "the nation constructs gender, sexuality, and their racial meanings through moments of nation building, such as the Gulf War, when the nation became a [patriarchal] family" (43). Hill Collins clarifies how the traditional family ideal is, in fact, an ideological construction and "a fundamental principle of social organization" (1998, 63). "Families constitute primary sites of belonging to various groups: to the family as an assumed biological entity; to geographically identifiable, racially segregated neighborhoods conceptualized as imagined families; to so-called racial families codified in science and law; and to the U.S. nation-state conceptualized as a national family" (63).

It is within this translation of the patriarchal family to the "national family" that violence, torture, and rape of women and girls are better understood and situated. In fact, many critical feminists have associated patriarchal familial attitudes and violence with militarism. Moreover, a number of feminist studies demonstrate increases and changes in modes of family violence during wars and wartimes (Kesic 2001, 26). "The forms of violence inflicted against women in wars vary in form, scale, and intensity from killing, rape, torture, forced impregnation, body searches at checkpoints, imprisonment, settlement in concentration camps and refuges, and forced prostitution to verbal insults and degradation, psychological suffering for losses, and the burden of responsibility that women carry as survivors" (25).

Eisenstein argues that "war rape is sexualized violence that seeks to terrorize, destroy, and humiliate a people through its women":

> Genocidal rape has its own horrors. It takes place in isolated rape camps, with strict orders from above to either force the woman's exile or her death. Rape is repeat-

edly performed as torture; it is used to forcibly impregnate; it is even used to exterminate. Women in the camps are raped repetitively, some as many as thirty times a day for as long as three consecutive months. They are kept hungry, they are beaten and gang-raped, their breasts are cut off, and stomachs split open. (1996, 59)

Yet, even under these conditions, women cannot be perceived as universal in that, as Enloe reminds us, rape in war is often structured by class, ethnic, and racial "inequalities between women" (1993, 168). The commoditization and colonization of different women, become evident in that the rape of these women, in times of war, upheaval, or political disputes "represents conquered territories" (Eisenstein 1996, 41).

In other words, women and girls are treated as possessions of husbands, fathers, sons, and brothers and their violation, torture, and murder is intended to demoralize and humiliate their enemy. Not to forget that boys and men are wounded, killed, and often tortured in these kinds of contexts, "the women's mediating role finds its basis in that the external enemy is imagined to other men, men who would defile or denigrate the nation" (Enloe 1993, 239) This was also the strategy of the Japanese during World War II, when they "conscripted" at least 200,000 girls and women from Korea, China, Taiwan, Indonesia, and the Philippines as sex slaves or "comfort women." Countless impoverished Asian girls and women were snatched from their homes to serve Japanese soldiers, who beat, raped, and murdered them. Some were recruited by force, coercion, and deception into sexual slavery from 1931 to 1945 (Kang 2001).[21] It would be absurd to deny the elements of patriarchal violence involved in these kinds of militaristic outrages and sometimes genocide, especially given that the Japanese recorded these sex slaves as "ammunition," and refused to even acknowledge that its military ran the program until 1993. Some of these women are finally receiving reparations from a private fund, although they have been treated as pariahs in their own communities and families but are receiving nothing from the Japanese government, which has yet to apologize (Kang 2001).

Indeed, respect for the human rights of these Othered women and/or compassion are absent in that during war, raped, battered, and butchered women are considered the familial property of enemy men. Indeed, this is only one example of how the hierarchical structure of family terrorism is interconnected with the patriarchal family and is embedded into the relations of the public sphere. In fact, "A primary reason why forms of violence against women, not just rape but also domestic violence and prostitution, have been kept off the international legal agenda is that so many governments, the principal players in United Nations human rights and war crime tribunal negotiations, are opposed to any outside agency being given authority to intervene in any activity deemed to be related to the 'family'" (Enloe 1993, 243).

However, transnational feminists and human rights activists, point out that "women also frequently experience sexual abuse when they are political prisoners or as an aspect of racial ethnic, or religious persecution" (Bunch 1991, 13).

Family terrorism, in reality, involves a vast set of dominant and often invisible relations and as Charlotte Bunch points out much of that violence against women and children "is part of a larger socioeconomic web that entraps women, making them vulnerable to abuses that cannot be delineated as exclusively political or solely caused by states" (13). Hence "patriarchal family terrorism" seems appropriate for describing the interrelated and hierarchical, multidimensional, forms and levels of violence perpetuated against many different women and children. This transformed notion of the family transcends the bifurcated mythical distinctions between the public and private and subverts the notion of traditional family values within a patriarchal, nuclear context. This new idea and metaphoric family resides within the Borderlands which transcend the public, private, local, global divides. The envisagement of the meaning and representation of "patriarchal family terrorism" has much in common with Zillah Eisenstein's reconceptualization and reclamation of the public realm that "presumes the interconnectedness of people and their responsibility for each other": "The *idea* of 'public' allows that individual needs are met socially and collectively, and collective needs are identified individually. . . . My notion of 'public' then is both a process—of thinking through and beyond the self—and a place where this happens" (Eisenstein 1998, 6).

The notion of "patriarchal family terrorism" thus provides for critical pedagogues a transformative notion that points to more radical and dialectical understandings of both the ideas and realities of family and family terrorism. This form of epistemology allows for both the critique of and transcendence of patriarchal familial relations. This becomes especially necessary given that, "Just as reworking the rhetoric of family for their own political agendas is a common strategy for conservative movements of all types, the alleged unity and solidarity attributed to family is often invoked to symbolize the aspirations of oppressed groups" (Hill Collins 1998, 63). It can also be reappropriated to subvert traditional, ideological interpretations, as well as false distinctions between domestic relations and public life. The importance of this kind of dialectical understanding of family, according to Hill Collins, draws on the "emerging paradigm of intersectionality" writing, "As opposed to examining gender, race, class, and nation, as separate systems of oppression, intersectionality explores how these systems mutually construct one another, or, in the words of Black British sociologist Stuart Hall, how they 'articulate' one another" (63).

It is in this sense that I argue that the metaphor "family violence" does not go far enough, and that the word *violence* is often overused and so liberally applied that it has lost its real meaning and become neutral and flat. Amnesty International's *Global Campaign against Torture Report* (2001) makes little distinction between violence and "torture," in relation to abuse of women and children, nor does it recognize the rights of governments, states, or bodies to distinguish between private and public violence. The report "urges governments to commit themselves to protecting women and girls from torture. Governments that systematically fail to take action to prevent and protect women from violence in the home and community share responsibility for torture and ill-treatment."[22] The report goes on to articulate and contextualize torture within a framework of global violence in that it maintains that: "Torture is fed by a global culture which denies women equal rights with men, and which legitimizes violence against women" and that the "perpetuators are agents of the state and armed groups, but most often they are members of their own family, community, or employers. For many women, their home is a place of terror."

Even less-progressive organizations are defining male violence against women as "systemic terrorism." For example:

> The NVAW survey provides compelling evidence of the link between violence and emotionally abusive and controlling behavior in intimate relationships. Women whose partners verbally abused them, were jealous or possessive, or denied them access to family, friends, and family income were significantly more likely to report being raped, physically assaulted, and/or stalked by their partners, even when sociodemographic factors such as race and education were controlled. These findings suggest that many women in violent relationships are victims of *systemic terrorism*; that is, they experience multiple forms of abuse and control at the hands of their partners. Future research should focus on the extent to which violence perpetrated against women by intimate partners consists of systemic terrorism and the consequences of this type of victimization. (Tjaden and Thoennes 2000, 56)

Moreover, even the traditional notions of battery are being reevaluated and recognized in systemic terms of pathology. "Battering is not usually an isolated incident, but rather it tends to be a cycle that increases in frequency and severity over time."[23] Feminist human rights activists like Charlotte Bunch go on to explain many of these kinds of violent relations also in terms of "terrorism" and "torture" and argue that abusing women physically is a reminder of the patriarchal territorial domination or colonization of women's bodes (and minds, perhaps) "and is sometimes accompanied by other forms of human rights abuse such as slavery (forced prostitution), sexual terrorism (rape), imprisonment (confinement to the home), or torture (systematic battery). Some cases are extreme such as the women in Thailand who died in a brothel fire because they were chained to their beds. Most situations are more ordinary like denying women decent education or jobs which leaves them prey to abusive marriages, exploitative work, and prostitution" (Bunch 1991, 14). In fact Amnesty International strongly recommends "the public condemnation of violence against women [and children], criminalizing violence against women [and children], investigating all allegations, and prosecuting and punishing the perpetrators."[24]

Escalating relations of global slavery and trafficking, often through the collaboration of the parents of these women and children intensifies the demand for involvement in global feminisms and human rights movements at every level. Amnesty International expands upon these kinds of relations:

> Women who have been *bought and sold* for forced labor, sexual exploitation, and forced marriage are also vulnerable to torture. Trafficking in human beings is the third largest source of profit for international organized crime after drugs and arms. Trafficked women are particularly vulnerable to physical violence, including rape, unlawful confinement, confiscation of identity papers, and enslavement.[25]

CONCLUSION

To recognize the ideological nature of family terrorism and patriarchal violence combats popular myths regarding feminism's alleged antimale bias and demonstrates that critical feminists have always recognized that "men were not the problem, that the problem was patriarchy, sexism, and male domination" (hooks 2000, 67). It is, however, essential to recognize that as there is no one feminism, nationalism, or colonialism, there is no one patriarchy. "They take different shapes, are defined by different contexts, and have different histories" (Eisenstein 1996, 139). The relationships of patriarchal family terrorism and globalization-from-above can be analyzed within this kind of critical, transformative pedagogy that highlights the dimension of gender within terrorism and globalization.

Deleterious effects of patriarchal values and beliefs on men in a variety of cultural, localized, and global environments have been a significant part of critical transformative feminisms and feminist pedagogies. Because violence is systemic and hierarchical, rigid bifurcated descriptions of gender violence must be retranslated into a more complex and contextual analysis of violence at a variety of levels.

I believe that the term *patriarchal family terrorism* is even more appropriate given the nature of the devastating effects of September 11 and the manipulation of this event as an excuse for contemporary global terror wars.[26] This is especially relevant given that certain forces are appearing to restrict the meaning of *terrorism* to exclude particular Western actions, as well as different dimensions of patriarchal violence and terror. It is imperative that the dialectical relationship between personal, familial, individual/group, organizational, religious/ethnic, national, state, and global terrorisms be analyzed and discussed in academic and public forums. Hence, feminists, critical scholars, and radical pedagogues need to better address and begin to further develop critical definitions and studies of terrorisms which go beyond identifying it as purely individual and collective crimes, but as a phenomenon also connected to gender and patriarchy. It is within this context that describing particular patriarchal relations of abuse, rape, murder, starvation, poverty, exploitation, torture, and genocide is especially relevant.

NOTES

1. Please see Rhonda Hammer (2002) for more expansive discussion of this notion.

2. It is important to note that scholars like bell hooks draw a distinction between "radical pedagogy" and "critical pedagogy" in regard to privileged critiques and to recognize that the term *critical pedagogy* has been a contested terrain within educational debates. For example, hooks points out that: "The scholarly field of writing on critical pedagogy and/or feminist pedagogy continues to be primarily a discourse engaged by white women and men. . . . But the work of various thinkers on radical pedagogy (I use the term to include critical and feminist perspectives) has in recent years truly included a recognition of differences—those determined by class, race, sexual practice, nationality, and so on" (hooks 1994, 8).

3. The master–slave dialectic finds its foundations in the work of nineteenth-century philosopher G. W. F. Hegel. It has been employed and translated from critical scholarship that attempts to understand the complexities of power relations and relations of domination and subordination. Alexandre Kojeve provides for an indication of Hegel's interpretation, and explains that a seminal aspect of this relationship is characterized by the needs of the dominant member to be recognized by the slave as the master. To do so: "He must overcome him 'dialectically.' That is, he must leave him life and consciousness, and destroy only his autonomy. He must overcome the adversary only insofar as the adversary is opposed to him and acts against him. In other words, he must enslave him" (Kojeve 1969, 15).

4. Attorney General John Ashcroft demonstrates the vagarious and ambiguous nature of this denotation of "evil," which allows for serious abuse of power in this regard. Ashcroft describes this "evil" in his prepared remarks to the U.S. Mayors Conference: "The men and women of justice and law enforcement are called to combat a terrorist threat that is both immediate and vast; a threat that resides here, at home, but whose reporters, patrons and sympathizers form a multinational network of evil" ("Prepared Remarks for the U.S. Mayors Conference," October 25, 2001).

5. Editors' comment, "A Roll of the Drums," *Progressive,* November 7, 2001.

6. Mark Weisbrot. 2001, November 6. *Common Dreams News Center.* Available online: www.commondreams.org/views.

7. Todd Gitlin, who has been castigating members of the Left that are in opposition to the war in Afghanistan and elsewhere, is on this list for "the highly inflammatory statement, 'There is lot of skepticism about America's policy of going to war'" (Clinton 2002, 11).

8. As Matthew Rothschild reports: "Attorney General John Ashcroft is rounding up or interrogating thousands of immigrants in what will go down in history as the Ashcroft Raids. The FBI and Secret Service are harassing artists and activists. Publishers are firing antiwar columnists and cartoonists. University presidents are scolding dissident faculty members. And rightwing citizen's groups are demanding conformity" (2002, 19).

9. "I am convinced," Representative Lee said on the House floor, "that military actions will not prevent further acts of international terrorism against the United States." Her position, in fact, is hardly at odds with widespread professional, military, academic, and intellectual critics who argue that not only will it not prevent further terrorist attacks but possibly will incite them (which has been demonstrated by numerous threats and attacks on the United States, western coalition countries, as well as an escalation of kidnapping of westerners, in a variety of nations). Moreover, Lee's objections would seem more than rational and appropriate given that several aspects of the resolution "did not identify who we were fighting" nor "did not identify an end strategy!" (Nichols 2001, 28). She also objected to Congress abdicating its constitutional role. "Congress," she argues, "has a responsibility to step back and say, 'Let's not rush to judgment.' Let us insist that our democracy works by ensuring the checks and balances are in place and that Congress is part of the decision-making process in terms of when we go to war and with whom. This resolution really took away that ability of Congress to play a role, and I don't think that's a good thing. I think we disenfranchised the American people." Indeed, it would seem in any other world but Alice's Looking Glass world, which seems to characterize much of the contemporary realities of the "war on terrorism," this woman would be recognized as a true patriot.

10. Editor's comment, "Assault on the Constitution," *Progressive,* January 2002, 8.

11. Editor's comment, "Assault on the Constitution," 8. Moreover, "The order does not precisely define these 'acts' of international terrorism, or acts in preparation therefore. Conceivably, non-U.S. citizens who are protesting the U.S. war on Afghanistan, or demonstrating against the World Bank and IMF, or objections to sanctions on Iraq could be labeled terrorists, since Bush may say he has 'reason to believe' they are aiming to affect U.S. foreign policy in an adverse way. He has given himself the power to arbitrarily apprehend, try, convict, and execute any number of people." For detailed critique of the Bush administration terror war policy and its Orwellian language, see Kellner (2003).

12. See *Los Angeles Times,* October 27, A1.

13. Chomsky goes on to note that "the Democratic-controlled Congress reacted by instantly escalating the crimes while the Court was roundly denounced on all sides as a 'hostile forum' that had discredited itself by rendering a decision against the United States. The Court judgment itself was

scarcely reported, including the words just quoted and the explicit ruling that U.S. aid to contras is 'military' and not 'humanitarian'" (1999, 73). State Department legal advisor Abraham Sofaer explained that "when the United States accepted World Court jurisdiction in the 1940s, most members of the United Nations 'were aligned with the United States and shared its views regarding world order.' But now 'a great many of these cannot be counted on to share our view of the original constitutional conception of the U.N. Charter,' and 'this same majority often opposes the United States on important international questions'" (Chomsky 1999, 75). Hence, as Sofaer explains it, "The United States does not accept compulsory jurisdiction over any dispute involving matters essentially within the domestic jurisdiction of the United States as determined by the United States." This assessment would seem to appropriately describe the U.S. position on "terrorism" and the escalation of military action throughout the globe.

14. See Kellner (2003) for an astute discussion of the analogies of Orwell's *1984* to Bush's terror war.

15. The official delineation is the Domestic Security Enhancement Act of 2003, informally known as Patriot Act II.

16. "Even feminist advocates for women, who called their cause 'the battered women's movement,' eventually succumbed; they adopted 'domestic violence' in their fund-raising proposals, so as not to offend men controlling the purse strings by suggesting that men were in any way to blame for this 'social problem.' So well does the phrase 'domestic violence' obscure the real events behind it that when a Domestic Violence Act (to provide money for battered women's services) was first proposed to Congress in 1978, many thought it was a bill to combat political terrorism within the United States" (Jones 1994, 82).

17. For example, the *National Violence against Women (NVAW) Survey on the Extent, Nature, and Consequences of Intimate Partner Violence*, cosponsored by the National Institute of Justice and the Centers for Disease Control and Prevention (Tjaden and Thoennes 2000).

18. Marcia Ann Gilespie, "Editorial," *Ms*, November/December 1994, 1.

19. Barbara Ehrenreich, *Los Angeles Times*, June 15, 2001.

20. Moreover, "One of every 20 people over 65 will become a victim of elder abuse, most at the hands of adult children or caregivers, according to the State Bar of California. . . . Officials estimate that each year as many as 2 million older Americans become the victims of crimes such as physical and mental abuse, neglect, abandonment, and financial exploitation" (Akilah Johnson, *Los Angeles Times*, August 1, 2003, B1).

21. As one officer of the Japanese Army Corps describes and justifies this practice: "This desire [for sex] is the same as hunger or the need to urinate, and soldiers merely thought of comfort stations as practically the same as latrines" (cited in Eisenstein 2004).

22. "Broken Bodies, Shattered Minds—the Torture of Women Worldwide," *Amnesty International News Release*, March 6, 2001, www.amnesty.org.

23. National Center for Victim Crime Virtual Library, 2000, www.ncvc.org.

24. "Broken Bodies, Shattered Minds."

25. "Broken Bodies, Shattered Minds."

26. Robert Scheer provides an insightful explication of Bush's technique in response to his 2003 demand for U.S. taxpayers to "cough up $87 billion more to enable him to sink us deeper into the Iraq quagmire of his making. Once again Bush is using the Big Lie technique, continuing to slyly conflate those responsible for the September 11 attacks with Saddam Hussein and Iraq, despite there being no evidence of such a relationship" (*Los Angeles Times*, September 9, 2003).

REFERENCES

Ahmad, Eqbal. 1998. *Terrorism: Theirs and ours*. Presentation at the University of Colorado, Boulder, October 12.

Amnesty International. 2001. "Broken bodies, shattered minds—the torture of women worldwide." *Amnesty International News Release*, March 6, 2001.

Bahar, Saba. 1996. Human rights are women's rights: Amnesty International and the family. *Hypatia* 11, no. 1 (Winter): 105–34.

Barsamian, David. 2001. The *Progressive* interview: Edward W. Said. *Progressive* 65 (11): 41–44.

———. 2002. The *Progressive* interview: Tariq Ali. *Progressive* 66 (1), at www.progressive.org/0901/intv0102.html.

Bartky, Sandra. 1990. *Femininity and domination: Studies in the phenomenology of oppression.* New York: Routledge.

Bunch, Charlotte. 1991. Recognizing women's rights as human rights. *Response* 13 (4): 13–16.

Castells, Manuel. 1997. *The information age: Economy, society and culture.* Vol. 2, *The powers of identity.* Malden, Mass.: Blackwell.

Chang, Nancy. 2001. *The USA Patriot Act.* Center for Constitutional Rights. Available at www.ccr-ny.org/whatsnew/usa_patriot_act.asp.

Chomsky, Noam. 1999. *Profit over people: Neoliberalism and global order.* New York: Seven Stories Press.

———. 2001. *9-11.* New York: Seven Stories Press.

Clinton, Kate. 2002. Dressed for surveillance. *Progressive* 66 (1): 11.

Conniff, Ruth. 2002. Patriot games. *Progressive* 66 (1): 14–18.

Douglas, Susan. 2001. The media fall in line. *Progressive* 65 (11): 23–25.

Eisenstein, Zillah. 1996. *Hatreds: Racialized and sexualized conflicts in the 21st century.* New York: Routledge.

———. 1998. *Global obscenities: Patriarchy, capitalism and the lure of cyberfantasy.* New York: New York University Press.

———. 2004. *Against empire.* New York: Zed Books.

Eisler, Riane. 2001. The school for violence. *LA Weekly,* September 28–October, 433–35.

Enloe, Cynthia. 1990. *Banana beaches and bases: Making feminist sense of international politics.* Berkeley: University of California Press.

———. 1993. *The morning after: Sexual politics and the end of the cold war.* Berkeley: University of California Press.

Freire, Paulo. 1972. *Pedagogy of the oppressed.* New York: Herder and Herder

Gillespie, Marcia Ann. 1994a. Editorial: Family values. *Ms.,* July/August, 1.

———. 1994b. Editorial: Where's our passion? *Ms.,* November/December, 1.

Gordon, Linda. 1988. *Heroes of their own lives: The politics and history of family violence—Boston 1880–1960.* New York: Viking.

Hammer, Rhonda. 2002. *Antifeminism and family terrorism: A critical feminist perspective.* Lanham, Md.: Rowman & Littlefield.

Hill Collins, Patricia. 1998. It's all in the family: Intersections and gender, race, and nation. *Hypatia* 13, no. 3 (Summer): 62–63.

hooks, bell. 1994. *Teaching to transgress: Education as the practice of freedom.* New York: Routledge.

———. 2000. *Feminism is for everybody: Passionate politics.* Cambridge, Mass.: South End Press.

Jones, Ann. 1994. *Next time she'll be dead: Battering and how to stop it.* Boston: Beacon.

Kang, Connie K. 2001. Apology sought for Japanese atrocities. *Los Angeles Times,* July 22.

Keeting, AnaLouise. 2000. *Gloria E. Anzaldua: Interviews.* New York: Routledge.

Kellner, Douglas. 2003. *From 9/11 to terror war: The dangers of the Bush legacy.* Lanham, Md.: Rowman & Littlefield.

Kesic, Vesna. 2001. From reverence to rape: An anthropology of ethnic and genderized violence. In *Frontline feminisms: Women, war, and resistance,* ed. Marguerite R. Waller and Jennifer Rycenga, 23–36. New York: Routledge.

Kinsley, Michael. 2001. Defining terrorism. *Slate,* October 4.

Kojeve, Alexandre. 1969. *Introduction to the reading of Hegel.* New York: Basic Books.

Martin, David. 2003. With a whisper, not a bang. *San Antonio Current,* December 24.

Moghadam, Valentine. 2001. *For gender justice and economic justice: Transnational feminism and global inequalities.* Annual meetings of the International Studies Association, Chicago, February.

Mohanty, Chandra. 2003. *Feminism without borders: Decolonizing theory, practicing solidarity.* Durham, N.C.: Duke University Press.

Nichols, John. 2001.The lone dissenter. *Progressive* 65 (11): 28–29.

Paul, Ron. 2002. Quoted in the film *The truth and lies of 9-11.* Sherman Oaks, Calif.: FTW.

Rothschild, Matthew. 2002. The new McCarthyism. *Progressive* 66 (1): 18–23.

Rycenga, Jennifer, and Marguerite Waller. 2001. Introduction. In *Frontline Feminisms: Women, War, and Resistance,* ed. Marguerite R. Waller and Jennifer Rycenga, xiii–xxvii. New York: Routledge.

Soto-Aquino. 1999. *Elder abuse: Incidence and prevention.* Congressional Research Service report. Derwood, Md.: Penny Hill Press.

Tjaden, Patricia, and Nancy Thoennes. 2000. *Extent, nature, and consequences of partner violence: Findings from the national violence against women survey, NIJCDC.* Washington, D.C.: U.S. Department of Justice, Office of Justice Programs.

Zinn, Howard. 2001. A just cause, not a just war. *Progressive,* December, 16–19.

———. 2002. Operation enduring war. *Progressive,* March, 12–13.

III

RADICAL PEDAGOGIES

14

Whose Lady of Guadalupe? Indigenous Performances, Latina/o Identities, and the Postcolonial Project

Bernardo P. Gallegos

Recently a former student asked if I would speak to her second-graders at a public school in a predominately Mexican (and working class) community in a Chicago suburb, as she and two other second-grade teachers were doing a unit on Native Americans. The student (Mexican) had recently completed a course (Policy Issues in the History of American Education) which I begin with a session on early educational policy in (Meso) America immediately after the European conquest. The assigned readings, lectures, and discussions focus on education as an instrument of colonization in the European subjugation of indigenous territories, bodies, and narratives. As a part of my lecture I sing Comanche songs performed by families in Albuquerque's South Valley (New Mexico), which I use as examples of the hybrid cultural forms and texts that emerged from colonial educational policies and practices (Gallegos 1994a, 1994b). Moreover, I discuss the interpretive complexities of the narrative of Our Lady of Guadalupe and its relation to colonial pedagogy. I assume that along with my discursive location in a hybrid Native American identity and occupation of an indigenous body, the invitation to speak was related to my pedagogical performance and perspective on these topics.

After a brief time in the classroom with my former student and her pupils (mostly Mexican or Latina/o), we all walked to the library where the presentation was to take place. En route I met the other two (white) teachers that form the second-grade team and we all filed into the library with sixty or so children whose bodies had to be arranged for the occasion. As I contemplated the performance, I gazed at the audience of small brown indigenous bodies (with the exception of perhaps five whites) waiting for my presentation/performance and noticed them looking curiously at my drum, one of the props that I assume, along with my indigenous body, and songs, would lend legitimacy to my words.

I began by telling the children that this area (Chicago) was populated by a great many Native American people who, I was careful to point out, "looked like most of you." I glanced over at the two white teachers, keenly aware of the possible power relations (institutional context) and the repercussions my words could have on my former student's employment situation. I told them (students) that most of them (Native Americans) died, were pushed away, or were killed. Aware of the performative nature of my presentation I looked regularly at the two white teachers for body language that might indicate their discomfort. I also looked to my former student for cues as to what else I should say or how far I could go. I wanted to say that white people killed them (Native Americans) and drove them away so that they could steal their land, but I hesitated, and limited myself to a softer more passive voice, as in "they were moved," "they died," or "they were killed," without identifying why or by who.

I soon began to sense restlessness among the children. One of the (white) teachers apparently also noticed, and informed me that they had taken a field trip to a museum to see a Native American exhibit and then turned to the students and asked: "What did we learn kids?" The children responded in a seemingly well-orchestrated chorus, "Native Americans ate corn." I asked them what else they learned, and they repeat (in chorus), "Native Americans ate corn." I told them energetically and as pedagogically correctly as I could (using the high, soft, and gentle voice that is so much a part of the elementary teacher performance) that, "some Native American foods are still widely eaten today." I told them that they may even eat some Native American foods themselves, and asked if they can guess what some of these are. Hands flew up and several responded eagerly, "corn." I could see that "corn" was the most I would get so I decided to help them. I asked (pretty much knowing the answer) if any of them had ever heard of "taquitos?" Not surprisingly almost all of them raised their hands but they appeared puzzled and looked at me in way that led me to interpret that "taquitos" were not a part of their Native American unit. I emphasized that "taquitos"—along with "tamales," "frijolitos" (beans), "papitas" (potatoes), and chocolate—are some of the Native American foods that are still eaten all over America.

I then began a discussion of Native American religions. I told them that there were many Native American goddesses and gods who were mostly forgotten because almost all of the Native American religions were destroyed. I told them about the Corn Goddesses of New Mexico (Gutierrez 1991), Huichilopochli the Hummingbird God, and Tlaloc the God of Rain (Leon-Portilla 1962). I told them that while most of the Native American gods and goddesses had been forgotten by the people, one goddess is still remembered; that people all over America still pray to her; and that she is very important to those Native Americans who call themselves Mexicans. I told them that she was the Mother of all the gods and goddesses and that she was called "Tonantzin Coatlalopeuh" and that she had a temple where people came from all over America to visit her at a place called El Cerro de Tepeyac in Mexico City (Ricard 1966, 191; Anzaldúa 2000). I told them that when the Spanish (I wanted to say whites, but refrained) priests came to Mexico they did not allow the Mexicans to continue praying to their own goddesses and gods and forced them to pray to the Catholic god (Ricard 1966). But, I explained, the Mexicans would not give up their own Goddess Tonantzin whom they considered their Mother (Castillo 2000; Ricard 1966). I told them that the priests let the Mexicans continue to go to pray to Tonantzin at El Cerro de Tepeyac but they made them call her by a different name. I asked the kids to guess what Tonantzin's new name is. A flurry of hands waved and several kids, hardly able to contain themselves, blurted out "Mary, Mary." I gently said no and called on another student and again several kids answered, "Mary!" I glanced over at one of the white teachers and sensed a discomfort in her body language. I told them that it is not Mary, and finally after I could see they could not guess, I told them that Tonantzin's new name was "Our Lady of Guadalupe" (Castillo 2000; Ricard 1966). Immediately I saw excited smiles and discovered (I don't know why I was surprised) that several of the kids were named Guadalupe. I emphasized that they were named after a great Native American goddess. I glanced at the teachers and now began to read much discomfort in the body language of one of them. I imagined that I was at the frontiers of this performance, that I had gone about as far as the context would allow so I brought out my drum and showed them how to sing a Comanche song.

As I reflected on the event, I wondered why I was censoring myself and monitoring my words and the body language of the teachers? After all, I am a tenured professor, published author, and knowledgeable about the topic. Moreover, my interpretation of their body languages was being played out in my own imagination and I may have been misreading the cues. To explore this point, I will examine the event in the context of current theoretical conversations in the areas of postcolonial and performance studies. More specifically I will use the work of postcolonial and performance theorists to explore the political contours of indigenous identities and the authoring of Latina/o histories in classrooms, on the pages of academic and popular texts, and more recently in museums. My intention, in short, is to explore the relationships between "taquitos," "corn," "Mary," "Our Lady of Guadalupe," and the politics of discursive production in the colonization of Native America.

As I spoke to the children, I wrestled internally with myriad voices and deliberated intensely over what to say and how to say it. Why couldn't I say that white people killed the people who lived here "who looked like you all?" The obvious answer is that there were contextual boundaries. It could have put my former student in a potentially problematic situation, with the guest speaker she invited saying something that could be construed as out of bounds. I was aware of the potentially disruptive character of my presentation/performance and the boundaries, which I should not cross lest I create a problem for my student. The negotiation over what I should/could say as I performed/presented is akin to the deliberations at play in the process of writing of histories in general. The process of textual production, including this very essay, is much like that which Homi Bhabba discusses in reference to an "originary" moment which, he explains, is "redolent with possibility, productivity, and agency" (Bhabba, quoted in Pollack 1998, 24).

Recently a body of scholarship has emerged that examines the performative nature of historical writing. Like other performances, the writing of history is framed as a bodily practice and as such characterized by an agency of a limited sort. There are, if you may, conceptual boundaries surrounding our imaginations, in addition to the more obvious rules and regulations governing the production of academic texts. Speaking to the limitations and possibilities of agency, Della Pollack (2000) employs the term *historicity* to explain how "the body practices history as it incarnates, mediates, and resists the metahistories with which it is impressed . . . [and] wrestles with the totalizing and legitimizing power of such historical tropes as telos and progress" (4).

Pollack, moreover, utilizes the term *intertext*, drawn from Bakhtin's concept heteroglossia, to describe historical texts "as the residue of performative pressures and exchange, as the messy, noisy conjunction of multiple and competing voices" (23). Her notion of "intertext" in the writing of history, or any academic project for that matter, is akin to the internal deliberation which I was experiencing in my presentation to the second graders. I was at that moment, aware of the relationship between the interplay of the text, context, and subtext and of the power relations governing them.

I was fully cognizant that my performance/lecture with the second graders was about imposing a particular story/interpretation for a particular purpose. In short, I had an agenda. I was, to use Pollack's analysis, "wrestling" with, in this case, metanarratives that disappear huge numbers of Native Americans by authorizing them into categories such as Latina/o, Hispanic, or various national identities (Gallegos 1998; Kobayashi 1985; Luykx 1996; Pérez 1999; Vaughan 1982, 1997). I was acutely aware of the agenda that I brought to the presentation and I assumed my former student was as well, for why else would she have invited me, knowing my take on Native American history, my framing of Mexicans as Native Americans, and my thoughts on Our Lady of Guadalupe.

I was attempting to disrupt a dominant narrative that frames the second graders, my student, and countless other Mexicans as outsiders (aliens, immigrants), to this geographical (and discursive) space. I told a different story, one in which the second-graders were representative of the Native American repopulation of that space that we currently name the United States. These conflicting stories, both legitimate in an academic sense, have a great deal to do with current social and educational policies and practices. California propositions 187 and 227 that respectively limit access to services and impact bilingual education programs are examples of this point (Gallegos 1998). Tamsin Spargo (2000), in a discussion of historiographical politics, posits that "arguments about the past are often explicitly and, I would argue, always implicitly interventions in debates about the present and the future" (2).

There is in fact a substantial body of literature addressing the politics of producing history, its propagandistic nature and its relation to current configurations of power (Jenkins 1997; Spargo 2000). Much of it is reliant on the work of Hayden White (1987) and his problematization of "objectivity" in the authoring of histories. White examines the ways that subjectivity is inherent in the production of narrative. As humans, we are at the same time products and producers of narratives. We live in and produce narratives that are populated by a myriad of agendas that serve to support, resist, or legitimate, particular social, cultural, and economic arrangements. The production of text then, whether it be a book or a simple statement is never disinterested (58–82). In a discussion of the impossibility of free speech, Stanley Fish (1999) reinforces this point by noting that every utterance is in some way connected to an agenda of sorts. Speech, he argues,

> is always at once constrained and constraining. Speech is constrained because one does not think to speak (or write) independently of some vision or agenda that, quite literally, *compels* assertion; speech therefore is not free because one is in the grip of compulsion—the softer word would be belief or conviction—at the moment of its production. (93)

Telling these second-grade Mexican kids that they in fact were Native Americans, and that Our Lady of Guadalupe was a Native American goddess was (if their responses to my questions were an indication) not a story that they were used to hearing in school. I was well aware of the potentially disruptive nature of my every word and their potential effects. Fish addresses this notion of discursive displacement as follows:

> if utterance always works to advance some interest as defined by some agenda, its effectiveness will always be achieved at the expense of some other interests as defined by some other agenda. Someone always pays when free speech takes. (1999, 93)

Aware of the power relations involved on that day of the presentation I was monitoring body languages in part, because I did not want my former student to pay for my "free speech taking!" Yet, I fully intended to make explicit the students' relationship to the earlier Native Americans who lived in the Chicago area. The conflict of narratives that are represented in my performance are in fact part of broader conversations that involve the politics of interpretation, and as I discussed earlier have a great deal to do with current power relations a point which I will now examine in more detail.

WHOSE LADY OF GUADALUPE?

Our Lady of Guadalupe emerges as central to this essay because of the phenomenal power that her story/image has had and continues to have in indigenous, Mexican, and now Latina/o lives and consciousness (Castillo 2000).

Moreover, the narrative of Our Lady of Guadalupe is and has historically been at the center of multiple and often conflicting interpretations. The conflict rests in large part on the identity of the "Our" in "Our Lady of Guadalupe." Or, to put it another way, is there an "Our"?

A recent controversy in New Mexico over ownership of the image of Our Lady of Guadalupe will be helpful in exploring this point. In the winter 2001, the Museum of International Folk Art featured an exhibit that contained a digital rendition of Our Lady of Guadalupe in a rose bikini by artist Alma Lopez. The controversy was complex and the limitations of space prevent me from going into detail, but generally some Native New Mexicans were outraged at what they perceived to be a blasphemous depiction of "Our (Their) Lady of Guadalupe."

The artist "who was born in Mexico and grew up in a Catholic family in northeastern Los Angeles" stated that her piece was "inspired by 'Guadalupe the Sex Goddess,' an essay by Hispanic author Sandra Cisneros" (*Albuquerque Tribune,* March 21, 2001). The Archbishop of Santa Fe's lending institutional support to the protestors derided the artist and the museum personnel for what he perceived as an affront to the "Blessed Virgin Mary." The controversy was of great interest to me in part because it involved my homeland and of equal importance because of the interpretive politics involved. I was aware of the historical co-construction and subsequent coproductions of the Guadalupe narrative and had in fact written about it (Gallegos 1994a, 1994b). Moreover, I was bothered by what I perceived as the appropriation of the narrative (His Lady of Guadalupe) by the Archbishop, and by the subsequent attempt to censor Alma Lopez's Lady of Guadalupe. I in fact wrote a letter to the editor of the *Albuquerque Tribune,* outlining the origins of the narrative of Guadalupe, which after much internal deliberation and consultation with friends and family I did not send. In the letter I supported the artist and derided her critics who, ironically were for the most part poor and working-class natives of New Mexico, a point which, in large part, led to my decision not to send the letter.

More recently, as I labored over this chapter in the kitchen of my mom's house in Albuquerque, the interpretive conflict surrounding Our Lady of Guadalupe once again presented itself. It was December 12, the day that "Our" (?) Lady of Guadalupe is honored. The December 10, 2001, issue of the *Albuquerque Journal* that lay on my mother's table had on the front page a large picture of a young indigenous girl dressed in neo-Aztec attire carrying an image of "Nuestra Senora" (Our Lady), followed by several Azteca dancers. Above was another photo of the (white) Archbishop of Santa Fe (Michael Sheehan) dressed in his costume holding a large staff in one hand and appearing to be performing a blessing with the other. In large bold print next to the photos a headline read: "Parade of Faithful, Roman Catholics gather in South Valley to honor Mary's appearance to a poor Indian in Mexico." Our/My/Their Lady was being framed by the newspaper as the Catholic "Mary." After explaining my essay and the idea of conflicting interpretations to my mother (since she asked), she stated that she did not ever consider "Our/Her Lady of Guadalupe" to be the Blessed Virgin Mary. She said she "always thought they were two separate persons."

This ambiguity over the identity of our lady was not new and in fact the narrative was controversial and open to multiple interpretations from its very origins. In the decades following the European conquest of America and the subsequent creation of the Guadalupe text, there was much controversy and deliberation among the religious authorities regarding what they referred to as "the cult of Guadalupe." Bernardino de Sahagun, advocate of higher education for the Indians, and teacher at the Colegio de Santa Cruz de Tlaltelolco (Kobayashi 1985), the first college for indigenous peoples in the Americas,

> was particularly uneasy about the cult of Guadalupe. He was acutely afraid lest the Indians, on the pretext of worshiping the Holy Virgin, [Mary] whom the preachers had erroneously given the name of Tonantzin, would really continue to render homage to the pre-Hispanic goddess Tonantzin, whose shrine had been at Tepeyac itself. (Ricard 1966, 191)

The pedagogical utility of the indigenous Mexican narrative of Tonantzin and the pilgrimages of the Mexicans to her shrine at Tepeyac, did not become clear to the missionaries until well into the colonization (Ricard 1966). "Our Lady" has, it seems, over the centuries metamorphosed, but the question of whose "Lady" she was apparently remains unresolved (Castillo 2000). In the following section I will briefly outline aspects of Postcolonial theory and its relation to indigenous identities, Latina/o histories, the politics of textual production, and the "Our" in "Our Lady of Guadalupe."

A detailed review of postcolonial studies, the broad territory traversed by its theorists, and its related range of interpretive frameworks, is outside the spatial limitations of this essay (Ghandi 1998). There are some important categories, however, that mark the postcolonial analytic project, which I will briefly review to establish a context for examining the politics of interpretation. The European conquest and colonization of much of the world was multifaceted and included but was not limited to forced labor, economic disruptions, genocide, and territorial appropriation. One of the most salient features of colonialism however, and the one of concern here, was the authoring of the colonized into Western narrative structures.

Colonization of course had different characteristics in particular regions of the world and changed over time. Gyan Prakash (cited in Ghandi 1998) characterizes the colonial project as evolutionary, beginning with the "bandit mode" of colonialism, which she describes as "simple minded in its physical conquest of territories." "Modern" colonialism, more advanced and reliant on institutional uses of force and coercion, enacted another kind of violence by instituting, according to Prakash, "enduring hierarchies of subjects and knowledges—the colonizer and the colonized, the Occidental and the Oriental, the civilized and the primitive, the scientific and the superstitious, the developed, and the developing" (15).

The advent of modernity moreover ushered in new forms of colonialism characterized by elaborate classificatory systems that were ultimately put to the purpose of human subjugation. The post-Enlightenment (modern) world according to race theorist Zygmunt Bauman (2000), was

> distinguished by its activist, engineering attitude toward nature and toward itself. Science was not to be conducted for its own sake; it was seen as, first and foremost, an instrument of awesome power allowing its holder to improve on reality, to reshape it according to human plans and designs. . . . Human existence and cohabitation became objects of planning and administration; like garden vegetation or a living organism they could not be left to their own devices, lest should they be infested by weeds or overwhelmed by cancerous tissue. (219)

Modernity then functioned to relegate the "other" (colonial subject) into the classificatory system of science. It had the effect of inscribing and later containing the colonial subject in discourses that were burdened with metanarratives such as "the progress of the human race" which championed the superiority of Europeans (after all it was their story). Darwin's theory of evolution for example became more than a narrative of the emergence and development of human beings. It was utilized to support narratives that distinguished between them (humans) in terms of place in the evolutionary hierarchy. Academic disciplines such as anthropology and history began authoring the rest of the world (colonized) into the epistemic system of the West, classifying us through elaborate theoretical lenses and myriad categories.

Anthropology in fact ushered in the era of the "primitive" who could perhaps be civilized by the intervention of the white race, a belief that was central to the forming of educational policy and practice for colonized peoples (Watkins 2001). "Assimilation" emerged as a powerful analytical concept that has most often signified the movement of less developed (primitive) peoples into more highly developed "Western culture." The construct has governed a great deal of educational policy and practice and has been central to a great many pedagogical campaigns, including that of the Spanish in the Americas (Gallegos 1992; Kobayashi 1985; Ricard 1966). Educational campaigns were organized for the purpose of transforming the "primitive other" into a familiar, docile, and more manageable "other" (Gallegos 1992; Spring 1996, 2000; Watkins 2001). Various national educational projects such as the Post Revolutionary campaign in Mexico were undertaken with the intent of integrating the large indigenous population into the national "imagined community" (Luykx 1996; Vaughan 1982, 1997).

People who occupy the category Latina/o were/are greatly impacted by these hierarchical evolutionary discourses that in effect supported imperialist and expansionist policies. The United States conquest and appropriation of the northern half of Mexican territory in fact was governed by these discourses which gave legitimacy/support to a war which would (theoretically) put a more advanced (evolutionary) peoples (Anglo-Americans) in charge of territories that were not being used to their full potential by a less-advanced peoples (Mexicans; Almaguer 1994; Horsman 1981). In a discussion of the rationalizations supporting the United States' conquest of Mexico and appropriation of its territories, Reginald Horsman cites various examples of perceived racial inferiority of Mexican and other non-European peoples. The discourses of Western racial and cultural superiority, he explains, were so pervasive that even staunch anti-war activists such as Theodore Parker expressed them. "In respect to *power of civilization*," wrote Parker, "the African is at the bottom, the American Indian next" (cited in Horsman 1981, 179). "Parker," explains Horsman, "had no doubt that the Caucasian was the superior race" (178).

Postcolonial scholarship seeks to examine and disrupt the multiple effects of colonization. In particular, postcolonial theorists are concerned with understanding discursive colonial disciplinary practices and their effects on the subaltern. As Gyan Prakash (1994) explains, the critique of colonization and dominance of the West is not limited to the "colonial record of exploitation and profiteering but extends to the disciplinary knowledge and procedures it authorized—above all, the discipline of history." Reflecting on the project of the postcolonial critic, Prakash writes:

> If the marginalization of "other" sources of knowledge and agency occurred in the functioning of colonialism and its derivative, nationalism, then the weapon of critique must turn against Europe and the modes of knowledge it instituted. (1,483)

Laboring in the very institutions that have been (and continue to be) employed in the service of the colonial project, however, the postcolonial scholar is left in the quandary of having to articulate an "impossible 'no' to a structure, which one critiques, yet inhabits intimately" (Gayatri Chakravorty Spivak, cited in Prakash 1994, 1,487). As descendants of Spanish as well as U.S. colonialism, Latina/o scholars likewise are in the position of having to exert agency within the classificatory categories that emerged from European domination.

Latina/o is in fact itself one such category. In the Americas during the sixteenth, seventeenth, and eighteenth centuries, Ladino/Latino was widely used to refer to an educated (in the Western sense) Native American, or to one who could read and write. The archival records of the Spanish colonies are replete with many references to "Indios Ladinos." Indigenous education in New Spain (Mexico) in fact was mainly concerned with incorporating native peoples into a Western (Catholic) worldview (Gallegos 1992, 1994a, 1994b; Kobayashi 1985; Ricard 1966). This entailed the systematic eradication of indigenous epistemologies and texts, often in public rituals. In sixteenth-century Mexico City, for example, "autos de fe," which consisted of the destruction of pre-Columbian indigenous texts were quite common (Ricard 1966). Fray Juan de Zumárraga, the first bishop of Mexico (City) reported in 1531, "that he had destroyed more than five hundred temples and twenty thousand idols" (Ricard 1966, 37).

The conquest however was not monolithic and colonial subjects also resisted (like the Guadalupana artist Alma Lopez) and performed in ways that functioned to provide a semblance of continuity to preexisting indigenous discourses and practices such as the Mexica (Aztec) dance steps in Matichine dances, or the pilgrimages to El Cerro de Tepeyac, mentioned earlier. The politics of interpretation, evident in the persistence of interpretive conflict regarding "somebody's" Lady of Guadalupe, were played out in various ways throughout the colonial period across the Spanish colonies.

The following event that occurred in eighteenth-century New Mexico illuminates this point and moreover speaks to the politics of classification, Fish's previously cited discussion of the relationship of utterance and agenda, and the power of the colonial classificatory system on native peoples. The event moreover, lends itself to an examination of the complexities of writing "Latina/o" histories and the utility of performance theory and its privileging of agency.

In 1746, in the Villa of Santa Fe in New Mexico, two Kiowa Apaches appeared before the governor with a letter from a representative of the viceroy of New Spain. The letter urged him (the governor) to respect the rights of the Indians of the Pueblo of Belen (forty miles south of Albuquerque) whom they (the two Kiowa Apaches) as war captains represented. Antonio Casados and Luis Quintana, both Genizaros (detribalized Plains Indians), had secured the letter in person while they resided in Mexico City, where they had, ironically, met for the first time. Both were at the time fugitive servants who had escaped from their masters and the province of New Mexico illegally. The petition that they had presented to the representative of the viceroy urged that their rights as Indians should be respected and noted that they were ready to defend the king, God, and their representatives, against the "infidel" nations that surrounded the province (New Mexico). The Indians of Belen, they explained were being caused great harm by the presence of the Spaniards in their pueblo (two in particular), and they wished to have them banned.

In their testimonies, the Spaniards of Belen argued that the petitioners and those whom they represented were people without a language or semblance of culture, and that there was no such pueblo as Belen, but only a small hamlet populated by some Spanish families and their Indian servants. Casados and Quintana, they argued, were fugitives from their masters and moreover, were shamelessly attempting to slander the very men who had rescued them from paganism and educated them in the Spanish religion and customs. Moreover, they contended, these people were liars, knaves, and thieves (Spanish Archives of New Mexico 1746).

The conflict of stories evident in this event illuminate the relationship between utterance and agenda. Casados's and Quintana's interpretation (had it taken) would have provided the Genizaros in the Belen area with land and a semblance of autonomy which the Pueblo Indians in eighteenth-century New Mexico possessed (Gutierrez 1991; Jones 1966). Their story however was rejected and not only did they lose the case, but they were imprisoned and punished for being fugitives from their masters and for attempting to incite the friendly Indians against the Spaniards.

As colonial subjects, Casados and Quintana were unable to shift identities from the category of "servants" to that of "Pueblo Indians." The event however, demonstrates a sophisticated attempt to negotiate the colonial categorical system in which they functioned. Their story speaks to a subaltern consciousness of colonial power relations and an attempt to disrupt the entrenched narrative in the promotion of their own interests and that of the people they claimed to represent. Prakash (1995) argues that one of the projects of postcolonial scholars entails rescuing the agency of the colonial subject. "We have several accounts of the resistance of the colonized," she explains,

> but few treatments of their resistance as theoretical events; there exist fine descriptions of the "people without history," but their conceptions are frequently treated as myths and "ethnohistories" left for anthropologists to decode and interpret; and while there are scrupulous accounts of Western domination, we have yet to fully recognize another history of agency and knowledge alive in the dead weight of the colonial past. (5)

It is at this very point I would argue, that performance theories most strongly intersect with the postcolonial project.

In an essay that, in part, explores indigenous identities, Los Angeles writer Ruben Martínez (1999) aptly captures this point. Martinez privileges the agency of the subaltern and in so doing captures the essence of the performative nature of identity. His rejection of "assimilation" as an organizing category, with its subsequent erasure of indigenous identities works, much like Alma Lopez's art, toward the disruption of discursive aspects of colonialism. For Martinez, one does not stop being an Indian just because one owns Western products. "El Indigena," he writes,

> es el que chambea al otro lado y regresa cargando un telivisor y una videocasetera neuevos para disfrutar de las películas de Steven Seagal. Mas que perdida de indentidad, vemos la continuacion del proceso de mestizaje, en donde el indigena— y el chicano tienen voluntad propia para armar el paquete cultural a su antojo. (159)
> [is Indian who labors on the other side (United States) and returns (to Mexico) with a new television and videocassette recorder to enjoy the films of Steven Seagal. More than loss of identity, we see a continuation of the process of hybridization in which the Indian and the Chicano exercise their agency to supply their cultural baggage at their own discretion.]

El Joven Mixteco (the Mixtec boy), Martinez explains,

> que vive en Fresno, California, y que ya no habla su dialecto, sigue seindo Mixteco precisamente porque la cultura es un organismo que para mantenerse vivo debe adaptarse a su nuevo entorno, seguir creciendo. (160)
> [who lives in Fresno, California, who no longer speaks his native dialect, continues being Mixtec, precisely because culture is an organism that in order to maintain itself and grow, must adapt itself to its new context.]

Martinez's privileging of the agency of the Spanish (and now U.S.) colonial subject demonstrates a discursive repositioning of identity that is central to the
postcolonial project. Moreover, his text, along with Lopez's art, and the case of
the two Kiowa Apaches, Antonio Casados and Luis Quintana, demonstrate the
importance of interpretive politics in the construction of indigenous identities
and Latina/o performances.

As postcolonial indigenous and Latina/o scholars, we are engaged in a discursive war of positioning of sorts. We carry out our work in institutional contexts that privilege certain stories and confer legitimacy on our own scholarly
work. In that respect our own pedagogical work can be conceptualized as a sort
of postcolonial performance to the extent that we are aware of the discursive
politics that envelop our scholarly work (Villenas 1996). As historian Emma
Pérez (1999) explains, "This means that even the most radical Chicano/a histori-
ographies are influenced by the very colonial imaginary against which they
rebel" (5). That is, we work within a discursive framework to resist it. But we do
it tactfully, and carefully, always reading the cues, paying great attention with the
knowledge that our own existence in the academy is always in jeopardy.

In effect as postcolonial scholars we are "at risk," by the very nature of our
political project. We struggle to articulate Spivac's "impossible no," in what is often the most difficult of institutional contexts characterized by a culture of surveillance. We are expected to publish in refereed journals and subject ourselves
to peer reviews (most often blind), student evaluations, and decisions by com-
mittees whose members may not share our project at best and at worst, may be
hostile to it. We are in a sense working under the "colonial" gaze within the very
institutions and academic disciplines that were central to the development of
modern colonialism.

James C. Scott in a discussion of political resistance within the context of
asymmetrical relations of power such as that represented by the slave/master or
peasant/lord, explains the conditions under which agency is exercised by the
subaltern in the following way:

> The undeclared ideological guerilla war that rages in this political space requires
> that we enter the world of rumor, gossip, disguises, linguistic tricks, metaphors, eu-
> phemisms, folktales, ritual gestures, anonymity. For good reason, nothing is en-
> tirely straightforward here; the realities of power for subordinate groups mean that
> much of their political action requires interpretation precisely because it is intended
> to be cryptic and opaque. (Scott 1990, 137)

The relations of power and institutional/disciplinary contexts that govern the
work of indigenous scholars, including those who perform Latina/o identities,
I would argue, require a scholarship that is of necessity "cryptic and opaque."
Our performances in the academy are not in fact very different from what I described in my presentation to the second graders in that we are always paying
attention to the relationship between texts, contexts, and subtexts. As critical
subaltern scholars we engage in the theoretical work of locating our work out-

side of the realm of colonial discourses. We function in what Pérez (1999) refers to as the "de-colonial imaginary" which she describes as "that time lag between the colonial and postcolonial, that interstitial space where differential politics and social dilemmas are negotiated" (6).

For the subaltern scholar engaged in the decolonial imaginary, the intersection of postcolonial scholarship, with its resistance to the discursive dominance of the "West" albeit from within, and performance theory's focus on the body as the ultimate site of hegemonic reproduction/disruption, forms a powerful analytical space from which to engage imperialist representations. Moreover, it provides a location from which to rescue the agency of the colonial subject and, more important, carries the potential to rescue the indigenous scholar from the colonial performance.

REFERENCES

Almaguer, Tomas. 1994. *Racial fault line: The historical origins of white supremacy in California.* Berkeley: University of California Press.

Anzaldúa, Gloria. 2000. Coatlalopeuh, la que domina a las serpientes. In *La diosa de las Américas,* ed. Ana Castillo. New York: Vintage Books.

Bauman, Zygmunt. 2000. Modernity, racism, extermination. In *Theories of race and racism: A reader,* ed. Les Back and John Solomos. New York: Routledge

Castillo, Ana. 2000. *La diosa de las Américas.* New York: Vintage Books.

Fish, Stanley. 1999. *The trouble with principle.* Cambridge, Mass.: Harvard University Press.

Gallegos, Bernardo. 1992. *Literacy, education, and society in New Mexico, 1693–1821.* Albuquerque: University of New Mexico Press.

———. 1994a. Schools and schooling in the Spanish borderlands. In *Encyclopedia of the North American colonies,* ed. Jacob Ernest Cooke et al. New York: Macmillan.

———. 1994b. Theories of education in the Spanish borderlands. In *Encyclopedia of the North American colonies,* ed. Jacob Ernest Cooke et al. New York: Macmillan.

———. 1998. Remember the Alamo: Imperialism, memory, and postcolonial educational studies— 1997 presidential address. *Educational Studies Journal* 29 (3): 232–47.

Ghandi, Leela. 1998. *Postcolonial theory: A critical introduction.* New York: Columbia University Press.

Gutierrez, Ramón A. 1991. *When Jesus came, the corn mothers went away: Marriage, sexuality, and power in New Mexico, 1500–1846.* Stanford, Calif.: Stanford University Press.

Horsman, Reginald. 1981. *Race and manifest destiny: The origins of racial Anglo-Saxonism.* Cambridge, Mass.: Harvard University Press.

Jenkins, Keith. 1997. *The postmodern history reader.* New York: Routledge.

Jones, Oakah, L. 1966. *Pueblo warriors and Spanish conquest.* Norman: University of Oklahoma Press.

Kobayashi, José Maria. 1985. *La educación como conquista.* México: El Colegio De Mexico.

Leon-Portilla, Miguel. 1962. *The broken spears: The Aztec account of the conquest of Mexico.* Boston: Beacon Press.

Luykx, Aurolyn. 1996. From Indios to profesionales: Stereotypes and student resistance in Bolivian teacher training. In *The cultural production of the educated person,* ed. Bradley A. Levinson, Douglas E. Foley, and Dorothy C. Holland. Albany: State University of New York Press.

Martinez, Ruben. 1999. Más allá de las mamonerías: Cultura, migración, y desmadre en ambos lados del Río Bravo. In *Urban Latino cultures: La vida Latina en L.A.,* ed. Gustavo Leclerc, Raul Villa, and Michael Dear. Thousand Oaks, Calif.: Sage.

Pérez, Emma. 1999. *The decolonial imaginary: Writing Chicanas into history.* Bloomington: Indiana University Press.

Pollack, Della. 1998. Introduction: Making history go. In *Exceptional spaces: Essays in performance and history,* ed. Della Pollack. Chapel Hill: University of North Carolina Press.

Prakash, Gyan. 1994. Subaltern studies as postcolonial criticism. *American Historical Review* (December).

———. 1995. Introduction: After colonialism. In *After colonialism: Imperial histories and postcolonial displacements,* ed. Gyan Prakash. Princeton, N.J.: Princeton University Press.

Ricard, Robert. 1966. *The spiritual conquest of Mexico: An essay on the apostalate and the evangelizing methods of the mendicant orders in New Spain, 1523–1572.* Berkeley: University of California Press.

Scott. James C. 1990. *Domination and the Arts of Resistance: Hidden Transcripts.* New Haven, Conn.: Yale University Press.

Spanish Archives of New Mexico. 1746. Series 1, reel 1: frames 1302–1327. Twitchell 183.

Spargo, Tamsin. 2000. Past, present and future pasts. In *Reading the past, literature and history,* ed. Tamsin Spargo. New York: Palgrave.

Spring, Joel. 1996. *The cultural transformation of a Native American family and its tribe, 1763–1995: A basket of apples.* New Jersey: Erlbaum.

———. 2000. *Deculturalization and the struggle for equality: A brief history of the education of dominated cultures in the United States.* Columbus, Ohio: McGraw-Hill.

Vaughan, Mary Kay. 1982. *The state, education, and social class in Mexico, 1800–1928.* DeKalb: Northern Illinois University Press.

———. 1997. *Cultural politics in revolution, teachers, peasants, and schools in Mexico, 1930–1940.* Tucson: University of Arizona Press.

Villenas, S. 1996. The colonizer/colonized Chicana ethnographer: Identity, marginalization, and co-optation in the field. *Harvard Educational Review* 66 (4): 711–31.

Watkins, William H. 2001. *The white architects of black education, ideology and power in America, 1865–1954.* New York: Teachers College Press.

White, Hayden. 1987. *The content of the form: Narrative discourse and historical representation.* Baltimore, Md.: Johns Hopkins University Press.

15

Critical Revolutionary Pedagogy after September 11: A Marxist Response

Peter McLaren and Ramin Farahmandpur

CITIZENSHIP AND REFLECTIVE IMPOVERISHMENT

The political fallout from the unforgiving and unforgivable attacks of September 11, 2001, have ushered in new realm of citizenship where the once inseparable connection between democracy and justice has been irreparably fractured. Reason has been sacrificed at the altar of unreflective action. Hatred of the Other that has been gestating for decades since the Reagan era has now been unleashed with the Bush/Cheney junta's furious assault on terrorism and all things turbaned, with the terrorists substituting for our former enemies: the Red Menace from the Georgian Steppes. Members of the ruling class have been the frontline defenders of the war on terrorism and are all-too-willing to sacrifice civil rights if it will protect their position in the global division of labor. The already complicated equilibrium of our cities has gone into frenzied fibrillations at the prospect of death and destruction suddenly raining down upon our innocents. The ever-imminent but undefined hope that the world is getting better has been forever silenced by September 11. The reflective impoverishment of the American public, raised for generations on sound-byte philosophy, K-mart realism and Diet Pepsi minimalism has proven an advantage to President Bush, whose popularity as the Christian Crusader whom God instructed to remove Saddam from power remains steady among evangelicals and Christian Zionists. Bush's mental glacier is in no danger of being shrunk by global warming. It continues to float the most hawkish ideas since Ronald Reagan, ideas that frighten even many conservatives. The public appears convinced that only Bush has the mettle to wipe the planet clean of Muhammed's holy militia.

In the current juncture of Bush and Bennett, it has become dangerous to think, to ask too many questions, or to look beyond the face value of whatever commentary is served up to us by our politicians, our military, and our so-called intelligence agencies, and those who have disingenuously become their Beverly Hills lap dogs: the media. Among most media commentators, dialectical thought has been lamentably undervalued and shamefully underpracticed. It is a world where it is safer to engage in rehearsed reactions to what we encounter on our television screens. It is less dangerous to react in ways that newscaster/entertainers big on acrimonious scapegoating and short on analysis define for us as patriotic: applaud all actions by governmental authorities (especially those of the president) as if they were sacerdotal or morally apodictic. During the invasion of Afghanistan, CNN declared it was "perverse" to focus on civilian suffering, exercising a racist arithmetic that deems civilian casualties in the United States to be superior to those in Afghanistan (and now Iraq). And it is clear that Fox television is little more than the *Pravda* of the Bush administration protecting George Bush Jr. from public scrutiny and steadfastly supporting his "enemy-of-the-month club."

Former Secretary of Education, and candidate for president in the 2000 Republican primaries, William Bennett, has become one of Bush's most outspoken public defenders and has assumed the mantle of "philosopher king" of the Republican Party. Bennett, has recently published *Why We Fight: Moral Clarity and the War on Terrorism* (2002). An angry and indomitable cheerleader for the American war machine, Bennett, continues to serve as a despotic mouthpiece and polemical hack for the most self-righteous and morally apodictic wing of the Republican far Right, mixing religious triumphalism (in Bennett's case, Catholic) with an overwhelming sense of his own importance and an absolute exclusion of any possibility of doubt or disillusionment on the issue of United States moral superiority in the world. Philosophically bankrupt, morally indignant, intellectually suspect, unburdened by an excess of imagination, and stamped with the temptation of careerism, *Why We Fight* is a half-baked criticism of the peace movement and what Bennett believes to be its benighted and morally dysfunctional leaders whom he blames for the failure of the United States to defeat the North Vietnamese and for aiding the enemies of civilization through their ongoing criticism of President Bush's permanent war on terrorism. Determined to give revenge by carpet bombing a moral justification and "payback" a philosophical warrant—not to mention the imprimatur of the Republican elite—Bennett's book rewrites bald imperialism as a democratic obligation to free the world from evildoers. Bennett's unwavering support for the U.S. war machine and its politics of preemptive strikes is as blinkered as it is pernicious. His unforgiving absolutism and elitist adulation for Plato's Republic betrays a contempt for dialectical reasoning and a blind allegiance to conservative dogma. For Bennett, merely raising the question of why the terrorist attacks of September 11 happened is an act of moral turpitude and a betrayal of the homeland. Bennett fails to connect the history of global capitalism to the history of U.S. foreign policy, or note the contradiction between its supposed leadership in the fight for democracy with its support for Latin American dictators, its training of death squad leaders in the (recently refunded) School of the Americas (now called WHISC: Western Hemisphere Institute for Security

Cooperation), its clandestine overthrow of democratically elected socialist governments, its buttressing of anti-Communist warlords in Southeast Asia, its slavish dedication to moneyed interests and its willingness to punish all those who resist the encroaching salvation of global corporatism.

CORPORATE TERRORISM AND THE NEW IMPERIALISM

With the U.S. government busy waging war against terrorism and the enemies of free-market capitalism both at home and abroad, a terrorism of another kind has recently swept across the social and political landscape of the United States: corporate terrorism. The scandals of Enron, WorldCom, AOL-Time-Warner, and Merck have made a mockery of democracy. Staffed by former oil executives, the Bush administration personifies the model of *corprocracy*: exclusive democratic rights for corporations and their subsidiaries. While corporations and fifth amendment CEOs, who have prospered from "corporate welfare"—the concentration of vast amounts of wealth and profits in the hands of greedy corporate executives and their large shareholders, and the socialization of the costs of corporate theft that average American taxpayers are forced to pay—are now the object of public scorn, there is little evidence that the capitalist ideology that drives their greed will be seriously challenged anytime soon.

As you read this, an estimated five billion men, women, and children are forced to subsist on two dollars a day. Meanwhile, the two hundred largest corporations in the world who have a combined 28 percent monopoly over global economic activities, merely employ a quarter percent of the global workforce. To put things into perspective, the combined wealth of the 84 richest individuals in the world exceeds the GPD of China, which has a population of 1.3 billion.

The staggering disparities between the rich and the poor can no longer be cast aside. The contradictions inherent within capitalist social relations of production are transparent for those who are brave enough to face the truth about the current crisis of global capitalism. To cite one example, between 1997 and 1999, the average wealth of the rich who were lucky enough to be listed on the Forbes 400 increased by $940 million. In sharp contrast, in the last twelve years, the net worth of the bottom 40 percent of the households in the United States declined by a dramatic 80 percent. Or take the example of the CEO of Disney, Michael Eisner, whose annual salary in 1998 was estimated to be $575.6 million. Compare that with the average annual salary of Disney employees, which stands at $25,070. We must question why, for example, the hourly wage of a worker in Guatemala is 37 cents an hour while Phil Knight, the CEO of Nike, has amassed a fortune of $5.8 billion.

By a sheer will to obliterate the past, modern day capitalists of the Enron school of ethics have unburdened history of its complexity and temporality and purified it of the stench of its victims. Capitalist accumulation can be experienced as an eternal "now," forever self-fellating and pleasure giving, never reneging on its promise of eternal happiness. If there is any justice folded into the transcendent order of things, it is this: When Bush's chief Bubba, "Kenny Boy" Lay is invited to drink at Plato's River of Forgetfulness, he'll be persuaded by the prophet of Necessity to return to the Republic in his most unvarnished incarnation: a hog squealing at the trough, waiting to be served up as Sunday dinner for all those "whose pension funds were pumped dry to provide the hog wallow with loot" (Cockburn 2002, 8).

The United States is by far the most powerful capitalist country in the world. Consider the list of 497 billionaires (down from 551 before 2001 as a result of global recession) in the world; 216 of billionaires are Americans, followed by Germany with 35 and Japan with 25. The combined wealth of these 497 billionaires equals the incomes of the most impoverished half of the human population Yet, in the wealthiest nation on Earth, the United States, one out of every six children lives in poverty. According to a published report by the progressive think tank, the Economic Policy Institute, one in four Americans were making poverty-level wages in 2000, and while major health care providers such as John Hopkins Hospital in Baltimore are developing special healthcare coverage programs that offer "platinum service" to the rich (complimentary massage and sauna time with physical exams in state-of-the-art testing labs), nearly forty million Americans lack health insurance.

The United States has declared the September 11 attacks to be an act of war. While these acts were indeed brutally warlike and a loathsome and despicable crime against humanity, clearly they did not constitute an act of war—an armed attack by one state against another—but rather acts of terrorism (which surely makes them no less hideous). Having failed to get authorization for the use of military force from the U.N. Security Council, Bush Jr. and his administration tried to get a formal declaration of war from the Congress but instead was given a War Powers Resolution Authorization (only one member of Congress, Barbara Lee, an African American representative from Oakland, demonstrated the courage to vote against it as a matter of principle). The Bush administration then convinced NATO to invoke Article 5 of the NATO pact in an attempt to get some type of multilateral justification for U.S. military action. After failing on two attempts to get Security Council approval for military action, the U.S. ambassador to the United Nations, John Negroponte, sent a letter to the Security Council asserting article 51 of the UN Charter, claiming that the United States reserves its right to use force against any state that it wishes as part of its fight against international terrorism (Negroponte was former U.S. ambassador in Honduras during the Contra war and oversaw the funding of Battalion 316 that all but wiped out in the democratic opposition; his confirmation was rammed through the day after the attacks).

President Bush now has his war mandate and is operating with a blank check for arming the military machine to its depleted uranium teeth. He is prepared to unleash Shock and Awe against any group of individuals or sovereign state that he alleges was involved in the attacks on September 11 or else sheltered, harbored, or assisted individuals in those attacks (see Boyle 2001). President Bush has made it unequivocally clear: those who are not with him are against him.

Chalmers Johnson's (2000) model of *blowback* (a term first used by the CIA but adopted by some leftists to refer to actions that result from unintended consequences of U.S. policies kept secret from the American public) offers a lucid framework for analyzing the attacks of September 11. Johnson argues what the mainstream media reports as the malign acts of "terrorists" or "drug lords" or "rogue states" or "illegal arms merchants" often turn out to be "blowback" from earlier covert U.S. operations (see Kellner 2003). Blowback related to U.S. foreign policy is directly related to the history of active support that the U.S. has given to terrorist groups or authoritarian regimes in Asia, Latin America, or the Middle East, before its clients turned on their sponsors. In Johnson's sense, September 11 is a classic example of blowback, in which U.S. policies generated unintended consequences that had catastrophic effects on U.S. citizens, New York, and the American and, indeed, global economy. The events of September 11 can be seen as a textbook example of blowback since bin Laden and the radical Islamic forces associated with the al Qaeda network were supported, funded, trained, and armed by several U.S. administrations and by the CIA. The CIA's catastrophic failure was not only to have failed to uncover the terrorist plot and taken action to prevent the attacks, but to have actively contributed to producing those very groups implicated in the terrorist attacks on the United States on September 11 (see Kellner 2003).

The United States imposes severe economic sanctions on Muslim countries that commit human rights abuses and that accumulate weapons of mass destruction. At the same time the United States ignores Muslim victims of human rights abuses in Palestine, Bosnia, Kosovo, Kashmir, and Chechnya. Through vast weapons sales, the United States props up its economy. Yet it insists on economic sanctions to prevent weapon development in Libya, Sudan, Iran, and Iraq. And, as Steve Niva points out, "The U.S. pro-Israel policy unfairly puts higher demands on Palestinians to renounce violence than on Israelis to halt new settlements and adhere to U.N. resolutions calling for an Israeli withdrawal from Palestinian lands" (2001, 3).

More broadly speaking, we believe that the events on September 11 should be examined in the context of the crisis of world capitalism. Here we are not so much referring to corporate executives—"the Ebola viruses of capitalism"—as we are the globalization of the productive forces under free-trade liberalization. We follow a number of the central assertions of William Robinson (2001), namely, that in recent decades the capitalist production process itself has become increasingly transnationalized. We have moved from a world economy to a new epoch known as the global economy. Whereas formerly the world economy was composed of the development of national economies and national circuits of accumulation that were linked to each other through commodity trade and capital flows, today national production systems are reorganized and functionally integrated into global circuits, creating a single and increasingly undifferentiated field for world capitalism. We are talking about the transnationalization of the production of goods and services (globalization) and not just the extension of trade and financial flows across national borders (internationalization). The new global financial system disperses profits worldwide as the world becomes unified into a single mode of production. The consequences of the restructuring of the world productive apparatus are staggering. We agree with Robinson that technological changes are the result of class struggle—in this case, the restraints on accumulation imposed by popular classes worldwide. Global class formation is occurring, with supranational integration of national classes accompanying the transnational integration of national productive structures. This has accelerated the division of the world into a global bourgeoisie (the hegemonic global class fraction) and a global proletariat. That is, dominant groups fuse into a class or class fraction within transnational space. There is an emergent capitalist historic bloc sustained by a transnational capitalist class and represented by a transnational bourgeoisie. The United States is playing a leadership role on behalf of the emerging transnational elite; that is, the United States is taking the lead as a rabid economic Alpha male in developing policies and strategies on behalf of the global capitalist agenda of the transnational elite. It follows from this that revolutionary social struggle must become transnationalized as power from below in order to counter transnationalized capitalist power from above.

Today, the marketplace is really a continuation of the core ideology of Reaganism, what Manning Marable (2001) describes as free markets, unregulated corporations, an aggressive militarization abroad, and the suppression of civil liberties and civil rights at home. In a sense, the United States is now closer to the Reagan ideal of the national security state "where the legitimate functions of government were narrowly restricted to matters of national defense, public safety, and providing tax subsidies to the wealthy." It is the flourishing of Reagan's "military Keynesianism"—"the deficit spending of hundreds of billions of dollars on military hardware and speculative weapons schemes such as 'Star Wars'" (4).

It is also clear that today world capitalism is trying to reestablish itself in transnationalized formations, since its current forms are virtually unsustainable. In other words, the transnational capitalist elites are seizing opportunities to use military force to protect their markets and create new ones. In fact, a more dangerous threat than individual acts of terror today are the multifarious contradictions internal to the system of world capitalism and the responses to these contradictions by the capitalist class. Throughout its history, U.S. capitalism has tried to survive in times of crisis by eliminating production and jobs, forcing those in work to accept worse conditions of labor, and seizing opportunities that might arise in which the public would support military action to protect what the United States defines as its vital interests. Developed and underdeveloped population groups occupying contradictory and unstable locations in an increasingly transnational environment coupled with cultural and religious antagonisms among the capitalist actors, creates conditions of desperation and anger among the fractions of the oppressed. We do not say this to give credibility to terrorism as a response to such anger but to seek to understand and prevent the conditions in which terrorism is ignited. Marable warns: "The question 'Why do they hate us?' can only be answered from the vantage point of the Third World's widespread poverty, hunger, and economic exploitation" (2001, 1).

Given this daunting global challenge, it is important that educators ask the following: Is there a viable socialist alternative to capitalism? What would a world without wage labor be like? Without living labor being subsumed by dead labor? Would a world without the extraction of surplus value and the exploitation that accompanies it be a safer and more just world, a world less likely to be infested with the conditions that breed terrorism?

UNMASKING NEOLIBERAL GLOBALIZATION

Contrary to the myths that have been circulated by the corporate-owned media, globalization does not, in any sense of the word, bring about the conditions for political harmony or economic stability. Nor does it furnish mutual economic growth for those nations, particularly Third World countries, who are forced to participate in the global economy under the leadership of the United States. The big scandal of our time, write Petras and Veltmeyer (2001), is that globalization fabricates the ideology that all countries benefit equally from the internationalization of trade. Yet, globalization is not by any stretch of the imagination, what we have been repeatedly told by corporate pundits: an "irreversible" and unstoppable process that arose from certain evolutionary social and historical conditions. In fact, we contend that economic globalization is a process orchestrated by advocates of neoliberal social and economic policies. Yet, we do not have to resign to the inevitability of neoliberal globalization.

Under the banner of globalization, corporate overworlders claim that the internationalization of capital is the solution to the declining rate of profit. For the cheerleaders of the free market, which include Milton Friedman, globalization is the cure to the accumulation crisis of capital. However, we unequivocally dismiss the claims that globalization represents, by and large, a qualitative leap in capitalist production. In our view, globalization represents a number of fundamental developments in capitalist economic crisis that include, among other things, a short-term solution to the long-term declining productivity; the intensification of competition among the leading imperialist nations, most notably, the United States, Japan, and Germany (the largest Western industrial economies who have shifted part of their production to Third World countries); the internationalization of investment and speculative capital; the international division of labor created by the integration of new technologies in an effort to raise productivity; the employment of new methods of flexible production largely derived from post-Fordist regimes of accumulation, and last but not least, the surging attacks on the working class and the poor by the Right on behalf of the ruling classes.

In our opinion, the concept of globalization serves to detract attention from the broader objectives of U.S. imperialism: to establish political domination; to facilitate economic exploitation; and to loot the natural resources of Third World nations. In other words, the concept of globalization serves as a smoke-screen to conceal the main objectives of U.S. imperialism's quest for global hegemony. As such, we believe that the concept of imperialism better reflects U.S. foreign policy objectives.

Finally, one of the objectives of neoliberal social and economic policies is liberating capital from any regulations that may be imposed upon it by government agencies. Part of the neoliberal social and economic policies is carried out through *privatization*—the e-Baying of state-owned enterprises, industries, and publicly-owned goods and services to the private sector, which is largely carried out under the banner of "efficiency" and "productivity"—two buzzwords that are employed to mask corporate theft of social resources. Furthermore, *deregulation* acts as a "buffer zone" to ward off any formidable threats against corporate profits in spite of the growing unemployment and environmental damage that neoliberal economic and social policies have caused, not to mention the reduction of reducing public expenditure on social services that include public education, health services, and child care to cite a few examples. In the end, what it all comes down to is that the objective of the Right is to abolish the concept of "public good" and to replace it with the ideology of "personal responsibility" of George Bush's compassionate conservatism.

THE NEW NICHE MARKET: GLOBAL SLAVERY

Capitalism is more than a sobering lesson for historians; it provides the ideal showcase for the tragedy of the human species. It not only includes men and women who are forced to work in hazardous working conditions, for barely endurable hours, and for much less than a living wage, but also children who labor perilously inside factories and sweatshops manufacturing numerous consumer goods (such as Nike shoes) that are shipped to consumer markets located in advanced capitalist countries. Capitalism does not screen its victims, anyone is fair game. It "sizes up" everyone. Anyone is ripe for exploitation. It should therefore surprise no one that capitalism is happily at war with children. Worldwide, nearly 250 million children are presently working (some estimate it is as high as 400 million). Nearly 90 million of the 179 million children in India work. Children in the southern region of India work sixteen hours a day, six days a week for a meager $1.30 a week salary. In Bangladesh, the number of working children is 6.1 million. In Thailand, there are nearly 13,000 child prostitutes (some estimate the figure to be closer to 800,000). In Nairobi, 30,000 children live in the streets. In Colombia, 28 percent of Bogota's prostitutes are young girls between the ages of ten and fourteen. In the United States nearly 290,000 children are illegally employed in various industries; this includes 59,600 children who are younger than fourteen (Kameras 1998). For the profiteers of capital, the children's war is a famously lucrative one.

Slavery is far from dead. Approximately twenty-seven million people worldwide are paid no wages and their lives are completely controlled by others through violence. According to Kevin Bales, "Slavery itself keeps changing and growing" (2000, 36). Slavery has largely disappeared as "the legal ownership of one person by another" but it remains inescapably true that slavery is a growing industry worldwide, from the brothels of Thailand, to the charcoal mines of Brazil, to women in the West who have been kidnapped from Eastern Europe. According to Bales:

> At US $2,000 the young woman in a Thai brothel is one of the world's more costly slaves. People, especially children, can be enslaved today for little as US $45. The 11-year-old boy I met in India six weeks ago had been placed in bondage by his parents in exchange for about US $35. He now works 14 hours a day, seven days a week making *beedi* cigarettes. This lad is held in "debt bondage," one of the most common variations on the theme of slavery. Debt bondage is slavery with a twist. Instead of being property, the slave is collateral. The boy and all his work belong to the slaveholder as long as the debt is unpaid, but not a penny is applied to the debt. Until his parents find the money, this boy is a cigarette-rolling machine, fed just enough to keep him at his task. People may be enslaved in the name of religion, like the *Devdasi* of India or the *trokosi* of West Africa. They may be enslaved by their own government, like the hundreds of thousands of people identified by the International Labour Organisation in Burma. Whoever enslaves them, and through whatever trickery, false contract, debt or kidnap method, the reality for the slave is much the same. (2000, 38)

The reason slavery escapes our notice and global initiatives to combat it are always exiguous is that Western jobs are not threatened and multinationals are not undercut by slave-based enterprises. In fact, citizens of 74 percent of countries with high international debt load are regularly trafficked into slavery. For countries with a low international debt load, the figure is 29 percent. In 50 percent of countries with high international debt load, slavery is a regular feature the economy, compared with just 12 percent of countries with low international debt load (Bales 2000). A recently leaked CIA report notes that as many as fifty thousand women and children are forced to work as slave laborers in the United States each year. They are lured to the United States from Asia, Africa, Latin America, and Eastern Europe and serve largely as prostitutes, domestic servants, or bonded workers. In 1995, seventy-two Thai clothing workers were found imprisoned in a Los Angeles sweatshop. They were forced to work twenty-two hours a day for sixty-two cents an hour (Grey 2000).

Those who naively believe that slavery has disappeared in the United States may be surprised to learn that in many prisons across the United States, slavery has been upgraded to "bonded labor." A number of corporations, including

JC Penney, IBM, Toys "Я" US, TWA, and Victoria's Secret have shamelessly prof-
ited from prison labor. And what about the close to fifty thousand women and
children who are forced into prostitution, domestic servitude, and sweatshop
labor each year?

The deteriorating working and living conditions for laborers in Third World
countries is comparable to—and in many respects exceeds—the horrid working
and living conditions of the English working class as described by Frederick Engels in his book, *The Conditions of the Working Class in England* (1847). In Sri
Lanka many workers must work fourteen hours per day; in Indonesia and the
Philippines they work twelve-hour days; and in the southern regions of China
sixteen-hour workdays are the norm. Working conditions for many women in the
United States is not much better than in developing countries. In Little Saigon, located in Orange County, California, the average minimum wage for undocumented immigrants working in illegal sweatshops has been reported to be one
dollar an hour (Parks 1997). Inside sweatshops and factories around the world,
young women are placed under incessant surveillance and subjected to humiliat-
ing working conditions by plant managers to ensure the efficient operation of production lines. For instance, young women are frequently given amphetamine to
prolong working hours, and their menstrual cycles are placed under continual su-
pervision to prevent pregnancy, a condition that is detrimental to business because
it slows down production lines (Parks 1997). In the *maquiladoras*, women's biological reproduction is regulated and synchronized to the pulse of new methods
of lean and flexible production to maximize profitability and minimize labor costs.
Young women are forced to provide evidence that they are menstruating each
month by participating in "monthly sanitary-pad checks" (Klein 1999). As part of
the contingent labor force, women are employed on twenty-eight-day contracts
that coincide with their menstrual cycle. Those who are found pregnant are automatically fired and summarily released from the factory premises.

In 1998, the Nike corporation, with its global army of a half-million contingent semiskilled workers in Third World countries, managed to amass a record
revenue of $6.4 billion dollars with the "assistance" of environmental laws pro-
moting deregulation and nonunionized cheap labor. In poor underdeveloped
countries such as Haiti, hourly wages are reported to be twelve cents an hour,
while in Honduras, workers' hourly wages are thirty-one cents an hour. The
cost of manufacturing a pair of Nike shoes—whose retail cost is $120—is esti-
mated to be seventy to eighty cents in the dank sweatshops of Indonesia.

The recent assaults on welfare programs, bilingual education, multicultural
education, and affirmative action boldly illustrates the incompatibility of capitalism with democracy. Mark Dery paints an eerie picture of contemporary capitalism at the end of twentieth century:

> Communism may have been consigned to the desktop recycle bin of history, as
> free-market cheerleaders never tire of reminding us, and Marx may be an ironic
> icon of nineties retro chic, but the old bearded devil may have the last laugh: As we
> round the bend to the millennium, class war and the percolating rage of the "work-

ers of the world" are emerging as the lightening-rod social issues of the coming century. Growing income inequality, accompanied by the hemorrhaging of U.S. manufacturing jobs because of automation or their relocation in the low-wage, nonunion "developing world," is sowing dragon's teeth. The disappearance of even unskilled factory work at time when economic growth is insufficient to absorb dislocated workers is dire enough; that it is happening at a moment when traditional safety values no longer function—owing to the wasting away of the labor movement, the conservative dismantling of social services in favor of 'market solutions' to social ills, and the ongoing buyout of representative government by corporate power—has created fertile soil for the apocalyptic politics of the disaffected. (1999, 262–63)

Contrary to popular mythology, money is not the source of capitalism's wealth; rather, its source is the sweat and blood of exploited workers. It is the savage manipulation of their labor power that creates revenue for the money moguls of the advanced capitalist West. Daniel Singer writes: "The obscene equivalence between the wealth of the world's top few hundred billionaires and the income of nearly three billion wretched of the earth illustrates this point" (1999, 216).

The contradictions of capital in general, and the imperfections of the market in the advanced capitalist countries of the West in particular, are especially evident throughout the United States. Today, nearly seven hundred thousand people are homeless at any given night in the United States. Annually, two million experience homelessness. Tragically, one out of every four homeless persons is an innocent child. In the majority of large metropolitan cities across the United States, homelessness is considered a crime. A number of innovative methods have been implemented to make homeless people invisible. In Chicago, for example, homeless people are arrested and prosecuted daily. These are the casualties of unceremonious economic ex-communication. Before he became reinvented as the purebred embodiment of New York City itself, Rudolph Giuliani—a potential presidential candidate—initiated a "quality of life" campaign in New York City that involved nightly sweeps and crackdowns on homeless people to ensure that they did not transgress the boundaries dividing the wealthy neighborhoods from the poor neighborhoods.

THE CIA–UNIVERSITY PARTNERSHIP

After September 11, the intelligence community has become one of the country's largest growth industries. A recent article by David Gibbs in the *Los Angeles Times* (January 28, 2001) raises a number of disturbing questions regarding the CIA's role and influence in public universities and colleges across the nation. Of course, the CIA–university partnership is nothing new. It has been a well-known fact that for some time now Ivy League universities such as Yale have collaborated with the CIA in the past. Since the late 1940s, and the early 1950s, universities have served as recruitment centers for future CIA operatives as well as drop-off points for the distribution and circulation of CIA propaganda. More recently, in 1991, Congress passed the National Security Education Act, which offers a $150 million trust fund that is overlooked by the Defense Intelligence College. The fund offers undergraduate scholarships and graduate fellowships to promising U.S. nationals who are encouraged to pursue scholarly activities and research both in the United States and abroad. The program also offers grants to participating universities who wish to develop and enhance their foreign language and area studies programs (MacMichael 2002). Funded by the CIA, universities and colleges that are interested can take advantage of the CIA officer-in-residence program. Under this program, CIA officers are hired as faculty members in history, political science, and economics departments where they teach courses and provide seminars on various pressing topics. The purpose of this program is for CIA officers-turned-academics to share the experience, knowledge, and skills that they have gained in the course of their career in the CIA with college students. David MacMichael (2002) further elaborates on this development and writes that

> the CIA offers to willing institutions of higher education the opportunity, at no cost to the institution, to have a CIA officer of appropriate academic attainment (advanced degrees, foreign experience, etc.) serve for a period of three years or so in a relevant department—history, political science, area studies—as a faculty member, teaching courses and holding seminars under, of course, the direction of the concerned department chairperson. Arguably, the CIA officer-in-residence will bring, besides his or her academic skills, the experience he or she has gained working in the field of intelligence and covert operations throughout the world. (47)

Moreover, citing a 1996 article in the academic journal *Lingua Franca*, Gibbs notes that prominent social scientists such as Columbia's Robert Jarvis, former president-elect of the American Political Science Association, and Harvard professor Joseph S. Nye, have openly admitted to working for the CIA. If this is true, then there is ample reason to believe that the pursuit of scholarly research by social scientists in universities is often politically motivated in the service of American imperialism. As Gibbs remarks:

> The CIA is not an ordinary government agency; it is an espionage agency and the practices of espionage—which include secrecy, propaganda and deception—are diametrically opposed to those of scholarship. Scholarship is supposed to favor objective analysis and open discussion. The close relationship between intelligence agencies and scholars thus poses a conflict of interest. After all, the CIA has been a key part to many of the international conflicts that academics must study. If political scientists are working for the CIA, how can they function as objective and disinterested scholars?

If Gibbs's account of the behind-the-scenes CIA–university partnership does not sound convincing, then the recent spy scandal involving a Fulbright doctoral student who was presumably engaged in "scholarly research" in Russia should raise some eyebrows. According to John Daniszewski of the *Los Ange-*

les Times (February 28, 2001), the twenty-four-year-old Fulbright scholar John Edward Tobin was arrested in Russia allegedly on marijuana possession. The Federal Security Service—Russia's intelligence service—has linked Tobin to the U.S. intelligence services. Furthermore, Daniszewski writes that during its investigation, the FSB learned that Tobin had studied Russian at the Defense Language Institute in Monterey, California. He had also received training as an "interrogation expert" at the Army Intelligence Center at Ft. Huachuca, Arizona. At the same time that Tobin was preoccupied with research for his dissertation on "Russia's political priorities" at the Voronezh State University, which also allegedly served as his cover, he was also training to become a proficient and fluent Russian language speaker for future covert espionage and intelligence assignments. If these allegations are proven to be true, then it would be interesting to inquire on how many other scholarship programs and research projects at major universities are directly or indirectly linked to the intelligence community.

SPIES "R" US

On another front, in a frighteningly Orwellian fashion, the so-called war on terrorism no longer restricts itself to Third World countries like Afghanistan, Iraq, Iran, North Korea, Colombia, or Indonesia; it spills over into the domestic frontier, reaching out to our very own neighborhoods. James Petras perhaps says it best when he argues that we inhabit a veritable police state, at the cusp of a totalitarian regime. He writes:

> One of the hallmarks of a totalitarian regime is the creation of a state of mutual suspicion in which civil society is turned into a network of secret police informers. The Federal Bureau of Investigation (FBI) soon after September 11 exhorted every U.S. citizen to report any suspicious behavior by friends, neighbors, relatives, acquaintances, and strangers. Between September and the end of November almost 700,000 denunciations were registered. Thousands of Middle Eastern neighbors, local shop owners, and employees were denounced, as were numerous other U.S. citizens. None of these denunciations led to any arrests or even information related to September 11. Yet hundreds and thousands of innocent persons were investigated and harassed by the federal police. (2002, 10)

Another recent example of Talibanizing of the public sphere is the Justice Department's proposal to have eight hundred thousand postal workers participate in a program called Operation TIPS (Terrorist Information and Prevention System). While Operation TIPS was cancelled by the Homeland Security Act, this does not mean similar programs are not in the process of being created. Under that program (redolent of Stalin's Soviet Union), letter carriers would voluntarily report any suspicious activities or individuals or groups to the Justice Department. Letter carriers could report "terrorist-related activities" that may occur on the "home front" in their neighborhood via a toll-free hotline or they could go online and report it on the Internet. But the program was not limited to postal workers. Truckers, train conductors, ship captains, and utility workers (i.e., cable, gas, and electrical workers) were among those asked to participate in the program. The main objective of this program was to encourage Americans to become government informants. In our opinion, the objective of gathering information in an efficient manner is not restricted to reporting terror-related activities, but it is also intended to target any political organization or social movement that are foolish enough to oppose neoliberal social and economic policies. In fact, as many legal scholars have forewarned, such undemocratic tactics will seriously threaten and jeopardize our constitutional rights such as free speech and free assembly.

Yet this is only one of the numerous shrewd and undemocratic tactics that the Bush administration is planning to deploy against the so-called war on terrorism. More alarming is a proposal spearheaded by Homeland Security Chief Tom Ridge, who wants to employ the military (air force, navy, army, marines) for the war on terrorism on the domestic turf. Ridge is hard at work to overturn *posse comitatus,* a law that was passed in 1878 that bars the military from interfering with domestic policies. Initially, the purpose of the law was to stop the use of federal troops to overlook elections in the former Confederate states. The law ensures that the military does not intervene in domestic law enforcement. However, under the pretext of the "war on terrorism," Tom Ridge is making a concerted effort to annul this law. Again, the broader objectives of Homeland Security is not only to wage war on terror, but to target any form of dissent that may oppose the interests of the ruling classes.

THE U.S. PATRIOT ACT

George W. Bush and his administration will now have more power to use political and economic repression to squash democratic protests by the working class against an economic crisis that was beginning to lurch out of control long before September 11, 2001. To suggest that they will refrain from doing so is naïve at best. Also forbidding is the wave of repressive actions, including a full-frontal assault of civil liberties by the Justice Department. Doug Kellner (2003) comments:

> On October 31, Attorney General Ashcroft ruled that the government could eavesdrop on phone calls between lawyers and clients if it was deemed there was "reasonable suspicion" to justify such a move. By November, over 1,200 people had been arrested and detained, usually Arabs or Muslims, and mostly without legal representation. When these massive detentions failed to produce any new evidence of the Al Qaeda network or terrorist plots, a discussion began about whether the U.S. should engage in torture to extract knowledge from suspects. The Bush administration was thus carrying out a Jihad on civil liberties and those who had supported the appointment of the Talibanesque John Ashcroft as head of the Justice Department were complicit in the systematic assault on democracy and constitutional balance of powers. Ashcroft claimed that, like the Taliban, he never read pa-

pers or watched television and began the day with group prayers and bible readings with his close associates. The Attorney General reserved for himself and his rightist associates to determine who was a terrorist, whose e-mail, telephone and computer communications could be monitored, who could be arrested without warrant and held without charges, whose conversations with their lawyers could be monitored, and who in effect would lose all civil liberties if suspected of being a terrorist.

The so-called USA Patriot Act is setting the stage for propaganda trials once reserved for military dictatorships who were our Cold War adversaries. The establishment of secret military tribunals to prosecute suspected terrorists amount to little more than legitimizing a network of ad-hoc, "drumhead," or "kangaroo" courts that can safely bypass both Congress and the judiciary. If, for instance, President Bush believes that a long-term resident of the United States has aided a terrorist in some way, that resident can be tried in secret by a military commission and sentenced to death on the basis of hearsay and rumor without any appeal to a civilian court. Even the Supreme Court will be out of reach.Without consulting with Congress, Bush signed executive order 13233 by which he seeks to modify the law and make it more difficult to make presidential papers and records available to the public. He appears to be grasping beyond his executive powers under the Presidential Records Act of 1978 most probably to prevent the public from gaining access to information during his father's vice presidency and presidency. Not only does he want to protect his father but also others—like Dick Cheney—now working in Bush Jr.'s administration.

ORGANIZING FOR RESISTANCE

Critical educators have often disagreed on the forms in which social revolution should be carried out. Despite their disagreements, all critical educators support the idea that organizations and forms of organizing are crucial in the struggle for social justice. Max Elbaum (2002) writes that "without collective forms it is impossible to train cadre, debate theory and strategy, spread information and analysis, or engage fully with the urgent struggles of the day. Only through organizations can revolutionaries maximize their contribution to ongoing battles and position themselves to maximally influence events when new mass upheavals and opportunities arise" (335). Yet at the same time, Elbaum warns that we must avoid what he calls "sectarian dead ends" in our struggle for social justice. Reflecting on his experiences with the New Communist Movement of the 1970s, he explains that when a movement becomes a "self-contained world" that insists upon group solidarity and discipline, this can often lead to the suppression of internal democracy. The rigid top-down party model is obviously a problem for Elbaum. On the one hand, social activists need to engage with and be accountable to a large, active, anticapitalist social base; on the other hand, there are pressures to put one's revolutionary politics aside in order to make an immediate impact on public policy. There is the impulse to "retreat into a small but secure niche on the margins of politics and/or confine oneself to revolutionary propaganda" (334). Elbaum cites Marx's dictum that periods of socialist sectarianism obtain when "the time is not yet ripe for an independent historical movement" (334). Problems inevitably arise when "purer-than-thou fidelity to old orthodoxies" are employed to maintain membership morale necessary for group cohesion and to compete with other groups. He reports that the healthiest periods of social movements appear to be when tight-knit cadre groups and other forms are able to coexist and interact while at the same time considering themselves part of a common political trend. He writes that "diversity of organisational forms (publishing collectives, research centers, cultural collectives, and broad organising networks, in addition to local and national cadre formations) along with a dynamic interaction between them supplied (at least to a degree) some of the pressures for democracy and realism that in other situations flowed from a socialist-oriented working-class." It is important to avoid a uniform approach in all sectors, especially when disparities in consciousness and activity are manifold. Elbaum notes that Leninist centralized leadership worked in the short run but "lacked any substantial social base and were almost by definition hostile to all others on the left; they could never break out of the limits of a sect." The size of membership has a profound qualitative impact on strategies employed and organizational models adopted. Elbaum warns that attempts to build a small revolutionary party (a party in embryo) "blinded movement activists to Lenin's view that a revolutionary party must not only be an 'advanced' detachment but must also actually represent and be rooted in a substantial, socialist-leaning wing of the working class" (335). Realistic and complex paths will need to be taken which will clearly be dependent on the state of the working-class movement itself.

It is axiomatic for the ongoing development of critical pedagogy that it be based upon an alternative vision of human sociality, one that operates outside the social universe of capital, a vision that goes beyond the market, but also one that goes beyond the state. It must, in our view, reject the false opposition between the market and the state. Massimo De Angelis writes that "the historical challenge before us is that the question of alternatives . . . not be separated from the organisational forms that this movement gives itself" (2002, 5). Given that we are faced globally with the emergent transnational capitalist class and the incursion of capital into the far reaches of the planet, critical educators need a philosophy of organization that sufficiently addresses the dilemma and the challenge of the global proletariat. In discussing alternative manifestations of antiglobalization struggles, De Angelis itemizes some promising characteristics as follows: the production of various countersummits; Zapatista Encuentros; social practices that produce use values beyond economic calculation and the competitive relation with the other and inspired by practices of social and mutual solidarity; horizontally linked clusters outside vertical networks in which the market is protected and enforced; social cooperation through grassroots democracy, consensus, dialogue, and the recognition of the other; authority and social cooperation developed in fluid relations and self-constituted through interaction; and a new engagement with the other that transcends locality, job, social condition, gender, age, race, culture, sexual orientation, language, religion, and beliefs. All of these characteristics are to be secondary to the constitution of communal relations. He writes:

> The global scene for us is the discovery of the "other," while the local scene is the discovery of the "us," and by discovering the "us," we change our relation to the "other." In a community, commonality is a creative process of discovery, not a presupposition. So we do both, but we do it having the community in mind, the community as a mode of engagement with the other. (14)

But what about the role of the national state? According to Ellen Meiksins Wood (2002), "the state is the point at which global capital is most vulnerable, both as a target of opposition in the dominant economies and as a lever of resistance elsewhere. It also means that now more than ever, much depends on the particular class forces embodied in the state, and that now more than ever, there is scope, as well as need, for class struggle" (291). Sam Gindin (2002) argues that the state is no longer a relevant site of struggle if by struggle we mean taking over the state and pushing it in another direction. But the state is still a relevant arena for contestation *if our purpose is one of transforming the state.* He writes:

> Conventional wisdom has it that the national state, whether we like it or not, is no longer a relevant site of struggle. At one level, this is true. If our notion of the state is that of an institution which left governments can "capture" and push in a different direction, experience suggests this will contribute little to social justice. But if our goal is to transform the state into an instrument for popular mobilisation and the development of democratic capacities, to bring our economy under popular control and restructure our relationships to the world economy, then winning state power would manifest the worst nightmares of the corporate world. When we reject strategies based on winning through undercutting others and maintain our fight for dignity and justice nationally, we can inspire others abroad and create new spaces for their own struggles. (11)

John Holloway's premise (2002) is similar to that of Gindin. He argues that we must theorize the world negatively as a "moment" of practice as part of the struggle to change the world. But this change cannot come about through transforming the state through the taking of power but rather must occur through the dissolution of power as a means of transforming the state. This is because the state reproduces within itself the separation of people from their own "doing." In our work as critical educators, Holloway's distinction between power-to (potentia) and power-over (potestas) is instructive. Power-over is the negation of the social flow of doing. Power-to is a part of the "social flow of doing," the construction of a "we" and the practice of the mutual recognition of dignity. We need to create the conditions for the future "doing" of others through a power-to. In the process, we must not transform power-to into power-over, since power-over only separates the "means of doing" from the actual "doing" which has reached its highest point in capitalism. In fact, those who exercise power-over separate the done from the doing of others and declare it to be theirs. The appropriation of the "done" of others is equivalent to the appropriation of "the means of doing," and allows the powerful to control the doing of others, which reaches its highest point in capitalism. The separation of doing from the doers reduces people to mere owners and nonowners, flattening out relations between people to relations between things. It converts doing into being. Whereas doing refers to both "we are" (the present) and "we are not" (the possibility of being something else) being refers only to "we are." To take away the "we are not" tears away possibility from social agency. In this case, possibility becomes mere utopian dreaming while time itself becomes irrefrangibley homogenized. Being locates the future as an extension of the present and makes the past into a preparation for the present. All doing becomes an extension of the way things are. The rule of power-over is the rule of "this is the way things are" which is the rule of identity. When we are separated from our own doing we create our own subordination. Power-to is not counterpower (which presupposes a symmetry with power) but antipower. As Holloway maintains, we need to avoid falling into identification, to an acceptance of what is.

Holloway also reminds us that the separation of doing and done is not an accomplished fact but a process. Separation and alienation is a movement against its own negation, against anti-alienation. That which exists in the form of its negation—or anti-alienation (the mode of being denied)—really does exist, in spite of its negation. It is the negation of the process of denial. Capitalism, according to Holloway, is based on the denial of "power-to," of dignity, of humanity, but that does not mean power-to (countercapitalism) does not exist. Asserting our power-to is simultaneously to assert our resistance against being dominated by others. This may take the form of open rebellion, of struggles to defend control over the labor process, or efforts to control the processes of health and education. Power-over depends upon that which it negates. The history of domination is not only the struggle of the oppressed against their oppressors but also the struggle of the powerful to liberate themselves from their dependence on the powerless. But there is no way in which power-over can escape from being transformed into power-to because capital's flight from labor depends upon labor (upon its capacity to convert power-to into abstract value-producing labor) in the form of falling rates of profit.

We are beginning to witness new forms of social organization as a part of revolutionary praxis. In addition to the Zapatistas, we have the important example of the participatory budget of the Workers Party in Brazil and in Argentina we are seeing new forms of organized struggle as a result of the recent economic collapse of that country. We are referring here to the examples of the street protests of the *piqueteros* (the unemployed) currently underway and which first emerged about five years ago in the impoverished communities in the provinces. More recently, new neighborhood *asambleas* (assemblies) have arisen out of local street-corner protests. Numbering around three hundred throughout the country, these assemblies meet once a week to organize *cacerolas* (protests) and to defend those who are being evicted from their homes, or who are having their utilities shut off, etc. The *asambleistas* (assembly members) are also coordinating soup kitchens to feed themselves and others. This antihierarchical, decentralized, and grassroots movement consisting of both employed and unemployed workers, mostly women, has taken on a new urgency since December 2002, when four governments collapsed in quick succession following Argentina's default on its foreign debt. According to a editorial report (2002) in *News and Letters,*

> What is remarkable is how ferociously opposed the *asambleas* are to being controlled, and to any hint of a vertical, top-down hierarchy. They insist on independence, autonomy, self-determination, encouraging all to learn how to voice their opinions and rotating responsibilities. They are explicitly for individual, personal self-development at the same time as they are for fighting the powers that be with everything they've got at their disposal. (6)

The larger *asambleas interbarriales* (mass meetings of the various *asambleas*) elect rotating delegates from the *asambleas* to speak and vote on issues that have been generated in their local communities. In addition, workers have occupied a number of factories and work sites such as Brukman, Zanon, and Panificadora Cinco. Workers have also occupied a mine in Rio Turbio. Clearly, new revolutionary forms of organization are appearing. As Ernesto Herrera (2002) notes:

> The experiences of the piquetero movement and neighborhood assemblies allow the possibility of the construction of a revolutionary movement, a democratic popular power with a socialist perspective. The "great revolt" has put on the agenda the question of a strategy that links resistance and the struggle for power, representative democracy and/or the principle of revocability, the "saqueos" as acts of self-subsistence in food. (10)

Of course, there are many problems with the assemblies in that they are composed of members of different class factions, with their many different political agendas. Yet all of the assemblies hold the restatification of recently privatized industries as a top priority (even as they reject vanguardist parties). At the same time, in this new rise of popular mobilization, as subjectivities are becoming revolutionized under the assault of capitalism, there needs to occur a programmatic proposal for political regroupment of the radical and anticapitalist forces. There must be more options available for organizers of the revolutionary left. Herrera (2002) writes:

> In Mexico, the Zapatista movement could not translate its capacity of mobilization in the Consultas and Marches into a political alternative of the left. There was no modification of the relationship of forces. The theory of the "indefinite anti-power" or "changing the world without taking power" has produced neither a process of radical reforms, nor a revolutionary process. (13)

From a Marxist humanist perspective, what needs to be emphasized and struggled for is not only the abolition of private property but also a struggle against alienated labor. The key point here is not to get lost in the state (nationalized capital) versus neoliberalism (privatized capital) debate. As the resident editorial board of *News and Letters* has made clear, the real issue that must not be obscured is the need to abolish the domination of labor by capital. Capital needs to be uprooted through the creation of new human relations that dispense with value production altogether. This does not mean that we stop opposing neoliberalism or privatization. What is does mean is that we should not stop there.

One of the major tasks ahead is the breaking down of the separation between manual and mental labor. This struggle is clearly focused on dismantling the current capitalist mode of production and setting in motion conditions for the creation of freely associated individuals. This means working toward a concept of socialism that will meet the needs of those who are struggling within the present crisis of global capitalism. We need here to project a second negativity that moves beyond opposition (that is, opposition to the form of property, i.e., private property)—a second or "absolute" negativity that moves toward the creation of the new. This stipulates not simply embracing new forms of social organization, new social movements, and so on, but addressing new theoretical and philosophical questions that are being raised by these new spontaneous movements. We need a new philosophy of revolution, as well as a new pedagogy, that emerges out of the dialectic of absolute negation.

TEACHERS AS IRREVERANT INTELLECTUALS

Public educators (and academics specially) face increasing difficulties in building a united anticapitalist front. In discussing responses to the current imperial barbarism and corruption of the empire, Petras (2001) distinguishes a pattern of responses which we have also noticed among our colleagues and students alike. Petras identifies stoics, cynics, pessimists, and critical intellectuals (categories that encompass those who serve the hegemony of empire, from the prostrated academics who bend their knees in the face of capitalism while at the same time denouncing its excesses, to the coffee-sipping intellectuals of Soho) from what he refers to as irreverent intellectuals (who serve the cause of developing revolutionary socialist consciousness and a new internationalism). The *stoics* are repulsed by the "predatory pillage of the empire" but because they are paralyzed by feelings of political impotence, choose to form small cadres of academics in order to debate theory in as much isolation as possible from both the imperial powers and the oppressed and degraded masses. The *cynics* condemn both the victims of predatory capitalism and their victimizers as equally afflicted with consumerism; they believe that the oppressed masses seek advantage only to reverse the roles of oppressor and oppressed. The cynics are obsessed with the history of failed revolutions where the exploited eventually become the exploiters. They usually work in universities and specialize in providing testimonials to the perversions of liberation movements. The *pessimists* are usually leftists or ex-leftists who are also obsessed with the historical defeats of revolutionary social movements, which they have come to see as inevitable and irreversible, but who use these defeats as a pretext for adopting a pragmatic accommodation with the status quo. The have a motivated amnesia for new revolutionary movements now struggling to oppose the empire (i.e., movements by militant farmers and transport workers) and use their pessimism as an alibi for inaction and disengagement. The pessimists are reduced to a liberal politics which can often be co-opted by the ideologists of empire. Critical intellectuals frequently gain notoriety among the educated classes. Professing indignation at the ravages of empire and neoliberalism and attempting to expose their lies, critical intellectuals appeal to the elite to reform the power structures so that the poor will no longer suffer. This collaborationist approach of critical intellectuals "vents indignation that resonates with the educated classes without asking them to sacrifice anything" (15). In contrast to all of the above, the irreverent intellectual respects the militants on the front lines of the anticapitalist and antiimperialist struggles. Petras describes them as "self-ironic anti-heroes whose work is respected by the people who are activity working for basic transformation." He notes that they are "objectively partisan and partisanly objective" and work together with intellectuals and activists involved in popular struggles:

> They conduct research looking for original sources of data. They create their own indicators and concepts, for example, to identify the real depths of poverty, exploitation and exclusion. They recognise that there are a few intellectuals in prestigious institutions and award recipients who are clearly committed to popular struggles, and they acknowledge that these exceptions should be noted, while recognising the many others who in climbing the academic ladder succumb to the blandishments of bourgeois certification. The irreverent intellectuals admire a Jean-Paul Sartre, who rejected a Nobel Prize in the midst of the Vietnam War. Most of all, the irreverent intellectuals fight against bourgeois hegemony within the left by integrating their writing and teaching with practice, avoiding divided loyalties. (15)

Petras's concept of the irreverent intellectual is one that holds promise as a model for progressive teachers. Drawing upon Petras's ideas stipulates supporting workers' movements, landless peasants' movements, and anticapitalist/ globalization movements worldwide in their struggle against structural formations of empire while at the same time developing workable coalitions and joint actions that will involve teachers and students in local and regional contexts in solidarity with community activists to bring about social and economic justice.

Keening the death of Marxism will do little more than momentarily stir the ghost of the old bearded devil. Clearly, present-day left educationalists need to rethink the state as a terrain of contestation while at the same time reinventing class struggle as we have been doing in the streets of Seattle, Porto Alegre, Prague, and Genoa. We have to keep our belief that another world is possible. We need to do more than to break with capital or abscond from it; clearly, we need to challenge its rule of value. The key to resistance, in our view, is to develop a revolutionary critical pedagogy that will enable working-class groups to discover how the use value of their labor power is being exploited by capital but also how working-class initiative and power can destroy this type of determination and force a recomposition of class relations by directly confronting capital in all of its multifaceted dimensions. This will require critical pedagogy not only to plot the oscillations of the labor/capital dialectic, but also to reconstruct the object context of class struggle to include school sites. Efforts also must be made to break down capital's creation of a new species of labor power through current attempts to corporatize and businessify the process of schooling and to resist the endless subordination of life in the social factory so many students call home (Cleaver 2000; see also, Rikowski 2001). Novel ingressions toward rebuilding the educational left will not be easy, but neither will living under an increasingly militarized capitalist state where labor power is constantly put to the rack to carry out the will of capital. While critical pedagogy may seem driven by lofty, high-rise aspirations that spike an otherwise desolate landscape of despair, where pock-marked dreams bob through the sewers of contemporary cosmopolitan life, they anchor our hope in the dreams of the present. Here the social revolution is not reborn in the foam of avant-garde antifoundationalism, which only stokes the forces of despair, but emerges from the everyday struggle to release us from the burdens of political détente and democratic disengagement. It is anchored, in other words, in class struggle.

KEEPING ANALYSIS ALIVE

It is crucially important that the left not shut down analysis of the war for fear that it will be seen as a justification for the terrorist attacks. An analysis of U.S. imperialism is not a justification for what happened. If anything, it is designed to have a prophylactic effect by removing the poison from the political soil that nourishes potential acts of terrorism. On this point, Ollman (2001) warns the Left:

> You cannot allow yourself to simply stop thinking, which some of my comrades have done because they are so angry and want to confront what they see as Muslim fascism. Some of them are willing to make concessions to capitalism to confront this fascism, but I don't think such concessions are necessary. Right now we are bombing Afghanistan and undoubtedly killing civilians. We are making a bad situation much worse. . . . Some people don't understand that it is always possible to make a bad situation worse. The bombing could swell the ranks with volunteers. Aside from that, as leftists we cannot trust that this is the Bush administration's main aim. There are other aims, having to do with securing oil resources, keeping certain vassal states in line and spreading American influence, that leftists must see. One must view this as, in part, the application of a military Keynesianism to forestall the mounting crisis of American capitalism. At the same time as we do not support the Taliban, we cannot support any criminal actions the U.S. government takes. (8)

Ollman's call for critical thinking was echoed recently in remarks Fidel Castro made in a televised presentation in Havana. Here Castro (2001) remarked: "I think that the way to show solidarity with the American people that lost thousands of innocent lives, including those of children, youths, and elders, men and women to the outrageous attack, is by frankly speaking our minds. The sacrifice of those lives should not be in vain, but rather it should be useful to save many lives, to prove that thinking and conscience can be stronger than terror and death."

Again, one has to apply critical analysis to the historical contradictions faced by world capitalism, as well as the role played by U.S. policies and interventions as contributing factors to these contradictions—all of this constitutes part of the process of understanding these events, because they contribute to the environmental backdrop against which these acts of terrorism occurred and will continue to occur as long as there exists such a disparity of wealth between nations. We would want to argue, however, that the context in which Islamic fundamentalism or Islamism arises is a lot broader than simply a reaction against U.S. foreign policy, although as we mention once again, this is surely one among several other factors that creates a climate of hatred against the United States with respect to certain radically political Islamic factions and a blowback *potential* for terrorism. And the problem of understanding the attacks of September 11 is certainly greater than attributing it to bin Laden's hatred of modernity.

Again, while we rightly condemn bin Laden's puritanical Islamism, at the same time we cannot ignore the U.S. policy of unilateralism and preemptive strikes that it is currently dragging onto the stage of world history. Our approach needs to be guided by a dialectical understanding of global events linked to the larger social relations of U.S. imperialism.

It is time to think about the pedagogical implications for understanding the role of imperialism—both covert and overt—and the globalization of capital on the world scene today. The issue is not to argue that U.S. military actions and U.S. support for brutal dictatorships in the past—and we could include Vietnam and Cambodia as well—somehow provide a justification for terrorism. Only a monster like bin Laden could make such a case for terrorism. There is no justification for terrorism. Absolutely none. The point we are making is a pedagogical one: Can we learn from capitalism's role in world history? Can we explore the relationship between capitalism and nationalism, between capitalism and nation building? Between U.S. foreign policy and the interests of transnational corporations—such as the oil conglomerates? What is the relationship among U.S. foreign policy, the United States as a declining hegemon, and the emergent global capitalist historic bloc at whose center is the transnational capitalist class? How are the particular forms in which capitalism developed historically related to the current crisis of capital? Can students in the United States learn from the role of the United States in world history? How can we strive to create a world where terrorism and oppression in all of its forms cease to exist? What would a world look like in which terrorism would not be a choice? Some would say that the United States has a responsibility as an empire. Others, like us, would say that we have a responsibility to create a social universe without empires.

We have criticized U.S. imperialism not to create an excuse or rationale for the terrorist acts, but to provide a context for discussing world history in light of the globalization of capitalism and contemporary geopolitics. We in the United States must share the burden of history. We cannot exempt our history from discussion and debate simply because it is *our* history. We are not morally or politically above the fray. To share the burden of history we need to become critically self-reflexive about our political system, its economic, domestic, and foreign policies in the context of the globalization of capitalism or what we have called the new imperialism. The problem is that students in the Untied States rarely are given the opportunity to discuss the above events because the media mostly avoids discussing them in-depth. And now, in the present climate, it is entirely possible—in fact it is more than likely—that you will be branded a traitor if you do discuss them. The point is that we need to be self-reflective as a citizenry—we owe it not only to ourselves as U.S. citizens, but as world citizens—and provide spaces for critical dialogue about these events. This is where critical pedagogy can be extremely important. The current generation has been sacrificed in advance to the globalization of capital. This poses a major dilemma for the future of the globe. And pedagogically, it places a heavy challenge in the hands of teachers and cultural and political workers worldwide.

To make the claim that if the United States is held accountable to the definition of terrorism it has established, then its backing of repressive Latin American regimes whose death squads massacred hundreds of thousands of civilians in Guatemala, Chile, El Salvador, and other countries makes high-ranking members of former White House administrations vulnerable to charges of terrorism, is to be challenged by the question: "Whose side are you on?" We would answer that we are on the side of justice for the poor and the oppressed and that it is our patriotic duty to criticize those regimes—even if it means our own government—who are not.

A PRIMER FOR A POST–SEPTEMBER 11 CRITICAL PEDAGOGY

Given the current crisis of global capitalism, and the uncertain future we face, it is crucial for teachers to lead students into discussions on terrorism. It is important to create pedagogical spaces inside classrooms in which students can express their concerns about the September 11 tragedy and their fears about the possibility of future attacks. One way to approach this task is to discuss, debate, analyze, and reflect upon the social and historical construction of such concepts as terrorism and patriotism. We believe that such concepts are not only ideologically constructed, but they are also intended to represent a narrow vision of the complex social world in which we live. Teachers can assist students to develop a "language of critique" (Giroux 1988) that can guide them to investigate how such concepts are "selectively" employed by the ruling class to represent and reproduce existing relations of power among dominant and subordinate groups in society. For example, teachers can help students to understand how contemporary right-wing forces have taken advantage of the September 11 tragedy by making patriotism synonymous with the ideology of Americanism and U.S. exceptionalism, and how terrorism is portrayed to represent violence by Arabs against Westerners and not vice versa.

We believe that educators have a moral and ethical obligation to provide a forum in which students can question and critique the right-wing's efforts to rally people around its domestic and foreign U.S. policy initiatives. This demands scrutinizing efforts by the media punditocracy and the right-wing elements, who make patriotism synonymous with capitalism, democracy, and consumerism. In this context, critical media literacy can play an important role in deepening students' understanding of the tragic events surrounding the September 11 attacks by providing them with the necessary pedagogical tools to decode and interpret images, sound bites, and texts produced by the mainstream media. To unmask the contradictions between patriotism and consumerism, between patriotism and democracy, and between patriotism and Americanism requires students to have access to a language of critique.

The root cause of terrorism, Bob Kumamoto (1993) writes, is violence. Terrorism is not only crafted into a media spectacle, but it is also deployed as a propaganda tool to rally marginalized groups to support their political causes. But it should be mentioned that the definition of terrorism is a subjective matter that depends on who is on the receiving end of violence. As Kumamoto explains,

> terrorism is political in nature, but more importantly, directed at a "target group" Terrorism is "theatre" aimed not at airline passengers, nor even presidents and Kings, but at the masses via media coverage. Terrorism relies on the "propaganda of the deed:" that is, it relies not so much on the act of violence itself, but on the exploitation of that violence to promote a revolutionary cause that will presumably stir the masses into political action. "Calculated yet random violence as politics" is what separates terrorism from murder or mayhem. Still, whether or not an act of violence is "terroristic," largely depends on which side of the bomb you are sitting— whether you are a deliverer or unwitting victim.[1]

Understanding the causes of terrorism is the first step that students and teachers can undertake in its eradication. We believe that the study of terrorism can be and should be integrated as part of a broader multidisciplinary curriculum in classrooms (Kumamoto 1993). Kumamoto has offered a number of steps that teachers can use part of their curriculum to help students explore terrorism in a systematic fashion. Kumamoto's approach involves the study of history, economics, political science, geography, anthropology, social psychology, and sociology. Teachers can begin this project by dividing their students into several groups. Each group concentrates on one of the factors, or one of the major area related to terrorism. For example, one group of students can examine how oil from the Middle East and the United States' arms sales to Israel contribute to the ongoing conflicts and tensions in that region of the world. From a sociological standpoint, students can study how the harsh and brutal living conditions that the Palestinians in refugee camps must endure contributes to terrorism. In addition, students can also investigate geographical complexities of the Middle East region that have ignited disputes and quarrels over the Holy Land and the occupied territories. In the political arena, students can find connections between the rise of Palestinian and Arab nationalism and U.S. economic and political interests in the region. Students can also examine Islamic fundamentalism and Zionism through their historical opposition to Marxism and their embrace of capitalist social relations of production. From a historical perspective, students can explore the root causes of both Palestinian terrorism and Israeli state-sponsored terrorism in an effort to discover alternatives to both. Finally, by drawing upon the literature in social psychology, students can investigate the various motivating factors that cause individuals and groups to engage in terrorism and violence against innocent men, women, and children.

After their initial investigation, each group can report back to the class and share their findings. Teachers can then guide students to make connections between their findings and social and historical processes which have shaped that region of the world. For instance, teachers can assist students in making connections between acts of terrorism and practices such as colonization and imperialism. Second, students can explore the relationship between new media technologies and how acts of terrorism are reported to the public in specific geopolitical contexts. Third, students can examine how new "weapons of mass destruction" (biological, chemical, and nuclear), which may fall in the hands of terrorist organizations, can pose new threats to world peace and global stability. Others areas and topics that students can connect their findings to, among other forms of terriosm, state-sponsored terrorism, narcoterrorism, and ecoterrorism (Kumamoto 1993). For example, students can explore which states actively promote terrorism to protect their social, economic, and political interests.[2]

Contextualizing the September 11 terrorist attacks mandates that we also question United States' foreign policy along with its vital political and economic interests in the Middle East region, not to mention its support for the Israeli state. We believe that U.S. foreign policy has generated deep-seated bitterness and resentment among Arabs, and in some instances, it has been a motivating factor in the rise of Palestinian extremism (Kumamoto 1993). This is not to suggest that criticism be deflected from the anti-Semitism, sexism, and homophobia exhibited by some Islamic fundamentalist groups (or by Christian fundamentalists, for that matter). Students of history can also see whether they can find connections between their findings and the causes for the longstanding tradition of "Yankeephobia" in Latin American and South American countries. Further, students would do well to investigate how unjust labor practices of multinational corporations in Third World countries make U.S. citizens easy targets of anti-American sentiments. Finally, we want to remind students and teachers that the purpose of such activities is not to find justification or a rationale for terrorism and violence, but to understand what motivates individuals and groups to resort to political terrorism.

Finally, we should remind teachers that exercising democratic rights demands that they engage their students in meaningful dialogues and discussion over social, economic, and political issues that affect their lives. As such, we want to differentiate between *formal* citizenship and *substantive* citizenship (Petras and Veltmeyer 2001). Whereas formal citizenship is linked to the legal dimensions of citizenship under capitalist democracy in which political rights are disjoined and severed from economic rights, substantive citizenship is intimately connected to the "capacity of individuals to exercise those powers in actual debate, and in the resolution of political issues." We believe that it is important for teachers to broaden and strengthen pedagogical spaces whereby students can exercise "substantive citizenship." Within the parameters of these social and political pedagogical spaces, teachers, students, and workers can undertake the task of self-empowerment by their direct participation in the decision making processes over issues that have an immediate impact on their daily lives at both the local and community level. These include, but are certainly not limited to, engaging in discussions and debates over issues such as housing, taxation, education, health services, and social programs.

TOWARD A CRITICAL REVOLUTIONARY PEDAGOGY

Critical educators across the country must continue to oppose what we are now seeing throughout the United States: a senseless xenophobic statism, militarism, erosion of civil liberties, and a quest for permanent military interventions overseas within the fracture zones of geopolitical instability that have followed in the wake of the attacks, all of which can only have unsalutary consequences for world peace. This is particularly crucial, especially in light of the history of U.S. imperialism, and in light of one of Said's trenchant observations (2001), that "bombing senseless civilians with F-16s and helicopter gunships has the same structure and effect as more conventional nationalistic terror" (3).

As critical educators we are faced with a new sense of urgency in our fight to create social justice on a global scale, establishing what Karl Marx called a "positive humanism." At a time when Marxist social theory seems destined for the political dustbin, it is needed more than ever to help us understand the forces and relations that now shape our national and international destinies. As Bertell Ollman (2001) opines:

> I think what Marxism is about is to avoid the temptation of taking a stand based
> solely on our emotions. Marxism encourages us not to moralize about good and

evil and who is more good or evil when you are confronted with many people capable of such actions. Marxism encourages us to contextualize what happened and who is involved; of how this happened in our world today and how it fits into history, into time. When you do that you can't avoid dealing with and trying to make sense of the role that the US has played in its foreign policy and also in global capitalism. One must look at that and figure out ways of dealing with it so that we can handle not only September 11th but all of the September 11ths which are coming up ahead. (7)

One of the purposes of critical/revolutionary pedagogy is to work to bring about a global society where events of September 11, 2001, are less likely to occur. It does this through creating contexts in which revolutionary/transformative praxis can occur. Critical pedagogy is a politics of understanding, an act of knowing that attempts to situate everyday life in a larger geopolitical context, with the goal of fostering regional collective self-responsibility, large-scale ecumene, and international worker solidarity. It will require the courage to examine social and political contradictions, even, and perhaps especially, those that govern mainstream United States social policies and practices. It also requires a reexamination of some of the failures of the Left, as well.

In the face of such an intensification of global capitalist relations, rather than a shift in the nature of capital itself, we need to develop a critical pedagogy capable of engaging everyday life as lived in the midst of global capital's tendency toward empire, a pedagogy that we have called revolutionary critical pedagogy. The idea here is not to adapt students to globalization, but make them critically maladaptive, so that they can become change agents in anticapitalist struggles. The revolutionary multicultural unity sought by proponents of critical pedagogy is unflaggingly opposed to its class collaborationist counterpart represented by Bush, Powell, and Rice.

Without question, the attacks of September 11 have handed the capitalist ideological offensive and imperialism a major and unexpected victory. Parasitical capitalism under the banner of neoliberal globalization, and spearheaded by the WTO, IMF, and World Bank, has been disastrous for the world's poor. The struggle ahead for leftist educators will be a difficult but there are some signs of hope. In her book, *Students Against Sweatshops*, Liza Featherstone (2002) writes:

> The triple extremities of war, terror, and recession could distract the public from capitalism's everyday inequities. On the other hand, they certainly dramatize the system's problems: Bush's tax breaks to corporations; the way every national burden, from economic slowdown to anthrax, is disproportionately shouldered by the working class. (104)

It is more likely now that people are willing to question more seriously the present system. One encouraging development that we are witnessing is a progressive radicalization of youth. Featherstone (2002) reports that many activists say that the September 11 attacks have left people ever hungrier for forward-looking, optimistic social action. The global economic justice movement in particular may stand a better chance of being heard, at a time when Americans are suddenly looking at the world and wondering, "Why do 'they' hate us?" . . . For many, September 11 underscored the need to rethink America's role in the world, and to redress global economic inequality. (104–5)

The defeat of U.S. imperialism will require teachers to join antiwar efforts and peace movements across the nation. Inaction on this front may lead to escalating acts of terrorism both here and in the "homeland" as well as throughout the world. Given the uncertainty that looms in our collective future, it is more important than ever before that educators participate in popular social movements—regional, national, and international—to resist the military adventurism and Enronization of the global lifeworld fueled by U.S. imperialism. As Michael Parenti (2002) has eloquently expressed elsewhere: "Those who believe in democracy must be undeterred in their determination to educate, organize, and agitate, in any case, swimming against the tide is always preferable to being swept over the waterfall" (111).

NOTES

Thanks to Routledge for permitting us to publish a modified version of the chapter: McLaren, P. and Farahmandpur, R. (2003). *Critical Revolutionary Pedagogy at Ground Zero: Renewing the Educational Left after 9-11*. In D. Gabbard and K. Saltman (Eds.), *Education as Enforcement: The Militarization and Corportization of Schools* (pp. 311–26). A portion of this chapter appears in Peter McLaren and Ramin Farahmandpur, *Teaching Against Globalization and the New Imperialism: A Critical Pedagogy*, Rowman & Littlefield Publishers.

Some sections of this chapter appeared in Peter McLaren and Nathalia Jaramilo, *Critical Pedagogy in a Time of Permanent War*, in Jeffrey R. Di Leo and Walter Jacobs, eds. *If Classrooms Matter: Progressive Visions of Educational Environments* (pp. 75–92). New York and London: Routledge, 2004; and Peter McLaren, *Critical Pedagogy in the Age of Neoliberal Globalization: Notes from History's Underside*. Democracy and Nature, volume 9, no. 1, 2003, pp. 65–90.

1. But we would take Kumamoto's thesis one step further by saying that the root cause of systematic violence is the contradiction within global capitalism between capital and labor.
2. These examples have been drawn from Kumamoto (1993).

REFERENCES

Bales, Kevin. 2000. Throwaway people. *Index on Censorship* 28 (1): 36–45.
Boyle, Francis. 2001. Speech at Illinois disciples. October 18. Available at http://msanews.mynet?Scholars/Boyle/nowar.html.
Castro, Fidel. 2001. Televised presentation by Fidel Castro Ruz, president of the Republic of Cuba, on the present international situation: the economic and world crisis and its impact on Cuba. Havana, November 2, 2001.
Cleaver, Harry. 2000. *Reading capital politically*. Leeds, Engl.: Antitheses; and Edinburgh, Scot.: AK Press.
Cockburn, Alexander. 2002. The hog wallow. *Nation* 275 (5): 8.

De Angelis, Massimo. 2002. From movement to society. *Commoner,* no. 4 (May). Available at www.commoner.org.uk/01-3groundzero.htm.

Dery, Mark. 1999. *The pyrotechnic insanitarium: American culture on the brink.* New York: Grove Press.

Editorial report. 2002. *News and Letters* 47, no. 6 (July 2002): 5–8.

Elbaum, Max. 2002. *Revolution in the air: Sixties radicals turn to Lenin, Mao and Che.* London: Verso.

Featherstone, Liza. 2002. *Students against sweatshops.* London: Verso.

Gindin, Sam. 2002. Social justice and globalization: Are they compatible? *Monthly Review* 54 (2): 1–11.

Giroux, Henry. 1988. *Teachers as intellectuals: Toward a critical pedagogy of learning.* South Hadley, Mass.: Bergin & Garvey.

Grey, Barry. 2000. Leaked CIA report says 50,000 sold into slavery in U.S. every year. *World Socialist* website. Available at www.wsws.org/articles/2000/apr2000/slav-a03.shtml.

Herrera, Ernesto. 2002. Latin America: The current situation and the task of revolutionaries. *Fourth International Press,* July 17, 1–16.

Holloway, John. 2002. Twelve theses on changing the world without taking power. *Commoner,* no. 4 (May). Available at www.commoner.org.uk/04holloway2.pdf.

Johnson, Chalmers. 2000. *Blowback: The costs and consequences of American empire.* New York: Owl Books.

Kameras, D. 1998. Bringing home child labor: What it takes to buy the products we buy. *America@work* 3 (5): 12–16.

Kellner, Douglas. 2003. *From 9/11 to terror war: The dangers of the Bush legacy.* Boulder, Colo.: Rowman & Littlefield.

Klein, Naomi. 1999. *No logo: Taking aim at the brand bullies.* New York: Picador.

Kumamoto, Bob. 1993. The study of terrorism: An interdisciplinary approach for the classroom. *Social Studies Review* 33 (1): 16–21.

MacMichael, David. 2002. CIA and RIT fundamentally incompatible: Intelligence and higher education. *Covert Action Quarterly,* no. 73: 13–17, 47.

Marable, Manning. 2001. The failure of U.S. foreign policies. *ZNET.* Available at: www.zmag.org/sustainers/content/2001-11/17marable.cfm.

Meiksins Wood, Ellen. 2002. Contradictions: Only in capitalism. In *A world of contradictions, socialist register,* ed. L. Panitch and C. Leys. London: Merlin.

Niva, Steve. 2001. *Addressing the sources of Middle Eastern violence against the United States.* Common Dreams news center, September 14. Available at www.commondreams.org/views01/0914-04.htm.

Ollman, Bertell. 2001. *How to take an exam and remake the world.* Montreal: Black Rose Books.

Parenti, Michael. 2002. *The terrorism trap: September 11 and beyond.* San Francisco: City Lights Books.

Parks, J. B. 1997. This holiday season no sweat. *America@work* 2 (10): 11–12.

Petras, James. 2001, September–December. Notes toward an understanding of revolutionary politics today. *Links,* no. 19. Available at www.dsp.org.au/links/back/issue19/petras.htm.

———. 2002. Signs of a police state are everywhere. *Z Magazine* 15, no. 1 (January): 10–12.

Petras, James, and Henry Veltmeyer. 2001. *Globalization unmasked: Imperialism in the 21st century.* Halifax, N.S.: Fernwood Publishing.

Rikowski, Glenn. 2001. *After the manuscript broke off: Thoughts on Marx, social class and education.* Paper presented at the British Sociological Association Education Study Group, King's College London, June 23.

Robinson, William. 2001. Social theory and globalization: The rise of a transnational state. *Theory and Society* 30: 157–200.

Said, Edward. 2001. *Observer,* September 16. Available at www.observer.co.uk/comment/story/0,6903,552764,00.html.

Singer, Daniel. 1999. *Whose millennium? Theirs or ours?* New York: Monthly Review Press.

16

Paulo Freire and Digital Youth in Marginal Spaces

Colin Lankshear and Michele Knobel

This chapter explores aspects of Paulo Freire's pedagogy in relation to computer-mediated learning activities in a community setting. It draws on recent work done with marginalized young people and Aboriginal elementary school students within a community-based space called GRUNT (Brisbane, Australia). Workers at GRUNT employ a range of media and cultural forms, including the use of various new technologies associated with the World Wide Web. We will focus mainly on an ongoing project called Virtual Valley, making particular reference to Freire's development and use of codifications as a pedagogical device for promoting critical consciousness. This account will suggest ways in which web page production in the Virtual Valley project could be developed further as a problem-posing pedagogy for indigenous inner city youth.

BACKGROUND: THE VALLEY AND GRUNT

The Valley

Fortitude Valley—the "Valley"—is located in Brisbane's inner city. It is a well known part of town which, in the past, has been associated with marginal life and activities. On one hand, it is the location of Brisbane's Chinatown, a bustling and thriving center of restaurants and businesses serving the long established Chinese community. More recently, other Asian ethnic groups have also established a cultural presence there, and different Asian communities find in the Valley a zone of ethnic familiarity and comfort. On the other hand, it has also for decades been a magnet for displaced, homeless, drifting folk, many of whom have addictions or histories of substance abuse. In addition, the Valley was formerly a well-recognized site of vice: prostitution and various forms of racketeering. In the late 1980s, the Criminal Justice Commission inquiry into corruption at high levels resulted in some of the Valley's best known personalities being convicted and imprisoned.

These days, however, the heart of the Valley has undergone a dramatic "facelift." The mall has been upgraded, new shopping centers established, and existing businesses revitalized. The mall is now home to many outdoor cafés, sidewalk bars, tourist-related businesses, and trendy nightclubs. This caters in part to a new clientele of tourists, as well as to more affluent social groups who are wanting something "a little exotic" and "on the edge." At the same time, the Valley retains its traditional gritty base. Street kids, aged alcoholics, young unemployed men hanging out in video game parlors, bag ladies, lingering mafia-like groups, and the like maintain a visible presence, albeit a lower profile presence than previously.

One consequence of these recent changes has been the "rewriting" and "sanitizing" of the Valley for sale as a tourist destination and yuppie playground. As a result, the longstanding marginal youth users of the Valley—who are among the traditional "owners" of this space and its activities—have been written out of the new official representations of the Valley and pushed still further to the margins.

GRUNT

GRUNT began its life in 1992 as an idea about creating a safe and welcoming space for young people in the Valley area. The driving forces behind GRUNT were two cultural animateurs, Michael and Ludmila Doneman (www.mwk16.com), committed to supporting socially based performance art—especially for disadvantaged youth—cultural development, and training. At the time of the Virtual Valley projects described below, GRUNT was both a physical production and meeting space *and* an agenda for cultural productions of meanings and identities. In part, GRUNT aimed to equip youth with skills and strategies to earn a living. GRUNT was also, however, heavily involved in offering activities which would promote a sense of self-identity and interconnectedness with other identities and contexts in a world where these young people seemed increasingly to have no place.

As a physical space, during its years of operation (approximately 1992 until 1997) GRUNT comprised three distinct areas set within one hundred square meters of warehouse space on the first floor of a building in the center of Fortitude Valley. One area was used mainly for regular art exhibitions and performances. A second was a general-purpose place to hang out, meeting room, and administrative space, furnished with deep comfortable chairs and decorated with paintings and collages done mostly by members of the GRUNT collective, plus the occasional eye-catching prop from previous performances. The third space was GRUNT's main production area with its two adjoining offices.

This space was spray-painted *Star Trek* silver, and was equipped with ten high-speed desktop computers. A local area network wired each computer to common online storage areas as well as to the Internet. An urban–industrial "feel" was given to the monitors by the placement of unpainted, galvanized iron garbage bins over them, with screen-size holes cut into the metal of each bin. The resulting flap of metal was peeled up and back like the peak of a baseball cap, with the screen of each monitor shining like a well-scrubbed face from the hole in each converted bin. The computer boxes themselves sat on tables and were covered completely by synthetic green sward, leaving only each keyboard and mouse visible. Making the space as "un-school-like" as possible was an explicit operating principle. Multimedia equipment available to GRUNT users included color flatbed scanners, state-of-the-art sound, text, and image authoring software, multimedia-capable Internet browser software and hypertext markup language (HTML) editors, data panels and projectors, digital cameras, conventional cameras, video cameras, and the like. The overall emphasis throughout the GRUNT projects was on support for enterprise and self sufficiency. Unlike drop-in centers and similar facilities, GRUNT, with its online telecenter and multimedia laboratory, worked at providing inner city youth with "training in vocational skills, in the mastery of the new information technology and in planning, management and life skills" (Stevenson 1995, 4).

GRUNT's cultural production agenda included a range of web-based projects as well as visits to marginal communities in rural and isolated areas of Australia—especially traditional indigenous communities in central Australia—and subsequent performance and artistic productions were based on what participants learned through these visits about others and about themselves. Web-based projects covered diverse interests and identities. Prior to forming GRUNT, the Donemans had established Contact Youth Theatre to undertake a series of indigenous and cross-cultural projects. Initially, these took the form of touring performances and created the need for a physical base, which became GRUNT. At the same time, similar groups were operating in other parts of Australia. It was decided to make known and connect the work of these groups by creating a common web space: Black Voices. The Black Voices website broadcast information about these theater groups and their performance-based projects. For example, the Contact Youth Theatre production *Famaleez* (a phonetic rendition of "families") was "based on the extremely sensitive issue of alcohol and substance abuse in indigenous communities" (Black Voices 1991). The project focus was on "the traditional aboriginal construction of 'family' and the way it was used to give people structure and meaning," and built on the historical reality of the invasion of Australia by Europeans which had resulted in "a whole range of social dislocations and problems through the destruction of the extended family structures of many groups." Another project that exemplifies the diversity of GRUNT projects is the ongoing Digitarts project (Digitarts 1998). Digitarts is an online multimedia project space constructed originally by young women for young women, but now also encompasses disadvantaged youth and people with disabilities (2001). The Digitarts' website explores different conceptions and constructions of female identity through poems, narratives, journal pages, how-to texts, and digital images, and presents alternative perspectives on style, food, everyday life, and commodities. The Australian-based project is "dedicated to providing young women who are emerging artists and/or cultural workers with access to the knowledge and equipment necessary for the development of their arts and cultural practices in the area of new technologies" (1998, 1). It aims to challenge "the 'boys toys' stigma often associated with electronic equipment," and to "provide young women with access to information technology in a nonthreatening 'girls own' space, to encourage involvement in technology-based artforms."

THE VIRTUAL VALLEY PROJECTS:
VIRTUAL VALLEY I AND VIRTUAL VALLEY II

Between 1995 and 1997, GRUNT conducted two projects, each with an online component. These projects were Virtual Valley I and II, and they focused on the way in which young people who have strong affinities with the Valley and whose identities were bound up with it, were being pushed out of its redefinition and gentrification (Virtual Valley 1996a).

Virtual Valley I

This version of the overall project ran in the months of May and June 1996 (Virtual Valley 1996b). It aimed at producing an alternative user's guide to the Valley, which would provide different readings and writings of the Valley from those in official municipal promotions and tourist brochures.

As an oppositional cultural response, Virtual Valley I presented work by nine young people who used the Valley on a daily basis for work and recreational purposes. These youth clearly held strong opinions about the Valley's role in the life of Brisbane, which at the time of this project was being promoted by the State government as "Australia's most liveable city." Participants' work was presented in two formats: a website, and a booklet of black-and-white images as postcards, and street maps with paper overlays that showed participants' ways of walking through and using the Valley (cf. de Certeau 1984) to help guide visitors through the Valley, according to how these young people saw themselves in relation to the Valley. Thus, the maps and images were based directly on these young people's identities, values, worldviews, experiences, and ways of locating themselves in time and space within the Valley. The focus was on encouraging young people "to map the Valley area in ways that are culturally relevant to themselves and their peers" (Virtual Valley 1996b, 1). Places of interest presented on the Virtual Valley I website include the location of a large clock (used by people without watches to check the time), and favorite places for dancing, eating, getting coffee, finding bargains, and meeting friends. These were incorporated into web pages built around an online street map which contrasted graphically with tourist maps, such as an official "heritage trail" which mapped points of interest from a colonial history mindset. The hard copy booklet provided a postcard picture collage of images—including some from the website—which ranged from snapshots of a gutter and a tidy line of garbage bins, to a crowded Saturday market scene in the mostly open-air mall.

Virtual Valley II

Virtual Valley II is an ongoing project involving students from two elementary schools near the Valley at the time of the start of the project (August 1996). One of these is an Aboriginal (Murri) and Torres Strait Islander independent community school, which aims to provide a pedagogical balance between Aboriginal funds of knowledge and culture and those of mainstream white Australians. This school has recently purchased a large, surplus-stock primary school from the state government and moved some distance from the Valley. Nonetheless, many of the school's families remain living in and near the Valley. At the time of first participating in this project, students (most about twelve years old) would walk to the GRUNT building and spend half a day each week exploring aspects of identity using conventional artistic means of painting, drawing, and collage, as well as learning technical aspects of web page construction—including basic HTML and web page design principles, using digital cameras, manipulating digital images and anchoring them to web pages, and using flatbed scanners. Students gathered material for their web pages on walks through the Valley, using digital and disposable cameras, sketchbooks, and notepads. They began putting together their individual web pages by creating large-scale annotated collages of aspects of the Valley that were significant to them. These collages comprised photocopies of digital and camera images they had taken of themselves, their friends, family members, and the Valley area, along with drawings they had done and found objects (e.g., food labels, ticket stubs, and bingo cards). They were then pared back to key images and passages of text as each student prepared a flowchart depicting the layout and content of their web page. During the last month of the project these flowcharts were used to guide the design and construction of web pages (see Virtual Valley 1996c).

The result is a series of compelling and evocative readings and writings of everyday cultural (re)productions of the Valley seen through the eyes of these Murri and Torres Strait Islander children. The web pages combine photographic images of themselves in relation to the Valley's topography and elements that serve as icons or tropes for the multicultural life of the Valley. For example, one image shows a Murri student—identified as the writer's cousin—sitting in the lap of a large statue of a Chinese figure in the heart of Chinatown. Others capture distinctive Chinese architectural shapes in the form of pagodas and symbolic gates, or shop windows displaying the headless bodies of plucked ducks ready for cooking. These pictures graphically portray the enacted identity of these Aboriginal and Torres Strait Islander young people "rubbing up against" key elements of Asian ethnic identities. Further images capture elements more directly involved in their own identities, such as photographs of Aboriginal mosaic designs set in the sidewalks, and others bring kinship together with vital aspects of popular youth culture and taste, such as the photograph of a Murri student drinking a McDonald's milkshake purchased by an Aunty he met on his walk with his class. Additional images of popular culture abound: such as pictures showing students lined up at a McDonald's counter, and photographs taken while playing video games at Time Zone and Universal Fun City. All of these photographs are accompanied by vivid texts. Justin's page is typical. His virtual tour of the Valley begins with a short poetic description of images and activities he sees around him.

> People allsorts
> Ice-cream parlour allkinds
> Timezone fun
> Dragons
> Temples colourful
> China Town lots of people

Justin's text is printed in large multicolored fonts (Courier and Times New Roman). Capital letters and italicized words, plus two photographic images, add further details to his stripped-down text. The first image captures the cultural diversity of the people in the Valley. The second underscores fun experiences at Time Zone by showing a video game in action. Following this description of his response to the Valley, Justin shifts to a recount genre and recalls the highlights of a particular stroll through the Valley with his class and activities at GRUNT, which included a role play about issues facing Aboriginal people in the Valley.

> susan pretended to be opal
> winney [Oprah Winfrey] and we was the audience
>
> one group was police the others
> was murries and shop owners after all
> that we did some drawings
>
> then we had lunch I had two banans
> and three sandwhiches
>
> I also had a drink of coke cola
> there was plenty for us to have
> seconds. My friend Louis ate lots of
> cakes and so he had an belly
> ache. After that we went for a walk
> in the valley we saw dead ducks
> with their heads still attached. (Virtual Valley 1996a)

FREIREAN PEDAGOGY AND CODIFICATIONS

As explained in other chapters, Freire's literacy pedagogy was housed within a larger pedagogy of liberation. Participants learned to read and write the *world* as well as the *word*, and to understand the relationship between word and world. For education to be liberatory, according to Freire, it must be critical and dialogical. As Nina Wallerstein (1987, 34) notes, human liberation occurs

> to the extent that people reflect upon their relationship to the world in which they live . . . In conscientizing themselves, they insert themselves in history as subjects . . . Learners enter into the process of learning not by acquiring facts, but by constructing their reality in social exchange with others.

Freire himself observed that "studying is a form of reinventing, recreating, rewriting, and this is a subject's, not an object's task" (Freire 1985, 2). If humans are to live humanly, to realize their ontological vocation (1972, 41), they must *name the world*, by making and remaking reality through a transformative praxis of action–reflection (Peters and Lankshear 1994, 179). This transformative praxis is, for Freire, *dialogue*: "the encounter between [human beings] mediated by the world, in order to name the world" (Freire 1972, 61). Dialogue is both active and critical. This is captured in Freire's notion of conscientization as a process within which learners are encouraged to analyze their reality so that they become aware of constraints acting on them in their lives and can undertake courses of action to change their situations. Pursuing liberation and becoming more critically conscious involves learners in becoming aware of their own incompleteness, as well as the incompleteness of the world itself. It also involves identifying constraints to attaining this awareness and to actively entering the process of creating the world and our own selves on equal participatory terms with others. These are key insights of critical consciousness, as defined by Freire. Bearers of naïve consciousness perceive the world/reality as complete, static, "given." They see the quality of their lives and the circumstances they inhabit as unalterable and inevitable. They believe they can only be what they already are (Peters and Lankshear 1994, 180).

In dialogical pedagogy, learners face challenges to naïve consciousness within tasks and activities organized to engage them in critical thinking, and in actively testing the efficacy of critical consciousness against the world itself.

Critical thinking starts from perceiving the root causes of one's place in society—the socioeconomic, political, cultural, and historical context of our personal lives. But critical thinking continues beyond perception—toward the actions and decisions people make to shape and gain control over their lives. True knowledge evolves from the interaction of reflection and action (or praxis) and occurs "when human beings participate in a transforming act" (Wallerstein 1987, 34; the reference is to Freire 1985, 104).

In dialogue, learners undertake collective transforming action on the world informed by collective reflection upon an aspect of reality important to them.

In the very process of testing reflection against the world by means of a transforming act, learners perform and achieve acts of liberation.

Within pedagogy as dialogue, codifications play an important role. In classical Freirean pedagogy, codification took the form of graphic representations—drawings, photos, slides—of typical existential situations of the learners. "These representations," says Freire (1973, 51), "function as challenges, as coded situation-problems containing elements to be decoded by the [learning] groups with the collaboration of the coordinator." In elaborations of Freirean pedagogy, codifications often take the form also of written stories, skits, collages, songs, and so on (Wallerstein 1987, 38). In all instances, however, codifications (or codes) re-present learners' reality back to the group. A code "'codifies' into one depersonalized representation, a conflict or problem that carries emotional or social impact in people's lives. It is more than a visual aid or a structured language exercise, as its purpose is to promote critical thinking and action."

Freire's pedagogy employed codification at three points. The first was before literacy activity per se took place. Codes were used to stimulate learners to see themselves as makers of culture; as being already actively involved in cultural creation. The purpose here was to challenge fatalistic orientations toward the world, and to encourage explicit recognition that learners *can* and *do* transform the world in various ways within the normal course of their daily lives. If they already work to transform reality in certain ways, surely they can also work to transform it in other ways—by challenging culturally created and maintained institutions, norms, structures, and processes which position them as marginal beings within the social order. At the second point in the pedagogy—the literacy phase—codes were associated with the generative words chosen to serve as the building blocks for learning to read and write. As a prelude to reading and writing words, learners in the culture circles (or learning groups) discussed existential situations associated with words such as *favela, comida, terreno, trabalho,* and *salário.* They tried to identify social and political forces at work in creating and maintaining these situations, as well as envisaging "limit acts" (Freire 1972, 74) through which they could attempt to challenge these forces and transform the historical and lived circumstances associated with them. At the third point in the pedagogy—the postliteracy phase—codes could be employed with generative themes.

The operating principle for codifications is the same at all points. For people to understand their reality critically, they need to be able to stand outside it—to get some objective distance from it, in order to reflect upon it and conceive strategies for acting upon it transformatively. When we are immersed in "reality," we often cannot see it for what it is, and we cannot create space to make it the object of our reflection. Still less can we make it the object of collective or group reflection within contexts where different points of view can be brought to bear upon it. Codifications "stand in" for reality here. Once codes for significant elements of learners' realities have been produced, participants can focus their "knowing energies" upon themes, and pursue deeper understandings of them in terms of causes and effects, institutionalized processes and structures, the interests they sustain and undermine, and so on—drawing on the range of perspectives, beliefs, information, and experiences of members of the learning group (which, of course, included "outsiders," in the form of the educator–educatees, as well as the "insider" educatee-educators). In this way, codifications stimulate and focus critical thinking and analysis, and transformative critical practice.

BEYOND VIRTUAL VALLEY I AND II: IMAGINING A PEDAGOGICAL DEVELOPMENT FROM TEXT PRODUCTION TO NAMING

The Virtual Valley projects were not conceived as any kind of Freirean project. They were about making space for marginal "voices" and validating identities that are typically marginalized within the normal routines and values of dominant groups in daily life, as distinct from fomenting transformative action or limit acts against limit(ing) situations. They were concerned more with producing alternative readings and texts from those vaunted in dominant discourses of tourist-oriented representations than about *naming* the world in Freire's extended sense. At the same time, the projects definitely stimulated the beginnings of critical engagement with master narrations of reality. They took strong steps toward enacting powerful literacies in the manner defined by James Paul Gee (1996). Gee defines powerful literacy in terms of using a literacy as "a meta-language or a meta-Discourse (a set of metawords, metavalues, metabeliefs) for the critique of other literacies and the way they constitute us as persons and situate us in society" (144).

In developing alternative textual readings and writings of the Valley, participants produced artifacts that could serve very well as codes, or codifications, for a Freirean approach to dialogical pedagogy. In this respect, the production of codifications differs in at least one significant way from that described by Freire in his early texts. As described in *Education for Critical Consciousness* (Freire 1973), the codifications used in the pedagogy were produced not by the participants themselves, but by artists who were working to specifications provided on the basis of observations and discussions grounded in the learners' daily realities. Numerous critics of Freirean pedagogy have noted—often ingenuously or by means of overstatement—the potential for manipulating learner consciousness through selective interpretation on the part of Freirean pedagogues. A strong point of codifications based on artifacts produced in the Virtual Valley projects is that no such allegations could credibly be advanced.

The work undertaken in the pedagogy of the Virtual Valley projects holds enormous potential for providing a base from which to launch a full-fledged Freirean pedagogy of dialogue. With texts representing dominant accounts of Valley reality already in place, and with Murri youth having produced their own representations of existential situations steeped in their lived realities, it would be possible to use the web page and other cultural artifacts produced in the Virtual Valley pedagogy as resources for problem-posing education—and to introduce dominant representations as problematic texts which in turn encode problematic situations.

From this point we can begin to envisage possibilities for cultural pedagogy built around the use of new technologies. In the case of the Murri School students this work could proceed in various directions. The following is a preliminary account of some directions a problem-posing pedagogy could take, drawing on the use of student artifacts or cultural investments as codifications.

1. The text of Justin's poem could be taken as codifying problems concerning constructions of school-based literacy in relation to wider cultural practices of meaning making. If we look at Justin's story-poem in terms of "official" constructions of school literacy it becomes problematic. In the state of Queensland, and in Australia more generally, there has been a strong, government-led rush toward national student profiles and benchmarks for English language literacy. Teachers are required to assess students using pre-set tests in grades three, five, and seven; report their performances against the benchmarks; and then to identify "at risk" students and enroll them in prepackaged, one-size-fits-all, commercial remedial literacy programs. Justin's text, despite its evocativeness, would almost certainly fail against the national benchmarks for his grade level.

   Of course, the problem with official constructions of literacy framed in terms of such benchmarks is that they "domesticate" literacy, reducing it to matters of technical accuracy, and to the ability to encode and decode text (even if that was never the intention of the benchmark writers). The uptake of benchmarks generally negates constructions of literacy in terms of relating word to world, of learning to read both word and world, and so on (cf. Knobel 1999, 2001). This is not to say that matters of technical accuracy are not important, because to a considerable extent they *are*. It is, however, to say that Justin's text—like others on the Virtual Valley website—is a powerful expression of meaning; a powerful statement of cultural understanding and of the relationship between language and identity/ies. It is also to say that this power is very often *absent* in technically accurate and "proficient" texts.

   A problem-posing pedagogy could use work like Justin's to investigate the values and norms underlying "benchmark-based" accounts and indicators of literacy, and contrast these with the values and norms underlying other social practices of literacy—including some of those which may be very powerful, but where the power has little to do with technical accuracy and more to do with breaking rules and conventions (such as in advertising, various popular cultural forms—e.g., gangsta rap, zines—and so on). Tensions between individualized and commodified constructions of literacy (as certified by test scores, recorded in student performance profiles, etc.) and more traditional and indigenous constructions of literacy could be investigated. Out of such problem-posing dialogue it might be decided to contest dominant/official constructions by developing and pro-liferating alternative textual norms and conventions of print-mediated meaning making in a range of public cyberspaces and meatspaces (see Knobel and Lankshear 2002; Lankshear and Knobel 2000). These alterna-tive texts could be used to claim and "inhabit" a distinctive "Murri space" or "Islander space" on the Internet; one that could be used for educating others about Murri or Islander ways. Indeed, the use of artifacts like the Murri students' web pages could become icons to be used in broad-based movements to contest the narrow, constraining, and technicist versions of "official" literacy being imposed by technocratic regimes of educational administration in many countries.

2. The students' artifacts could be used to problematize other aspects of school knowledge and school-based pedagogy. For example, the Virtual Valley web pages graphically contest the banking model of classroom learning, and the construction of learning as an interaction between teacher and learner that occurs within classrooms. The presence of kin—especially Aunties (not necessarily blood kin in the Anglo-Saxon sense of the "kin")—in so many of the students' photographs and drawings stimu-late wider conceptions of learning resources and learning guides than teachers and conventional classroom materials alone. They remind us that the gates and walls between the traditional classroom/school and the community are artificial barriers that serve to enclose official learning within particular sites and under the subjection of particular regimes of truth—resulting in learning grounded in school discourses which gener-ally have very little to do with "mature" (or "insider") versions of social practices in the world beyond school; inviting the question of what school learning is *for* (Gee, Hull, and Lankshear 1996, 1–23; Knobel 1999, 2001). They remind us also that subject boundaries are themselves in many ways artificial demarcations which can impede our efforts to know the world in ways which relate "parts" to "wholes."

Despite strong shifts in primary education away from time-tabled sub-ject lessons and toward cross-curriculum planning and teaching, our ex-periences in the many classrooms we have visited suggest there is still a very strong tendency to compartmentalize subject areas by means of timetables. At best, we find classroom practices that attempt to interweave different subject areas by using a theme or topic to bind them together. Here we can ask the following: What is gained and who benefits when knowledge is compartmentalized? What is gained and who benefits when what we can know about the world geographically becomes divided from what we can know sociologically? What is gained and who benefits when certain perspectives are ruled out of official definitions of school subjects? What is lost, and who loses as a result, when knowledge becomes timetabled into subject slots and when what students learn in one subject area is not developed further in other subject areas? When the Murri students went out into the school community, were they doing "language arts," or "social studies," or "art"? A mix of all three, or something more? What would have been gained or lost if the students had been instructed to go into the Valley to gather information for only one or other of subject areas? What would have been gained or lost if literacy benchmarks had been imposed externally on the products of their time at GRUNT?

As codifications, various components of the students' web pages have the potential to support problem-posing pedagogy that opens up crucial epistemological themes related to questions of power and advantage in ways learners and teacher–facilitators together can relate to their own circumstances as members of socially marginalized groups. Such codes could stimulate questions about how conventional school-based learning opportunities differ from learning opportunities available in GRUNT space. They could also provide opportunities for asking whether it would be effective—or possible—to try and reinvent their school learning in ways that are more like learning opportunities at GRUNT within the Virtual Valley project, and how this might be done. Of course, participants could experiment with reinventions of school learning, as a strategy for answering their own reflection-based questions.

3. The students' cultural investments themselves contain problematic elements which could be codified for closer investigation. Time Zone is commodified entertainment, part of a commercialized youth culture, which costs regular players—usually young people—large amounts of money each year. At the same time, the video games at Time Zone and similar parlors contain values and storylines which are very often highly sexist, racist, and violent. They often mystify power—reducing power to considerations of physical strength—and encourage vicarious living. In many ways these genres operate on the "logic" described by Freire as "taking the oppressor within": individuals who experience disempowerment in many areas of their lives are encouraged by video game playing to enter virtual worlds where they experience illusions of power. This process diverts attention and energy away from reflection–action to address issues of social power in the real world. It can often be a form of "bread and circus" diversion. It is also an invitation into conceptions of power as individualized property—the winners and heroes in the games are very often "heroes" (and sometimes "heroines") working and winning alone.

Part of what is attractive to youth who hang out at game parlors like Time Zone is the opportunity to meet as a group, to belong to a community of practice where they achieve success and status. Student-produced codifications of cultural practices in spaces like Time Zone could be used as a stimulus to explore issues of community as well as issues of power, and to decode the ideologies of the games and relate the various elements of these ideologies to larger social processes—particularly, processes which create and sustain hierarchies of dominant and marginal social groupings. Indeed, for many of these young people new electronic technologies memberships in quite different communities of practice which are grounded in quite different purposes and possibilities. Within Time Zone, the technologies provide a focus for alliances and practices associated with youth culture, street culture, hanging out, and being entertained. Within GRUNT the technologies mediated opportunities to acquire new technological skills and understandings within contexts of exploring cultural identity and creating spaces for expressing this identity to and among audiences who will accept and relate to it on its own terms.

By rubbing different elements of these codifications against each other, it becomes possible to identify and analyze possible options made available by engaging with new technologies. Given the crucial significance of electronic technologies in postmodern times, enabling learners to understand and access different options for using these technologies becomes a major educational purpose.

CONCLUSION

Of all the elements which shape and reshape postmodern times, few are more palpable than new digital technologies. Yet, as critically informed commentators increasingly observe, new technologies can be employed for very different purposes. Freire, of course, made exactly the same observation about education—which can be seen as an age-old, albeit evolving, technology. Like education, new information and communication technologies can be turned to purposes of oppression or liberation: both in their own right and in their more specific roles as *educational* or *learning* technologies. These who are interested in the theory and practice of liberatory education in current times cannot afford to ignore this new dimension of educational mediation and engagement. This chapter has attempted to explore in a preliminary way some of the points at which new technologies can be employed for critical, dialogical, and liberatory purposes within education.

REFERENCES

Black Voices. 1991. *Famaleez*. Brisbane, Austr.: Contact Youth Theatre.
Brown, C. 1975. *Literacy in thirty hours: Paulo Freire's process in North East Brazil*. London: Writers and Readers.
de Certeau, M. 1984. *The practice of everyday life*. Berkeley: University of California Press.
Digitarts. 1998. Welcome. Available at http://digitarts.va.com.au/welcome.html.
———. 2001. Front page. Available at http://digitarts.va.com.au.

Freire, P. 1972. *Pedagogy of the oppressed*. Harmondsworth, Engl.: Penguin Education.
——. 1973. *Education for critical consciousness*. New York: Seabury.
——. 1985. *The politics of education*. London: Macmillan.
Gee, J. 1996. *Social linguistics and literacies: Ideology in discourses*. 2nd ed. London: Taylor and Francis.
Gee, J., G. Hull, and C. Lankshear. 1996. *The new work order: Behind the language of the new capitalism*. Boulder, Colo.: Westview Press.
Knobel, M. 1999. *Everyday literacies: Students, discourse, and social practice*. New York: Peter Lang.
——. 2001. "I'm not a pencil man": How one student challenges our notions of literacy "failure" in school. *Journal of Adolescent and Adult Literacy* 44 (5): 404–19.
Knobel, M., and C. Lankshear. 2002. Cut, paste, publish: The production and consumption of zines. In *Adolescents and literacies in a digital world*, ed. D. Alvermann. New York: Peter Lang.
Lankshear, C., and M. Knobel. 2000. Mapping postmodern literacies: A preliminary chart. *Journal of Literacy and Technology* 1, no. 1. Available at www.literacyandtechnology.org/v1n1/lk.html.
Peters, M., and C. Lankshear. 1994. Education and hermeneutics: A Freirean interpretation. In *Politics of liberation: Paths from Freire*, ed. P. McLaren and J. Giarelli, 173–92. London: Routledge.
Shor, I. 1980. *Critical teaching and everyday life*. Boston: South End Press.
Stevenson, P. 1995. *Making space: For those who invent tomorrow, a report on the feasibility of a multi-purpose youth facility for Brisbane*. Brisbane, Austr.: Queensland Department of Tourism, Sport, and Racing; and Queensland University of Technology Academy of the Arts.
Virtual Valley. 1996a. Justin. Available at www.odyssey.com.au/ps/GRUV/vvalley/mis/justin.htm.
——. 1996b. Phase one. Available at www.mwk16.com/perfectstrangers/GRUV/vvalley/phase1.htm.
——. 1996c. Phase two. Available at www.mwk16.com/perfectstrangers/GRUV/vvalley/phase2.htm.
——. 1996d. *Virtual Valley: Brunswick and beyond* . . . . Available at www.mwk16.com/perfectstrangers/GRUV/vvalley/welcome.html.
Wallerstein, N. 1987. Problem-posing education: Freire's method for transformation. In *Freire for the classroom: A sourcebook for liberatory teaching*, ed. I. Shor, 33–44. Portsmouth, N.H.: Boynton/Cook.

17

Intercultural Education: A Contribution to Peace in the Developing Global Society?

Erika Richter

THE POTENTIAL FOR PEACE AND THE ABSENCE OF PEACE IN THE WORLD

The Evolution of Western Civilization

In *The Civilizing Process* (2000), Norbert Elias described the history of Western civilization since the early Middle Ages as a process of increasing control over people's "inner nature," as an increasing confinement of their emotional economy and—as a result—gradually increasing self-control.

Centuries earlier, feelings of desire and hate were expressed much more unevenly, vehemently, and directly than today; it seems that human feelings were capable of sudden and—compared with contemporary norms—irrational reversals: from happy cheerfulness to murderous rage, for example. The documents of the period reveal an unbridled and permitted lust for killing, fighting, and torture, which our contemporary society would define and understand as pathogenic sadism. This lust for fighting was at the time still, so to speak, innocent, because it had not yet become socially sanctioned.

Elias's scholarly interest in his historical studies focuses on the connection between the structures of society and the emotional makeup of the individuals, which, in turn constituted these societies. He explains this earlier roughness or "savagery of feeling" (2000, 162) as follows: at that time there was still no central instance of social control and punishment which was powerful enough to protect the individual. Everyone was pitted against everyone else—perhaps with a few friends or allies on their side. The "permanent readiness to fight, weapon in hand, was thus 'a vital necessity' in medieval times" (166). Elias then identifies an important condition for the collective transformation of behavior within the historical process. Namely, as soon as "in this or that region the power of a central authority grows, of over a larger or smaller area the people are forced to live in peace with each other, the moulding of the affects and the standards of the drive-economy are very gradually changed as well . . . the reserve and the 'mutual consideration' of people increase, first in normal everyday social life" (169).

What I have briefly reported on in relation to the beginning of the segment of the civilizing process described by Elias, with a quick exemplary reference to aggressiveness, was further demonstrated by him with a variety of aspects of behavior in everday life as well as the "fate" of instinctual life in the course of history.

One of Elias's central general insights—which I also regard as very important in relation to the problem of peace—is as follows: it is the respective "structure of society that required and generated a specific standard of emotional control" (2000, 169). And it seemed impossible to decide which of the two sides: the society or the individual—be the motor of social development.

At this point I would like to argue that Elias interprets the history of civilization in the Western world up to the present in evolutionary terms—that is, as the higher development of human beings in the wake of the gradual taming, sublimation, and refinement of their affects, resulting in what is in comparative historical terms an immense pacification of the instinctual economy of the civilized person of today.

How, then, are we to explain the relapses—such as the barbarism of National Socialism—below the achieved standards of civilization?

Elias himself gives an explanation for possible collective regressions: "And immense social upheaval and urgency, heightened by carefully concerted propaganda, are needed to reawaken and legitimize in large masses of people the socially outlawed drives, the joy in killing and destruction that have been repressed from everyday civilized life" (2000, 170; cf. van Krieken 1998).

The Breach in Civilization

On the basis of the high point of German cultural and spiritual life—because of the glittering products of the Enlightenment, Idealism, and Romanticism, the Germans were seen as "the" cultured people—how was it possible to descend so far into the deepest barbarism? Adorno and other members of the "Frankfurt School" have investigated this difficult to understand phenomenon with the help of empirical social research, motivated additionally by an interest in preventing similar potential civilizatory breaches.

How was it possible, then, to arrive at "Auschwitz," and what conditions are required to ensure "that Auschwitz not happen again" (Adorno 1998, 191)? The critical theorists of the Frankfurt School also investigate (as Elias did before them) the mediations of societal with individual–psychological forms and dynamics. However (unlike Elias) they place the primary emphasis on the side of the individual, because it is only there that they see a chance of mutability. Since the possibility of changing the objective—namely societal and political—conditions is extremely limited today, attempts to work against the repetition of Auschwitz are necessarily restricted to the subjective dimension (192).

The analysis runs as follows: It is the so-called petty bourgeois, or rather the petty-bourgeois character form which Hitler and National Socialism made possible which—as the large majority—helped carry them along. The studies show the petty bourgeois as the type of the collaborator; the manipulable collective character which is authoritarian and at the same time submissive to authority; their consciousness reveals itself as reified, that is, captured by prejudices, stereotypes, and schemata; their emotional life reveals itself as determined in a fundamentally negative way, as a combination of hardness and coldness, people, all in all, "who cannot love" (Adorno 1998, 200).

Adorno sees great potential in Enlightenment pedagogic intervention, even the only chance of changing such individual–psychological and at the same time social–collective personality forms. Enlightenment of people through these mechanisms and thus creating a general consciousness are necessary conditions for the prevention of further relapses. He is thus committed to education for "autonomy," "the power of reflection, of self-determination, of not cooperating" (1998, 195).

"Spaceship Earth": The "One World"

Here I would like to extend the perspective to include the question of peace.[1] The metaphor, introduced by Goldschmidt (1982), of the Earth as a "spaceship" gave colorful expression to ideas of global interdependence, the worldwide networks and mutual dependencies of states, much like the resulting mutually dependent search for solutions to the global population problem.

Without wanting to relativize the National Socialist terror—since, as will become clear, this barbarism is to be judged precisely against the background of the standard of civilization reached in the West—it remains true that discord, violence, and domination are worldwide phenomena among human beings. It no longer seems to make an enormous difference where the local crises or wars break out, we sense and know that in this small "One World" (Nolte 1982) we are all equally threatened. This produces our collective responsibility. The existence of millions of refugees is symptomatic of the worldwide absence of peace. According to the United Nations Humanitarian Committee on Refugees nearly two hundred million people took flight in the twentieth century, having thereby been named the "century of refugees."

A brief outline of this unpeaceful world situation looks as follows. In the 1970s, Johan Galtung and, following his analysis in his findings of the structures of "Third World" societies, Dieter Senghaas, characterized global discord as "structural violence"—which can be captured diagramatically in a coordinate cross, symbolizing the world-geographical relationships, the horizontal arm representing the (former) West–East rivalry, the finally overcome good–evil schema of the persistently maintained Cold War rhetoric; the vertical the so-called North–South gradient, representing the "structural dependency," colonial and neocolonial exploitation and domination of the Third by the First World.[2]

In the competition for the better system, the East had shut itself up in a huge, self-constructed prison which seemed to fulfill the purpose to protect the State from its own citizens than the other way around, since it was, concerning the standards of living and the possibilities of freedom, impossible for the system of the so-called Socialism, that is, the real, existing Communism, to keep up with the Western modifications of societal capitalist system, which offered, far from being unproblematic in itself, indeed the better opportunities in the above respects, since they had passed through quite different historical conditions of development.

In relation to the North–South division, I would support the thesis that the "North"—that is, Europe and North America—owes its traditional economic superiority and its well-being to colonial exploitation and its extension through imperialistic and neocolonial policies—including industrialization and development politics in the form of arms supply. The fierce struggle over spheres of influence and niches in the world market "generates disaster in the Third World" (Nuscheler 1984, 206). And despite, or as critics claim, because of foreign aid, there has in the course of the last two decades taken place a shift to the worse in the relations between the "core"—and the "periphery"—countries of the globe,[3] that is, between the industrialized and the underdeveloped nations of the Third World, marking a deterioration in the living conditions for those people making up roughly three-quarters of the global population.

RESPONSIBILITY FOR THE "ONE WORLD"

World History and World Domestic Politics

In the 1960s and 1970s Carl Friedrich von Weizsäcker put forward for public discussion his conception of world peace. World politics is—because of international dependencies—more than ever before to be understood as "world domestic politics."[4] This was to be a politics

> in which, through the use of supra-national institutions to clearly restrict sovereignty, power is managed in such a way that through transcending warfare a thoroughly pluralistic world system as a whole can be established and extended in the pursuit of a world order of reason.[5]

The realization of this idea is, however, dependent on an underlying "transformation of consciousness."

The development of Weizsäcker's suggestions rests on the distinction between "culture" and "civilization" as it is portrayed in German philosophy and critical theory.[6] "Culture" is understood as the essence of all rational products of the human mind, while "civilization" in contrast is seen as pure technical advance, which is often not identical with the advancement of reason. In the name of this normative understanding of culture, Weizsäcker criticizes the fundamentals of modern technical civilization: the automatism of technical civilization is the automatism of a will operating without the benefit of reason.

The prospect of restricting or abolishing war is thus dependent on the further development of human culture. Unfortunately Weizsäcker fails to identify any explicit theory of culture. The dilemma is, namely, that the process of the uniform spread of modern technology and civilization over the whole globe seems irresistible. How is a "pluralistic world system" to be developed in the face of this danger of the universal extension of industrial civilization? Is there another way, can the agony of the ever-increasing discrepancy between rich and poor, between material welfare and material as well as psychic misery, be stopped? Is there any chance of rescuing traditions, reason, and freedom, or will the "world state" of culturally cloned parts of the world, including for members of the developed nations, one in which freedom will be lost? Are we still to realize Orwell's *1984*?

Cultural Universalism and Cultural Relativism

Reflections on culture are currently widespread. What is the background to this renaissance of the concept of culture, and what is the "struggle between culturally relativistic and universalistic social science" (cf. Schöfthaler 1983) about? Probably as an expression of the global experience of crisis, the "new culturalism" (cultural relativism) constitutes an attempt at a worldwide "revaloratization of national, ethnic, and local associations" (335). Western alternative and countercultures find themselves driven by one and the same cultural imperialism toward solidarity with the peoples of the Third World (cf. Geertz 1973; Lévi-Strauss 1992). The "dominant culture" has cultural meaning only for the ruling class; for the ruled classes and peoples, however, it has only an ideological meaning. Gramsci's distinction (1983) between "objective" and "subjective" culture becomes important here: what creative space do individuals have for subjective appropriation of culture within the framework of handed-down institutions?

The conflict between "cultural universalism" and "cultural relativism" reflects the competing positions that the diversity of "objective cultures" are either arranged "in terms of a model of individual and social development" or have to be seen "also as a multiplicity of conditions of subjection acquisition" (cf. Steinmann and Scherer 1998). The concept of universalistic development is thus grounded in a normative–evolutionary approach.

It is worth noting that since the early twentieth century, three paradigm shifts have taken place in the relevant social sciences between the two positions, and that today, as an expression of the *Zeitgeist* (cf. Williams 1984), they lie on the

312   *Erika Richter*

side of relativism (cf. Huntington 1996; for the discussion with reference to the American Society, cf. Sleeter and McLaren 1995; Gordon and Newfield 1996; McLaren 1997).

Schöfthaler's identification of the central problem of the relativistic standpoint, characterized by critics as "paternalism," is the danger of avoiding analyses and diagnoses of the *real existing* "colonization of the life world" (Habermas 1981)—and thus a failure to pursue forms of resistance. Ultimately, then, it amounts to the "legitimation of social inequality" (336).

The position of cultural universalism, in contrast, is branded by its critics, because of its "eurocentric" perspective, as "cultural imperialism." However, it is explicitly defended by its advocates because of its defence of European cultural values. This does not mean, though, that they should be regarded as uncritical propagandists for Western culture as the only true, correct, and best way.[7] Yet for the critical theorists of the society it is the essential criterion of progress, in modern as opposed to traditional societies, which allows for criticism at all, criticism made possible on the basis of similar principles making up this culture: the "potential for rationality embedded in communicative action" also constitutes the possibility of criticism of the "pathologies" of modern society (cf. Habermas 1981; also Finkielkraut 1987; Kymlicka 2000; Taylor 1993); it thus also opens up the prospect of human emancipation from social constraints, toward self-realization, so that humans become what they are capable of becoming (cf. Heydorn 1979).

The Future of Education

What role can pedagogy and education play here in addressing these questions and in the development of problem-solving strategies? Given the disillusionment what has accompanied a century identified as "the century of the child," can any hope be placed in pedagogy? Skepticism is justified, and yet: Precisely because of the experience of powerlessness in a modern technologically determined world, being more the object than the subject of decision-making processes, we are left only with the search for new starting points and possibilities for transforming and overcoming alienation. This means learning from the mistakes of established pedagogy. The approach of reform pedagogy, following a conservative cultural critique, of withdrawing into a supposed haven from the "hostile" social environment, turned out to be false, since pedagogy then had nothing with which to resist the later manipulative interventions of society and state, indeed failed to even notice these conditions. The "future of education" (Peukert 1984) must be one in which the critical rationality of the concept of education is mediated with political education. Adorno pointed this out in his piece on "Education after Auschwitz." For Peukert, too, the current crisis provides an encouragement to reconstruct the educational dimensions of the classical tradition. It is on this basis that he wants to construct our understanding of education, on which "the future of our society" appears to depend (129).

It is thus a matter of transcending the historical institutional form taken by education—which aims at human emancipation, self-realization, and subjectification—to become a form of capital or bourgeois status privilege. Education in the epoch of neohumanism sought an answer to the feeling of being "alienated" associated with early industrialization. It was opposed to education as adaptation to these modern relationships. "With the concept of education, the antithesis to the process of upbringing was developed. . . . Education understands itself as liberated autonomy, as consummated emancipation. It allows the individual to understand themselves as their own author, to understand that the chains which cut into their flesh are made by human themselves, and that it provides the prospect of breaking those chains" (Heydorn 1979, 10).

Peukert builds on Heydorn's reconstruction of the meaning of education with a demand that all learning and thinking, if it is to transcend its cognitive–instrumental form, be once again associated with ethics as responsible, creative human action. The idea of education then takes on a universal perspective: we can only resist radical threats

> if we set out from a linkage of our knowing and acting with an ethics of intersubjective creativity within a universal horizon . . . and only when we are able to realise a comprehensive and differentiated concept of education in the realms of politics and economy and to avoid regressions of consciousness. (Heydorn 1979, 129–30)

The modern experience of the civilizing process has led philosophers—and not only them—to ask whether the dominant form of human rationality within the Occidental tradition does not contain self-destructive tendencies. Opposition to such tendencies, then became a matter of reconstructing rationality to the extent that it represented the capacity to position oneself in a relationship to the totality—and to this extent it also concerns education (cf. Richter 1994). What other hopes and tasks await us?

It strikes me as productive also to draw on another tradition, namely, the considerations of the poet of German romanticism/classicism Friedrich Schiller's anthropology, which he conceived as a pedagogic–aesthetic–political project, in his 1794–1795 letter "On Aesthetic Education" (1966). Here Schiller thematizes the comprehensive internal conflict of contemporary life in all its arenas: the disintegration of society into estates and classes, the narrowing of human experience into professional specializations, the splitting of human capacities themselves between reason and emotion. "The culture itself" (453) was what Schiller identified as the cause of these developments; but he described and analyzed them as the result of an increasing social division of labor and specialization in the wake of the industrialization process.

To what extent, then, is what Schiller had already identified as responsible for social injustice, the noninvolvement of the "heart" in the enterprises of the "head," causally involved in people's current energetic attempts at self-destruction?

THE PERSPECTIVE OF WORLD PEACE

Even if we accept that utopia is possible, the road to any longed-for paradise is by no means guaranteed. In an interview with Carmen Thomas in 1985, the eighty-seven-year-old Elias felt it was entirely possible that the civilizing process would advance so that later generations would wonder how their ancestors could have inflicted violence on each other in the name of differing, ideologically determined world views. This astonishment would be comparable to the strangeness we attach to earlier and temporary religious wars.

The advance of civilization—as we would then experience it—might thus be hopeful. However, the denouement of the interview included something more bitter: Elias feared that it would be more difficult for people as they are currently constituted to manage an extended period of peace than the current situation of crisis.

In conclusion I would like to refer to Immanuel Kant's mildly self-ironical thoughts (1968) on the conditions necessary for the establishment of an "eternal peace." The preface ("Perpetual Peace") to this tract, in which he addresses the relationship between statesman and philosopher in this particular, as well as in more general respects, shall be quoted in full:

> Whether this satirical inscription on a Dutch innkeeper's sign upon which a burial ground was painted had for its object mankind in general, or the rulers of states in particular, who are insatiable of war, or merely the philosophers who dream this sweet dream, it is not for us to decide. But one condition the author of this essay wishes to lay down. The practical politician assumes the attitude of looking down with great self-satisfaction on the political theorist as a pedant whose empty ideas in no way threaten the security of the state, inasmuch as the state must proceed on empirical principles; so the theorist is allowed to play his game without interference from the worldly-wise statesman. Such being his attitude, the practical politician—and this is the condition I make—should at least act consistently in the case of a conflict and not suspect some danger to the state in the political theorist's opinions which are ventured and publicly expressed without any ulterior purpose. By this *clausula salvatoria* the author desires formally and emphatically to deprecate herewith any malevolent interpretation which might be placed on his words.

NOTES

1. See Galtung (1971, 1977); Senghaas (1971, 1974); Gerdes (1984); Röhrs (1984). According to Gerdes, peace research distinguishes between two definitions for peace, a negative one in terms of "absence of war" and a positive one in terms of "transcending structural violence." The condition the latter arrived at would be one of social justice (Galtung 1977). Long-term peace research aims at the study and elimination of the causes of structural violence. On the basis of structural relations of violence between unequal opponents, the current state of the world can be characterized as one of "organised unpeacefulness" (223–24).

2. Elsenhans (1984, chap. 1), Geiger and Mansilla (1983), Sturm (1984). "They are so poor because we are so rich" was the general theme of a big conference on the topic at the University of Bielefeld in the 1980s. See also the analyses of the "politics" of international corporations and cartels in Müller (1983) and Mirow (1979).

3. See Senghaas (1974) and Sivanandan (1980).
4. See von Weizsäcker in Goldschmidt (1982). Central issues here include hostility to outsiders and racism; see Bayer (1985).
5. See Goldschmidt (1982, 120).
6. See Elias (2000); Marcuse (1968).
7. See Schöfthaler and Goldschmidt (1984), regarding problems of the cross-cultural research, inspired by Piaget.

REFERENCES

Adorno, T. W. 1998. *Education after Auschwitz in critical models: Interventions and catchwords*. New York:

Bayer, M. 1985. Weltweite Fremdenfeindlichkeit: Erklärungsansätze und Versuche interkultureller Erziehung. In *Im Schatten des Fortschritts. Gemeinsame Probleme im Bildungsberiehc in Industrienastionen und Ländern der Dritten welt*, ed. C. Wurf (Hg.). Saarbrücken: Breitenbach.

Elias, N. 2000. *The civilizing process*. Oxford: Blackwell Publishers.

Elsenhans, H. 1984. *Nord-Süd-Beziehungen. Geschichte-Politik-Wirtschaft*. Stuttgart.

Finkielkraut, A. 1987. *Die Niederlage des Denkens*. Reinbek.

Galtung, J. 1971. Gewalt, Frieden und Friedensforschung. In *Kritische Friedensforschung*, ed. D. Senghaas (Hg.). Frankfurt: Suhrkamp.

———. 1977. *Strukturelle Gewalt*. Reinbek: Peter Lang.

Geertz, C. 1973. The interpretation of cultures. New York: Basic Books.

Geiger, W., and H. C. F. Mansilla. 1983. *Unterentwicklung: Theorien und Strategien zu ihrer Überwindung*. Frankfurt.

Gerdes, D. 1984. Friedensforschung. In *Lexikon "Dritte Welt,"* ed. D. Nohlen. Reinbek: Rowohlt.

Goldschmidt, D. 1982. Raumschiff Erde. Nachdenken über "Wege in der 'Gefahr.'" In *Physik, Philosophie und Politik. Festschrift für Carl Friedrich von Weizsäcker zum 70*, ed. K. M. Meyer-Abich (Hg.) Geburtstag: München.

Gordon, A. F., and C. Newfield, eds. 1996. *Mapping multiculturalism*. Minneapolis: University of Minnesota Press.

Gramsci, A. 1983. *Marxismus und Literatur: Ideologie, Alltag, literatur.* Hamburg.

Habermas, J. 1981. *Theorie des kommunikativen Handelns. 2 Bde*. Frankfurt: Suhrkamp.

Heydorn, H. J. 1979. *Über den Widerspruch von Bildung und Herrschaft: Bildungtheoretische Schriften, Bd. 2*. Frankfurt: Syndikat.

Huntington, S. P. 1996. *Kampf der Kulturen: Die Neugestaltung der Weltpolitik im 21*. Jahrhundert. München.

Kant, I. 1968. Zum ewigen Frieden: Ein philosophischer Entwurf. In *Schriften zur Anthropologie, Geschichtsphilosophie, Politik und Pädagogik*. Darmstadt.

Krieken, R. V. 1998. *Norbert Elias*. London: Routledge.

Kymlicka, W. 2000. *Multikulturalismus und Demokratie: Über Minderheiten in Staaten und Nationen*. Frankfurt.

Lévi-Strauss, C. 1992. *Strukturale Anthropologie*. Frankfurt: Suhrkamp.

Marcuse, H. 1968. Bemerkungen zu einer Neubestimmung der Kultur. In *Ders, Kultur und Gesellschaft, Bd. 2*. Frankfurt.

McLaren, P. 1997. *Revolutionary multiculturalism: Pedagogies of dissent for the new millennium*. Boulder: Westview Press.

Mirow, K. R. 1979. *Die Diktatur der Kartelle: Zum Beispiel Brasilien. Materialien zur Vermachtung des Weltmarktes*. Reinbek: Rowohlt.

Müller, M. 1983. *Heile und herrsche: Gesundheit in der Dritten Welt und die Politik der Pharma-Industrie*. Berlin.

Nolte, H. H. 1982. *Die eine Welt: Abriss der Geschichte des internationalen Systems*. Hannover.

Nuscheler, F. 1984. *Nirgendwo zu Hause: Menschen auf der Flucht*. Baden-Baden.

Orwell, G. 1961. *1984*. New York: Harcourt, Brace.

Peukert, H. 1984. Über die Zukunft von Bildung. In *Frankfurter Hefte, FH-extra 6*. Reinbek.

Richter, E. 1994. Intercultural education as the responsibility of the school. *Education* 49/50.

Röhrs, H. 1984. Frieden/Friedenspädagogoik. In *Lexikon "Dritte Welt,"* ed. D. Nohlen. Reinbek: Rowohlt.

Schiller, F. 1966. Über die ästhetische Erziehung des Menschen in einer Reihe von Briefen. In *Ders., Werke in 3 Bänden, Bd. 2*. München.

Schöfthaler, T. 1983. Kultur in der Zwickmühle zwischen Relativismus und Universalismus. Zur Aktualität des Steits zwischen kulturrelativistischer und universalistischer Sozialwissenschaft. *Das Argument* 139 (25).

Schöfthaler, T., and D. Goldschmidt, Hg. 1984. *Soziale Struktur und Vernunft: Jean Piagets Modell entwickelten Denkens in der Diskussion kulturvergleichender Forschung*. Frankfurt: Suhrkamp.

Senghaas, D., Hg. 1971. *Kritische Friedensforschung*. Frankfurt: Suhrkamp.

———, Hg. 1974. *Peripherer Kapitalismus: Analysen über Abhängigkeit und Unterentwicklung*. Frankfurt: Suhrkamp.

Sivanandan, A. 1980. Die neue industrielle Revolution: Arbeitsmigration, Imperialismus und disorganische Entwicklung. In *"Dritte Welt" in Europa: Probleme der Arbeitsimmigration,* J. Blaschke and K. Greussing (Hg.). Frankfurt: Syndikat.

Sleeter, C. E., and P. McLaren, eds. 1995. *Multicultural education, critical pedagogy, and the politics of difference*. Albany: State University of New York Press.

Steinmann, H., and A. G. Scherer, Hg. 1998. *Zwischen Universalismus und Relativismus: Philosophische Grundlagenprobleme des interkulturellen Managements*. Frankfurt.

Sturm, R. 1984. Neokolonialismus. In *Lexikon "Dritte Welt,"* Hg. D. Nohlen. Reinbek: Rowohlt.

Taylor, C. 1993. *Multikulturalismus und die Politik der Anerkennung*. Frankfurt.

Williams, R. 1984. *The long revolution*. New York.

18

The Work of Performativity: Staging Social Justice at the University of Southern California

Donna Houston and Laura Pulido

This chapter explores the connections between labor, community, and memory as they were imagined, performed, and articulated by low-wage service workers at the University of Southern California (USC). From 1996 to 2000, food service workers, represented by the Hotel Employees and the Restaurant Employees (HERE; Local 11), waged a protracted struggle against USC's unfair labor practices. The conflict centered on the university's desire to subcontract work, which would have a negative impact on an already highly marginalized workforce, including a reduction in wages, the loss of family health care, tuition remission, and a general exclusion from the "Trojan Family," the much-vaunted community of USC workers, students, and alumni. The workers' struggle at USC speaks directly to the ways in which difference is constructed through place, notions of justice, citizenship, community, and everyday social practices (Shields 1997, 95). We are particularly interested in how the workers used performative strategies as part of their struggle for better work conditions. Our analysis centers on two performances by HERE Local 11 workers, *The USC You Never See*, a street-theater skit performed at USC and in Pershing Square in downtown Los Angeles; and *The Hungry for Justice Campaign*, a rolling fast that traveled throughout California. The workers' performances contributed a great deal to their campaign in several important aspects. First, the performances revealed problematic and contradictory notions of "community" and "place" deployed by USC in its effort to represent and contain the labor conflict in particular ways. Second, they played a pivotal role in increasing workers' consciousness, organizing skills, and sense of efficacy. And finally, the performances were crucial to generating broadbased community support, which was instrumental in resolving the contract dispute.

317

The primary purpose of this chapter is to argue for the importance of collective politics within the realm of performativity in geography. In this regard, we question the ways in which social agency and political action have been articulated by contemporary geographic work on the role of performativity in everyday life (Bell, Binnie, Cream, and Valentine 1994; Nash 2000; Thrift 1997). Particularly influential in much contemporary research on performativity in geography and elsewhere, has been Judith Butler's groundbreaking work (1990, 1997, 1999) that revealed the extent to which identity formation is inscribed by the reiterative (performative) and regulatory power of discourses. Indeed, Butler's work on the compulsory performances of gendered identities has been both critiqued and extended by social theorists and has contributed significantly to the popularity of performativity across the humanities and social sciences, including geography (see work by Bell et al. 1994; Diamond 1996; Kondo 1997; Lott 1995).

While the trope of performativity has provided a necessary corrective to formulaic notions of identity and resistance, we also feel that there is an urgent need to reconnect performativity to historical materialism and collective social action. Indeed, despite providing many useful and imaginative insights, we argue that poststructural and postmodern theories of performativity, while often claiming to be about the everyday practices of ordinary people, has become increasingly abstract. It is in this context that we explore the performativity of the workers' struggle at USC and the ways in which theories of performativity in general might be resituated within the larger literature and politics of oppositional social movements, which are currently undergoing a resurgence in the United States and other parts of the world today. While we are cognizant that much contemporary work on performativity has little to do with theatrical performance in the conventional sense (see Thrift and Dewsbury 2000), we turn to the tradition of radical theater grounded in Marxist theory and practice, to help us make the connections between work and imagination outlined above. Research for this project was conducted over the course of several years, as one of the authors helped organize campus support for the workers. In addition to extensive ethnographic fieldwork and participant observation, a survey and series of interviews were conducted with workers and activists regarding union participation (Pulido 1998). In the first part of the paper we discuss recent debates concerning performativity within human geography. In the second part, we describe the political and economic context of the workers' conflict and discuss how USC responded to it. In the third section, we analyze the workers' performance in terms of memory, identity, resistance, and collective social action.

Performing Resistance or Resisting Performance?

The trope of performativity in human geography has been used to understand the movement or "play" between bodies, texts, identities, and space (see Bell et al. 1994; Nash 2000; Nelson 1999; "Performance" 2000; Rose 1997; Thrift 1997).

There is no denying that understanding how the body inscribes and is inscribed with discourses, representations, and practices is pivotal to an analysis of resistance, in this paper, we consider the continued relevance of performance as an oppositional, critical, and collective form of political and social action. Instead of thinking of performativity in a postmodern sense as being "radically inclusive"— that is, the idea that the self is constituted through compulsory social performances that can be either coercive or enabling—we think of performativity as a dialectical operative—that makes connections between labor, work, and the practices associated with the material production of everyday life with imaginative work as a means of engaging in political action and resistance.

Our emphasis on performance as dialectical practice demonstrates the importance of thinking about cultural politics and performance from a radical materialist perspective. As we demonstrate in the third part of this paper, the workers' performances of *The USC You Never See* and the *Hungry for Justice Campaign*, demonstrate the work of performativity in its historical, geographical, social, and imaginative contexts. The workers at USC engaged the performative not only to expose the ruptures and contradictions of the university's unfair labor practices, but also to enact social justice as the work of collective action and imaginative intervention by intentional social agents. Consequently, we understand performativity as a dialectical set of practices, which are enacted in specific historical and geographical contexts, and that expose the dynamics of power and exploitation while at the same time producing and rehearsing strategies for social and personal transformation.

As such, we are somewhat critical of postmodern theories of performativity that tend to locate both identity formation and resistance on either a discursive or a "nonrepresentational" terrain, where subjects are inscribed by regulatory discourses and normative power relations, or, governed by a set of contingent localized practices (see for example Butler 1990; Thrift 1997). To be fair, Judith Butler and Nigel Thrift's theorizations of performativity differ substantially in that Thrift sees nonrepresentational theory as a means of grasping "performative 'presentations,' 'showings' and 'manifestations of everyday life'" that extend well beyond the realm of discourse and which are clearly enacted within specific spatial contexts (Thrift 1997). However, Butler and Thrift, despite their differences, do share a certain debt to a Foucauldian analytics of power, which maintains that since discourses are fundamentally unstable, so too are the power-knowledge regimes, networks, and practices that give rise to them.

Resistance, in this sense, becomes an increasingly slippery concept to grasp since political action arises at moments of indeterminacy and through nonintentional everyday practices (no matter how insignificant or small) that carry the potential to disrupt normative geographies (Hennessy 1995). In Butler's work, this mode of theorizing is indebted to an uneasy linking of Derrida's deconstructive textual strategies (1976) with Foucault's discursive materialism (1976).[1] Such a reading maintains that since discourses are constantly repeated and performed, they can always be undermined, exposed, and/or subverted. As Foucault suggests "discourse transmits and produces power; it reinforces it, but also undermines and exposes it, renders it fragile and makes it possible to thwart it" (101). Moreover, resistance not only arises from what is inadvertently exposed through the reiterative performance of power, but also by what remains hidden in the gaps of, or supplemental to, the dominant cultural logic. What is important here, is that postmodern theories of performativity offer a nonintentionalist account of the world where identity formation and modes of resistance are decentered and rendered intelligible through multiple networks of power, signification, and embodiment.

Thus from a postmodern perspective, it is precisely "the unstable improvisations within our deep cultural performances," that "can expose the fissures, ruptures and revisions that have settled into continuous reenactment" (Diamond 1996, 2). John-David Dewsbury (2000, 472) also takes up this notion of performativity when he argues that, "the performative is the gap, the rupture, the spacing that unfolds the next moment allowing change to happen." In this regard, performativity is not about what one is (especially in a radical humanist or empirical sense), but rather, what one does, or more specifically, by what is rendered visible in the act of doing (Dewsbury 2000; Thrift 1997). The continual movement or play between discourses, bodies, identities, and places registered by the performative gesture, continually troubles hegemonic social and spatial relations which appear to us as "natural," by threatening to expose the performance of power as a performance. For human geographers, particularly Daniel Bell and colleagues (1994), Dewsbury (2000), Longhurst (2000), Thrift (1997), the performative provides an important connective between identity, power, and the construction of normative geographies, what Catherine Nash (2000, 656) calls "microgeographies of habitual practices," in which the body becomes a performative site upon which multiple social identities are continually encoded and potentially resisted.[2]

Positing subjectivity, or more specifically, the processes of subject formation as performative, however, is not without its difficulties. As we have already suggested, the emphasis on nonintentionality in postmodern accounts of performativity, whether they are inspired by Butler, Thrift, or Foucault, mark the move toward a conception of human agency as the product of the compulsory "play" of discourses and practices. In line with this, moments seized for resistance emerge when ruptures in deeply embedded cultural performances appear at times of uncertainty or indeterminacy. Since resistance can only take place when the fiction of identity is exposed as a fiction, this implies a notion of human agency that is the product of cultural inscriptions and habitual practices increasingly abstracted from social, spatial, and economic production. This has the effect of mystifying material relations and radically reduces the scale of resistance to the site of the individual body, thereby diminishing the power and viability of collective political and social action.

The resulting reification of discursive representations as a form of materialism, which is particularly evident in Butler's work, has been well documented (Ebert 1996; Hennessy 1995; Nelson 1999). However, nonrepresentational accounts of performativity also run a similar risk in that they reify the minituae of everyday practices and replace materiality (historical and embodied praxis) with a fluid and contingent notion of "embodiment," which implies physicality and sensuous experience, yet is suspiciously disconnected from the laboring body and contradictions of economic and social production (see, also, Callard 1998).

Moreover, while we do not wish to deny the power of discourse, embodied practice or disavow the many forms that resistance may take (Cresswell 1996; Miller 2000; Nagar 2000; Pile and Keith 1997; Robinson 2001; J. Scott 1990), postmodern configurations of performativity can run the risk of fetishizing resistance to the point of encompassing everything and nothing. Such theorizing tends to conflate the discursive with the social, while at the same time devaluing oppositions, and thus oppositional politics, as being oppressive and totalizing. This has the effect of emphasizing the politics of cultural difference (which is concerned almost exclusively with issues of representation and embodied practices) at the expense of an analysis of the politics of economic difference "as the struggle of the exploited and oppressed for systemic social *emancipation*" (Sahay 1998, emphasis in original). This distinction is crucial because the social reality of late capitalist cultures is that daily life continues to be structured by the biggest binary of all: the division between capital and labor. Indeed, for many people throughout the world, questions regarding the body and resistance are life and death struggles, embedded in the very material struggle of how to keep one's body alive (Price 2000).

As David Harvey (2000) has suggested, "the body is not monadic nor does it float freely in some ether of culture, discourses, and representations" (130). For low-wage workers fighting for job security, improved wages, dignity, and better opportunities for their children, Harvey's point is not insignificant. Given that the vast majority of Local 11 workers are Latino immigrants, they are acutely aware of the migrations their bodies have made from the "Third" to the "First" world; of the racial and class geography of Los Angeles which restrict their bodies to the ghetto and barrio; as well as the social boundaries which destine them to be low-wage workers rather than faculty or administrators at USC. It is within this political and economic context that workers' performances must be understood as not only a form of embodied social critique, but also a struggle over the means to reproduce one's body. While some postmodern theorists might critique the workers' performances at USC for their "metaphysics of presence," we believe that such a presence, secured through the performance of work, place, and memory, not only exposed asymmetrical power relations, but also posited workers as historically and geographically specific subjects with multiple social identities as workers, immigrants, and Latino/as. The performances were thus crafted with a number of goals in mind, including challenging the administration, engaging the audience, empowering and inspiring workers, and locating their campaign within the larger historical context of Latino workers' struggles in the region.

REVOLUTIONARY BODIES AND POPULAR PERFORMANCE

To bridge the gap between postmodern performative theory and oppositional forms of collective action, we turn to Marxian theatrical practices, which have emphasized a long tradition of embodied social critique and imaginative political intervention. Some critics, such as Carlson (2000), have argued that few contemporary performances fall within the tradition of such explicitly oppositional theatre as Boal's *Theatre of the Oppressed*, Luis Valdez's *El Teatro Campesino* (Broyles-Gonzalez 1994), or the guerrilla theater of the 1960s. Instead, in keeping with the rise of new social movements (Handler 1992; Jasper 1997), contemporary theater focuses largely on the various tensions and dissimulations of postmodern identity politics. While this may be true to a large extent, it overlooks many class-based struggles, including those that manage to link material and identity-based politics and their practices (Anner 1996). For example, in Los Angeles, one of the best examples of Marxian theatrical praxis has been embodied by the Bus Riders Union (BRU; Sindicato de Pasajeros), in their much-popularized struggle against transit racism. BRU members performed skits on Los Angeles Metropolitan Transit Authority buses and on city streets as a way of both demonstrating the racial and class biases of Los Angeles's transportation system and as a means of encouraging people to join the BRU (Mann and Dutton 1996; see also www.thestrategy-center.org). The workers' performances at USC fall within this tradition of performance and labor activism in Los Angeles, and in fact, there is a class and racial overlap between the BRU and USC's low-wage workers.

Performance as embodied social critique has enjoyed a long and lively tradition in Marxist-inspired theatrical practice (Boal 1993; Brecht 1964; Case and Reinelt 1991; Valdez 1971). The performative goal of radical theater is to serve as social critique and to articulate alternatives to the oppressive regimes of capitalism, imperialism, patriarchy, and white supremacy. In this approach to theatre, the performative operates dialectically with the material relations of production. As we have already suggested, dialectical and revolutionary theatrical practice makes explicit connections between economic and social production. For example, writing on Bertold Brecht's *Epic Theater*, Walter Benjamin (1968) observed that revolutionary performance seeks to develop actions as the representation of social conditions. Brecht achieved this by breaking down bourgeois theatrical conventions (especially those exemplified by Naturalist theater) that mystified class power relations. He achieved this by constructing minimalist and mechanical sets that were designed to expose the actual workings of theatrical production, and by challenging the passivity of the audience by transforming spectators into actors. Brechtian theatre exposed the operational and ideological contexts of performativity, in other words, the production of the production. As Bryant-Bertail (1991) explains:

> Epic theater should not only naively reflect our images of historical change, causality, and agency, but expose these images as ideological discourse, to catch them in the act of mechanical self-reproduction, so to speak. The "dialectical" theater

would demonstrate human existence as a work-in-progress by openly pointing to itself as an operating model of that work. (20)

Brecht's performativity resonates with embodied revolutionary praxis in at least three important ways. First, it maintains that "radical social change begins with the actions and gestures of everyday life" (Hyman 1997, 81). Such an observation is in keeping with the burgeoning literature on everyday forms of resistance, which is sometimes the only avenue available to subordinated populations (de Certeau 1984; Enstad 1998; Mullings 1999; J. Scott 1990). Second, it situates performance as both critical and imaginative praxis. By interpreting performance as a form of political practice, workers/actors are given the opportunity to rehearse resisting the boss/landlord/police, or whoever the oppressor may be. Paulo Freire's observation (1990) that praxis entails "reflection and action upon the world in order to transform it" (33), is central to understanding the development of worker consciousness and the performances themselves. Finally, revolutionary performance, as Raymond Williams (1989) suggests, exposes asymmetrical power relations and contradictions while presenting the bourgeois world as "domineering" and "grotesque" (93). This underscores Bakhtin's notion in *Rabelais and His World* (1984), of performance as a social inversion that temporarily turns "the world upside down" in order to critique or parody dominant power structures. Performativity as dialectical praxis, understood in this sense, operates simultaneously as a space of possibility and becoming, and as a mechanism for working through existing social contradictions by making them visible. As it can be seen, proletarian performance and theatrical productions function both as a "weapon" of class struggle and as a vehicle for educating audiences about oppressive and exploitative situations, sustaining worker consciousness and organizing efforts, and supporting campaigns and strikes (Hyman 1997, 2).

As we discuss in detail in the third part of this paper, the performances of *The USC You Never See* and the *Hungry for Justice* campaign illustrate the fluidity and dynamism of the workers' identities and social space, without severing them from the larger historical and geographical processes that shape the social realities of race, class, and gender formation. In both cases, workers' theatricalized protest served to perform, imagine, and bring into being an alternative configuration of social justice. The workers and activists were thus able to assert their presence as social agents, and in doing so (re)inscribe racial and class politics onto the social and material landscape of the campus. In particular, they revealed the contradictions embedded in definitions of community, place, and memory as imposed by USC's official culture. In addition, the workers connected their struggle with the wider labor movement of Southern California, which has been at the forefront of social movement unionism (Cleeland 1996; Savage 2000; Silverstein 1996). By engaging the performative as a form of social critique, the workers at USC linked their political struggle with other workers in California both past and present, and demonstrated the ways in which labor activism and unionism in Los Angeles has been transformed both politically and culturally in recent years.

(RE)PLACING LABOR: THE POLITICAL
ECONOMY OF USC'S LABOR CONFLICTS

USC was established in 1880 and is currently the largest private university in the western United States. Originally built on the periphery of downtown, USC is now located in what has become known as South Central, and is the largest private employer in Los Angeles County. Despite being situated in one of the poorest areas of the region, USC has been derisively dubbed as the "University of Spoiled Children," as it has, for most of its history, served a white, wealthy, conservative constituency, and was considered academically inferior to its cross-town public school rival, UCLA. Figure 18.1, published by the university, seeks to subvert this pejorative title by emphasizing not only the extent to which the institution has changed, but also the supportive environment that it provides for its students.

And USC has indeed changed. Beginning in the 1980s, USC sought to remake itself by becoming a serious research institution, attracting a more diverse and better-prepared student body, and renegotiating its relationship with the surrounding neighborhood (Sample 2001; see the spring 2001 issue of *USC Trojan Family Magazine,* 33). The contemporary social and political landscape of USC has been described as follows:

> Though it is a largely white, prosperous enclave surrounded by the impoverished black and Latino neighborhoods of South Central Los Angeles, USC has developed a remarkable form of protection—by bonding with inner-city residents in one of the most ambitious social outreach programs of any university in the nation. (Hornblower 1999, 71)

USC's efforts to cultivate a positive relationship with the local residents of South Central was felt to have paid off in 1992 when during the civil unrest that erupted after the Rodney King verdict, USC emerged unscathed. The university responded in two telling ways. First, it built a wrought-iron fence around the campus to further insulate itself from the neighborhood. Second, and to the university's credit, it decided to increase its "good neighbor" efforts to enhance the community's investment in USC. Such efforts were recognized when USC was named "College of the Year 2000," largely due to its extensive community outreach (Hornblower 1999).

Such shifts cannot be understood outside of the dramatic demographic and economic changes that southern California underwent in the 1980s and 1990s. Although southern California has always been ethnically diverse, Asian and Latino immigration grew significantly during this period and changed the face of Los Angeles (Allen and Turner 1997). Factors including the Mexican debt crisis, Central American civil unrest, the 1965 Immigration Reform Act, as well as already-existing networks, all contributed to increased immigration (Ethington 2000; Sabagh and Bozorgmehr 1996). According to the 2000 census, Latinos now constitute 44.6 percent of Los Angeles county, whites compose 31 percent, while Asian/Pacific Islanders and Africans registered 10 percent and 12 percent,

UNIVERSITY OF SPOILED CHILDREN?

A favorite stunt of rival football fans from UCLA, Stanford and Notre Dame is to wave their car keys and credit cards in cadence to the Trojan Marching Band as it plays "Tribute to Troy," a march our opponents love to hate. This amusing ritual is meant to symbolize their contention that USC is the "University of Spoiled Children."

If you have heard the myth promoted by students at other colleges that USC's student body is rich and spoiled, **consider this:**

· *Among the nation's most selective universities, our student body is also one of the most ethnically and racially diverse,* and draws students from all fifty states and more than one hundred countries.

· *USC distributes $200 million in financial aid; over 60 percent of our students receive assistance.*

· *More than 60 percent of USC students volunteer in community-service programs in neighborhoods around campus and throughout L.A.*

And consider this:

· *The student-to-faculty ratio is 14-to-1;*

· *The average class size is 26 students;*

· *Full-time faculty teach the vast majority of our courses;*

· *Students can get all the classes they need in order to graduate in four years;*

· *USC grads get great jobs, attend the best graduate and professional schools in the country (including our own) and are supported by the Trojan Family, a network of nearly a quarter million alumni.*

So, maybe we do spoil our students—and we intend to keep it that way.

USC

Figure 18.1. University of Southern California Advertisement Subverting the School's Image as the "University of Spoiled Children." http://homer.ssd.census.gov/cdrom/lookup.

respectively. One major consequence of these changes has been a large supply of low-wage, nonwhite labor (A. Scott 1996; Los Angeles Alliance for a New Economy 2000).

These demographic changes have also been accompanied by geographic shifts, with important implications for both USC's workforce and its relationship with the surrounding community. Whites, sustaining a shift begun in the post–World War II era, have continued to move toward the outer suburbs (Allen and Turner 1997, 51; *Los Angeles Times* 2001; Pulido 2000). People of color have also participated in widespread suburbanization (Johnson and Roseman 1990; Li 1998; Texeira 2001), however, due to immigration, economic polarization and continued housing discrimination, segregation is still a serious problem (Ethington 2000). The end result of these many changes has been the creation of a dynamic South Central, a poor area that is not only growing in size, but is home to both a large African American and Latino population (Allen and Turner 1997).

While popular representations of South Central Los Angeles, as seen in music, film, and television often depict a solidly black community, such is not the case (Valle and Torres 2000, chapter 2). Parts of South Central, are in fact, 50 percent Latino (Tobar 1990). This is important when considering USC's nonacademic workforce. While the faculty and administration are overwhelmingly white (and reside in the suburbs), the staff is racially mixed, and low-wage workers are almost exclusively black and brown, with the majority being Latino. Many of these workers come from the surrounding community.

The composition of USC's workforce reflects the economic and racial polarization that characterizes the region as a whole (Ong and Blumenberg 1996). Like other major cities, Los Angeles's economy has become increasingly polarized with the rise of the service sector, which produces both high- and low-paying jobs. Southern California is unique, however, in that manufacturing is still important to the region. While on the one hand, an abundance of low-wage labor has contributed to a partial reindustrialization, there has also been a simultaneous downgrading of manufacturing employment (A. Scott 1996). As a result of all these shifts, Los Angeles is now the "capital" of the working poor in the United States. Although Latinos constitute 40 percent of the workforce, they make up 73 percent of the working poor. In contrast, whites are 39 percent of the workforce, but only 13 percent of the working poor (Los Angeles Alliance for a New Economy 2000, 17). In short, despite the existence of a stable middle-class community of color, whites are clearly the most privileged group, while people of color and immigrants constitute the majority of those in poverty.

IMMIGRANTS, LABOR, AND POLITICS IN LOS ANGELES

Commentators frequently dismiss Los Angeles's poverty and inequality as simply a function of immigration. There is strong sentiment that immigrant poverty and hardships are entirely justifiable and acceptable, since they are, after all, immigrants (Hondagneu-Sotelo 1995). For example, in discussing the fact that undocumented children do not qualify for resident college tuition, one woman wrote in a letter to the editor, "Regardless that they came here as children with their parents, it does not erase the fact that they are criminals who think nothing of flouting our laws. They should be grateful for the education they have already received. Why these people [are referred to] as Americans is beyond my comprehension. One does not become a citizen simply by living here for a long time" (Lieberman 2001, B9; see also, Leovy 2001). This practice of rationalizing extreme inequality reached its highpoint with Proposition 187, in which California voters sought to exclude undocumented residents from all social services, including education and health-care. Though many decried such a hostile move, often overlooked was the extent to which such a political project is predicated upon *not* acknowledging immi-grants as *workers*. By focusing attention solely on immigrants' legal status and con-sumption of state services, a highly racialized picture has been created of an ex-ploding mass of Latino parasites that burden communities and institutions: Latino immigrants are not constructed as workers, or members of the working class—they are "illegals," and thus not deserving of consideration.

While it is easy to blame such initiatives on unethical individuals, such as then governor Pete Wilson, or a racist electorate, significant responsibility lies with the labor movement itself. During the 1980s, unions continued a long-standing tradition of treating immigrants as the enemy of organized labor. This, coupled with resistance to accepting women and people of color into its ranks, despite their growing numbers ("Building on Diversity: The New Unionism" 1993; Needleman 1993; Savage 1996), left the door wide open for a series of bitter at-tacks. Immigrants became, in effect, the scapegoats for California's economic woes during the 1980s and 1990s (Davis 1995). The following anecdote suggests the level of resistance on the part of organized labor to its new constituency:

> In L.A. labor's prize moment of idiocy, the leadership of the Hotel Employees and Restaurant Employees Union spent $100,000 in a 1984 lawsuit to ensure union meetings would *not* be translated into Spanish for their membership—70 percent of whom were Latino. (Gardetta 1993, 23)

Shortly after this debacle, María Elena Durazo, a Latina union organizer, was elected president of Local 11 and radically reoriented the organization to meet the needs of its members (Milkman and Wong 2000; Siegel 1993; Spichen 1997).

Though one cannot ignore the structural problems that confronted labor in the 1980s, including deindustrialization and attacks by then-president Ronald Reagan, it must be recalled that long ago organized labor consciously chose "bread and butter" unionism over social movement unionism, thus precluding the building of a radical politics (Davis 1986). This shift included the abandon-ment of serious organizing. Only when unions were willing to embrace a di-verse workforce, return to the nuts and bolts of organizing, and adopt a more democratic and activist model, did its situation improve. Key to the rebirth of organized labor have been service unions, including the Service Employees In-ternational Union (SEIU) and the Hotel Employees and the Restaurant Employ-ees (Banks 1991; Johnston 1994; Lerner 1991; Savage 2000; Wial 1993). Partly because their membership is overwhelmingly female, nonwhite, and immi-grant, both unions have had to devise new ways of operating and appealing to its membership (Savage 1996). It is also these unions that have been at the cutting edge of a revival of social movement unionism, which includes direct action and militant protest, democratic participation, worker leadership, and fostering ties to the community (Hoyos 1994; Johnston 1994; Scipes 1992). This new type of union culture was exactly what was needed to wage a successful campaign at USC.

ERASING LABOR FROM THE USC "COMMUNITY"

That USC sought to subcontract its low-wage service workers should not be surprising. Not only is subcontracting becoming a preferred means of organizing labor ("Privatization and Contracting Out" 1988), but institutions of higher learning are becoming increasingly like private corporations in their management styles (Nast and Pulido 2000). The first indication that the university wished to alter its more Fordist work arrangement came in the summer of 1994 when the university experimented with subcontracting.[3] The food-service workers have been represented by HERE for approximately twenty-five years, when they fought a bitter battle for the right to unionize. Many of these workers are routinely laid off for the summer simply because there is less to do. Though the university and workers disagreed on several important issues during contract negotiations in 1995, the stumbling block was subcontracting (Deemer 1995). USC wanted the right to subcontract out summer work, rather than ensuring that Local 11 members be given any available employment. Local 11 decided to fight this move for at least two reasons. First, subcontracting was becoming a rampant problem and could potentially undermine union contracts. Second, given that USC is the largest private employer in the county, its labor practices help set the standards for the region, thus it was a battle worth taking on, despite the fact that it lasted over four years.

Given that USC desired to subcontract its low-wage workforce, its opposition to workers' demands was perhaps inevitable. Nonetheless, *how* the university sought to sway public opinion and workers' response to it, is worth examining in brief. USC invoked several distinct social and spatial strategies to dismiss workers' claims, including abstracting labor from the operational contexts of the university, and defining the "Trojan Family" in an exclusionary way. In this section, we consider how universities in general may be interpreted as nonwork sites, and how USC deployed its community initiative as a substitute for addressing labor issues and its role as an employer.

Universities as Nonwork Sites

The university as both a real and imagined space represents a site where institutional and cultural power is inscribed and embedded in the very architecture of place (McDowell 1999). Universities are not only extremely powerful institutions, but their particular role as sites of education, knowledge, and truth, contribute to their hegemonic position. With its long association with the production of masculine and European forms of knowledge, the space of the university is the virtual embodiment of instrumental reason. This is especially true of USC, which until recently, has been considered the school of choice for wealthy whites. Not only was USC's early history marred by anti-Semitism, but traditionally it has not been receptive to working class communities and people of color. Despite such clear exclusions and biases, it is precisely because the university is represented as a place of "progress" or as a repository of enlightenment values, that it has been able to naturalize its own privilege while maintaining invisible boundaries that exclude "Others."

By presenting itself as a modern site of education rooted in the enlightenment project, USC was able to pretend it was not engaged in the *business* of higher education, and thus, not a site of a labor conflict. As the Reverend James Lawson, a member of Clergy and Laity United for Economic Justice, who actively supported the workers, commented, "unlike a normal corporation, USC is able to clothe its actions as natural because it is an institution of learning" (quoted in Medina 1999, 19). The representation of USC as a modern and enlightened institution also served to disavow the university's role in producing economic and cultural differences. Essentially, power only becomes explicit to those who do not feel they are permitted "to enter," either on the basis of race, gender, sexuality, class, and/or ability.

This dynamic of exclusion and the erasure of labor was illustrated dramatically at a fundraiser when USC alumni and friends confirmed that the "Trojan Family" was defined as wealthy white alumni and not low-wage service workers. This particular event, which targeted alumni, was attended almost entirely by white, upper-class guests. Local 11 activists decided that it was a valuable opportunity not only to alert members of the "Trojan Family" that an unresolved labor dispute existed, but also to remind the administration that workers would make their presence known at inopportune moments, until the conflict was resolved. As the master of ceremonies, entertainer Steve Allen, was greeting the guests, approximately twenty-five workers interrupted his monologue as they burst across the stage carrying union banners, chanting "no justice, no peace!" and distributing leaflets. To show their support for the administration, the audience, almost as if on cue, rose and began singing the USC Trojan's fight song. This was a remarkable display of how "Family" status was reserved for alumni, students, donors, and properly behaved faculty and staff, rather than low-wage, nonwhite workers.

As parts of its effort to ideologically exclude workers, USC developed a highly spatialized conception of "community" centered on USC's relationship with the surrounding neighborhood. The notion of community deployed by USC was highly selective and served to reinforce the separation of production and reproduction, which in turn, reinforced the image of the university as a site of "enlightened" abstract space. Our purpose here is not to critique the efforts of students, administrators, and faculty at USC to forge a better relationship with the residents of South Central. However, we are critical of the ways in which such efforts were repackaged by USC's official culture and deployed as a strategy to obfuscate the university's own unfair labor practices.

The university's community initiatives are indeed numerous and impressive (Holland 2001; Hornblower 1999), but it is perhaps most proud of its community education projects. This includes its extensive service-learning program (Joint Educational Project), the Neighborhood Academic Initiative, which helps prepare local children to attend USC by offering them supplemental training plus scholarships, and the Family of Five Schools:

> USC's "Family of Five Schools" [is] an unprecedented effort, begun in 1994, to target the university's vast resources on a close-in area. The aim is to transform five nearby schools . . . with a total of 8,000 students into no less than, the best schools in the entire city of L.A. . . . The intense focus, with one program layering on another, has woven a safety net around the children, their families, and their teachers. (Hornblower 1999, 73)

USC is understandably proud of its record and should be commended for engaging with the ghetto and barrio in a positive way.[4] Nonetheless, there remains a number of profound contradictions between USC's community outreach and labor policies that warrant interrogation. First, USC deployed the notion of "community" as an inclusive term that served to suppress difference under a rhetoric of "common goals." This was an important strategy for the university administration who consistently represented the labor dispute as disruptive toward the achievement of common goals, and which subsequently constructed the striking workers as being "out of place" (Cresswell 1996). This was vividly demonstrated when USC secured a restraining order against both HERE Local 11 and SEIU Local 1877, both of whom were organizing campus workers at the time. Arguing that the unions' activities were disruptive to the primary function of the university, the union activists were only allowed to congregate in groups of four or fewer on campus and the surrounding streets (*University of Southern California v. Local 11* 1996). Not only was worker organizing considered contrary to USC's purpose, but so too were students who wished to learn about economic justice by supporting the workers. According to the chief of campus security, "student labor . . . supporters can't demonstrate with union members and claim not to be on the union's team" (in Trendowski 1997, 6). Consequently, for a period of time, the university threatened to apply the court injunction against students, and on one occasion a student activist (a geography student, no less) wearing a bright red union T-shirt was held by campus security for several hours and questioned (Whang 1997). In short, the idea of "community" implied a false inclusivity, since it was USC that defined what should be valued and how. This was not lost on either the workers or students:

> There is something your university administration wants you to know . . . the message is . . . "USC is not an elitist institution. USC is not a school whose sole purpose

is for rich kids to meet each other and forge lifelong business connections." A message to this affect appears every year in the brochure distributed to potential applicants. And of course, it's true.

It sometimes makes you wonder, though. . . . What are these university administrators trying to hide? A possible answer is revealed by their recent actions toward a student group that has vocally supported USC janitorial workers. . . . The student support committee, instead of being allowed the free-speech rights given to students . . . has been placed under the restraining order on union representatives, with its markedly lower free speech parameters. (*Daily Trojan* 1997, emphasis in original)

In what follows, we show how Local 11 workers actively challenged official versions of "community" and "the place of labor" at USC at multiple geographical scales by relying upon performative strategies.

SCALING PERFORMANCE: LABOR, MEMORY, AND THE STRUGGLE FOR JUSTICE AT USC

As we have seen, USC sought to erase labor from public representations of the campus, and to reframe the conflict as one centered on an ideal of "community." Given this situation, Local 11 realized it had to reassert the centrality of labor to the conflict. Fortunately, a renewed labor movement, plus widespread community support were available to the union (Hondagneu-Sotelo and Lemma 2001). The workers realized that "jumping scales" (see Herod 1996), was one of the most effective ways that they could take control of the discourse and redefine it as a *labor struggle*. Engaging in a politics of resistance that deployed both performance and forms of cultural memory was central to this effort. Since USC was intent on erasing workers from its institutional landscape, the union's performance dramatically reinscribed the social relations of an exploitive employer (USC) and oppressed workers (Local 11 members).

Acknowledging that workers are complex individuals occupying multiple subject positions, the union and its members forged a political culture appropriate to a workforce comprised overwhelmingly of Latino immigrants. Though the union never sought to portray the conflict as a strictly racial one (whites versus Latinos), it actively exploited the racial/ethnic power differential to further malign the image of USC. Not only did USC's policies contribute to the racial polarization and economic inequality that characterize Los Angeles, but the union used the workers' identities as a resource in mobilizing both workers and supporters. Consequently, while this was very much a labor issue, it was also a Latino one, enabling the union to draw on ethnic specific support from organizations like the student group, el Movimiento Estudiantil Chicano de Aztlán, Latino politicians and community leaders as well as the prominent Mexican American Legal Defense and Education Fund. Local 11 essentially implemented Neil Smith's observation (1993) that scale can be used to either constrain struggles within fixed borders, or expand them into new spaces (106). In this case, the workers' performances were intended to jump scales in two distinct but related spheres: among labor activists and among Chicanos/Latinos.

The degree to which union culture has changed is readily evident in places like Los Angeles (Cleeland 1996). Because of its racial and ethnic diversity, large immigrant population, and economic structure, the city has emerged as a leader in the new, militant, social movement unionism (Milkman and Wong 2000; Pulido 1998; Savage 2000; Waldinger et al. 1997). As evidence of the region's growing labor prominence, for example, the AFL-CIO executive committee switched its annual meeting from Florida to Los Angeles in 1996 (Cleeland 1996). Key to the transformation of the labor movement has been the development of close ties with the larger community. Local 11's connections with social justice, civil rights, student, environmental, clergy, and peace organizations have served to create a dense fabric of resistance that was able to take on USC.

THE PLACE OF LABOR: PERFORMING SOCIAL JUSTICE AT USC

We now present two theatrical interventions enacted by USC workers. In both cases, workers' theatricalized protest served to perform, imagine, and bring into being an alternative configuration of social justice. In particular, the workers and activists purposefully enacted racial and working class politics on the social and material landscape of the university, and demonstrated the contradictions embedded in USC's official version of community, place, and memory. In the skit *The USC You Never See* (Haitsuka 1995, 1), workers challenged the progressive and enlightened image of the university by emphasizing the class and exploitive nature of the relationship between administrators, faculty, and students on the one hand, and the workers who serve food and clean offices and bathrooms on the other. They did this by exposing the naturalization of race and class oppression in the USC "community." The play was performed in three parts by members of HERE Local 11 and enacted workers' frustrations with the contract negotiations. Indeed, this performance clearly exposes exploitative economic conditions and presents USC's articulation of "community" as domineering and grotesque. The first scene was performed in English and the second and third scenes performed primarily in Spanish, with English narration. Below is a short summary of the performance:

> In the first scene, two members of the "USC Administration" discussed the ramifications of employing union members all year:
> The audience booed the administrator dressed in a black graduation gown and rainbow cowl, who used phrases such as, "We need to run this place more like a business," and, "Let's get some cheap workers in here . . . these people can live on air."
> The second scene depicted non-union workers as slaves, chained to a contractor. The robed administrator clapped the well dressed, cigar-smoking, whip-toting man on the back.

In the final scene, the union workers confronted the administration. The administrator in the graduation gown held up a sign, which represented USC's "Strategic Plan," a 15-page document that, among other things, touts the university as "the largest private employer in Los Angeles."

One of the union workers snatched the sign from him, crumpled it up and threw it back in his face, accompanied by a roar of applause and cheering.[5] (Haitsuka 1995, 1)

The skit was performed at both USC and in downtown Los Angeles. In both cases large numbers of students, union members, and staff and workers were the audience. Because administrators did not attend such performances there was an open and celebratory air to the events. Not only was a diverse group of individuals working together and forging a new community, but people felt energized and positive about empowering themselves and others. Indeed, taking over public space and participating (either as actors or spectators) was one of the genuine pleasures of the campaign (see Jasper 1997). Though we are focusing on formal performances, it must be recalled that they were just one part of a much larger campaign that included petitions, strikes, slow-downs, community pressures, civil disobedience, and fasts. Figures 18.2 and 18.3 hint at the size of the mobilization that Local 11 was able to organize and the context in which the performances were "consumed."

In *The USC You Never See*, theater quite literally becomes a site of ethical engagement that clearly troubled USC's official definition of community by explicitly rendering the university as a site of employment. Power was made explicit

Figure 18.2. Workers' Protest in Pershing Square, Downtown Los Angeles, with Police in Foreground. Photo courtesy of Local 11.

Figure 18.3.   Local 11 Supporters Holding a Banner Referring to Cesar Chavez and the United Farm Workers. Photo courtesy of Local 11.

via the symbolism of the administrator in the black graduation gown, a marker of privilege and cultural capital, and the figure of the contractor, who is represented as a slave owner. Significantly, the skit with its references to "we need to run this place more like a business" and the cigar-toting slave owner, fore-grounded the ways in which the university sought to abstract labor and focus the dispute around the economic bottom line. Moreover, the actors saw the degree to which university practices drew on a heavily racialized discourse. The university's justification of cheap labor is based on racist assumptions that African Americans and Latinos "can live on air." The idea that the university is a site of the production of abstract space (that is, a space of capitalist accumulation) was abundantly clear to the workers who attempted to expose power hidden in the architecture of the university, and the specific strategies deployed by USC in order to erase the signs of its own production.

The USC You Never See challenged the aggressive self-promotion of the university that touted community outreach, economic prosperity, and notions of justice on the one hand; and naturalized exploitation and reduced the workers' struggle as simply disruptive to the "Trojan Family" on the other. The comparison of the workers' struggle at USC with the institution of slavery resonated with the long history of racialized labor exploitation in the United States and with the sentiment of many workers that the political economy of USC's "enlightened self interest" in the neighborhood of South Central Los Angeles, perhaps more closely resembles the political economy of the plantation.

While *The USC You Never See* was a highly formalized performance, *The Hungry for Justice* campaign drew primarily on both ritualized performance and oppositional cultural memory as a way of engaging in and embodying a politics of resistance. Marita Sturken (1997, 19) defines cultural memory as "memory that is shared outside the avenues of formal historical discourse," yet is entangled with cultural products and cultural meanings. While *The USC You Never See* was intended to challenge the university's identity and representation of work and community, the primary purpose of *Hungry for Justice* was to expand the scale and visibility of the workers' struggle, as well as to actively build broad-based support for Local 11 workers throughout California. This was achieved by the workers who actively drew upon the memory and history of labor activism in the Southwest, particularly that of the United Farm Workers (UFW).

In 1998 the workers decided to engage in an *ayuno*, or fast. This form of protest was familiar to USC workers because not only is fasting a regular part of Catholicism and indigenous spirituality, but it also has a long history in oppositional Mexican struggles. A group of workers, union organizers, and supporters (including USC faculty, students, and staff), participated collectively in a five-day fast. Each day included a service held at the University Church, as well as vigils and rallies to support the fasters (Rorlich 1998). The workers believed that the fast was not only an effective publicity and organizing tool, but also recognized the personal and spiritual benefits it generated for the fasters and the larger community. Consequently, they initiated a second fast in the spring of 1999. Durazo, the president of Local 11, participated in the fast, but then decided to pursue a hunger strike until the conflict was resolved. After eleven days and facing irreparable harm, she ended her strike, but not wanting to lose momentum, union organizers decided to transform the hunger strike into a rotating fast. Under this scenario, the fast was rotated from person to person every twenty-four hours for a four-month period. This allowed the fast to travel geographically to various parts of the city and state, as well as among diverse groups, including politicians, clergy, unions, Latino groups, and Hollywood celebrities.

Large institutions and organizations committed to maintaining the fast anywhere from a few days to several weeks. So, for instance, the faculty, staff, and students of USC maintained the fast for three weeks, which, not coincidentally, turned out to be the final weeks of the campaign, as the contract was settled while the USC community was fasting (Luna 1999; Medina 1999). The result of the rotating fast was that it expanded the scale of the workers' struggle by reaching out to an ever-larger audience and by transforming spectators into performers.

Since fasting is the act of *not* eating, organizers had to devise a way to collectivize and ritualize this form of protest. "As forms of enacted meaning," Peter McLaren writes that "rituals enable social actors to frame, negotiate, and articulate their phenomenological existence as social, cultural and moral beings" (1999, 50). Thus, for the workers and their supporters at USC, not only was it necessary to *perform* the fast for the sake of publicity, it was also necessary for the sake of the fasters themselves. Maintaining a water only diet from one to three days is not easy, and the organizers quickly realized that collective action was necessary to raise the spirits of the fasters and remind them of the larger political reason for their sacrifice. Part of this was accomplished by the "transition ceremony," a form of ritualized performance that was enacted when the fast was rotated from one person, or set of people, to the next.

During the three weeks that the USC community fasted, all fasters and union supporters would meet in the center of campus at noon. This site, which is frequently depicted in university promotional brochures as emblematic of the Trojan Family, became instead, the site of resistance on behalf of USC's most subordinated workers. At the transition ceremony, fasters would introduce themselves, explain why they were fasting, offer updates on the struggle, and conclude with a series of chants and claps in support of the workers. This was accompanied by a passing of a simple wooden cross that Cesar Chávez, cofounder of the UFW, had worn during his numerous fasts. The cross had been lent to Local 11 by Helen Chávez (Cesar's widow), and one faster would be chosen to wear the cross for twenty-four hours as emblematic of the group's commitment and solidarity. Given the significance and symbolism of Chávez's cross, there was a friendly competition to see who would get to wear it, with the wearer solemnly acknowledging the responsibility of caring for this historical artifact. Such collectivized rituals were essential to breaking the individual experience of fasting.

The presence and memory of the UFW and Chavez was constant throughout the fast and is worth considering in some detail, as it raises important issues about the politics of cultural memory. Indeed, the memory and acknowledgement of the UFW not only allowed workers to draw political sustenance from the protests staged by Chavez and the UFW, but also offered a degree of moral authenticity to the campaign.

To a certain degree, both performance and memory operate through technologies or mechanisms that mediate human relations (Sturken 1997). Chavez's cross represented such a "technology of memory" that linked the USC workers to "past performances" of regional labor politics. Specifically, it represented the historical exploitation of Mexican workers and acknowledged the extent to which they are no longer confined to the agricultural sector, but are central to the manufacturing and service industries. In short, the staging of cultural memory became a strategic site of political intervention and praxis, which Durazo makes explicit in the following quote:

> Fasting nourishes the soul, even as it weakens the body. The memory of the sacrifices of my parents, immigrants who worked in the fields to see that their children would have a better life, returned to inspire me. Conversations with Dolores Huerta, co-founder of the United Farm Workers, brought to life again the work and teaching of Cesar Chávez, which gave me strength. How could I ask others to work harder in the labor movement, to take even greater risk for their children and their co-workers, unless I was willing to fast side by side with them? (Durazo 1999, B9)

It is important to understand that most of the USC workers do not necessarily have any personal memory or connection to the UFW. The UFW is most closely associated with the Chicano movement of the 1960s and 1970s, while most of the workers are more recent immigrants from Mexico and Central America. Nonetheless, they had learned the significance of Chávez and the UFW through HERE organizers, many of whom are Chicana/o and initially became involved in labor through the UFW (Pulido 1998). By consciously referencing the UFW in their political practice, Local 11 transformed this memory into a living and breathing politics of resistance. But this is not a one-way street. Local 11 workers themselves are building on this tradition by becoming the stuff of legend and memories that will inspire future generations. Indeed, one observer has suggested that the urban labor movement, led by Justice for Janitors and Local 11, is in fact, replacing the UFW as the contemporary "touchstone" for this generation of Latino, labor, and social justice activists.[6]

> The janitors, in tandem with Local 11 of the Hotel Employees and Restaurant Employees, have supplanted the United Farm Workers as the political powerhouse and moral beacon of local Latino politics. It was the UFW's legendary Dolores Huerta who coined the slogan, "Si, se puede" (Yes, we can!) for a union of immigrants who'd come to rural California. Today, the slogan has been picked up by the unions representing, at least in spirit, the millions of immigrants who've since settled in urban California; and it is these unions whose members have shown, in fact, that they can do it—win good contracts and amass political clout. Today, the janitors and hotel workers . . . have caught the imagination and won the allegiance of a new generation of immigrants. (Meyerson 2000, 20)

While there were many factors that contributed to the success of USC workers, including broad community support and a vibrant labor movement, the role of theatre and performance should not be underestimated. The performance of both formalized skits with scripts and costumes, as well as actors/spectators enacting their individual and collective identities as activists, were powerful forces contributing to the workers' success.

CONCLUSION

In this chapter we have argued for the need to rethink questions of performativity and materiality. Our analysis has focused on how the performance of community, labor, and memory is always linked to the material and economic processes in which gender, race, and class formations are constructed, located, and negotiated within specific circuits of power. For workers at USC, the performance of their identity as workers allowed them to not only make their struggle visible and garner support, but it also allowed them to challenge USC's attempt to separate notions of community from work practices and labor politics. In addition, the workers' performances demonstrate the importance of symbolic and imaginative work in social struggle, and its potential for helping to create solidarity amongst proletarian constituencies. This has been especially true in Los Angeles, where labor activism and unionism have been radically transformed by cultural and demographic shifts in the urban landscape in recent years. Significantly, the workers' performances at USC were all about mobilizing a collectivized and critical oppositional politics against an oppressive situation. The workers thus deployed the performative strategies both to expose and undermine USC's unfair labor practices and to transform an exploitative situation into a socially and economically just one. Importantly, the workers emphasized *both* economic and cultural politics in their struggle for better work conditions, showing that the two cannot be separated. This enabled the workers to ground their struggle in a history of labor activism and economic struggle in the region. Moreover, the workers were able to represent themselves as complex political subjects with multiple identity formations—as workers, immigrants, and Latino/as. Such representations enacted by the workers allowed them to creatively and critically intervene in USC's attempt to abstract their labor and reroute the struggle for fair wages and conditions around the economic "bottom line."

Ultimately, USC Local 11 workers were successful in securing a better contract. Soon after in 2000, Justice for Janitors, in a dramatic strike, won a regionwide contract that offered improved wages and working conditions. We end this paper on this note in order to make two points. First, we need to appreciate the extent to which the success of Local 11 workers was partly a function of the larger, regional political culture. The struggle they waged would have been impossible if organized labor had not invested significant resources into organizing workers and promoting worker leadership. The whole issue of regional political cultures is something that we feel is often neglected in more esoteric studies of performance, bodies, and resistance. These events do not occur just anywhere, they are located in particular geographies that can make all the difference in the world. Second, the urgency and importance of the workers' victories and losses stand in stark contrast to many of the concerns raised by geographers and others (the present authors included) interested in questions of resistance and politics. We wish to point out such contradictions because this chasm can be seen as both an opportunity and a challenge to make our work and ourselves more relevant. This is not to suggest that there is not room for abstract theorizing about the body, space, performance, and resistance, but rather to urge all of us to consider how we can actively contribute to such struggles, and if our theories and research are, in fact, truly liberating.

NOTES

The authors would like to thank Richa Nagar and two anonymous reviewers for their thoughtful comments and Local 11 for their support. The authors remain responsible for all shortcomings. Versions of this chapter have been presented by Donna Houston at the Annual Meetings of the Association of American Geographers in Pittsburgh and New York.

1. For a detailed discussion of Butler's use of Derrida and Foucault in her work on performativity and her theoretical impact on human geography more generally, see Nelson (1999).

2. Felicity Callard (1998) in her essay on "The Body in Theory" provides an excellent discussion of theoretical perspectives on the body and the tensions between discursive and material approaches to transgression and resistance.

3. It should be noted that in addition to HERE Local 11, there was a second, simultaneous labor conflict at USC, involving Justice for Janitors, which is beyond the purview of this paper. In the spring of 1996, USC summarily contracted out its janitorial workforce. Most workers were rehired by the subcontractor Service Master, but at lower wages, with decreased benefits and without the privileges associated with being a USC employee, including tuition remission. The janitors responded by organizing themselves and voted to join SEIU, Local 1877, Justice for Janitors (Chuang 1996). As members of Justice for Janitors, USC janitors are now covered under the master contracts that SEIU negotiates on behalf of all janitors in the area.

4. There are, nevertheless, some serious contradictions with the university's practices. Consider the following quote from a USC student: "I first became disgusted with my educational institution's treatment of its workers two years ago, when I learned that Habitat for Humanity, which helps the impoverished build new homes, was helping a university employee" (Trendowski 1997, 6).

5. The Strategic Plan, first developed in 1994, is a university document that identifies the following four initiatives as areas of focus and development: undergraduate education, interdisciplinary activities, Southern California, and internationalization. Proposed projects and policy initiatives are routinely scrutinized in light of the Strategic Plan. Available at www.usc.edu/admin/provost/strategicplan.

6. Witness the recent Ken Loach film *Bread and Roses*, which depicts the struggle of Los Angeles janitors.

REFERENCES

Allen, J., and E. Turner. 1997. *The ethnic quilt: Population diversity in Southern California*. Northridge: California State University, Center for Geographical Studies.

Anner, J. 1996. *Beyond identity politics*. Boston: South End Press.

Bakhtin, M. 1984. *Rabelais and his world*. Bloomington: Indiana University Press.

Banks, A. 1991. The power and promise of community unionism. *Labor Research Review* 10 (2): 17–32.

Bell, D., J. Binnie, J. Cream, and G. Valentine. 1994. All hyped up and no place to go. *Gender, Place and Culture* 1: 31–47.

Benjamin, W. 1968. *Illuminations*. New York: Schocken Books.

Boal, A. 1993. *Theatre of the oppressed*. London: Pluto Press.

Brecht, B. 1964. *Brecht on theatre: The development of an aesthetic*. New York: Hill and Wang.

Broyles-Gonzalez, Y. 1994. *El teatro campesino: Theatre in the Chicano movement*. Austin: University of Texas.

Bryant-Bertail, S. 1991. The good soldier Schwejk as dialectical theater. In *The performance of power: Theatrical discourse and politics*, ed. S. E. Case and J. Reinelt. Iowa City: University of Iowa Press.

Building on diversity: The new unionism. 1993. Special issue of *Labor Research Review* 20.

Butler, J. 1990. *Gender trouble: Feminism and the subversion of identity*. New York: Routledge.

——. 1997. Imitation and gender insubordination. In *The second wave: A reader in feminist theory*, ed. L. Nicholson. New York: Routledge.

——. 1999. Performativity's social magic. In *Bourdieu: A critical reader*, ed. R. Shusterman. Oxford: Blackwell Publishers.

Callard, F. 1998. The body in theory. *Environment and Planning D: Society and Space* 16: 387–400.

Carlson, M. 2000. Resistant performance. In *The Routledge Reader in Politics and Performance*, ed. L. Goodman and J. de Gay, 60–65. New York: Routledge.

340 *Donna Houston and Laura Pulido*

Case. S. E., and J. Reinelt, eds. 1991. *The performance of power: Theatrical discourse and politics.* Iowa City: University Iowa Press.

Chuang, A. 1996. 100 janitors walk off jobs at USC. *Los Angeles Times,* December 5, B1.

Cleeland, N. 1996. L.A. area now a model for labor revival. *Los Angeles Times,* September 6, A1, A20.

Cresswell, T. 1996. *In place/out of place: Geography, ideology and transgression.* Minneapolis: University of Minnesota Press.

Daily Trojan. 1997. Editorial. January 15.

Davis, M. 1986. *Prisoners of the American dream.* New York: Verso.

———. 1995. The social roots of proposition 187. *NACLA report on the Americas* 29, no. 3.

de Certeau, M. 1984. *The practice of everyday life.* Berkeley: University of California.

Deemer, S. 1995. Union upset with USC hiring policies. *Daily Trojan,* June 4, 1, 15.

Derrida, J. 1976. *Of grammatology.* Baltimore: Johns Hopkins University Press.

Dewsbury, J-D. 2000. Performativity and the event: Enacting a philosophy of difference. *Environment and Planning D: Society and Space* 18: 473–97.

Diamond, E., ed. 1996. Introduction. *Performance and Cultural Politics.* New York: Routledge.

Durazo, M. E. 1999. Fasting to right worker injustices. *Los Angeles Times,* May 25, B9.

Ebert, T. 1996. *Ludic feminism and after: Postmodern, desire, and labor in late capitalism.* Ann Arbor: University of Michigan Press.

Enstad, N. 1998. Fashioning political identities: Cultural studies and the historical construction of political subjects. *American Quarterly* 50: 745–82.

Ethington, P. 2000. Segregated diversity: Race-ethnicity, space and political fragmentation in Los Angeles County 1940–1994. Final report to the John Randolph Haynes and Dora Foundation. Los Angeles. Available at www.usc.edu/college/historylab.

Foucault, M. 1976. *The History of Sexuality.* Vol. 1. London: Penguin Books.

Freire, P. 1990. *Pedagogy of the oppressed.* New York: Continuum.

Gardetta, D. 1993. True grit: Clocking time with the janitors' organizer Rocio Saenz. *LA Weekly* 15 (3): 16–24, 26.

Haitsuka, A. 1995. Union rallies for better contract. *Daily Trojan,* April 7, 1–3.

Handler, D. 1992. Postmodernism, protest and the new social movements. *Law & Society Review* 26: 697–731.

Harvey, D. 2000. *Spaces of hope.* Berkeley: University of California Press.

Hennessy, R. 1995. Queer visibility in commodity culture. In *Social postmodernism: Beyond identity politics,* ed. L. Nicholson and S. Seidman. Cambridge, Engl.: Cambridge University Press.

Herod, A. 1996. Labor's spatial praxis and the geography of contract bargaining in the U.S. east coast longshore industry 1953–89. *Political Geography* 15: 1–25.

Holland, G. 2001. The kids are all right. *USC Trojan Family Magazine* 33: 53–57.

Hondagneu-Sotelo, P. 1995. Women and children first: New directions in anti-immigrant politics. *Socialist Review* 25 (1): 169–90.

Hondagneu-Sotelo, P., and K. Lemma. 2001. *Economic justice: A case study of clergy and laity united for economic justice.* Paper presented at the Pacific Sociological Association Annual Meeting, Cathedral Hill Hotel, San Francisco, March 29–April 1.

Hornblower, M. 1999. College of the year 2000: The gown goes to town. *Time/Princeton Review,* 70–78.

Hoyos, L. 1994. Workers at the center. *Crossroads,* July/August, 24–27.

Hyman, C. A. 1997. *Staging strikes: Worker's theatre and the American labor movement.* Philadelphia: Temple University Press.

Jasper, J. 1997. *The art of moral protest.* Chicago: University of Chicago Press.

Johnson, J., and C. Roseman. 1990. Increasing black outmigration from Los Angeles: The role of household dynamics and kinship systems. *Annals of the Association of American Geographers* 80: 205–22.

Johnston, P. 1994. *Success while others fail: Social movement unionism and the public workplace.* Ithaca, N.Y.: ILR Press.

Kondo, D. 1997. *About face: Performing race in fashion and theater.* New York: Routledge.

Leovy, J. 2001. Bill seeks to legalize immigrant students. *Los Angeles Times,* May 21, B1, B9.

Lerner, S. 1991. Let's get moving: Labor's survival depends on organizing industry-wide for justice and power. *Labor Research Review* 19 (2): 1–16.

Li, W. 1998. Anatomy of a new ethnic settlement: The Chinese ethnoburb in Los Angeles. *Urban Studies* 35: 479–501.

Lieberman, S. 2001. Letter to the *Times*. *Los Angeles Times,* April 21, B9.

Longhurst, R. 2000. "Corporealities" of pregnancy: "Bikini babies." *Environment and Planning D: Society and Space* 18: 453–72.

Los Angeles Alliance for a New Economy. 2000. *The other Los Angeles: The working poor in the city of the 21st century.* Los Angeles: Author.

Los Angeles Times. 2001. Whites: In many areas, no longer the majority. April 21, U6.

Lott, E. 1995. *Love and theft: Blackface minstrelsy and the American working class.* New York: Oxford University Press.

Luna, C. 1999. Labor contract signed. *Daily Trojan* October 6, 1, 14, 19.

Mann, L. H., and T. Dutton. 1996. Subverting the avant-garde: Critical theory in the practice of architecture. In *Architecture: Critical discourses and social practices,* ed. L. Hurst Mann and T. Dutton. Minneapolis: University of Minnesota Press.

McDowell, L. 1999. *Gender, identity and place: Understanding feminist geographies.* Minneapolis: University of Minnesota Press.

McLaren, P. 1999. *Schooling as a ritual performance: Toward a political economy of educational symbols and gestures.* Lanham, Md.: Roman and Littlefield.

Medina, J. 1999. Jackson urges student activism. *Daily Trojan* October 7, 1, 19, 21.

Meyerson, H. 2000. The red sea: How the janitors won their strike. *LA Weekly,* April 28–May 4, 17–20.

Milkman, R., and K. Wong. 2000. *Voices from the front lines: Organizing immigrant workers in Los Angeles.* Los Angeles: Center for Labor Research and Education, University of California, Los Angeles.

Miller, B. 2000. *Geography and social movements: Comparing antinuclear activism in the Boston area.* Minneapolis: University of Minnesota.

Mullings, M. 1999. Sides of the same coin? Coping and resistance among Jamaican data-entry operators. *Annals of the Association of American Geographers* 89: 290–311.

Nagar, R. 2000. I'd rather be rude than ruled: Gender, place, and communal politics among South Asian communities in Dar es Salaam. *Women's Studies International Forum* 23 (5): 571–85.

Nash, C. 2000. Performativity in practice: Some recent work in cultural geography. *Progress in Human Geography* 24 (4): 653–64.

Nast, H., and L. Pulido. 2000. Resisting corporate multiculturalism: Mapping faculty initiatives and institutional-student harassment in the classroom. *Professional Geographer* 52: 722–37.

Needleman, R. 1993. Space and opportunities. *Labor Research Review* 20: 6–20.

Nelson, L. 1999. Bodies (and spaces) do matter: The limits of performativity. *Gender, Place, and Culture* 6: 331–53.

Ong, P., and E. Blumenberg. 1996. Income and racial inequality in Los Angeles. In *The City,* ed. A. Scott and E. Soja, 311–35. Berkeley: University of California Press.

Performance. 2000. Special issue of *Environment and Planning D: Society and Space* 18.

Pile, S., and M. Keith, eds. 1997. *Geographies of resistance.* New York: Routledge.

Price, P. 2000. No pain, no gain: Bordering the hungry new world order. *Environment and Planning D: Society & Space* 18: 91–110.

Privatization and contracting out. 1988. Special issue of *Labor Research Review* 15.

Pulido, L. 1998. *The roots of political consciousness among militant unionists and worker activists in Los Angeles.* Los Angeles: Center for the Study of Southern California, University of Southern California.

———. 2000. Rethinking environmental racism: White privilege and urban development in Southern California. *Annals of the Association of American Geographers* 90: 12–40.

Robinson, A. 2001. Framing Corkhill: Identity, agency, and injustice. *Environment and Planning D: Society and Space* 19: 81–101.

Rorlich, T. 1998. USC workers launch fast in job dispute. *Los Angeles Times,* November 19, B1, B5.

Rose, G. 1997. Performing inoperative community. In *Geographies of Resistance,* ed. S. Pile and M. Keith, 184–202. New York: Routledge.

Sabagh, G., and M. Bozorgmehr. 1996. Population change: Immigration and ethnic transformation. In *Ethnic Los Angeles,* ed. R. Waldinger and M. Bozorgmehr, 79–107. New York: Russell Sage Foundation.

Sahay, A. 1998. Transforming race matters: Towards a critque-al cultural studies. *Cultural Logic* 1, no. 2. Available at http:eserver.org.clogic/1-2/sahay.html.

Sample, S. 2001. *State of the university address.* Los Angeles: University of Southern California.

Savage, L. 1996. Negotiating common ground: Labor unions and the geography of organizing women workers in the service sector. Ph.D. diss., Clark University, Worcester, Massachusetts.

———. 2000. Geographies of organizing: Justice for janitors in Los Angeles. In *Organizing the landscape,* ed. A. Herod, 225–52. Minneapolis: University of Minnesota.

Scipes, K. 1992. Understanding the new labor movement in emergence of social movement unionism. *Critical Sociology* 19 (2): 81–101.

Scott, A. 1996. The manufacturing economy: Ethnic and gender divisions of labor. In *Ethnic Los Angeles,* ed. R. Waldinger and M. Bozorgmehr, 215–44. New York: Russell Sage Foundation.

Scott, J. 1990. *Domination and the arts of resistance: Hidden transcripts.* New Haven: Yale University Press.

Shields, R. 1997. Spatial stress and resistance: Social meanings of spatialization. In *Space and social theory: Interpreting modernity and postmodernity,* ed. G. Benko and U. Stroymayer, 186–202. Oxford: Blackwell.

Siegel, L. 1993. LRR voices: Local 11 takes on L.A. *Labor Research Review* 20: 21–23.

Silverstein, S. 1996. Going to work on L.A. *Los Angeles Times,* February 22, D1, D3.

Smith, N. 1993. Homeless/global: Scaling places. In *Mapping the futures: Local cultures, global change,* ed. J. Bird, B. Curtis, T. Putnam, G. Robertson, and L. Tickner, 87–119. New York: Routledge.

Spichen, B. 1997. Labor of love. *Los Angeles Times,* March 9, E1, E8.

Sturken, M. 1997. *Tangled memories: The Vietnam War, the AIDS epidemic, and the politics of remembering.* Berkeley: University of California Press.

Texeira, E. 2001. Migrants from L.A. flow to affordable suburbs such as in Inland Empire. *Los Angeles Times,* March 30, U2.

Thrift, N. 1997. The still point: Resistance, expressive embodiment and dance. In *Geographies of Resistance,* ed. S. Pile and M. Keith, 220–43. London: Routledge.

Thrift, N., and J. D. Dewsbury. 2000. Dead geographies—and how to make them live. *Environment and Planning D: Society and Space* 18: 411–32.

Tobar, H. 1990. Changing face of South L.A." *Los Angeles Times,* March 30, A1, A32, A33.

Trendowski, N. 1997. Letter to the editor. *Daily Trojan,* January 30, 6.

University of Southern California v. Local No. 11 of the Hotel Employees and Restaurant Employees Union, AFL-CIO et al. 1990. Preliminary injunction, Superior Court of the State of California for the County of Los Angeles, May 14.

Valdez, L. El Teatro Campesino. 1971. *Actos.* San Juan Bautista, Calif.: Cucaracha Press.

Valle, V., and R. Torres. 2000. *Latino Metropolis.* Minneapolis: University of Minnesota.

Waldinger, R., C. Erickson, R. Milkman, D. Mitchell, A. Valenzuela, K. Wong, and M. Zeitlin. 1997. Justice for janitors. *Dissent* (Winter): 37–44.

Whang, J. 1997. Supporters angry over restraining order. *Daily Trojan,* January 15, 1, 11.

Wial, H. 1993. The emerging organizational structure of unionism in low-wage services. *Rutgers Law Review* 45: 671–738.

Williams, R. 1989. *The politics of modernism: Against the new conformists.* New York: Verso.

19

Is There Any Space for Hope? Teacher Education and Social Justice in the Age of Globalization and Terror

Gustavo E. Fischman and Peter McLaren

GLOBAL/LOCAL CRISIS AND TEACHER EDUCATION

In this final chapter we want to argue that the current calls to restructure public schooling systems according to the demands of corporate sectors and the market presents one of the most threatening assaults to the possibilities of schools of contributing to the creation and sustainment of more democratic solutions to the current worldwide problems of illiteracy, poverty, inequity, and oppression.

Current neoconservative policies of social and economic restructuring—what otherwise can be known under the rubric of imperialism—have profound implications for reforming the public education sector and have involved the application of tighter systems of accountability in the context of the de-skilling, standardization, and changing rationales of the teaching profession (Popkewitz 1991). Pressure to do more work in the same amount of time, to do more work for less money, or to increase the number of students per classroom are clear manifestations of what has been termed the "intensification of teaching" (Apple 1997).

Both de-skilling and intensification are phenomena well-known to United States teachers. Because much of the "schools are failing" literature blames teachers for the so-called current decline in student achievement, the relationship between teachers and educational authorities are under increased pressure (Whitty 1997), and teacher education programs in particular have been under severe scrutiny. Plans to reform these institutions have frequently become key agenda items worldwide (Darling-Hammond 1998; National Commission on Teaching America's Future 1996).

Even where there is less focus on blaming teachers, attention is directed toward issues involving the control of teachers, as in the case of teacher competency testing, certification, and national exams. In short, diverse attempts are being made to improve aspects of teachers' activities judged as central to the quality and excellence of instruction. However, in this context, excellence becomes tantamount to attempts at reducing expenses of financially overburdened school districts and to make these systems more cost-effective. This process usually involves layoffs and the substitution of fully trained, more expensive teachers for lower-paid instructional personnel (Carnoy 1995; Whitty 1997). Within such a scenario, public schooling has been reduced to a subsector of the economy, as cost–benefit analysis and the maximization of profits have emerged as the major components for the manufacturing of educational "excellence" according to the needs of the triumphant global society. Globalization, which has been framed as a dramatic yet, unstoppable "new era" appears on the stage of the public discourse as an autonomous entity, as the new divine agent of salvation through which society's destiny will be realized, while we the audience, sit in the back rows, waiting for the miraculous power of technocapitalism to defy death on behalf of struggling humanity. Here capitalism is conceived as both generating and containing its own excesses, borrowing from the future and forever deferring its payments (Zizek 2002).

As educators, as students, and as citizens in the making (in structural conditions not always of our own choosing), we are living amidst a major crisis of capitalism and the concomitant changes that new capitalist formations have brought about in social, political, and cultural life.

THINKING AGAINST THE GRAIN 1: REFLECTING ON THE NEOLIBERAL MODEL OF GLOBALIZATION

The unregulated system of private power that we are now witnessing on a global basis—under the sobriquet of "globalization"—imposes severe restrictions on political decision making in the interests of social equality in both the so called "developed" and "underdeveloped" nations (Mander and Goldsmith 1996). Most of those changes are justified by ruling classes worldwide as the only possible solution to the economic disarray into which most of the world's societies had become plunged only because these policies were attuned to the worldwide process of global integration. For many people living Latin American, Asian, and African countries, "globalization" is equated with "modernization" and implies the acceptance of the expansion of transnational capital, the supranational character of productive decision making, increasing trends pressuring in the direction of the homogenization of information and cultural consumption, and the connection of geographically and culturally distant places in such a way that local events are shaped, as well as influenced, by events occurring in remote places.

Although we recognize that globalization is one of the most contentious and most argued about concepts, both in terms of its meaning and outcomes among social scientists (Rhoten 2000) it is also important to emphasize that the "global market" has not delivered all the benefits its public defenders have promised. In fact, the globalized economy is largely been a disaster of staggering proportions and there are consequences for the world's oppressed peoples. Given this scenario, how can a well-meaning government in the Third World use tax revenues to bring about a more equitable distribution of the national product when it was the use of tax breaks and tax concessions that attracted capital to the country in the first place? A more equitable distribution will eliminate the current advantages which attract investors and induce them to settle in countries who in order to sustain these dynamics need to lower even more the salaries of the workforce.

For the most part, the globalization of capital is administered through the hydraheaded operations of multinational corporations (MNCs) and guided by the mutual interests of the G-7 countries (United States, Canada, France, Japan, Italy, Germany, United Kingdom), international financial institutions, and supranational organizations (see McLaren and Farahmandpur 1999a, 1999b, 2000). Since the mid-1970s the MNCs have grown more rapidly than the world economy. In 1976, the fifty largest industrial corporations worldwide had sales of $540 billion and received $25 billion in profits. In 1990, sales figures for the top fifty had climbed to $2.1 trillion and their profits had reached $70 billion. In real terms, whereas the U.S. economy was growing at an annual rate of 2.8 percent (the Organization for Economic Cooperation and Development's average was 2.9 percent), the MNCs' annual sales growth was about 3.5 percent during the 1975–1990 period (Brown and Lauder 1997, 444).

And it is precisely now, when the drums of war are sounding at the rhythm of Western imperialist need for oil and geopolitical advantage, the global divide between rich and poor is widening at a staggering rate. Arundhati Roy (2002) writes:

> In the past ten years, the world's total income has increased by an average of 2.5% a year. And yet the number of the poor in the world has increased by 100 million. Of the top 100 biggest economies, 51 are corporations, not countries. The top 1% of the world has the same combined income as the bottom 57%, and the disparity is growing. Now under the spreading canopy of the war against terror, this process is being hustled along. The men in suits are in an unseemly hurry. While bombs rain down, contracts are being signed, patents registered, oil pipelines laid, natural resources plundered, water privatized and democracies undermined.

At a time when the Bush administration is equating the "American way of life" with financial market liberalization unencumbered by regulatory structures, with subordinating industrial development to the operations of financial capital, with championing the economic rationality of neoliberalism to the detriment of the social rationality of the global economy, with curtailing civil liberties in the name of protecting freedom and fighting terror, with the threat of preemptive military strikes against sovereign nations, the faultlines of the American Empire are beginning to strain. The stress of being the world's surrogate governement is causing its walls to rupture. Its veins rupturing like an impacted bowel, the empire is choking on its own refuse. Roy (2002) writes:

> Fortunately, power has a shelf life. When the time comes, maybe the mighty empire will, like others before it, overreach itself and implode from within. It looks as though structural cracks have already appeared. As the war against terror casts its net wider and wider, America's corporate heart is hemorrhaging. A world run by a handful of greedy bankers and CEOs whom nobody elected cannot possibly last.

Social policies—from housing and economic development to health and education—have been subordinated to a neoliberal rationale that demands structural competitiveness and a growing internationalization of capital. Such policies arrogantly disregard the enormous amount of data denouncing the increased pathological mixture of social inequalities that neoconservative and neoliberal proposals have inflicted upon countries throughout the world (Fischman 1998; Kabeer 1994; Sammoff 1994).

Neoliberal and neoconservative discourses in education have been theoretically and ideologically fueled by the corporatist logic of the free market. As part of a neoconservative discourse of efficiency and accountability, neoliberalism has taken a vicious hold on today's societies, particularly affecting state-sponsored programs such as public schooling. In this urgent sense, we are faced with what Pierre Bourdieu (1998) refers to as the "gospel" of neoliberalism. This gospel is one that serves as a clarion call to combat "*by every means,* including the destruction of the environment and human sacrifice, against any obstacle to the maximization of profit" (126). Bourdieu describes neoliberalism as:

> a powerful economic theory *whose strictly symbolic strength, combined with the effect of theory, redoubles the force of the economic realities it is supposed to express.* It ratifies the spontaneous philosophy of the people who run large multinationals and of the agents of high finance—in particular pension-fund managers. Relayed throughout the world by national and international politicians, civil servants, and most of all the universe of senior journalists—all more or less equally ignorant of the underlying mathematical theology—it is becoming a sort of universal belief, a new ecumenical gospel. This gospel, or rather the soft vulgate which is put forward everywhere under the name of liberalism, is concocted out of a collection of ill-defined words—"globalization," "flexibility," "deregulation" and so on—which, through their liberal or even libertarian connotations, may help to give the appearance of a message of freedom and liberation to a conservative ideology which thinks itself opposed to all ideology. (126)

These ideological forces described by Bourdieu are operating in a context in which the public continues to witness a dramatic assault on the social and personal rights of the working classes, ethnic and social minority groups, and the social, political, and economic infrastructures that have traditionally supported them. And here we want to note that by recognizing and criticizing these attacks, we in no way wish to suggest that the traditional structures of the welfare state were always successful in promoting more egalitarian societies.

It would be a mistake, nevertheless, not to examine the complex and contradictory histories of personal and collective struggle which have contributed to and benefited from the redistributive policies developed under the welfare state model. To dismiss the fact that, accompanied by severe contradictions, the condition of public schools as a component of the welfare state did vastly improve—in relative ways—the social conditions of economically and socially oppressed groups is not only politically disingenuous, but also an inadequate exercise in historical reasoning.

Free market fundamentalism and its unholy alliance with informational society has catapulted democracy onto the brink of an abyss, comodifying its logic and transforming it into an "authorized" language of neocapitalist technoculture, bureaucratic high-tech developmentalism, infotainment, and teledemocracy (Garcia Canclini 1995). In the face of the historical resiliency of the ruling class, democracy has become reduced to spray-painted slogans on decaying buildings, or airbrushed sentiments invoked in public by stern-faced corporate leaders in partnership with government initiatives to privatize the lifeworld of the entire planet.

Workers' rights diminish, as the progressive collapse of the welfare state is followed by a rising tide of homeless populations, diasporic movements of immigrants looking for work, a vicious private sector and government assault on unions, and the political neutralization of the labor movement and other alternative voices in the political spectrum.[1]

We do not believe that history follows a succession of stages from particular ideologies to universal ones. Nor do we believe that history is at an end. It is obvious that ideological conflicts still characterize much of public life in the United States and elsewhere. Even if capitalist market principles of economic organization do predominate, restrictive forms of liberal democracy do not go uncontested. Bold, small, and grand narratives of human emancipation still struggle on. And while there is a permanent contestability to historical narratives, Marx's analysis of the fundamental oppressive characteristics of capitalism has far from exhausted itself as an essential diagnostic tool and utopian narrative even as we acknowledge, with regret, its residual attraction among mainstream teachers and its leavened attachment among progressive and radical educators.

MORE THINKING AGAINST THE GRAIN: REFLECTING ON THE PEDAGOGICAL USE OF MARX'S LABOR THEORY

Capitalism may not be an all-embracing totality that mediates all aspects of social, cultural, and political life, but its circuits, flows, networks, and social relations undeniably play a central exploitative role in our contemporary existence and need to be critically interrogated as part of any progressive teacher education program. Notwithstanding, some might view any attempt to engage in Marxist analysis as either an expression of nostalgic scholarship, or as the will of renewal of an authoritarian and homogenous discourse preoccupied by a single-minded and narrow focus on only one set of explanatory terms. We believe that such descriptions are inaccurate.

There exists no pure Marxist problematic, no unitary and cohesive Marxist epistemology, no pristine ontology, no "official" Marxist philosophy or unsullied devotional methodology (McKay 1995–1996). There are many Marxisms, and we are urging that a dialogue begin not only among competing Marxisms (which after all, is one of the great legacies of Marxian thought) but that educators begin a dialogue with Marxian approaches to education in a nonrecriminatory and productive manner.

In our view, the Marxian problematic in general possesses, a singular capacity to formulate new perspectives whose dimensions are always situation-specific and reflect the class-determination of practitioners. We do not see Marxism as imprisoned by the ironclad dogmatism historically associated with it or as a total philosophy of social evolution.

While clearly Marxist programs and proposals have not solved the problems of bureaucracy, surveillance, hierarchy, and state control, we believe that they still carry great explanatory power for developing a framework and foundation for the multiple anticapitalist, antisexist, and antiracist struggles ahead. And, more importantly, for making history in addition to theorizing about capitalist social realities (Rikowski 2000, 2001a, 20001b; Hill and Cole 2001). In this regard, we point to the necessary emphasis teacher and researchers need to place on the politics of capitalist domination as well as working-class resistance—or what Antonio Negri (1991) has called working-class self-valorization.[2]

In our work in critical pedagogy, we have noticed that few, if any, contemporary North American critical educators ground their pedagogical imperatives in the concept of labor in general, and in Marx's labor theory of value in particular. We believe that this concept has to be central in theorizing any school/society relationship. We follow the premise that value is the substance of capital. Value is not a thing. It is the dominant form that capitalism as a determinate social relation takes. Following Dinerstein and Neary (2001), capital can be conceived as "value in motion." Marx linked the production of value to the dual aspect of labor. Workers do not consume what they produce but work in order to consume what has been produced by others. Labor is thus grounded in both use-value and exchange-value. Domination in this view is not by other people but by abstract social structures that people constitute. Labor, therefore, has an historically specific function as a social mediating activity. Labor materializes itself both as commodified forms of human existence (labor power) and structures which constitute and enforce this process of generalized social mediation (such as money and the state) against the workers who indirectly constituted them. These determinate abstractions (abstract labor) also constitute human capital and the class struggle against both the exploitation of living labor and the "capitalization" of human subjectivity.

We are using the term *class struggle* after Rikowski (2001a), as a social relation between labor and capital. It is one of the phenomena integral to the existence of capitalist society, "an element of the constitution of a world struggle" (1) that exists everywhere in capitalist society. We share Glenn Rikowski's perspective that the class relation is the capital–labor relation that forms the "violent dialectic" that generates all value. Class struggle is born out of the antagonistic relation between capital and labor. In fact, Rikowski argues that class struggle occurs intersubjectively as well as collectively as a clash of contradictory forces and drives within the social totality. Rikowski notes that

> the class relation *runs through our personhood*. It is internal to us; we *are* labor, and we *are* capital. We are social beings incorporating antithetical social drives and forces. This fact sets off contradictions within our lives, and their solution can only come from the disintegration of ourselves as both capital and labor and our emergence as a new, non-capitalised life-form. (20)

This split within capital–labor itself is founded on the issue of whether labor produces value directly or labor power. Following Dinerstein and Neary (2001), we adopt the premise that abstract labor is underwritten by value in motion, or the expansive logic of capital (referring to the increases in productivity required to maintain capitalist expansion). This value relation—captured in the image of the capitalist juggernaut driving across the globe for the purpose of extracting surplus value (profit), reflects how the abstract social dimension of labor formally arranges (through the imposition of socially necessary labor time) the concrete organization of work so that the maximum amount of human energy can be extracted as absolute surplus value. Here, concrete labor (use value) is overwhelmed by abstract labor (value in motion) so that we have a noncontradictory unity. That is to say, capital's abstract–social dimension dominates and subsumes the concrete material character of labor and becomes the organizing principle of society—the social factory where labor becomes the constituent form of its own domination. This helps to explain how workers become dominated by their own labor. Labor becomes the source of its own domination. The subsumption of concrete labor by abstract labor or value in motion is what Dinerstein and Neary (2001) refer to as Disutopia. They write:

> disutopia is the most significant project of our time. It is not the temporary absence of Utopia but the celebration of the end of social dreams. Social dreams have become a nightmare in which it is impossible to materialize our desires into a collective thought. Disutopia should not be confused with the form in which it appears: indifference. Disutopia entails an active process involving simultaneously the struggle to control diversity and the acclamation of diversity; the repression of the struggles against Disutopia and celebration of individual self-determination. The result of this is social schizophrenia. In so far as diversity, struggle and contradiction cannot

be eliminated by political or philosophical voluntarism, Disutopia has to be imposed. The advocates of Disutopia spend a huge amount of time in de-construction, repentance, denial, forgetfulness, anti-critique, coupled with academic justifications and the scientific classification of the horrors of our time. Whilst the reality of capitalism is destroying planet earth, Disutopia pictures Utopia as a romantic, naïve and old-fashioned imaginary that is accused of not dealing with the real world. However, our point is that Disutopia can only be sustained by denying the real content of life, that is, the foundations of the real world. The result of all this together is mediocrity. (4)

Yet the contradictory logic of this production of real abstraction takes concrete forms—such as workers fighting for their jobs or antiglobalization protesters demanding substantive and formal democracy. However, these types of struggles disconnect themselves from the struggle they claim to be representing because they are still positing capital against labor. Following Dinerstein and Neary, we are making an immanent critique derived from the idea of the subsumption of concrete labor by abstract labor and claim that capital is not against labor but rather capital constitutes an impossible human society. Thus, it is not enough to critique capital but we must critique in and against capital. Our struggle must be anti–value in motion. In sum, class struggle has to be linked to the relation internal to all labor, the split or rift within labor as a form of social existence within capitalist society. Class struggle is implicated in the tragic truism that labor creates its own opposite (capital) that comes to dominate it. The issue of class struggle needs to be approached from the perspective *of a critique of capital and its value form of labor*.

We believe Rikowski's adaptation of Marx's value theory of labor which reveals how education is implicated in the social production of labor power in capitalism. Glenn Rikowski's premise, which is provocative yet compelling (and perhaps deceptively simple), can be summarized as follows: Education is involved in the direct production of the one commodity that generates the entire social universe of capital in all of its dynamic and multiform existence—labor power. Within the social universe of capital, individuals sell their capacity to labor—their labor power—for a wage. Because we are included in this social universe on a differential and unequal basis, people can get paid above or below the value of their labor power. Because labor power is implicated in human will or agency, and because it is impossible for capital to exist without it, education can be redesigned within a social justice agenda that will reclaim labor power for socialist alternatives to human capital formation.

According to Rikowski (2001a), education is a key process in "the generation of the capital relation." Education "links the chains that bind our souls to capital. It is one of the ropes comprising the ring for combat between labor and capital, a clash that powers contemporary history: "the class struggle" (2). Schools therefore act as vital supports for, and developers of, the class relation, "the violent capital-labor relation that is at the core of capitalist society and development" (19).

As a consequence of this, we need to devise forms of labor power expenditure and development *not tied to the value form of labor.* In the meantime, teachers are in a structural position to subvert the smooth flow of labor power production by inserting principles in opposition to the domination of capital (Rikowski 2001b). Rikowski asserts that while teachers are surely helpful in reproducing the ideological fabric of capitalism, they are also potentially "dangerous to capital and its social domination" (38). He argues that educators constitute the "guardians of the development of the one commodity that keeps capitalism going (labor power), whilst also being in a structural position to *subvert the smooth flow of labor power production* by inserting *principles antagonistic* to the social domination of capital. Such principles include social justice, equality and solidarity for progressive social change" (38, original italics).[3]

TOWARD A RENEWED TEACHER EDUCATION CURRICULUM

Critical educators committed to social justice, in our view, should focus on problematizing the production of value through the work experience, and teacher education programs are key spaces to expand and reflect on this perspective. Teacher education is about extending the pedagogical appreciation of the ability of students to act autonomously within the larger political context of class struggle in such a way that students identify themselves not only as students but also in solidarity with workers, unwaged workers, and all those struggling against myriad class, race, and gender forms of oppression.

Teacher education needs to meet the educational tasks demanded by the challenge of the global informational age: from the development of new Marxian, feminist, and anticolonial inspired languages of criticism and interpretation to a praxis that refuses to compromise its commitment to the imperatives of emancipation and social justice.

We do not have space to do much more than to offer a brief sketch of what a teacher education curriculum committed to social change would look like. Thus, we want to end our discussion in this section by offering some general recommendations that capture the fundamental elements of utopic–heterotopic teacher education programs.

First, it is fundamental to reaffirm the democratic promises embedded (yet, never fully accomplished) in systems of public education and to rethink the purposes of schools so they can be framed within the context of antiracist, anticapitalist, and feminist pedagogies. We believe that this can be most effectively accomplished when those perspectives are linked to shifting patterns of capitalist accumulation. Teacher education students need to engage in an analysis of the mechanisms of capitalist production and exchange, and develop research methodologies that will facilitate such analyses. In this context students should be introduced to theories of power and be encouraged to pursue sociological investigations of administrative control, bureaucratic manipulation, the process of commodification, the creation of violence in nation-states, and the destructive patterns within the earth's ecosystems.

Second, we believe that existing teacher education programs be reconsidered in light of the shifting patterns of globalization and how these patterns effect local communities. This means that prospective teachers need to be actively involved not only in their professional struggles for better learning and teaching conditions but also connect their professional needs with the local community struggles for better jobs, better working conditions, daycare facilities, housing, medical treatment, and so on. This implies that teachers and teacher educators must take the leading role in developing a coherent pedagogical, philosophical, moral, and political vision of school reform in such a way that their efforts are connected to the needs of their local communities.

Third, the efforts for reimagining and reforming public education need to be rooted in the ongoing production and revision of socially and scientifically relevant knowledge, emerging from the manifold pedagogical encounters of teacher–teacher, student–teacher, teacher–community coupled with the information derived from the academic disciplines. At the same time, it is fundamental that the pedagogical encounter includes the recognition and critical incorporation of what have heretofore been devalued and excluded: subjugated and indigenous knowledge. Teachers and teachers educators need to move beyond white, Anglo-Saxon, middle-class, and heterosexual educational norms and explore the subjugated knowledges of women, minority groups, and indigenous groups. Such a move will advance the possibilities of forging active alliances with social movements so that what transpires in their methods classes, or classes in social sciences, or with teacher–mentors in classroom sites, is grounded in a well-articulated political project aimed at the transformation of asymmetrical relationships of power and privilege (McLaren 1995).

Fourth, teacher education programs need to emphasize a media literacy curriculum. Today it is necessary to acquire multiple literacies in order to critically engage in the production of counterhegemonic discourses through the use of print, television, film, photographs, and computer technologies. Students and teachers need to be able to become critically literate in many different sites, genres, modalities, and styles of knowledge production as well as learn to employ a multiplicity of innovative technological devices in the service of resistance to all forms of discrimination and processes of exploitation. Underwriting this critical pedagogy of media literacy must be a commitment to social justice articulated in a pedagogical language that enables relationships of domination, exploitation—and in certain instances, relations of equality—to be identified and critically engaged.

Teacher education needs to make available to students a multiplicity of critical languages developed within literature, sociology, anthropology, political science, and cultural studies, so that the epistemologies and social practices that support mainstream pedagogy and research in teacher education can be interrogated, rearticulated, and transformed if they are shown generally to reproduce existing social relations of inequality (McLaren 1997). In order to assure this, the former teachers and teacher educators need to struggle and abandon formalized modes of thinking. Whereas formal thinking involves scientific procedure and the certainty it produces, postformal thinking involves understanding the production of one's own knowledge and includes etymology; the exploration of culturally validated knowledge; and understanding the patterns and relationships that support the lived world.

While it is clear for us that the current language of educational research is largely neglecting its potential for exercising social power, for resisting and creating alternatives to today's economic injustices, we are not suggesting that all is needed is a Marxian rewriting of the language of educational theory. But we are calling for a renewed emphasis on a critique of political economy and the irreducibility of politics and the economy. As Slavoj Zizek notes (2002), one of Marx's key insights is how the political struggle constitutes a spectacle that can only be understood from the sphere of economics. That is, the whole problem of freedom can be uncovered in the social relations that are often characterized as nonpolitical by bourgeois liberals. For Marx, capital is not just an empirical sphere but "the matrix which generates the totality of social and political relations" (271). The field of economy is nor reducible "in its very form" to politics and cannot be reduced to one of several social spheres, but remains "the key that enables to decode political struggle" (272). Zizek sees the relationship between the political spectacle and the economy in terms of a Mobius strip: First, we have to progress from the political spectacle to its economic infrastructure; then, in a second step, we have to confront the irreducible dimension of the political struggle at the very heart of the economy." We cannot grasp both the economy and politics from the same "neutral" or prototrascendental vantage point.

In addition to calling for a reengagement with Marxist theory, we are asking educators to reconsider their understanding of social and political power within educational arenas from the perspective of a critique of the globalization of capital, and to recast teacher education programs as integral parts for the extension and deepening of the democratic project; in other words, we seek to explore utopian possibilities within a socialist optic. Furthermore, teacher education programs should be committed to the development of critical epistemologies as well as be grounded in ethics of caring, compassion, and solidarity.

THE STRUGGLE AHEAD

The struggle, as we see it, from the standpoint of socialist, democratic pedagogy, is to work at the macropolitical level against the injustices of global capitalism—by working *within* and *against* the social universe of capital—and locally to construct sites—provisional sites—in which new structured mobilities and forces can be created that suture political agency to the larger problematic of social justice. We do not envision social justice here from the perspective of redistributing material resources within the current rule of capital.

Rather, we are using social justice in the sense of fundamentally abolishing the rule of capital (the noncontradictory unity of labor and capital) and capitalist social relations through socializing the productive structures and increasing the control of production and distribution by independent workers' organizations. The Marxist humanisim that informs our understanding of justice distances itself from the concept of distributive justice since distributive justice reduces the process of exploitation and alienation of labor endemic to capital to an allocation of corporative advantage. Thus, what appears as a "cure" for capitalist exploitation is, in effect, an embellishment. We believe that any state structure that emerges from anticapitalist struggle must encourage both formal democracy (focusing on political rights) and substantive democracy (focusing on economic justice). One type of democracy cannot be sacrificed for or subordinated to the other.

In our view, one essential way that schools can be more democratic and encouraging of civic life is to offer students and teachers the possibility of dialogical interaction based on a value system that, while not ignoring social realities, will expose the ideological traps of a system that has converted even adults into indifferent citizens or cynical players. The "real world," we contend, is dominated by the frenzied logic of the capitalist market, and so far schools have, with marginal success at best, navigated the messy contradictions between the utopic logic of democracy and that of corporate capitalism. Here we need to be wary that in many respects civil society is little more than an appendage of the state and to presume that "civic life" can bring about democracy without at the same time a drastic restructuring of the social relations of production, is naïve at best, and foolhardy at worst.

The notion that "culture" is the communal soil that precedes the economy is wrongheaded and leads to the erroneous notion that all we need is a common space of cultural understanding that can shape the production and exchange of merchandise. The concept that what we need is a new balance between culture and the market is a pseudosolution. The key question is finding the organizational structure which will strengthen the antiglobalization movement in the firm political demand of liberation from capitalism. Unless we have the ability to develop such an organizational form, we are going to be left with a revolution without revolution. We cannot simply supplement economic globalization by a political globalization.

To create school sites that speak to the utopian and heterotopian democratic imperatives we believe that schools should be detached from the requirements of the "real world," where reality has been collapsed into a function of the market. If we want schools to reinvent democracy, they need independence from the market. We share the sentiments of Paulo Freire (1998), who writes:

> An economy that is incapable of developing programs according to human needs, and that coexists indifferently with the hunger of millions of people to whom everything is denied, does not deserve my respect as an educator. Above all, it does not deserve my respect as a human being. And it is not well to say, "Things are the

way they are because they cannot be different." They cannot be different because if they were, they would be in conflict with the interests of the ruling class. This cannot, however, be the determining essence of the economic practice. I cannot become fatalistic in order to meet the interests of the ruling class. Neither can I invent a "scientific" explanation to cover up a lie. (36)

Finally, we want to argue that imagining schools as utopic–heterotopic spaces is impossible without acknowledging the crucial role of teachers in any educational change. Teacher education in this regard is perhaps a key site for initiating practices aimed at opening new spaces of democratic practice and for transforming school sites into centers of possibility (Fischman 2000). Schools as centers of possibility means to understand them as spaces of transmission and creation of meaningful knowledge and as political laboratories that can deepen participation and dialogue about the larger social, political, and economic relations and practices that are transforming this planet into a toxic sewage dump and mass graveyard for the victims of Fascism, terrorism, and imperialism.

Democracy requires the realm of freedom and the constant development of an ethic of social justice as its two fundamental premises. No realm of freedom or ethics of social justice worthy of the name can continue to be defined by social relations constructed to assure privileges for whiteness, capitalistic relations of exploitation, patriarchal forms of family organization, and forced heterosexuality. In the same vein, we need to denounce and continuously create alternatives to those structures of exploitation and discrimination as the markers of the "good society," therefore allowing them to keep being the dominant values for the education of today and tomorrow's teachers.

We lack optimism but that does not make us pessimists, because we have hope. Capital feeds false hope but it cannot displace hope altogether. There is hope as long as we have the capacity insurgency, that is, as long as we have the knowledge that we *can* act when the opportunity arises, and that we *will* act. Without hope, there cannot be resistance. Hope is not coterminous with life but can be generated only when we recognize our capacity and acknowledge our determination to make our own history.

Understanding teaching in a global context of increasing violence, poverty, and horror requires a considerable dose of hope, and even more if the attempt is to develop alternative proposals to the current process of intensification of teachers' work. We contend that this challenge requires not only a hopeful attitude, but also to rethink traditional categories of analysis, remembering Raymond Williams's worthy advice and "speak for hope as long as it doesn't mean suppressing the nature of danger" (cited in Apple 2000, xv). Paulo Freire (1998) reminds us that we cannot generate hope from the past but must set our sights on tomorrow. For it is tomorrow that holds the promise of today's vision and promise of a new world. He writes:

> Without a vision for tomorrow, hope is impossible. The past does not generate hope, except for the time when one is reminded of rebellious, daring moments of flight. The past, understood as immobilization of what was, generates longing,

even worse, *nostalgia*, which nullifies tomorrow. Almost always, concrete situations of oppression reduce the oppressed's historical time to an everlasting present of hopelessness and resignation. The oppressed grandchild repeats the suffering of their grandparent. (45)

In our struggle to defeat capital, we must ensure that hope is not left as a metaphysical or mystical abstraction. Hope must be made practical and despair impractical. What is currently lacking among the educational left is what Daniel Bensaid (2001) calls "strategic reason" and the "strategic art of the possible." He writes:

The art of decision, of the right moment, of the alternatives open to hope, is a strategic art of the possible. Not the dream of an abstract possibility, where everything that isn't impossible will be possible, but the art of a possibility determined by the concrete situation: each situation being singular, the instant of the decision is always relative to this situation, adjusted to the goal to be achieved. (cited in Callinicos 2001, 55)

In other words, hope in global times mean that both teachers and students have no other possibility but to struggle to affirm themselves against the internal contradictions generated by the capital relation and the "capitalization" of human subjectivity as well as external pressures to strip them of their democratic rights. It is up to them and to us as scholars and practitioners to create spaces for hope and the strategic art of the possible, in order to bring about those extraordinary times in which collective action can demonstrate that history is always in the making.

NOTES

1. This is especially true now in the United States after the terrorist attack on Washington and New York City. Under the cover of a state of permanent "war on terrorism" the government has instituted new laws that will enable increasing surveillance of any organization at odds with corporate America and the military/industrial complex that protects it.

2. Working-class self-valorization implies new autonomous ways of organizing, ways of being, forms of self-activity, autonomous cultural and political activities against the centralizing power of national and international capital, and the creation of social relations outside of the social universe of capital.

3. Marx's value theory of labor does not attempt to reduce labor to an economic category alone but is illustrative of how labor as value form constitutes our very social universe, one that has been underwritten by the logic of capital. Value is not some hollow formality, neutral precinct, or barren hinterland emptied of power and politics but the very matter and antimatter of capitalism's social universe. It is important to keep in mind that the production of value is not the same as the production of wealth. The production of value is historically specific and emerges whenever labor assumes its dual character. This is most clearly explicated in Marx's discussion of the contradictory nature of the commodity form and the expansive capacity of the commodity known as labor power. For Marx, the commodity is highly unstable, and nonidentical. Its concrete particularity (use value) is subsumed by its existence as value in motion or by what we have come to know as "capital"

(value is always in motion because of the increase in capital's productivity that is required to maintain expansion). The issue here is not simply that workers are exploited for their surplus value but that all forms of human sociability are constituted by the logic of capitalist work. Labor, therefore, cannot be seen as the negation of capital or the antithesis of capital but the human form through and against which capitalist work exists (Rikowski 2000). Capitalist relations of production become hegemonic precisely when the process of the production of abstraction conquers the concrete processes of production, resulting in the expansion of the logic of capitalist work. Class struggle has now been displaced to the realm of the totality of human relations, as abstract social structures such as labor now exist as the transsubstantiation of human life as capital (McNally 1998). So when we look at the issue of educational reform, it is important to address the issue of teachers' work within capitalist society as a form of alienated labor, that is, as the specific production of the value form of labor that culminates in the production of social agents as transhuman, capitalized as subjectivity.

This becomes clearer when we begin to understand that one of the fundamental functions of schooling is to traffic in labor power, in the engineering and enhancement of the capacity to labor so that such labor power can be harnessed in the interests of capital. Glenn Rikowski has put forward an important argument on the topic of schooling and the production of value. In a capitalist society we are inescapably embedded in the social universe of capital. The substance of our social universe of capital is value. Value in this sense operates as a social energy field. The fluid movements of capital in its various forms and the social relations between capital and labor mediate the social forces of this energy field.

This value, or social energy, is always in motion and is variously transformed into forms of capital. They key term for Rikowski in this process is "labor power." Labor power—the capacity to labor rests upon the energy, skills, knowledge, physical and personal qualities that we, as laborers possess—constitutes what Rikowski calls the "cell form" of value or "the primordial form of social energy within capital's social universe." Labor power is transformed into labor in the act of laboring (i.e., through living labor) and this process powers social life as we know it. While value is the substance of capital's social universe, labor power (expended as abstract labor or living labor) is the substance of value.

Labor power is always expended in a dual mode as both concrete and abstract labor. But since value's substance is labor power and since labor power is a living commodity labor power constitutes capital's *weakest link*. Why? This is because labor power has to be manipulated or coerced into action as workers must be forced to produce more value than that which covers their subsistence (i.e., socially necessary labor time). Labor power is purchased as a capacity for generating and creating value. Labor power expenditure can create value over and above its own value. From this perspective critical educators are in a unique position to play in struggles over the privatization and business takeover of education—and ultimately in the struggle for a socialist future. Since teachers are involved in the reduction of humanity to a capital as they socially produce the human as capital, human capital, they need to develop pedagogical approaches that can resist the capitalization of human subjectivity. Labor power—capital's weakest link—needs to be channeled into non- and anticapitalist social forms.

REFERENCES

Apple, Michael. 1997. Introduction. *Review of Research in Education* 22: xi–xxi.
———. 2000. Foreword in *Teachers' work in a globalizing economy,* ed. John Smyth, Alastair Dow, Robert Hattam, Alan Reid, and Geoffrey Shacklock. London: Falmer Press.
Bensaid, Daniel. 2001. *Les Irreductibles*. Paris: Gallimard.
Bourdieu, Pierre. 1998. A reasoned utopia and economic fatalism. *New Left Review*, no. 227: 125–30.
Brown, P., and H. Lauder 1997. Observations on global/local articulations of the re-gendering and restructuring of educational work. *International Review of Education* 43 (5–6): 439–61.
Callinicos, Alex. 2001. Tony Negri in perspective. *International Socialism* 92: 32–61.

Carnoy, Martin. 1995. Is privatization the answer? *Education Week,* July 12, 29–33.

Darling-Hammond, Linda. 1998. Teachers and teaching: Testing policy hypotheses from a national commission report. *Educational Researcher* 27 (1): 5, 17.

Dinerstein, Ana, and Mike Neary. 2001. Marx, labor and real subsumption; or, How *no logo* becomes *no to capitalist everything.* Unpublished paper.

Fischman, Gustavo E. 1998. Donkeys and superteachers: Popular education and structural adjustment in Latin-America. *International Review of Education* 44 (2–3): 191–213.

———. 2000. *Imagining teachers: Rethinking gender dynamics in teacher education.* Lanham, Md.: Rowman and Littlefield.

Freire, Paulo. 1998. *Pedagogy of the heart.* New York: Continuum.

García Canclini, Nestor. 1995. *Hybrid cultures: Strategies for entering and leaving modernity.* Trans. Christopher Chiappary and Silvia L. Lopez. Minneapolis: University of Minnesota Press.

Hill, D., and M. Cole. 2001. Social class. In *Schooling and equality: Fact, concept and policy,* ed. D. Hill and M. Cole. London: Kogan Page.

Kabeer, Nalia. 1994. *Reversed realities: Gender hierarchies in development thought.* New York: Verso.

Mander, Jerry, and Edward Goldsmith. 1996. *The case against the global economy.* San Francisco: Sierra Club Books.

McKay, Ian. 1995–1996. The many deaths of Mr. Marx: Or what left historians might contribute debates about the "crisis of Marxism." *Left History* 32 (4): 1, 9–83.

McLaren, Peter. 1995. *Critical pedagogy and predatory culture: Oppositional politics in the postmodern era.* London: Routledge.

———. 1997. *Revolutionary multiculturalism: Pedagogies of dissent for the new millennium.* Boulder, Colo.: Westview Press.

McLaren, P., and R. Farahmandpur. 1999a. Critical multiculturalism and globalization. Some implications for a politics of resistance. *Journal of Curriculum Theorizing* 15, no. 3: 27–46.

———. 1999b. Critical pedagogy, postmodernism, and the retreat from class: Towards a contraband pedagogy. *Theoria,* no. 93: 83–115.

———. 2000. Reconsidering Marx in post-Marxist times: A requiem for postmodernism? *Educational Researcher* 29, no. 3: 25–33.

McNally, David. 1998. Marxism in the age of information. *New Politics Symposium: The Relevance of Marxism on the 150th Anniversary of the Communist Manifesto,* n.s., 6, no. 4 (Winter): 99–106.

National Commission on Teaching America's Future. 1996. *What matters most: Teaching for America's future.* New York: Author.

Negri, Antonio. 1991. *Marx beyond Marx: Lessons on the Grundrisse.* New York: Autonomedia; and London: Pluto.

Popkewitz, Thomas S. 1991. *A political sociology of educational reform.* New York: Teachers College Press.

Rhoten, Diana. 2000. Education decentralization in Argentina: A "global-local conditions of possibility" approach to state, market, and society change. *Journal of Education Policy* 15 (6): 593–619.

Rikowski, Glenn. 2000. *Messing with the explosive commodity: School improvement, educational research and labor-power in the era of global capitalism.* A paper prepared for the symposium "If We Aren't Pursuing Improvement, What Are We Doing?" British Educational Research Association Conference 2000, Cardiff University, Wales. September 7, session 3.4.

———. 2001a. *After the manuscript broke off: Thoughts on Marx, social class and education.* Paper presented at the British Sociological Association Education Study Group, King's College London, June 23.

———. 2001b. *The battle in Seattle: Its significance for education.* London: Tufnell Press.

Roy, Arundhati. 2002. Not again. *Guardian,* September 27.

Samoff, Joel. 1994. *Coping with Crisis.* London: UNESCO-ILO.

Whitty, Geoff. 1997. Creating quasi-markets in education. *Review of Research in Education* 22: 3–49.

Zizek, Slavoj. 2002. *Revolution at the gates: Selected writings of Lenin from 1917.* London: Verso.

Index

About the Contributors

Dr. Mike Cole is senior lecturer in education at the University of Brighton, England. He has written extensively on equality issues. Recent publications include *Red Chalk: On Schooling, Capitalism and Politics; Schooling and Equality: Fact Concept and Policy; Education Equality and Human Rights; Marxism against Postmodernism in Educational Theory;* and *Professional Values and Practice for Teachers and Student Teachers.* He is the author of *Marxism, Postmodernism, and Education: Pasts, Presents and Futures.*

Antonia Darder is professor of educational policy studies and Latino/a studies at the University of Illinois Urbana-Champaign and an associate editor of *Latino Studies.* Her teaching and scholarship focus on critical issues related to schooling, society, racism, and the economy. Her publications include *Culture and Power in the Classroom; Reinventing Paulo Freire: A Pedagogy of Love; After Race: Racism after Multiculturalism;* and *The Latino Studies Reader: Society, Politics, and the Economy.*

Ramin Farahmandpur is assistant professor in the Department of Educational Policy, Foundations and Administrative Studies at Portland State University. His research in education encompasses globalization, imperialism, neoliberalism, Marxism, and critical pedagogy. He is the coauthor of *Teaching against Global Capitalism and the New Imperialism: A Critical Pedagogy.*

Gustavo E. Fischman is assistant professor in the ASU College of Education Division of Curriculum and Instruction. His areas of specialization are comparative and international education, gender studies in education, and the development of participatory and action-oriented research programs. Dr. Fischman obtained his Ph.D. in social sciences and comparative education from the University of California, Los Angeles. His doctoral dissertation won the 1998 Gail P. Kelly Outstanding Dissertation of the Year Award of the Comparative and International Education Society. He actively collaborates on projects in the United States, Brazil, Argentina, and Mexico and is the author of several books and numerous articles on critical pedagogies, teacher education, and gender issues in education. In addition, Dr. Fischman serves on several editorial boards and is the editor of the Spanish and Portuguese sections of *Education Review* and *Educational Policy Analysis Archives*.

Robert FitzSimmons teaches English at the University of Lapland. He received his Ph.D. in education in 2004. His dissertation,"Toward a Critical Revolutionary Pedagogy: Inquiries into Karl Marx, Vladimir Lenin, Mao Tse-Tung, and Fidel Castro," was assessed by professor Peter McLaren.

Bernardo Gallegos is Distinguished Professor of Multicultural Education at Washington State University. He is the author of *Literacy, Education, and Society in New Mexico, 1692–1821,* as well as several articles, chapters, and reviews. He has coedited as well as contributed to *Performance Theories in Education; Power, Pedagogy, and the Politics of Identity; The Handbook of Research in Social Foundations;* and *Indigenous Education and Epistomologies in the Americas: a Special Issue of Educational Studies.* Professor Gallegos writes about education, identity, and power, especially in relation to nontribal Native Americans, Hispanics, and Mixed-bloods.

Henry A. Giroux holds the Global Television Network Chair in Communications in the faculty of humanities at McMaster University. His most recent book is *Take Back Higher Education* (coauthored with Susan Searls Giroux) and *The Terror of Neoliberalism.*

David Theo Goldberg is director of the system-wide University of California Humanities Research institute and professor of African American studies and criminology, law and society at the University of California, Irvine. He is the author of *The Racial State* and coeditor of *Companion to Gender Studies; Relocating Postcolonialism; Companion to Racial and Ethnic Studies;* and *Race Critical Theories.*

Rhonda Hammer is research scholar at the UCLA Center for the Study of Women and lecturer in women's studies and education at UCLA. Her publications include: *Rethinking Media Literacy: A Critical Pedagogy of Representation* (coauthored) and *Antifeminism and Family Terrorism: A Critical Feminist Perspective.*

Dave Hill is professor of education policy at University College Northampton, U.K. and senior visiting research fellow at Sussex University, U.K. He is the founding editor and chief editor of the *Journal for Critical Education Policy Studies* (www.jceps.com) and founding director of the Institute for Education Policy Studies (www.ieps.org.uk), an independent radical Left policy research unit. For twenty years, he was an elected labor union leader and organizer/agitator in England and an elected labor political representative on the Left of the Labour Party. He has written and/or edited nine books on issues of equality, Marxism and education, and policy, with three more forthcoming in 2005. He cofounded the Hillcole Group of Radical Left Educators in Britain (with Mike Cole) and is an active member of the U.S. Left educators group, the Rouge Forum.

Donna Houston is a doctoral student in the Department of Geography at the University of Southern California. Her research interests focus on radical perspectives on landscape, history, and the environment. She is currently completing her dissertation on "Topographies of Memory and Power: Environmental Justice in the 'New' Nuclear West."

Michele Knobel is associate professor at Montclair State University, where she is also the coordinator of the undergraduate and graduate literacy programs. She has worked within teacher education in Australia, Mexico, and the United States. Her research interests focus principally on school students' in-school and out-of-school literacy practices and the study of the relationship between new literacies and digital technologies.

Douglas Kellner is George Kneller Chair in the Philosophy of Education at UCLA. He is the author of many books on social theory, politics, history, and culture. His recent books include a study of the 2000 U.S. presidential election, *Grand Theft 2000: Media Spectacle and the Theft of an Election,* and *The Postmodern Adventure: Science, Technology, and Cultural Studies at the Third Millennium* (coauthored with Steve Best). His latest books are *Media Spectacle* and *September 11, Terror War, and the Dangers of the Bush Legacy.* His website is available at www.gseis.ucla.edu/faculty/kellner/kellner.html.

Colin Lankshear is professorial research fellow at the University of Ballarat, a freelance educational researcher and writer based in Mexico, and adjunct professor at Central Queensland University. His current research interests are mainly in the areas of literacy and social practices mediated by new computing and communications technologies.

Peter Mayo is associate professor in the Department of Education Studies in the faculty of education at the University of Malta. His books include *Beyond Schooling: Adult Education in Malta* (coedited with G. Baldacchino), *Gramsci and Education* (coedited with Carmel Borg and Joseph Buttigieg), *Gramsci, Freire and Adult Education: Possibilities for Transformative Action* (translated in both Catalan and Portuguese—a German translation is forthcoming), and *Liberating Praxis: Paulo Freire's Legacy for Radical Education and Politics.*

Peter McLaren is a political sociologist in education and an activist. He is professor in the Division of Urban Schooling at the Graduate School of Education and Information Studies, University of California, Los Angeles. He is the author and editor of over forty books. Professor McLaren lectures worldwide and his works have been translated into fifteen languages.

Michael A. Peters is research professor of education at the University of Glasgow (U.K.), adjunct professor in the school of education at the University of Auckland (NZ), and school of communication studies at the Auckland University of Technology. He has research interests in educational theory and policy and contemporary philosophy. He has published over twenty-five books in these fields, including: *Poststructuralism and Educational Research; Critical Theory and the Human Condition* (editor); *Futures of Critical Theory* (editor); and *Poststructuralism, Marxism, and Neoliberalism: Between Theory and Politics.*

Dr. Ludwig A. Pongratz is professor of general pedagogy and adult education at the Darmstadt Technical University. His publications and research concentrate primarily on the history of educational theory, the methodology of pedagogy, critical theory, educational philosophy, and adult education. Recent publications include: *Zeitgeistsurfer. Beiträge zur Kritik der Erwachsenenbildung; Kritik der Pädagogik—Pädagogik als Kritik* (coedited with W. Nieke and J. Masschelein. Opladen); and *Nach Foucault—Diskurs- und machtanalytische Perspektiven der Pädagogik* (coedited with W. Nieke, M. Wimmer, and J. Masschelein).

Laura Pulido is an associate professor in the Department of Geography and program in American studies and ethnicity at the University of Southern California. Her research focuses on race, social movements and political activism, Chicano/Latino studies, and Los Angeles. She is the author of *Environmentalism and Economic Justice* and *Black, Brown, Yellow, and Left: Radical Activism in Los Angeles, 1968–1978* (forthcoming).

Erika Richter, M.A., teaches in the Department of Education at the University of Wuppertal. Her main fields of interest and publication include intercultural education, multiculturalism, migration, philosophy of education, and critical pedagogy.

Dr. Albert Scherr teaches sociology at the University of Education (Pädagogische Hochschule Freiburg). His publications include: *Subjektorientierte Jugendarbeit; Soziologie der Sozialen Arbeit;* and *Bildung für die Einwanderungsgesellschaft.*

Dr. Heinz Sünker is professor of social pegaogy and social policy in the Department of Education at the University of Wuppertal. His main interests include critical social theory, critical pedagogy, theory and history of social work and social policy, and childhood studies. His books in English include: *The Politics, Sociology, and Economics of Education* (edited with R. Farnen) and *Education and Fascism: Political Identity and Social Education in Nazi Germany* (edited with H.-U. Otto).

Juha Suoranta is professor in the Department of Education at the University of Joensuu (Finland). In 2003, he worked as a senior researcher in the Academy of Finland and as a visiting professor at the University of California, Los Angeles. His recent book is *Children in the Information Society.*

Tuukka Tomperi is a professional philosopher and works as researcher in the teacher education department at the University of Tampere (Finland). His most recent publications are a textbook and a teacher's guide for citizenship education.